second edition

the Complete Adoption book

Everything You Need to Know to Adopt a Child

**Laura Beauvais-Godwin
& Raymond Godwin, Esq.**

Adams Media Corporation
Holbrook, Massachusetts

We dedicate this book to our dear children, Erika and Elizabeth,
who have taught us that a true family is one based on love, openness,
and honesty. We also thank their birth mothers, who made this all possible.

Published by
Adams Media Corporation
260 Center Street, Holbrook, MA 02343 U.S.A.
www.adamsmedia.com

1-58062-334-4

Printed in Canada

J I H G F E D C B

Library of Congress Cataloging-in-Publication Data
Beauvais-Godwin, Laura.
The complete adoption book : choosing an agency, independent adoptions, international
adoptions, state-by-state requirements / Laura Beauvais-Godwin & Raymond Godwin.
p.   cm.
ISBN 1-58062-334-4 (pb)
1. Adoption—United States. I. Godwin, Raymond. II. Title.
III. Title: Everything you need to know to adopt the child you want in less than one year.
HV875.55.B45   1997
326.7'34—dc20   96-43250
CIP

The authors have made every effort to ensure that the information contained in this book is current
and up to date; however, matters relative to adoption often change quickly. Because adoption involves
people and changing information, the authors have found that each adoption scenario is unique and
different to some degree. This book therefore should not be a substitute for an adoption professional's
involvement in your specific adoption matter.

This publication is designed to provide accurate and authoritative information with regard to the
subject matter covered. It is sold with the understanding that the publisher is not engaged in rendering
legal, accounting, or other professional advice. If legal advice or other expert assistance is required, the
services of a competent professional person should be sought.
— From a *Declaration of Principles* jointly adopted by a Committee of the
American Bar Association and a Committee of Publishers and Associations

This book is available at quantity discounts for bulk purchases.
For information, call 1-800-872-5627.

Contents

Acknowledgments

This book could not have been written without the many professionals who provided us with their expertise. We would like to thank the staff at Adoption Information Clearinghouse and the North American Council on Adoptable Children. Thanks also to the professionals at the South Carolina Department of Social Services, who have provided immeasurable information regarding children with special needs.

We appreciate the many attorneys who provided us with legal and practical advice regarding their states' laws. Also, several therapists have given us insight into issues that must be faced by all involved in adoption.

Pam Liflander, our editor at Adams Media, was committed to this book and provided much inspiration and support. Her suggestions helped to make the technical information more palatable and kept what is truly important in perspective. Thanks for all your encouragement and hard work.

Our very special thanks goes to the countless friends, adoption professionals, adoptive parents, birth parents, and adoptees whose lives have demonstrated that adoption is a loving choice and have made so many dreams come true.

Preface

In America today there are about 200,000 couples who want to adopt. This dream is said to be very costly and difficult to achieve. Yet nearly all the people we know who have actively and diligently sought to adopt had a baby or child in their home within eighteen months.

Nine years ago my husband and I did not know this. In fact, we were not aware that there were choices in the area of adoption. We did not know that a couple could adopt and have a baby within months. When we seriously began to consider adoption, we gave little thought to independent adoption. The idea of advertising for a baby made us uncomfortable; more important, we did not know anyone who had adopted independently. We had heard that independent adoption was risky and that it usually required the assistance of an expensive attorney.

So for a couple of years we pursued adoption through more traditional channels. Like many prospective adoptive parents, we spent years examining applications, and finally completed the forms for a few adoption agencies. This was a rather complicated process, as some applications were quite lengthy, and even after completing forms and sending in application fees, we had no guarantee of becoming parents. After attending a meeting conducted by an international adoption agency, we finally decided that we would adopt through an agency that placed Korean babies in a matter of months.

Then, on the day that we mailed our final application to the international agency, an acquaintance called us and asked whether we would be interested in meeting with a pregnant woman who wanted to place her baby for adoption. We were stunned. In a reversal of all our expectations, we became parents in four short months through independent adoption.

Moving from that fateful phone call to our daughter Erika's arrival was trying, despite the fact that our adoption was relatively simple and uneventful. So after we became adoptive parents, my husband decided to use his experience in family law and his personal experience as an adoptive parent to provide independent adoption services. Two and a half years later after Erika was born, an agency for whom Ray worked as a consultant asked whether he would be interested in adopting a baby that was soon to be born. Three weeks later, Elizabeth was in our arms.

Our goal in writing this book was to provide you, the prospective adoptive parent, with a step-by-step resource to guide you through a process that can sometimes feel overwhelming. Couples often tell us that they feel bewildered—that they do not even know where to begin. We have been there, too. In fact, when we were researching the adoption laws and practices of Canada, we were reminded of what it was like to begin the adoption process for the first time. When we started to look at adoption, we were helped tremendously by adoptive parents associated with a local chapter of RESOLVE, an infertility support and referral organization. They understood adoption issues and knew how to give us good, practical advice. Simple things like encouraging the birth mother to stay on a nonmaternity floor if she wished proved to be invaluable information at a time when our emotions were running high. In fact, knowing people who had experienced all the emotions that we were about to embark upon was very comforting.

Still, even with this advice we often felt unsure about how to handle certain situations. Unfortunately, we knew of no book that could help us with issues like talking with birth mothers, meeting with obstetricians, and when to pay medical expenses. Nor did we know of a book that could prepare us for the perplexing situations that my husband and I would encounter: the obstetrician who told my daughter's birth mother that the adoption was illegal, or the hospital staff who made insensitive remarks.

Our experience has taught us that nearly every adoption unfolds a little differently from what is expected. Adoption—like all other miracles—has its quirks and unpredictable moments. Nevertheless, there are some constants in the process, and preparation can alleviate a great deal of uncertainty. If you follow our advice, there's no reason pursuing adoption shouldn't be a positive experience for you, and for the birth parents too, if they are involved in the process.

As with any process, the more you know about adoption at the outset, the more confident you can be. There is a lot of information contained in the following pages, and there are a lot of choices to make. Do not become overloaded. Find what is best for you. As you will see, adoption can be broken down into manageable steps. In the chapters that follow you will find much of the legal and practical information you will need to make you comfortable with the process. We have experienced many different adoption situations and learned a great deal about the nuances of the process. We also remember how *we* felt when we first got involved in adoption. We hope this book reflects that.

All information offered in this book is true to the best of our knowledge. Information, however, especially legal information, can change rapidly. Rely on an adoption attorney for updates.

Names have been changed throughout, unless otherwise stated, and certain facts altered to protect anonymity.

Attorneys, state agencies, newspapers, support groups, books, newsletters, professionals, and organizations mentioned in this book *are not* endorsed by Laura Beauvais-Godwin or Raymond Godwin. It is up to the reader to investigate the credentials of any person or organization before using its services.

Chapter One

Is Adoption for You?

I f you are reading this book, chances are you are considering adoption. Perhaps you are in the middle of infertility treatment, or nearing the end of that treatment and wondering, "Where do I turn now?" Or it may be some time since you ended your treatments, and now you are ready to proceed with adoption. By now you know that the world of adoption is far from simple. There's a lot to learn. The good news is, that also means a lot of choices.

At the beginning, the process will probably seem confusing. Should you hire an attorney and adopt independently, or go with an agency? Is it better to adopt internationally or simply go through the local social services department? No one can answer these questions for you. You must consider the advantages and disadvantages of each route and decide which risks you can live with and which ones you cannot.

Even after you have decided on the method you want to pursue, approaching the adoption itself can feel overwhelming at first. There are so many fees and unknown expenses, so much paperwork. You have to think about getting through a home study, possibly meeting a birth mother, or even traveling to another country. You may create worries of your own by presuming that you must look a certain way, weigh a certain amount, and earn a certain income.

All adoptive parents go through this process, and they should. After all, this is a major life decision. With so many avenues to explore, it is important to take your time and ask as many questions as you can. Emotionally, you are bound to have a lot at stake, so proceed cautiously; get all of your facts in order and try not to let your feelings run ahead of your wallet or reality. Remember, proceeding cautiously does *not* mean proceeding slowly.

Many couples spend a year or two or three just "thinking about adoption" and making a few contacts. Some are still trying to conceive; others are just not quite ready to make the decision. It is very easy to fall into this routine. Each month may hold some promise that you may conceive, making it difficult to commit wholeheartedly to the adoption process. Without the actual promise of a real live baby, you may find it hard to put much effort into completing forms, getting the paperwork together for a home study, and writing out your life stories. The thought of talking to a birth mother may unnerve you, and when you consider traveling to another country, you remember the friend who got malaria while in Africa.

And so you say to yourself, "Let's wait another couple of months and see whether anything happens." This is understandable. What we hope to do in this book is show you that the tasks are not insurmountable. Sure, it is unfair. Biological parents do not have to go through the research, assemble documents, submit to a home study, or pay the fees. But if you are considering adoption, it is worth it. There are babies and children to adopt, and it does not take years to do it or tens of thousands of dollars. Most adoptions cost less than $10,000 and take a matter of months. You do not have to be perfect, either—just normal and stable and loving.

THERE *ARE* CHILDREN TO ADOPT

There is a widespread myth that adoption choices are limited because there are too few babies and children to adopt. It is true that a few years ago your options were more limited. Things have changed: There are many babies and children available. In fact, when international as well as domestic adoptions are considered, there are far more babies and children available than there are parents seeking to adopt.

So how many parents *are* looking to adopt? You will sometimes see the figure of two million couples being bandied about. That figure, though, really relates to the number of infertile couples, not all of whom are pursuing adoption. Elizabeth Bartholet, author of *Family Bonds*, writes that at any given time there are approximately 200,000 women looking to adopt, while two million have at least investigated the process. This figure seems closer to the true number of prospective adoptive couples. That means that in any given year about one prospective couple in three will adopt. Those are very promising numbers.

The number of adoptions by nonrelatives has fluctuated over the years. In 1951 there were 33,800; in 1961, 61,600. Adoptions reached a peak of 89,000 in 1970, then fell to 47,000 in 1975. Today there are probably about 63,000 adoptions by nonrelatives every year. However, there is a real lack of concrete data regarding numbers of couples hoping to adopt and numbers of children placed for adoption. Even the numbers of adoptions taking place can be hard to measure. Intrafamily adoptions (grandparents adopting grandchildren, aunts adopting nieces and nephews) and stepparent adoptions account for about half. The exact number of private agency and independent adoptions is not known because there is no centralized way of collecting data. In general, international adoption statistics are accurate. All that is really clear is that adoption figures vary dramatically from state to state—influenced not only by population but by the various state laws surrounding adoption. So hard numbers are elusive. We do know this, however: People *are* adopting. Statistics prove it.

WHO CAN ADOPT?

Nearly anyone who can provide a child with a stable, loving environment can become an adoptive parent. You do not have to be under thirty-five, have a large income, own a home, have money in the bank, or be married, childless, or infertile. Unlike any other group of parents, however, you will be required to provide information that indicates that you are stable and loving; that you are healthy enough to meet a child's needs; that you have a normal life expectancy; that you have a sufficient income to provide for a child; that you have adequate space for the child to live; if you are married, that your marriage is healthy and that you do not have an extensive divorce history; and if you do have children, that they are not exhibiting problems related to poor parenting.

Many people worry that they will not be approved to adopt. Most states do require that you be evaluated by a social worker or caseworker, who will then prepare a preplacement report known as a *home study*. Regulations as to what is included in this study are established by each state, but the basic standard is really one of common sense. What does it take to be a fit parent? Basic financial wherewithal, stability, and love. The home-study process is designed to screen out those who would not make suitable parents because of serious medical problems, mental illness, insufficient income, criminal history, a record of child abuse, or a current drug or alcohol addiction. Unless you have a serious problem, chances are good that you will be able to adopt.

You may run into other restrictions, depending on what avenues you decide to explore. Some licensed agencies have restrictions as to who can adopt as a means of limiting the number of prospective adoptive parents. Public agencies have requirements that those adopting children with special needs be able to meet the challenge of raising a child who has physical, mental, or emotional disabilities or illnesses. Every foreign country has its own guidelines as to who can adopt.

HOW TO BEGIN

Many people begin investigating adoption by looking under "Adoption" in the yellow pages of their telephone book and calling up the agencies listed, both public and private. Initially, this can be very discouraging. If you are looking to adopt a healthy infant, most social services departments have years-long waiting lists. Private agencies may also have long waiting lists, and in addition they may have many requirements and restrictions, not to mention high fees. For many the next step is to call an attorney's office, where they are asked to advertise for a birth mother, meet her, and possibly pay her living expenses for several months. Those who then turn to an international adoption agency learn they must travel to a foreign country and stay there for at least two to three weeks. All these options seem to have a downside. All you want is a baby or child, and suddenly you must consider what route you want to take, whether you will be accepted, whether you can afford it, and whether you are ready to take the risk. For many, it can feel overwhelming.

No matter what avenue you choose, there will be risks, whether they are financial risks, risks relating to the child's health, or risks associated with birth parents' rights. But these are calculated risks—not blind risks. For some, the risks associated with certain kinds of adoptions are enough to keep them away from that route. Others decide to go ahead. Only you can make the choice.

WHAT KIND OF CHILD DO YOU WANT?
In deciding which route to take, you may first want to consider what kind of child you want to adopt. Initially most people think of adopting a healthy newborn infant or a very young baby of their own ethnic background. But as people begin to consider adoption, the categories of adoptable children they will consider can broaden. This does not mean that a couple who had their heart set on a healthy Caucasian infant but could not afford the fees decides to "settle" for a two-year-old of another ethnic background. It is far more complex than that. All adoptive parents must carefully consider their background, resources, family, neighborhood, church, and available schools in considering what kind of child would be best suited for their family.

WHAT ROUTE DO YOU WANT TO TAKE?
There are two broad categories of adoptions: domestic and international. Within each of those two categories there are two general types of children to be adopted: those who are healthy and those who have special needs.

When adopting domestically, most people are interested in adopting healthy infants. There are two routes taken toward achieving this goal. One is private, or what is called *independent*, adoption. This entails hiring an attorney who will either locate a birth mother for you or instruct you on how to find one yourself through advertising or networking. The other route is to go with an agency, either public (a state agency) or private. The advantages, disadvantages, and legal issues associated with these two routes are discussed at length in the chapters that follow. For now, you may simply find it helpful to know that state agencies do have some healthy children to place for adoption—that applying to a state agency does not necessarily mean applying for a child with special needs, as many people believe. Many couples begin as foster parents and then learn as much as possible in order to be in the right place at the right time for a permanent placement. The success of this approach depends on the state and the timing. Not many infant adoptions take place through these state agencies, but your local state agency may present an opportunity. Some attorneys specialize in representing foster parents who aggressively push for adoption.

Most state agencies and a few private ones focus on placing children with special needs in the homes of adoptive couples. The special needs category includes both physical and psychological needs, with the label "physical needs" covering a wide range of medical conditions. Special needs children often come from abusive homes. Having been surrendered voluntarily by dysfunctional birth parents or taken from such homes by court order, they have usually been placed in foster homes for a time. The state agency operating the foster care system also has an adoption unit, which attempts to place the children for adoption. Again, the severity of the need, whether physical or psychological, varies greatly.

MOVING FROM INFERTILITY TO ADOPTION

If you are choosing adoption because you cannot have biological children, then before you begin the adoption process, you will want to explore your feelings about infertility and adoption. If you have been undergoing infertility treatment, you have probably felt out of control. Not only have you not achieved a successful pregnancy, but other areas of your life have probably been very much affected. You may not have taken the vacation you wanted because it conflicted with your infertility treatment. Or infertility has affected the way that you relate to others. For example, you may find it difficult to be around pregnant women, and attending a baby shower has become nearly intolerable. The self-doubts and out-of-control feelings that accompany infertility may remain with you as you approach the adoption process.

It is important to try and resolve some of the negative feelings associated with infertility, and also to examine your true feelings toward adoption, both positive and negative. Infertility treatment is an exhausting, time-consuming undertaking, and you may feel that you do not have the emotional energy to pursue these issues diligently. If you choose adoption, however, now is the time to begin resolving your feelings. If you pursue a private adoption, you may be parents quickly—perhaps even before you have had time to search within yourself and feel whole again. On the other hand, couples pursuing agency adoptions may be required to attend infertility and adoption workshops for several weeks. They also may be on a waiting list for three to five years—plenty of time to explore their feelings.

Adopting a baby does not necessarily alleviate all the insecurities that accompany infertility. We recommend that you join an adoption support group or an infertility support group, such as RESOLVE, to learn more about infertility and adoption issues. Read this and other books that deal with adoption after infertility. Not only will you be better prepared to be in charge of your adoption plans, you will be more comfortable in talking with others about your desire to adopt.

WHEN INFERTILITY IS NOT THE ISSUE

Many people do not adopt because they have no children or because they cannot have children. Many adoptive parents have chosen this route because they want to add to their family and make a difference in a child's life. In my experience, about 50 percent of the families seeking to adopt internationally, as well as those who are adopting through the social services department of their state fall into this category. If you fall into this category, you may not have to deal with issues of infertility; however, you must still address many of the same issues because although you do not feel that you have "lost" the opportunity to have biological children, the child and the birth parents have had a loss.

Also, in looking at your adoption choices, you must still go through your idea of what an adopted child will be like and still come to the decision as to what route you want to take and what resources you have to parent a child. Generally, those already with a few children do not look to adopt newborn infants. Perhaps because they feel that birth mothers are more drawn to those who cannot have children or because now that they have successfully parented children, they now want to provide a child with a loving home who may otherwise be in a group home or orphanage. Also, these parents can accept the fact that a child may have some developmental delays or other health problems. Again, you still need to explore if you want to parent through adoption. As you continue reading, although you may have had children and already know that they do not necessarily look like you or have your interests and talents, remember, however, that you too may be giving up a dream about what an adopted child may be like. You may also need to move to another stage in deciding what type of child you can parent and what you can realistically expect a child to be like.

ARE YOU READY TO ACCEPT PARENTHOOD THROUGH ADOPTION?

You have probably invested much time, money, and energy in attempts to have a biological child. Somewhere in the middle of your infertility treatment, you probably began to ask yourself why you so desperately wanted to have a child. As you thought about that question and underwent more invasive procedures, you may have been more convinced than ever that you wanted a biological child. As a successful pregnancy began to seem less and less likely, however, you had to move from your dream of having a biological child to considering child-free living, or adopting. Now, as you think of beginning the adoption process, you need to establish your reasons for becoming parents and to realize that an adopted child can fulfill your need to be parents. The first step, then, is to explore why you really want to be a parent.

Life is a constant series of decisions. Some are minor, such as what to have for breakfast; some are major, such as choosing a college or a partner, or deciding to have children. Nearly all the decisions we make are reversible. We can change our jobs, get a divorce, or transfer to another college. But one decision is never considered reversible, and that is the decision to have children.

That is why it is crucial to answer the question, "Why do we want to have children?" Although your reasons do not have to be completely logical, they should be defined, because of the tremendous responsibility and expense that come with being a parent. You need to establish some rational and sensible motives for having children if you are about to adopt.

People who set out to have biological children have many reasons for doing so, some more important than others. Here are the most common reasons people give for wanting children. Each is followed by a response suggesting why an adopted child would most likely meet a couple's needs.

To have the perfect child. Many people fantasize about having the "perfect" child. They think, "He will have my nose, my hair, my husband's eyes and lashes, my family's mind, and his family's language skills."

Response: Now imagine the worst possible genetic combination and ask yourself how "perfect" such a child would be. Don't forget to consider the worst traits of your family and in-laws. In other words, the "perfect" biological child might not be so perfect. There are many genes your child could inherit.

To continue your family lineage. Some people do not want to create the "perfect" child; rather, they feel the need to perpetuate the "perfect" family. Perhaps your family is one that believes that "blood is thicker than water." In fact, you may feel a great responsibility to pass on certain characteristics of your family or yourself to a child.

Response: Again, children can draw from a very large gene pool. There is no guarantee of passing on any single characteristic to your child. It may be that the characteristics you want to perpetuate have more to do with your values than with your family genes, however, and these are passed on to your child through your nurturing, not your genetic role. An adopted child will have the same opportunity to develop strong, positive values that a biological child would.

To have a child with your interests, talents, and abilities. The reasons for wanting a child who shares your interests are similar to those for wanting the "perfect" child: your desire to pass on the best of the family's traits. For example, you may be a wonderful pianist. Music may always have been a great love in your family. You might fear that an adopted child would not have the same innate musical ability that a biological child would have.

Response: First, acknowledge that even a biological child will not necessarily inherit your musical abilities. Second, be aware that you can seek out and select a birth mother who is musically inclined, if you believe that musical ability is inherited. Finally, remember that even a child born without innate musical ability can be coached to play a musical instrument and to appreciate fine music.

Of course, we must accept our children for who they are, not for what we want them to be. Whether our children are born to us or adopted by us, they are ours to love for themselves, not for what they do.

To pass on the family name. When people think of perpetuating a family heritage, the "family name" is often the first thing they think of. Viewed in this light, it becomes almost an obligation to keep the family name moving.

Response: If you are a Louis Johnson III, can you feel comfortable naming an adopted child Louis Johnson IV? Some people's initial response is negative. Yet when they think further about what it means to name a child after themselves or another family member, they realize that it does not really matter whether the child is biological or adopted. The feelings that parents have for their adopted children are the same as for biological children. Feelings of love make the connection between the parent and the child; the name can just be an extension of that connection.

To have your child accepted by other family members. Many couples fear that other family members will not love and accept an adopted child, particularly one of a different ethnic background.

Response: Research indicates that even relatives who are opposed to the adoption develop very strong feelings for the child once the child is placed.

To experience pregnancy and birth. Some women believe that to feel truly feminine, they must experience pregnancy, giving birth to, and breastfeeding a baby.

Response: If these reasons for having a child are very important to you, then you need to grieve the loss of these opportunities. If you cannot move past the grieving stage, then perhaps you need to continue infertility treatment.

Joining an infertility support group, such as one offered by RESOLVE, can help you through the grieving process, as well as assist you and your spouse in deciding when to continue infertility treatment or when to end it. Knowing when "enough is enough" can help you and your spouse move toward resolving your infertility and accepting adoption or child-free living.

Control of mother's health during pregnancy. Another reason to want biological children is to have as much control as possible during your pregnancy. As a conscientious person, you would eat well, take prenatal vitamins, avoid alcohol and drugs, and seek proper medical care.

Response: Adoptive parents are right to be concerned about the birth mother's well-being and health during her pregnancy, since we know that her health can influence a child's development. Actually, depending on what route to adoption you follow, control of the birth mother's health is not entirely out of your hands. Nevertheless, for some couples considering adoption, the risks are too great. Perhaps you and your spouse need to put your fears into words. Sometimes identifying fears can help you face them. Then you can determine what risks you are willing or not willing to take. For more about medical issues, see chapter 18.

To rear a child that you love. This should be your number-one reason for wanting to be a parent: to provide a loving and stable environment for a growing child. To make this investment in a life, you want the child to be truly yours. Indeed, some people believe that the love you have for a child is a result of the biological connection and not the relationship; therefore, an adopted child can't be truly theirs.

Response: Adoptive parents, some with both biological and adopted children, unanimously say that they love all their children the same.

For most, the decision to adopt follows infertility treatment. You may take comfort in knowing that although adoption may be your second choice, it is not second-best.

WHAT ARE YOUR REASONS FOR WANTING A CHILD?
Having thought about some of the things that motivate people to have children, you and your spouse need to explore your reasons for wanting to be parents. Here is an exercise designed to help you do just that.

1. Working independently, write out the reasons you want a child.
2. Now identify the reasons you have in common. Are there answers that are important to both of you? Is there one that is very important to you but not to your spouse?
3. Now write out the needs that you believe having an adopted child can fulfill.

Chapter Two

Agency Adoption

An adoption agency is a business incorporated as either a nonprofit or a for-profit entity. It is licensed by its state to place children for adoption and to conduct home studies; some agencies only conduct home studies. The director of the agency must also have certain qualifications, such as a master's in social work and several years' experience in the adoption field. The social workers or caseworkers working for the adoption agency generally have at least a college degree, if not a master's in social work. Sometimes years of experience in social work or adoption will allow someone to work for the agency without having a specialized degree. There are numerous directors and social workers involved with adoption agencies who *are* highly qualified and professional. Many are themselves adoptive parents, and so can bring a special touch of empathy to the process.

However, being qualified by state standards does not guarantee that the worker is knowledgeable about adoption issues or highly sympathetic to your or a birth mother's concerns and needs. Like many attorneys, adoption caseworkers may not have the skills to interact with birth parents.

Each state has its own laws and regulations as to who can form an agency and what guidelines must be followed to maintain an agency license or certification. Remember, just because an agency is incorporated as a nonprofit entity does not mean that the owner of the agency is not profiting from the organization; the owner will profit by drawing a salary. Nor does another agency's for-profit status imply that those who operate the agency are money-hungry and unscrupulous. Whether an agency is nonprofit or for-profit has more to do with tax and legal considerations than anything else.

Some people still believe that operating as a nonprofit organization gives an agency the appearance of being more ethical, since almost all well-known charities and religious organizations are nonprofit entities. No matter what your take on this issue, it is important to question an adoption agency about its experience and professionalism, no matter what umbrella the agency is incorporated under. The agency's written policy and the way it really functions can sometimes be quite different.

Most agencies have a policy stating that their purpose is to provide suitable homes for children—not to find children for couples. Their focus is often on the birth mother, with the agency in essence acting as her advocate; the agency does not represent the adoptive couple, nor are the couple's interests as highly regarded as they may believe. To use an extreme illustration, in one case an agency informed an adoptive couple on the weekend they were to pick up their baby, that the birth mother wanted an open adoption after placement, and that the couple had no choice in the matter. This would mean visits with the birth mother on a regular basis. The agency director informed the couple, who had received no prior warning about open adoption and had been given no information about their rights, that this was the way adoptions were now done, and that if the couple could not consent to such an arrangement, they were not ready for adoption. The couple declined to go forward with the placement.

Birth mothers and children do need advocates. But adoptive parents also have rights and feelings. An ethical agency will be clear as to its purpose and up front as to its policies from the very beginning.

PUBLIC ADOPTION AGENCIES

Public, or government-operated, agencies are usually a part of the state social services department. Most states operate several adoption agencies, generally on the regional or county level. To locate the public adoption agency in your area, contact the adoption specialist in your state (see the Appendix) or look in the government section of your telephone directory.

Couples seeking to adopt will often begin their adoption research by opening up the telephone directory and calling their social services department. If they are looking for a healthy Caucasian infant, they may be discouraged to be told that the wait is seven to nine years. For those who are truly flexible, however, who have researched the possibility of adopting a child with special needs or one of another ethnic background, going through a state adoption unit may be a very good choice. It is estimated that there are at least 50,000 U.S. children in need of adoptive homes; these are children placed in the states' foster care systems.[1]

AVAILABLE CHILDREN

Public agencies primarily place children who have been in the foster-care system, even if the children have no physical health problems. These children have often been abused or neglected; many have been in multiple foster homes. Their biological parents' rights have usually been involuntarily terminated (or are in the process of being terminated) because of the abuse or neglect.

Many of these children placed for adoption are older. However, as more laws are passed to get children into permanent homes at a faster rate, more babies and preschool children are becoming available. Many of these children are physically healthy. If the children are young, they are less likely to have the degree of emotional scarring found in older children. If you are willing to be a "foster-adoptive" parent and to have a child in your home who is considered a moderately high legal risk (because of issues such as the biological parents' rights), you may also have more opportunity to adopt a child at a younger age.

Although the trend in government is to provide permanency for children instead of allowing them to go from foster home to foster home, it may still take months or years before both biological parents' rights are terminated and the actual adoption can go through. The length of the waiting time varies from state to state and according to individual circumstances. In any case, you can be the child's foster parents until the adoption is finalized.

PUBLIC AGENCY ADOPTION: PROS AND CONS

Few of life's accomplishments provide the same level of reward as adopting a child with special needs. Also, you can adopt quickly—in six to twelve months—if you desire to adopt a minority or school-age child. Another important advantage of using a public agency is cost. Adoption expenses are usually minimal, and often state and federal subsidies are available. Support services are usually available and public agencies usually network with other government agencies to provide counseling services to children and adoptive parents.

Concerning the disadvantages of using a public agency, several important—but not insurmountable—challenges must be highlighted.

1. There's no denying that working with the bureaucracy can be difficult. You may agree to take a child who is considered a moderate-to-low legal risk and find that because of the law it takes years to terminate a missing parent's rights. You may also have to interact with social workers who have a bias against transracial adoptions. In one case, two African-American children were kept in foster care for a full year after the rights of the birth parents were terminated because the social worker involved was seeking only a college-educated African-American couple with a certain income as the prospective adoptive couple.

2. The agency may expect you to attend twenty-five hours or more of pre-adoption seminars.

3. The public agency's home-study process may be more demanding than a home study done for a private placement. Because you are requesting a child with special needs or of a different ethnic background from your own, the agency may ask you numerous personal questions about your upbringing and your attitudes on many issues. These questions may be necessary, but they can also feel invasive.

4. The child that you are adopting will not be a newborn, and the quality of care he or she received during the first year or more of life may be relatively unknown.

5. You will need to become educated about the kinds of emotional problems the child may suffer as a result of his past experiences.

6. You may need to advocate for yourself to even get a social worker to contact you and discuss children available for adoption, although many children are listed. Families with good credentials have not always received encouragement from the social workers, leading to these families feeling frustrated. You may have to regularly contact the agency regarding a specific child/ren. It is best if you establish a personal contact with one social worker who knows you and the type of child you are seeking to adopt.

STATE- AND FEDERALLY-FUNDED PRIVATE AGENCIES

Some agencies operate much like public adoption agencies, receiving government monies, networking with their state's social services department, and placing exclusively special needs children. Such agencies usually accept children for adoption and assume legal responsibility for them. Often they will function to fill a need not covered by the public agencies. For example, a specialized agency may place older African-American children, whereas a social services department might not have the resources to reach out aggressively to the African-American community for potential adoptive parents. Such agencies do not usually charge a fee, because they are serving waiting children, but if they do charge one, it is made considerably lower by the provision of government grants.

Sometimes an older or special needs child may be placed with a private agency that is working with the biological parent or guardian of the child to keep the social services department from getting involved and placing the child in foster care. In cases like this, the agency itself may be hindered by the bureaucracy in attempting to establish a permanent placement.

RELIGIOUS AGENCIES

Some agencies providing adoption services have a specific religious affiliation. These include Catholic Charities, Lutheran Social Ministries, and Bethany Christian Services. From this group, some take applicants only from certain religious affiliations, while others have more flexible policies, especially for special needs or minority children. These agencies receive charitable donations and so can often keep their expenses lower. Moreover, they often do not charge directly for the birth mother's expenses, because so many birth mothers change their minds when working with these agencies. (Religious agencies are more likely to counsel birth mothers to raise their own children.) These agencies usually have a set fee or have sliding-scale fees based on your income. If the birth mother changes her mind, you are not charged for her living expenses. Sometimes services are provided to the birth mother through the agencies' own organizations. For example, they may allow or require her to live in a home for unwed mothers or with a family who will care for her during her pregnancy.

Religious agencies network with churches, synagogues, crisis pregnancy centers, hospitals, private religious schools, and other organizations that often refer birth mothers to them. Because some of these agencies are well-known names, they are often the first place a birth mother will go when she learns she is pregnant.

Other religiously affiliated adoption agencies are offshoots of homes for unwed mothers. These homes may have been created as conscious alternatives to abortion, and their staffs may provide career training and counseling services. Such agencies often provide strong emotional support for choosing an adoption plan. When a woman places a child for adoption, the fees charged to the adoptive parents often pay for the upkeep of the home and services to other pregnant women.

Like birth mothers, many adoptive couples often turn first to an organization affiliated with their religion. This can work to your advantage if the agency is selective and you meet its requirements. Some religious agencies, however, can be overly controlling in their approach to adoptive parents, insisting on significant paperwork, attendance at several workshops, a home study that can feel invasive, and excessive initial fees. These requirements can limit the number of applicants and slow down the adoption process so that it takes six months to a year just to complete all the requirements. But if you are patient, you can adopt.

PRIVATE AGENCIES THAT PLACE INFANTS

For years private adoption agencies that placed primarily infants were the chief vehicle for couples seeking a placement. Indeed, up until the mid-seventies, private agency adoption was virtually the only system used. Things have changed now, but many of the old impressions and fears about private agencies persist. A birth mother may worry that an agency caseworker will interrogate her or pass judgment about her unplanned pregnancy, or that her baby will be placed in foster care for a week or more, then adopted by a couple she knows little about. Some adoption agencies may still operate like this, but not many.

Adoptive couples may suffer from equally outmoded ideas. They may think that all they have to do is apply to an agency, and after a short time, they'll receive a phone call that a baby is waiting to be picked up. This picture no longer matches reality. Today, the birth mother's cooperation is often actively sought during the process of making a placement. Couples applying for adoption compile portfolios about themselves, complete with photographs and a letter to the prospective birth mother, on the basis of which she makes the selection. Some agencies may allow the birth mother to meet with the couple before the birth. Thus, the decision as to placement is very often left up to the birth mother, not the agency. Of course, the agency controls which portfolios it presents to the birth mother. But placements are no longer simply made on the basis of first come, first served.

Agency adoptions take several different forms. Let's begin with the traditional agency adoption.

TRADITIONAL ADOPTION

Traditional adoption is a closed adoption in which the birth and adoptive parents never meet. An agency calls you to take home a baby who has been released for adoption. This often means that the child has been in foster care for a few weeks. Why? Because depending upon the state, the birth mother may have a set period of time after the baby is born in which to change her mind about placing the baby for adoption. This waiting period may be anywhere from ten to ninety days, and some agencies will not permit a child to be placed in an adoptive home before the waiting period has elapsed. In some states, in fact, it is against the law to do so because the child is considered a "high legal risk." If he or she is permitted to go home with the adoptive parents, they may be referred to as the "foster parents" until the waiting period has elapsed and the birth parents' rights are terminated. Unquestionably the worst-case scenario is for an infant to be placed in a couple's home, only to have one of the birth parents change his or her mind and remove the child. This happens only rarely, but when it does, the heartache is immense.

The scenario just described occurs only in states in which birth parents' rights are not terminated when they sign the consent to the adoption. (The consent is usually signed a few days after the child's birth.) States have such laws for a reason. Their point is not simply to favor birth parents but to avoid the often thorny legal challenges associated with adoption. However, they can have unintended consequences. Birth mothers find themselves in a dilemma: Should their child be placed in foster care or not? Most birth mothers do not want their babies in foster care; they very much want the baby to go home from the hospital with the adoptive couple. Because agencies are usually not willing to place a baby with a couple until the birth parents' rights have ended, birth mothers often end up avoiding agencies altogether. Agencies that are able to comply with the birth mother's wishes by making the adoptive couple the foster family until the birth parents' rights are terminated probably offer the best solution.

FACILITATED AGENCY ADOPTION

With a facilitated agency adoption, the agency introduces you to a birth mother before the baby's birth. This option is much like a private adoption (see chapter 3) and therefore is now much more prevalent than a traditional agency adoption. You take on essentially the same involvement that you would in a private adoption, and unless the agency receives outside funds, you will be paying the birth mother's legal, living, and counseling expenses in addition to the agency fee.

Some agencies now require their clients to advertise for their own birth mother. Once you find a birth mother, the agency will handle her concerns, provide her with counseling, and sometimes make arrangements for her housing and medical care.

The chief difference between this type of agency adoption and private adoption has to do with cost. The up-front costs of the agency adoption may be much higher—in many cases, several thousand dollars before you even start. Moreover, once you make such an investment in an agency and locate a birth mother, you and the birth mother are pretty much committed to working with this agency.

There are risks with this approach. If a birth mother changes her mind and decides to keep her child, the couple are not only heartbroken, they may be several thousand dollars out of pocket as well. If a child is placed with you as a result of your finding a birth mother on your own, and for some reason the birth mother cannot or does not want to work with the agency, the agency may require that you forfeit all of your initial fees. This arrangement is usually spelled out in the agency-client contract. Be very cautious of such a contract; it means that you can lose substantially. Some agencies will allow you to put the money toward a second adoption, while others will not.

THE MIDDLE ROAD

The most typical agency adoption is the one in which you are informed that a birth mother has chosen you after viewing your portfolio, and you wait to pick the baby up from the agency immediately after the birth mother has signed the documents terminating her parental rights. Like a traditional agency adoption, the fees are generally higher than if you find the birth mother yourself.

Many agencies have taken this middle road, as it were, between an independent adoption, in which you meet the birth mother, and a traditional agency adoption, in which the placement is completely anonymous. Taking this in-between route can protect the emotions of both the birth mother and the adoptive couple, in the event that the birth mother changes her mind.

The caveat with this method of adoption is that you must be very careful in working with an agency that requires large payments for a specific birth mother's living and counseling expenses. If she changes her mind, you will probably not be reimbursed for the monies paid to her and for her benefit.

Unfortunately, it is too easy for an agency to charge its nonrefundable fees for matching you with a birth mother that the agency should have had reservations about. If you do not meet with the birth mother, you will not pick up on the warning signs. Meeting you, furthermore, can force a birth mother out of denial and lead her to make a concrete decision about an adoption plan. Otherwise she may continue to draw monies from the agency as she works through certain issues about the adoption—at your expense. If you know that there is some hesitation, articulated or not, then at least you can decide whether to risk your money and your emotions. The same scenario can also happen with attorneys who match couples with birth parents.

IDENTIFIED AGENCY ADOPTION

Identified agency adoption, also called designated agency adoption, is essentially an independent adoption that becomes an agency adoption. Usually the prospective adoptive parents and a pregnant woman have made some form of contact with each other before involving an agency. An identified adoption proceeds much like an independent adoption, except that the agency provides guidance and support. Also, the laws governing an agency adoption are followed, rather than those governing an independent adoption.

Agencies recognize that more and more people are choosing independent adoption, and therefore they are providing more identified adoption services. Actually, this compromise can offer the best of both worlds: the personal control the birth and adoptive parents seek in an independent adoption, and the emotional and sometimes legal advantages permitted in an agency adoption. Some agencies even counsel prospective adoptive parents on how to proceed with an independent adoption.

In the four states where private adoption is illegal, an identified adoption is one of the few options available. In a few more states it can be advantageous (see the Appendix). In most states, however, an identified adoption offers limited benefits.

WHY CONSIDER AN IDENTIFIED ADOPTION?

If you are thinking about private adoption, there are a number of reasons why an identified adoption could make sense. For instance:

1. *Counseling for birth and adoptive parents.* The counseling that birth parents receive through an agency can help determine whether they are quite sure of their decision to place the baby for adoption. Counseling can also help prepare them for the feelings they will experience once the baby is born. Adoption creates many highs and lows for everyone, birth and adoptive parents alike, and it can be reassuring to have a counselor on hand to provide support and encouragement, to give the feeling that someone is "holding their hand" throughout the process.

2. *Birth mothers' expenses.* Expenses that adoptive parents cannot legally pay for in an independent adoption, such as rent, may be permitted in an agency adoption, although state laws vary considerably on this point. Paying expenses can help facilitate the adoption process and provide an incentive to the birth mother to work with you. But be careful! You do not want to fall into the trap of paying for excessive expenses.

3. *Fewer legal complications.* In some states the birth parents' rights are terminated earlier in an agency adoption than they would be in an independent adoption. This provision usually prevents the removal of a child from a couple's home if a birth parent changes his or her mind, saving much heartache for everyone involved.

   Knowing that her parental rights are terminated once the baby goes home with the adoptive couple can actually give a birth mother greater peace of mind. There is no temptation to second-guess her decision or agonize about whether to change her mind. She is also more secure knowing that the birth father's rights have been terminated and that he cannot interfere with the adoption plans.

   Although placing a child for adoption can be very sad for birth parents, having the process reach closure allows them to grieve their loss and then to get on with their lives.

4. *More legal options.* In states in which independent adoption is illegal, a couple can essentially pursue a private adoption and then contact an agency to make it into an identified agency adoption. An agency can also serve as an intermediary in states where intermediaries are not permitted. This means contracting with an agency so that an intermediary or a birth mother can contact the agency instead of you. For example, you may wish to write to obstetricians and enclose your adoption business cards. Instead of putting your name and telephone number on the card, you can supply the agency's name and telephone number, along with your first names.

5. *Protection of privacy.* When advertising in newspapers and through adoption cards, you can use the agency's name and phone number instead of your own. By doing so, you remove some of the anxiety associated with screening phone calls, especially prank calls.

    Note: This does not always work to your advantage. Many birth mothers will not want to deal with an agency. *Be sure to specify in your ad that the phone number belongs to an agency. Birth mothers will hang up if they feel they are being deceived*—and rightfully so. No birth mother wants to hear "Happy Land Adoption Agency" when she is expecting to reach Arlene and Peter at a private home.

6. *Support system for birth mother.* For adoptive couples who do not wish to meet and talk with the birth mother on a weekly or even a monthly basis, the agency social worker assigned to the birth mother can "hold her hand" in a positive sense.

IDENTIFIED ADOPTION: SOME DISADVANTAGES

With an identified adoption, problems sometimes arise if you or the agency is not clear in your expectations. As identified adoptions become more common, long-established traditional agencies that primarily place babies may decide to go along with the trend and offer identified adoption services. The problem is that such agencies are historically biased against independent adoptions, and this strong bias can eventually show.

An example of agency bias has to do with foster care. Some agencies will encourage a birth mother to place the baby in foster care for six weeks or longer. Even if you have met the birth mother yourself and have begun to work out an arrangement, the agency may have its own agenda, insisting, for instance, on repeatedly contacting the birth father and getting him to relinquish his rights even when the father is completely unresponsive and the state laws provide an adequate way to terminate his parental rights without his having to formally sign them away.

Most states require that agencies discuss alternatives to adoption with the birth mother whether she wants to or not. That's not necessarily bad. A woman seeking to place a baby for adoption has a right to consider all her options. When she does so and still chooses adoption, she is less likely to change her mind after the baby is born. However, if you have met with a birth mother who is resolute in her decision to place the baby for adoption, she may feel very uncomfortable having to discuss in detail why she is not planning to raise the child, or even why she is not considering an abortion. Repeated probing about feelings and family backgrounds can make a birth mother feel she is guilty of something. Understanding counselors will respect a woman who is very firm in her decision and not press her for an elaborate explanation.

Before committing yourself to an identified adoption, *find out what the expenses will be.* The cost of this kind of adoption varies greatly from one agency to the next, as do the billing systems used. Some agencies charge one fee; others bill by the hour. Circumstances make a difference: If you meet a birth mother when she is nearly nine months pregnant, she will probably not receive as many hours of counseling as a woman who contacts you when she is three months pregnant.

Other factors that can increase the cost include the level of the birth father's involvement, his counseling, the distance the social worker has to travel to meet with the birth mother and father, and whether she communicates with the birth mother and father by long-distance telephone.

Watch out! If you have not personally met the birth mother, an agency may want to charge you for a direct placement instead of an identified adoption. One couple had spoken with a birth mother and then contacted an agency to conduct an identified adoption. The cost was $2,000 one day, $14,000 the next. Because the couple had not met the birth mother face to face, the agency wanted to charge them the higher rate.

In states in which private adoption is illegal, such as Massachusetts, agency fees for an identified adoption can be astronomical—$4,000 just for the home study. It may be less expensive to adopt in another state. Even if you have to live in a hotel for two weeks after the baby is born, it will still be much cheaper than an agency fee of $10,000 plus the birth mother's expenses.

Finally, find out whatever you can about an agency's reputation. Some agencies will "steal" a birth mother from you and steer her to one of its own couples. A dishonest agency would find this very profitable, because when an agency finds a baby for someone, the fee is almost always more than for an identified adoption. Consult your attorney before making a commitment. Be aware, however, that some attorneys discourage identified adoptions, since they usually make less money when an agency takes on more responsibility.

IS AN IDENTIFIED ADOPTION FOR YOU?

Now that you know the pros and cons of an identified agency adoption, the question becomes one of individual circumstances. For some situations an identified adoption may be the best way to go. Consider the following scenarios:

Scenario A. You live in a state in which the birth parents' rights are terminated at a later date in an independent adoption than they are in an agency adoption.

For many couples this is the most important reason to go with an identified adoption. They could not bear to have a birth mother change her mind after the baby is already placed with them. In New Jersey, parental rights can be terminated only two to three months after placement if the birth mother does not appear in court shortly after birth. The agency's involvement, however, ensures that rights are terminated earlier, usually within days after birth, providing security for the adoptive couple and closure for the birth mother.

Scenario B. You want to adopt a baby from another state, and the law requires an agency in an out-of-state placement.

If you adopt a baby from Florida, for example, and you are not a Florida resident, the baby must be released to an agency before he is given to you. Even in states that do not require an agency, you may want to use one as a security measure. You want to make sure everything is signed and sealed before the adoption proceeds through Interstate Compact (the branch of the state department of social services that oversees interstate adoptions). Also, having a sensitive, knowledgeable social worker in the same city as the birth mother can be a comfort to her, especially if you live miles away yourself.

Scenario C. You are unsure about a birth mother and believe that counseling will help her become more secure in her decision.

Of course, an agency is not necessary for a birth mother to receive counseling. If everyone agrees, a social worker or therapist not affiliated with an agency can counsel birth parents.

Scenario D. A birth mother needs to have more expenses paid than are permitted by law in an independent adoption.

Some states restrict the expenses that a couple can pay in order to prevent the practice of "buying" babies by paying excessive expenses. For example, until recently, in North Carolina an adoptive couple could not even pay for the medical expenses of a birth mother. Such laws usually allow agencies to pay for more of the birth mother's expenses than are permitted in an independent adoption. The couple is in essence paying for the birth mother's expenses; the monies are just going through the agency first.

A final note before moving on to agency services. An agency, as has been pointed out, can represent both adoptive parents and birth parents. Many will make it clear that they do not represent the interests of the adoptive couple; others give the appearance of regarding the concerns of the adoptive couple by assigning them a social worker separate from the one assisting the birth mother. Because of some of the financial and emotional risks discussed earlier, it is suggested that a couple hire an attorney to represent them even if they are seeking a placement through an agency. The attorney will be the couple's advocate, emphasizing the concerns of the couple and seeing to it that an inexperienced social worker does not disrupt an adoption plan. Also, the attorney will be needed to process the adoption paperwork with the courts after placement.

WHEN AN AGENCY TURNS YOU DOWN

Agencies do not have an unlimited number of children for placement; therefore, some establish criteria for adoptive parents beyond what is mandated by the state. These criteria may be related to geographic area, age, marital status, educational level, and religion, and must be applied equally and without bias to all applicants.

Some agencies also have a screening process separate from the mandatory home study. *Remember, being refused by an agency that makes direct placements and conducts home studies is not the same thing as not having an approved home study.* You may simply have failed to get through the agency screening for direct placement purposes.

Once the screening process is completed, the agency will conduct a home study, if one has not already been conducted by another agency. If an applicant is rejected, the agency should provide detailed information as to why. In New Jersey, for example, the agency must offer services to help the couple adjust to the decision, as well as give information about the agency's grievance procedure.

ADOPTIVE PARENTS' RIGHTS: GETTING ALL THE INFORMATION

As prospective adoptive parents, you do have certain rights, and one of the most important is the right to information, especially about the adoptive child. Agencies are required to provide any medical information about the child that is available, as well as any genetic and social background. Sometimes this information will be part of the placement agreement; at other times it will be a separate document. Some states require in-depth information, including the child's diet and feeding habits. If the child has special needs, the agency may be required to provide the applicant with a list of long-term needs and available community resources for coping with them.

Remember, clients have the right to refuse a child. This is not so adoptive parents can "shop"—that is, pick and reject children; it is to encourage them to make an intelligent decision, based on full information, as to whether they can appropriately meet a child's needs.

Sometimes couples will state that they are open to adopting, say, a toddler with certain physical disabilities, when what they really want is a healthy infant. Do not try this. There's no point in going through an agency that places many special needs children unless you are willing to be honest about what kind of child you can care for.

PRIVATE AGENCIES: WHAT TO LOOK OUT FOR

Although there are many excellent agencies that truly support both the birth parents and the adoptive parents, some agencies are set up in a way that makes the process difficult for everyone involved. Here are some of the problems you could find yourselves running into:

1. *The agency is not sufficiently aggressive in recruiting birth mothers.* Many adoption agencies are not even listed in the yellow pages. Some long-established traditional agencies do not appear to be what one might expect. We did consulting work for one agency that gave no indication that it was in the adoption business. Because the agency also provided a broad range of social services, a birth mother coming into the office would be hard-pressed to find brochures or other information that explained the advantages of adoption. This agency, like many others, simply did not emphasize adoption services.

2. *The agency expects you to find the birth mother.* Some agencies require you to pay a sum of money up front—up to $10,000, in some cases, and the couple must then find their own birth mother! The agency fee is for taking care of all the details and some of the expenses after a couple finds the birth mother.

3. *The agency does not encourage adoption.* In an October 14, 1991, article in *Forbes* magazine, William Pierce of the National Committee for Adoption noted that many social workers appear to do as much as possible to talk a woman out of placing a baby for adoption. This is a common bias among social workers and religious counselors. The question is, does it have any place in an adoption agency?

    You might suppose that adoption agencies would have to place a certain number of babies each year in order to stay in business, but this is not necessarily so. Agencies have other ways to raise funds, including donations, conducting home studies, and requiring couples to attend adoptive parenting classes and counseling. Charging prospective adoptive couples a fee, as some agencies do, to have their portfolio placed on file and shown to birth mothers generates further income. Once a birth mother selects a couple based on their portfolio, the couple may be responsible for paying all of her medical expenses, counseling fees (for counseling provided by the agency), and the agency's administrative costs, even if the birth mother changes her mind.

Adoptive parents may also be allowed to use an agency's phone number in their newspaper ads—for a fee. The agencies may charge for the service, as well as for each phone call made to the office.

All of this is not to say that agencies that provide such services do not support adoption—usually they do. Just be aware that the cost of the actual adoption is only one means of collecting revenue. It is important to note that although thousands of agencies conduct home studies and provide other adoption-related services, only about 250 are directly involved in the majority of placements that occur each year in the United States.

Some social workers are paid a salary regardless of the number of adoptions they oversee. Often working on a limited budget, they have neither the time nor the resources to market the agency and its services. Furthermore, some social workers who work for an agency that provides many social and charitable services often do not take a positive view of adoption. They look on it as a last resort, believing that there are enough social programs available for single mothers. Also, women who choose adoption may be viewed as "unfit mothers"—either because they have not accessed the available social programs or because they have the audacity to choose not to parent and to move on with their lives.

4. *The agency has restrictions regarding who can adopt.* Agency restrictions usually relate to age, religion, weight, ethnic background, income, educational level, marital status, and an infertility diagnosis. Some agencies are so restrictive that they have two applications: one to determine whether you meet the initial standards, and a second for the adoption itself. Even when a couple meets all the standards, success is not automatic.

5. *The agency permits limited contact, if any, between adoptive parents and birth parents.* Some agencies still take the old-fashioned approach to arranging adoption. Many, however, are beginning to allow more communication, so that the birth mother and adoptive parents may meet in person or through pictures and biographical sketches. Most parents see this as a step in the right direction.

6. *The agency has a long waiting list.* An agency may claim that the wait is two to three years, but this may be after the home study is completed—and you may wait six months to a year for the home study. One agency is listed as having a waiting time from application to homecoming as two to four years. Yet I know couples who waited four to five years for the arrival of their baby. Not surprisingly, the waiting period for special needs children and non-Caucasian infants in the statistics is often much shorter than that for healthy Caucasian infants.

CONTRACTING WITH AN AGENCY: WHAT TO ASK

Before you decide to use an agency, you will want to investigate it thoroughly. Talk with the staff; if you can, talk to other parents who have dealt with them. Many agencies will provide the names and numbers of couples who will gladly talk with you about their experience.

Before you visit an agency, call and ask the counselor or secretary about its philosophy on adoption. What you ask will depend on what kind of child you are seeking to adopt. If you are looking for a healthy infant, and the agency requires that you do at least part of the work of advertising and networking for a child, then you will want to ask questions about their relationships with birth mothers and what support systems they provide. If you want to adopt a toddler-age child with special needs, you may want to ask questions about what birth family background they usually provide and what services and subsidies are available to meet the child's special needs.

Trust your instincts. If you call an agency and feel that you are being treated as an irritant, even though you are asking the questions very politely, take it as a warning. Remember, a birth mother is going to feel even worse if she contacts the agency. On the other hand, do be reasonable; agency personnel have limited time to talk on the phone.

Some of your more in-depth questions might better wait for an initial interview or for one of the seminars that the agency gives on a regular basis.

No matter what kind of agency you are contacting, you will want to ask these questions:

1. *What are their requirements and restrictions?*
2. *What kinds of children does the agency place?*
3. *How many children did the agency place last year?*
4. *What are the agency's fees?* If there is a standard flat fee, ask:
   - What is the payment schedule?
   - If the birth mother changes her mind, is any money refunded?
     If the fee is based on the number of hours the parties spend in counseling and on the nature of the adoption, then ask:

- Is there a cap on the fees?
- Do the fees include the birth mother's living and medical expenses?
- How much do the home study and postsupervisory visits cost? An agency's adoption fees may sound reasonable, until you hear that the agency requires a social worker to visit your home eight times at a cost of $2,000, when your state requires only two visits. A reasonable fee would be well under $200 for each visit.
- What is the initial fee? Some agencies charge large up-front fees and then expect you to play an active role in finding your own birth mother. Retaining an agency the way you retain an attorney is fine. However, paying $10,000 or more to an agency and still having to find your own birth mother is too risky. If an agency asks you for more than $1,000 up front, ask whether that money is returned if it turns out you do not need the agency.

5. *What is the agency's home study process like?* If you have already had a home study completed, ask whether the agency accepts home studies conducted by other agencies.
6. *Does the agency provide you with a copy of the home study?*
7. *Does it release the home study to attorneys or other agencies upon request?* If so, ask whether there is a fee. A small fee is reasonable—$100 per copy is not.

These are the questions that are appropriate to ask at the beginning of your investigation. Once you get more serious about an agency that places infants, you can schedule an interview to ask more in-depth questions. For example:

1. *What roles do the agency and the birth mother play in selecting a couple?*
2. *Do you get to meet the birth mother during her pregnancy?*
3. *How does the agency feel about dealing with an attorney or another agency, if you find a birth mother in another state?* (If you find a birth mother on your own in another state, there may be no need to use the agency.)
4. *Does the agency discuss all of the woman's options with her?* You want a birth mother who is firm in her decision to place the baby for adoption. You want her to feel comfortable, not pressured to make a decision or to defend her choice.
5. *How does a social worker determine whether the birth mother is sincere?* This is especially important to ask if an agency identifies a birth mother for you and then asks you to pay her living expenses and counseling fees.
6. *If the agency senses that the birth mother is uncertain about her adoption plans, how does it respond?*

- Does it notify the adoptive parents of the apparent uncertainty?
- Is it made clear to a birth mother that to have a couple pay for her medical and other expenses when she has no real intention of placing the baby for adoption is fraud, and that she could be prosecuted?

7. *At what hours are agency personnel available?* If you are working directly with a birth mother, and the agency is involved, it is very important that you be able to reach someone at the agency during nonbusiness hours. What if the birth mother goes into labor earlier than expected? What if the hospital personnel are giving you problems about visiting the birth mother or baby? What if the birth mother wants to meet with you immediately, along with a counselor? Many agency personnel believe that phone calls after five P.M. are an intrusion and that few emergencies warrant this invasion. For the most part this is true. Be reasonable. But remember, you are paying for a service.

When investigating an agency that places special needs children, other questions and concerns arise. Begin by telling them what kind of child you are interested in adopting. If you are very specific, saying you want a one-to-two-year-old blind Asian girl, the agency staff person may offer to put you on the waiting list; however, the opportunity to adopt such a child may range between limited and nonexistent. If you are very specific about the kind of child that you want to adopt, you should apply to many agencies and work with the large adoption exchanges.

Here are some important questions to ask.

1. *How many and what kinds of legally free (or almost legally free) children are in the agency's caseload?*
2. *Does the agency place children only from its county (or other geographic region), or does it place children from other parts of the state?*
3. *What is the average wait for a child?* Is this from the time of the home study or from the time the application is completed?
4. *What kinds of pre- and postadoption services does the agency provide?*
5. *If the child is in foster care, would you be allowed to visit the child there once he or she was assigned to you?*
6. *What is the agency's policy toward adoption subsidies?* Are most of the children it places eligible for federal or state subsidies?
7. *If you decline a child that is offered, what is the agency's policy about future placements?*
8. *What if a situation does not work out; how is this handled?*

9. *What level of openness is expected with the birth family?* You will want to raise this question before committing to an agency. If the agency believes that birth families and adoptive families must maintain some level of openness no matter what the circumstances, then you will want to find out what they mean and whether they have any exceptions. Or you may find an agency that wants to bar all contact; this, again, is not an appropriate response.

INVESTIGATING AN AGENCY'S REPUTATION

Except with some international adoptions, agencies have legal custody of the child until the adoption is finalized and can use this as leverage with the adoptive parents before and after placement. Expenses are one area in which they can exert control—occasionally through deception. No matter how many questions you ask the agency staff directly, one of the best ways to find out about an agency's reputation is to ask others about the agency and how it handled their adoption. Joining a RESOLVE support group or an adoption group is one of the best ways to find out about an agency's reputation. Don't ask just the support group leadership. Ask couples who have worked with the agency what their experience was.

You can expect to hear from people who are somewhat disgruntled. Adoptive couples sometimes complain about costs even when they knew up front what the expenses were going to be. And couples who have sought to adopt a child with special needs may not have "heard" the agency staff tell them all the possible legal risks involved or the child's potential problems.

Chapter Three

Independent Adoption

Although independent adoption has been legal in most states for the last ten or twenty years, only recently has it begun receiving public attention. Over the past five years, stories on adoption have finally begun appearing prominently in newspapers and magazines like *Time* and *Forbes,* especially during November, national adoption month. *Immediate Family,* a film about independent adoption, generated much interest in how a couple finds a birth mother without waiting for years on an agency list, and the film *Losing Isaiah,* with Jessica Lange, explored the theme of an independent interracial adoption.

Many people have at least an idea about what independent adoption is, without quite understanding its legal and practical meaning. Some people think it is baby buying or black-market adoption. After watching some talk show segments on the topic, viewers across the nation become convinced that every other independent adoption fails, leaving a devastated couple in its wake. The reality is, if every talk-show host presented a success story a day, they would still not run out of happy placements to share.

In an independent adoption—also called a private, or self-directed, adoption—the birth parents and the adoptive couple find each other through advertising, through a personal referral—usually by a mutual friend or acquaintance—or through an adoption attorney. There is no agency involved.

Often the birth parents and the couple will meet to become acquainted and discuss the adoption. For birth parents or adoptive couples who do not wish to meet, communication can take place by telephone or letter, or it can be handled by a third party, provided this is legal in their state. From these contacts an understanding develops that the birth parents' child will be placed with the adoptive parents. The adoption statutes of various states refer to this kind of adoption as a nonagency adoption, to distinguish it from an agency or stepparent/family adoption.

The time frame is the most dramatic difference between an agency and a nonagency adoption. In an independent adoption you can start the adoption process immediately and have a newborn baby in your arms within several months. Things do not always go this smoothly, of course, and yet we know many couples who have adopted within three to six months after beginning their adoption endeavors. Whether it works this way for you will depend on certain factors outside your control. There are couples whose adoption search has taken much longer than months, and in some cases has been totally unsuccessful. But with independent adoption you are in charge of the process, and the effort you put forth will largely determine how much time it takes before you become a parent.

To get started, contact an adoption attorney to make sure you are on the right legal track. Do not worry that you will have to fill out mountains of forms; your attorney will take care of the paperwork. While you are waiting for an appointment with your attorney, read Chapter 4 of this book and begin to follow some of the steps it outlines for getting the word out. Write your broadcast letters. Assemble your portfolio. Install a second phone line. Your adoption adventure is underway!

THE INDEPENDENT ADOPTION PROCESS

The first thing to know is that independent adoption is illegal in some states. Laws regulating adoption vary considerably from state to state; therefore, you will need to find out what your rights are before proceeding.

Where independent adoption is legal, the basic steps are as follows. A couple hires an attorney. This attorney will act as an unpaid intermediary; that is, she will charge fees for legal representation but not for serving as an intermediary. The couple may give her a portfolio containing photographs of themselves, a letter, and other material that gives a picture of their lives, which their attorney can then show to birth mothers.

At this point a couple will often have a second telephone line installed in their home to take phone calls from prospective birth parents. They may begin advertising in newspapers and networking with friends and family to try to meet a prospective birth mother.

If they have not already done so, they may arrange for a home study at this time. Every state requires that adoptive parents undergo a home study to determine their parental fitness. In most states the task is delegated to licensed adoption agencies and independent social workers, who then submit the home study to the court. To initiate this process, contact an agency or social worker.

In nearly all states the home study is conducted before the child is placed in your home; in a few states, you can wait until afterward. If you live in a state in which a home study is required beforehand, you should probably have it done when you first start to seek a birth mother. If you network or advertise out of state for a birth mother, then you should begin the home study process, regardless of whether your state requires a home study prior to placement. Any interstate placements are governed by the Interstate Compact Act, which requires a home study prior to placement in any state.

The next thing that is likely to happen is that a pregnant woman (or a parent with a child) will call in response to your advertisement or letter to discuss her intentions to place her child for adoption. If you and she are comfortable about meeting, you discuss this possibility. If one of you is not comfortable with meeting face to face, you will talk about keeping in touch by telephone, letter, or through your attorney, who will most likely meet with the birth mother.

Next, the birth mother or birth parents meet with you at a restaurant or other public place or at your attorney's office. If both of you are comfortable with each other, you and she will probably make a verbal commitment to each other. If you do not meet, this commitment will take place by telephone.

Depending on the circumstances, you and the birth parents will decide whether the adoption is to be an independent or an identified agency adoption. An identified agency adoption is one in which an independent adoption is converted into an agency adoption. The agency may provide counseling for the birth parents, in addition—at least in some states—to obtaining surrenders of parental rights in a shorter time frame than with an independent adoption. Because an identified adoption is considered an agency adoption, the laws that govern agency adoptions apply. Your attorney can help you sort out the pros and cons of either choice.

Be careful not to discuss the possibility of agency involvement with the birth parents until you have built a relationship with them. Many birth mothers do not want a third party, such as an agency social worker, asking them a lot of questions.

If you and the birth parents agree to an identified agency adoption, contact an agency that provides such services. The one you choose will probably conduct your home study too, if you have not already done one.

Again, discuss your choice of agencies with your attorney. It is vital that the agency staff work well with birth parents. Birth parents know that they have choices; the newspapers are full of adoption advertisements. If you have not built a solid rapport with the birth parents, and the agency staff are condescending or lacking in sensitivity, the birth parents may well go elsewhere.

If you do not get an agency involved, then you or your attorney should discuss with the birth parents the advantages of counseling. The benefits are twofold: (1) Some states require birth parents to have counseling or at least to be offered counseling; and (2) more important, counseling may assist the birth parents in understanding adoption issues and their feelings about them.

Also, your attorney should discuss with the birth parents the opportunity to be represented by their own attorney. In some states, such as New York, a birth parent must be represented by an attorney who is not representing the adoptive couple.

Now you or the birth mother will contact an obstetrician or clinic and the hospital where the baby is to be delivered, if this has not been taken care of already. Finding a physician who is open to adoption is very important. It is also important, if possible, that your attorney become involved in choosing the hospital, as some are actually hostile toward adoption; he will contact the hospital's social services department to determine its policy on adoption.

Next, depending on where you live, the birth parents will give up their parental rights by signing legal documents referred to as "surrender of parental rights." This is different from a consent-to-adoption document, which is not a surrender of rights but simply indicates the birth parents' approval of you as adoptive parents. Confusingly, some agencies and attorneys refer to the termination document as a consent form, so you must ask what purpose the consent document serves in your state. Depending upon state laws, the documents may be signed either before the baby's birth or in the hospital after birth. Each state has different laws as to when birth parents' rights can be terminated, how long birth parents have to change their minds and revoke their surrenders, and whether the birth parents must also appear in court to have their rights terminated officially (even after signing the surrender documents). Check with your attorney, since these laws can change.

Now the baby is born. Your attorney may visit the birth mother in the hospital so that she can sign legal forms. Before the birth you should find out what documents are needed by your insurance company to ensure immediate coverage for the baby.

You and possibly your attorney go to the hospital, where the baby is given to you. Often a birth mother will discharge herself before the baby goes home. In this case she must sign documents allowing the baby to be placed directly with you. Many hospitals, however, require the birth mother or her relative to place the baby in your arms. If the birth mother does not wish to see the baby, and the hospital requires her to be there at the baby's discharge, then your attorney can arrange legally for her to avoid this situation by filing legal documents in the county court.

Your attorney next files the adoption petition, or what is sometimes called an adoption complaint, with the court. Some time later, depending upon the state's regulations, you go to family court to gain parental rights to the child (an adoption hearing). Unless the parental rights of the birth parents have already been terminated, they must be provided notice of this hearing, but they are not usually required to attend unless they have changed their minds about the adoption.

If you reside in one state and the baby is born another, then your attorney must also complete Interstate Compact forms and file them in both the "sending state" (the state that the child was born in) and in the "receiving state" (the state where you reside). There are specific forms that the birth mother and the adoptive parents must sign for interstate purposes.

As a final step, your attorney accompanies you to court and presents your testimony, including how you came in contact with the birth parents, what monies you have paid, and why you wish to adopt the baby. The adoption agency or social worker (independent investigator) that conducted your home study will have provided your home study to the court, including a favorable recommendation as to your fitness as parents. The judge hearing the adoption will generally review the home study to ensure that the agency has recommended you as adoptive parents.

Each of these steps will be discussed in detail in the chapters that follow, so if you have any questions, just read on.

WHY PURSUE AN INDEPENDENT ADOPTION?

Adoption can be a wonderful experience for the birth parents who are placing the baby in a loving home, for the baby who is going there, and, of course, for the couple who has longed for the baby. With an independent adoption, the experience can be especially positive. Both sets of parents can feel more in control, because they are the decision makers. They meet and decide together what is best for the baby. A birth mother feels very secure in knowing and approving of the adoptive parents. The decision about the couple is made by her alone, not by an agency. Although she will still feel sad about placing her child for adoption, she will have seen firsthand that the child will be reared by a mother and father she has chosen and who can provide love and stability, an impression she will carry forever.

Indeed, independent adoption is usually a birth mother's first choice. Twice as many birth mothers choose independent adoption as agency adoption. Birth mothers choose this approach because they want to be in control. They do not want agency personnel questioning their motives for choosing adoption or explaining their "options" to them. Often they have already made an adoption decision and are ready to go ahead. They want to choose the adoptive parents themselves. In fact, the level of control a birth mother has is often what determines whether she will place the infant for adoption.

Most birth mothers select adoption because they are young, are in school, know they can provide little for themselves and the child at this point in their lives, and want a better future for everyone. They're not after a better career for themselves or a swimming pool and trips to Disney World for their child. They want the child to have a stable, loving home life. A 19-year-old woman with few resources in her second year of college cannot provide a home for a child if she must work full-time in a minimum-wage job. Most birth mothers care enough to make a decision that is best for themselves and the baby. A birth mother chooses adoption because of her love for her child.

Many adoptive couples start out believing a certain stereotype of the birth mother: that she is ignorant, unfeeling, on welfare, and basically a "low life." The reality is, the average birth mother is "the girl next door who got pregnant." No one kind of person is more likely than another to be a birth mother. Almost all, however, want what is best for their child, and direct involvement in the decision-making.

Empirical data on private adoption are difficult to find, partly because states are not required to keep track of how many adoptions take place, and so many do not. But based on the data from the National Council for Adoption, it would appear that at least two-thirds of the infant adoptions finalized in the United States each year are independent adoptions. Some believe the figure is closer to 80 percent.

In any case, in the majority of situations that we have known, couples who pursue independent adoption have a baby in about one year or less. The process takes commitment, but once a couple commits, they become parents. If you work diligently, very likely you will have a baby in your home sooner than you thought possible. The advantage of private adoption is that it works, and it can work quickly.

Here are some other advantages to think about:

- *The infant is placed directly with the adoptive couple.* In traditional agency adoptions, an infant will often be placed in a foster home for a period of time, weeks or even months. Many birth mothers strongly oppose this arrangement. An independent adoption satisfies the birth mother's concern for her child's welfare and allows an adoptive couple to experience the first days of infancy with their child.
- *The adoptive parents may share in the pregnancy experience and in the baby's delivery.* If a birth mother lives nearby, the adoptive mother may take her to doctor appointments and may even act as her coach during labor and delivery. A birth mother may want the adoptive parents to be a part of

her life. This can often help her to see past her own difficult circumstances and focus instead on the benefits of her unplanned pregnancy.

- *An adoption agency is not in control.* Independent adoption increases the likelihood that a pregnant woman will choose adoption. Between 50 and 80 percent of pregnant women using an agency do *not* release the baby for adoption, whereas 75 to 90 percent of pregnant women using private channels do. A very active agency in Arizona (now out of business) arranged for the adoptive parents and the birth parents to meet when the birth mother was eight months pregnant. This meeting reduced the risk that a couple would meet a birth mother who would change her mind. Even then 50 percent of the birth mothers changed their minds.

  In states that do not permit independent adoption, the number of adoptions per capita is usually lower. In 1960, when Connecticut outlawed independent adoption, the number of adoptions taking place dropped by half.

- *Independent adoption is less expensive.* In an article in *Forbes* magazine entitled "How Much Is That Baby in the Window?" an independent adoption is stated to cost about $50,000, while Cynthia Martin, a California psychologist and adoption expert, is quoted as saying that adoptions for healthy Caucasian infants cost about $20,000. Our experience is that few adoptions in which the couple find the birth mother cost anywhere close to $20,000. *The total expenses for an independent adoption, including medical expenses, attorney fees, and some living expenses, need not be more than $10,000.* In an article in *Smart Money* (April 1993), a couple quotes their total expenses for private adoption at $6,000. (The magazine mistakenly said that $6,000 was the attorney's fee. These fees were actually $3,200.)

  The administrative and personnel costs involved in a single agency adoption can range from $10,000 to $15,000, and that may not cover the birth mother's medical, living, counseling, legal, and transportation expenses. Even adoption attorneys who handle the process from beginning to end do not usually charge this much. In certain sections of the country, such as New York City, the fees and expenses associated with a private adoption can easily total more than $20,000.

  Some agencies have the adoptive parents pay a birth mother's expenses indirectly as part of the agency's fees, in which case the fee will range from $20,000 to $30,000. In an independent adoption, it is often possible to find a birth mother who has her own medical insurance or who qualifies for Medicaid coverage and so does not need medical expenses. In such cases the adoptive couple pay only for the medical expenses of the baby and any counseling requested by the birth parents, in addition to necessary living expenses. In many adoptions the couple's medical insurance will cover the baby's hospital costs.

INDEPENDENT ADOPTION: SOME DISADVANTAGES

Not every couple has a positive experience with independent adoption. Sometimes the problem is the attorney. Although most adoption attorneys are straightforward and reasonable in their fees and practices, there are some dishonest ones around. Some will charge for expenses never incurred by the birth mother and engage in other illegal practices. In other cases, the attorney is honest but does not assist his client with sufficient one-on-one attention; he does not get directly involved with the birth mother or hospital or agency (if one is needed). Basically, the couple is on their own. Needless to say, this gives independent adoption a bad name.

For other couples the personal involvement in an independent adoption is simply too difficult. Putting in a phone line and waiting for "that call" is too intense an experience, while actually talking to or meeting with a birth mother is more than some couples can take on emotionally. This may be especially true for a couple who has been through the wringer of infertility treatment or experienced multiple miscarriages.

One other potential difficulty with independent adoption is that birth parents who could really use some counseling may not get it. Even in an independent adoption a birth mother has every right to receive counseling. Of course, most adoptive parents will pay for a woman's counseling expenses if she requests it. She does not have to go to an adoption agency to receive counseling. Call your local adoption support groups for the names of therapists, counselors, or social workers specializing in adoption.

An attorney is not, of course, an adoption counselor. Nevertheless, a compassionate attorney should be able to discuss with a birth mother her reasons for placing the baby for adoption. This will give him a sense of whether the woman is sincere or whether she is being coerced by someone or is emotionally confused. A sensitive attorney can also determine how well she is coping with her adoption plans. These discussions help a woman verbalize her feelings, helping her further solidify her reasons for making adoption plans. Again, an attorney should never be a substitute for competent counseling. Your attorney must make sure a birth mother has access to counseling. Any attorney involved with adoption has a list of capable therapists.

Note: In nearly every state you are permitted to pay for counseling fees, but double-check to be sure it is legal before you do so.

IS AN INDEPENDENT ADOPTION FOR YOU?

Agency adoptions are not suited to everyone, any more than independent adoptions are. Many people assume that couples who pursue independent adoption do so because they've been rejected by the agencies, perhaps because of their age or personality. This is unfounded. People who have difficult personalities or overwhelming problems are usually no better candidates for independent adoption then they are for an agency adoption. After all, in most states, in either independent or agency adoption, adoptive parents must undergo a home study conducted by a licensed adoption agency or certified social worker to determine their suitability as parents.

Some people, it is true, do pursue independent adoption because an agency will not accept them, especially when age is an issue. Others, however, never decide whether independent or agency adoption is right for them. They just happen to learn of a pregnant woman, sometimes through a mutual acquaintance, and the parties come to an agreement. In such cases they may have no contact with an agency, except perhaps during the home study.

Following is a list of some of the tasks and stresses associated with independent adoption. Discuss with your spouse how each makes you feel. If you feel negatively about one aspect of independent adoption, do you believe that you can overcome these feelings?

1. *Placing an advertisement telling of your desire to adopt in various newspapers and responding to calls the ad generates.* (Note: Not all states that allow independent adoptions allow such advertisements.)
2. *Having a special "baby telephone line" placed in your home and waiting for it to ring.*
3. *Receiving prank phone calls.*
4. *Speaking articulately and compassionately with a woman who calls in answer to an advertisement or letter.*
5. *Meeting with a birth mother.* Most couples who pursue adoption do meet with the birth mother to share some information. In some states, such as Virginia, identifying information (complete names and addresses) must also be shared between the adoptive and birth parents.

    At first many couples are afraid of that initial meeting. Yet no adoptive couple we have ever known was sorry they met with their child's birth mother. Most likely you will be glad you did, not only before the baby is born but long after.
6. *When you meet the birth mother, presenting yourselves as "normal" people.* Many kinds of people meet with birth mothers and complete the adoption.

However, there are special considerations to be aware of and adjustments that may have to be made if:

- *The prospective adoptive parent has an obvious disability.* We know of one wonderful man who lost his legs in military service. Despite his disability, he and his wife had no problem getting a birth mother to select them. In fact, they now have a beautiful baby boy. If you have an obvious disability, tell the birth mother before you meet her, but do not mention it immediately in your first conversation.

- *The husband has long hair and earrings and dresses for shock value.* Some birth mothers are looking for the home with the "white picket fence." On the other hand, if the husband has long hair because he is, for example, a musician, and in your newspaper ad you state, "professional jazz musician" or "nature lover," a birth mother probably will not expect a couple dressed like June and Ward Cleaver. In fact, many birth mothers would find long hair and an earring appealing and would be delighted by a "funky couple." In general, however, a man with shorter hair and no earring has a better chance of appealing to a birth mother—even a birth mother who likes to dress in the latest fad.

- *The husband or wife is obese.* Unless the birth mother is a real fitness or sports buff, she will probably not care if one of you is overweight. Yet we must all acknowledge that people do discriminate against overweight individuals, and a birth mother could be turned off if you are extremely overweight. If this is your situation, you may want the birth mother to know your positive attributes before she meets you in person. And before you do meet, you may want to mention that you are working hard to lose weight.

  We know of women and men who were overweight, however, who have adopted without their weight ever being an issue. In two of the cases the birth mothers themselves were overweight. Moreover, being overweight appears to be less important if one spouse is of average weight. In short, do not wait until you lose the weight to pursue an adoption.

7. *Meeting with a birth mother and making arrangements with her, knowing that she may change her mind.*

8. *Taking a limited financial risk with a birth mother, such as paying some of her medical expenses and/or living expenses.*

9. *Becoming emotionally involved with one or both birth parents.*

10. *Pursuing an adoption in which the baby may be born with medical problems; if it is, deciding whether you can go through with the adoption.*
11. *"Working" with more than one birth mother at a time.* Making arrangements with two or more birth mothers, knowing that you want only one baby, can be very emotionally taxing.

INDEPENDENT ADOPTION: ONE COUPLE'S STORY

My husband, Richard, and I were happy with the differences in our ages and our religious and ethnic backgrounds. We had been married for four years. I had been married before, and that marriage had ended in divorce. My marriage to Richard signaled a new beginning, a chance to have a family, even though I was now older than I would have preferred to be as a prospective mother.

Sadly, nature and the state of technology at the time of my experience were defeated by my "advanced" age. I was in my early forties. A biological child seemed an impossibility, and we were unsure about taking the step toward adoption. Even if we decided to adopt, agencies might turn us away for having an unconventional profile.

Richard felt that I needed to be absolutely sure about the decision to adopt, since he would undoubtedly be content without children. This placed the responsibility for making the "right" decision on me, and I lingered for months with the possibilities, the fears, and the longing, while becoming more and more discouraged by the imagined failure ahead.

At last, after reading an article in their newsletter about independent adoption, I called RESOLVE of central New Jersey and spoke to a woman who was planning an independent adoption information session. She spoke at length about her own experience, which seemed miraculous.

Feeling a burst of hope in spite of my misgivings, I announced tearfully to her, "We're thinking about adoption, but I'm afraid we won't qualify because I'm too old, we're of different religions, and I've been divorced."

"It only matters to the birth parents," the woman said. "If they like you and want you to be their child's parents, then you won't have any other significant barrier." My uncertainty disappeared with this new information. "I'm now sure that we should try to adopt a child," I told Richard that evening. "I don't look forward to the next twenty years without a child."

"Are you really sure?"

"Yes!"

Within two weeks my friend phoned me with the news that someone knew a pregnant woman who wanted to place her baby with a nice couple.

This was too much good fortune to be believed. Yet later in the week, the young woman, Linda, called and confirmed that she hoped to find a nice couple for her baby, since it was too late in the pregnancy to have an abortion.

She was nineteen. She had had another child whom she relinquished to her in-laws when she and her husband divorced. Because of her pregnancy they had had a "shotgun" wedding when they were sixteen. Things had gone from bad to worse, and she did not want to repeat her mistake this time with another man.

Richard and I met Linda in person. We reviewed her health history with the aid of a questionnaire supplied by our attorney. Linda and I went to the obstetrician together. We also went to a social service agency in case Linda wanted counseling, financial support, or Medicaid.

Linda called frequently. She used me as her lifeline, she said, and she was very appreciative of my time and the monies spent on her medical care. I felt that I had developed enough of a relationship with Linda that I would be alert to a difficulty or a change of heart. When she told me that she had located the address of her boyfriend's parents in New York, an alarm went off.

Would Linda actually make contact with them or with her boyfriend with the idea of reuniting and keeping the baby, perhaps even using the pregnancy as leverage (again)? While such a plan seemed foolhardy, it was entirely possible, given Linda's past experience.

Was she feeling reluctant to part with this potential bundle of love, silky skin, and gurgles that was growing inside her? Did she wish that her boyfriend would see the error of his ways and love her again?

Sure enough, with just two weeks remaining, Linda phoned to say, simply, "I've decided not to give you the baby, so I won't be talking to you again." Good-bye, little love. Good-bye, hope. Good-bye to the settled situation.

Richard cried with grief, surprising me with the intensity of his feelings, since I had been the one to initiate the adoption and carry on the relationship with Linda. He said that somehow his stake in adoption had crept up on him, with its promise that he would soon be a daddy, that we would experience the joy that a new baby brings, that this long wait would finally end. He had been unprepared emotionally to feel much one way or another. Now he could see that this unexpected disappointment could happen again and again, even if we found another birth mother.

With renewed determination, I proposed contacting the attorney about this change in plans and about placing ads in the newspaper. Using suggestions from the attorney and from people at a RESOLVE meeting, I phoned in the first of several advertisements to run in New Jersey newspapers, while Richard made arrangements to install another phone line in our home.

The ad read "Everything is ready for a baby." I didn't see any other ads like that. Maybe it would catch someone's eye.

The ad appeared the following weekend. Nothing happened. I used call forwarding during the days that I went to work. My new friend from RESOLVE, Karen, who had recently adopted, had agreed to take calls during those times. She had a vibrant phone personality and was deeply sensitive and caring. She was so kind to do this for us. However, no calls came.

Three days later, when I arrived home, I phoned Karen just to check in.

"You just got a call!" Karen said. "You better call back fast before she calls someone else!"

"Hello. This is Ellen," I said. "I understand you just called about our ad in the paper. . . . Yes, we are ready to adopt a baby immediately. How wonderful! A baby girl!"

Richard and I brought home our little girl within a week. She was born the weekend our ad ran, and her birth mother, Sandy, still had the newspaper.

Sandy had made earlier adoption plans with an agency but changed her mind because of a negative experience with a social worker. Ultimately she had resolved her problem by requesting information about independent adoption. Her requirements were to have the adoptive parents pay for medical expenses, since she did not want to involve an agency of any kind, and to have the adoptive parents— us—take the baby home right away without resorting to foster care, despite the sixty to ninety days that would elapse before she could surrender her parental rights under New Jersey law.

Sandy was delighted that we resided in a certain county in New Jersey because she knew it from her childhood experiences with her family. She was going back to college and wanted no further contact. She preferred not to meet with us prior to our taking custody of the baby because she wanted to protect herself from additional involvement.

Her mother and sister wanted to speak to me on the phone. It felt like the embrace of a family.

"What a great family our daughter comes from," I said to Richard later. The miracle of adoption had happened to us too, just nine months from the start of our quest. Would it last? It did.

It was a beautiful resolution for all concerned. In fact, Richard and I are sure that the reason it took nine months was that we had to wait for our daughter to be born!

Chapter Four

Choosing an Adoption Attorney

I f you decide you want to adopt through private channels, one of the first steps is to contact an adoption attorney. Your attorney is by far the most important professional in the adoption process. He or she will guide you through your state's adoption laws and provide you with practical tips. Your attorney is also someone the birth mother can contact to discuss legal and financial matters.

Many people have a trusted attorney who has completed their wills, conducted the closings on their homes, and provided legal advice on other matters. He may be likable and competent in the areas of wills, real estate closings, and general law; he may even have assisted others with one or two agency adoptions in the past. However, this is not necessarily the same attorney you want to guide you through a private adoption. Not only must an adoption attorney be very knowledgeable about your state's adoption laws and the nuances of Interstate Compact requirements, he must also have a comfortable manner with clients and people in general. This is especially important because the attorney will be talking (and often meeting) with birth parents, social workers, and sometimes the parents of birth parents. It is better to find a good adoption specialist.

Perhaps you've had the experience of engaging a professional (a doctor, a dentist, an infertility specialist, a CPA) who was extremely competent but not very personable. You may have overlooked any boorish or rude behavior because she was a "good doctor" or an "excellent endocrinologist." The adoption attorney *must* be someone you like and feel genuinely comfortable with. If you like him, the birth parents will probably also like him and feel comfortable with him. This cannot be emphasized strongly enough. Adoption plans have ended because an attorney was condescending or rude to a birth mother. A birth mother wants to be treated with respect and sensitivity and will look for another couple if your attorney is lacking in these areas.

If you have friends or acquaintances who have hired adoption attorneys, ask for a recommendation. RESOLVE or an adoption support group is an even more likely source. If you are not involved with your local RESOLVE chapter, call the national number at (617) 643-2424 or write to 1310 Broadway, Somerville, MA 02144. Staff members can give you the names of attorneys listed in the American Academy of Adoption Attorneys, as well as the address and phone number of the RESOLVE chapter nearest you.

SERVICES AND FEES

In states where this is legal, an attorney can serve as an intermediary, matching a prospective adoptive couple with a birth mother. In California, for example, which permits attorneys to bring birth mothers and couples together, birth mothers as well as adoptive parents often hire attorneys as intermediaries. Not surprisingly, California has one of the highest numbers of infant adoptions each year compared with other states, most through private placement.

Attorneys who work as adoption intermediaries often advertise in the yellow pages under "Adoption," using ads explicitly directed at birth mothers. Some advertise in states where intermediaries are permitted, even if their practice is not in that state. It is not unusual to find a California attorney placing an ad in a Louisiana newspaper.

An independent adoption always begins with finding a birth mother. In some states this task may be carried out by an adoption attorney for an additional fee, but many other states forbid the practice, regarded as too much like "baby selling." Find out what the rules are in your state and make sure your attorney's fees are in accordance with them. Of course, even assuming that they are, you will do well to remain cautious—especially of an attorney who claims he has located a birth mother and then immediately asks for monies related to the woman's needs, such as traveling, hotel rooms, rent, food, medical fees, and counseling. Remember, *at this point your emotions and your checkbook may not balance.* At the very least, obtain documentation for all expenses before paying for anything. Not only is it unethical for an attorney to ask you to pay for a woman's gynecological visits without proof of a bill, it is also illegal. Once you have disbursed substantial expenses and lawyer's fees "up front," you may feel compelled to continue sending more money; otherwise, you will have forfeited your initial investment. Find out your attorney's total fees before committing, including the expenses you will be reimbursed if no birth mother selects you within a reasonable period of time—usually eighteen months.

THE ATTORNEY AS INTERMEDIARY

How does an attorney arrange for birth mothers and adoptive parents to select one other? An ethical attorney usually uses the same system employed by many adoption agencies, allowing a birth mother to select adoptive parents from an assortment of portfolios. A portfolio is a three-ring binder containing biographical information, pictures, a letter to the birth mother, and sometimes your home study (without last names or other identifying information). For advice about putting together a portfolio, turn to the end of this chapter.

Once the birth mother has decided upon the couple or couples she may be interested in, the attorney may suggest that she meet them. If she prefers not to meet with anyone, the attorney will simply contact the couple himself and describe the birth parents to them.

Sometimes a birth mother will want to meet more than one couple before she makes up her mind. Of course, only one couple will ultimately be selected, which can lead to disappointment.

Some attorneys are unethical. Be cautious of the following scenarios:

- *An attorney places several prospective adoptive couples in one room at the same time and then allows a birth mother to pick one.*

- *You are at an introductory session with other prospective parents to find out about an attorney's services, and the attorney suddenly states, "A birth mother has just called, and someone will soon receive the infant."* This actually happened to a friend of ours!

- *The attorney claims that a birth mother is interested in you, then asks you for money for her expenses.* Although this is not necessarily a sign of trouble, the couple may find themselves paying money for weeks before their attorney tells them that the birth mother has "changed her mind." The attorney gives no explanation about your money. You just lost a few thousand dollars. Unfortunately, this experience is not uncommon.

  During the year after one couple first retained an attorney, for example, he "found" them two birth mothers. The first time he immediately asked the couple to send money for expenses. They sent $3,000. A few weeks later the couple received a call from the attorney's office telling them that they would not have wanted this birth mother because she was using drugs. (The couple never met the birth mother.)

  A few months later the couple received another phone call from their attorney about a second birth mother. Of course they were expected to send more money, which they did. By this time, with the attorney's expenses continually rising, they were borrowing money from relatives. (Once someone spends $6,000, it is hard to say, "I do not want to go through with this adoption.") A few weeks later they were once again told, "The birth mother changed her mind." The couple is not even sure whether these birth mothers ever existed. They had only one "documented" adoption expense from their attorney—furniture for the birth mother. (Incidentally, it is usually considered illegal to pay this kind of expense.)

If anything like this should happen to you, call the State Bar Association or State Supreme Court immediately and file an ethics complaint against the attorney. Then call the attorney and demand your money back—*all* of it.

One final note of caution: When an attorney is acting as an intermediary to link you up with a birth mother, the usual wait for a placement is a year to a year and a half. If the attorney says, "I can guarantee you a baby within three months," be very careful. It is nearly impossible for an attorney to do this. Remember, price does not guarantee success.

YOUR ATTORNEY'S ROLE IN A DOMESTIC OR INTERNATIONAL AGENCY ADOPTION

In an agency adoption, the attorney's role is more limited than in an independent adoption, but not less important. Normally, the attorney will not interact with the birth parents or assist you when the baby is placed in your arms at the hospital. However, your attorney is a resource person and must be aware of state laws regarding agency policy and procedure. Your attorney should review all documents that the agency has you sign, including the application, placement agreement, and especially the surrender documents, to ensure that they comply with state law. For example, you want your attorney to make sure all paperwork is filed with the local court in states where parental rights are revocable until filed. This is particularly important if you are dealing with an out-of-state agency. Also, the attorney will assist the agency in complying with Interstate Compact requirements. In addition, an attorney can often get through the bureaucracy and confirm that all necessary paperwork is filed.

Remember, an agency is usually representing the birth mother and child; you need an attorney to represent you. Therefore, share with your attorney your interactions with the birth mother and agency social worker. The attorney's goal is to determine if the agency is doing its job. For example, one agency never asked the birth mother's mom how she felt about the adoption—a critical question, especially if the unborn child will be the first grandchild.

Your attorney's role in an international adoption is usually limited and may be unnecessary when working with very large agencies such as Holt International—an agency with years of experience and an excellent reputation. However, if you are dealing with a small agency or with an intermediary, your attorney can ensure that the foreign translation of the Judgment of Adoption or the termination of parental rights documents contain the correct legal language to satisfy your local court. Also, your attorney can help you complete the various international documents and put you in touch with the right person.

In any adoption—domestic or international—your attorney can also guide you so that you pay only expenses that are permitted by law.

PUTTING TOGETHER A PORTFOLIO: A QUICK OVERVIEW

As discussed, an attorney and many agencies will ask you to provide a portfolio so that birth mothers can "see" you and possibly select you. A portfolio is a picture story of your life as a couple or as a family with children. It is like a scrapbook or picture album containing pictures of you, any children, close relatives and friends, pets, your home, important occasions, and favorite activities. Its purpose is to tell your "story" to a birth mother.

Even if you plan to do your own advertising and are not expecting your attorney to find a baby for you, a portfolio can be a useful thing to have. It can be shared with your birth mother at any point to give her an idea of who you are and what your lives are like.

One couple met a birth mother just after she gave birth. When they went to the hospital to meet her, they were able to present their lives very succinctly by showing her their portfolio. Once the baby is placed with you, a birth mother may want to keep the portfolio as a keepsake.

Portfolios are *not* beauty contests. They are not designed so that a birth mother can select the family with the largest home, nicest furnishings, or prettiest smiles. They are meant to provide a picture description of you as a couple and family. If your home is very large or elegant, try to minimize this. It may only intimidate a birth mother.

Designing Your Portfolio

Choose an album book in which pages can be rearranged and added. Avoid bulky, fabric-stuffed books, which are difficult to store and mail. We recommend using low-acid paper for the original to ensure that it will last a lifetime—or several lifetimes. Someday it will be a precious keepsake for your family.

Once you have your album, you may wish to select a theme, usually one related to childhood. For example, the cover may have motifs of Beatrix Potter,

Disney, Winnie the Pooh, or other storybook characters, or baby animals such as bunnies, ducks, or teddy bears. These motifs may then be sparingly placed throughout the rest of the album. Avoid motifs involving babies—booties, diaper pins, pacifiers, etc. These are *not* appropriate.

The next step is to place pictures of yourselves, special people in your lives, and important life events in chronological or thematic order. You might include pictures of your wedding; holidays with family and friends; vacations, outings, and picnics; your home; and favorite activities or hobbies, such as your art collection, crafts, woodworking productions, or activities like horseback riding, skiing, and gardening.

Select photographs that are homey and provide a feeling of comfort, warmth, and responsibility. Do not include pictures of the two of you in your bathing suits or in skimpy outfits, or pictures that show alcoholic beverages. If your favorite cousin looks as if he belongs to a motorcycle gang, you may want to leave him out. Not all birth mothers and fathers care about issues like smoking, drinking, or style of dress, but even if they do not, the birth mother's parents might see the portfolio and influence the birth mother to select a more "wholesome" couple. Play it safe. No one is *not* going to select you because you weren't pictured drinking alcohol, but they may exclude you if you were.

Place no more than six to ten pictures on a page. This may sound like a lot of pictures, but if you trim them, you can fit about eight comfortably. Using heart-shaped, round, and oval cookie-cutters as stencils makes for nicely trimmed pictures.

Write captions for each picture or set of pictures. It is better to write or print, if your handwriting is legible; otherwise, type your labels and attach them to the pages. When referring to yourselves, use your first names. Personalize the information as much as possible while still maintaining your anonymity. Be creative but not too cutesy.

Include no more than twenty pages of pictures in the book—ten pages front and back.

The next item to prepare is a "Dear Birth Mother" letter. This letter describes your feelings toward the birth mother who is reading the letter and also how you feel about the decision she is making. It says something about the two of you and why you want to adopt. The letter goes on the first page of the portfolio. A sample birth mother letter can be found on page 59.

These are the essential features of the portfolio. Many couples also include a copy of their home study. Home studies usually highlight people's positive characteristics. If yours is like this, place what is called a "sanitized" home study (with all identifying information taken out) in the back of your portfolio. Accompanying your home study are letters of reference; these add a nice touch to your portfolio as well.

If you do not include a home study, an alternative is to write a one-page "resume," or biographical sketch, that highlights your life and some of your positive assets, such as your stability, love, financial security, home, family, hobbies, and favorite activities. In fact, even if you do include a home study, a birth mother may be more likely to read a one-page outline of your life than a multipage home study. Place the biographical sketch in the front of the portfolio, after the "Dear Birth Mother" letter.

Now your portfolio is finished. But can you be sure it looks right? Have a few trusted friends look it over and give their feedback. If you can, send a copy to your agency or attorney's office for suggestions.

When you are satisfied with your finished portfolio, take it to a shop that does color copying and have two copies made. Keep at least one copy at home and send one or more to your attorney. Remember, if you or your attorney identifies a potential birth mother and a portfolio is mailed to her, you may never get that portfolio back again. Keep the original at home. Once you adopt a child, the portfolio makes a lovely beginning to a baby book! That's one reason why doing a portfolio is never a waste of time. You can always use the original to tell your child the story of how you adopted him.

Some people like to include a video with their portfolio. If this appeals to you, the guidelines are fairly simple. Share the kind of information you included in your birth mother letter and biographical sketch. In other words, talk a little about yourselves and her. You may also want to include a special occasion that captures you at your best. Keep the video short—about five to ten minutes.

Chapter Five

Finding a Birth Mother

Now that you have decided to adopt, should you share your desire to find a baby with people you know? Telling others about your decision essentially means publicizing your infertility, and that makes many people uncomfortable. Try telling a few people in your "safe zone" first—people whom you trust, like close friends or relatives. Later you may feel ready to share your plans with coworkers or acquaintances.

If you are truly serious about adoption, however, it is best to tell nearly everyone. The more people you inform, the more you will increase your chances of finding a birth mother. As you explain your situation, never sound desperate. Let people know that you and your spouse have chosen to go on to this next step in your lives, emphasizing your interest in adoption in a casual, matter-of-fact tone. Most couples are rewarded with sincere empathy.

Sharing your desire for children often opens the doors of people's hearts, leading them to go out of their way to pass on the word about your adoption plans. Do, however, be prepared for a few negative reactions. Some people will respond with surprising ignorance. Fortunately, this group is likely to be in the minority.

Your job is to throw the "pebble"—the news that you want to adopt—into your "pond" of friends and acquaintances, and wait for the ripple effect to take place. Your friends and acquaintances will tell their friends and acquaintances—often people you do not even know—who will tell their friends and acquaintances, resulting in your contact with a birth mother. Perhaps you have had this experience when searching for a job. If you tell 25 people that you are interested in adoption, and they each tell another 25, you will have "told" 625 people. This "ripple effect" does work.

NETWORKING

Establish a network for spreading the word about your decision to adopt. Remember, though, that a contact from a birth mother usually comes from the most unexpected sources, not necessarily from your "planned" efforts.

Here are some good places to start your networking campaign.

People in Adoption or Infertility Support Groups or Organizations

Infertility and adoption support groups can provide a strong network of people who are also pursuing adoption. At first you may be tempted to view these couples as your competition. Sometimes, though, they may have contact with more than one birth mother and will be able to refer one to you. We know of a couple who had contact with three birth mothers. After adopting two of the babies themselves, they referred the third birth mother to another couple, who adopted a beautiful baby boy.

In another situation a woman named Michelle casually mentioned at a RESOLVE board meeting that she would like to adopt an older baby. A few days later, an adoptive mother named Betty, who had also attended the meeting, received a phone call from a birth mother who had an eighteen-month-old baby. Betty told the birth mother that although she was not interested, she knew of someone else who might be. Two days later the birth mother contacted Michelle and her husband. Ten days later Michelle and her husband brought home a baby girl.

Another benefit of knowing other prospective adoptive couples is being able to make referrals to them. If you are not interested in adopting a particular baby, it is comforting to be able to give the birth mother another couple's name. Betty, for example, did not have to just say no to the birth mother. She successfully referred her to another couple.

Friends and Relatives

Telling friends and relatives, especially those far away, that you want to adopt can extend your likelihood of locating a birth mother by tapping resources that you would otherwise not have been able to reach. One couple's friend was at her obstetrician's office for a routine visit when she struck up a conversation with a pregnant woman. The woman was experiencing a crisis pregnancy and intended to place the child with an adoption agency. The friend referred the birth mother to the couple, who successfully adopted her baby.

In another example, a couple's friend's cousin knew a nurse who knew a birth mother. The nurse referred the birth mother to the cousin's friends—the adoptive couple. The adoption was a success. Yes, it sounds confusing, but this is how you make contact with birth mothers. The moral of a complicated story? Don't overlook anyone.

Coworkers, Clients, and Customers

Telling coworkers, colleagues, and sales representatives, for example, can also provide you with a far-reaching network. However, a woman who plans to remain at home once her baby arrives should be cautious about broadcasting this information too freely. She does not want to jeopardize her job or career advancement.

If your job involves routine contact with clients or customers, mention that you are seeking to adopt when they ask, "Do you have children?" Ray was weary of the "You've been married ten years and still no kids?" comment from those at his office. He finally told them that we were infertile and hoped to adopt soon. Not long after that disclosure, a secretary telephoned him with a birth mother contact that resulted in our adopting Erika.

Hairdressers, Manicurists, and Barbers

Consider the broad range of people you come into contact with each week. Your hairdresser probably sees hundreds of clients a month. One of these contacts just might be a pregnant woman, her mother, or her friend, who happens to share information about her adoption plans while getting her hair cut. Do you think this couldn't happen? It does.

Your Dentist or Other Health Professional

Medical forms include questions about your general health and whether you are taking any medication. These may provide an opening for you to share your situation with the health care professional.

Some people try to adopt through obstetricians, sending countless letters to every ob-gyn in the yellow pages. This effort is usually in vain. In some states it is even illegal for a doctor to assist a nonfriend in meeting a birth mother. In any case, ob-gyns are inundated with letters from couples hoping to adopt. Unless you know a physician personally or are in the medical field yourself, you will seldom get a lead in this department.

If you are in the medical profession, however, you will probably have some opportunities for adopting a baby. One physician and his wife adopted a baby just three days after they first began to consider adoption seriously. This came about because the wife had casually mentioned to one of her husband's colleagues that they were now considering adopting. "That's interesting," the physician said. "I know of a baby who was just born who is going to be placed for adoption."

Clergy

If you are religiously affiliated, the network you maintain through your denomination or affiliation can be a wonderful way to find a prospective birth mother. There are many birth mothers who want to select a couple of a particular faith.

Talk with your pastor or clergy person. Explain your infertility and your desire to adopt. (Do not be surprised if he or she is unaware of the emotional impact of infertility.) Let the clergy person know that if he learns of a pregnant woman from another church who wishes to have her child adopted, you would be glad to be contacted. He may be able to spread the word to his colleagues and associates.

Pastors, priests, and rabbis need to know about potential adoptive parents, since they are often the first to counsel a family whose daughter is experiencing a crisis pregnancy. How reassuring it would be for a pastor to tell the parents of a pregnant teenager, or the teenager herself, that he knows of a wonderful couple who could provide a secure and loving home for the baby.

Ask your clergy person for the names of other clergy who may be interested in talking with you or receiving a letter from you. Send them each a letter, enclosing copies of letters that can be given to birth mothers.

If your faith places an emphasis on the sanctity of unborn life, let the woman know this in your letter. Emphasize the attributes of your faith that will make you a better parent. One note of caution about discussing your faith, however: Do not assume that the birth mother places a great emphasis on her religion or that she expects you to do so just because the referral was through her clergy person. A birth mother's main concern is probably that appropriate family values are taught to the child—the kinds of values that often come through religious teachings.

BROADCAST LETTERS

Sending out letters is a relatively inexpensive way to make contact with a birth mother. Although writing one takes time and forethought, once one letter is written, duplicates are the easiest things in the world to produce. Here are some likely people to send letters to:

- *Friends.* When you send out your holiday cards, you may want to share with your friends your desire to adopt. Of course, you do not have to do this at Christmastime, but the holidays are a time for children and babies, and people tend to be extra responsive.

- *Professional or volunteer associates.* If you belong to a professional or volunteer organization, you may consider sending letters to some or all of its members. There are print shops listed in the yellow pages that handle mailings if you give them your organization's list. In one situation, two birth mothers contacted a couple who used this method. Apparently, people are very receptive to these letters.
- *Clergy.* As noted earlier, contact with clergy can be a good way to locate a birth mother. Sometimes it is better to contact a clergy person outside your own church or synagogue. You probably do not want to adopt a baby whose birth mother attends your church or synagogue.

Here's a list of where *not* to send letters. Although sending letters to these organizations will not do any harm, the likelihood of finding a birth mother this way is next to zero.

Crisis Pregnancy Centers (CPCs). At first CPCs might seem like a likely source for pregnant women seeking to place their babies for adoption. However, the staff at these centers are usually not permitted to give birth mothers the names of couples who are interested in adoption. CPCs get many letters from couples who want to adopt, which they have no choice but to throw away. When a woman considers adoption, they usually send her to an adoption agency of the same religious affiliation as the center.

If you know someone who works at a CPC, you may mention to her your desire to adopt. She might be able to provide your name to a pregnant woman, if this is not viewed as a conflict of interest.

Planned Parenthood. Planned Parenthood and other clinics already receive many letters from prospective adoptive parents. Even if they had a policy of responding to them, they wouldn't have the resources to do so.

Obstetricians. Ditto. Don't waste your time.

Writing the Letters

Separate letters should be written for friends, associates, clergy, and potential birth mothers. Examples of three letters can be found on pages 59–61.

Make sure that your letter to the birth mother expresses your special understanding of what she is experiencing and also that it tells her something about you: your hobbies, home, talents, interests, and positive attributes. Follow these guidelines:

- *Keep it easy to read.* Remember, she may be a teenager. Keep the language simple and the sentences short. You are trying to impress her not with your command of the English language but with your genuine desire for a child and the love that you can provide to that child.

- *Be sensitive to her needs.* Let her know that you are sympathetic about her unplanned pregnancy and that you realize she does care about her unborn child. This woman did not choose abortion. Without directly saying so, let her know that you respect her for choosing to carry her pregnancy to term.

- *Mention your infertility.* You do not have to mention your specific infertility diagnosis, but vaguely addressing the problem can help a birth mother feel for your situation as well. Never say, "We cannot have children of our own." Adopted children *are* your own.

- *Mention your livelihoods.* It is fine to state your professions, but keep the reference to them general.

- *Mention your favorite hobbies and activities, especially ones that a child may enjoy.*

- *Share the positive points of your marriage.* For example, you may want to mention long walks and talks, suggesting a warm and communicative relationship.

- *Share your religious faith.* When talking about religious involvement, however, it is usually best not to mention your denomination, unless you are targeting pregnant teenagers or women who share that denomination or belief. If you are not part of an organized religion, then you will want to share the values that will make you a good parent, such as commitment to family and community, honesty, hard work, and acceptance of others.

- *Show that you are willing to have some level of "openness" in adoption.* Suggest your willingness to maintain an "open" relationship. If you are not willing to see the birth mother after the baby is placed, do not mention this. Please note, however, that most birth mothers do not expect to see you or the baby after placement. Whatever degree of openness you are comfortable with, let her know. Every birth mother should at least be given the opportunity to receive pictures and progress notes about the baby. Do let her know that you will send these to her. It is very comforting to a birth mother to know that she is not just handing a baby over to someone, never to hear about the couple or the baby again.

- *Make it personable.* Do not greet the birth mother as "Dear Birth Mother." Just say hello, or use some other informal salutation. Use your first names in letters and portfolios. Do not refer to yourselves as Jane and John Doe or "The Adoptive Couple." You are two real, living human beings with feelings: Let this come through.

SAMPLE LETTER TO BIRTH MOTHER

Hello,

You and I are in very different circumstances, and yet in some ways we are in very similar circumstances. We both find ourselves in a situation that we wish we could change. You have an unplanned pregnancy, yet love the child that you will give birth to. I cannot bear a child, but would love to have a baby for our family. My husband and I have longed for a child for three years. But I had four miscarriages, and the doctors cannot give me any treatments that will help me carry a child to term. Like you, I value unborn life and do not feel that it is right to keep trying to give birth to a baby while risking another miscarriage. My husband also cares about my health and that of the unborn child. Besides, our goal is to be parents, and through adoption we can love and cherish a child.

Just to let you know a little about us, I will tell you about our home and our activities. We live in a lovely ranch home with four bedrooms. Outside is a large yard with apple trees. There are two parks within walking distance of our home. My husband has a management job with an oil company. He was recently promoted. I am a third-grade schoolteacher. I enjoy my job, but I would like to be home with a child. If we are blessed with a child, I plan to stay home full-time. Both my husband and I love snow skiing and take about four or five trips to Vermont each winter. During the year we enjoy bike riding and long walks and talks together. Sometimes we take a picnic basket to the beach or park and then walk for hours. We also love to socialize with our friends. Many of our friends have small children. David and I both teach Sunday school at our church. Our lives are very full. There is only one thing missing—a child.

We would love to meet with you, if that is your desire. Or if you are more comfortable, we could exchange information over the telephone or through letters and pictures. David and I are also willing to maintain a relationship with you, even after the baby is born. If you select us as parents, we would be happy to send you pictures and letters to let you know what the child is doing at each age. We would even consider a more open relationship if you are comfortable with that. Of course, we also want to respect your privacy and the life ahead of you.

We also could pay for your medical expenses if you do not have insurance. All information between you and us would remain confidential. We have an attorney so that everything is legal.

Please let our friends who have given you this letter know what you would like best. They can then contact us. Or you can contact us directly at (800) 123-4567.

We wish you the best, whatever you decide. I know it is a difficult time in your life. We do care and are willing to help.

Susan and David

SAMPLE LETTER TO FRIENDS

Dear Friends,

As you may already know, David and I have longed to have children and have been unable to do so. This time of year is especially hard for us, as we would love to have presents under the Christmas tree for our child.

Recently we have decided to adopt and are letting all of our friends know in case they may know of someone who wants to place her baby for adoption.

We have everything that a child could want. Most of all, we want to provide a child with love, stability, and acceptance.

Our jobs are going well. In fact, David was recently promoted to northeast director of marketing. I do enjoy my job, but I would rather be at home with a child.

If you hear of anyone who is pregnant and knows this is not the best time in her life to raise a child, please let her know that we would be interested in meeting with her, talking with her, or making whatever arrangement she finds comfortable. Our number is (222) 555-1234.

Dave and I have also enclosed some "Adoption" cards. If you feel comfortable with distributing them, you could help us by placing them by public telephones and in the women's rooms at shopping centers.

We appreciate your help, and we'll keep you posted about our progress.

Wishing you all a Joyous Christmas and Happy New Year,
Sue and Dave

SAMPLE LETTER TO COLLEAGUE OR ASSOCIATE

Dear Fellow Rotary Member:

This may seem like an unusual appeal, but I hope you consider it seriously. As a fellow volunteer, I know that you are in contact with many people, and therefore may know of a woman who is experiencing a crisis pregnancy and is interested in placing the baby for adoption.

If you do, my wife, Gloria, and I would be most interested in contacting her. For five years now we have longed to become parents but cannot. Our lives have gone well, and sometimes it seems as if we have everything—everything except a child to love.

Please contact us at (555) 123-4567 (collect) if you know of someone who is considering adoption. If you can, please pass the enclosed letter on to her.

Thank you.

Terry Harkins

BUSINESS CARDS AND FLIERS

Business cards are yet another way to get the word out. They can be designed so that the front of the card presents a color photograph of a baby and the word "Adoption." Or you could place a picture of you and your spouse on the front of the card. On the back of the card, write a message similar to one that you would put in a newspaper advertisement (see page 66). As with an ad, you also include an 800 number or "Call collect." Place these cards in malls, restrooms, restaurants, and other public places. You also may want to mail several to each of your friends with the letters described earlier.

Because fliers are larger and inexpensive—you pay only for paper and photocopying—you can add more information than you would in a classified advertisement. Fliers can be placed at bus stops, college campuses, and other public places where young women may be.

NEWSPAPER ADVERTISEMENTS

The most common way for adoptive parents and birth mothers to make contact is through newspaper advertising. Writing an advertisement for a newspaper takes a little work, but the rewards can be great. Like all ads, adoption ads should be short, convey an important message, and immediately attract the reader. You are not only presenting yourselves, you are seeking a most important person—your baby. Your ad should display warmth and compassion as well as your unique characteristics.

Listed below are some tips on writing an advertisement. But before you write your own, read other adoption advertisements. Which ones grab your attention? Decide why that advertisement makes a positive impression on you. If you can, fashion your ad in a similar way, yet make yours unique. You want a birth mother to see your ad and say to herself, "They sound like a nice couple who could provide a good home."

What should you include in your ad? Following is a list of what to cover—and what not to cover.

1. *What kind of child you are interested in adopting.* How much should you say about what kind of child you would like to adopt? Most couples seeking to adopt through private channels are interested in a healthy Caucasian newborn infant. If these are the limits you are placing on the child you seek to adopt, you should *not* mention it in your ad. Most birth mothers who are calling you will be Caucasian and pregnant and planning to place the baby with you immediately after birth. If you state that you are willing to pay for medical expenses, you are in essence saying you want a newborn baby.

    Here are some other issues parents have to consider in wording their ad:

    - The child's health status. Don't mention that you want a healthy baby. A birth mother may think you are looking for a "doll" and not a real child who will get sick throughout his life. Most birth mothers who respond to advertisements are pregnant and believe that the baby is healthy.
    - The child's racial/ethnic background. Many newspapers have policies that prohibit you from mentioning ethnic background or age. The best thing to do is wait until you talk with the woman on the telephone to determine her ethnic background and that of the birth father. If you are interested in adopting an African-American or biracial child, you may choose to mention this in your advertisement. Part of your ad may read, "interested in infant of any racial background."

        If you are of a specific nationality and state that you want only a child from that ethnic background, you may find yourself waiting a long time for a birth mother to respond. Instead of stating that you want, for example, a baby of Irish descent, you may say in your ad "Irish-American couple seeking to offer a child happiness." You may also want to advertise in a newspaper that targets those of your specific nationality.

Some couples do not want to adopt a child of a certain ethnic heritage. Even if you feel strongly about this matter, do not mention it in your ad. Screen your telephone calls to find out what the birth parents' ethnic backgrounds are.

■ The child's age. If you want an older baby or young child, placing an advertisement in the newspaper probably is not a good way to find such a child. Yet if you are willing to adopt a child from birth to three years of age, your ad may read like this: "Couple seeks child for adoption."

2. *Your first names.* We advise against using false names. In the first place it is unethical, and in the second, impractical. Once you meet with the birth parents, it will be very difficult for you to keep calling your husband "Harry" if his name is "Massimo," and for him to call you "Sue" when your name is "Angelina." On the other hand, a birth mother may not respond to an ad if she has never heard of your first names before. She may feel more comfortable calling a Mary and John than a Xenia and Archibald. If your names are particularly ethnic-sounding, you *may* want to Anglicize them a bit. "Mordecai" could become "Mort," and "Raymondo" could become "Ray."

If your name comes from another language, just change it to English. Instead of being "Jose," call yourself "Joseph." Then if you inadvertently call your spouse by his or her more ethnic-sounding name in the presence of the birth parents, at least your spouse can honestly say, "That's what my family calls me."

The point is not to misrepresent yourselves. If you are Jewish and your names are very ethnic, you would not want to select traditionally Christian names like "Mary" and "Christopher."

Some adoptive parents are very concerned about retaining their anonymity and do not want a birth mother to find out their full identity. If your names are "Archibald" and "Penelope," you may fear that a birth mother will be able to figure out who you are. "How many couples are there named 'Archibald' and 'Penelope' in the state of Iowa?" you may be thinking. Or you may fear that your specialized profession will be a dead giveaway to a birth mother intent on finding out who you are. After all, how many "Samantha and Jacks" are there in which the wife is an orthopedic specialist?

The truth is, no combination of first names is either common or unique. We do not know any other "Ray and Laura" combinations, although neither of these names is unusual. What you should really consider is what you could lose by using an alias. It is too easy for you or your attorney, legal secretaries, physicians, or anyone else involved in the adoption to make a mistake and call you by your real names. If this happens, the whole adoption could fall through.

Apart from that, it is morally wrong to try to deceive a birth mother about your names. When the truth is discovered—and it probably will be—the birth mother's trust will be diminished, if she does not immediately change her mind about placing her baby with you. Besides, you may have an ongoing relationship with this woman for the rest of your lives, even if just through letters and pictures. If your child seeks out his birth mother when he is eighteen years old, how will everyone feel when it is discovered that you had lied about your names all these years?

3. *Your unique characteristics.* Nearly every couple who advertises claims to be "a loving, happily married couple who will provide a child with much security." You therefore want your advertisement to stand out. Emphasize some unique characteristics that make you special. For example, if you are gifted as an artist, musician, baseball player, or tennis pro, you may want to include these details in the ad. One prospective adoptive father was a mechanic and did not want to include this in his ad. It turned out he had many interesting hobbies, such as hiking and woodworking. The couple included this information in the ad instead and soon had a response from a birth mother. They are now parents.

Your profession is a unique characteristic that can serve to your advantage, and sometimes disadvantage. Birth mothers seem to respond most favorably to teachers and nurses, and less favorably to physicians and attorneys.

Activities that revolve around animals, beaches, mountains, and other outdoor activities are especially appealing.

Be careful of setting yourself too far apart from a birth mother. You may be very well educated, have a large home, and take many vacations, but don't call attention to it. The following will *not* do: "Harvard graduates who love tennis, golf, and yachting in the Caribbean seek to provide a child with much love. Call Biff and Buffy." Most birth mothers are intimidated by such a show of education and wealth.

4. *Your religion.* Again, your religion, or a profession that may suggest your religion, can work either for or against you. In many cases, however, mentioning a religious affiliation will only serve to screen out birth mothers. Use your judgment.

Many Jewish couples worry that they may have difficulty finding a birth mother who will work with them, since very few birth mothers are Jewish. Actually, experience shows that this is not an obstacle. Birth mothers are usually more interested in whether you practice a religion and will make good parents.

5. *Your financial status.* If you are financially comfortable or a member of a respected profession, you may *discreetly* mention these facts in the ad.

6. *Medical expenses.* If you are willing to pay for medical and other expenses, instead of directly stating this in your ad, simply say, "We care and want to help."

7. *Legality of independent adoption.* Even in states where it is legal, which includes most, you will be surprised how many people think that independent adoption is illegal. You may want to mention that the adoption plans are *legal* and confidential if no other adoption ads are in the newspaper.

8. *Your telephone number.* At the same time that you plan to place an ad in the newspaper, have a separate phone line installed in your home for responses from birth mothers. Order a toll free number from the telephone company, or state in your ad that the birth mother can call you collect. *Do not place ads in newspapers that permit only a PO box number and no phone number. Birth mothers will not write to a box number.*

OTHER CONSIDERATIONS

Start your ad with the letter A or with the word "Adopt." This will put your ad at or near the beginning of the adoption ads or "Personals" column of the newspaper. One couple told me that a birth mother confessed to them, "I called you because your ad was one of the first of thirty ads, and I am not going to call all thirty ads." We do suggest that you not compete with more than four other adoption ads. Although having other adoption ads can be a good sign—it probably means this is a newspaper in which adoption ads are read by and responded to by birth mothers—it is hard to make an ad stand out. Make sure yours is unique.

Be succinct. Cut superfluous words and phrases. Just don't go overboard! Saying that you are a loving couple sounds superfluous, but you must say it. Leaving it out is like not putting "attractive male/female" into a singles ad; if you do not say it, it is assumed you are unattractive.

The truly adventurous may want to experiment with a very unusual ad, testing it out in one newspaper to start with. Make sure the newspaper or magazine fits your style. Do not say you are a Rush Limbaugh fan in the "Personals" section of *Rolling Stone* magazine.

SAMPLE ADVERTISEMENTS

ADOPT Manager and piano teacher want to share the love that we have for each other and our joy in music with a child. We care and want to help. Fred and Wilma at (800) 123-4567.

ADOPT Professional yet fun-loving couple desires to share our love of life with a child. We enjoy camping and horseback riding. Call Martha and Harry at (800) 333-4444.

An accountant and teacher—financially secure—want to offer child a wonderful home by the beach, but most of all—lots of love. Call Blair and Lois collect at (333) 123-4567.

A successful broker and loving at-home artist seek infant. We can provide child with many blessings, but most important, lots of love and happiness. Call Steve and Jane at (800) 123-4567.

Physician and nurse who cherish quiet walks, friends, and family want to share our love with a child. Dave and Sue, at (800) 123-4567.

We want to share our large home and small farm in the country—but most of all our love and happiness with a child. Call Susan and Jim at (800) 555-6543.

Teacher dad, loving at-home mom, and big sister long to share our love with a child. Call Tony and Pam at (800) 123-4567.

Adoption is a loving choice, as three-year-old brother knows. Dad, loving at-home Mom, and Grandma and Grandpa all can't wait. We care and want to help. Call Mike and Lisa at (888) 765-1234.

Loving dad and mom want to provide a child with strong family values and security plus fun days at the beach with lots of cousins. Call Mark and Pam at (800) 123-4567 PIN 1234, or our attorney John Smith at 800-555-1313.

WHERE SHOULD YOU ADVERTISE?

Perhaps you've been wondering how far from home it is best (and safest) to advertise for a child. Here are some options you may or may not have thought of already.

Out of State

As a general rule, the state where you advertise is the state where the baby will be born. (Note: Not all states that permit independent adoptions allow advertising. See the Appendix.) This means that if you live in New Jersey and advertise in Iowa, you must correspond with someone in Iowa and possibly visit the birth mother there at least once before the baby's birth, in addition to the trip to Iowa to receive the baby. Of course, many trips to another state can be expensive. Laws differ from state to state, too, resulting in possible complications. But even without complications you will need to either retain an attorney or engage an adoption agency in each state. Before you decide to advertise in a state other than your own, therefore, ask yourselves these questions:

- Am I willing to travel there at a moment's notice?
- Can I afford to make more than one trip to that state?
- Am I willing to incur the expense of living in a hotel before and after the baby is born? (You will usually live in a hotel for one to two weeks while all the Interstate Compact paperwork is filed.)
- Am I willing to incur the expenses of maintaining a long-distance relationship by telephone?

If you decide that advertising out of state is still a good idea, then the question becomes "Where?" Some couples find that they get a better response advertising in less densely populated areas of the United States, like the Midwest and the South, than they do in the Northeast. A couple seeking a Caucasian infant is more likely to find a birth mother in a rural area than in a cosmopolitan or urban area.

In Your Own State

If you advertise in your own state, select a small hometown newspaper about fifty miles away from where you live. Do not advertise in a newspaper that is distributed too close to your home. You probably do not want to live in the same town as the birth mother.

Although birth mothers and adoptive parents and children are maintaining closer relationships these days, living in the same area and having mutual acquaintances may infringe on everyone's privacy.

What Kinds of Newspapers?

Once you have decided which state(s) to advertise in, decide which area of the state to target. Some say the best place is near a college campus or military base. In other words, advertise in a community where there is a high concentration of young women.

This does not necessarily mean a college newspaper, although you might assume this would be the perfect place to advertise. Unfortunately, these young women often choose abortion over adoption. However, there are couples who have advertised in campus newspapers and received positive responses.

If you do choose a campus newspaper, select a college that is rural and, if possible, of a religious affiliation that does not condone abortion. If you think of this newspaper as one means of locating a birth mother but not your only means, you will have nothing to lose.

What about a large daily paper? It is true that a large newspaper goes to more homes. However, the "Personals" section of a small newspaper is more likely to be read by a birth mother or her friend or family member. Weekly newspapers are also more likely to stay in the home longer than a large daily newspaper; and since advertising in a small newspaper is usually less expensive, you can afford to do it more often.

Call the various newspapers to determine their rates. Ask to have the papers mailed to you so that you get a "feel" for the area and so you can see how many other couples are advertising in each paper.

Remember, with a daily newspaper it is best to place your ad every day. If this is too expensive, try placing it twice a week and once on the weekends. Similarly, if you place the ad in a weekly newspaper, plan to do so for a few weeks running.

Newspaper Networks

If your finances are limited, you can still get broad coverage in some states by advertising in the Newspaper Network Association in your state. Then your ad will go in both daily and weekly newspapers. For $100 to $250 per week you can place an ad of twenty-five words or less (extra for each additional word) in all the newspapers that belong to that association. About 90 percent of the newspapers will place your specific ad.

In New York State only 50 percent of the newspapers in the Classified Advertising Network accept adoption ads. However, the response you receive from birth mothers can still be very good, depending on what region of the state you choose. By selecting, for example, only the Metro, Western, or Central region, you may pay less than $150 to have your ad placed in thirty-five to sixty newspapers.

For a larger sum of money you can place your ad in several networks simultaneously, giving you multiple-state coverage. Again, this can be done with one call to a local network association. For more information, see the Appendix.

An obvious but important note: If you have invested several hundred dollars in placing ads, you, the wife (birth mothers are more comfortable talking woman-to-woman), should either have a cellular phone and much privacy at work, or stay home for a week or two to answer the phone. That's too much money to spend only to have a prospective birth mother reach an answering machine.

Finally, if you want to go nationwide, advertise in *USA Today* or in the *TV Guide*. Yes, it is expensive (about $1,500 a week), but you will probably find a birth mother in a matter of two or three weeks. Again, if you do this, *stay home to answer the telephone.*

Note: If you advertise in a national newspaper or in a different time zone from yours, you may receive phone calls at odd hours. For most people this poses only a minor inconvenience.

How Long Should You Run Your Ads?

It is easy to be discouraged if you place an ad in a weekly newspaper and have not heard from a birth mother in a month. If you still have not had any calls after two or three months, this may not be a good source.

If you do get a few phone calls from one newspaper, continue advertising, even after a birth mother contacts you and decides that she wants to place the baby with you. If you have paid for a certain period of time, such as a month, keep the advertisement for that time period. You could get a call from another birth mother. It can sometimes help to have more than one option.

INTERNET ADOPTION SERVICES

Now that it seems nearly everyone is on the Internet, it makes sense to consider advertising on a Web site. There are Internet sites that will place information about you so that birth mothers can find you. Because nearly 50 percent of American homes are linked to the Internet, there is a good chance that a pregnant woman will be on the Internet. And if she does not have a computer at home, she may have one at school or work.

Instead of a birth mother contacting you by phone after reading a classified ad, she can contact you through e-mail any time of day or night—and so can agencies and attorneys who may know of a birth mother or child who needs a specific type of adoptive family. Time zone differences do not interfere with anyone reaching you. Also, contacting you by e-mail can be a lot less intimidating for the birth mother than calling you directly. Plus, you never miss a "call" because you and the birth mother can check your e-mail at your convenience. Her contact with you is also not being screened by others in her home. And for you, reading e-mail can be a more relaxed approach to being contacted by a birth mother than waiting for the phone to ring.

Unlike placing ads in newspapers, a Web site is a great way to gain national and even international exposure to potential birth mothers. You can "meet" birth mothers in states where advertising is not permitted. Of course, the financial and logistical disadvantages of dealing with a birth mother who lives thousands of miles away must also be considered when communicating with birth mothers all around the country. If you live in Maine and find a birth mother on the West Coast, will you want to travel so far to meet her and then travel again when the baby is born?

No matter where the birth mother lives, eventually you will want to talk with her on the phone and most likely meet her in person. "Talking" through e-mail, however, allows one more level of anonymity until both parties decide that they would like to work with each other. Although "meeting" a birth mother through the Internet may be a good way to start, you will need to find out more about her before you assist her with any living expenses. Also, you will want your attorney or agency to have at least some telephone contact with her before sending her any assistance.

The disadvantage to this level of anonymity is that swindling prospective adoptive parents out of money is probably more easily done through the Internet than through any other means. However, if you are using a registry, a birth mother cannot be taking money from multiple couples on the same site because contacts made by a birth mother are screened.

So how do you begin getting on the Internet? There are hundreds of sites, and selecting just the right site for you can be a bit daunting. Amy Miller of the Link National Adoption Registry in North Carolina recommends that you investigate each site to see if it meets your needs. Some sites allow photos, others do not. Some sites also allow short biographies. According to Miller, a good "Dear Expectant Mother" letter should include the prospective adoptive family's biography, and sites that permit you to place just one paragraph describing yourselves do not provide enough information to a birth mother.

If you do decide to seek a birth mother through a Web site registry, be sure that your biography and birth mother letter are written so that they will appeal to young women. Use easy-to-read language and short sentences. The site sponsor should also critique your letter.

Miller further suggests that you select an Internet site that is promoted to crisis pregnancy centers and other places such as homes for unwed mothers. Certain Web sites may also be advertised in magazines that appeal to young women. Find out to what extent the Web site on which you will place your letter and picture is advertised or promoted.

According to Rachel Marks of Adoption.com, one of the most dominant adoption Web sites, the Adoptive Parent Registry is the site's largest section. There are more than 150 couples/singles listed. Each prospective adoptive family must meet all state requirements to legally adopt a child, so you should have completed a home study and be working with an attorney or adoption agency.

At Adoption.com, the Web page includes your "Dear Birth Mother" letter, four color photographs, profile information, and a feedback page. For an additional fee your photo will be featured on a rotating basis on the site's home page. Other perks include a guide and business cards with your Web page address on them to give to friends and family. For a one-time fee, your Web page will be posted for six months. These fees are paid up front, and there are no additional fees that you will encounter. Both packages can also include a link to other Web pages, so if you have created a Web page on your own that is adoption related, Adoption.com can provide a link.

For those who are successful on the Web, Marks states the average wait is about three to four months.

Although you will want to appeal to many birth mothers, if you do have unique strengths or if you are interested in adopting a child with special needs, then you may want to let this be known on your Web page so that attorneys and agencies can contact you if they have a birth mother who wants a particular type of couple.

For more information contact:

Adoption.com
4700 S. McClintock Drive, Suite 120
Tempe, AZ 85282
(888) 962-3678
(480) 897-8500
rachael@adoption.com

Advertising on the Web site can be relatively inexpensive. Fees range from a $150 donation to thousands of dollars per year. Some Web site registries charge an initial fee and then a monthly service fee; others charge just a one time fee for a specific period of time—usually six months. More money does not necessarily mean more exposure, so shop around. Also, do not be tempted to place yourself on lots of Web sites. This can get very expensive. Instead, vary your methods of finding a birth mother.

Will you find a birth mother through the Internet? Perhaps. As the Internet becomes more popular and user-friendly, the potential of finding a birth mother increases. Even if you do not find a birth mother directly this way, you could find out about other people who are also looking to adopt, and by connecting with them as you would with an adoption support group, you may find a child another couple is not interested in adopting.

If you do advertise through the Internet, most likely you will also want to have a separate telephone line installed so that the birth mother can call you at a toll free number. This telephone number, as well as your e-mail address, should be listed on your Internet site.

Likewise, if you are also advertising in classified ads, mailing letters or handing out "adoption cards," be sure to list your Web site address. Then when a birth mother sees your ad in the newspaper, she can look up your information on the Internet, and if she is too nervous to call you, she can e-mail you instead.

SETTING UP A TELEPHONE LINE ("BABY PHONE")

Most couples pursuing private adoption have a telephone line installed in their home just for calls from birth mothers. Your first contact with a birth mother, after all, is usually by telephone. Having a separate telephone line can provide you with some emotional control as well. Every time your regular phone rings, you will not assume it is a birth mother. If you are seeking a birth mother by the means of advertising, sending out "adoption cards," or letters to acquaintances, you will definitely want to set up a special line.

When you contact your telephone company to install the line, you may want to explain why you are installing a second line and ask that the second line be billed to your original phone number so that the telephone company has no separate record of the second phone line, and so that your address is not connected with the second line. The representatives are usually very understanding, although some personnel at the telephone company are not knowledgeable about adoption and think that "baby phones" are illegal.

Also, ask for a "lock" to be placed on the number. That way a birth mother cannot call the phone company when she gets her phone bill and ask for the name of the person associated with your number. *A second telephone line is no guarantee, however, that a prospective birth mother will not discover your last name and address.* Computerization of data means that this information is available to marketers and others. A birth mother who lived in the Midwest, whose parents had access to a large computer system, was able to learn the last name and address of a couple in the Northeast.

Installing a telephone is a moderate expense and well worth your peace of mind. Following are some other phone options you might consider.

- A *toll free number.* A birth mother is more likely to call a toll free number. Many long-distance carriers such as Excel now allow you to order a toll free number without installing a second line. The toll free number simply overrides your regular line. The cost is about $3 per month, and all incoming phone calls on the toll free line are billed at the regular long-distance rate and not the collect-call rate.
- *Voice mail and answering machines.* If you use an answering machine, be sure the outgoing message tells the birth mother the best time to call back. Don't state that collect phone calls are permitted unless your machine is the kind that allows the caller to leave only a three-minute message. Otherwise, prank phone callers can use all the recording time available at your expense.
- *Distinctive ring.* Another option is a distinctive ring service, which costs about $4.50 per month. This system allows you to have up to three different telephone numbers and three different ring patterns on one line. If you have "call waiting," a special tone that matches the special ringing pattern assigned to each telephone lets you know which number the caller is trying to reach. All outgoing phone calls, however, are from your main number.
- *Phone block.* Using "Caller ID," technology that identifies an incoming call by phone number, a birth mother could potentially learn your main home number. To avoid this, you might consider having a block placed on your number, especially if you are using a toll free number that overrides your existing telephone number. Then your number will not be traceable.
- *Call forwarding.* Call forwarding can be used to send calls from your home to a friend's or relative's home. This may be something to consider if both of you are going to be away from home all day. The friend or relative can take messages and have you contact the birth mother in the evening.
- *Cellular phones.* Cellular phones are very inexpensive, and you may want to purchase one and obtain a toll free line so that you can be reached nearly anywhere you go.

- *Attorneys and agencies.* Attorneys and agencies can also take phone calls for you. If you arrange this, make sure you list the attorney's or agency's number in the ad along with your own.

We should say that the advice offered so far about how to maintain your anonymity is not intended to imply that having a birth mother know your tele-phone number and address is risky or even inappropriate. These measures are really for protection from pranksters and criminals, not well-meaning young women. We should note that none of the adoptive couples that we know have had any problems with criminals and pranksters beyond an occasional crank call. Once you establish a relationship with a woman and are certain she will place her baby with you, you may choose to share more identifying information.

SEARCHING FOR A BIRTH MOTHER: ONE COUPLE'S STORY

The quest for a birth mother can sometimes involve a few unexpected twists and turns, as Leslie and Paul discovered. Here's the way Leslie tells the story.

> It seems as if a large chunk of my life was spent thinking about getting pregnant, trying to get pregnant, and then worrying about it— I'd been an infertility patient for more than eight years. At last my hus-band, Paul, and I decided to end the treatments and focus our energies on adoption. Reaching this decision lifted a huge burden from our shoulders. Finally we could share our secret.
>
> Apart from our immediate families, no one was aware of our situ-ation. We had felt it would be easier to keep our infertility under wraps. That way there would be no pressure and no nosy questions from well-meaning friends and acquaintances.
>
> The response to our adoption plans was wonderful. I'll never forget how immensely pleased our families were when we broke the news. Until then they had just figured we didn't want to have children. It's funny—I went from telling no one to telling everyone. When people would casually ask, "So, do you have any children?" I'd say, "No, but we're hoping to adopt." Even on airplanes I started asking other passengers how many kids they had. Invariably they'd turn the question around and ask me, which was the perfect entree.
>
> We had already decided to pursue an independent adoption, for several reasons. Because Paul was in his early forties and I was in my late thirties when we started the process, we would probably not have met the age requirements for many agencies. In addition, a number of

agencies are religiously-based, usually Christian. We're both Jewish, so this would not have worked for us. We also considered an international adoption, but dismissed the idea after speaking to our rabbi and other Jewish friends. We agreed that it would be difficult for a child of a different ethnicity to fit into the Jewish community.

Having made this decision, though, we barely knew where to begin. We figured it was best to speak with an attorney first and proceed from there.

Unfortunately, the first attorney we talked to left us cold. We were uncomfortable with what we perceived as her lack of integrity. I feared that if we used her, some day down the road someone would knock at our door and demand our baby back because the adoption wasn't conducted legally. So I found another attorney who seemed much more credible and kept him on retainer. He immediately recommended that we install a separate phone line and begin our newspaper campaign. We placed ads in papers all over the country. Our ad was short, and we ran it daily for thirty days in roughly four to six papers a month.

It worked. We received calls from all twelve states in which the ads appeared. The calls ranged from the serious to the ludicrous—like the man who guaranteed that I'd become pregnant if I spent a week with him! After all, when your phone number is appearing all over the country, you are bound to attract some weirdos. But we attracted serious callers, too. Like the Louisiana college students, newly married and shocked to discover that the young wife was pregnant. Knowing that they couldn't possibly raise a child now, they began seeking out adoptive parents. They said they were instantly drawn to our ad.

In fact, after I'd spoken to the young woman a few times, she asked for more information about us—what we were like as a married couple, our careers, and what we'd be like as parents. She also wanted to speak to our attorney. Things were looking quite promising, and I was starting to feel excited. So was Paul. With the Louisiana woman five months pregnant, we might have a baby in four months! Shortly after we sent them our biographical sketches, however, the couple called to say they could no longer work with us. They didn't like the abrupt manner with which our attorney treated them on the phone. They felt he was unsympathetic and brusque. I was stunned. They also admitted they'd been in contact with other couples, and, frankly, why should they deal with a condescending attorney when plenty of other couples out there have warm and thoughtful attorneys?

At first, I didn't know whether their concerns were legitimate or whether they were politely refusing us. Of course I was upset; it was very discouraging. Yet I had been warned that these things happen. Paul and I continued on. We placed more ads and took more calls.

I had decided early in the process to quit my engineering job and concentrate on the search. Paul's job as a marketing analyst would allow me to be a full-time mom once the baby arrived. Since the adoption process required so much energy, it made no sense to keep working. It was far better for me to be available to answer the baby phone myself than hook it up to a phone machine. What birth mother wants to pour her heart out to a machine?

Certainly not Annie, a sixteen-year-old Iowa girl who was expecting twins. Annie liked our ad, called us, and struck up a friendly rapport with me. A needy young woman, Annie would sometimes call me as often as three times a day. I spent hours and hours on the phone with her. We discussed virtually everything. After several months of dialogue she verbally committed to placing her babies with us. Naturally, Paul and I were elated! Not one, but two babies! It seemed too good to be true. It was.

The first setback came after Annie talked with our attorney. There was a mix-up with some paperwork, and she said the attorney was so mean and rude to her on the phone, she never wanted to speak to him again!

This was the second time we had heard negative remarks about our attorney. It was the last straw! If you are going to be an adoption attorney, you have to be prepared to do a lot of hand holding for young girls who are nervous, even hysterical. Our attorney's abrupt "New York" manner was not what these Midwestern girls wanted to hear. We immediately fired him.

Not long afterward, Annie confided that she had severe epilepsy. This did not pose a problem, until she mentioned that she was taking an antiseizure drug on a daily basis. I immediately phoned my pediatrician and discovered that there was a very high chance that the twins would be born with multiple birth defects—spina bifida, a cleft palate, even brain damage.

Could we take this chance? Paul and I were forced to do some serious soul-searching. What would it be like to care for not one but two babies, possibly with very high needs? Could we do it? In the end, we decided we could not take the chance. Birth defects are a terrible thing. When it's your biological child, you cope wonderfully because you have to, but Paul and I felt that we had a choice.

Then came the hardest part of all—telling Annie that we had changed our minds. It was one of the most difficult things I've ever had to do. We had developed a very close relationship over the phone, and I knew she was going to be devastated. She was. I tried to be as gentle and as loving as I could. I did not mention the possibility of birth defects. I felt this information should come from her doctor. Instead, I told her we were simply not equipped to care for twins.

We both cried on the phone. Annie sobbed uncontrollably. I tried to reassure her that with hundreds of couples out there looking to adopt, surely she would find someone to provide a loving home for her babies.

As it turned out, Annie went into labor the very next day, six weeks before her due date. She delivered a girl and a boy. Sadly, the boy died a month later. Annie ended up raising the girl herself. Surprisingly, she continued to call me from time to time. We had a strong emotional connection, and she looked to me for support. She ended up going away to college, only to become pregnant again within five months! Since then I have not heard from her.

After Annie we had a few calls, but nothing promising. The next few months were totally uneventful. I was feeling discouraged and wondered whether it made sense to continue the ads. I questioned what we could have been doing wrong.

Around this time we hired a new attorney on the recommendation of the state agency that handles adoptions. The new attorney, Ray Godwin, suggested advertising in a newspaper in an urban area about forty miles from our home. I was skeptical, but figured we should give it a try.

Within three days after the ad ran, a pleasant, articulate woman named Hayley phoned us. Unlike the other callers, Hayley was not a birth mother. She was the best friend of a woman who was due in exactly two days. This young woman wanted very much to place her baby for adoption, yet could not bring herself to make the calls or even talk about the situation. Hayley was very generously acting on her nineteen-year-old friend Diana's behalf.

Well, Hayley and I just hit it off fantastically. Here we were, two strangers talking on the phone, yet it felt as if we were old friends. At the end of our conversation Hayley said she felt as though we had just gone out together for a long, chatty lunch. More important, she couldn't wait to tell Diana about us!

Later that night Hayley called again and spoke to Paul. Initially, he'd been skeptical, but like me he started to get excited about the possibility. Things were looking very promising—yet I didn't want to get my hopes up too high. I'd already seen how easily things can fall through.

The next step was to speak to Diana herself. Hayley warned us that Diana was a very shy, very insecure young woman. She was a bank teller who lived at home with her mother and brother, neither of whom had been supportive of her decision. She had a long-term boyfriend who had fathered the child, but they were not ready to marry or raise the child themselves.

Hayley was very much on target—her friend was extremely shy. Our phone conversation was strained. I tried to get as much detailed information from her as I could the two times that we spoke: Was she right, or left-handed? What were her likes and dislikes? What did she and her family members look like? During our second talk she agreed to place her baby with us!

We were thrilled! Soon, very soon, we'd be parents. Paul assembled the crib, relatives loaned us a bassinet, we bought diapers, formula, and bottles. The anticipation, the excitement, the thrill of it all were just overwhelming. In a matter of days we'd actually have our baby! Or so we thought.

About a week later (like many first-time moms, Diana was late), Hayley called with some grim news. Another couple had offered Diana $10,000 for her baby. (Although it's illegal to "buy" a baby, many desperate couples are said to do so.)

Paul and I thought long and hard before we came up with a strategy. We got Diana on the phone and asked her outright, "Is your child's life worth money?" And, "Do you really want to turn your baby over to a couple who would buy him?"

Our tactic worked! A day later Hayley called to say that Diana definitely wanted us as parents. Whether the other couple had ever existed, we'll never know. Needless to say, these ups and downs were emotionally draining. We were exhausted.

A few days later, on a Thursday—it was the first day of Rosh Hashana, the Jewish new year—Diana delivered a healthy baby boy! We were ecstatic. We had a son! Ray Godwin assured us our baby would be home within a few days.

Once again, however, trouble loomed. Mysteriously, the hospital staff would not allow Ray inside to see the baby. The staff began pressuring Diana to turn the baby over to Catholic Charities and told her they would not release her unless she carried the baby out herself.

Like most birth mothers, Diana had been under the impression that the adoptive couple would be taking the baby home directly. Neither did she expect to have to feed and change the baby, which the hospital required her to do.

In the meantime, we were at home, pacing, worrying, and praying, waiting for Diana to call. Ray urged us not to panic or lose faith. Diana would call us. We kept hoping in our hearts that he was right. But Saturday came and went with no calls. We called it Black Saturday—it was a horrible day. Late that night, truly alarmed, we slowly began resigning ourselves to the reality that we'd lost another baby.

When Ray called the hospital on Sunday, he found that both Diana and the baby had been discharged. No one answered when he phoned her home. We had no idea where she might have gone. Did she take the baby and flee? Did she accept the $10,000 offer from the other couple? By Sunday afternoon Ray still hadn't had any contact with Diana. Gently, very gently, he told us that we might as well just forget it.

Paul and I couldn't stop crying. We knew in our hearts this was *our* baby. We had already named him David. How could this be happening? To be so very close and have the baby just slip away was devastating.

Sunday, ironically, was sunny and crisp, an absolutely gorgeous day. We drove to the beach, where we walked for miles and miles, all afternoon. At times I would just collapse in a heap and cry. Paul would stop and console me, and I did the same for him.

As the afternoon went on, we decided to take a few weeks off, go away somewhere, grieve a little, and then renew our energies. We'd come back and resume our search.

When we finally got home from the beach that night, I couldn't even bear to walk past the baby's room. I asked Paul to take down the crib and bassinet and put them away in the basement. I didn't want to look at them.

I had started to prepare some dinner when the phone rang. It was Hayley.

"What's the matter?" she asked. "Don't you want the baby?"

I was speechless.

"I've been calling you all afternoon, and no one's been home," Hayley explained. "Diana figured it would be easier for her to just go home, rather than deal with the hospital. She's staying here at my apartment."

This was unbelievable! These two young girls had simply brought the baby home and were playing "Mommy" for a day.

While I kept Hayley on the "baby phone," Paul called Ray Godwin on the other line. Ray, his wife, Laura, and daughter Erika were at a party that afternoon, and we reached him through his beeper. He told us to get to Hayley's apartment immediately. He'd follow with all the paperwork.

I'd been crying all day and I looked terrible. I needed a complete makeover, but there was hardly enough time to change clothes. Instead, we sped off to Hayley's to pick up our baby. Everything had an edge of unreality to it. Just hours earlier, we'd phoned all our relatives with the bad news.

Paul and I kept each other calm during the thirty-minute drive. I hoped and prayed that nothing would go wrong this time. Ray did warn us about one thing. Diana did not want to meet us face to face. Although she would be there in Hayley's apartment, the thought of meeting us was overwhelming, too much for her to handle. But she did want to see what we looked like.

It would have been wonderful to meet her, to be able to thank her for all she'd done for us. But we understood how she felt.

When we arrived at the apartment complex, Ray, Laura, and their daughter had already gotten there. Diana had completed all the paperwork.

Just as we stepped into the apartment, Hayley slowly walked out of the bedroom, holding a tiny baby swaddled in a blanket. "This is your son," she said, and handed David to me.

When I saw the baby's beautiful little face, tears flowed down my cheeks.

It was wonderful, it was all you could imagine. Hayley and I gave each other a huge hug. But there was no time for heavy emotional exchanges. Ray had urged us beforehand not to dilly-dally. He recommended keeping the exchange as brief as possible.

As we bundled the baby into the car, I glanced back up at the window and saw the curtains fluttering. I knew Diana was watching us.

David, now nearly three years old, is a happy, rambunctious toddler who brings great joy to his proud parents.

Chapter Six

Who Are Birth Mothers, Fathers, and Grandparents?

Exactly who are birth mothers, and why do they place their babies for adoption? As you begin your search for a birth mother, you'll probably be wondering about what kind of person she might be and why she has chosen to place a child with an adoptive family. You might be anxious about meeting her. But the more you know about the birth mother, the more comfortable you will be when you do meet each other. Even more important is the fact that usually, if the birth mother is comfortable with you, she will be more likely to go through with the adoption.

In most independent adoptions, the prospective adoptive couple will meet with the birth mother, and possibly the birth father, before the baby's birth. Most encounters that we know of go very smoothly. The personal contact that you have with her is one of the main reasons that a birth mother chooses the independent adoption route. You are not adopting an anonymous woman's baby; you are meeting a person who will give birth to your child. A birth mother deserves much respect. She is not a commodity or merely a person who is a means to an end—a birth mother is a woman who has gone through nine months of pregnancy, labor, and birth, and has probably agonized over her decision.

A HISTORICAL PERSPECTIVE

Adoption has not always been viewed in a positive manner. It was once a solution for "bad" women who got pregnant, for couples who could not "have children of their own," and for "illegitimate" children. In other words, it was considered a second-rate choice for all parties involved. While adoption has certainly become more mainstream, the myths of the birth mother still linger. The following are examples of reasons why birth mothers have been stereotyped. As you read them, keep in mind the impact that such attitudes could have on the adoption process.

1. Birth mothers were told to "forget" their babies. Pregnant women were told to have their babies, surrender them to the agency, go home, forget what happened, and get on with the rest of their lives.
2. Birth mothers were treated as though they were shameful. Some were sent away to a home for unwed mothers so that no one would know about their pregnancy and adoption plans.
3. Birth mothers did not see their babies at birth or ever again. In the delivery room, physicians sometimes instructed nurses to cover the birth mother's eyes so that she would not see the baby.

   Once the baby was relinquished, a woman did not know what gender the child was or what he looked like, much less what happened to him. She also had to bear a secret for many years in her attempt to "forget it all." This level of secrecy led to much anguish.
4. It was believed that a birth mother was a poor judge of what was best for the child. Not only was it assumed that the less a birth mother knew, the better, but it was also assumed that a woman who allowed herself to get pregnant could not possibly be a good judge in selecting adoptive parents. Therefore, agency workers selected the best parents for the child.
5. It was believed birth mothers cared very little about their children. This attitude is probably best expressed in the term "unwanted child," but birth mothers in general do care very much about their children.

Today, we know that many birth mothers are simply women whose birth control method failed. These women believe that their child can be given a better life with other parents than with themselves or their families. Generally, they have chosen placing their child for adoption over abortion or the possibility of raising the child alone without financial support.

PREDICTING THE LIKELIHOOD OF PLACEMENT

Only a few studies have been conducted to determine the likelihood that a birth mother will actually proceed with adoption plans after the baby is born. These studies have examined birth mothers who have used agencies. Yet, for the most part, the same factors that determine if a woman is more likely to place her baby with an agency for adoption can also be applied to an independent adoption.

According to studies conducted in the late 1950s and 1960s, birth mothers who placed their babies for adoption were primarily white, middle to upper-middle class, with white collar or professional employment. They generally lived in a shelter for unwed mothers during their pregnancies, where they received group counseling.[1] A 1971 study analyzed data from 1967 to 1968 and came to similar conclusions—birth mothers with fewer emotional, social, and economic resources were more likely to retain their babies.

In a study published in 1988 by Steven McLaughlin, birth mothers who chose to give their children to adoptive parents were more likely to marry later and less likely to be unemployed. These findings are confirmed by Christine A. Bachrach of the National Center for Health Statistics. She stated that birth mothers who retained their children had fewer educational or career goals, whereas birth mothers who placed their babies for adoption had significant life goals. Bachrach also found that birth mothers who made adoption plans were similar in income and education to birth mothers who married before giving birth or who had abortions. More often, it was middle-class women who were more likely to place a newborn for adoption, contrary to the popular opinion that only lower-class women place babies.[2]

According to a 1993 study done by Medoff, it was found that women who were also religious fundamentalists and had a high school education were more likely to place a child for adoption, whereas women receiving Aid to Families with Dependent Children (welfare) were less likely to place a child for adoption.

In applying these statistics to private adoptions, there are certain "red flags" that can indicate whether or not a birth mother will relinquish her baby. Usually, these women who ultimately decide to keep their child are on public assistance, or have unmarried friends who have children and are also on public assistance. On the other hand, women who are likely to place a baby for adoption communicate frequently with the adoptive parents beforehand and have family members who are supportive of the adoption.

Six percent of women who have children out of wedlock place them for adoption. One study has indicated that over 12 percent of white birth mothers place their children for adoption, while less than 1 percent of black birth mothers choose this option. However, other studies have shown that black women are not more or less likely than white women to place a child for adoption.[3] In our experience, black women will consider adoption but seldom go through with the decision. Therefore, it is very difficult to adopt a black newborn through a private agency or attorney. However, white women expecting biracial children frequently place their children for adoption.[4]

The women who choose to place their babies for adoption are generally sixteen to twenty-nine years old. Many of them already have children. A birth mother may already have had two children in or out of wedlock, is now single, and just cannot afford or manage another child.

CHOOSING TO PLACE A BABY

In general, birth mothers care very much about their children. It takes a lot of love to make adoption arrangements to ensure that a child goes into a loving, stable home in which her emotional and material needs can be met. Birth mothers do not make their decision lightly. Even the woman who knows right away that she cannot have an abortion or rear the child usually spends time soul-searching and agonizing over her decision.

According to Anne Pierson of Loving and Caring, Inc., a Christian organization that provides counseling for birth mothers considering adoption, the advice her clients would give to others in the same situation includes the following:

1. Make a decision that benefits the child as well as you.
2. Look at the future and outline your goals and plans.
3. Think of the consequences of your decision.
4. Pray and seek God's help.
5. Think of the adoptive couple.
6. Never forget your child and always think of him/her.
7. Choosing adoption with the right intentions is positive and rewarding.

In Pierson's 1989 book, *Helping Young Women Through the Adoption Process*, she lists some conditions and attitudes that help birth mothers:

1. The knowledge that the child is going to a parent or a couple who would love the child as much as the birth mother would
2. Loving support from friends and relatives
3. Faith in God
4. Counseling
5. Having much information about adoption and the adoptive couple
6. Exchanging letters, gifts, and pictures with the adoptive couple
7. Surrounding herself with understanding people who do not condemn her
8. Being able to see the baby and say good-bye
9. Meeting other birth mothers and adoptive couples
10. Having her physical needs (e.g., clothing, medical) provided for

However, Pierson also mentions some experiences that birth mothers say are not helpful:

1. Acquaintances approaching them and confiding in them that they would have adopted the baby

2.   Not being treated with the same respect as other mothers in the hospital
3.   The awkwardness they encountered with friends and acquaintances when discussing the baby
4.   Being told, "You're doing the best thing"
5.   Not being given enough time to say good-bye to the baby, and being ignored by the adoptive couple once the baby is placed

Qualities Birth Mothers Look for in Adoptive Couples

Because most birth mothers care about their children, they want to be part of the adoption process. A birth mother usually wants to know the couple and wants some contact after placement to assure her the baby is doing well.

Pierson's book lists certain traits birth mothers seek in adoptive couples:

1.   Financial security and good jobs
2.   Some type of spiritual commitment to provide the child with a religious upbringing and strong family values
3.   Emotional stability and readiness for a child
4.   A strong marriage of at least four to five years
5.   No history of substance abuse
6.   Nurturing and loving qualities
7.   Being supportive of the birth mother
8.   Willingness to send letters and pictures to the birth mother
9.   Willingness of adoptive mother to stay home with the child
10.   Infertility
11.   A good sense of humor

For more on the kinds of questions birth mothers will ask you, see Chapter 7.

BIRTH FATHERS

A survey completed by the Catholic Charities Adoption Services found that

1.   Most birth fathers (81.8 percent) are more than "casually" involved with the mother.
2.   Most (62.5 percent) are committed to the relationship.
3.   Most (52.3 percent) dated the birth mother for more than six months.
4.   Most (73.9 percent) acknowledge paternity.

Based on our experience, these statistics are representative of birth fathers involved in independent adoption.

However, the birth father is often not part of the adoption decision. Frequently, the birth mother and her family do not want him to be part of the process. Usually, the less romantically involved the birth mother is with the birth father, the more likely she is to place the baby for adoption.

Until 1972 birth fathers had no legal rights. Today birth fathers can gain custody of their child based on their emotional and financial commitment to him or her. (See Chapter 8, "Birth Fathers and Their Rights," and the Appendix for the laws of each state that relate to birth fathers' rights.)

BIRTH GRANDPARENTS

Prospective adoptive parents may find themselves dealing with not only the birth parents but with the birth grandparents. If the birth mother is living at home, it is more likely that her parents, particularly her mother, will want to meet with you and discuss the adoption plans. Jeanne Warren Lindsay, in her book *Parents, Pregnant Teens and the Adoption Option*, cites cases that describe the experiences and emotions that birth grandparents often have throughout the process.

1. When parents hear of their daughter's pregnancy, they are usually in shock. Then they often react with anger and bitterness before they move to the next stage of love and acceptance.
2. Many parents of pregnant teenagers never consider adoption. Most parents believe they and their daughter must rear the baby.
3. Birth grandparents feel very alone in what is happening to their family. Some want to talk with friends and family, while others want to be left alone.
4. Of those families that consider adoption, the birth grandparents need to allow the birth mother to feel secure in her own decision. Although it is difficult for birth grandparents not to give advice, the birth mother must ultimately be the decision-maker.
5. No matter what the birth mother's age, by law she has the right to have an abortion, to select adoption (in some states if she is under 18, a guardian is appointed), or to rear the child herself. This can make the birth grandparents feel very powerless, especially when they are still responsible for many of their daughter's other actions.
6. No matter how disturbed the birth grandparents are about the pregnancy, their daughter and the baby's father need much support during this time.
7. When parents say to their teenage daughter, "You can keep the baby, but you cannot live with us," they are, in essence, not giving her a choice.
8. Often the baby is their first grandchild.

9. When adoption is the choice, the birth grandparents need to grieve, just as the birth parents need to grieve, for the loss.
10. Birth grandparents need to consider the hopes and dreams they have for their daughter as she considers whether to raise the baby or to make adoption arrangements.
11. Often the younger the birth mother, the more difficult it is for the birth grandparents to go through with an adoption plan, as they feel more compelled to raise both their daughter and the baby. In fact, most birth mothers that Ray talks with are between nineteen and twenty-four years of age. Other statistics also indicate that most birth mothers are between these ages.
12. Often the birth grandparents are younger than the adoptive parents. This can cause the birth grandparents to feel guilty, for if the adoptive parents can rear the child, they ask, "Why can't we?"
13. Some birth grandparents do help their daughters interview prospective adoptive couples. The questions they ask are often more sophisticated than a teenager's would be.

Lindsay recommends that the birth grandparents receive counseling as well as the birth parents.

Talking with Birth Grandparents

The ideas listed above can provide you with some understanding about birth grandparents. By recognizing their situation, you can better communicate with them if the occasion or need arises.

These pointers will help you talk with birth grandparents:

Provide a listening ear. Unfortunately, they may not have many other people who are supportive of their daughter's/son's decision. Often people seek counseling from those who are most understanding of their situation. You may be the most understanding person in their lives.

Let them talk out the option of rearing the child. As they discuss this option and the details involved, they probably will realize that adoption is the best plan. If they do not bring up the subject, you may ask, "Why did your daughter choose adoption instead of deciding to raise the child herself?"

At first this may seem like a question that could cause the family to change their minds, but actually their answers will reinforce their reasons for making adoption plans. The reasons birth grandparents and birth parents give you for making adoption plans will later provide them with rational guidance once the baby is born—a time when everyone's emotions take over.

If they really have no reasons for adoption, then perhaps they may be considering raising the child. It is better to find out during the pregnancy than afterward.

Discuss with them their hopes and plans for their daughter. When birth grandparents begin to discuss their children's college education and other matters, they realize that she would have difficulty achieving her goals while raising a child.

Let them know that you appreciate their involvement and commitment as well as their daughter's. Everyone wants to be appreciated and understood. Also, this is an opportunity to let them see that an unplanned pregnancy can touch other lives in a miraculous way.

By understanding the families' feelings about adoption, you have a better idea of whether the birth parents will go through with the adoption plans once the baby is born. For example, if a birth mother wants to place the baby for adoption, but the birth father is ambivalent and the birth grandmother thinks the baby should not be placed for adoption, there could be trouble ahead.

In situations in which an adoption is questionable, counseling could be useful. It could help guide all the parties involved so that they can manage their emotions and understand the facts. Also, counseling will assist all the family members to consider their options and find out who is going to be emotionally and financially responsible for the child if she is not placed for adoption.

Ray always counsels a birth mother that family pressure should not influence her ultimate decision. The decision to rear a child, or to place a child for adoption, must be made by the birth parents.

In some states birth parents' rights are terminated shortly after birth, whereas in others it could take months. If birth parents can change their minds after the baby is with you, you may not want to take the baby home unless the birth parents and other family members are secure in their decision. The birth grandparents and other family members can strongly influence a woman who has just had a baby and may convince her to change her mind. Perhaps if the family seems uncertain, ask your attorney about the possibility of foster care placement until the birth parents' rights are terminated.

If you are older than the birth grandparents, do not make an issue of it. Explain your situation. Tell them how you tried for years to conceive a child and how much you long to become parents. If you are wealthier or have a position with more status, do not flaunt this. Let the birth grandparents know that you want to provide the child with the best in life, especially time and love.

Because birth grandparents can ask sophisticated questions, be prepared. Often the birth grandparents are looking for the same traits in adoptive parents that more mature birth parents look for: a stay-at-home mom, financial security, lots of love and warmth, a stable marriage, and some commitment to a religious faith.

Chapter Seven

Meeting the Birth Mother

I n most cases the first contact with a birth mother is by telephone. This is an emotionally fraught moment for everyone. You and she will both have many questions; both of you will be wanting to present yourselves in a favorable light. After all, this could be the beginning of an important relationship.

The birth mother is considering you to be the parents of her child, and so she is likely to be curious about your home, other family members, your religion, and your employment. Answer her questions honestly, but do not feel you have to provide more information than is necessary. For example, she may ask if you go to church. If you do, say yes. You do not need to go into detail about your religion and the tenets of your faith.

If you get the feeling that one of your answers is not the "correct" one, and you cannot change the situation, then ask her if the issue is a problem. For example, perhaps she asks whether you have any other children, and you say yes. If you sense that this is not the answer she wants to hear, then simply ask her kindly, "Is that a problem?" You cannot change certain factors in your life, such as your religion, your age, or where you live, but depending on how she responds when you ask, "Is that a problem?" you may be able to tell her other things that help her feel more comfortable.

WHAT TO TELL HER, WHAT TO ASK
Early on you will want to let the birth mother know what your level of openness is toward an adoption arrangement. A birth mother usually cares very much about the child's welfare, although she may not know how to express that she is interested in knowing about the baby after it is born. You may want to offer to send photos and letters to her.

Do share a special interest, hobby, or sport. Sometimes one common interest is the reason a birth mother pursues you as parents.

There are several things you will probably want to ask a birth mother in your first conversation with her. For example:

Why she wants to place the baby for adoption. She will probably confide her reasons before you even ask. If she does not, try to determine her reasons and whether they appear to be valid.

Her health history. It is not easy to ask someone outright, "What is your medical background?" You may instead ask, "How is your pregnancy going?" Be cautious in asking direct questions. Your attorney will also be asking her these questions, and you may want to wait for him to do so.

Needless to say, asking someone point-blank about possible drug use is not tactful during a first conversation. Asking about school, work, hobbies, and interests may help you get a sense of how well this birth mother is caring for the unborn child. If she says she spends most of her spare time in pool halls with the guys in a rock band, or at bars, you may have cause for concern. On the other hand, if she says she spends her time studying, swimming, and participating in a church youth group, she is probably living a clean life.

Asking someone about her life without prying also demonstrates that you are a caring person. Your concern for this unborn life can indicate that you will care about the baby later.

The birth parents' ethnic backgrounds. If you want a Caucasian infant, or any other kind, then it would be appropriate to find out early on about the parents' ethnicity. You may simply ask, "What ethnic background are you and the birth father?" Don't make this your first question, but do raise it the first time you talk with her.

Money. Do not bring up the subject of money unless she does. A woman who is just looking for someone to pay her medical and living expenses and has no plans for adoption will probably ask for money in the first conversation. A woman who mentions that she does not have insurance and would like to receive money for medical care, on the other hand, is not necessarily insincere.

When you are ready to end the telephone conversation, you might say something like, "I've really enjoyed talking with you, Jane. Perhaps we can meet each other so that we can talk further and you can get to know us a little better. Would you like to meet in a diner somewhere between our location and yours, or at our attorney's office?"

Here are a few more pointers about telephone contacts with birth mothers.

Don't pose questions as if you are reading from a list. Ask in a conversational manner, and listen to her responses carefully and thoughtfully. It is a good idea to practice this with a friend before you actually talk with a birth mother.

Jot down any questions that occur to you while she is speaking so that you are not tempted to interrupt her. You will probably be nervous (and so will she); however, give her time to complete her statements before you ask another question.

Maintain good records so that you can give any information you have to your attorney.

Do not expect to complete a full interview with every birth mother. Some women call many ads. Some are just thinking about adoption and are still unsure. Other calls will be pranks.

Always ask the birth mother for her phone number. This is a good way to find out whether the person is sincere or just someone making prank phone calls. Most genuine callers will leave a phone number, whereas most prank callers will say they can't or that they are calling from a phone booth.

If a woman gives you a phone number, call her right back after you end your conversation with "just one more" comment or question. This lets you know whether she really is at that number. When you do call back, you may say, "I just wanted you to know my lawyer's number in case you also wanted to talk with him. Or if you would prefer, I can have him call you at a convenient time." (Of course, if she is very far along in her pregnancy, she *must* talk to your attorney as soon as possible. Most birth mothers are unsure of the legal process and do want to know what to expect.)

Following is a list of questions you will want to ask in your first few telephone conversations with a birth mother. It is a good idea to copy this list and post it near your baby phone so that you will not have to think about what to ask when you are under pressure. Do not try to ask every question on the list during your first conversation. Concentrate on the ones that seem the most important, and be sure she has a chance to ask all her questions, too.

1. Birth mother's name. (She may choose to give just her first name.)
2. Why do you want to place the baby for adoption?
3. How do you feel?
4. How did you find our number? (Friend, ad, business card? If newspaper, which one?)
5. How old are you?
6. Is the birth father involved in your life?
7. How does he feel about your adoption arrangements?
8. Does your family know that you are pregnant?
9. [If yes] How does your family feel about your adoption arrangements?
10. How many months pregnant are you?
11. Where do you live? (state or general area of a state)
12. Where do you plan to deliver the baby? (hospital and state)

13.   What medical care have you received? Did it include an ultrasound?

14.   What other results did you get from the obstetrician?

15.   Are you taking any medications?

16.   How has your pregnancy gone? Are there any complications?

17.   Do you live with your family, by yourself, in a dormitory, with friends...?

18.   What nationality are you?

19.   What ethnic background is the father?

20.   May I call you back? (if she is comfortable giving you her phone number)

21.   Where can we meet? (if she wants to meet)

22.   Other relevant information:

MEETING

Once a birth mother has called and seems sincere, arrange to meet her, if this is what everyone wants. You will probably not agree to meet after the first phone call—more like the second or third.

You will need to decide where to meet. If you made contact through a mutual friend, relative, or acquaintance, then you may want to meet at that person's home for the first time. For more confidentiality, meet at a park, library, or restaurant. Make sure you describe yourselves on the phone so you can identify each other easily. If you meet at a restaurant, pick up the tab!

If she selects a place that is familiar to her but not to you, visit the destination (if it is not too far away) so that you know that the place really does exist and so you will not get lost when it comes time to meet her.

You could agree to meet at your attorney's office, but this might be a bit intimidating for a first meeting.

Overcoming Your Fears about Meeting

Meeting a birth mother is important for your peace of mind. It will give you at least a sense of the kind of person she is. If she is neat, clean, and dressed in a turtleneck, khaki jumper, and penny loafers, chances are slim that she is taking drugs. If she is disheveled and smells of tobacco and liquor, she is probably not taking care of herself, and she may be taking other substances. Seeing her and speaking to her will go a long way toward allaying your anxieties—or may warn you if something isn't right.

There's no question, however, that meeting a birth mother face to face is difficult for all parties. Everyone is nervous. To relax yourself, think of all the other firsts in your life and how nervous you were: your first day of kindergarten, your first date, your first good-night kiss, and so on. This is just another first—the first time you have ever met a birth mother. For additional reassurance, talk to other people who have met with a birth mother and adopted.

Be yourself. Isn't that what your mother told you as you went on your first date with the guy that you were crazy about? But being yourself and knowing what to say are not always easy.

Birth mothers are no different from other people: Some are talkers and some are quiet and reserved. If the birth mother is shy, making conversation can be difficult. Do not feel that you have to make great conversation. It should be pleasant and polite.

You could start the conversation by asking her how she is feeling. If you begin to feel comfortable with her, and you both agree, you can go on to give identifying information such as your place of employment, the town you live in, and your last names. If you've met through a mutual acquaintance, she may already have this information.

Some birth mothers have no idea what to ask. You may have to take the initiative. Explain why you want to have a baby, and ask her why she is making this decision. A teenage mother may be accompanied by one of her parents, who will usually know what to ask, even if the teenager does not. Be aware of the birth mother's behavior if she is young and accompanied by her mother. Sometimes the adoption is her mother's idea, not hers, and she does not want it to happen.

If you have talked on the telephone with a birth mother, you have probably already shared some facts about your lives. As birth parents become more sophisticated about adoption, seeking greater control, some will want to know very specific facts about you. Naturally, you will present your finest points and discuss your interests. Be honest but not controversial. Birth mothers are looking for assurance that you will be a good parent—not that you are a Democrat or a Republican.

Here are the questions about your life that birth mothers usually want answered:

- What is your family like? Your parents, brothers, sisters, etc.?
- How do you spend the holidays? Birth mothers find it reassuring that the child will be in a home in which extended family members share important occasions together and where warm traditions are carried on.
- What activities do you enjoy? Sharing your interests in sports, music, and community activities indicates that you will probably share these interests with a child.
- What kind of a community do you live in? The kind of community you live in says something about what kind of life a child will have. Talk

about any parks, beaches, mountains, or other recreational sites close by. Tell her if there are other children in the neighborhood.

- Will a parent be staying home with the baby? For how long? Some birth mothers feel that if you are going to place the child in a day care center, she might as well raise the child herself and make the same arrangements. No matter how untraditional her life may be, chances are she wants a traditional home for the baby. A birth mother wants to know that the mother (or father) is going to be home to care for the child for as long as possible. If you know that staying home full-time is not possible, you may want to share your intention to have the child cared for at your home by a motherly figure or a relative of yours. Never lie about your plans. If you are unsure, tell her that you plan to stay home as long as possible. If you tell the birth mother that you plan to stay home full-time to care for the baby when you really plan to go back to work, you will probably feel guilty once you return to work. Going back to work and leaving a baby in someone else's care can be difficult enough. Do not add extra guilt to the situation.

Remember, if you choose not to meet face to face, you will want to keep in contact through telephone or letters. This happens often. Some birth mothers avoid emotional involvement by making all arrangements through a third party—the person who told you about each other or an attorney. You will simply want to do your best to stay aware of how she is feeling about her adoption arrangements, and whether she is getting the care and counseling she needs.

TALKING TO BIRTH MOTHERS

When talking to a birth mother, take cues from her about her conversational comfort level. If she is a soft-spoken Midwesterner, do not overpower her with your Northeastern accent. If she is animated and lively, then you will want to be positive as well.

It is appropriate to ask questions and make statements like these:

- What plans do you have for your future?
- Why do you want to place the baby for adoption?
- Have you discussed your plans with anyone else? What do they think?
- Why do you think adoption plans are best?
- I understand that placing a baby for adoption is a difficult decision; if you need counseling, we will be glad to assist you financially.
- I believe that you want what's best for the baby. As a couple, we want what's best for the baby too.

- It must be difficult not to have your parents support your decision (if this is the case). Is there anyone else who supports you? (If not, then offer to provide her counseling from a professional, if she so desires.)
- We will be praying for you as you go through this difficult time in your life.
- From what I understand, placing a baby for adoption can be painful and fulfilling at the same time. I know of a group of other women who are facing the same issue. I can give you the phone number of this support group.

Such statements acknowledge that the adoption decision is difficult, while offering her constructive means for making and accepting that decision.

SUPPORTING A BIRTH MOTHER EMOTIONALLY

You may well become part of the birth mother's support system, and you do want to be a considerate, thoughtful friend. As with any relationship, however, there are appropriate limits. You may not mind becoming "counselors" for the birth mother—many couples do—but you will not want to provide a twenty-four-hour-a-day counseling service. That can drain you and make you feel negative toward the birth mother. If you begin to dread the ringing telephone for fear that you will have to listen to a birth mother's problems for another two hours, you will need to set limits. Similarly, if you are uncomfortable about the discussions you are having, perhaps you can offer to pay for counseling for the birth mother.

Let her know that you will do what you can to make each part of the adoption process as easy as possible. If you can, help her set up her doctor and counseling appointments. If she needs transportation, make arrangements for this as well. Let her know that you understand her need to get on with her life while demonstrating that you are willing to maintain a certain level of openness within the relationship.

SUPPORTING A BIRTH MOTHER FINANCIALLY

Expenses that an adoptive parent legally can pay for vary according to state law, so you may be limited by more than your own finances. Even if there were no such limits, however, you would not want to be taken advantage of by an insincere woman who has no plans to place a baby for adoption, or one who believes that doing so entitles her to a nine-month luxury vacation.

Living Expenses

Paying for a birth mother's living expenses is a very delicate balancing act. Some couples resent paying anything, making the adoption process difficult. Some attorneys offer birth mothers excessive living expenses, making it difficult for couples who cannot afford to pay, for example, $1,000 a month in living expenses for seven months.

Some birth mothers ask, while others expect, to be assisted with rent, phone, utilities, food, gas, car repairs, and so on. All such financial assistance should be handled through your attorney or agency. Your attorney should give the final approval, with funds coming through his trust account. In most states a judge must approve these expenses, usually at the time of the adoption hearing. You do not want your adoption questioned because living expenses were excessive or inappropriate. Having your lawyer handle the finances also keeps you from having to say no to a birth mother when expenses cannot be paid. Instruct your attorney to contact you before sending out monies that were not prearranged. One attorney sent a birth mother in California $1,500 to have her car fixed without first asking the couple whether it was all right.

Medical Expenses

It is appropriate to support a birth mother by allowing her to see a private physician (if she has no health insurance or does not qualify for Medicaid) or by purchasing vitamins and healthy foods. It shows you care about her and the baby.

Counseling

Paying for counseling also shows that you care about her emotional needs. Sometimes a birth mother has more difficulty after she places the baby than before. Many adoptive parents pay for her counseling fees during this time.

Legally, most expenses can be paid only up to six weeks after birth. Yet counseling may be required for an extended period of time. If your birth mother needs counseling, try to see whether you can get special court approval through your attorney to pay for counseling beyond six weeks if necessary.

Lost Wages

In some states birth mothers are permitted to be reimbursed for lost wages resulting from pregnancy and postnatal recuperation. This can be very expensive and is sometimes used as a "legal" way to "pay" a birth mother for placing her child with you. If a birth mother earns, for example, $300 a week and is out of work for six weeks before birth, some attorneys will tell her that she can be given $1,800 at birth and another $1,800 after if she is out of work for another six weeks—possibly even on top of whatever she receives in living expenses.

This is an area where paying lost wages can look like baby selling. If you are giving a birth mother this kind of assistance, be sure she is not also receiving disability or paid sick leave.

RELATING TO MORE THAN ONE BIRTH MOTHER

What do you do when you receive calls from more than one birth mother? If you have advertised diligently, especially in the newspapers, you can have more than one birth mother who is interested in placing a baby for adoption. This offers you more options but also means you must make some difficult choices. It is not unethical to be making arrangements with more than one birth mother for a very short time period without disclosing that to both birth mothers; you have the right to change your mind, just as she does. However, it is unfair to string someone along for more than a couple of months. Here are some scenarios that could arise, and some suggestions for handling them:

A birth mother calls you on Tuesday and another calls you on Wednesday. One has a delivery date in two weeks; the other is due in six months. If both women seem sincere, agree to meet both of them. If both agree to place a baby with you after meeting with you, your choices are as follows:

a. Decide which birth mother you would rather deal with based on her background and interests.
b. Select between the birth mothers based on the earlier delivery date. All other things being equal, if one birth mother's due date is in two weeks and the other's is six months away, it is best to make adoption arrangements with the former while maintaining communication with the latter. If the first birth mother changes her mind, you can then make arrangements with the birth mother whose delivery date is in six months.
c. Agree to make arrangements with both women, and if neither changes her mind, be ready to have two babies—five to six months apart. Good luck!

Two birth mothers call, and each one has a delivery date about five to seven months away. You meet each birth mother and agree that you like both equally.

a. Continue arrangements for a few weeks with each woman until you sense which one you would prefer and which seems most sure of her decision.
b. Make arrangements with both birth mothers, and if both place the babies, be prepared to have two babies a few weeks apart!

Here are some general guidelines for relating to more than one birth mother at a time. *Note:* Should you become pregnant while pursuing adoption, you may want to use similar strategies, given the uncertain outcome of your pregnancy.

1. While you are still choosing between two birth mothers, never let one know about the other.

2. If you cannot bear to call a birth mother to tell her that you did not choose her, have your attorney do so for you.

3. Have a network of other prospective adoptive parents so that you can give their names to a birth mother if you are not going to commit to her. Alternatively, if your attorney is permitted to act as an intermediary, he can provide another couple.

Chapter Eight

Birth Fathers and Their Rights

PUTATIVE FATHER REGISTRIES

To deal with contested adoptions by birth fathers, some states have established putative father registries. A putative father registry allows the biological father (the "presumed" or "reputed" father) to record his interest in the child. The state is then required to notify the birth father of any legal proceedings that relate to the well-being of his child. About 32 states have laws related to putative father registries. (See Appendix to learn if your state or the state from which you may adopt has a registry.)

The moment Mary and John had long awaited finally arrived when they took home their beautiful baby girl. They had not expected problems, since both of the sixteen-year-old birth parents supported the adoption. In fact, both the birth mother, Sally, and her ex-boyfriend, Tom, had responded well to counseling. Then Tom unexpectedly threw a wrench into the works. He decided that the only way to win Sally back as his girlfriend was to insist upon having the baby back. Surprisingly, Tom's mother supported his wish, even agreeing to help raise the baby. Tom hired a high-profile attorney he had seen on television who argued that the "natural" parents are always best for the baby.

Sally knew that Tom's family had many problems and that this was not the ideal household for the baby. Her only choice was to raise the child herself. Naturally, it was not her first choice. Sally had hoped to go to college. Nor were her parents able to help. Her mother worked full-time, and her father was partially disabled.

Ray and I will never forget having to pick up the one-week-old infant from John and Mary's home and take her back to Sally. Of course, Ray could have taken the case to court. But with no guarantee of winning their case, the adoptive parents would have risked losing the baby after she had been in their home for nine months or more, an even worse scenario.

Ironically, two weeks later, Sally, the baby, and her family moved to a new city 800 miles away from Tom. Now Tom has visitation rights that he has yet to exercise. The baby is with the birth mother, and her life goals have been severely limited. If Tom's goal was to punish Sally, he succeeded.

LAWS AND PRECEDENTS

These events took place in New Jersey, where Tom has the same right to change his mind about an adoption as Sally does, provided he has a means of caring for the baby. Birth mothers in New Jersey do not have the right to say they want their child to be placed for adoption instead of being raised by a birth father, even a birth father who has not been supportive of her during the pregnancy. The story illustrates the impact of various state laws on adoption outcomes. Had Sally agreed to take part in an identified adoption, working with an adoption agency, she and Tom would have been asked to sign a termination of rights seventy-two hours after the baby's birth. If Tom had refused, the baby would never have gone to Mary and John's home, saving them untold heartache.

If Mary and John had lived in South Carolina, the birth parents' rights could have been terminated immediately after birth in either an agency or private adoption. Across the border in North Carolina, on the other hand, where parental rights are terminated twenty days from birth whether the adoption is agency or private, getting an agency involved would not have changed the circumstances. There is no national policy on adoption. Every state has its own laws, and invariably there are unintended consequences.

One area in which state adoption statutes have been affected across the board, however, is that of birth fathers' rights. Until 1972, "unwed" or "putative" fathers had relatively few rights. States did not include an unwed father in the definition of "parent," meaning that his consent was not needed for adoption placements. These laws cut both ways. An out-of-wedlock child could not demand support or inheritance from his birth father; the birth father had no legal status to influence the child's upbringing. Not only was the birth father's consent not needed in many states, but he was often not even entitled to notice of any adoption hearings or proceedings. Unless he took the extraordinary step of asserting his paternity, an adoptive couple had no need to worry about the birth father. An adoption was routinely initiated and finalized without any regard to him.

Since 1971, however, the Supreme Court has rendered several decisions that provided, under certain circumstances, the same rights to a birth father as are given to a birth mother. All state adoption statutes must provide these rights so long as the birth father meets certain conditions or takes certain steps to establish his paternity. Usually this means taking one or more of the following actions:

1. Establishing paternity by obtaining a court order
2. In states with a putative father registry, submitting his name to the registry
3. Having his name placed on the child's birth certificate or similar document
4. Maintaining a relationship or attempting to maintain a relationship with the child to be adopted—including providing financial and emotional support. New Jersey law, for example, emphasizes maintaining an emotional relationship with the child. Many state laws stipulate that this relationship must be maintained during the six months (or some part thereof) following birth.

Which of these steps are regarded as indispensable varies from state to state, but in most, if the birth father puts his name on a putative father registry or on the birth certificate without attempting to "act like a father," it will probably not be enough to prevent an adoption. Similarly, if he tries to establish paternity just prior to or just after the adoption finalization, his rights are limited unless he can show that his inability to assert his parental rights was the result of circumstances beyond his control, such as being incarcerated in a state prison. A birth father who "sits" on his rights as time goes by and fails to show paternal interest weakens his position to contest the adoption.

In 1979 the United States Supreme Court stated that an unwed father who has "manifested a significant paternal interest in the child" must be allowed the right to veto his child's adoption. What constitutes "significant paternal interest," of course, is left to the interpretation of the states. Let's consider a 1983 case involving a New York birth father. In *Lehr v. Robertson*, a putative father attempted, after the fact, to contest the final adoption of his daughter by the birth mother's husband. The birth mother consented to the adoption. The case went all the way to the Supreme Court, which stated that an unwed father who had failed to establish and maintain "any significant custodial, personal, or financial relationship" with his daughter was not entitled to notice of the adoption proceedings.

The birth father had lived with the birth mother before the child's birth and had visited the hospital several times after birth. However, he provided no financial support, nor did he offer to marry the birth mother. Of equal importance, he did not take the steps required under New York law to establish his paternity, which included putting his name on the birth certificate or mailing in a postcard to New York's putative father registry. Noting further that the birth father did not live with the birth mother and child after birth, the Court declared that "the mere existence of a biological link does not merit" constitutional protection when the birth father in essence "sat on his rights." This decision incorporates the principles of all recent Supreme Court decisions pertaining to the putative father's rights to contest an adoption. As Justice Stevens noted in the *Lehr* decision, "The rights of the parents are a counterpart of the responsibilities they have assumed."

These principles have been incorporated into the laws of every state. In any adoption situation, the adoptive couple and attorney must determine what role the birth father desires to play, if any, and to what extent he will be involved. His involvement should be addressed at an early stage to avoid any "surprises" at the time the baby is discharged from the hospital. Many birth mothers, of course, do not want the birth father to be involved, particularly if they have parted ways. However, once a birth mother learns that the birth father has equal rights and could cause the adoptive couple problems, she will usually agree to provide information about him. She, a family member, or the adoptive couple's attorney must then approach him, perhaps for the first time, with the issue of his interest in the child to be born.

The couple's attorney must be aware of the state statute and case law dealing with the birth father's rights. In situations like the *Lehr* case, where state law and the facts allow, the attorney and couple can abide by the birth mother's wishes not to notify the birth father of the adoption proceedings because the birth father has not asserted his rights by following state law.

Unless an adoption has a *Lehr* birth father, the United States Supreme Court has required in general that if a birth father's rights are to be terminated, he must receive notice of the adoption proceedings. The notice must provide in clear language that unless the birth father communicates his opposition to the court, his rights will be forfeited forever. It must state how much time he has to act and how he can communicate his opposition. The time period in which to respond is usually ten to forty-five days, depending on the state. If he is opposed to the adoption, he must usually communicate this in writing to the court or appear at the adoption hearing. At this point the adoption is classified as a contested adoption.

WORST-CASE SCENARIOS

Most adoptions go through smoothly. Sometimes, however, questions about the identity or whereabouts of the birth father can lead to serious complications. One—fortunately rare—illustration has to do with the naming of the birth father. A birth mother can name any man as the birth father. So long as he signs the consent or surrender, and the true genetic father is not in the picture, there is no problem. But if she or the real birth father changes her or his mind, the birth mother who has given an irrevocable surrender (or whose rights have been terminated in court) can ask the "real" birth father to come forward and ask for the child back. In other words, a dishonest birth mother can ask her cousin Vinny or some friend to say he is the birth father, use his name on the birth certificate, and ask him to give consent or sign surrender documents. Then if she changes her mind, all she has to do is ask the true birth father to identify himself and say that the birth mother miscalculated her menstrual cycles and that he would like the child back. The birth parents' surrenders mean nothing if the genetic father is not the person giving surrender. This situation does not often come up, but it highlights the need to focus on a birth mother's honesty.

Another scenario that can create problems is when there is an unnamed "out of the picture" birth father. This is usually a man who had sexual relations with the birth mother but has had no more contact with her and did not know she was pregnant. If, fourteen months after conception, he suddenly finds out the child was placed for adoption, he may decide that he wants to raise the child himself.

This came up in New York in the case of *Robert O. v. Russell K.* The birth father had learned two years after placement that the birth mother, with whom he had sexual relations, had become pregnant, delivered the baby, and placed the child with an adoptive couple. He took the matter to court, stating that had he known she was pregnant, he would have wanted to parent the child. The court ruled that a birth father's "opportunity to manifest his willingness" to parent a child after his birth must be of short duration because of a societal need for adoptions to be finalized promptly and efficiently. It further declared that "promptness is measured in terms of the baby's life, not by the onset of the father's awareness" that a child was born to a woman with whom he had sexual relations. In *Robert O.* the court stated the birth father was too late; he had an obligation to confirm whether the birth mother became pregnant after the relationship. Since he did not, it was in the best interests of the child to remain with the adoptive couple.

In sharp contrast is a 1990 North Carolina case, *Adoption of Clark*, in which the birth father was in a Marine boot camp in another state and did not know of his child's birth and placement. The agency, which knew his identity but not his whereabouts, did not attempt to locate him and notify him of the proposed placement. The court recognized that the birth mother had withheld information from the adoption agency as to the birth father's whereabouts, but ruled that the agency had failed to exercise "due diligence" in seeking out the birth father and notifying him of the adoption proceedings. In other words, the agency hadn't tried hard enough. The horror of this case, as pointed out by one of the justices who disagreed with the decision, is that the litigation had lasted six years, during which time the child lived with his adoptive parents. The ruling did not consider whether it would be in the child's best interests to remain with the only parents he had ever known. Sadly, North Carolina is not the only state that fails to consider the child's best interests if the birth father's rights have not been properly terminated under state law, even when it can be shown that a child has bonded with a couple and will suffer psychological and emotional harm by being taken from his home. It seems to defy logic when a child who is flourishing with an adoptive couple for several years is turned over to a birth father she knows hardly, if at all.

The California courts have articulated a standard that a birth father's parental rights cannot be terminated if he is exercising due diligence in pursuing custody of his child, unless it can be shown that he is an unfit parent. In one case the California Supreme Court stated that it would not presume "either as a policy or factual matter, that adoption is necessarily in a child's best interest," going on to say that a child's best interest is not automatically enhanced because a birth mother places him with an adoptive couple instead of the birth father (*Kelsey S.*, 1992). Having made this judgment, however, the court then went on to say that all factors must be considered in deciding whether a birth father is fit, including a father's actions prior to and after birth. At the time he knows or should have known about the birth, he must present himself as one who can and will assume full custody. If there is any hesitation or lack of ability to parent, this will be held against him. Practically speaking, this covers most cases.

Nevertheless, it is clear that the birth father's rights cannot be ignored and that his status must be resolved as expeditiously as possible. Although his rights are as viable as the birth mother's, they weaken with time if he does not assert them or act upon them either during the pregnancy or after the birth of his child. As the Arizona Supreme Court stated, "an unwed father's parental rights do not attain fundamental constitutional status unless he takes significant steps to create a parental relationship...for, in the child's eyes, a valiant but failed attempt to create a relationship means little" (*Appeal in Pima County Juvenile Severance Action*, 1994).

Chapter Nine

Openness in Adoption

O penness in adoption means communication between you and the birth parents, primarily after the placement of your child in your home and after finalization of the adoption. This can range from sending your attorney pictures and progress notes about the baby for him to forward to the birth mother, to having the birth mother visit you and the baby at your home and perhaps even celebrate holidays with you. Openness can consist of contact for a very short period of time—six months—to contact for a period of several years.

In most adoptions openness is minimal, but attitudes are changing. More adoptive couples are becoming comfortable about sharing the details of their child's life with the birth mother. There are, it is true, situations in which openness would not be appropriate, some of which are discussed in Chapter 14, "Special Needs Adoption." And for many children who are adopted internationally, there is little, if any, possibility of maintaining an open relationship with the birth parents. But in most other cases, open adoption is coming to be seen as a healthy alternative to the anonymity and secrecy of the past.

IS OPEN ADOPTION FOR YOU?
Couples involved in an open adoption will want to attend workshops and read books to learn as much as possible. Although it is important to agree on a plan for openness before the adoption takes place, adoptive parents must be willing to allow the openness to be an evolutionary process and not a specific set of terms. In most cases the adoptive couple and the birth parents get together more when the children are young; the need for openness usually dissipates over time. You may want to ask yourself how you would feel if the birth mother visited the child the first year and then did not visit after that. Or, to turn the question around, how would you feel if the birth mother wanted to visit more often than originally

planned? Would you feel a sense of entitlement to your child? Would you worry that the birth mother might interfere too much?

OPEN ADOPTION: ADVANTAGES

Open adoptions are a relatively new phenomenon, and we lack models for them. Advocates point out that the secrecy associated with closed adoptions has been detrimental to all involved—concluding that if closed adoptions are bad, open adoptions must be good. However, there is more anecdotal information than hard evidence to back this up. Indeed, there is no question that open adoption can sometimes be difficult. The fact that a birth mother chooses you does not guarantee that you and she will have a wonderful, communicative relationship, even if you all initially agree on the level of openness you want.

This is why it is best to allow the relationship to evolve gradually. For example, you may initially agree that you will talk on the phone and send letters and photographs. If you and she find that the relationship is very comfortable, you may want to meet without the baby. From that meeting you may decide that she can come to your home to meet the baby.

Open adoption offers psychological advantages for everyone concerned: birth parents, adoptive parents, and child. To the birth mother, for instance, it offers the opportunity:

- To resolve many of her feelings as she grieves placing her child for adoption
- To have peace of mind
- To see firsthand the kind of family the child lives in
- To know the status of the baby's health
- To minimize her fears and insecurities
- To be part of the adoption process
- To have an honest and realistic picture of the child, not an idyllic fantasy

It allows the adoptive parents:

- To see the birth parents' traits firsthand, including physical appearance, intellectual abilities, personality, and skills
- To assess the birth parents accurately instead of fantasizing about them
- To have fewer fears and insecurities about the birth mother
- To answer the child's questions about why the birth mother placed the child for adoption and about the birth mother's love for her child

Finally, it allows the adoptee:

- To understand her biological roots.
- Not to feel that her life is filled with "secrets."
- To know the circumstances surrounding her placement. This allows her to move beyond the sense of rejection that can occur in a closed adoption.
- To grieve the loss of biological parents. Unlike adoptive parents, who choose to adopt, the child does not choose to have no biological link with her family. It just happens.
- To have a more realistic picture of the birth parents instead of fantasizing about an ideal parent.
- To know that she was born and did not just arrive on planet Earth. This may seem simplistic, but it is very important for a child to know that she was born as well as adopted.
- To have a medical family history. As the birth parents' families age, their medical histories can give the adoptee a better picture of her genetic history. The child's birth parents and grandparents will probably be healthy at the time of the child's birth because they are young. But they may later develop genetically linked health problems. This knowledge could help save an adoptee's life down the road.

OPEN ADOPTION: DISADVANTAGES

Given the emotional factors associated with adoption, it is not surprising to learn that there may be stress in most open adoption relationships. Expectations, for example, can sometimes evolve to an uncomfortable point. You and the birth parents may both agree to one set of expectations at the baby's birth, only to find the birth parents pushing for more openness than you want later on. Especially if the birth mother is a teenager, she may have unrealistic expectations about her role in your family, expecting in some way to become a part of your family—to be "adopted" herself. These expectations may be more apparent in girls who have families with profound problems and who view the adoptive couple as the perfect family.[1]

Another problem associated with open adoption is that the birth mother may not properly grieve for the loss, because she does not fully experience the adoption as a loss.[2]

Of course, there is always the possibility that the birth mother will not want an open relationship; many do not. If so, you cannot coerce her into one. A birth mother does have the right to place a child for adoption, grieve the loss, and move on with her life. In fact, in a survey of fifty-nine biological mothers (aged sixteen to forty-five years) who placed a child for adoption through an agency, it was found that those who chose an open adoption felt *more* social isolation and despair, and expressed more dependency, than those who opted for a confidential adoption.[3] Although it could be that these particular women simply had more difficulties, it could also be that open adoption prevented them from "moving on" in their lives.

Finally there's no denying that some birth mothers are more "together" than others. Although we have enjoyed working with nearly all of our birth mothers, not all have been stable people. Having said that, not one who knew the address and phone number has ever yet shown up at the adoptive parents' home. One birth mother, who does have a mental illness, did call the adoptive parents once and harass them, but after that incident, all other limited communication between them was cordial.

In other words, even when there was a history of mental illness or instability, no birth mother has ever caused problems in any of the adoptive couples' lives. Even so, just knowing that a birth mother's mood can swing can cause some people so much consternation that they find themselves living in a state of "what if."

LEGAL CONSIDERATIONS

In most states a signed agreement between you and the birth parents to maintain an open adoption is not legally binding. Where states have addressed the issue of open adoption rights, only one-third have held that open adoption agreements are valid and that they do not go against public policy so long as the openness is in the child's best interest. The cases in which openness was allowed came as a result of a lawsuit in which birth parents wanted to challenge the adoption. In these cases visitations were allowed in exchange for dropping the lawsuit.[4]

HOW OPEN IS OPEN?

When you first make contact with a birth mother, all you will know about each other is your first names. As you become more comfortable with each other, you and she may want to share last names too. Then, if you decide to correspond directly with each other, you will exchange addresses and perhaps telephone numbers. (Note: In a few states you are legally required to reveal your last names and addresses to the birth parents, in which case anonymity is no longer an issue.)

If you are not comfortable sharing such information, or if the birth mother is from another state, you may arrange for all contact to be handled through your attorney's office. Your attorney may include this service as part of the adoption arrangement, or he may charge extra each time his staff handles correspondence and telephone calls. The fee for such services should be reasonable.

Remember, no matter how careful you and the birth parents are about retaining your anonymity, it is all too easy for a professional to slip and reveal your last names. If your attorney's staff is accustomed to addressing you as Mr. and Mrs. Sanders, for example, they will have to change gears to refer to you as Chuck and Doris when speaking to the birth mother. Forgetting to conceal last names on documents is another common slip. Mistakes do get made. We've often known the judge who presides over the court hearing to reveal the last names of the birth parents.

STAYING IN TOUCH
There are various ways to maintain openness in an adoption arrangement. Here are some of the most common.

Correspondence
Many couples exchange letters and photographs with birth mothers. Most birth mothers want to maintain some level of correspondence, at least for the child's first year of life. Letters telling of the baby's progress are usually sent at Christmas and the baby's birthday. You may want to send a note once a month along with a picture, especially during the baby's first year.

Sending Pictures
Nearly all birth mothers want pictures and letters sent to them. Even those who did not make an adoption decision but had the child removed from them want to know that the child is all right, and pictures are the most obvious way— short of seeing the child in person—of knowing that she is alive and well. Videotapes are very easy to produce, and a growing number of adoptive parents and birth parents exchange them.

The birth mother may likewise send you pictures of herself, her family, and the birth father. These can be important keepsakes for your child.

Telephone Calls
Calling the birth mother, or having her call you, will probably occur more spontaneously than an arrangement to send letters and pictures, but adoptive parents could agree to call the birth mother once a month or so to let her know how they and the baby are doing. The birth mother could also have permission to call the adoptive parents for information about the baby. If this is too personal, she could call your attorney's office for information about the baby; then the attorney's office personnel could call you and get a verbal progress report to pass along.

Sometimes a birth mother just does not want to communicate with the adoptive parents. Perhaps she is living with a boyfriend or husband, someone she does not want to know about her past. In such cases it is sometimes a relative of the birth mother who stays in touch.

Exchanging Gifts

A birth mother or her family may want to give the baby a special gift, perhaps one with sentimental value. This can be a special keepsake to share with your child to let her know that the birth mother cared very much about her.

After the adoption is finalized, you are permitted to send the birth mother a gift. (It may be illegal to do so before then in your state.) You may want to give her a token to remember you by.

Exchanging Other Mementos

Some birth mothers may request other sentimental tokens from you. Our younger daughter's birth mother asked that we send her a lock of hair when she got her first haircut. Other personal tokens can be the child's artwork, or one of the child's favorite dolls or rattles after she has outgrown it. Some people like to send a special book, a Bible, or jewelry.

Sample Letters

Following are samples of the kinds of letters that you or your child's sibling may want to send to the birth mother. *Always respond to a letter sent to you from the birth mother.*

LETTER FOR BIRTH MOTHER WHEN SHE RELINQUISHES THE CHILD TO YOU

Dear Cindy,

Thank you so much for all that you have done for us. Your love and commitment to David's well-being are magnificent, and the joy that he will add to our lives is immeasurable.

We loved David before we even met him, and we look forward to caring for him and sharing our lives with him. He will truly be a special person—not just for the love that we will provide him, but for the love that you have expressed in making plans for his life.

Christopher is already so excited about the campsites and ball games that he wants to take David to. I have to remind him that it will be a few years before David will be playing ball and camping.

Cindy, Christopher and I wish you well in your education. You have been so diligent in all that you have done. I trust that you will find just the right job when you graduate from school next year.

You will certainly always be a part of our lives and in our prayers. We truly love you for all that you have done. Do keep in touch. As we have promised, I will send you lots of pictures of David each month. (I can hardly wait to start photographing our beautiful baby.)

Do take care, Cindy, and I will write to you next month.

All our love,

Sharon, Christopher, and David

LETTER TO A BIRTH MOTHER WHEN THE CHILD IS SIX MONTHS OLD

Dear Jenny,

I can hardly believe that James is six months old. He is now starting to creep and to make the funniest sounds. He is very alert and loves to watch his older sister play. James especially loves music. When Jodi's singing her favorite nursery rhymes, he nearly hums along with her while his body rocks back and forth. Sometimes I play some lively classical music, and again, his body sways to the music. Everyone says James is very good-natured.

Enclosed are pictures from Thanksgiving. We had a wonderful day at my parents' home in the country. All thirteen of James's cousins were there. My favorite picture is Tom holding James next to the turkey. The turkey and James weighed about the same—20 pounds.

We and all the relatives will be back at my parents' house again for Christmas. As soon as we get pictures of James's first Christmas, I will send them to you.

Jenny, I trust you are doing well. I was very pleased to hear about your new adventures. Please continue to keep us updated about your activities and plans.

Thank you so much for the letter and pictures you sent James. We will keep them in a very special place for him. Someday James will know how blessed he is that you loved him enough to make adoption plans for his life.

John and I trust that you will have a warm and special Christmas. We understand that this time of year may be difficult for you. You have made a very difficult but loving decision, and I hope you are especially comforted knowing that James is loved immensely by us and his relatives.

We'll look forward to hearing from you.

Love,

Sandy and John

LETTER FROM THE CHILD'S SIBLING TO BIRTH MOTHER

> Dear Stephanie's birth mother,
>
> Thank you for giving us a baby sister. She is so cute. We love her and we love you. Mommy and Daddy said you are a really nice person. We will take good care of her.
>
> Love,
>
> Jason and Brian

SEARCHING FOR BIRTH FAMILIES

Although open adoption has received much attention over the last ten years, the reality is that most adoptions have not been open. Even in cases where letters and pictures are initially exchanged between the birth parents and adoptive family, as the years pass, the contact may diminish or end. Even so, adoptions that have been somewhat open provide at least some identifying information exchanged between birth and adoptive families. As a result, there will be a future generation of adoptees who will be able to find and meet their birth parents if they so choose.

Currently, however, nearly all adult adoptees and those now reaching adulthood were never given detailed information about their birth parents. Sometimes the agency or attorney did not obtain the information. Many times adoptive parents, for whatever reason, did not share what information they had with their children. Other times adoptive parents did not share birth family information with the adoptee because they considered it superfluous; but this information could be essential to finding a birth parent. In fact, most adult adoptees feel that their parents withheld information surrounding their adoption from them.

Although parents and relatives should be the first place that adoptees go to get information, adoptees often say that if their parents ever knew that they were searching for their birth parents it would "kill" them. The tone that was set in the home may let the adoptee know whether searching for information about his birth history is or is not "open for discussion."

First, a word about terms often used in searching for a birth family—*reunion* and *triangle*. When, for example, a birth daughter and birth mother find each other, this is sometimes called a reunion. Yet others find this term to be inappropriate, because a reunion is usually *a celebration when family gets together because they share a heritage.* Those who search are not necessarily looking to reunite with their birth families; they may just want to have some questions answered or find out some information. Or they may seek and find the birth relatives, but these encounters may be not positive and could hardly be called reunions. Therefore, the term *meeting* rather than the word *reunion* is used when two birth relatives meet. If they continue to see each other, then they have an ongoing relationship.

Another misnomer is the term *triangle*—meaning adoptive parents, adoptee, and birth family; the word *triad* is more appropriate to describe the three parties involved in the adoption.

So Why All of the Interest in Searching?

As one adult adoptee said, "I never thought it was possible until I had seen a television program where a birth mother and daughter met each other." In this day of sensational talk shows, the meeting of birth parents and children is probably not very titillating, but just a few years ago, it was news! Now there are search support groups all over the country, and laws have been passed to help those in the adoption triad find each other. The Internet has also made the logistics of such a search more affordable and likely.

How Many People Search?

The numbers vary greatly, but one Web site, the Adoptee Search Center Registry, which has been in existence since 1996, currently has more than 27,000 people registered who are looking for birth relatives and growing at a rate of 1,000-1,500 persons per month. According to Merry Block Jones, who wrote *Birthmothers: Women Who Have Relinquished Babies for Adoption Tell Their Stories*, when she interviewed birth parents, she found that nearly all of them continue to wonder how the child they relinquished for adoption is doing. These feelings surface especially when the child reaches the age that he or she would be starting school, graduating, getting married or having children.

Who Searches?

Anecdotal evidence suggests that mostly female adoptees and birth mothers are searching. It is understandable that more birth mothers than birth fathers would be searching—after all, the woman is the person who gave birth and the birth father may not even know that he has a biological child. Why more women adoptees search is not so well understood. People who search are from all age ranges, but as may be expected, many are in their early twenties. If adoptees are under eighteen years old when they search, they usually have the support of their adoptive parents

Why Do People Search?

The most prevalent reason given is to obtain medical histories—*this is reasonable as most of us know our genetic and medical background*. However, for adoptees who were placed as infants, there may be a limited medical background because their biological grandparents may only have been in their early forties, and certain diseases may not have manifested themselves. Also, the birth mothers and their siblings were probably healthy at the time the adoptees were placed for adoption. However, as the birth parents' parents age, and the birth parents and their siblings go on to have children, it is very likely that someone is going to have a medical condition that has genetic component. Even as open adoptions become more prevalent, most adoptees will not have updated, ongoing medical information. Obtaining a medical history is not just about what is happening now. It's about going to a health professional and the adoptee always having to say, "I don't know my family history; I'm adopted." Health information can also provide insight as to what may happen in the future and may mean taking measures to prevent a disease. If this were not so important, then why do medical forms ask about family history?

Although adoptees often identify wanting their medical family history as the primary reason to search—perhaps because it sounds acceptable and is the most tangible reason that can be expressed—the real reason may be curiosity. Although "curiosity" does not sound very meaningful, it is reason enough. Yet others may not understand this concern.

Some people advise that if the adoptee has no compelling health problem, and if the search is going to hurt the adoptive parents, then the adoptee shouldn't do it. But this advice can be missing the whole point. The person may really be saying, "I want to know why my hair is red and my eyes are blue." Also, when an adult adoptee considers having children, she may begin to grieve the fact that she does not know the genetic history she is passing on to her child. It's not just the medical background that she is passing on, but hair color and height, and even personality traits.

But beyond wanting to know their medical and genetic history, adoptees say that they want to know why their birth mother placed them for adoption. Likewise, birth mothers search for their birth children so that they can see that they are happy and to tell them why they were placed for adoption.

Because the outcome of the search is not always favorable, being emotionally prepared for who and what you will find is very important. One birth mother who belonged to a support group in which the group discussed all the possible outcomes was not prepared for the fact that her birth son had died a few years previously from a genetic disease that she did not even know she carried.

Two other birth mothers who searched and found their birth children discovered that each child lived in a home where one parent was an alcoholic and that the adoptive parents had divorced. Even with this information, one birth mother said that adoption was the right choice, but she wished that she had had more input into the selection of the family. She even said, "I wish that I could have made them sign a paper that the couple would never divorce." The other birth mother has a warm ongoing relationship with her adult birth daughter. She also wishes that she had had more control in the selection of a family.

Of course, not all searches are so heart wrenching. Birth parents often find that the adoptive parents were good parents and that the birth children are doing fine.

HOW ARE SEARCHES CONDUCTED?

The first place to start is a support group. Beyond emotional support, other searchers can give advice as to how to search. Also, their successes probably will encourage you if you have snags in your search. Whether your support group is people that you talk to on the phone or through e-mail, or who you meet at a group meeting, be careful about the information you get and of others' reasons for searching. For example, someone you meet or e-mail may try to convince you that something is wrong with you if you have doubts about searching for your birth parent or child. Perhaps all you want is information and do not necessarily want to meet the other person. When some people join an organization, the "cause" becomes their focus in life, and they may try to convince you that this should be your whole focus as well. Others who are searching are very angry about being adopted and may project their anger onto you. A support group should provide common sense advice and let you know that your feelings are "normal." You do not need to have someone causing you angst about your past.

Next, you may want to contact the adoption agency or attorney who handled the adoption. Larger agencies may even have a registry and someone on staff who assists those who are searching. If they do not have a registry, they may at least give you nonidentifying information about your birth family. Also, ask them if you can sign "a waiver of confidentiality" statement giving your birth child/parent permission to contact you should he/she contact the agency.

There are now national and state-level registries. You can contact the National Adoption Information Clearinghouse to find out if your state or the state you were born in has a registry. Getting your name on a registry can be an active way to find a birth relative. On the other hand, a registry can be for those who are not actively searching but who are willing to be contacted by a birth relative.

The Internet is probably a great place to search if you are not able to contact an agency. The search is done using date of birth, social security number, addresses, and other types of information. At the Adoptee Search Center site the staff and volunteers are also searchers. First priority is given to those who have a demanding medical need. This site and others have links for other mailing lists, other registries, prison sites, and telephone databases. So if the person you are looking for is not listed, the site's resources may help you find that person.

If your search is getting nowhere, you may consider hiring a private investigator. The fees can be high, so start your own search first and see where this leads. Keep good notes. Then if your search is not going anywhere, share what information you do have with the investigator. Be sure to use someone who is experienced and is familiar with looking for birth relatives.

POTENTIAL OUTCOMES

What can you expect to find when you do a search? If you were placed for adoption through the foster care system, you can probably expect your parents' lives to be still in turmoil. If you were abused or neglected and you find that one of your parents is working and leading a seemingly "normal" life, you may be angry that you received abuse and now their lives are "fine."

Rachel, who is now a teenager, was adopted along with her two older brothers by her foster family when she was a baby. She recently began to search for her birth family. She already knew that her birth mother had used drugs and permitted men to sexually abuse her. However, she also knew that her birth mother was a nurse and could still be employed as one.

Her biological brother, who knew that she was going to search with the support of their adoptive parents, asked that she not share any information with him unless it was part of his medical history. Rachel discovered that the man whom she thought was her biological father was not, but rather the man who had sexually abused her and her brothers. Within a matter of days, Rachel went from searching for a birth mother to finding out that she was not her brother's full biological sibling but had a different biological father than he did. She also found out that she had five other birth siblings who were also placed for adoption with other families.

Because Rachel and her adoptive mother were permitted to read the file that social services maintained, and because most of the social workers involved in the case when Rachel was placed for adoption were still working for social services, they were also able to get a full report of the abuse that occurred in her birth family. These reports confirmed what her older brother had said when he was a child. The adoptive mother said that she had always believed her oldest son's reports of what happened in his birth home; however, she felt that because he was only five or six years old when he shared this information that his story was clouded by a six-year-old child's perception and limited ability to relay the facts.

As a result of her search, Rachel did not just learn what her birth mother looked like and what she was doing now in her life. She also learned a lot about her past—all in a very short period of time. Of course without the right support from her family and social workers, this information could have been overwhelming.

With this support she will continue her search, knowing that more questions will arise as more information is gathered.

Rachel knew that she was most likely never going to connect with her birth parents, and based on the circumstances of her adoption placement, this is understandable. Others who have searched, however, have said they have found "another" family. Not that a birth family is there to replace the adoptive family, but sometimes birth siblings find that they actually can enjoy each other's company and want to see each other a few times a year.

Like other adoption-related stories, the ones with more colorful details are the ones that get media attention and are more memorable. The story of a birth mother and daughter who find each other, visit each other a few times a year, and have a pleasant, cordial relationship is not exactly the plot for a movie. But in reality this is probably what is lived out.

WHAT ABOUT INTERNATIONAL ADOPTION?

When you read about the compelling need for some to find their birth parents or at least information about their backgrounds, you may wonder, "What about children who are adopted internationally? Will they be able to even consider searching?"

The fact is that when adoptions are conducted today, the birth mothers are usually known. In fact, a birth mother often signs a relinquishment. Most adoptive parents are given their child's original birth certificate, and much of the information on that can be used to find a birth mother.

Perhaps the greatest barriers to searching for a birth relative in another country are language and custom. Birth mothers in other countries may not be familiar with the concept of open adoption and may never expect that children they have given up for adoption may look for them. Internet searches and registries probably just do not exist in many countries. But for those being adopted now, the chances of finding a birth mother will improve. Countries in Eastern Europe are becoming more "Westernized," English is spoken by the young people, and computers and the Internet are also growing.

If you feel that your child will never be able to find his birth family overseas, then you may want to at least encourage your child to visit his country of origin. Those adopted from Korea have formed groups that visit the country. If a group of teenagers and those in their twenties have a shared experience of traveling to Korea, this may also provide a support group of people who share the limited possibility of ever finding their birth parents. The group can be a place where your child can share the losses and the gains that he has experienced.

CONTACTING A BIRTH RELATIVE

How do you handle that initial contact? Making that first phone call to a birth parent or child can be worse than standing before a crowd of a thousand. You will be very nervous. Ideally, it would be great if you first e-mailed each other. When you call, of course, you will be very nervous. So have a pen and paper ready. If you are calling your birth mother, she may expect you to be angry. She may immediately tell you why she placed you for adoption and sound apologetic. One adoptee who had a wonderful life with her adoptive family made an effort to reassure her birth mother that she grew up in a great home. One adult adoptee said that when she got ready to call her birth mother after much time spent searching, she made sure her children were not around; then when she made the call, she realized the voice sounded familiar—it sounded like her own voice.

Perhaps the happiest search story I have come across concerns clients who are now adopting themselves. This couple, John and JoAnn, were high school sweethearts, and JoAnn became pregnant when she was about sixteen years old. JoAnn's parents forbade her to ever see John again. JoAnn went on with her life and married. Her daughter, Claire, had never known her biological father but wanted to find him. JoAnn supported Claire's decision to search and gave her as much information as she had about John. After Claire found John, who had also been looking for her, the father and daughter communicated regularly. Then Claire's mother and John remet each other. Both of them had been divorced, and they started dating. They are now married and are in the process of adopting children with special needs. Claire now has both her mother and biological father in her life, and John and JoAnn are finally able to have a family together.

LEGAL ASPECTS OF SEARCHING

Many groups have advocated at the state and national level that birth and adoption records be opened. For those advocating, progress is slow. Florence Fisher, founder of the Adoptees Liberty Movement Association (ALMA), is outraged that she cannot have what is afforded to every other American—her birth certificate and records. Most states will not give an adoptee her birth certificate and records without some compelling reason to do so. The reason given for not changing the laws is that women and men who placed children for adoption should be allowed privacy for the rest of their lives. Also, some feel that the adoptive family should not have to be concerned with birth families contacting them. The only states that allow open adoption records are Alabama, Alaska, Hawaii, Kansas, and Tennessee. However, adult adoptees have automatic access to their original birth certificate in some cases in Ohio and Montana. Access in these states depends upon which year the adoption was finalized.

People have access to medical and other family history without interfering with others' privacy in nearly all states except Washington D.C., Louisiana, and New Jersey. These states, however, allow adopted persons to have access to their nonidentifying information. Nonidentifying information is usually a description of the adoptees birth relatives. The information may include date and place of the adopted adult's birth; birth parents' age and physical description; birth parents' race, ethnicity, religion, and medical history; type of termination; facts and circumstances relating to the adoptive placement; age, sex, and health status of children of the birth parents at the time of the adoption placement; and educational levels, occupations, interests, hobbies, and skills of the birth parents. States usually place more restrictions on the birth mother than on the adoptee.

Some states have mutual consent registries that provide identifying information to the parties in an adoption only if all have agreed that they wish to be found. In some states the registry is centralized by the state, and in others it operates across the state through the agencies or courts that handle adoption. Some states will not release information to a requesting person if the other party is deceased. Sometimes information will not be released if the adopted adult has not received the permission of the adoptive parents. This, of course, gets ridiculous when a thirty-five-year-old adult cannot get information without his parents' consent. When requesting information about another birth relative, the person usually has to make the request in writing and provide identification, such as a copy of his or her driver's license.

Adoptive parents can receive nonidentifying information about the birth parents after placement in all states except Colorado, Connecticut, the District of Columbia, Idaho, Kentucky, Louisiana, Maryland, New Jersey, New York, and Virginia.

Birth parents can access nonidentifying information in Alabama, Arizona, Arkansas, California, Colorado, Connecticut, Delaware, Maryland, Michigan, Minnesota, Montana, New Mexico, North Dakota, Oregon, Rhode Island, South Carolina, Tennessee, Utah, Vermont, Washington, and West Virginia.

Passive registries, also called *mutual consent* or *volunteer registries*, require both parties to register before information is released and a match is made. Once a match occurs, both parties are notified. Passive registries in the United States currently have a match rate of about 10 percent. States that have a passive registry include Arkansas, California, Colorado, Florida, Georgia, Hawaii, Idaho, Illinois, Louisiana, Maine, Maryland, Massachusetts, Michigan, Missouri, Nevada, New York, North Dakota, Ohio, Oklahoma, Pennsylvania, Rhode Island, South Carolina, South Dakota, Texas, Utah, Vermont, West Virginia, and Wisconsin.

Active registries do not require that both parties register their consent. Once one party is registered, an agency or court representative usually contacts the other party being sought and finds out if it is all right to release information. These registries have a match rate of 50 to 90 percent. States with active registries include Connecticut, Indiana, Kentucky, Minnesota, Nebraska, New Jersey, and Oregon.

Search and Consent authorizes an agency to assist a searching party in locating a triad member and to find out if information can be released or if they want to meet. If, for example, a birth mother agrees that information can be given to a birth child, the court then authorizes this. In many states counseling is required before information can be received.

Some states have confidential intermediaries who are permitted to get court-sealed information and then contact the parties involved. These states include Alabama, Arizona, Arkansas, Colorado, Illinois, Indiana, Michigan, Minnesota, Montana, New Mexico, North Dakota, Oklahoma, Oregon, Virginia, Washington, Wisconsin, and Wyoming.

Affidavit System, also called a *consent, waiver,* or *authorization.* In an affidavit system, each party gives written permission to release identifying information. The affidavit system is often used along with the search and consent system. The states that have this system include Alabama, California, Delaware, Hawaii, Indiana, Iowa, Louisiana, Massachusetts, Michigan, Minnesota, Mississippi, Nebraska, Ohio, Oklahoma, Vermont, Washington, and Wisconsin.

Veto System. When someone in the adoption triad does not want to be contacted or have her identifying information released, she files a veto document. Tennessee is the only state with contact veto.

Court Orders. In most states in which adoption records are sealed, an adoptee can petition the court to receive identifying information. Usually "good cause," such as a health reason, must be present for the information to be given. Alabama's statute lets parties with a "compelling need" for medical information petition the court for permission to make contact in order to get that information.

In many states, new adoption laws only affect the adoptions finalized after the date the law is passed. This means in one state there can be two set of rules.

See the appendix for a state-by-state guide of registries and what documents and information are available to those in the adoption triad.

The District of Columbia seals all adoption proceedings and makes no provision for releasing any information to any party except by order of the court.

Illinois allows adoptive parents to ask the court to appoint a confidential intermediary to locate birth parents to request information necessary for medical treatment for the adoptee.

Iowa requires the person to show "good cause," but the court may deny the request for information if releasing it may harm a minor sibling.

Kentucky allows the adopted adults to petition the court to open closed records if the birth parents are missing or deceased.

North Carolina requires a court order to release identifying information.

Virginia will release identifying information if "good cause" is shown.

Hawaii: The state utilizes a "notice and consent" provision for adoptions before 1991, where parties being sought are sent notice through certified mail. If the party does not respond, confidentiality is assumed to have been waived, and identifying information is released. For post-1991 adoptions, an access veto system is in place.

Indiana: Those whose adoptions were finalized through 1993 are serviced through an active registry system, while post-1993 adoptions are subject to an access veto system.

Michigan: The state system combines access veto and passive and active registry systems. Use of these plans is determined by the date of termination of parental rights, with division between those whose rights were terminated before 1945, between 1945 and 1980, and after 1980.

Montana: The state passed a bill allowing those born before 1967 to obtain their original certificates. Those born between 1967 and 1997 must go to court to obtain their records. Those born after October 1997 will have access to their original birth certificates unless a birth parent has filed a nondisclosure request.

Nebraska: An access veto system applies for adoptees placed after 1988. For adoptions prior to that date, there is an active registry. A birth parent registry, to which affidavits may be submitted, also exists.

Ohio: Ohio has different access provisions for pre-1964 adoptions, adoptions finalized 1964–96, and those finalized after 1996. Pre-1964 adoptees have full access, an affidavit system is in place for adoptions 1964–96, and an access veto system applies to post-1996 adoptions.

Tennessee: The state enacted a statute in 1995 granting access to all records to those adopted before 1951 and providing a contact veto system for other adults starting in 1996. As of April 1998, the statute is under an injunction and is being appealed to the Tennessee Supreme Court.

Legislative Activity

Colorado: House Bill 1188 allows for adoption records of adoptions finalized after July 1, 2001, to be available to an adopted adult, birth parent of an adopted adult, adoptive parent, adult sibling or half-sibling, or the adult descendant of an adoptee or adoptive parent. In adoptions that were finalized prior to July 1, 2001, adoption records should remain confidential and access is allowed only through the appointment of a confidential intermediary.

Delaware: House Bill 522 allows adopted adults aged twenty one or older to receive a copy of their original birth certificate. House Bill 522 has been passed and signed into law.

Resources:

Adoptee Search Center Registry
P.O. Box 281223
Memphis, TN 38168-1223
www.adopteesearchcenter.org

Adoption Connection
(508) 532-1261

Adoption Connections Project
www.sover.net/~adopt
Contact Susan Wadia-Ellis at adopt@sover.net.
The Adoption Connections Project is a group of women dedicated to bringing together birth mothers, adopted daughters, adoptive mothers, foster mothers, and stepmothers.

Adoption Support Newsletter
Adoption Circle
P.O. Box 290581
Brooklyn, NY 11229-0581
Attention: Susan Balloqui
www.adoptcrle@aol.com

Infomax, Inc.
4600 Chippewa, Suite 224
St. Louis, MO 63116

Internal Revenue Service
Disclosure Office, Stop 1020
300 N. Los Angeles St.
Los Angeles, CA 90012-3363
The IRS requires that you provide the name and social security number. It is unlikely that adoptees know their birth parents' social security number, but is possible. The adoption agency or attorney you used may know the social security number, and you can ask the staff to forward a letter.

International Soundex Reunion Registry
P.O. Box 2312
Carson City, NV 89702
(702) 882-7755
It is best to send them a self-addressed, legal-sized envelope with your written request. This organization does not charge a fee, but it does accept donations.

National Adoption Information Clearinghouse
naic@calib.com

Open Adoption Mailing List
majordomo@chrystal.com

Chapter Ten

Special Families: Special Considerations

SINGLE-PARENT ADOPTION

If you have made the decision to become a single parent through adoption, you are joining a growing group of people. About twenty years ago, it was nearly unheard of for a single woman to adopt. Now even single men are increasingly being considered seriously as adoptive fathers.

According to Shirley Roe, a single mother who adopted from China and the former co-president of RESOLVE of Greater Hartford, Connecticut, adoption, even adoption of young babies, is now very possible for single people. Whereas in the past unmarried individuals may have been required to adopt only older children, new flexible policies in China and other countries mean that babies are available to single parents. In fact, 40 percent of those adopting from China are single. And now men as well as women are permitted to adopt. Furthermore, even domestic agencies are broadening their policies and allowing singles to adopt.

Mature single parents can offer a child many benefits. At least one study suggests that being single has little, if any, effect on adoption outcome. Single-parent families were shown to be as nurturing and loving as dual-parent families. In fact, without the demands of a marital relationship, a single parent may be better equipped to give the level of involvement and nurturing needed by a child who has had difficult life experiences.

Having said that, no study is needed to highlight the fact that being a single parent has many drawbacks as well. Juggling a full-time job and a child is a daunting task requiring both maturity and resources. Single parents can often provide these things, and certainly from the child's standpoint having one stable, loving parent is better than living in an orphanage or institution, or being bounced from one two-parent foster home to another. But the challenges are considerable, and it is essential to consider them carefully before taking this step.

WHAT TO ASK YOURSELF

Jane Mattes, founder of Single Mothers by Choice, recommends that you begin by asking yourself whether you are ready to become a parent and whether you are seeking parenthood for the right reasons. The following questions are ones she has drawn up to help singles explore these issues. Whether you are a man or woman, or even if you are married, answering the questions can help to make you more prepared for the home study process and eventually for parenthood.

1. Have you accomplished all the personal and career goals that are necessary for you to feel good about yourself? How will you feel if you are not able to achieve some of these goals?

2. How will you feel about others' criticism of your decision to be a single parent?

3. Are you able to support yourself and a child emotionally and financially?

4. Do you have elderly parents who may need your assistance just at the time that you will be devoting yourself to a baby or young child?

5. Are there particular reasons why you are not with a partner, and will these reasons affect how you parent your child?

6. If you date often, can you manage working, dating, and caring for a child? How will a child affect your likelihood of finding a mate? Can you make a distinction between which needs can be fulfilled by a child and which ones can be fulfilled only by a spouse?

7. Do you have a good support system of friends, family, church/synagogue, and work to help you during stressful times? If you do not have family who can care for the child, are you prepared for the twenty-four-hour-a-day responsibility of caring for a child with no assistance except from friends and paid child care?

8. Does your job have the flexibility to allow you to meet a child's needs when he is sick, has a special event, or needs extra attention?

9. How do you handle stress? Will you be able to meet the challenge of caring for a baby while working? Will your coping skills enable you to deal with the stressful situations that having a child will bring, like a baby crying all night because of an ear infection?

10. If you are considering adopting an older child, are you prepared to meet the child's special emotional needs and issues? Do you have time to take a child to a therapist in addition to Girl Scouts and other school and community activities?[1]

OPTIONS FOR SINGLE PARENTS

Although some courts have stated that to promote the welfare of the child, parents should be married, most agencies and courts do not make marital status alone the basis for assessing parenting skills. Yet some adoption professionals have difficulty placing children in single-parent homes. One reason is that statistically, single-parent families produce children who have far more problems than children who are raised by a mother and father. Although these statistics are based on the experiences of poor, undereducated teenage moms with minimal parenting skills and inadequate plans for the future, rather than those of older, well-educated women with well-paying jobs, these statistics and generalizations can make it hard for a birth mother to accept a single woman as a potential adopter. (Men are virtually never even considered by a birth mother as an adoptive parent.) After all, if the agency professional has been making the case that the birth mother's child needs to be raised in a more stable environment with a mother and father, it is not so easy for her to turn around and present a single mother as a potential adopter.

The argument about whether a child is better off with an adoptive mom than his teenage birth mother has become a class issue, diverting participants from focusing on what is better for the child. Many articles have been written to suggest that adopters are in a class tugs-of-wars with women who cannot afford their children. From the agency's standpoint, presenting a two-parent family to a birth mother is a way of staying out of this battle. The practical reality, however, cannot be glossed over by talk of "class tugs-of-war." More often than not, single adoptive mothers have the maturity, the financial wherewithal, and the support system to provide a healthier environment for a child than a teenage mother.

Of course, even if the single adoptive mother has these things, a birth mother is still likely to be concerned. She may wonder, "What's wrong with this woman, and why couldn't she find a husband?" Birth mothers are more open to a single adoptive mother if she is divorced, widowed, or presently involved with a man. If the birth mother senses that the adoptive mother will eventually marry, she may be more open to placing her newborn child with her. These same factors hold true for single men also, except the person who is concerned about his lifestyle and ability to parent is not a birth mother but agency social workers.

Agency Adoption

In their book, *How to Adopt a Child*, Connie Crain and Janice Duffy warn that some domestic agencies will accept the single person's up-front fees and then stall the adoption process. They will seldom show your profile to birth mothers, so that there will not be an opportunity for a birth mother to select you. Duffy and

Crain suggest talking to other single parents who have adopted through the agency you are considering to see how long it took them to adopt.[2] Lois Gilman further cautions that "Singles often find that agencies will not allow them to apply to adopt healthy infants and younger children. Many agencies will tell them bluntly that these children are reserved for two-parent families and will encourage them to consider special needs children instead."[3]

Independent Adoption

Single adoptive mothers will encounter roadblocks in the independent adoption process as well, and single men have even more hurdles to leap over. A typical birth mother's attitude is, "If she (the adoptive mom) can raise a child by herself, then so can I." When a birth mother makes the decision to place a child, she wants a home with more resources than she can provide, and to her this usually means a father and a mother.

Some birth mothers, however—especially those who grew up in single-parent homes or who already have one child and are able to maintain a family life of sorts—believe that the stability of family life is determined solely by income. Their experiences tell them that a single mom can provide a suitable home for a child if her income level is adequate to do so. In fact, many birth mothers' experiences are positive enough that they would parent the children born to them if their cash flow warranted it.

The reality is that very, very few successful agency and independent adoptions involve single mothers. Although it is not impossible, prospective adoptive mothers need to know that the image of a "June and Ward Cleaver" family strongly dominates the typical birth mother's thinking.

Special Needs Adoption

It should surprise no one that agencies that place children with special needs are usually very accepting of single adoptive parents, as long as they have an income sufficient to meet the child's needs. Most social services departments will not allow an adoption if the child's monthly subsidy from the state is going to be the main source of household income.

Single people parenting special needs children may have fewer resources than a two-parent family, and yet these children usually require extra resources. Many single people, however, can meet the demands of a special needs child very well, especially one whose behavior improves as a result of the one-on-one attention and understanding single parents can provide. Indeed, children who come from chaotic backgrounds and have been physically and sexually abused often do better in single-parent homes where the family dynamics are simplified.

International Adoption

The great majority of adoptive single parents have adopted internationally. In fact 40 percent of all adoptions from China are done by singles. Most countries now permit single people to adopt, and many more are allowing single men to adopt. As with any adoption, you must prove to the Immigration and Naturalization Service that you can afford the child and provide adequately for him. When adopting a child, you may be encouraged to adopt a child who is a little older—two to three years old. Usually agencies believe it will be easier for you as a single person not to have to care for a very young baby. Also, in-country officials want the healthy babies to go to two-parent households. However, as Mary Hopkins-Best states in the book *Toddler Adoption*, singles should not assume that caring for a toddler is any easier than caring for a baby; a toddler can be more demanding—only in a different way from a baby. Toddlers require a great deal of time and attention.

THE HOME STUDY PROCESS

If you are a single person about to arrange for a home study, you can expect to be asked to address issues related to marriage, including what plans, if any, you may have for marriage, how marriage would change your relationship with the child, and how being a single parent might change your prospects for marriage. If you answer that you would consider marriage, the caseworker may want to know what kind of a person you would seek to marry, or the caseworker may ask you about your living arrangements and whether you are gay or lesbian.

It is crucial that you understand as quickly as possible during the home study process if the caseworker may be biased. Tune in to any common theme in the caseworker's questions. General questions about your employment, for example—your hours, responsibilities, stress level, etc.—may lead to the all-important issue of child care arrangements, and you may be expected to address arrangements in greater detail than a married couple, even when both of them plan to work. The caseworker will want to know whether you will have any time and energy left for your child after a long day at work.

UNIQUE CHALLENGES FOR SINGLE MEN

Men usually experience more difficulty than women when adopting children. First, they are not perceived as nurturing, and second, their motives are questioned. To put it bluntly, they are suspected of being child molesters. After all, most known child molesters are men. Single men over thirty years of age are often assumed to be gay. To get around these detractors, Crain and Duffy suggest that you take a psychological assessment or personality test so that you can prove you are "normal." One single male client was required to take a battery of tests, which was standard practice for all clients using a particular home study agency. Because he is "normal," the results of these tests were especially useful in allowing him to adopt. It is not just the agency that may screen males more carefully, but the facilitators and officials in other countries will want more detailed information to show that the man can parent a child. For example, in this client's case, after seeing his home study, the agency staff were comfortable with his adopting. It is the agency's responsibility to make sure that the in-country officials and facilitator are also comfortable with his motives to adopt and his ability to parent.

Although such "psychological" information is deleted from the home study sent to the foreign country, this information should be kept in when a single man is adopting. Expect the in-country facilitator or officials in the country to want a more detailed home study. For example, if the man is divorced, the reasons for the divorce may have to be addressed more fully in the home study than if a man who is remarried is adopting with his second wife. In addition, information about his church activities and child care arrangements should be carefully addressed, especially in the dossier home study.

Certainly men can make excellent parents, especially for boys who need a strong male role model, firm discipline, and guidance. Social service agencies usually do in-depth home studies, and this can serve to your advantage. You may feel like you are being "poked and probed" to make sure you are all right. However, when it is all finished and everyone is satisfied with the results, including you, you can then use your home study to search for children all around the world.

When adopting internationally expect the agency to encourage you to adopt a toddler or older child. Again, proving that you are nurturing and can care for a young baby may take added effort. Even though it is well established that the earlier a child is adopted, the less likely it is that he will suffer from being in an institution, there may still be a bias that young babies should be placed only with couples and single women.

Also, plan to adopt a boy—nearly everyone else involved in the adoption process will be expecting this. Because most families want to adopt girls, there are usually many more boys waiting to be adopted, which can serve to your advantage as a single man. If you plan to adopt from Eastern Europe, it is unlikely that the agents and officials in those countries will permit you to adopt a girl.

As for adopting an infant born here in the States, realistically, it would be difficult for a single man. Most birth mothers want the child to be reared by a two-parent family. Yes, there are exceptions, but the process could be exhausting and frustrating. If you are single, you may find that you spend a lot of money just to be on attorneys' and agencies' waiting lists.

If you are a single man, adoption is a very viable option and the barriers are eroding. Yes, you will have to prove that you are "normal" and that your motives are sincere, but if you can accept the fact that you will be scrutinized more closely than the average couple choosing to adopt, then you can most likely adopt quickly if you choose international adoption.

Resources:

Adoption Resource Exchange for Single Parents
ARESP
P.O. Box 5782
Springfield, VA 22150
aresp@aol.com
www.aresp.org/
(703) 866-5577
(703) 912-7605 (fax)

Committee for Single Adoptive Parents
P.O. Box 15084
Chevy Chase, MD 20815

National Council for Single Adoptive Parents
www.adopting.org/ncsap.html
Provides help and support for single women and men looking to adopt

Single Mothers by Choice
P.O. Box 1642
New York, NY 10028
(212) 988-0993
This national organization provides support and information to single women. It publishes a quarterly newsletter and local membership directories.

Single Parents Adopting Children Everywhere (SPACE)
6 Sunshine Ave.
Natick, MA 01760
(508) 655-5426

Single Parents with Adopted Kids
Dannette Kaslow—SWAK
4108 Washington Road #101
Kenosha, WI 53144
A newsletter for singles with adopted children that is produced four
times a year.

SingleMOTHER
P.O. Box 68
Midland, NC 28107
(704) 888-KIDS
Publishes a bimonthly newsletter for divorced, widowed, and never mar-
ried mothers. Has local chapters.

Curto, Josephine J. *How to Become a Single Parent: A Guide for Single People
Considering Adoptions or Natural Parenthood Alone.* Englewood Cliffs, NJ:
Prentice-Hall, 1983.

Mattes, Jane. *Single Mothers by Choice.* New York, NY: Random House, 1994.

ADOPTION FOR GAYS AND LESBIANS

Court cases involving adoption by gays and lesbians have made news headlines.
Most of these situations involved one partner adopting the biological child of the
other. Some courts have ruled, for example, that a lesbian may adopt the child of a
partner who became pregnant through donor insemination.

Although there are books that specifically address gay and lesbian adoption,
the fact remains that it is rare for two same-sex partners to adopt a child of no
biological relationship. First, gays and lesbians make up only about two percent of
the population, and second, only a small percentage are interested in adopting.

Although most states do not permit unmarried couples to adopt, only two
states—New Hampshire and Florida—have an outright ban on gay adoptions.
Some states, like New York, New Jersey, Vermont, Minnesota, and California,
allow gay adoption. Although some gays and lesbians adopt children—usually
harder-to-place children—as single parents, their partners usually do not adopt
the children. If the partner does not adopt, she may seek, however, to be the
child's legal guardian.

Most agencies that place infants with adoptive parents allow the birth
mothers a role in the selection of the adoptive parents, and most birth mothers
want a traditional two-parent family for their children. An agency whose policy is
to present a few prospective adoptive parents' portfolios to a birth mother will

often hesitate to offer a portfolio of a gay or lesbian couple for fear of giving offense. It is a rare birth mother who walks into an agency and says that she wants to place the child with a gay couple. The few agencies that place infants with adoptive parents without much input from the birth mothers are traditional organizations, usually ones with a strong religious orientation. This kind of agency is not likely to approve a gay or lesbian couple to adopt a child.

Attorneys who do direct placements will experience the same kinds of responses from birth mothers. Finding a birth mother who feels enthusiastic about gay or lesbian adoptive parents is difficult. Sometimes gay and lesbian couples place ads in some of the more avant-garde newspapers, hoping to attract a birth mother, and this is not a bad strategy, although probably still a long shot.

A gay or lesbian couple will have to find an agency/social worker willing to approve their home study. Regardless of the social worker's view on homosexuals' adopting, many social workers feel that they must honestly address the adoptive parents' living arrangements and the role the nonadopting partner will have in parenting children. If someone is gay and has a live-in partner, the adoptive parent must either lie about the relationship or tell the truth. Even if the prospective adoptive parent does not reveal the sexual relationship she has with her live-in partner, she must reveal that another adult lives in the home. In virtually all states, regardless of who is adopting, any adult eighteen years or older living in the adoptive home must have a criminal background check. Therefore, it is considered highly unethical not to mention that someone else lives in the home.

In most states gays and lesbians can adopt through a public agency, though an exception may have to be made with a child who had a known history of sexual abuse. Then an agency may feel that the child would be better off in a traditional two-parent home or a single-parent home, so that as he deals with the difficulties in overcoming his abusive background, he does not also have to deal with the issues of coming from a lesbian or gay home. In all cases, the agency will want to consider how living in a nontraditional family will impact the child. Further, special needs children have usually lived chaotic lives filled with emotional pain. To place them in gay or lesbian homes may mean more emotional challenges as they seek to integrate their adoptive home experience with their past.

What about international adoption? At first this might seem like an option for gay and lesbian couples; there are so many children who need a home, and single parents are now permitted to adopt in many countries. However, no country permits gays or lesbians to adopt. Certainly there are lesbian women who adopt children without disclosing their sexuality in the home study.

The National Adoption Information Clearinghouse has on its Web site the Child Welfare League of America's Policy Regarding Adoption by Gay or Lesbian

Individuals. Essentially, the League states that all applicants should have an equal opportunity to apply and should be assessed on their abilities to successfully parent a child and not on their appearance, differing lifestyle, or sexual preference. Agencies should consider each applicant based on the best interests of the child. Such considerations should include personality and maturity and the ability of the adoptive applicant to meet the child's needs.

Gay/lesbian adoptive applicants should be assessed the same as other adoptive applicants. The Welfare League further states that that sexual orientation and the ability to nurture and care for a child are separate issues.

Adoptive applicants should know that their sexual orientation will be shared with the birth parents and that the birth parents may or may not select them based on this information.

ADOPTION FOR UNMARRIED COUPLES

Except in rare cases, unmarried couples are usually not permitted to adopt. Unlike gay and lesbian couples, for whom marriage, as of this writing, is not an option, marriage for heterosexual couples usually is as simple as getting a license and saying "I do." For this reason, even where unmarried couples are permitted to adopt, the question of why two people do not get married will be a focal point in the home study process, and the commitment level of the two prospective adoptive parents will be closely scrutinized. Because the stability of the couple's relationship is essential to approving a home study, an agency caseworker would find it difficult to approve such a home study. A social worker conducting a home study for a private adoption, however, may simply write up the home study without strongly addressing these issues.

However, courts are beginning to allow unmarried couples to adopt in certain situations. This is particularly true in states that recognize common-law marriages; that is, if a couple has been together for a certain time period, then the state recognizes their relationship as a marriage. The key components in evaluating an unmarried couple's fitness for adoption are the longevity of their relationship and whether they are stable people and committed to each other and to having children. For example, one court judge in South Carolina approved an adoption of a hard-to-place child with an unmarried couple who had lived together for seven years.

MILITARY FAMILIES

Special considerations need to be given to military families. Traditionally, if military families wanted to adopt a child through the social services department, they experienced difficulty—not necessarily because they were in the military but because they did not live in one place long enough to get through the trainings, the home study, and the waiting for an assignment of a child.

This barrier has prevented military families from adopting, even though they may be the ideal candidates. What makes them ideal? First, they are often a racially diverse group, and 40 percent are minority families. If a family were to adopt transracially, they would most likely find that other military families are very accepting. This could be one of the most ideal settings, especially for a biracial child.

Also, military families usually have ready access to no-cost medical resources, including occupational and physical therapists, speech pathologists, and mental health professionals. The military covers even pre-existing conditions. If treatment is not available at a military medical site, then the patient is referred to a civilian hospital. If a patient receives treatment at a civilian hospital, then his/her health care is covered under CHAMPUS, a health insurance program; however, using this insurance policy requires a copayment.

If a military family pays a copayment, it can easily add up to thousands of dollars. Therefore, it is advised that when a adopting a child in the U.S. with special needs, the family should apply for their child to receive any special benefits—even if the family does not receive adoption subsidies. It is a wise precaution to take these benefits even if they are never used. Mounting medical bills can be devastating.

If a child has special medical needs, the child will be permitted to stay in an area where medical treatment is available. This dismisses another concern adoption professionals may have—that the military personnel may be transferred to an area where adequate medical services are not even available. Fortunately, the Exceptional Family Member Program states that no member of the military can be transferred to an area where specialized medical care is not available for a family member. Of course, these provisions include adopted children.

As special employees of Uncle Sam, military families can receive adoption benefits of up to $2,000 a year. Although it is not a great deal of money, the benefits are broad and even include medical expenses incurred by a birth mother. Military families, like all other Americans who fall within the income age, are eligible for a $5,000 tax credit, or $6,000 if the child has special needs.

The Home Study

Military life is not always considered "normal" life, and there are positives and negatives associated with the lifestyle. If you are in the military, you will want to acknowledge to the social worker conducting your home study the realities of being in the military and how this could impact a child. You will also want to address what you do already to compensate for the downside of this life—regular moves, one parent being absent in a time of war, and so forth. For example, you may state the support system you have through other military families, that you make friends easily, and that you get involved in community activities. You will also want to share with the social worker the advantages of a child being reared in a military family. For example, if you are adopting internationally, you may want to discuss how diverse your neighborhood is and how comfortable your family is in traveling.

What If You Are Transferred Overseas?

If you are transferred overseas, there should not be a problem. But you may have to educate your agency about this. Those living on military installations can adopt children from the United States through the Interstate Compact on the Placement of Children because U.S. military bases are considered U.S. territory. You are simply conducting an interstate adoption. A social worker or clergy member on the overseas base can do the home study or postplacement follow-up visits once the child is placed with the family.

Some agencies, such as the Pearl S. Buck Foundation in Perkasie, Pennsylvania, have worked with military families in Asia for years. The Buck Foundation has branches in countries with large U.S. military populations. The agency even employs social workers to work with the military personnel stationed in these countries. If an agency does not have an overseas branch, however, it can use the services of International Social Service, American Branch (ISS/AB) in New York City. ISS/AB is an international network of professional social work agencies working in more than thirteen countries where U.S. military personnel are often stationed, including Germany and France. ISS/AB can help agencies monitor families who have been transferred before an adoption has been finalized. See the resource section at the end of this chapter for the address and telephone number of ISS/AB.

Resources:

Military Family Resource Center
> The center provides resources for military members and their families.
> mfrc.calib.com/
> mfrc@hq.odedodea.edu

Ellen W. Carey
> Adoption Specialist
> U.S. Department of Health and Human Services
> Children's Bureau
> P.O. Box 1182
> Washington, DC 20201
> (202) 205-8652

Kelli Harris
Program Coordinator
Welcome House Social Services of the Pearl S. Buck Foundation
P.O. Box 181
Green Hills Farm
Perkasie, PA 18944
(215) 249-1516

Stephanie Henderson
Project Coordinator
Porter Leath Children's Center
868 N. Manassas St.
Memphis, TN 38107
(901) 577-2500

International Social Service
American Branch
95 Madison Ave.
New York, NY 10016
(212) 532-5858

Melody Jameson
Project Director
Fairbanks Counseling and Adoption
P.O. Box 71544
Fairbanks, AK 99707
(907) 456-4729

Carolyn Johnson
Executive Director
National Adoption Center
1500 Walnut St., Ste. 701
Philadelphia, PA 19102
(215) 735-9988

Dr. Hubert Kelly
Project Director
Recruitment of Military Families
DC Department of Human Services
Randall School, First and I St., S.W.
Washington, DC 20024
(202) 727-5947

Brenda Kerr, Program Specialist
Jacquelyn Kidd, Program Coordinator
Virginia Dept. of Social Services
730 E. Broad St.
Richmond, VA 23219-1849
(804) 662-1291

Joe Kroll, Executive Director
North American Council on Adoptable Children
970 Raymond Ave., Ste. 106
St. Paul, MN 55114-1149
(612) 644-3036

Marcie Velen, Project Director
Arizona Children's Home Association
2700 S. Eighth Ave.
Tucson, AZ 85725
(602) 622-7611

Military Personnel with Knowledge of Adoption Issues

Iris Bulls
Family Programs Manager
Office of the Assistant Secretary of Defense
Force Management and Personnel
Office of Family Policy, Support and Services
The Pentagon 3A280
Washington, DC 20301-4000
(703) 697-7191

Master Sergeant Bob Cornyn
Fort Lewis Army Base
7807 50th St.
Puyallup, WA 98371
(206) 922-2751

Sydney Hickey
Associate Director
National Military Family Association
6000 Stevenson Ave., Ste. 304
Alexandria, VA 22304
(703) 823-6632

Jane Johnston
Military Family Resource Center
Military Family Clearinghouse
4015 Wilson Blvd., Ste. 903
Arlington, VA 22203-5190
(703) 385-7567

Col. James Schlie
Office of the Assistant Secretary of the Army Manpower
and Reserve Affairs
111 Army Pentagon
Washington, DC 20301-0111
(703) 693-7618

Al Smith, Deputy Director
Family Service Center
Naval Air Station
South Weymouth, MA 02190
(617) 786-2581/2983

In Summary

Many families are not traditional, but in general a birth mother will seek to place her own child with a more traditional family regardless of what her own lifestyle is like. Essentially she is looking for a two-parent family. Yes, there are exceptions, but they are just that—exceptions. A nontraditional family may believe that attracting a birth mother requires deception, but this is unfair to everyone involved in the adoption process. Someday, the child might discover that you lied in your home study or to the child's birth parent.

For some children, a nontraditional family still may be very suitable if not better than a traditional two-parent family. Certainly considering the conditions of orphanages around the world and the gloomy statistics of what happens to these children once they reach seventeen and are released into the world, nearly any home in the United States that is not abusive is far better than what a child would experience. That is not to say that homes should not be screened and the parents properly prepared for the children to be adopted. But the home that a birth mother in the United States may *not* select for her newborn child is still a good option for a child who is living with less than enough food and little hope for the future.

Resources:

National Adoption Information Clearinghouse
   naic@calib.com

Chapter Eleven

Relative and Stepparent Adoption

The most common form of adoption in the United States is a stepparent adoption, in which the child of the biological parent is adopted by that parent's spouse. A relative, or "intrafamily," adoption is usually defined as one close relative, and possibly that person's spouse, adopting another relative. This child can be related to the wife or the husband (as is the case with a niece or nephew) or to both (as with a grandchild). The degree of relationship permitted varies from state to state.

Unlike in other adoptions, one generally does not plan to become a parent through stepparent or intrafamily adoption; the adoption occurs because of other circumstances in your life. Neither do people set a goal for themselves of becoming stepparents. Instead, marriage to a particular person is a package that includes children. A stepparent often wants to make an investment in the child's life, and the child and parent believe that it is important to cement that commitment through adoption.

About 8 percent of all adoptions in the United States are relative adoptions. According to statistics gathered from the National Center for State Courts, 42 percent of all adoptions are stepparent adoptions and just over 50 percent are either stepparent or intrafamily adoptions.[1] The two kinds, although quite different from each other, follow similar laws within each state.

In many states a home study is not required for a relative or stepparent adoption. When one is required, it is often conducted in a simplified form and is mainly intended to confirm that the placement was voluntary and that the adoptive family is functional and can provide for the child. The adoption is viewed as a family matter. Having children is a fundamental right that extends to family members who adopt the child, so long as the child is not abused or neglected. However, one very important component of the home study is educating the adoptive couple about adoption-related issues. If the home study is not done, the educational opportunity is missed. That education may be all the more important in a relative or intrafamily adoption because the adoption issues may be more complex. Since families involved in stepparent and intrafamily adoptions do not usually seek out adoption information, there may be no other such opportunity.

ADOPTION BY RELATIVES

As a rule, the relatives included in the definition of an intrafamily adoption are the child's grandparents, aunts, uncles, and siblings. Children are placed with relatives at different ages and for different reasons. Often a girl or woman becomes pregnant and wants to place the child for adoption, and another family member who cannot have a biological child adopts him. As with any other infant adoption, in this situation the birth mother (and perhaps the birth father) makes a decision to place a child for adoption because her life circumstances make it difficult to raise a child.

There are obvious advantages and disadvantages to relative adoptions. One long-term benefit is that the child can grow up with his biological relatives and have a stronger connection to his genetic background—so long as the child is aware that he has been adopted within his biological family. It may also be easier to have more consistent contact with the birth mother so that the child can know his birth mother's health history.

A legal advantage to a relative adoption is that the adoption itself is usually less complicated than an independent or agency adoption, and in some states the laws are more lax. In the four states where independent adoption is illegal, it is all right to pursue a relative adoption, although a home study may be required, and if the child is born in one state and you live in another, you will not have to go through Interstate Compact.

The disadvantages of relative adoption can be more or less pronounced depending on the birth mother's location and situation and how the rest of the family handles the adoption. If she is a close relative and lives very close by, you may be concerned that she will want to share in parenting decisions. If you have a difficult relationship with her, you may worry about her interfering or saying inappropriate things to your child. A woman's reasons for placing a child for adoption can also influence how she feels about setting boundaries. For example, an older sister who is divorced and already has four kids would probably have a very different attitude from the fifteen-year-old cousin who places a baby with you. Your sister, because she is older and a mother already, may feel that she has a right to give input about the raising of your adopted child—her birth child.

If you have such concerns, they need to be discussed up front. Sometimes attitudes can be deduced from comments by the birth mother and other family members and from the way the birth mother has handled other situations. If she is very unstable, you may need to create some distance between her and your immediate family once the child is born. Remember, unlike other birth mothers, she will probably always know where you live.

Other family members may feel the need to give their advice as well. You may find yourself pressured by suggestions and negative comments made by other family members. Although you want your family's support in your adoption decision, all communication should be between you and the birth mother. For example, if your mother tells you that she was talking to your Aunt Edna, and Aunt Edna mentioned that her teenage daughter, your cousin Tracy, is pregnant and wants to make adoption plans, and your mother told Aunt Edna that you may be interested, your Aunt Edna and Mom may feel that they should be privy to all future conversations between you and your cousin. It is nice that your mom took the initial step to "feel out" the situation, but the remaining communication needs to be between you and your cousin. Of course, her parents, your aunt and uncle, may be involved because of the birth mother's age. This no longer is an issue between your mother and aunt, however; it is between you and the birth mother.

If you were adopting a nonrelative, you might well share with your parents details of your conversations with a birth mother and how all the plans were going. In an intrafamily adoption, you need to protect your privacy as well as the birth mother's. This means setting up very clear boundaries, if possible without hurting anyone's feelings. Let family members know, very tactfully, that you are glad they are concerned but that you want your cousin Tracy to be able to make her plans as she sees best. You would not want to say anything to anyone that would influence her decision or make her upset. Remind them that it is important to protect Tracy's privacy. If she wants to share information with others, that is her decision.

You will also want to establish some boundaries with the birth mother if she does live close by and if you normally see her for family gatherings and holidays. Having her remain in your life as much as she was before the child was placed with you can be appropriate, but because you will need to feel entitlement to the child, there may need to be limited contact initially.

What if the birth mother changes her mind? A woman named Katie who was in her late thirties wanted to have another child with her second husband, but infertility problems prevented her. When her son's girlfriend became pregnant, it was decided that the child would be placed with Katie and her husband. Toward the end of the pregnancy, however, the birth mother changed her mind. Katie and her husband were very disappointed. It was difficult, because they felt they could not express their disappointment to the girlfriend since they wanted to have a relationship with the child as the child's grandparents. They had already prepared a nursery in anticipation of adopting the child. They kept the nursery instead in anticipation of their grandchild. Once the child was born, the grandparents had to be careful that they maintained appropriate boundaries. Otherwise, in time, the child's mother might have come to see the grandparents as full-time babysitters, rationalizing leaving the child with them for extended periods by saying to herself that they were going to adopt the baby anyway.

How to Tell Your Child

Unfortunately, because a relative adoption is so close, some adoptive parents do not share with the child that he is adopted. Perhaps they assume it is not important, since the child is already "family" and he already "knows" his birth mother—even though he does not know, for example, that his older sister is also his biological mother. Or they tell the child that he is adopted but leave out the fact that his aunt Jane is also his biological mother. However, this can create problems in the future, since the lie conceals the child's genetic background.

When children are adopted, a birth mother has a dual role: one of biological parent and one of relative. According to Sharon Kaplan Roszia, it is best in these cases that a child call the adoptive parents "Mom" and "Dad" and the birth mother "Aunt" or whatever relation she is to the child based on the child's adoption.[2]

Using a Private Attorney

Nearly all stepparent and intrafamily adoptions are handled independently. An agency cannot file papers for you, so most people file the necessary legal documents through their attorney. Because most stepparent and relative adoptions are uncomplicated, nearly any competent attorney can facilitate the adoption. However, if you think that the adoption may be contested, you will want to retain an experienced adoption attorney. These are the steps that must take place before the adoption can be finalized:

1. Depending on what state you live in, you, the adoptive parents, may need to have a home study, a child abuse clearance, a criminal clearance done by your local police department or your state agency, and possibly an FBI clearance, carried out through a fingerprinting check.
2. If you are adopting an infant who will be placed with you upon her release from the hospital, the biological parents must sign consents that terminate their parental rights.

3. If the child is older and you have been caring for her but the birth parent(s) have not signed consents, they must be contacted for their consent or at least notified of an adoption hearing so that they have the right to object to the adoption if they so choose. You may need to employ a process server to serve the papers on the biological parents. They do not have to sign anything; the papers are simply to inform them that their rights are about to be terminated and an adoption is about to take place, and that they can contact your attorney or be at court if they want to contest the adoption. Some states require consents unless the child has resided with you for at least six months.
4. Legal papers, including a Judgment of Adoption, are filed with the court-house in your county. A date is then given to your attorney as to when the adoption will take place.
5. You go to court to adopt the child.

Young and Older Child Placements

Most adoptions among relatives start as informal arrangements. A relative may serve as a guardian for a time, then eventually adopt the child. Knowing each other and having a blood connection can make intrafamily adoptions both easier and harder. The common heritage, family lifestyle, and traditions are already known to the child, smoothing the transition; however, in most situations in which a young or older child is placed with a relative, it is because of the parent's inability to care for him. The birth parent may be viewed negatively in the family, an attitude that can extend to the child. The relationship can be even more com-plicated if, for example, the husband has a very negative attitude toward his wife's sister—the biological mother of the child. When a woman adopts her incarcerated sister's baby, for instance, the husband may have ambivalent feelings over the decision, a tension that will be heightened if the wife adopted her sister's child because it was the "right" thing to do—not because she especially wanted to expand her family.

Why Relatives Choose Adoption

Adoption is not always a choice, especially in cases where it will be difficult to terminate the parents' rights. However, if the parents are willing to have their rights terminated, or if their lives are in such disarray that they would have trouble making a case for their suitability as parents, or if the social services department has declared that the relatives are the permanent foster parents, then adoption may be considered. The great advantage of adoption is permanency. Permanency not only benefits the child; the relatives are also reassured to know that the parents, whose lives are not together, cannot remove the child from the home on a whim. If the child was removed from his biological parents because of neglect or abuse, and the parents have not complied with the requirements for getting him back, adoption can be a message to the child that someone is going to take care of him and love him unconditionally. It also means an end to intervention by the social services department, which will no longer have the power to separate the child from the relative's home or otherwise interfere in the life of the family.

Because adoption is permanent, it usually means a severing of relationship between the child and his biological parents. Depending on the situation, this step may be too extreme. A *kinship adoption* can allow some aspects of the birth parent and child relationship to stay intact, if appropriate, by establishing a certain level of openness between the child and biological parents.

Kinship Adoption

"Kinship adoption" is an informal term used when a parent can no longer parent a child and a relative takes over that role. When children are removed from their homes because of abuse or neglect, for example, and relatives who can adequately care for the child are called upon, the term "kinship adoption" comes into use. Usually a kinship adoption is an informal arrangement between the parent and the relatives; sometimes the arrangement is more formal. For example, a social service agency will often seek out relatives to care for a child instead of placing her in a foster home. Often this makes a great deal of sense, especially if the child has had regular contact with the relatives. According to a study by the National Black Child Development Institute in 1986, when an agency asked relatives to care for the children, more than 50 percent said yes. The care of children by relatives helps preserve families, traditionally one of society's most important support systems. "Traditionally grandparents have been viewed as the keepers of the family culture and the thread that ties the family together, by providing the wisdom and emotional support that serve as the forces for continuity."[3] When it comes to adoption, however, it is important to realize that relatives are no longer automatically awarded first preference. Although the courts may decide that a family relationship best fulfills the child's interests, the family relationship itself will not be the deciding factor. The ruling is based solely on what appears to be best for the child.

According to Ann Sullivan of the Child Welfare League of America, more and more children are living with relatives in general and grandparents in particular. The reasons for this go beyond parental divorce and death to reflect a range of social ills: teenage pregnancy; joblessness; child neglect, abuse, and abandonment; incarceration of the parent; drug addiction; and diseases like AIDS. Sullivan says that only 15 percent of relatives legally adopt the children who are placed into their custody by social services departments. Many family members believe that to adopt another family member's child would cause great conflict in the family, so they do not take this step. In informal situations, in which the family is being assisted by social workers but the child is not in the custody of the child welfare agency, adoptions are particularly rejected. Most relatives see adoption as unnecessary, since the child is already with family.[4]

If you have been caring for a relative's child because the child was abused or neglected, and you decide you would like to adopt her, the public agency that first got involved in the placement can usually handle the adoption. This agency and the court must believe it is in the child's best interest for the parents' rights to be terminated and for you to adopt the child. Talk with your caseworker about the possibility of the child becoming your full charge instead of the state's responsibility. You may need to hire your own attorney to get the process moving faster and to see that your rights and the child's are fully protected.

If the agency has legal custody of the child and you have been a foster parent and receiving subsidies, you most likely will be eligible for subsidies even after the adoption takes place.

Grandparents

"In 1999 more than 3.8 million children under the age of 18 lived with 2.5 million grandparent households." This number has grown 40 percent from 1992 to 1998.[5] In a third of these cases, the grandparent provided care without the assistance of the parents. One study found that 50 percent of the relatives caring for the children were grandmothers.[6]

If a girl has a child at the age of sixteen, and her parents are about twenty years older than she is, that means that her parents are in their early forties—an age when some couples today are beginning (or continuing) to have children. As lifestyles have changed, many grandparents in their forties and early fifties are able to take on the responsibility of caring for young children. Sometimes grandparents deliberately plan to adopt the child who is about to be born out of wedlock; for others, the decision evolves out of circumstances. If a daughter has a child at sixteen and over time realizes that the task is more than she can handle, her parents may assume more and more responsibility until they are making the major life decisions for their grandchild. At this point the grandparents may decide that adoption would be in their and the child's best interest. At least it would mean that the child could be covered by their health insurance and could receive benefits like social security.

One set of grandparents, for instance, adopted their fifteen-year-old daughter's infant, initially for legal reasons (the family was traveling internationally), even though both mom and grandparents were sharing in the parenting role. Over time, however, the grandparents took full responsibility for the child because the daughter—the child's biological mother—was doing other things in her life. Now the child is seven years old, and the grandparents are still his primary parents. He knows that he is adopted and that his "sister" is his biological mother. He calls his grandparents "Mom" and "Dad," and his birth mother by her first name.

Nancy, who is in her late thirties, says her grandparents adopted her because her mother was only fourteen years old at the time of her birth. Although her birth certificate was changed to name her maternal grandparents as her parents, her mother maintained a relationship with her, mostly by telephone, and she called her mother "Mommy." As Nancy got older and her mother matured, her mother was able to communicate with her and help Nancy make decisions. Today the two have a close relationship. They live near each other and see each other regularly.

ADOPTION BY STEPPARENTS

As divorce and out-of-wedlock birth rates rise, stepparenting is becoming more common. Remarriages accounted for nearly 46 percent of all marriages in 1990, compared with 31 percent in 1970. Every year more than one million children are involved in a divorce, and in several million families at least one spouse has had an out-of-wedlock child before getting married. As a result, more and more families will be made up primarily of a biological mom and stepdad. Today, nearly seven million children live in stepfamilies, making up 15 percent of all children living in a two-parent household.

Only a fraction of these stepchildren, however, are ever adopted. Why? One reason may be the ways in which general adoption laws are applied to stepparent adoptions. One study, for example, found that stepfathers wanted to adopt but thought it would be impossible because of the biological fathers' involvement in the children's life.[7] As the courts allow more flexibility in stepparent adoption, we may find more stepparent adoptions taking place.

Stepmothers/Stepfathers

Most stepparent adoptions are cases of stepfathers adopting their stepchildren. In 1988, only 11 percent of stepfamilies were made up of the biological father and the stepmother. Custodial stepmothers seldom adopt their stepchildren—even when the father is widowed.[8] Perhaps this is because the children and the stepmother all share the same last name, meaning that the stepfamily does not appear any different from a fully biological family. One study found that children tend to do better in mother/stepfather homes rather than in father/stepmother homes. Also, girls do not appear to be more disturbed than boys. The same study demonstrated that the stepparents' interpersonal relationship with the child played a crucial role in the child's academic achievement.[9]

Why Adopt Stepchildren?

Here are some of the reasons to consider adopting your stepchild or stepchildren:

1. *You will still be the child's parent should the biological parent die, become disabled, or divorce you.*
2. *Should you die or become disabled, the child will be entitled to social security benefits.*
3. *You can feel like a real parent.*
4. *The child can have a sense of permanency.* Children's security is often tied to being in a "forever" family. The adoption by a stepparent can provide this "foreverness." Adoption can provide other emotional benefits, too, if your child is from a previous marriage or relationship and you now have another child with your husband. In a situation like this, your older child may feel "second-best" because he is not your husband's child. Adoption can help him feel that he belongs permanently to both you and your husband.
5. *The child can take on her parents' last name.* If you are a woman and have taken your husband's last name, your children may still have your last name (if they were born out of wedlock) or their father's last name. Adoption means the whole family can have the same last name. If adoption is not feasible because your ex-spouse objects, you can still consider a name change. Conversely, if the child is older, she can be adopted without a name change. If the biological father has died, the child may see a name change as disloyal to the deceased parent.
6. *The child's birth certificate changes.* Unlike the simple name change that sometimes occurs in stepfamilies, with adoption the birth certificate changes to indicate the stepparent as the original parent. If the child is older (usually ten years and up), the child's permission is needed to do this.

Disadvantages of Stepparent Adoption

Here are some concerns to consider before taking the step to adopt:

1. *The stepparent may have to make child support payments in the event of a divorce.* If you are the primary wage earner and you and your spouse divorce, you will probably be responsible for child support payments if the child lives with her mother. If your spouse were to leave you for someone else and take the children, you could still end up being responsible for child support payments.

2. *The child may feel disloyal to her noncustodial parent.* She may feel that if she is adopted she can never have a relationship with her other biological parent, and that to proceed with the adoption would be to reject that parent. Such feelings are not easily overcome.

3. *The noncustodial parent could interfere.* Trying to gain the cooperation of the noncustodial parent could turn into litigation if the parent contests the adoption. Your family also runs the risk of counterclaims by your ex-spouse if you mention your adoption plans to him or her.

   Contrary to what many assume, adoption does not necessarily cut off all relationship with the parent who is not living with the child. The other parent can still have visitation rights as part of the adoption agreement. Indeed, most couples who want to proceed with a stepparent adoption are not trying to get the other biological parent out of the picture. Usually the father is already out of the picture and is not paying any child support.

   Many stepparents say that they want to adopt but believe that it is impossible because of the previous spouse's interference. Check with a lawyer in your state or where the parent lives to see what his rights are. Bear in mind, however, that no matter what those rights, there is always the possibility of a dragged-out family conflict in which the child will be exposed to the problems of both of his parents.[10]

4. *Any child support being paid by the noncustodial parent would stop.* A parent who is faithfully paying child support usually cares very much about his child and is involved in her life. Many stepparents prefer not to assume full financial and legal responsibility while the noncustodial parent still has this close relationship, especially if the parent and ex-spouse have had a bitter divorce.

Grandparent Issues

You and your children may have a relationship with their grandparents even if they have little contact with their noncustodial parent. This may be especially true if the parent lives in another state while his parents live close to you and your children, or if your first spouse has died. In either case, but especially the latter, the grandparents may feel that your husband's adopting the children is removing your late husband's place in the family. It would be wise to discuss the adoption plans with them before you proceed—not to get their permission but to reassure them of the important role that they will continue to have in your children's lives.

Parent-Stepparent Issues

If a stepparent has been married to the biological parent for a year or more (in some states six months), and the other biological parent is essentially not in the child's life, you can consider adoption. If the other biological parent is involved in the child's life, the adoption can be finalized only with that parent's consent.

Children in stepfamilies are likely to have known and to have had an emotional relationship with the parent who is not living with them. In such cases there is a strong argument for establishing what is called an "open arrangement"—proceeding with adoption, but continuing at least limited contact with the noncustodial parent. This allows children to express their preference for being adopted without breaking allegiance to the biological parent who no longer lives with them. Of course, if the child has not known the biological parent, if the biological parent abused or neglected the child, or if the biological parent has never paid any child support or provided any emotional connection to the child, then an open arrangement may not serve any purpose.

If parents are pressing for an adoption, the child may feel ambivalent and confused. You will want to discuss both sides with your child, even though you may feel strongly about proceeding with the adoption. A child over the age of eight should have freedom of choice about the adoption and what last name he will use, unless the adoption is sought in an emergency. An example of this is if the mother has a life-threatening illness and wants to solidify the legal relationship between her spouse and her children in the event of her death.

If the biological parent will not consent to the adoption, you may need to wait to find grounds for termination. If several years of non–child-support payment and lack of contact are grounds for involuntary termination in your state, it would be better to wait out the time period than to initiate an adoption that might only serve to draw the biological parent back into your lives.

The best stepparent adoptions occur when the whole family wishes for the adoption as a legal means of expressing their emotional security. The least successful are those in which a child has been coerced into the decision. Sometimes when there is friction between the stepparent and child, families may suggest adoption as a way of solidifying the relationship. This is a mistake. Adoption should take place when the relationship between the child and stepparent is positive, and always with the agreement of the child.

When a child reaches adolescence, as with any child who is adopted, he may want to reexamine his adoption and ask questions about his origins, identification, and original name. He may also want to search for his biological parent. During this time it is important for his parent and adoptive parent to reassure him of their commitment to him while allowing the child to explore his identity.

For a child, living in a household with only one biological parent represents a loss. Despite the commonness of divorce and remarriage, children are well aware that the "ideal" family is made up of two parents who stay together. The divorce itself is a loss for children. If the original marriage was horrible and the noncustodial spouse was abusive or deserted the family, divorce for the child represents the lost possibility of a good biological parent. Even if the next spouse is "Mr. Wonderful" and loves the child and wants to adopt him, the child may still need to grieve for the "lost" parent, the lost marriage, and possibly the lost "ideal" parent.

You may have very negative feelings toward the parent, and your child may share those feelings. Remember, however, that just as you may have wished that your first marriage could have been better, your child will probably wish the same thing. Try to acknowledge his loss. You may say, "I wish that your dad could have been more caring, and I know it hurts you that he was not kinder. One thing that I am glad about is that you are my child and that you have another dad who really does care about you."

If your child has never met her biological parent, then she may have a need to know about him as well as a desire to meet someday. This desire on the part of a child is comparable to what is felt by those conceived through donor insemination. It is not that she wants to change anything; rather, as she matures, she may need a greater understanding of her genetic background. She needs to know "who I am."

If a woman has a child out of wedlock and marries a man who is not the child's biological father when the child is still very young, and he adopts the child, then this adoption needs to be explained to the child from the earliest age possible, whether or not the birth father is in the picture. This may not feel comfortable at first. You may begin by saying to a one-and-a-half-year-old, "Mommy and Daddy love you so much, and Daddy adopted you because he loves Mommy and you so...o...o...o much." This may feel contrived and awkward, but the alternative is not saying anything until the child is older, which can be damaging. Finding just the "right" age may be awkward. If you wait until she is old enough to "understand" that she is adopted, she may have already found out through documents or through others' comments.

If your husband has legally adopted your child, you may want to place the paperwork and pictures associated with the occasion in the child's baby book. If you can find other mementos surrounding the adoption that demonstrate your husband's commitment to and love for the child, include these as well.

As with other types of adoptions, sometimes parents withhold information about the child's birth from her because it causes embarrassment to the parent—especially if the child was born out of wedlock. Some people would also prefer to forget a previous marriage, and in trying to re-create their new family, they never share with the child her relationship to the nonbiological parent. It is very important that parents share with their child that she has been adopted and that the child has a biological parent as well.

As difficult as it may be, share with your child the circumstances that led to her being adopted by your spouse. Of course, the information needs to be age-appropriate, but in general most information should be shared before the child hits adolescence.

Most adoption authorities agree that adoption information should be shared with the child, regardless of how much you want to protect your child. In the case of stepparent adoptions, your child will know eventually—first, your wedding date will come after the child's birth. Obviously other people will know that your husband, for example, is not the child's biological parent, and it is very unfair to your child to have others know about her parentage when she does not. My experience over and over again has shown that adoptees feel angry, betrayed, and hurt when information regarding their adoption is withheld from them.

One woman shared with me how upsetting it was for her after her mother died that she found out that her father was not her biological father; the woman seemed more hurt because her mother could not share a part of her life with her daughter. The adoptive father had always wanted to tell the daughter, but the mother was too ashamed to discuss this because she had given birth to her out of wedlock. When her mother died, so did her mother's story.

The woman had wondered about her biological father since she was in her twenties. This woman, now in her forties, went on the Internet and was able to locate her biological father. At first his name did not come up, and then a few days later she tried again. Her biological father had just been given a Web television, and she found him days after he set it up. When she called him on the telephone, she began by asking him questions to make sure she had identified the right person. In the conversation he said that he had always wondered what had happened to her and was very concerned about how she was. Since talking with each other, they have met and regularly communicate through e-mail. The woman's step/adoptive father understands and supports the relationship that this woman has with her birth father.

The Stepparent Adoption Process

Here are the basic steps toward a stepparent adoption:

1. *Depending upon the state and county in which you live, you may have to have a home study and a criminal and child abuse clearance conducted.*
2. *The other biological parent's rights must be terminated, or he must sign a consent to an adoption.* If the biological parent has been out of the child's life, he may be served legal papers (the adoption complaint or petition) informing him of the adoption hearing. If he objects, he can contact your attorney or show up at court to contest the adoption. If he does not respond by a specified number of days, usually twenty to thirty-five, he is presumed to have waived his right to object to the adoption.
3. *A hearing is held, usually two to six months after the filing of the adoption petition.* At the hearing the adopting parent must say why he wants to adopt the child; testify that he contributes to the financial stability of the home or that he and the biological parent together can provide financial support to the child; and state his belief that it is in the child's best interests to be adopted by him. The biological parent must testify that she consents and that she feels it is in the child's best interests to be adopted. If the child is over the age of ten (in some states twelve or fourteen), he is questioned by the judge either in the courtroom or in her chambers to confirm that he wants to be adopted. At the hearing the attorney must present to the court either the signed consent of the noncustodial parent or proof that he was served the legal papers and did not respond.

   If the noncustodial parent cannot be found, the attorney must place a legal notice of the adoption proceedings in a newspaper published in the last county in which the parent is known to have lived. If he does not respond, the effect is the same as if he had been served personally.

Resources:

Brookdale Grandparent Caregiver Information Project
Center on Aging
140 Warren Hall
University of California
Berkeley, CA 94720
(510) 643-6427
(510) 642-1197 (fax)

Foundation for Grandparenting
>7 Avenida Vista Grande, Suite B7-160
>Sante Fe, NM 87505
>(505) 466-1336
>www. grandparenting.org

Kids 'n' Kin
>Philadelphia Society
>415 South Fifteenth St.
>Philadelphia, PA 19146
>(215) 875-3400

Parenting Grandchildren: A Voice for Grandparents
>A free newsletter put out by the AARP
>Grandparent Information Center
>601 E. St., NW
>Washington, DC 20049

Stepfamily Foundation
>333 West End Ave.
>New York, NY 10023
>(212) 877-3244

Chapter Twelve

International Adoption

illions of children around the world need a family, not just for their emotional well-being but often for their very survival. Although only a fraction of these children are legally free for adoption, this fraction still translates into tens of thousands of children being available and waiting for adoption. During the 1980s the number of international adoptions rose from 5,700 in 1982 to nearly 10,000 in 1987. The numbers decreased in the early 1990s, mostly because South Korea reduced the number of children available. In 1992 about 6,500 orphans were adopted from other countries. In 1994 the number rose to 8,200, a 12 percent increase over 1993, and in 1999 the numbers jumped to more than 16,000. This growth is largely because of an increase in adoptions from China, Russia, and the countries of Eastern Europe. Currently, these countries account for about 66 percent of the international adoptions. Today international adoption makes up about 26 percent of the roughly 60,000 adoptions by nonrelatives in the United States every year and is the fastest-growing area of adoption.

The National Council on Adoption reports that these statistics are reliable because each child adopted can be tracked since he/she must have a visa for an intercountry adoption. These data include each child's age, gender, and country of origin as well as the adoptive parents' residence. Nothing comes close to this tracking system for U.S. adoptions.

INTERNATIONAL ADOPTION: ADVANTAGES
The advantages of international adoption are considerable. Here are several:

1. *There are plenty of children available.* There are significant numbers of healthy babies and children awaiting homes.
2. *Adoption requirements are often less restrictive.* Adopting from other countries can be a more viable choice than adopting domestically, especially

for those who are single or have other children. Because a birth mother is not screening you, you are not necessarily selected based on the number of children you have, your age (people in their fifties have successfully adopted), your marital status, or your economic ability.

3. *The wait can be shorter.* Because of the abundance of children available, a baby or child can be adopted as soon as your paperwork is completed. The paperwork usually takes three to four months to complete.

4. *Once you have an approved home study, you are virtually guaranteed a child.* Unlike adopting in the United States, where you can comply with all requirements and still not have a child, when you are adopting internationally, you are almost guaranteed success. You are not counting on a birth mother selecting you; instead, you and a child are matched, either through your own resources or through an agency or organization.

5. *The cost of an international adoption is well defined.* Although international adoptions as a whole vary drastically in costs, fees and expenses for your particular adoption should be specified in writing. The cost of an international adoption usually ranges from about $12,000 to $25,000, although some sources say it can be as high as $35,000.

Many people ask why an international adoption costs so much. First, domestic adoptions can cost nearly as much, depending upon the birth mother's expenses and the attorney's fees, the agency's fees (if applicable), and the area of the country where you or the birth mother lives. Second, if you adopt through a public agency (which places only children with special needs), you will incur little or no costs; however, these adoptions are not "free." Each adoption costs the taxpayer about $20,000 and instead of you personally paying for the adoption expenses, the government incurs the costs.

In an international adoption, many of the fees are the same as those incurred with domestic adoptions. The expenses for an international adoption include the home study, immigration and naturalization services, translation of documents, and the agency fee. The in-country facilitators make arrangements for the adoption hearing in court, supply interpreters in the country, and see that children are cared for before the finalization. Often, monies sent to the country go to maintain an orphanage and to maintain relationships with officials. Although not usually openly addressed, some monies are paid to officials. Additionally, in countries where government employees may go months at a time without a paycheck, there is often an expectation that some money will be given to them in exchange for services.

Nearly everyone whom INS approves for an international adoption will have a child within one year. In contrast, in a domestic adoption, the adoptive couple risks the birth mother's changing her mind and, consequently, losing all the money they have paid toward her support. With international adoption, expenses may unexpectedly increase but you are almost certain to end up with a child. True, there are horror stories of those who have gone overseas and been swindled out of large sums of money. Fortunately, laws have been changed, so there is less opportunity for exploitation. Of course, prospective adoptive couples should always consult with others who have used the agency or organization they are considering using before paying any fees.

6. *Healthy children are available.* Most of the medical problems international children suffer are related to living in an impoverished country, and these conditions are usually treatable.

Do not expect a child who has been living in an orphanage to fall in line with American standards for growth and development. However, once these children are in the United States with loving parents and proper medical attention, they quickly begin to grow and develop. In a matter of days, children's personalities begin to change. And in weeks to months most children begin to flourish. Indeed, notes Melinda Garvert, an adoption attorney who has placed over 600 international children, no family has called to say, "It's not working out."[1] Certainly there are those who have received children who have had deep emotional problems, but, in general, the children do very well.

INTERNATIONAL ADOPTION: DISADVANTAGES

Having considered the advantages of international adoption, let us turn to the disadvantages.

1. *You will probably have to travel to another country.* Couples with busy schedules often consider this a great disadvantage. If they already have children, staying a week or more in another country can mean making extensive child care arrangements or taking their children along. Traveling by plane and staying in hotels can also be expensive.

However, traveling can be an advantage as well. It is an opportunity to learn about your child's country. While you are there, you can ask the orphanage caretakers and medical personnel to give you more medical and social information than may actually be in your child's health records. Immediate adjustment issues can be handled by finding out little details, such as the temperature your child likes his bottle, his sleeping habits, and his food likes and dislikes. Also, some orphanages will allow you to feed, dress, and otherwise interact with your child during the time you wait for approval to leave the country.

2. *You cannot bring home a newborn infant.* The infants who are available are usually between a few months and one year old at the time of placement. Although many children are abandoned at birth, the regulations of the country and complications of international adoption make it difficult for a child to be placed with a couple right away.

3. *The child's background is uncertain.* There is usually a gap in the information available about the child and his family background. Even in domestic adoptions the child's biological parents' full medical backgrounds are often unknown; yet most couples in the United States have at least some medical and social background on the birth mother and could perhaps track down the birth father if necessary. Studies of adopted children do show that it is important for parents and professionals to obtain accurate and detailed information on the child's background whenever possible. Finding your child's birth parents in another country may not be possible.

4. *The child may have emotional and developmental delays related to being in an institution.* Studies indicate that institutional life can cause attachment disorders and other emotional problems in children similar to those seen in children in the foster care system. Usually the longer a child is in an orphanage, the more pronounced the problems. This is true even in orphanages where the care is good. Also, it is sometimes difficult to get an accurate assessment from the orphanage staff regarding the child's true personality and mental health.

5. *The child may have been prenatally exposed to drugs or alcohol.* As Eastern European countries, in particular, become more "Westernized," so does the growing influence of drugs and alcohol. Often little prenatal history is collected from birth mothers and since drug and alcohol screenings are not done, it is difficult to assess if a birth mother used drugs or alcohol while pregnant.

6. *The child is unlikely ever to know her birth parents.* Openness in adoption is considered an advantage to the child, especially when she comes to inquire about her genetic background. In an international adoption, no matter how much you share the child's culture with her, she will probably know little about her biological parents and may never have the opportunity to meet them.

Some people admit to choosing international adoption because they did not want to "worry" about the birth parents' interfering with the adoption. Although it is true that no birth parent has ever come back to the United States to take back a child in an international adoption, it is also true that fewer than 1 percent of all American-born children are removed from their adoptive homes by a birth parent.

Not wanting to involve yourself in a legally risky adoption is understandable no matter what route you take. Many couples choose international adoption to avoid dealing with birth parents before and after the placement of their child. If this is how you feel, you may need to give some more thought to the roles the birth parents will play in your child's life, whether or not they were directly involved with him or you. Birth parents matter to children, and this is true even in the thousands of adoptions in which there is no contact with a birth mother or father.

7. *The wait for a child, once he is identified as your child, can be very emotionally taxing.* Waiting for a child is always difficult, and in some countries it can take months before your identified child can come to the United States. Once you receive a picture or videotape of your child, you begin to long for that child and bond with him. Meanwhile, knowing that your child is in an orphanage with less than optimum care is difficult for you as a parent. Your child is somewhere where you cannot help him. This is one of the most difficult aspects of international adoption, as it is very emotionally taxing on adoptive parents. When couples are collecting paperwork and making travel arrangements, they feel as if they are "doing something." Then when all the paperwork is completed, all that adoptive parents can do is wait. Updated videotapes and medical reports can help alleviate the anxiety, but these pictures and reports can also make a couple long even more for their child.

If you must wait for your child while she is in one country and you are in the United States, you can comfort yourself with the knowledge that she is going to have the best life possible once she comes home to you. You did not do anything to cause your child to be in an orphanage, but you are doing something to bring her out of it. If you had never made plans to adopt her, and you did not allow yourself to experience the emotional agony of being separated from your child-to-be, then she might never have had the opportunity to live with a family.

8. *The paperwork and repetitive procedures can be difficult.* For some, the hardest requirement in adopting a child from another country may be completing what appears to be endless paperwork and dealing with

bureaucracies both at home and abroad. Nevertheless, it can be accomplished. One adoptive mother whose child is now twenty-five years old says that when she began to inquire about the process twenty-three years ago, she was told by a legal secretary that the paperwork was so overwhelming that she should not even bother to proceed. This mother thought that if a legal secretary, who deals with paperwork and forms all day long, found the paperwork burdensome, then she was in no position to tackle such a task. Then she met a woman who belonged to an adoption support group, Latin American Parents Association, who was planning to adopt in Colombia. This woman had done her paperwork and was so confident that she would be returning from South America with a child that she was already decorating the nursery. The prospective adoptive mom thought that if this woman could do it, so could she. And so can you! (Incidentally, both women adopted within months of their meeting each other.)

Fortunately, some countries, like China and Ukraine, have streamlined the paperwork so the process is relatively easy. To help minimize your paperwork, use an agency that you know will assist you with your paperwork. Find out from others how much help they received with the paperwork from the agency. Also, you want to make sure that the agency handles the paperwork carefully. Lost or misfiled paperwork can cause great delays in the process. Immigration and Naturalization Services or another country's policies can slow down the adoption process. However, your agency should not delay your process—they should help expedite the process to the best of their ability.

GETTING STARTED

When adopting internationally, you must meet the requirements of your state, the agency, the foreign country, and the United States government. You cannot change the requirements that your state places on you, unless you move to another state, and you have no say in the requirements imposed by the United States. But you do have a choice in the country you adopt from and the agency that conducts the adoption.

Before you receive your child, there are certain steps that you must take. Each country has different requirements and procedures, so chances are you will not necessarily follow the steps in exactly the order given. Even when couples adopt from essentially the same agency's program, they may have completed the process in a somewhat different order, but each step will eventually have to be completed.

1. Talk to others who have adopted internationally, join a support group if available, or check out what people are saying on the Internet (just don't take everyone's comments seriously—see if there is a consistent pattern).
2. Select a country from which to adopt
3. Select an adoption agency or facilitator
4. Get your passports
5. Fulfill Immigration and Naturalization Services (INS) requirements
    - Home study
    - I-600A Form
    - Get fingerprinted
6. Fulfill your state's requirements (home study)
    - Birth certificates
    - Marriage license
    - Divorce decrees (if applicable)
    - Financial statements
    - Medical exams
    - Police/FBI clearance and child abuse clearance
    - Letters of reference
    - Financial statements such as 1040 or W-2 Forms
7. Collect documents for your dossier
8. Have a child assigned to you and then have the videotape and medical report evaluated by an expert
9. Commit to adopting a particular child (These documents are usually similar to the ones collected for your home study. Each country, however, has different requirements.)
10. Make travel arrangements if you must go to get your child
11. Complete and take INS documents with you to the child's country
    - I-600
    - Affidavit of Support
12. Bring home your child!
13. Re-adopt your child
14. Complete INS Form I-643 so your child can become a U.S. citizen

SO LET'S GO: THE PROCESS

First, you should talk to a few people who have adopted internationally. Ask what their experiences have been like. Most agency referrals are made this way. Satisfied clients tell others about their experience adopting a child from another country and the agency that they used. You will want to join a support group of parents who have adopted internationally and those looking to adopt. (See the

Appendix for a list of support groups.) If no support group is available, you may want to use the Internet to link up with other people who have gone to the country that you plan to travel to. Or you may stay in touch with others who are using the same agency that you are so that you do not feel alone throughout this process.

If you are able to go to an adoption support group, find out how people in the group adopted their children. Not only can they tell you the best agencies or facilitators to use, they can also fill you in on all the little things you need to know about the process, the trip to the foreign country, what you need to pack, and what costs can be expected.

Often support groups will have speakers come in and discuss various aspects of international adoption. Agency personnel, for example, can offer very practical advice while promoting their services.

Special Note: Adoption for Non–U.S. Citizens

If neither you nor your spouse is a citizen of the United States, you absolutely cannot adopt internationally and reside in the United States with your internationally adopted child. This applies to those who are permanent residents with "green cards." So if you and your spouse are from England and are legally employed here and have green cards and adopt a child from Romania, you cannot enter the United States with that child until the child has lived with you for two years. This means you must live elsewhere with the child for two years before you and the child can enter the United States. However, if one spouse is a U.S. citizen, then the couple can adopt internationally. The American citizen is the petitioner on the I-600A Form and the sponsor on the Affidavit of Support.

Selecting an Agency, Organization, or Facilitator

To determine an agency's or facilitator's credibility, call the adoption unit of your state and ask about the agency or the organization, or call your Better Business Bureau or the Joint Council on International Children's Services.

Agencies range in size from small local organizations to large national institutions. As a rule, the safest and easiest way to adopt a child from another country is to involve an adoption agency in your own state. Of course, this is not always possible, since some international adoption agencies handle only certain countries. If you want to adopt a child from a certain country and the agencies in your state do not provide this service, or if the agency is very expensive, you will want to go through another agency, organization, or facilitator. There are many agencies, so gather lots of information. Although many people search for an agency on the Internet, this is not the best way ultimately to select an agency, just as you would not blindly select one out of the yellow pages. The Internet should serve as a guide to the types of programs available, the fee structures, and what the process is like. The best way to select an agency is by getting referrals and then contacting the agency yourself. After inquiring about an agency, use your instincts. Do you trust the staff? Are they warm and caring?

When you call an agency, do not expect the staff to have time to cover every last question. Begin with general questions and ask to receive their literature, or visit their Web site. Once you decide you would probably like to use a particular agency or organization, then you can begin to ask more in-depth questions that are not covered in its Web site or its literature.

Here are some questions to ask:

1. *What countries does the agency work with*, and what kinds of connections do they have with that country?
2. *What criteria must you meet?* (List the specific countries you are interested in adopting from.)
3. *What services does the agency offer?* Get very specific information. Some agencies actually assign and place children with you; others just help facilitate the adoption and guide you along the way.
4. *Does the agency provide help with the paperwork*, putting together a dossier, finding a translator, and making travel arrangements? What services does it help you obtain in the foreign country? Finding an interpreter and a lawyer? Finding the embassy? Getting the child's visa and passport?
5. *How is the agency aware of the children available for adoption?*
6. *What are the adoption laws of the country?*
7. *Can the agency provide you with the names of clients?* With the names of professionals who work with the agency?
8. *How many adoptions has the agency conducted in that country?* (If you are looking to adopt in Korea and you are dealing with a large organization such as Holt, this is an unnecessary question.) Also, some programs are just opening up in certain countries. The key is for the agency or facilitator to be honest with you in stating what she does and does not know.
9. *What are the fees and other expenses?* Agency quotes can often vary by thousands of dollars. Some of this discrepancy can be explained by what the agency includes in the cost and what it omits.
10. *How are monies for in-country expenses and fees handled?* Foreign country fees should, as a rule, be deposited into a separate escrow account and released when the adoption is completed. Because wiring money to

other countries costs a great deal, many programs require that you take money with you to the country.

11. *What can be known about a child's health and background?* In most countries, little may be known about the child's family. If this information is not usually available, the agency should say so.

12. *Must you travel to the country, and if so, for how long?*

13. *Once you complete your paperwork and receive approval from the INS, how long can you expect to wait for a child to be assigned to you?*

DECIDING ON A COUNTRY

Because you must meet the requirements of a particular country, you will want to begin by investigating which countries will accept you and what kinds of children are available. Most countries, however, have very open policies for single women and traditional families. You most likely will be the one who selects a country based on your desire, not based on whether or not you meet the country's criteria.

When prospective adoptive families ask for the advantages and disadvantages of adopting from different countries, I suggest to the couple that they really think through each program and what will best serve them and their family. Some people want a very young baby, so they choose a country such as Russia. Others want an Asian female so they choose China. Others want to adopt very quickly and want more than one child, so they select Ukraine. Families often want to adopt from Guatemala, where some of the babies are cared for in private foster homes instead of in an orphanage. The country selected is usually based on the age of the child the family wants, the cost of the program, the length of stay in the country, what the children look like, and how quickly the adoption process moves.

Sometimes the right country is obvious; sometimes families vacillate when deciding upon a country. Usually when prospective adoptive parents have great difficulty making up their minds, it is often because they also have some reservations about adopting.

Starting the home study process may help you sort through some of these issues as the social worker shares her insights about international adoption with you. You may want to start on the INS paperwork as well. Then when you are ready to select a country, you are not months behind in the process.

Other than paying the fees for a home study and Immigration and Naturalization Services, you will not want to commit any more money to an adoption program until you are absolutely sure that you want to adopt internationally and that you know which country you want to adopt from. Sometimes families get this far in the process and then adopt a child in the United States. The only monies "lost" are those spent on Immigration and Naturalization

Services. No one ever complains that they spent $455 for INS approval and in the meantime, a birth mother selected them to adopt a baby. In this scenario, the international adoption-style home study is simply revised to be a domestic home study.

Also, you may decide to use the Internet to research various countries. Looking at sites such as those put out by Friends of China, Latin American Parents Association, Friends of Russia, and Ukrainian Adoptions can help you decide upon a country that you want to travel to and have a shared heritage with through your child.

Get some general information on each country before you begin to go to chat rooms and e-mail individual people. Although the Internet can help you reach people who are far away and get their perspective on the adoption process, you can have input from far too many people with too many variable circumstances. All the information can become confusing and conflicting. Try to narrow your search before you even start. If you decide to adopt from China, for example, then begin to "talk" with those through e-mail who have already adopted. This could also help you find the agency that you want to use.

If you truly do not know which country you want to adopt from, it is best to call a few agencies and find out firsthand what each country's program is like. What is presented on paper, no matter how clear a description, is not the same as talking with someone who understands the program and with adoptive parents who have actually done the adoption.

As you contemplate international adoption, keep several things in mind. If you are a Caucasian, adopting a child from another country—unless it is a European country—probably means that the child is not going to look at all like you. If you adopt a child from Asia, for example, your family is entering into a transracial adoption. For a Caucasian couple, adopting an Asian child is certainly a different cultural experience from adopting an African-American or biracial child, yet there are many similarities. You and your spouse need to review some of the issues involved in entering into a transracial adoption before deciding to adopt a child from another country.

Often the cost to adopt from a particular country can help you determine which one to select. Sometimes the cost of the adoption is due to the orphanage donation, traveling expenses, and the required length of stay in the country. However, agency and attorney fees can also vary quite significantly. Make sure you get an itemized list of all fees, in addition to expected traveling and lodging expenses.

Another consideration in choosing a country is what age child you want. Most countries do not allow children to be adopted until they are at least six months old. If you want a very young baby, you will want to choose a country that has a policy of releasing children as soon as the mother relinquishes the child, or as soon as the child is abandoned.

Another variable is a country's policies regarding who can adopt. Agencies may have few requirements, but the country from which you seek to adopt may impose restrictions related to age; marital status, including number of years you have been married; number of previous divorces; and the number of children you have. Find out whether you will be accepted before you set your heart on adopting a child from a particular country.

Finding a reputable agency or facilitator to handle the adoption is crucial. Make sure there is an agency that you feel comfortable in working with that will assist in adopting a child from the country from which you want to adopt.

Following is a list of countries that permit people from abroad to adopt their orphans. Bear in mind as you read this list that adoption laws in a particular country can change quickly.

Latin America

Bolivia. Infants eight months and older are available. Couples must be married for two years and be between twenty-five and fifty-five years old. Some agencies permit singles to adopt. Some agencies say that you must be infertile. It takes about six to eighteen months to get a child after INS approval. Both parents must travel for one week and one family member must stay in the country for another four weeks.

Brazil. In 1998, 106 children were adopted from Brazil by Americans, and Brazil was the sixteenth most popular country from which to adopt. Couples married two years and single men and women may adopt. There are no age restrictions. The husband and wife must stay with the child in Brazil for two weeks before beginning the adoption process, and the mother must stay a total of five weeks. Only approved agencies can represent adopting parents. Many of the children available are of African descent or of mixed race.

Chile. Couples should be twenty years older than the child and have been married for at least three years. Singles are seldom accepted. No more than two children already in the family. Nonresident foreigners cannot adopt, so they are given guardianship and authority to take the child out of the country; you cannot finalize an adoption there. Infants and older are available. The system is handled by private attorneys. Adopting parents must appear before a judge in Chile (sometimes only one spouse must appear). It takes about one to two years to adopt. The stay is for one to weeks.

Colombia. In 1999, 231 Colombian children were adopted into the United States, and Colombia was the eighth most popular country from which Americans adopted.

The age of children who can be adopted is based on the adoptive parents' age. If you are thirty-six to forty-five years old, you can adopt a child three to seven years old. Essentially, family members should not be more than thirty-five years older than the child. Toddlers and siblings are available. Children must stay in the country until the final adoption is completed. Both parents must stay for about one to two weeks; the mother must stay for another one to two months before the child can be brought home. Families are randomly assigned to one of twelve family courts; the wait is between three and eight weeks before a hearing is scheduled.

Only sources licensed by the Colombian Family Welfare Institute and licensed Colombian adoption agencies can offer children for adoption. The Colombian Family Welfare Institute and most private agencies will work only with United States adoption agencies, not individuals. It takes about twelve to eighteen months to get a child after INS approval.

Dominican Republic. In 1998, 140 children were adopted by Americans from the Dominican Republic, and this was the fourteenth most popular country from which to adopt. Couples must be married for at least ten years, and one spouse must be thirty-five years or older. Primarily biracial infants of African/European descent are available. Private adoption attorneys can arrange adoptions as well as agencies. Traveling to the country is required. You may also have to wait three to six weeks after placement to come home.

Ecuador. The husband must be between the ages of thirty and fifty-five, and the wife must be between twenty-five and forty and have been married at least two years. Singles over thirty may adopt a same-sex child. Infants, toddlers, and children as well as sibling groups are available. Adoption can take place from either an Ecuadorian or an American-based agency. The wait for an assignment of a child is about six to twelve months, but the wait between getting an assignment and receiving the child is about a week.

Guatemala. In 1999, 1,002 children were adopted by Americans from Guatemala, making it the fourth most popular country from which to adopt. Singles or couples married at least one year between the ages of twenty-five and fifty are eligible. A private adoption in Guatemala usually takes between six and twelve months after documents are submitted. Children usually have warm skin tones and dark hair and eyes. Mostly healthy infants—more boys than girls—are available. Abandoned children or those whose parents have died can also be adopted. Agencies can work with birth mothers; thus, very young babies can be adopted. The adoptive family stays in the country about three to four days or the child can be escorted home.

Haiti. In 1998, 121 Haitian children were adopted by Americans. The country can be relatively easy to adopt from as long as you are using an attorney approved by the U.S. Embassy in Haiti. Babies and young children are available, and the children are of African descent. There are very few biracial children available. Getting all of the dossier documents authenticated can cost well over $1,000. The other adoption fees are usually very reasonable. If you receive your child, you will stay only a few days. Escorting is often permitted.

Honduras. Singles and couples married at least three years who are between twenty-five and fifty-one years old may adopt. Both spouses must be in the country for the initial assessment. After this session, the prospective adoptive parents may leave the country and let the attorney handle the final adoption. Only one parent needs to return to get the child, and the stay is about one week. Only licensed agencies may place children from Honduras.

Jamaica. Singles may adopt. The wait for a child is about eight months. Black infants and older children are available. Travel is optional.

Mexico. This is a very limited program and in 1998, 168 Mexican children were adopted by Americans, making Mexico the twelfth most popular country from which to adopt. Considering that Mexico is geographically the closest country from which to adopt, it would seem to be a country to seriously consider adopting from, especially if you live in the Southwest. The adoption programs are changing and becoming more promising.

Two trips are usually required to adopt. Because adoption procedures vary widely through the thirty-one Mexican states, the time required to complete an adoption can be anywhere from one month to two years. The cost can also vary widely. Using a private attorney is more costly but usually less time consuming.

Nicaragua. Singles and those who have been married for one year may adopt. Applicants must be between twenty-five and forty years old. Children are between three months and six years old. Placement takes about six months. Parents must stay in the country about two weeks. New programs are opening up.

Paraguay. Single women and couples who are at least thirty-five years old or who have been married five years or more are eligible. Infants and toddlers in foster care are available. Some agencies allow skin and hair color preference. The only age limits are those imposed by the agencies. Travel is for about four weeks, or two trips. Cost: about $15,000, not including travel. Other agencies list $21,500, including travel and local service.

Peru. Couples under fifty-five years old may adopt and single women thirty to forty-five years old may adopt children three years old and older. Although infants are available, most children are between two and five years old. The country's programs work with licensed agencies only. Two parents must usually stay two weeks and one parent may have to stay longer.

Latin America Parents Association
LAPA New York
P.O. Box 339
Brooklyn, NY 11234
(718) 236-8689
LAPA.com
This organization is an extensive support group that provides information about countries and will recommend a program after three successful adoptions. Anyone contemplating an adoption from Latin America will want to contact LAPA.

Africa

Couples married at least two years and single women may adopt. Ethiopia had an excellent adoption program, but as of this writing the program is not going well. About seventy children from Africa are adopted each year. Many are older and have lived through war or refugee camps; some have experienced sexual abuse and have chronic hepatitis B.

Asia

Cambodia. In 1999, 248 children were adopted from Cambodia and it was the ninth most popular country from which to adopt. Single women who live alone or with relatives, and couples married at least two years may adopt if they are twenty-five to fifty years of age. Christians, nonsmokers, and small families are preferred. One parent must be at home at least six months after placement. Travel is optional, and if you do go, you need stay only one week.

China. China was the second most popular country from which to adopt in 1999, and 4,101 children came to the United States. In 1995, when China was the most popular program, 2,130 Chinese children were adopted by Americans. Adoptions can only go through agencies approved by China.

It takes about six months after all your paperwork has reached China for a child to be assigned to you and then you wait another two months to travel to get your child. The China Centre for Adoption Affairs tells the agency of your approval and then selects which province your dossier will be sent to. The dossier translation is also done by China Centre. When a child is assigned to you, you will get medical information and a small black-and-white photo of the child. You must accept the child in writing before traveling.

After arriving in Beijing, you then travel to meet your child the next day. After completing the paperwork necessary to finalize the adoption, you travel to Guangzhou to obtain the child's visa. The following day the families go to the medical center, where the children are examined. Next you obtain photos for your child's visa and then go over to the American Embassy for the visa interview. The visa is issued in a few hours, and you can be on your way home the next morning.

Adoptions are finalized directly in China, and at least one parent must travel to receive the child and finalize the adoption. The stay is about ten days.

Overall, the Chinese government has been very cooperative about adoptions, and the paperwork required is relatively easy to understand and follow. For the most part, the children are healthy: Chinese women usually do not smoke, and AIDS and other sexually transmitted diseases have not been a concern so far. The children available are for the most part infant girls. Sibling groups are not available.

China has lifted its age restrictions on adoptive families and the number of children that you can have. It takes about six to nine months to get a child after INS approval.

Families with Children from China, an adoptive parent organization, has a Web site at *http://www.catalog.com/fwcfc/*. This is an excellent source of information and lists support groups throughout the country and the world.

Families with Children from China
255 W. 90th St. 11C
New York, NY 10024
Caugh@aol.com

Hong Kong. Couples must be married for at least three years or five years in cases of remarriage after only one divorce, and be between twenty-five to forty-five years of age. More males are available and children are one year old and older. The wait for a child is about one year after INS approval. Currently Hong Kong has its own administrative procedures, but it is believed that eventually Hong Kong will operate in the same way as China.

India. In 1998, American adopted 478 children from India, making India the sixth most popular country from which to adopt that year. Couples married for two years and single women may adopt. Couples can have only two children and singles can have one child. Many agencies place primarily low birth weight infants, although toddlers and sibling groups are available. Parents do not have to travel. If you do travel, the stay is one to two weeks.

Ichild is an Internet mailing list for families who have adopted children from India. To join the list, send a message to *ichild@ibm.net* with "subscribe" on the subject line.

Japan. Japan prefers couples of Asian descent, but the law does not prohibit foreigners from adopting. There are no specific government regulations. Traveling is optional. If you do travel, plan to stay anywhere from three days to three weeks. Visas are issued only on Tuesdays, so paperwork can be delayed by a week. The waiting period for a placement can vary from a matter of months to four years, depending upon what program is used. It is best to work directly with an orphanage. Costs vary widely but can be over $25,000. Having a personal contact can reduce costs considerably.

Korea. In 1999, 2,008 South Korean children were adopted by Americans, and Korea was the third most popular country from which to adopt. The following regulations apply only to couples who have been married for at least three years. Couples may not have more than four other children, unless they are adopting a special needs child; and children who are classified as abandoned must stay in Korea for six months in case a family member comes forward, unless one or both birth parents have signed relinquishments. If you want to adopt from Korea, you must go through a licensed agency that has a relationship with Korea and the agency must be licensed in your state. Exceptions are made if you want to adopt a child with special needs. Koreans are beginning to adopt within their own country, meaning that fewer children are available. Nevertheless, large numbers of orphans are still adopted in the United States every year. The children are brought to the United States, so traveling is unnecessary. It takes about one year after your documents are submitted to adopt a child from Korea.

Marshall Islands. The State Department does not maintain statistics on the Marshall Islands because visas are not issued. At present, you do not go through INS to adopt from the Marshall Islands because of their status with the U.S. government under the Compact of Free Association. The children have warm skin tones and dark straight hair. Usually the birth parents relinquish a child—even older children—directly to you. The children are usually well-loved but the parents want a better life for their child. Expect to meet and interact with the child's parents. Because children have usually lived with their birth families, the children do not suffer from attachment disorders. While on the main island you go to court, where the adoption is finalized. You cannot apply for citizenship for your child until he has lived with you for two years under INS regulations. Usually adoptions from the Marshall Islands are relatively inexpensive and are processed in just a few months.

Philippines. In 1999, 198 children were adopted by Americans from the Philippines, making this country the eleventh most popular country from which to adopt. Couples must be married three years and have no more than three children, and single women can adopt school-aged children. Mostly boys, aged six months to fifteen years old, are available. Rules are fairly flexible as to parents' ages. Travel is usually for three to nine days, but sometimes escorts can be arranged. The usual wait for a child is six months to two years. A committee selects the best family for each child, so you can wait on a list for a very short time or a long time.

Taiwan. Healthy infants who may have some previous medical problems are available. Couples twenty-five to forty-five years old with one or no children are eligible. The wait for INS approval is one to two years. Traveling is not always required; if you do go, plan to stay two weeks.

Thailand. In 1998, 84 children were adopted from Thailand by Americans. Childless couples under forty-five years of age are preferred. Mostly boys two years old and older are available. The U.S. State Department warns that an adoption from Thailand can be complex and lengthy and may take up to two years to complete.

All adoptions in Thailand must be processed through the Child Adoption Center of the Department of Public Welfare (DPW). Three organizations are licensed to deal with Americans through the DPW's Child Adoption Center:

Holt Sahathai Foundation
850/33 Sukhumvit 71
Bangkok 10110
P.O. Box Nana Nua 1478
Bangkok 10110
Tel. (66)(2) 381-8834

Thai Red Cross Foundation
Chulalongkorn Hospital
Corner of Rama IV Road and Rajdamri Road
Bangkok 10300
Tel. (66)(2) 252-8181 or (66)(2) 256-4178

Pattaya Orphanage
Pattaya City, Chonburi
P.O. Box 15
Pattaya City, Chonburi 20151
Tel. (66)(38) 422-745

For complete information and application forms, prospective adoptive parents should contact one of the above agencies or DPW directly at:

Child Adoption Center
Department of Public Welfare
Rajvithee Home for Girls
Rajvithee Road
Bangkok 10400
Tel. (66)(2) 246-8651

The wait for a child under three years old is about three months, and the wait is six to twelve months for an infant. Once a child is assigned to you, you must wait three to four months until the child can immigrate to the United States.

Vietnam. In 1999, 712 children were adopted from Vietnam by Americans, making Vietnam the sixth most popular country from which to adopt that year. Married couples and singles under sixty years old may adopt. More boys than girls are available and young infants and sibling groups can be adopted. It usually takes less than nine months from INS approval to receive a child.

Europe and Russia

Armenia. The U.S. State Department has no information on Armenian adoptions. Couples married for two years, under fifty-five years of age and of Armenian descent may adopt. Babies eight months old and older as well as sibling groups are available. The wait for a child is about six to twelve months after INS approval. Both parents must travel, and the stay is at least two weeks.

Belarus. Most of the children affected by Chernobyl are in Belarus. This would be a country to consider if you are looking to adopt a child with special needs. Single women and couples may adopt; the mother must be under forty-five years old for a child under five years of age. Many boys six months and older are available. According to the U.S. State Department, the process can be expensive, difficult, and time-consuming.

Bulgaria. In 1999, 221 Bulgarian children were adopted by Americans. Couples and single women who are forty-five or under may adopt and childless couples are preferred. Regulations prohibit foreigners from adopting children under the age of one. Most of the children available are over the age of four, especially those with minor physical problems and those of Romany (Gypsy) descent. The wait for a child is about six to twelve months. Escorting is possible. If you do travel, the stay is about two weeks.

Georgia. Healthy children must be on a registry for six months before non-Georgians can adopt them, unless the child's health is in danger. Unlike other countries, the day a child enters an orphanage, he is put on the registry.

Hungary. In 1996, 51 Hungarian children were adopted by Americans. Singles and couples may adopt. Parents must be no more than forty-five years older than the child. Toddlers and older children are available—especially boys. Some are of Gypsy descent. Orphanage conditions are good, and children come with thorough health records. According to the State Department, the wait for a baby could be years. However, those interested in adopting a child over three years old or a Gypsy may only have to wait about six months. Travel is required for both spouses. One may leave after one week; the other must stay two to four more weeks.

Kazakhstan. Although the State Department may say that adoptions are not permitted, adoptions are legal. The ethnicity of the children is very diverse, so some children are very fair and others are Asian. Babies four months and older are available, and almost as soon as your INS paperwork is complete you can travel. One parent must travel and stay in the country for about two to four weeks.

Latvia. In 1998, 76 Latvian children were adopted by Americans. Singles and couples married at least one year and under the age of fifty-five may adopt. Adopting from the country is relatively simple. Your stay there is comfortable and you can adopt babies as young as four months old. Sibling groups are also available. However, if you want to adopt a very young baby the wait is about two years. Some families begin two adoptions: one in another country, such as Russia, and the other in Latvia. After the couple adopts their first child in Russia, about one year later, the couple adopts a very young baby from Latvia. Because the in-country fees are not collected until right before you travel to Latvia, there is no loss of funds if you change your mind. Also you can start the adoption process in Latvia while you seek to adopt an infant in the United States. If you adopt through a domestic adoption, then in two years, you can adopt your next child. If you encounter a few failed adoptions, you know that at least this one will most likely go through. If for some reason Latvia were to close its adoption program, you would not lose your money. The stay in the country is ten to twenty-one days.

Lithuania. In 1997, Americans adopted 78 Lithuanian children. Singles and couples married at least one year can adopt. They must be under forty-five to adopt an infant. Children available are between one month and twelve years old. According to the U.S. State Department, the adoption process is rather complicated; therefore, prospective adoptive parents should contact the U.S. embassy in Vilnius and the U.S. Immigration and Naturalization Service early in the process, before you have identified a specific child to adopt.

Prospective parents must register with the Children's Rights Protective Service in Lithuanian *before* beginning any adoption proceedings. As children become available, the CRPS contacts parents according to their position on the list. The waiting period depends largely on the parents' flexibility in adopting a child. According to the State Department the wait for a child could be years.

Moldova. In 1994, four Moldovian children were adopted by Americans. According to the State Department, adopting from Moldova can be expensive, time consuming, and difficult. Adoptions are granted on a case-by-case basis by the Moldovian judicial authorities and American consular officers to ensure that the legal requirements of both countries have been met. Single women and couples may adopt. Most of the children available are healthy toddlers. One parent should be at home at least three months after placement. Travel for one parent is about three weeks.

Poland. In 1998, 77 children were adopted from Poland into the United States. The kinds of children available and the required length of stay are all subject to change. Poland works only with licensed agencies and prefers parents with a strong Polish background. The wait for a child can be less than six months. Both parents must travel for one week; the other then stays for three more weeks.

Romania. In 1999, 895 Romanian children were adopted by Americans; in 1998, 406 were adopted; in 1997, 621 were adopted. Romania has new adoption laws and the programs in general are operating very well. Romania is quite flexible as to the age of the applicants, and single women and sometimes men may adopt. Children are assigned at a very young age, but usually the children are not adopted and allowed to leave the country until they are at least six months old. The process is very simple, and the wait to adopt is about six months after INS approval. Romania has established an excellent foster care system so that adoptive families can adopt babies who have been cared for in foster homes rather than in orphanages.

Only one parent needs to stay in the country for about three days; in some areas the stay can be as long as ten days. Escorting is also permitted.

Russian Republic. In 1999, Americans adopted 4,348 Russian children, making Russia the most popular country from which to adopt. Infants and many sibling groups are available. Most of the children are between six months and six years old when placed. Tens of thousands of children are in institutions, but many do not fit the INS "orphan" definition. It is estimated that over 100,000 children will be abandoned in Russia in the next year.

The process of adopting from Russia is relatively simple, and once you receive approval from INS, you can be traveling in about two months or sooner, depending upon whether your child has been properly registered for adoption. One parent must travel. You must travel to your child's region for the adoption, and because Russia is so large (it has eleven different time zones), and because you must travel in and out of Moscow, your trip will take from one to two weeks— usually about ten days. In some regions the ten-day wait after the adoption hearing is not waived, so your trip could be as long as three weeks. As the child's age increases, the fees generally decrease. Also, if you adopt a child with a medical condition or disability, fees are again reduced.

Ukraine. In 1999, 323 Ukrainian children were adopted to the U.S. This is a growing program and the process has been streamlined considerably. Singles and couples may adopt. The children are usually one year and older, although babies can be adopted. In general, sibling groups are not available because accurate records are not kept. It is illegal for an agency to allow families to select a child based on a picture or videotape viewed here in the U.S. You must go to the Ukraine to select your child; this process is done by first looking at a picture of a child at the National Adoption Center in the capital of Ukraine and then visiting with the child at the orphanage. If you feel that the child is not right for your family, then you may select another child. The Ukrainians want you to feel very comfortable with your child before proceeding with the adoption.

Adopting from Ukraine is a relatively simple process, and about four to five weeks after you are approved by INS, you can travel to Ukraine. You will stay about two to three weeks. The child's visa is obtained in Warsaw, Poland.

For more information on children from Eastern Europe contact:
Families for Russian and Ukrainian Adoption
P.O. Box 2944
Merrifield, VA 22116
(703) 560-6184
(301) 474-4516 (fax)
www.frua.org
This organization focuses on countries beyond Russia and Ukraine.

Resources:
U.S. State Department. The Office of Children's Issues, within the Bureau, offers on its Web site country-specific information on the adoption procedures of 60-plus foreign nations.
travel.state.gov/
travel.state.gov/adopt

Immigration and Naturalization Service—recorded information for requesting immigrant visa application forms, 1-800-870-FORM (3676).

Automated fax—contains the full text of the office's international adoption information fliers and general information brochure, *International Adoptions*. From the telephone on your fax machine, call (202) 647-3000.

The Immigration and Naturalization Service Web site has laws, policy, and regulation information. INS provides downloadable forms online as well as online order forms for packet mailing (I-600, I-600A, and I-864 for international adoption and N-643 for naturalizing an adopted child) on its Web site: **www.ins.usdoj.gov/.**

Precious in HIS Sight maintains an extensive photolisting of children available for international adoption through a variety of agencies. Countries of origin include Russia, China, India, and Korea. The photolisting is updated at least once a month. You can reach this Web site at **www.adoption.com.**

Families for Russian and Ukrainian Adoption is a support group for adoptive families. They have a Web site at **www.serve.com/fredt/adopt.html.**

WHO CONDUCTS YOUR ADOPTION?

Sometime during the process of deciding which country you want to adopt from, you will also have to decide who is going to help you with your adoption. Very few adoptive parents do this process independently. Your agency, facilitator, or attorney will guide you through the process. Many of the steps and documents required will be the same no matter which program you go through, yet each country will be somewhat different. This is where your agency guides you.

There are hundreds of agencies and child-placement entities in the United States that handle international adoptions, as well as a number of attorneys. Most agencies or entities work with at least a few countries, because one country may suddenly ban adoptions. No one agency, however, can handle adoptions from every possible country. For example, if you want an Asian child, you will want to use an agency that operates adoptions from Asia. If you want a Caucasian child, you will want to work with an agency that conducts adoptions in Eastern Europe and Russia. Many countries, such China and Romania, require that adoptions be conducted only through a licensed child-placing agency. Therefore, if you want to adopt from one of these countries, you will need to adopt through an agency.

Also, in selecting an agency or facilitator you will want one that provides excellent services once you are in the child's country. Therefore, most families seeking to adopt use an agency that has a facilitator who is bilingual in the site country to guide you when you get there.

Other families do not use an agency, but have a personal contact in another country and just use an agency to do their home study, and then go to the country to adopt. Even if you lived in the country from which you are adopting, unless you know someone who knows how to proceed with the adoption in the country, that process can be difficult.

INTERNATIONAL AGENCY ADOPTION

Agencies in the United States facilitate an adoption by providing guidance, direction, and contact people overseas. Direct-placement agencies are licensed in the

United States and maintain a direct relationship with foreign placement services. Their function is to place international children directly with American families or to refer these children to American agencies.

A direct-placement agency handles the paperwork, including the foreign application; assigns a child to you; and communicates with those in the child's country by coordinating state, foreign, and emigration procedures. Once the child is assigned to you, the foreign child-placement organization sends the birth mother's relinquishment or abandonment decree and the child's birth certificate to your agency or gives them directly to you to take to the U.S. embassy affiliated with your child's country. Without these two documents, the adoption cannot take place. If the foreign country permits, the child may then be escorted to the United States.

Some agencies help facilitate the adoption and work with large organizations or are connected to other larger agencies that have facilitators in another country. Since there are many agencies that serve as facilitators, you may find one in your own state. This agency will probably conduct your home study and see that all the required documents are together. Once the home study is completed and the documents are together, the agency will assist you in putting together a dossier to send to the foreign country.

Agency personnel invest a great deal of time and money in paving the way for adoptions to proceed in a particular country. The fees you pay to the agency are for their knowledge and expertise in the culture, laws, procedures, and required paperwork of a given country. Generally, the service fees are about $4,000.

Remember that using a licensed agency does not mean that the people operating the agency are knowledgeable, scrupulous, and ethical. Some states are more lenient than others about issuing licenses to agencies. There's a chance that the licensed agency taking your money for an international adoption does not have the contacts and the expertise to facilitate an international adoption successfully.

CHILD-PLACEMENT ENTITIES AND ATTORNEYS

Some organizations, individual liaisons, and attorneys have contacts, or sources, in other countries and know how to proceed with an international adoption. Some of these liaisons are people who have adopted independently themselves, have learned what must be done, and are now assisting others to take the same route they have taken. They have established and maintained strong contacts in the foreign country and may work with contacts who prefer to work with an individual rather than an agency. Like agencies, these organizations handle the red tape, have contacts in other countries, and can help with the language barrier.

Sometimes a liaison organization is in the process of getting an agency license from its state. States can make it difficult to get a license until you can prove that you have children available and can show some record of success. In order for an organization to do that, it may have to coordinate several adoptions before it can become licensed.

A child-placement entity can be less expensive than an agency. Remember, though, always to get their fee schedule in writing. Licensed agencies, adoption organizations, and law firms are operated by individuals: Some are honest and some are not.

PARENT-INITIATED INTERNATIONAL ADOPTION

Some people do not use an agency or facilitators, but instead conduct parent-initiated adoptions, also called "direct" or "independent" adoptions. The prospective parents have a home study conducted by an agency or certified investigator, then take full responsibility for adopting a child. This kind of adoption occurs frequently in Latin American countries and may be the only way to adopt a child when there is no U.S. agency interacting with a particular foreign child care agency.

Some people like the high level of personal control they have with this method of adoption. It can actually speed up the procedure when you do not have to rely on agency personnel who must divide their time among many clients. You may also have greater control over the health, ethnicity, age, and gender of the child, though not necessarily. An agency or attorney will also give you the power of selection by providing you with a picture of the child and as much background information as possible; after all, they want the adoption to be successful as well.

A parent-initiated adoption can be less expensive than an agency adoption. However, if you make mistakes along the way, the financial and emotional costs can be far greater. Remember, no matter which method you select, you will have certain expenses: processing fees, a home study, translations, a donation to the orphanage in some cases, foreign attorney fees, air fare, and so on. If you are going to invest that much money, you may want to be assured that everything is going smoothly and to spend the few thousand dollars more to have an agency or attorney handle the red tape. If you do decide to conduct an adoption independently, make sure you seek guidance from others who have preceded you. There are plenty of horror stories circulating about bribes being taken and children being sold on the black market. The best way to avoid this is to join a support organization and talk to the people in it.

Before you proceed, you should certainly write to the U.S. State Department, to the Immigration and Naturalization Service, and to the embassy of the country where you are thinking of adopting and find out what the requirements are for adopting a child from that particular country. If you have a particular child in mind, make sure she is legally eligible for adoption. One of the worst situations in doing your own adoption or not using a reputable agency is that the child you select may not meet the legal definition of an "orphan" and might not be permitted to immigrate to the United States.

GETTING THROUGH THE PAPERWORK

In the process of selecting a country from which to adopt and an agency to conduct the adoption, you will also need to process some paperwork. Before you become overwhelmed just looking at the paperwork, remember that nearly everyone can get through it, and your agency should help you with it. So if you know which country you will be adopting from and the agency you are using, the following is just a guideline to make sure you are staying on track and you have not forgotten anything.

Passport

One of the first paperwork matters you should take care of is getting a passport. They're valid for ten years, and it's one less piece of paperwork to have to think about. In many countries your passport number is your identifying number; therefore, both spouses should get a passport, even if only one spouse will be traveling. If you are just thinking about adopting an international child, get a passport now. To obtain a passport, you must provide a certified birth certificate (a copy is not acceptable). Also, when you have your passport photos made, have an extra set of photos made if you need to get a visa to go to your child's country. If you are a member of AAA Auto Club, they will make passport pictures at a limited or no cost. The photos for your passport cannot be more than six months old.

You do not have to go to one of the main thirteen passport offices in the United States to get a passport; over 2500 courts and 900 post offices accept passport applications. You must apply in person to get a passport. If your child is thirteen or older, he must also go in person. You can apply for your child if he is under 13. Everyone needs a passport—even newborn infants. If you already have a passport that has not expired, you can renew it by mail. If your name has been changed since your last passport and you are renewing it, you must enclose a marriage certificate, divorce decree, or a court order. If your name changed for another reason, you must renew your passport in person.

Send your passport, Form DSP-82, and money order or check to:
National Passport Center
P.O. Box 371971
Pittsburgh, PA 15250-7971

If you want it expedited, use an overnight courier and enclose a prepaid, self-addressed courier envelope.

Passports are processed according to the expected date of departure that is written on your application. If you do not put a date down, the passport office will assume you are not planning a trip any time soon and you can then wait about six to eight weeks for your passport.

If you need to have a passport immediately, it can be done for an extra fee of $30. You must prove that you are leaving within ten days by showing your airline ticket or reservation. If you need a visa, and are departing within three weeks, you can also expedite the process.

If you are applying for a passport at a court or post office instead of one of the thirteen passport centers, it is best to provide prepaid overnight envelopes so that your application can be sent quickly to the passport office and back to you. The enclosed envelope should have your address on it.

Get Approval Through Your State and from Immigration and Naturalization Services

To adopt you must get approval from Immigration and Naturalization Services. INS consists of offices throughout the country that handle all immigrations and allow noncitizens to become citizens. The INS wants to ensure that you are following your state's laws and the laws of the foreign country and that you are suitable as indicated by your home study to adopt a child.

You must get the following to Immigration and Naturalization Services: your home study, your I-600A form, your check for INS processing, fingerprint clearance through the FBI, and a copy of your birth certificate, marriage license, and all divorce decrees.

To fulfill your state's requirements, you will need to get a home study and accompanying documents such as birth certificates and statements from your physician. Also, the home study that is written to fulfill Immigration and Naturalization Services is different from a domestic home study and certain sections, as would be expected, address issues related to adopting internationally.

Have a Home Study Completed

You can start the home study process even before you know which country you are adopting from or even which agency you will be using to facilitate the adoption. If you are using an agency to do your home study that is different from the international agency that you are adopting through, the agency conducting your home study will not usually place restrictions on you beyond those imposed by the INS and your state. If you are forty-five years old, for example, and both the country from which you are adopting and the child-placement agency accepts applicants of this age, then the agency doing your home study generally would not say that you are too old to adopt. Always double-check that a home study agency will not disapprove you because of your age or other factors that do not have a moral or legal basis. For example, if you want to adopt two unrelated children, some home study agencies do want to approve you for this.

As described in Chapter 17, a home study is a document completed by an agency employee or social worker to indicate that you are approved to parent a child. If the agency you are using to facilitate your adoption is not in your state, you will need to obtain an agency or social worker in your state to conduct your home study. The person who conducts your home study will complete a six- to twelve-page, single-spaced document, which is to be sent onto the Immigration and Naturalization Service. Some agencies take a long time to complete a home study, especially if there are only a few licensed agencies in your state. If your state permits individual licensed social workers to conduct home studies, make sure that the country from which you are adopting and the child-placement agency will accept a home study from a nonagency professional. Also, if you must have a home study conducted by your placing agency, find out how long it takes. It would be a shame to use an agency that has a good international program, but the agency takes six months or longer to complete a home study.

Expect the person conducting the home study to meet with you twice, and one of these meetings will be at your home. The purpose of these meetings is to get to know you and share with you the benefits and concerns associated with adopting internationally. Many states require at least two or more meetings with the social worker. Often agencies will require that you go to educational meetings as part of the home study process.

Certain documents, such as your marriage license, birth certificates, and criminal clearances must accompany your home study. In general, copies are acceptable for all documents. Only a home study dated in the last six months can be submitted to Immigration and Naturalization Services, which also must approve you to adopt. Therefore, all dated paperwork such as your health exams must also be dated within the last six months.

The INS requires that your home study indicate whether or not you or your partner has a history of substance abuse, sexual or child abuse, or domestic violence, even if no arrests have been made. This history includes whether or not you have been a victim of any abuse, including sexual abuse. If there is a history, the issues must be addressed. Because this information can be especially difficult if you have been a victim, your social worker should be sensitive to this and word the information very carefully. Also, ask that this information *not* be included in the dossier home study, which is the home study sent to the country from which you are adopting.

The home study must also include whether or not you have been rejected as a prospective adoptive parent or have had an unfavorable home study in the past. If you have, these also must be addressed. Again, if you have been denied a favorable home study, for example, because of a physical handicap or some other matter that is subject to a great degree of interpretation, this must be worded carefully. Again, this information should not included in the dossier home study.

If you have a criminal history, no matter how minor, tell your caseworker. If you are unsure how she will feel about the matter, discuss it with her *before* you pay for a home study. Most caseworkers will approve your home study if you have small violations in your past, especially related to teen drug or alcohol use or shoplifting. She will not be likely to approve you if it turns out that you lied to her. A past arrest does not necessarily disqualify you as an adoptive parent. If your home study agency approves you, in general, so will the INS. Although the INS has a policy of not approving you if you have committed a felony, there can be some flexibility on this depending upon when the felony was committed, the nature of the crime, and what your life is like now.

The INS requires that a court disposition accompany any reported crime. A court disposition is obtained at the courthouse in the jurisdiction where you lived at the time of the crime or where the crime took place. Even if you were arrested for a "bad" check and then you paid off what you owed, you must still get a court disposition about the crime. This disposition must state what the crime was; if no record is available at the courthouse, then the court must state that no record is available. One client's INS approval was held up for a few months because the INS wanted a court disposition from a person who had written a check ten years ago for $50 that would not clear because she had closed out her account. The check and fine were paid ten years ago and the state police report indicated this. However, INS still wanted a court disposition. Because of this, the couple's travel date was delayed. Another family was delayed because of a DUI years ago; the court dispositions did not clearly state that the crime was a DUI.

Your home study should include a summary of the preadoption counseling/education you have received. It should state that the counseling/discussion addressed the international adoption process and its possible expenses, difficulties, and delays.

If you seek to adopt a child with special needs, your home study must state that fact. Read adoption books and attend workshops to become acquainted with general and international adoption issues. This will help you feel more comfortable during the home study and adoption process.

Lastly, your home study should have one closing paragraph that specifically approves you for the type of child(ren) whom you will be adopting. It may read that you are approved to adopt two related or unrelated children from a certain country or region of either sex under the age of thirty-six months old who have minor correctable health problems.

Unless you know specifically the type of child you want to adopt, and you are not willing to go outside those bounds at all, do not have the social worker write too specifically the type of child you are willing to adopt. Many couples initially think that they want a girl, but then when they realize the wait may be much longer, they are more flexible—or a boy becomes available whom they want to adopt. If you want a child two and under, are you willing to take a twenty-five month old? If you only want one child, are you willing to take twins?

It is much easier to have a more broad approval from INS right from the start, than selecting a child of a different age or sex than was put in your original home study. I have sent many addendums to the INS because clients decided to adopt more than one child. If an addendum must be sent to the INS, this certainly can hold up the adoption process, because the INS must also forward this information to the U.S. embassy in the foreign country.

It is best to send the INS all the supporting documents that you give your home study agency, such as your physician's report and your 1040s as well as personal reference letters. Your documents do not need to be originals nor is there a need to have any of your documents notarized.

The agency doing your home study will know which INS office should receive the home study and accompanying documents.

Depending upon the country you are adopting from, the home study agency will also prepare a special dossier home study, which is usually shorter; this shortened home study is then translated into the language of the country.

Complete the I-600A Form

As soon as you know which country you want to adopt from, you will want to file the orange-colored, I-600A form with the INS. You can order the necessary forms by calling 1-800-870-FORMS, or the agency, organization, or attorney you are working with should also have them. Complete the I-600A form if you plan to adopt but do not have a specific child designated for you yet. It is best to know which agency you are using and which country you will adopt from. If you are unsure which country you want to adopt from, you can complete it anyway; however, once you do know, you will have to pay an extra $120 and let the INS know the country from which you are going to adopt, so they can send the approval to the proper American embassy in the foreign country.

When you have completed your I-600A form, you will send the form to the INS with copies of your birth certificate, marriage license, and any divorce decrees. The fee for filing the I-600A is $405 as well as $25 for each person eighteen years and older in your household who must be fingerprinted. Therefore, if you are married and one of your children in your home is nineteen years old, you will send the INS a total of $480 (as of this writing).

You can take or mail your I-600A form, even if your home study is not done, to your designated INS office. From that office you will be given a receipt and permission slip to get fingerprinted at the same or a different INS office. Again, ask your placing agency or home study agency for the easiest way to do this. You cannot get fingerprinted at your police department; it must be at a specially designated INS office. Also, even if you have been fingerprinted within the last year for employment purposes or any other reason, you must still get fingerprints done through INS. Each person eighteen years and older living in your home must be fingerprinted.

The fingerprints are processed through the FBI, and getting them cleared can take a few weeks. Lately this process has gone much more quickly than in years past.

On Block II of the I-600A form answer the questions as follows:

1. If you are married, the first person named should be whoever will be at the embassy in the foreign country. If you both plan to travel and be there the whole time, then it does not matter.
10. The name of your agency conducting the adoption (not the home study)
11. Yes, unless you know for sure your child will be escorted home
12. Yes
13. a. Unknown
    b. Unknown
    c. City that you will arrive in
14. Yes or no—ask your agency
15. Yes or no—ask your agency
16. City and country of the American embassy where you will obtain the child's passport
17. If you check off that you want to adopt more than one child, be sure that your home study also approves you for the same number of children. If you indicate a different number of children from your home study, INS may ask for further information and this can slow down your adoption process.

If you must talk with someone at the INS, you may need to call the office of your U.S. representative or senator and ask a staff member to contact the INS for you. If there is a problem, your agency often will contact the INS as well. Try to make a personal contact at your legislator's office if you think you will be dealing directly with the INS in the future. You will probably be calling this person at least a few times to double-check on everything.

Note: When you send documents to the INS, sending them Federal Express is no guarantee that they will get to the right person. It is essential that you designate that the documents go to the Adoption Unit or to a specific person. The agency doing your home study should know the exact address of the INS office. Never expect to get any documents back from INS—there is no need to. You or your agency representative will simply be sending them your home study and copies of your accompanying documentation.

Note: Some people complete an I-600 form, *Petition to Classify Orphan as an Immediate Relative,* before they receive their child if they know who their child is and have the proper paperwork to process it. Even if you know the name of the child whom you will be adopting, it may not advisable to file an I-600 form before you adopt your child, because the paperwork may not be available or you may not adopt that specific child. If you are applying to adopt a specific child, you can submit the same documents as with the I-600A: birth certificates, marriage certificate, and divorce or death decrees (if married before). Also, you will need to send in the home study and be fingerprinted. However, other documents about the child's status as an orphan are required, and they must be filed within a year of filing the I-600A form.

Obtaining Approval to Adopt

Once you have sent all your documentation to the INS, the office will send back to you form I-171H, *Notice of Favorable Determination Concerning Application for Advance Processing of Orphan Petition.* Form I-171H indicates that once a child is assigned to you, it is acceptable for you to proceed with an adoption. The I-171H document is valid for eighteen months. This means you have an extended period of time to get your child before your permission expires.

Nearly every country's officials require you to have an I-171H as one of your documents. The INS will also cable or fax this preapproval status to the U.S. embassy consulate in the child's country. It is necessary for the INS to cable the preapproval, so make sure they have done so. Your agency should take care of this matter for you.

The I-171H is one of the most important documents that you will get. **Copy it immediately.**

COMPLETING YOUR DOSSIER

The criteria of the foreign country. Nearly all countries require a set of specific documents. Together these documents are called a *dossier* (pronounced doss-ee-ay), and each country has different requirements. The documents must be translated into the country's language. In general, the dossier documents are certified copies or originals, such as an original birth certificate or marriage certificate. You need only prepare one set of original dossier documents, but some people put together two sets in case one gets lost in the mail. Usually you begin the process of compiling your dossier documents while you are waiting for approval from Immigration and Naturalization Services. Once you have this approval, your dossier should be ready to be translated and to be sent on to the country from which you are adopting.

Documents for your dossier are gathered by you (some documents may be forms that the agency provides to you) and then notarized by a notary public. Depending upon the country from which you are adopting, you may have to have the notary public's signature certified/verified or apostilled by the secretary of state in the state in which the documents have been notarized. This certification/verification apostille is simply a document that is attached to the dossier document, such as your birth certificate, indicating that the notary public is registered in that state. For an up-to-date list of secretaries of state contact **www.asststork.com.**

An Apostille. An apostille, like a verification, is a sheet of paper that states that the notary public's signature is valid. Only countries that belong to the Hague Convention can have the documents for the dossier have an apostille placed on them. For example, documents for a Russian dossier have apostilles attached because Russia belongs to the Hague Convention. The advantage of an apostille is that it saves you the further steps of having to have the documents authenticated by the secretary of state in Washington and then by the Russian embassy.

Note: In 1993 the Hague Conference on Private International Law adopted the Convention on Protection of Children and Cooperation in Respect of Intercountry Adoption, covering all adoption between countries that are members of the convention. As of June 1995, twenty-two countries signed the convention, including the United States, but it has not yet been ratified. The convention states that the best solution for an orphan is for the child to be adopted within her own country, but that international adoption is preferable to foster care or institutionalization in the child's country of origin.

Because this process of having documents verified/certified (or apostilled), then authenticated, and then sealed can be a bit complicated, your agency may take care of this for you. Also, it is best to use a courier service for taking care of this matter, as a good courier will see that documents are accurate and will get your documents to the right place and pick them up in a timely manner.

Whether or not you use a courier, always send your dossier documents by Fed Ex, UPS, or some other mail service that has a tracking system. If you are sending documents directly to government offices and not to a courier, then send them by Fed Ex, as other services may not be available at the State Department or embassy. Whenever you send your dossier documents to a courier or to the State Department and embassy, always include a prepaid return envelope.

Again, in the long run, it is safer and could be less costly to use a courier service than to rely on your dossier getting from one site to the next. An excellent courier service, the Assistant Stork, will guide you in using couriers in other cities around the country. The Assistant Stork will also assist you in obtaining any documents you need, such as birth and marriage certificates.

Courier
Laura Morrison
Assistant Stork
2144 Aquia Drive
Stafford, VA 22554
(540) 659-6845
Laura@asststork.com

What is included in a dossier? Although each country has its own standards as to what documents should be sent to the officials in that country, listed below are the usual type of documents. No one country requires all of these documents. These are listed as an example of what to expect. As you can see, many of these documents are the same ones required by your state with your home study and also required by INS. The difference is that most of these documents, such as your birth certificates, cannot be photocopies but must be originals or certified copies. Certain documents will be copies, such as your INS approval or the picture page of your passport. Usually you must sign these copies, state that these are true and accurate copies, and have your signature notarized.

Sample Documents Required for a Dossier

Medical Statements: Medical statements should include the dates of your last physical exams, one for each member of the household. Most countries are looking for a simple statement from your physician that you can expect to have a full life span; that you have no communicable diseases; that you are not infected with the HIV virus (you may have to take an AIDS test); and that you do not use drugs.

If you are just beginning to gather all of your documents and are still exploring options, you may want to wait until you have gathered all your other documents before getting a medical exam. When you do, ask the physician to have it notarized if possible.

Police Clearance Letter: Your agency or state may require that you get this from your local or state police system confirming that you and your spouse have no criminal records. When requesting this letter, ask that it also be notarized. This is *not* the same as being fingerprinted.

Child Abuse Clearance: Your social worker will ask you to sign a form that she will process with the social services department in your state. As of October 1995, the Immigration and Naturalization Service requires child abuse clearance on all adoptions.

Birth Certificates

Marriage Certificate

Divorce Decree or Death Certificate of late spouse (if applicable)

Letters of Reference: Foreign officials often like to see letters of reference from professionals and leaders, so try to have at least two letters of reference on professional letterhead from a lawyer, city council member, minister, teacher, or business owner, and at least one from a friend who will write a warm, descriptive letter. Ask each person to have the letter notarized.

Most other countries do not have a computerized system for checking on someone's credit history and possible criminal and child abuse record. Officials will be looking for documentation to confirm that you are an upright citizen. In the United States, where your history can be checked, references are much more personal and directed more toward your child-rearing abilities than your good citizenship.

Letter to the Agency or Entity That Is Finding Your Child: Write a brief description of yourselves, any children you may have, and the kind of child you wish to adopt, including the age, sex (if you have a preference), and any medical conditions you are willing to accept. If the agency that does your home study is the same agency that will be making arrangements for you to find a child, it will probably have you complete this information on their forms.

The Dossier Home Study: When pursuing an international adoption, you may end up with two home studies: one that meets the requirements of your state and the INS, and another, usually shorter, version for the country in which you will be adopting. Why is the dossier version shorter? First, because it must be translated, and second, because a home study that has too much "psychological" information in it may cause some foreign officials concern. On the other hand, the shorter version may address an issue or two of concern to the specific country that may not be asked on a standard United States home study.

Unless the country from which you are adopting requires state or FBI criminal clearance, do not include any criminal background information in the dossier home study—not because you are hiding information, but because you have already explained the situation to your home study social worker and to the INS. Your in-country facilitator will have difficulty explaining to authorities in another country sensitive information that may be in your home study, including a history of counseling, being an abuse victim, drug or alcohol treatment, or "criminal activity." In some countries, for example, child abuse is not recognized unless the abuse is severe, so the in-country officials may not understand your being a victim of abuse.

The Home Study or Child Placing Agency's License: The agency that conducted your home study may be required to have its license attached to the home study. Likewise, the agency placing the child may be required to submit its license.

Because an agency will only provide copies of these licenses, the agency director will usually state on the license, "This is a true and accurate copy," and then she will sign the document and her signature will be notarized.

Guarantee of Postplacement Services: Some countries, such as Russia and Romania, want the placing agency to state that they will make sure that postplacement reports and updated pictures of the child are sent back to the proper authorities.

Financial Statements: Different countries require different types of documents to indicate your income is sufficient. Your latest 1040 may be required or a letter from your bank. Since most people keep very little money in the bank due to low interest rates, not having large sums in the bank is not problematic.

Letter from Your Employer: This letter will usually state your length of employment, the type of work you do, and your salary.

INS Approval to Adopt (Form I-171H): Nearly all countries require the I-171H to be a part of your dossier.

Other Paperwork You May Need

Powers of Attorney: Some countries require a power of attorney be granted to the in-country facilitator so that he can represent you in court and possibly get your child's new birth certificate and passport.

Nonrecurring subsidies: If you are adopting a child and your state allows you to receive nonrecurring subsidies for the adoption of an international child with special needs, you will need to get the information to your state subsidies specialist and the agreement back to them *before* you adopt your child. For example, if your child is adopted in Romania before you receive your child, you must get this paperwork processed before your child is adopted, not before you receive your child.

Health Insurance Coverage: You will want to notify your medical insurance carrier that you will be adopting a child. Because they must provide benefits just as if you had given birth to the child, and they are not allowed to exclude pre-existing conditions, you will want to make sure this is taken care of before you bring your child home. Insurance companies do not always follow the law, and years after the law has been written, companies still try to get around it. Insist that the company give you the agreement in writing.

A Will: If you are adopting a child, you will probably want to change your will so that the child will become a beneficiary from the date that you receive her. Also, if you do not have a guardian named in your will in the event that you and your spouse became incapacitated or die, you will also want to take care of this matter.

Other Adoption Benefits: Usually companies will ask you to submit an expense account after your child is adopted and in your home. But before you ever gather your child, you probably have already incurred the adoption expenses that the company is going to reimburse you for; so go ahead and gather all your receipts, for, say, the $2,000 in supporting paperwork. Then when you adopt your child and are back home with her, just make a copy of the adoption decree, put it in the envelope with the other information, and mail it off to your benefits department.

WHEN A CHILD IS ASSIGNED TO YOU/SELECTING A CHILD

In general, once your home study is completed, you have received approval from INS, and your dossier is complete, you will be assigned a child. Sometimes a child is assigned to you before you receive INS approval, but, of course, you can never adopt or receive your child until you have such approval as stated on the I-171H form from Immigration and Naturalization Services.

Depending upon the program or agency you are using and the country from which you are adopting, there are different methods of having a child assigned to you. The countries placing children for adoption want to make sure you want the child you are adopting. That is one reason, for example, that in Russia one of the adoptive parents must visit the child before proceeding with the adoption. As with any adoption, the older the child, the more you will want to know about him in order to be fully aware of his physical and emotional needs.

Years ago prospective adoptive parents would go into an orphanage and select the child they would like to bring home. This is not the way adoption happens today—not even when there are scores of children in one orphanage. A child is generally assigned to you *after* all your paperwork is done and you are approved to adopt, but before you actually travel to the country.

Sometimes adoptive parents go to an adoption agency's workshop and see pictures of children available for adoption. They may want to know whether they can adopt a particular child. Usually the child cannot be held for a family while they are completing their paperwork and waiting for approval from the INS. Some countries do allow an assigned child to wait several months for the adoptive parents to complete their paperwork.

If at a workshop or on the Internet you see a picture of a child who is waiting to be adopted and you have some facts about her, go ahead and get all your paperwork done. The child may still be available; if she is not, there will be others. Some agencies try to get people to go with their program by getting prospective adoptive families attached to specific children. This method of attracting a family can be very emotionally devastating if the child, for whatever reason, is no longer available.

Because there are so many available children now posted on the Internet, some people are finding their children this way—especially older children. However, as a rule, babies and toddlers are assigned to families and do not get posted on the Internet. Once the family accepts the referral of a particular child, the parents wait for all the paperwork to be processed to get their child.

Usually when a child is referred to you, you will be given a report that includes details about the child and his background. Some reports are comprehensive, but most have minimum information because little is available. The younger the child, of course, the fewer details about her personality and milestones will be provided. In a country like China, where most of the children are assigned to you at about six to nine months old, you will just be given a picture of the child and as much information as possible about her and her parents' medical history.

People often worry about how they will react when they receive an assignment. They think, will I like the baby? Will she be cute or ugly? *Remember, you do have a choice.* Nearly all adoptive parents we have known have been pleased with the child assigned to them and considered him the most wonderful child ever. However, there are others who did not feel connected to the child in the video. That is all right. Unless a family starts to arbitrarily reject baby after baby shown on a videotape, an agency should accept the fact that the couple did not feel comfortable with a particular child. In some countries, such as Russia and Romania, the children can vary greatly in coloring, and sometimes after seeing videotapes a family will say they want a child who has lighter or darker skin and hair.

If the child is older, profiles of various children may be offered to you, or the agency may call you and say that a five-year-old girl is available for adoption, give you background information and a health report on her, and ask whether you are interested. It is expected that you will be more particular about the type of older child that you adopt. This can be a similar process to adopting an older child in the United States. You will see a picture of the child and possibly a videotape. Once you select a child, he will be tentatively assigned to you before you travel to the country. At that time you will be told more about him—his likes and dislikes, his temperament, his learning ability, and any health problems. Some parents do not want to proceed with the adoption of a particular child once they meet him; this usually occurs when the child has more medical or emotional problems than the parents had anticipated. For that reason, more care is taken in matching an older child with a family. If you plan to adopt an older child, it is highly recommended that you visit with the child first and then make a second trip when all the paperwork is completed and it is time to complete the adoption. Although this is not always practical, it could save you and your family regrets if you realize that the child has profound emotional problems that you are not prepared to handle.

If an agency refers a child to you who has severe medical problems, and this is not the type of child you are prepared to adopt, then clearly state so. One family contacted me after working with an agency that assigned two children to them who had severe neurological and medical problems. The family had given the agency $17,000. Then when the family said that they were not prepared to adopt such children, the agency tried to make them feel guilty and said that they had to take the children or their money would not be returned.

Do not allow an agency to do this. First, never give that much money to an agency without being assigned a child whom you truly feel comfortable adopting. Second, find out what the agency's risk statement includes and ask under what circumstances funds are returned or applied toward another adoption. Third, make it very clear to your agency the type of child you are approved to adopt. That is why the INS has it clearly stated in your home study the age range, sex, and type of child(ren) you are prepared to adopt. You cannot arbitrarily decide to adopt a twelve-year-old child with cerebral palsy when your home study has approved you for a child between six months and thirty-six months who has minor, correctable health problems. Yes, an addendum to your home study can be sent in to INS, but the home study will have to address more issues than just the fact that you want an older child. This is not like an addendum to a home study where you first state that you want to adopt a female child and then broaden it to a male.

When you receive the medical information on your child, it is recommended that you present the information to a physician for interpretation. If you give the report to your local pediatrician, she may see any health problem as a reason not to go through with the adoption. Sometimes if the child has a serious health problem you will not want to proceed with the adoption. However, that is not always the reason for an evaluation. Many adoptive parents just want to know what to expect and to be prepared. Therefore, it is best to send a videotape of a child to a specialist who regularly evaluates international children. These physicians see children before and after adoption and know what to look for. They can decipher the medical conditions described by the in-country physician. For example, some of the medical diagnoses of children from Russia sound like the child has gross mental and neurological problems. However, a physician who sees these diagnoses knows what they mean and if the child truly has a medical problem.

Also, unlike your local pediatrician, the physician will not make a judgment about adopting the child; he will just give you the facts and his perception.

Although these physicians can view hundreds of videotapes, and can make careful assessments, they are looking at only a videotape and a medical report. Therefore, the reports are usually not definitive but are meant to help you decide if the child is indeed healthy and if there are any serious medical or developmental concerns. Remember, the physician can describe a disease or condition and possible problems associated with a given condition, but do not expect her to make a full evaluation based on the notes presented.

For example, the Evaluation Center at Schneider Children's Hospital states that its goal is to help parents make as informed a decision as possible, based on the child's medical record and videotape.

According to Schneider Children's Hospital, the *medical evaluation* of the child assesses:

- past medical conditions
- child's current weight, height, and head size using age- and sex-appropriate norms and to see if these indicate malnourishment, failure to thrive, poor growth, or microencephaly
- (if photos or a video are available) the child's facial features, looking for signs of fetal alcohol syndrome or other medical or genetic syndromes
- medical problems or conditions
- the need for further medical evaluation
- the need for medical treatment
- how medical status will affect future health

The *developmental evaluation* of the child assesses the child's current level of functioning with respect to motor skills, cognitive development, adaptive skills, speech/language development, and personal-social skills. In particular it identifies:

- any developmental disabilities or delays
- whether the child's environment has caused developmental delays
- factors that are likely to have a long-term impact on the child's development

Because most agencies ask that a family make a decision about a child in about ten days, these medical centers are sensitive to adoptive families' time constraints. Usually results are sent by e-mail or fax; however, when there are questions, usually the adoptive family will want to speak with a physician. These centers may also suggest that the adoptive parents ask more detailed questions about the child so that further assessments can be done. In addition to verbal feedback, parents will be provided with a typed list of medical and developmental concerns.

The staff at Schneider Children's Hospital will also communicate directly with other physicians and agency personnel about a particular child's medical and developmental status and needs. If a family is overseas, they may also call the hospital if questions arise. This is especially important for families who go to a country and select their child there. Other times, a child's health status may change, and the family may need to have a consultation before taking a child home.

If the child is very young, making an assessment is relatively easy; most problems, if they exist, are medical, not developmental. True, infants in orphanages often do not receive the emotional love and stimulation that they need, which can cause some developmental delay. However, most catch up quickly. A child under the age of one will not have moved from one caretaker to another. Nor will he suffer from the emotional problems associated with abuse or gross neglect. The physical examination he will have before leaving the country will tell you whether he has any congenital health problems or other medical conditions. The major risk is that of unknown genetic factors, which is true with domestic adoptions too—especially when a birth father is not identified.

Adopting an older child is invariably more of a challenge. For one thing, it can be difficult to make an accurate assessment, since her exact age may not be known. Malnutrition and lack of emotional attention can influence growth, so that tooth eruption and head circumference are sometimes the only measurements available to estimate age. If the child was abandoned, moreover, her history before being placed in an orphanage or with a foster family can be completely unknown.[2]

If you choose to adopt an older child, you will want to know more about her environmental background. If she has been raised in an orphanage, she may be very developmentally delayed and may even have an attachment disorder. Such a child may have a host of emotional and behavioral problems and may never develop properly. Unlike with the adoption of a child with special needs in the United States, where his background is likely to be well documented, with international adoption the child's background may be unknown or undisclosed.

Many couples seeking to adopt never "hear" what the social worker is telling them about the child's problems. They see the beautiful child's picture and "fall in love with her face." As difficult as it may be, try to be objective. Listen carefully and understand what problems the child may have. Yes, you can make a difference in a child's life, but a very disturbed child can also make a difference—for the worse—in your life. You must be prepared to handle the potential problems.

For example, even very young children who have grown up in poorly staffed orphanages may have attachment disorders. This condition is not going to be documented, and the only way you may be able to tell whether the child is going to be able to bond with you is by visiting him and seeing what he is like. Such a child will generally not respond to you, and when you look at him, his eyes will appear to be "hollow." Agencies may gloss over such conditions, insisting that within a few months of living with you, the child will be very normal. However, attachment disorders are very difficult to treat, and the course of treatment can be extensive—and expensive.

If you were to adopt such a child in the United States through a social services agency, the child would probably be entitled to special services paid for by Medicaid and other funds. Not so with an international adoption; if your health insurance does not cover extensive mental health counseling, the cost can be very high, although there are limited state funds available. (See Chapter 15, Special Needs Adoption.)

WHY DO SO MANY FAMILIES WANT TO ADOPT A GIRL?
Why are more girls adopted than boys? In 1996, 64 percent of the children adopted by Americans were girls. Part of this high percentage is due to the fact that in 1996, China, which has mostly girls available for adoption, was the most popular country from which to adopt.

The availability of more girls explains these percentages, but agencies report that couples request to adopt girls much more often than they request boys. Often families who already have boys will want to adopt girls. This is understandable. But why are there not the same number of families with only girls seeking to adopt boys? In fact, many families choose international adoption over a domestic adoption because they can definitely know that they can adopt girls. Sometimes people feel that girls are easier to handle and cuter to dress. Yes, couples expecting biological children also express these same reasons for wanting girls, but many express their desire for boys. Perhaps, families want a boy to carry on the family name and value system and do not think of adopting children for that reason.

Another reason more girls may be placed is that international adoption is usually a single person's first choice. Because most singles adopting are women, who usually seek to adopt a same sex child, it is only natural that more girls would be placed with singles.

Except for China, more boys are usually available than girls. If you do not have a strong preference for a female child, then seriously consider adopting a boy. If you cannot consider adopting a boy, perhaps you need to ask yourself why.

If you feel that you can only accept a girl from a particular country because of the child's ethnicity or race, remember that child may someday have sons who will be your grandsons. Certainly you have the right to request whatever sex you desire, and the agency should not judge you; however, for your sake and the child's you may need to examine why you feel this way.

DECIDING TO ADOPT MORE THAN ONE CHILD

Usually your personal finances and the INS will keep you from bringing home a planeload of kids, as some clients threaten to do. Naturally, if you are concerned about children, you may feel that you want to adopt as many as your finances allow. But as our eleven-year-old daughter so wisely said to me, "Mommy, even if we were millionaires, we would not adopt a lot of kids because then our home would just be an orphanage." So in reality, how many children are too many?

First, unless you are adopting a sibling group, you probably do not want to adopt more than two children. Three or more children being siblings doesn't make the task of child care any easier, it is just that it seems only fair to try to keep siblings together if at all possible. But children who are biological siblings do not necessarily have a sibling bond. They may be in different foster homes or orphanages while in their country.

If the children are not related, you probably do not want to adopt more than two children together unless they have bonded with each other in a special home-like setting.

If you have no children, you may be tempted to adopt two or three young children at one time. You may have longed for children for some time, and now you feel you are ready to settle down into a large family. However, you need to think hard about the impact this decision will have on your life. Adding just one child to a childless home changes life completely. Babies are a lot of work, but they do sleep a lot, and it is possible to adjust to their schedule. If you suddenly find yourself with a nine-month-old baby, a two-year-old, and a three-and-a-half-year-old, you will have three children all going through a cultural adjustment while you yourself are going through a major life adjustment. If you plan to be a stay-at-home parent, staying at home and caring for children will be your life. Lots of people, of course, have three children close in age, but they've had time to grow with the job—and their children are not making the cultural and emotional adjustments that yours will be.

This is not to discourage you from considering adopting more than one child, or siblings, but only to help you think about what it might involve. Actually, the decision to adopt sibling groups can be good for you and certainly for the children. A study shows that international children who are adopted as siblings actually have fewer disruptions and behavior problems than those adopted singly.[3] If you are seriously considering this option, we suggest you offer to have two or three of your nieces and nephews over for a few days or more and see how you cope. If it feels manageable, and you have good support systems and the financial resources to meet their needs, ask your social worker to approve you for up to the number of children you want to adopt at the same time. Within reason, the INS does not place restrictions on the number of children you can adopt as long as you earn more than 125 percent of the poverty level for your family size.

ADOPTING TWO CHILDREN OF NEARLY THE SAME AGE
With more and more babies and children available internationally, it is possible to adopt two children of nearly the same age. One family was going to adopt just one child and then decided to adopt a baby girl who had severe but correctable medical problems. The children are three days apart. When the babies are in their stroller together, it seems nearly everyone in the mall must come up and ask the parents, "Are they twins?" The parents found that if they said, "No they're three days apart," they would be in the mall forever trying to explain their story to people.

Some adoption experts will argue against adopting two children of the same age because it means that the child will have to face even more questions than the average adoptee has to face. Throughout school, children and others will ask, "Why are you in the same grade?" "How can you be sister and brother and only four months apart?" Yes, it may be inconvenient at times to explain what does not happen in biological families, but most times it's just that—an inconvenience.

Just as a man and woman would not cancel their marriage plans because they have two children of nearly the same age, you should not necessarily forgo adopting another child because she will be the same age as the first child you are adopting. If my clients had not adopted the girl with a medical condition, she may have died in her country. Instead the child has a wonderful, loving home, excellent medical care and a brother who is three days younger than she. The family is careful to give each child his/her own identity, as you would with any two children, twins or not.

Also, adopting two children at the same time may make sense economically (see Chapter 18, Adoption Expenses). The home study, and your flight, lodging, and food are all the same regardless of how many children you adopt. Also, many programs reduce their fee for the second child.

SPECIAL NEEDS CHILDREN
Just as there are thousands of children in the United States with special needs waiting to be adopted, so it is in countries around the world. Just a few years ago, an agency would feature these children through newsletters and perhaps even its own Web site. Now there are Web sites such as Precious in HIS Sight that feature hundreds of babies and children, many with special needs, so that agencies can allow anyone with a computer and modem to see these children. Because so many people visit these sites, thousands of children are placed for adoption.

In general, agencies are eager to place older children or children with special needs. In their desire to place these children in homes, the agencies may or may not require you to attend workshops or read materials related to adopting a partic-ular type of child. If you were adopting a similar child through your social services department, you would be required to attend workshops about issues related to adopting a child who has experienced abuse or neglect. However, this is not always the case when adopting internationally.

Before you decide to adopt a child you see on the Internet, read books that relate to adopting an older child. Some of these children may be fine and adjust very well within a few months, but when they reach adolescence, they may start exhibiting behaviors that stem from their early backgrounds. Families who do best are those who are knowledgeable, well prepared, and have realistic expectations.

As discussed in Chapter 15, a child with a club foot or cleft palate has a dis-tinct diagnosis for which there is a fairly standard treatment plan. However, if a child grew up in an orphanage, you do not know necessarily what the child experi-enced in the orphanage or before she was placed there. Also, you do not know how her early experiences are going to affect her. Bringing a ten-year-old child from an orphanage into your family is wonderful if you are especially called to this, are well educated on the matter, and have the background and skills to deal with the issues this child may face. Talk to others who have adopted a child over two years old, including those who have had their children for a couple of years and those whose children are adolescents and older. Of course, if you talk only to those who have teenagers, you may get the same skewed results that you would get from any parents of teenagers. Find out from these parents how the children fared. When things got rocky, how did the family cope?

When adopting internationally, all children are essentially special needs because of their unknown backgrounds. However, usually for an agency to reduce its fee, there are three basic criteria that will qualify an international child as special needs:

1. *The child is preschool age—at least four years old.* Again, the age of the child is less of a determinant of the child's adjustment than her early experiences. Early neglect, abuse, and repeated changes in the caretaking environment increase the risk for later maladjustment.[4]

2. *The child has a correctable or noncorrectable medical condition.* "Correctable" covers the following:
   - club foot
   - cleft palate/cleft lip
   - need for open-heart surgery
   - malnourishment
   - medically controlled epilepsy
   - scars from burns
   - cataracts
   - tumors or cysts
   - delayed development

   Noncorrectable conditions include:

   - postpolio effects
   - cerebral palsy
   - spina bifida
   - blindness and deafness
   - unknown prognosis—child may be "slow"

3. *The child is part of a sibling group.* Some may consider adopting, say, a brother and sister. Sometimes children are available only as siblings, since an agency, orphanage, or government may be opposed to breaking up the family unit.

There are distinct advantages to adopting sibling groups: The children may have an easier time adjusting because they "have each other," and you can grow your family faster than if you adopt singly. Adopting more than one child at a time can be far less expensive in the long run, too, especially when you consider traveling expenses.

If you are considering adopting siblings or more than one child at the same time while you are in another country, your home study must qualify you for the exact number of children you wish to adopt. Just because you are qualified to adopt one child does not mean you are qualified to adopt three. A social worker doing the home study will want to know how many other children you already have, what experience you have with children if you do not have any children, how large your home is and how many bedrooms it has, and whether your income can support a larger family.

In some countries the stipulations as to who can adopt may be very narrow, and only those adopting a child with a medical condition may have the restrictions broadened. However, if the country happens to be one where there are far more children than adoptive parents—meaning that officials are eager to find placements—the definition of special needs may be very broad, covering such conditions as chronic ear infections. If you want to adopt in a particular country and you do not qualify because of an arbitrary guideline, you may indicate that you are willing to adopt a child with a minor, correctable disability or health condition.

Sometimes it turns out that children have been classified as "special needs" so that they can be placed for adoption. The officials in charge of the orphanage classify the child as having a health problem just so he can released for adoption.

Remember, fees can be reduced if you adopt a special needs child.

AFTER A CHILD IS ASSIGNED TO YOU

Once a child is assigned to you and you accept the child, the care of the child in a foster home or orphanage may become your responsibility. In some countries it can take several months before the child is actually placed with you (depending upon the country's regulations), so in the meantime you want to make sure that your child is as well cared for as possible. Although a seemingly large amount of money may be requested for foster care, bear in mind that these funds also take care of the administration of the program and the cost of disposable diapers and formula—which can actually be more expensive in another country. So even if the average family income in your child's country is $150 per month, you may be asked to send a few hundred dollars per month to a facilitator to help support the child. The extra funds are often used to support other children also in foster care. Just as some programs require you to donate about $3,000 to an orphanage, which actually goes to care for other children, so a foster care payment can actually be supporting the needs of other children as well as your own.

If you are concerned about poor foster care, make sure your facilitator or agency knows how you feel and that you want to make sure that the monies you are sending for the care of your child are doing just that.

While waiting for a child many families will want to buy clothes and lots of baby products. This, of course, is the exciting part. However, it may be wise to wait before purchasing very many items because your child may not fit into those clothes and you may have to take them all back. Also, wait to have baby showers until you are much closer to the time that you will get your child as people will know better what the child's needs are.

In the meantime, prepare the baby's bedroom. Also, do the all the necessary work such as getting a pediatrician and calling your health insurance company. This is not as exciting as baby clothes shopping, but when your child comes home, you will be very thankful you took care of these things.

GETTING READY TO TRAVEL

The main reason many Americans do not want to adopt a child from another country is fear of travel. People will cite the usual disadvantages of traveling—being away from your job, traveling with your children, or making child care arrangements. The real reason, though, has more to do with fear of the unknown.

Your fears will be minimized if you are as prepared as possible. The Internet is a great way to do research on a country. You can also check out hotel rates and airfares, find out what the currency exchange rate is, and even get the latest weather report. If possible, go during "tourist season." Tourists are particular and want to be comfortable—you will also want to be as comfortable as possible, especially with a new small child.

Many clients are concerned that when they get to their child's country no one will be there to meet them. The purpose of an agency is to have someone who is bilingual meet you at the airport and take you to your hotel. There should be a translator with you at regular times and someone to see that you get to all of the official places you need to so that your adoption can be processed.

Safety and Health

One concern in traveling to a poorer country is that the water may not be potable and there may be an increased risk of getting sick from the food. If you are staying less than three weeks, your chances of getting ill are slight. Most parents travel for less than two weeks, and they stay in large city hotels and eat at better restaurants. This minimizes the likelihood of contracting an illness. It is certainly essential, however, to get whatever immunizations are recommended for the country you will be traveling to. Start by making sure your childhood immunizations are all up to date. In addition, you may need the following immunizations:

Diphtheria. If you have not had a diphtheria/tetanus booster in the last ten years, get one. Diphtheria is a major health problem in all of the former Soviet Union.

The following vaccines are recommended to those who expect to be staying for a long time under adverse conditions:

Hepatitis A. Nearly everyone in the developing world has had it, and about 50 percent of American adults have been infected. If you are going to be in contact with a baby or will be eating in questionable places, get a shot of immunoglobulin, or ISG. This immunization is partially protective for several weeks and is very safe. Unfortunately, the dose is so big that you will have to get it in the thigh or buttocks, and you will be in some pain for a few days.

Hepatitis B. Hepatitis B vaccine is not usually considered necessary unless your child has the virus or you will be caring for children who carry it. There are two kinds of vaccines, each of which costs about $110 for three doses. Even one provides some protection if you do not have time to complete the series before traveling.

Influenza. The "flu" can be prevented by taking amantadine for the whole trip. If you are at risk for other diseases associated with the flu, get immunized instead.

Cholera. Cholera is an ongoing epidemic in Latin America and much of Africa, as well certain parts of Russia and is spread through contaminated food, water, and feces. Cholera is characterized by extreme diarrhea. The victim can go into a coma or shock because of dehydration. Because cholera vaccine is not very effective and has side effects, it is not recommended if you are traveling for a short time. Because the disease is caused by consuming large amounts of the organism in foods and water, boiling water will usually prevent the transmission of the disease. Also, grains and other foods should be refrigerated.

Typhoid. Typhoid has been reported in many parts of the former Soviet Union. New typhoid vaccines—both injectable and oral—are available, have few side effects, and are effective in preventing 50 to 75 percent of cases. Typhoid vaccine is recommended for those who expect to eat food or drink water at nontourist facilities.

To prevent serious illness and the gastrointestinal problems caused by viruses, bacteria, and parasites, you will have to take certain common sense precautions. Needless to say, do not have unknown sexual contact, blood transfusions, or contact with animals.

Avoid mosquito-ridden areas, and use mosquito repellent if necessary. Mosquitoes can carry malaria, Japanese encephalitis, yellow fever, and dengue. Malaria is a significant problem in many areas. Every year between 200 and 300 Americans contract the disease. If you are going to an area that has a high incidence of malaria, especially in the rainy season, you may need to take an anti-malaria drug, starting one week before you leave and continuing for six weeks after your return home. Depending upon where you are going and what kinds of malaria strains are present, you may have to take more than one drug. All can cause severe reactions, so you will want to discuss with an expert whether they are necessary.

If you are going to a big city and will not be going out much at night, your risk for getting a mosquito-carrying disease is very low. Even travel to the countryside poses little risk during the day. Stay in a hotel with air conditioning, and to be extra safe, bring an insect repellent and wear long pants and sleeves.

Contaminated food and water pose the greatest risk. Travelers' diarrhea can be a significant problem, so you may want to have a special prescription of antibiotic in case the need arises. Usually drinking only bottled water and eating carefully prepared foods can prevent this problem. Remember this motto: "Boil it, cook it, peel it, or forget it!" Use good bottled water and make sure the seal is not broken; drink only canned beverages or boiled water. If these are not available, use purifying tablets, which can be bought at camping stores. Use water that has been boiled for at least ten minutes and then cool it or use it to make hot drinks and formula. Rinse out the cup or container first with the boiled water (preferably while the water is still hot). You will also need boiled water for brushing your teeth. Beer and wine that have not been mixed with another beverage are safe. Do not use ice cubes.

As for food, if it is not steaming hot or peelable or dry (cereal, bread, crackers), you should probably not eat it. Eat hot dishes that have been made up fresh. Food eaten in a private home is usually safer. You may ask your hostess how she prepares such a wonderful dish before you eat it.

Finally, avoid contact contamination. Wash your hands, wash your hands, wash your hands.

Drive carefully! Accidents are the major cause of death and disability for travelers.

Resources:

HHS Publication No (CDC) 85-8280
Superintendent of Documents
United States Government Printing Office, Washington, DC 20402
According to Dr. Jerri Ann Jensita, this is a very authoritative book and the
most accurate source of information regarding immunization and malaria
risk. It is organized first by country, then by disease.

CDC's International Traveler's Disease Hotline
To obtain specific health documents call (404) 332-4565. Call this number
for information on disease risk and prevention for every country. Your
requested information is faxed back to you within minutes.

Consular Information Sheets
(202) 647-5225
(202) 647-3000 (fax)

State Department Electronic Bulletin Board
(202) 647-9225
www.stolaf.edu/network/travel-advisories.html

Documents for Traveling

Once your dossier is in your child's country, most likely you will need to be
ready to travel at short notice. Make sure you have all the proper documents,
including:

Passports. If you and your spouse are traveling together, always travel with a
copy of the other's passport as a precaution in case one of you loses a passport. If
your spouse is not traveling with you, take a copy of his or her passport's vital page
as identification.

A tourist card or visa. Some countries require adoptive parents to have tourist
visas, while others require business visas. Your agency will assist you with this.
Contact the consulate of the country you will be adopting from and find out what
documents are needed. You may want to call a travel agency or airline for this
information first. Verify what the cost and procedure are for yourself and your
child, if he will also be traveling. If you or your spouse is not a citizen, tell the consulate. Visas are usually attached to your passport, so the consulate most likely will
need your passport to issue the visas. Find out the best way to get it to them
directly—Federal Express is usually the safest.

First find out how long you can have the visa before it expires. Get it for at least three to six months in case of a delay. If it expires in a matter of months, you may not want to get one until your flight reservations are made. In this case, obtain visa application forms, but do not complete them until you have made all your reservations for the trip.

Power of Attorney. If you are not traveling with your spouse, you will need a legal document giving you power of attorney on behalf of your spouse. Talk to your agency about this. This does *not* need to be prepared by your attorney, but do get it notarized.

INS paperwork. These forms are taken to the U.S. embassy in your child's country. (For some countries such as Moldova and Ukraine, go to the U.S. embassy in Warsaw, Poland.)

I-600 Form (Petition to Classify Orphan as an Immediate Relative). You will need an I-600 form for each child you are adopting. The documents needed to accompany the I-600 form will be given to you when you adopt the child.

If you will be traveling to the child's country, you will take the I-600 form with you so that you can get the child a visa. Leave the child's name blank on the form and complete that information once the child is definitely going to be placed with you. If your spouse is not traveling with you, have him or her sign the document and have it notarized before you leave. Also, make sure that the spouse who is not traveling is listed as the second person on the I-600 form. If one of you may come back to the United States, complete two versions, one with each of you as the main petitioner. Always take two copies with you, with your spouse's signature on each, in case one is lost or the wrong information on the child is entered.

One petition is necessary for each child adopted. If more than one petition is filed on behalf of siblings, there is only one application fee.

All of the documents that you get in your child's country that support the child's status as an orphan must be typed and translated into English. An affidavit affirming that the translator is qualified to translate from the given language to English, and that the translated document is accurate, complete, and true, must accompany the translation.

The I-864 Form (Affidavit of Support). A letter from your employer and your individual federal income tax returns for the past three tax years must be submitted with form I-864. The letter from your employer should indicate your salary and that employment is permanent or temporary. If you are self-employed, you must have a CPA sign a statement indicating the earnings of your company. Be sure that you have your complete tax returns. Sign them and have them notarized. If you filed a joint tax form and are using only your income to qualify, you must also submit your W-2 forms. Or the other spouse can complete the second section of the Affidavit of Support. A good agency will assist you in completing these forms.

If you are traveling with your spouse it is best to have copies of all these documents. Keep one set on each person.

What to Pack

When preparing for your trip, remember to pack lightly. Let me say it again: pack lightly. If you cannot carry your luggage up two flights of stairs or for one-fourth of a mile, then you are carrying more than you can manage. You do not need many changes of clothes, even if you are staying for a few weeks. Remember, when you get to the country, you will have a child to carry as well as his belongings. What to take will depend on the country to which you are traveling, the time of year, and your child's age and size.

Many parents do not know what size clothes to take to their child; try to estimate or take a few different sizes. The sizes that do not fit can be left for the other children in the orphanage. In many countries you can purchase some outfits once you are in the country. The children generally do not leave the orphanage in their clothes; you must bring some for your child.

When packing for yourself, you will want to take basic toiletries and personal hygiene products. Some things are hard to get, such as mouthwash and antiperspirants, even in developed areas. Waterless hand-wash is great to have. Also, disposable baby wipes are great for washing hands and babies.

What to pack and bring for a baby or child:

- Baby carrier (cloth and lightweight)
- Baby bottles and nipples, preferably disposable
- Disposable diapers and baby wipes
- Tylenol
- Thermometer
- Pedialyte (or you can make it with bottled water and sugar and a dash of salt)
- Diaper rash ointment such as A&D ointment
- Hygiene products
- Benadryl

You will be surprised what you can buy in other countries. Check with your agency or others who have traveled as to what is available. It can be confusing to read the labels in another language on medicine bottles, so it may be best to bring a first-aid kit of sorts.

Also, because you will most likely be adjusting to time changes, it may be helpful to take a sleep aid such as Benadryl or Tylenol P.M. with you in case you have trouble falling asleep. Although such products may be available, it may be difficult to tell your translator what you need.

When checking in at the airport, there are restrictions as to how much bags can weigh. Each airline has its own guidelines, but in general, you can check two seventy-pound pieces of luggage and one twenty-two-pound carry-on bag. Even though you can carry on this much, do not take this much with you unless you are bringing in goods to the country to leave there, such as medicines or clothing for an orphanage. If at all possible, take suitcases that you do not mind leaving behind.

Carry on all products that you would want with you for the first few days. There are two types of luggage: carry-on and lost. If your luggage is delayed getting to you or is lost, can you live without what is in there? Place extra snack food, inexpensive gifts and used clothing in these carry-on bags. All of your medicines, documents, and hygiene products and a few days' worth of clothes should be in the carry-on luggage.

Carrying Money

Usually you will have to carry some money on your person so that you can pay the in-country facilitator. Most countries have a cash economy, so you will need to carry clean, crisp, usually $100 bills with you. Even the U.S. embassies usually require you to pay them in cash using clean, new, unmarred $100 bills.

If you must carry a few thousand dollars with you, divide it between you and your spouse or companion. Keep your money for the embassy very clean and try not to fold it.

To safeguard your money, place it in your passport holder and wear it on your body at all times. Stores sell special passport/money pouches on a string that you can tuck under your clothes.

Sometimes you can wire money to the facilitator so that you do not have to carry so much money with you. However, you may still be required to pay in cash at the U.S. embassy for the child's visa and for the purchase of other items. Unless you are staying in a Western-style hotel or eating at such a restaurant, credit cards or travelers checks are not accepted.

ISSUES RELATED TO HAVING INTERNATIONAL CHILDREN

Because children adopted internationally often look different from their parents, you may be subject to such unintentionally insensitive questions such as, "Where did he come from?" "When did you get her?" or "How old was he when you got him?" Holly van Gulden and Lida M. Bartels-Rabb suggest giving answers like, "We come from New Haven," "I pick her up after school," or "It seems she's been with us forever."[5]

When we are on the playground and spot a family that appears to have adopted children, because of our interest in adoption, we too are tempted to ask such questions. In adoption play groups, where some of the children are adopted and some are biological, such questions are considered perfectly acceptable. And sometimes people ask such questions because they are genuinely interested in adoption.

Gulden and Bartels-Rabb emphasize the importance of answering such questions so that your child feels like a part of your family and as as way to set an example so your child can set appropriate boundaries. In answering others' questions, never let your answer be sarcastic so that it makes your child and others uncomfortable about adoption.

Insensitive questions can happen to any parent of a child who is "different." When adopting internationally, you inevitably will be exposed to some racism. Gulden and Bartles-Rabb write, "Regardless of how you interpret such situations, your first response must be to validate your child's feelings." They suggest making the following points: that comments will happen and do hurt; that your child is worthy and good and does not deserve the comments; and that people who make such comments do not know your child and have no right to say such things.[6]

MEETING YOUR CHILD

When you get to the child's country, you will probably be meeting your child for the first time and then adopting her in the next few days. In some countries, such as Romania, you have already adopted your child before you meet her. In Russia, like Romania, you will have known your child only through a videotape. In the Ukraine, you will select your child once you are in the country and then adopt her.

Upon meeting their children, whom they have seen only on videotapes or pictures, some adoptive parents love their babies immediately and are very excited. Yet not all children look like the person in the pictures or videos. If the child is several months older, and has gone from being a newborn baby to a six-month-old, of course, the child will hardly look the same.

You do not have to adopt the child you have agreed to adopt based on a videotape and medical report if the agency or facilitator has not filled you in on other details about the child, or if the child has developed an illness that you were not aware of, or if the child appears to have emotional problems that seem more profound than other children in the orphanage. To change your mind would be very difficult and devastating, and perhaps sounds harsh, but if you have selected a child based on his health, and you were not told the truth or not given accurate updates when a problem arose, then you have a right to change your mind.

Before you sign up with an agency, find out what its policy is regarding a change of mind. Most of the time, if the child has a serious health condition of which you were not aware, you can adopt again with no extra fees; you will incur only travel expenses again.

This situation very rarely occurs, but I have heard of agencies withholding information from clients. In one case, a family was traveling to receive a child with a serious medical condition. The heart condition was serious but treatable, and the child was thought to possibly have other syndromes that may be associated with mental retardation. The parents were prepared to receive the child in whatever condition he was. The day before the clients were to leave to get their son, the agency called them and said that another medical diagnosis had been made, but the staff would not share the results with the parents. Needless to say, the adoptive parents were angry because information was being withheld. They were very worried but proceeded with their travel plans. Fortunately, when the family met their son, he was in good health, and a serious thyroid condition had been diagnosed and was beginning to be treated. The child is now two years old; he appears to be bright and his speech development is advanced for his age.

If you must select your child once you get to the country, be sure that a thorough medical exam is done and that a complete health history is given to you. Usually when you see your child, you can tell where he is developmentally compared with other children in the orphanage.

Make sure that the child begins to respond to you. For example, he should smile and his eyes should shine. When you go to meet your child, depending upon the child's age, you may want to bring a small, soft toy and some sweet crackers or plain sugar cookies. Often children in orphanages are not used to chocolate or other rich desserts, so keep the treats simple.

Because you will be spending a few days with your child, taking her to the U.S. embassy and other offices, have some light snacks and juices available. You may not be able to eat in certain offices, but a child could have a bottle. Also, have some small, entertaining toys to keep her occupied.

ADOPTING A CHILD IN ANOTHER COUNTRY

In some countries, such as Romania and Guatemala, the child is adopted before you even get there. However, in most countries, including China, Russia, and the Ukraine, you will actually go to court for your child's adoption. Certain documents will be given to you that you will then need to take to the U.S. embassy in the country from which you are adopting so that your child can be issued a visa.

If you are adopting without the assistance of a child-placement agency, you need to make sure the child is truly an orphan. The federal definition of an orphan is very narrow and somewhat ambiguous. An orphan is a child whose parents have both died or a child whose "sole parent" is placing the child for adoption. Under United States law, a "sole parent" is an unmarried person. This single parent can sign a release of parental rights for his or her "illegitimate" child to be placed for adoption. However, the other parent must have severed all ties to the child. If the child has two parents, her parents must abandon her, as two parents cannot sign a relinquishment.

In general, children are matched with parents by an agency, or the parents may have seen pictures of children and identified the one they want to adopt. Once you accept a child, the adoption process in the foreign country can begin. You may have to give power of attorney to a foreign lawyer or facilitator who will represent you in the other country's court. You are not responsible for obtaining these documents, only for processing them later.

The major documents needed to prove that the child you are adopting can come to the U.S with you, or with an escort, include the following:

The orphan's birth certificate. If this cannot be obtained, an explanation of circumstances needs to be submitted. The birth certificate should show the date and place of the child's birth. Some countries change the certificate to show the child's new name and the names of the adoptive parents. **Make sure you get at least two sets of certified copies.**

Statement of release of child for adoption. **Again, get at least two sets.** The statement of release shows that the orphan's only surviving parent cannot provide for the child and has forever and irrevocably released the child for adoption and emigration. The release must state why the mother (or possibly the father) relinquished the child. If the birth father's name is known, it should be listed. Certified copies of this form must be retained to use in adoption proceedings in the United States.

Certificate of abandonment (if the child has not been relinquished). **Get at least two sets.** The court issues this document after publishing for the child's parents. If the child was in an orphanage, it must show that she has been unconditionally abandoned to the orphanage. The certificate grants custody to an agency, legal placing entity, or the adoptive parents.

Death certificate of orphan's parents (if applicable).

Adoption decree, permanent guardianship, or custody transfer to adoptive parents. This should confirm the child's legal status as an orphan. **Get at least two sets.** A resolution is sometimes given instead of a final decree, which is issued later. The resolution is as acceptable as an adoption decree and will give the adoptive parents custody of the child.

The above documents represent the necessary evidence to substantiate the child's status as an orphan, which is required for processing the I-600 form. The complete list of documents needed for the I-600 is described below.

Supporting Documents for Form I-600

The requisite supporting documents include the following:

1. *The child's birth certificate, or proof of the child's age*
2. *Statement of Release of Child for Adoption or Certificate of Abandonment*
3. *Death certificate of orphan's parents* (if applicable)
4. *Evidence that the preadoption requirements of your state have been met.* This is usually just a home study and documents. The INS sends the U.S. embassy your approval, so the embassy knows that you have met your state's requirements.
5. *A filing fee of $405 if you are adopting a second unrelated child.*
6. *Background information on the child's biological parents, if any*

The consulate wants to make sure that the parents are fully aware of the child's medical problems or disabilities and are going to take full responsibility for the child. Once your child is examined, you will receive a medical form enclosed in a sealed envelope. Do not open the envelope; it will be given to the consulate when you apply for the child's visa.

Some consulates require additional documents, so call the consulate to make sure you have all needed documents.

Documents for Child's Visa

1. *Visa application form OF-230 or FS-510*
2. *Pictures of the child for the visa.* (This means three color photos on a white background. The photo must be one and a half inches square, the head size must be about one inch from chin to hair, and the child should be shown with three-fourths frontal view, with right face and right ear showing. Lightly print the child's name on the back of each photo and sign your name on the front side using pencil or felt pen.
3. *Child's birth certificate*
4. *Country's adoption decree or guardianship.* Must be translated into English. **Get at least two sets.**
5. *Passport.* You will need to obtain a passport for your child.
6. *Form 157, Medical Evaluation of the Child. The* U.S. embassy in your child's country will provide you with the names of U.S.-approved clinics or physicians who can complete this form.

YOUR CHILD IS HOME: WHAT YOU NEED TO DO

When your child comes home, you may want to have undisturbed time with him. You probably will be exhausted from jet lag and all the adjustments you have made. Plan to do absolutely nothing the day after you arrive. Tell people that you need time with your child even though everyone is going to want to come to your home and visit.

Medical Exam

Within two weeks after arriving home, your child should receive a thorough age-appropriate physical. Generally your child should have a full evaluation done by someone who is familiar with international adoption. One study concluded that many diagnoses were missed by pediatricians when the children were re-examined by specialists for international adoptees.

Because many international children harbor infectious diseases, which could not only be harmful now but have long-term effects if not treated, you will want to have your child tested for such. According to the *1997 Red Book: A Report of Infectious Diseases* published by the American Academy of Pediatrics, international children should be tested for the following diseases:

- CMV
- *Intestinal pathogens.* Fecal exams done on internationally adopted children found that fifteen to thirty-five percent had ova and parasites. The most common problems are *Giardia, Ascaris, Trichuris, Stronglyloides Entamoeba Historlytic,* and sometimes hookworm. If the child has diarrhea, he should also be tested for *Salmonella, Shigella, Yersinia, and Campylobacter.*
- *Tuberculosis.*
- *Syphilis.* Congenital syphilis is sometimes undiagnosed and not adequately treated.
- *Hepatatis.* Sometimes children classified as noncarriers of the hepatitis B virus are later shown to be carriers. To be considered as having chronic hepatitis B, the child must have hepatitis B antigens for six months.

Each child should also have a complete blood count to screen for anemia and hemoglobinopathies. In addition, your child should be screened for sickle cell hemoglobinopathies if he is adopted from India or Central or South America. Hemoglobin E can be found in children from Southeast Asia, and B-thalassemia occurs in children from India and Southeast Asia. If the child has anemia, the health care provider may then want to investigate a dietary deficiency, intestinal parasite or other infection or health problem.

Immunizations

The U.S. embassy will require you to have your child immunized before you leave the country, or you will be asked to sign an affidavit stating that you will have your child immunized when the child is in the United States. Unless your child has good immunization records, the child should be immunized in the United States.

According to Jerri Jenista, M.D., if the record is written in different handwriting and at different monthly dates, then the record is probably accurate. However, if your child has "perfect" immunization records, this is usually an indication that the records have been falsified.[7]

Although some vaccines may have reduced potency and therefore are not as adequate, most vaccines, even those in developing countries, are reliable.

ADOPTING YOUR CHILD IN THE UNITED STATES

Depending on the type of visa issued, you may be required to readopt your child in the United States. There are two types of visas:

An IR-3 (IR means "Immediate Relative") visa will be issued to the child who has been legally adopted by you in his country of origin and whom you have seen before he was adopted. (Seeing your child on video does not meet this standard.) Also, the adoption decree issued by the foreign court must give you and your child all the same rights as adoptive parents and child here in the United States. Although you do not have to reconfirm your child's adoption here in the United States unless your state requires you to do so, you may want to consider doing so, as discussed in the following section.

An IR-4 visa is issued if your child *was not adopted* in his country of birth, but instead you were given guardianship. This visa is also issued if you *did not see* your child before he was adopted or if the adoption decree *does not give you and your child the same rights* as a decree issued here in the United States. Federal law mandates that you must adopt or readopt your child.

Your child cannot become a U.S. citizen until he is adopted in the United States if he has an IR-4 visa. Also, you cannot receive a tax credit for the adoption of your child until he is readopted. Make sure your state permits you to "readopt" a child. In some states, there is no law.

Why Readopt?

If you do not have to readopt, why would you do so? First, in some states, where you can file the papers yourself, readoption is a very inexpensive and fairly simple procedure. In some states you may not be issued a new birth certificate unless you readopt. Your child can always use his birth certificate from his country of origin, but an official translation would always have to accompany it.

Also, readoption ensures your child better legal protection in the event complications arise between the child's country of origin and the United States.

If you are considering readopting, most likely you will be required to have postplacement reports done as required by your agency, your state, or the country from which you are adopting. This report, conducted by an adoption agency, can also be submitted to the court as part of the documentation required to conduct a readopt. Why wait until your child is here in the States for five years to readopt him, and then have to have another postplacement report done?

Furthermore, state courts are not required to automatically recognize a foreign adoption decree. This does not mean that the United States does not respect or recognize the authorities in the child's country, but rather, the status of the child potentially can always be challenged in a state court unless the child has an adoption decree from the United States. Thus, adoption experts usually recommend that the child be readopted as a precautionary measure. Following a readoption in the state court, parents can request that an amended state birth certificate be issued. This birth certificate is then recognized in all other U.S. states.

Moreover, some countries, such as Ukraine, require the child to keep his Ukrainian citizenship until he is eighteen years old. In such cases, the United States permits dual citizenship although it does not recognize it; however, a country such as Ukraine does, and thus could possibly call your child into military service because he is a citizen. Readopting helps to confirm that the child is a U.S. citizen first.

How to Readopt

When readopting your child, you will be required to have postplacement study reports and file for adoption in accordance with your state laws. Please be aware that your child will not automatically be a United States citizen once she is adopted in the United States.

Here is the procedure you will probably follow:

1. *Contact a knowledgeable attorney to file papers for adoption.* The cost of this adoption is a fraction of an independent adoption. The attorney is simply filing the appropriate papers. Some couples do this without the assistance of an attorney. However, getting a new birth certificate can be difficult unless all the required documents are submitted exactly as required.

Be prepared to provide the attorney with one or possibly two copies of your home study (one for state approval and one for foreign country approval), the child's birth certificates, documents indicating parental abandonment or relinquishment, and the adoption decree from the foreign country.

2. *Arrange with an agency or independent home study investigator to conduct postplacement visits.* This is not required in all states.
3. *Go to court for the child's final adoption.*
4. *Your attorney or the court submits a Judgment of Adoption or Adoption Decree* to your state's Department of Vital Statistics to obtain a birth certificate. Make sure the Judgment of Adoption lists your child's date and place of birth. Vital statistics offices do not like to have to look at any other paperwork.
5. *Obtain a copy of the child's birth certificate.* The new birth certificate will include the child's new adoptive name, you as his parents, and his date and place of birth. In some states, such as New Jersey, when a child is adopted internationally as opposed to domestically, the birth certificate says "Adopted" right on it. If your child was issued an IR-3 visa, in some states, he can receive a new birth certificate without his being readopted.

OBTAINING CITIZENSHIP FOR YOUR CHILD

According to the Joint Council on International Children's Issues, adoptive families should get U.S. citizenship for their internationally adopted children as soon as possible. Use form N-643, the Application for Certificate of Citizenship. This form can be downloaded from the INS Web site at **http://www.doj.ins.** The Joint Council cites instances in which adoptees who have committed crimes and who never received U.S. citizenship are awaiting deportation to their country of origin. Of course, you do not think of your child ever becoming a criminal, but what if he got into trouble while college-aged and was deported to a country where he knows no one and cannot even speak the language.

Applying for citizenship for your child is simple. File INS form N-643, *Application for Certificate on Behalf of an Adopted Child.* If your child has an IR-3 visa, you are allowed to immediately submit form N-643. If your child has an IR-4 visa, you will have to adopt him here in the States before applying for citizenship (see preceding section).

The INS does not require original documents, so send only photocopies. Attach a letter and state that they are true copies of the originals and have your signature notarized. According to Cynthia Teeters, who addresses this issue for the Eastern European Adoption Coalition, the INS may tell you that they want originals, but you can send copies. Also, you do not have to send in the child's "green card," and since it is not required, do not send it.

The first section of the N-643 asks, "Who can file?" It states that both parents must be U.S. citizens. This is wrong. Only one parent need be a citizen of the United States. The fee schedule is also probably wrong. Check with your agency as to the fee.

Documents That Must Accompany the N-643

- Child's alien registration card
- Child's birth certificate
- Final adoption decree
- If the child's name has been changed since coming to the U.S. submit evidence of legal name change if not in the adoption decree
- Evidence that one of the adoptive parents is a U.S. citizen.
- Marriage certificate of adoptive parents
- Divorce decree or death certificate (if applicable). If either parent has been widowed or divorced, evidence of termination of these marriages must be given.
- Photographs. You will need to submit three identical passport photos of your child; these photos must be no more than thirty days old.

Getting a Social Security Card

Whether your child has an IR-3 or an IR-4 visa, he can still get a Social Security card. Sometimes the person at the Social Security Office may not know that an "alien" is eligible to get a card; however, because your child is a permanent resident, he should qualify.

You cannot get an Adoption Taxpayer Identification Number for a child adopted internationally. However, you can get an Individual Taxpayer Identification Number (see Chapter 18, Adoption Expenses).

POSTPLACEMENT

Many countries require that follow-up documentation be sent to the foreign courts to monitor the child's progress. These reports, documents, and especially photos (send photos even if not asked), allow the placing organizations and agencies to prove to the courts and authorities that this child is in a wonderful environment and is not being exploited. Sending these reports and pictures can mean the difference between a country's keeping its adoption policy open or closing the doors. Even if the courts do not mandate that you send documentation, send letters, small gifts, a few dollars, and photographs to your child's caregiver or orphanage. In some countries you should not send large packages, since corrupt mail carriers and others will open packages that appear to have valuables in them. Keep your child's orphanage address on your Christmas list, and send photos and a letter at least once a year.

STEPS TO TAKE

So you are definitely interested in pursuing an international adoption? Congratulations! Following is a checklist of all the steps involved, from start to finish. You may find it helpful as you embark on this complicated but very worthwhile endeavor.

1. Join a support group or at least talk to a number of people who have adopted internationally.
2. Decide which country you want to adopt from.
3. Find an agency or facilitator that conducts adoptions from those countries.
4. Determine the requirements of that country and agency.
5. Call references about the agency.
6. Begin to gather paperwork—birth and marriage certificates, 1040s, and letters of reference.
7. Arrange for a home study.
8. Schedule a physical examination for every family member.
9. Call the INS and order your adoption forms; ask for at least two. (You can order up to five sets.)
10. Begin to have letters of reference done.
11. Complete all remaining INS paperwork (I-600A) and wait for their approval to adopt. You will need to submit copies of your birth certificate, marriage certificate, divorce decree, or late spouse's death certificate if applicable. Complete INS Form I-864, *Affidavit of Support* and submit with letter from your employer and last three years income taxes.
12. As soon as you can, get fingerprinted at an INS office.
13. While you are waiting for INS approval, gather all documents for your dossier.
14. When you have INS approval, have the approval and all other documentation notarized, and possibly apostilled or certified and authenticated.
15. Have translations done, if necessary.

16. Wait for a child to be assigned to you by your agency or facilitator.
17. Travel to the child's country and adopt the child in that country—this procedure will vary by country.
18. Take your child to the U.S. embassy-approved clinic for a physical examination.
19. Process INS form I-600 to get your child a visa to come to the United States. Also take to the embassy your I-171H form and your Affidavit of Support and accompanying documents.
20. Bring the child home.
21. Get your child's social security card.
22. Have the child adopted in the United States if he needs to be.
23. Arrange for the child to become a United States citizen.

ADOPTION FOR AMERICANS LIVING OVERSEAS

If you live overseas, an adopted child may also enter the United States if she is under the age of sixteen and has lived with you for at least two years. No home study is required, and the child does *not* need to meet the INS definition of being an orphan. Americans who are working overseas, including missionaries, often use this method of adoption. An American missionary family that lives in Romania adopted two Romanian children by having a home study conducted by the author's agency in the United States, applying with Immigration and Naturalization Services in Vienna, and complying with Romanian adoption law. The process went fairly quickly and the expenses were kept to a minimum.

Clinics That Assess International Children Via Video

There are several facilities across the United States where medical doctors specializing in the medical needs of intercountry adoptees, especially those in foreign orphanages, will review medical information (including videotapes and photographs) for prospective adoptive parents. These physicians are available for evaluation or medical treatment of adopted children upon their arrival in the United States.

These centers also provide postadoption assessments. The child should receive a general physical examination, a neurological examination, and a developmental assessment. Psychological testing may also be done. Based on the exam, the physician may recommend other tests or treatments.

Disclaimer: This information is offered as a public service and should not be construed as the authors' endorsement.

Andrew Adesman, MD
Director
Evaluation Center for Adoption
Schneider Children's Hospital
269-01 76th Ave.
New Hyde Park, NY 11040
(718) 470-4000
(718) 343-3578 (fax)
adoption@lij.edu
www.lij.edu/sch/
  dev-behavioral_ped/adoption/
  adoption.html

Jane Ellen Aronson, MD
International Adoption Medical
  Consultation Services
Winthrop Pediatric Associates
222 Station Plaza North
Mineloa, NY 11501
(516) 663-4417
jaronmink@aol.com

Deborah Borchers, MD
4452 Eastgate Blvd. Ste. 202
Cincinnati, OH 45245
(513) 753-2820

Dr. Sharon Cermak
Professor of Occupational Therapy
Boston University
Sargent College
635 Commonwealth Ave.
Boston, MA 02115
(617) 353-7500

Harry Chugani, MD
Pediatric Neurologist
Positron Emission Tomography
  Center
Children's Hospital of Michigan
PET Center
3901 Beaubien Blvd.
Detroit, MI 48201-2196

Ron Federici, MD
Developmental Neuropsychologist
400 S. Washington St.
Alexandria, VA 22309
(703) 548-0721

Dr. Boris Gindis
Center for Cognitive
  Developmental Assessment,
  Rehabilitation and Training
13 South Van Dyke Ave.
Suffern, NY 10901
(914) 357-2512
boris@J51.com

Dr. Margaret Hostetter
Yale Child Health Research Center
464 Congress Ave.
New Haven, CT 06510
(203) 737-5970

Jerri Jenista, MD
557 Second St.
Ann Arbor, MI 48103
(313) 668-0419
(313) 668-9492 (fax)
Editor, *Adoption Medical News*
Subscription Information:
1921 Ohio St. NE
Suite 5
Palm Bay, FL 32907
(407) 725-6379

According to the National Adoption Information Clearinghouse, the following clinics provide specialized services for international adoptees:

Dana Johnson, MD
International Adoption Clinic
University of Minnesota Hospitals
C432 Mayo Building
420 Delaware St. SE
Minneapolis, MN 55455
Mailing address:
Box 211
Minneapolis, MN 55455
(612) 624-1112
(612) 626-2928
(612) 624-8176 (fax)
johns008@maroon.tc.umn.edu
www.cyfc.umn.edu/Adoptinfo/
    index.html

Patrick Mason, MD, PhD
International Adoption Evaluation
    Center
Hughes Spalding Children's Hospital
35 E. Butler St., SE
P.O. Box 26020
Atlanta, GA 30335
(404) 727-9566
info@adoptionclinic.org
www.adoptionclinic.org

Laurie Miller, MD
Tufts University
NEMC # 286
750 Washington St.
Boston, MA 02111
(617) 636-8121
(617) 636-5080
(617) 636-8388 (fax)

Dr. Lisa Nalven
Valley Hospital's Center for Child
    Development and Wellness
505 Goffle Road
Ridgewood, NJ 07450
(201) 612-1006

Todd Ochs, MD
841 Bradley Place
Chicago, IL 60613-3902
(773) 975-5989 (phone and fax)
t-ochs@nwu.edu

Karen Olness, MD
Rainbow Center for International
    Child Health
11100 Euclid Ave. MS
Cleveland, OH 44106-6038
(216) 844-3224
(800) 755-6601
RCIC@po.cwru.edu
www.uhhs.com/toheal/rcic.html

PACMED Clinics
1101 Madison #301
Seattle, WA 98104
(206) 505-1101
www.pacmed.org

Post-Institutionalized Children
Thais Tepper, Codirector
PNPIC
P. O. Box 613
Meadowlands, PA 15347
info@pnpic.org
www.pnpic.org
(724) 222-1766
(724) 979-3140 (fax)

PNPIC is a support network devoted to understanding the medical, developmental, emotional, and educational needs of children adopted from hospitals, orphanages, and institutions throughout the world.

Schneider Children's Hospital
Evaluation Center for Adoption
Suite 139
269-01 76th Ave.
New Hyde Park, NY 11040
(718) 470-4000
(718) 343-3578 (fax)

Nina Scribanu, MD
International Adoptions Health
   Resource Center
Georgetown University Medical
   Center
Child Development Center
Department of Pediatrics

3307 M St. NW
Suite 401
Washington, DC 20007
(202) 687-8635
(202) 687-8669
(202) 687-8899 (fax)

Dr. Matthew Speesler
Center for Pediatrics
P.O. Box 6086
23 Clyde Road, Suite 101
Somerset, NJ 08875-6086
(908) 873-2229

Sarah Springer, MD
Adoption Resource Center of
   Pittsburgh
Department of Pediatrics
Mercy Hospital Pittsburgh
1515 Locust St.
Pittsburgh, PA 15219
(412) 575-5805

Department of State

The Office of Overseas Citizens Services of the Bureau of Consular Affairs advises and supports our embassies and consulates around the world in such matters as deaths, arrests, robberies, citizenship and nationality, federal benefits, notarization of documents, international parental child abduction, and international adoptions. The Office of Children's Issues, within the Bureau, offers on its Web site country-specific information on the adoption procedures of sixty-plus foreign nations.

The State Department lists the laws, requirements, and procedures for adopting from different countries on the Internet. Questions regarding a specific country may be addressed to the Consular Section of the U.S. embassy or consulate. You may also contact the Office of Children's Issues, U.S. Department of State, Room 4800 N.S., 2201 C St., N.W., Washington, DC 20520-4818, telephone (202) 647-2688, with specific adoption questions. Recorded information concerning significant changes in adoption procedures is available twenty-four hours a day at (202) 736-7000, or by automated fax (calling from the telephone on your fax machine) at (202) 647-3000. If the country you are interested in is not listed, procedures have not significantly changed. Information on immigrant visas is available from the State Department's Visa Office, at (202) 663-1225.

travel.state.gov/

travel.state.gov/children's issues.html#adoption

Immigration and Naturalization Service

The Immigration and Naturalization Service, a service of the U.S. Department of Justice, provides enforcement of and offers information about the immigration laws of the United States. Parents considering intercountry adoption should look into all applicable INS regulations.

www.ins.usdoj.gov/

The INS Web site has laws, policy, and regulation information. INS provides downloadable forms online as well as online order forms for packet mailing (I-600, I-600A, I-864 for international adoption and N-643 for naturalizing an adopted child).

www.ins.usdoj.gov/forms/download/formdown.html

International Concerns for Children publishes an excellent resource called the *Report on Intercountry Adoption*, which comes out once a year and includes ten updates annually. This book provides excellent information about international adoption and a country-by-country description of what is required to adopt and which agencies are assisting in the placement from that country.

International Concerns for Children
911 Cypress Drive
Boulder, CO 80303-2821
(303) 494-8333 (voice and fax)

Joint Council on International Children's Services
Maureen Evans, Executive Director
7 Cheverly Circle
Cheverly, MD 20785-3040
(301) 322-1906
(302) 322-3425
jcics.org
Mevans@jcics.org

Chapter Thirteen

A BRIEF OVERVIEW OF CANADIAN ADOPTION

CANADIAN ADOPTION

If there is one generally true statement that can be made about adoption in Canada, it is that no such comprehensive statement really exists! Adoption rules and regulations vary tremendously from province to province. Not only are the diverse provincial laws varied in their content and applications, they are also in a constant, almost day-to-day state of flux. According to Judy Grove of the Adoption Council of Canada, "It is a full time job, just keeping up with all of the changes."[1] Because of the fluid nature of Canadian adoption regulations, this chapter does not attempt to be a definitive guide for the Canadian adoptive parent. The goal here, instead, is to provide a brief but accurate overview of Canadian adoption. Adoptive parents are advised to take advantage of the list of resources at the end of the chapter where they will find people and organizations that can provide them with complete, up-to-the-minute information.

AN OVERVIEW OF DOMESTIC AND INTERNATIONAL ADOPTION IN CANADA

As more mothers consider single parenthood to be a viable option, and as birth control and abortion are becoming more accepted, the number of babies available for adoption has decreased dramatically. It is estimated that there are only about 1,400 babies available for adoption in Canada each year, but at least 16,000 couples want to adopt. This is one reason that international adoption has become a popular option. Intercountry adoptions now outnumber domestic adoptions by a ratio of three to two, according to adoption expert Michael Sobol.[2]

According to statistics provided in a phone interview with the Adoption Council of Ontario, between fifteen and twenty-five children were placed domestically for private adoption per month throughout Canada in 1999. However, one year earlier, in 1998, 2,222 children were adopted by Canadians from foreign countries.[3] This is an average of 185 foreign adoptions per month, a telling statistic that underscores the truth of Sobol's assertion that, increasingly, Canadians are opting to adopt abroad.

Despite the changes in Canada's cultural climate, married couples still have the easiest time completing both domestic and international adoptions. According to the Adoption Council of Canada, other Canadians may find adopting more difficult. Some foreign countries do not accept single applicants, while others place restrictions on the age of a child to be adopted by a single parent. Canadians living abroad are frequently denied access to Canadian resources for adoption, and as of February 2000, only British Columbia, Alberta, and Quebec allow adoptions by same-sex couples.

PRIVATE DOMESTIC ADOPTIONS IN BRIEF

There are essentially three different kinds of private domestic adoptions in Canada: independent, licensee, and direct placement (formerly known as identified adoption).

Independent Adoption

In an independent, or self-directed, adoption, the adoptive parents contact a birth mother who chooses to place her child directly with them without the assistance of an agency. The adoptive parents usually have to find the birth mother themselves. Independent adoptions are not allowed in some provinces, so check with your provincial government before undertaking such a procedure. As of this writing, independent adoptions are becoming less and less prevalent.

Licensee Adoption

According to Judy Grove of the Adoption Council, Ontario is the only province that uses the term "licensee adoption," but many provinces have licensed agencies. In a licensee adoption, the services of a "licensee," or adoption professional, are engaged. This licensee may be either an agency or a person. Licensed agencies employ social workers to coordinate adoptions and a lawyer to conduct the legal work. In cases where a licensed individual is used, the licensee is usually a lawyer, social worker, or physician.

Direct Placement

In direct placement adoptions, a birth mother chooses you, but a licensee conducts the adoption. The licensee may be associated with an agency or may be an approved individual. Direct placements can be quicker than independent adoptions, because the agency you are working with may find a child for you while you simultaneously conduct your own search for a birth mother.

Note: It should be emphasized that in many provinces in Canada, it is illegal for adoptive parents to pay a birthmother's expenses during pregnancy.

PROVINCIAL RULES AND REGULATIONS

Those interested in domestic adoption must acquaint themselves with their provincial laws. Private agencies are allowed for domestic adoptions in some provinces but not all. As of February 2000, the following are the provincial rules for adopting domestically:[4]

Alberta: Agency required, except in direct placement

British Columbia: Must use an agency

Manitoba: Agency required

New Brunswick: Must use a government-run agency and a lawyer

Newfoundland: Direct placement allowed. No private agencies; use a lawyer.

Northwest Territories: Private placement allowed. Use your own lawyer.

Nova Scotia: Direct placement allowed. There are private agencies, but you may also adopt directly using a lawyer.

Ontario and Prince Edward Island—No direct placement

Quebec: No private agencies, no direct placement

Saskatchewan: Direct placement allowed. Use an attorney, because there is only one private agency.

Yukon Territory: No direct placement

Who to Contact

As previously mentioned, provincial laws on domestic adoption are subject to constant fluctuation. To receive the most current information about your province, contact:

Judy Grove
Adoption Council of Canada
888-542-3678 (888-54-ADOPT)

The Adoption Council is a private organization, not a government agency, but it is mandated to keep up with changes in adoption legislation, both domestic and international.

INTERNATIONAL ADOPTION

In Canada, most international adoptions are conducted through private agencies. These agencies engage the help of provincial and national government ministries to complete the legalities of the adoption. One organization that may be of assistance in your adoption is the National Adoption Desk, an organization formed in 1975 that exists for the purpose of providing a liaison between foreign governments and Canadian national and provincial governments. "The Desk," as it is commonly called, tracks the adoption laws and politics of other countries, assisting in the dissemination of information to the provincial government and to the prospective adoptive parents. The Desk has official relationships with nine countries at this time: Colombia, Haiti, Hong Kong, Jamaica, Peru, the Philippines, Romania, St. Vincent, and Thailand.

It must be emphasized that the Desk is NOT an adoption agency. It does not place children. It simply serves as a clearinghouse for official, current adoption information about the countries with which it has official programs. Therefore, it is not possible to conduct a public adoption through the Desk, per se. However, the Desk may assist your agency in getting the most current adoption legislation in your child's country of origin.

Canadians may also adopt from other countries that do not have programs administered by the Desk. In such adoptions, it is the responsibility of the private agency to keep up with current legislation in the child's birth country.

Two Types of International Adoption

International adoptions fall into two basic categories: those which are finalized in Canada, and those which are finalized in the child's country of origin. In either, the first five steps are essentially the same:

1. An adoption home study must be completed, with medicals, references, and police clearance.
2. a—The home study is sent to the National Adoption Desk, if the desk has a program with the country, which then forwards it to the country from which you wish to adopt.

    b—If the Desk has no program, documents are sent directly by the agency to the foreign country.
3. The local Ministry of Community and Social Services issues a letter of recommendation.
4. All children entering Canada must be "sponsored," which means you must complete a form called Undertaking of Assistance. This form can

be obtained from your local Canada Employment and Immigration office.

5. Once the sponsorship form is returned, the immigration office contacts the provincial government and asks for a Letter of No Objection regarding the adoption. This letter states that your adoption plans are known and that the provincial government has no objection.

At this point, the processes between adoptions finalized at home or abroad diverge. When the adoption is finalized in Canada, both provincial and national government ministries play a major role. When the child's adoption is finalized in his/her own country, the procedure is somewhat simpler, as the involvement of a Children's Aid Society or licensee is not required. However, the authorities in the child's country may require supervision reports from Canada for a certain period of time. You should arrange for such reports with an approved social worker on a private basis.

The Canadian government, unlike that of the United States, does not place a restrictive terminology on the word "orphan." Often, in fact, when a child is not able to come into the United States because she is not an "orphan" as strictly defined by the U.S. Immigration and Naturalization Services, an immediate search will begin for a Canadian couple instead.

The Hague Convention on Intercountry Adoption was ratified in 1994 and is an important aspect of international adoption in Canada. If the country from which you wish to adopt is a country that has subscribed to the standards set forth by The Hague, you must meet these standards in order to be approved. For a current list of Hague and non-Hague countries, contact Judy Grove at Adoption Council of Canada (888 542-3678).

Canadians considering international adoption may consult the *Canadian Guide to Intercountry Adoption*. This book is an indispensable tool that helps parents choose the country that is best for them and assists in the process of choosing an agency. You may order the *Guide* by sending a check for $12.00 (Canadian dollars), made out to Robin Hilborn: 224 Morpeth St., Saugeen Shores, Ontario NOH 2LO. Robin Hilborn also publishes a quarterly magazine, *Adoption Helper*, which can be obtained by writing to the same address. A subscription for one year is $32.00 (Canadian dollars); two years is $64.00.

COUNTRIES FROM WHICH CANADIANS FREQUENTLY ADOPT

Here is a brief look at the countries, both Desk-approved and non-Desk-approved, from which Canadians may conduct international adoptions at this time.[5]

Countries That Have Programs with the National Adoption Desk

China. The Desk does not have a formal program with China, but at the request of Chinese adoption authorities, all adoption applications are channeled through the National Adoption Desk. International adoption applications are handled through the China Centre of Adoption Affairs in Beijing. Adoption applications are forwarded to the Centre by the Desk.

Colombia. There is no provision for private adoptions in this country. All adoptions must be channeled through the Desk and arranged by the Colombian Institute for Family Welfare. Adoptions are processed by the Canadian embassy, Apartado Aereo 052978, Santa Fe de Bogota, D.C., Colombia, South America.

Haiti. The Desk has made arrangements with the orphanage Rainbow of Love under the Foundation for the Children of Haiti (FCH) for Canadians to adopt from Haiti. Haitian children may be especially suitable for the French Quebecois, as there is no language barrier. The available children are from six months to five years (mostly two to four) and are of black racial background. The children will have been tested negative for AIDS. Most are from the Port-au-Prince area.

Hong Kong. The Desk works with Hong Kong through International Social Service, Hong Kong Branch, which is an agency coordinating the placement of children from Hong Kong. There are more males than females available, between the ages of one and fourteen years. Most are in good health, although their biological parents may be drug addicts, alcoholics, or mentally ill.

Jamaica. The Desk has a working arrangement with the Adoption Board in this country. The Adoption Board does not accept applications or home studies from adoptive parents directly.

Peru. This country established new adoption legislation in 1993, requiring foreign states/countries to have agreements with Peru before applications to adopt Peruvian children can be considered. Canada was the first country to negotiate such a working relationship with Peru. Only applications going through the Desk will be accepted; Peru does not permit adoption through private arrangements.

Philippines. Adoption applications are referred to the Government of the Philippines, the Department of Social Welfare and Development (DSWD) in

Manila. The DSWD has created the Inter-Country Adoption Board to act as the central authority in matters relating to intercountry adoptions.

Romania. New Romanian legislation has been passed that requires that adoptions in that country meet the standards set by the Hague Convention on Intercountry Adoption. All activities relating to adoption must be carried out by accredited agencies in Romania. Foreign authorities must either have implemented the Hague Convention or formally enter into a cooperation agreement with the Romanian Committee for Adoption (RCA) in order for adoptions to proceed.

St. Vincent. Applications for adoption are submitted to St. Vincent Adoption Board through the National Adoption Desk. Once a specific child is selected for applicants by St. Vincent Board, the adoption is processed and completed in a court in St. Vincent.

Thailand. The National Adoption Desk has had an adoption program with Thailand since 1990. The Department of Public Welfare in Thailand has expressed a strong preference for working with just one central office, the NAD, and they will not work with anyone else. To try to circumvent the system to speed up the adoption process is to seriously jeopardize the prospective parents' chances of adopting successfully, according to the Thai adoption authority. The Thai Red Cross, an approved agency in Thailand, has also agreed to accept adoption applications from the NAD. The Red Cross places children from infancy to three years of age. The wait for a child is approximately twelve to eighteen months but can be much longer, depending upon the number of children available for adoption at any given time.

Other Countries from which Canadians May Adopt

Brazil. International adoption in Brazil is a serious, complex, and very delicate matter, prone to a lot of misunderstanding and corruption, according to the Consulate General of Canada in Brazil. An adoptive parent may receive a child only from the hands of a judge, never from anyone else. A "Certificate of Eligibility" is issued by the Brazilian government, which allows a person to adopt a child in that state if and when a child is identified. After this certificate is issued, the adoptive parents may start searching for a child. The purpose of the certificate is to prevent the sale of children and the charging of extortive fees. Children available for international adoption are usually over the age of two years or are special needs children.

Cambodia. The Adoption Bureau is the only official office within the Cambodian government to process adoptions. Cambodia has subscribed to the Hague Convention. Many Cambodian children are orphans or are seriously deprived because of the extreme poverty of their parents or guardians. A Cambodian child must be under the age of eight to be adopted internationally.

El Salvador. Previous adoption agreements between Canada and El Salvador have been stopped. Currently, adoptions are arranged privately from this country. The Immigration section of the Canadian embassy in Guatemala is responsible for processing adoption applications for a child's permanent residence in Canada for a Salvadoran child.

Estonia. Currently there is a very long waiting list for the adoption of healthy children under the age of four.

Guatemala. The Canadian embassy has advised that adoptive parents must obtain the services of a Guatemalan lawyer or notary for processing adoption in Guatemala. In the recent past, there have been many incidences of baby selling and kidnapping. For this reason, the Solicitor General in Guatemala is very thorough in its investigations of the birth mother and her documents. Adoption in Guatemala can take six to eight months, if all goes well.

India. The National Adoption Desk is recognized by the Indian government as an approved foreign adoption agency. The Indian government has asked the Desk to deal with the agencies in India that are recognized by the government to handle intercountry adoptions. A list of the agencies recognized in India can be obtained by calling the Ontario Ministry of Community and Social Services. Before a child can be adopted internationally, three categories of families must be considered first: (1) Indian families living in India; (2) Indian families living abroad; and (3) Indian families living abroad where one spouse is non-Indian.

Korea. In March 1991, the Social Welfare Society of Korea discontinued its long-standing program with Canada. However, the National Adoption Desk is currently investigating the possibility of working with another agency in Korea.

Latvia. Adoption outside of Latvia is only allowed under certain conditions, which are: (1) the child is adopted by relatives; (2) the child will be provided with medical care that would not have been available to the child in Latvia; and (3) the child has mental or physical disorders and was not selected for adoption by a Latvian within one year of being registered with the Social Assistance Department.

Lebanon. As Lebanon is a Muslim country, it does not recognize adoption as Canadians know it. Children are not formally adopted, and the adoptive parents are regarded by the Lebanese government as just being *de facto* guardians of the child. Legal Christian adoption can occur via an orphanage or a children's shelter. There are few Lebanese children available for adoption.

Lithuania. Lithuanian couples have priority over international couples. There are about 150 Lithuanian couples on the waiting list for a child. If no Lithuanian couples wish to adopt a particular child, he/she becomes available for international adoption. At present, there are 230 foreign couples on the waiting list.

Mexico. Adoption of Mexican children by foreigners is very risky. The Canadian embassy has been informed that no more adoption applications will be entertained until a change of Mexican administration.

Nicaragua. Foreigners may only adopt Nicaraguan children if they intend to remain in Nicaragua until the child is eighteen years of age. This law appears to be strictly applied; the Canadian embassy is not aware of any exceptions.

Pakistan. Pakistan will only allow its own citizens to legally adopt children, as it is a Muslim country. Mohammedan Law does not allow for the creation of a parent-child relationship, as biological ties cannot be severed. A Pakistani child may be placed with a Canadian couple by obtaining a guardianship order from Pakistan and then proceeding with the adoption in Canada, but this adoption will not be recognized as binding by Pakistan.

Poland. International adoption falls under the jurisdiction of the Poland Ministry of Education. Private international adoptions are possible and are the responsibility of an accredited agency called the National Adoption Centre. This Centre is connected with the Ministry of Education. The NAC administers a database on children eligible for international adoption.

Russia. As of 1996, local courts have authority over adoption cases, whereas beforehand, regional governors had this responsibility. Informal applications are filed by the adoptive parents or by a designated representative with the local Ministry of Education office in the area where the adoptive parents wish to adopt.

Adoptive parents must provide personal information to the Ministry and make specific requests about the child they wish to adopt (i.e., age, gender, disabilities, sibling groups).

Rwanda. The massacres that have occurred recently in Rwanda have affected thousands of children who have been left without parents. There have been evacuations of Rwandan children to neighboring countries, deemed essential to save these children's lives. Adoption should not be considered until at least two years have passed, in which all feasible steps to trace parents or other surviving family members have been taken.

Taiwan. Applications for adoption are primarily taken by the Cathwel Service in Taiwan. This agency only accepts a small number of applications. Adoptive parents must be between thirty and forty years of age, unless they can accept a handicapped child.

Ukraine. At this time, only unhealthy children are available for international adoption. The Canadian embassy has been unable to obtain a copy of the decree detailing the diseases/conditions associated with these children. However, many children designated as unhealthy may have only minor, correctable problems.

ADOPTING A CHILD FROM THE UNITED STATES

Approximately 100 American babies are adopted by Canadians each year, according to the Adoption Council of Canada. Adopting from America is like any other international adoption in most ways. In a phone interview, Joanne Conlin, a licensee in Ontario, outlined the steps of the process. Bear in mind that some of these steps may be unique to Ontario, but overall, the process is fairly similar from province to province:[6]

1. An agency in the U.S. is chosen, and the home study package is submitted, with medicals, references, and police clearance.
2. The local Ministry of Community and Social Services issues a letter of recommendation. (Most agencies in the U.S. want to see both of the above.)
3. Adoptive parents fill out a sponsorship application and get approval from the government.
4. A child is selected.
5. Social and medical history of birth parents and child are obtained and given to the Canadian government.

6. The government issues a Letter of No Objection and an approval of the placement of this particular child with this particular family.
7. The Letter of No Objection is given to the Canadian embassy in Buffalo, New York, along with copies of the adoptive parents' passports, the approval for placement, and immigration medical on the child. This medical must be performed by a physician in the U.S. who is approved by the Canadian government to do adoption immigration physicals.
8. An application for permanent residence is filled out.
9. A visa is issued for the child. The usual lapse of time between the child's birth (or selection) and the issuance of the visa is three to four weeks.
10. After the child enters Canada, the adoptive couple is on probation for six months. Reports on the progress of the child are sent to the agency in the U.S.
11. The family goes to court to get an adoption finalization order and a new birth certificate for the child.

ADOPTION IN QUEBEC

The province of Quebec is distinct from the rest of Canada in many matters involving culture and law. Adoption is no exception to this separateness, both at the domestic and international levels. Quebec is a very adoption-minded province with almost 1,000 international adoptions per year amongst a population of just 7 million. Proportionately, many more Quebecois adopt than do U.S. citizens. Each year, there are as many adoptions in Quebec alone as in all the rest of Canada put together.

International adoptions are more popular in Quebec than domestic, for several reasons. Quebecois are not allowed to publish advertisements seeking a birth mother in their own province. They must advertise outside of Quebec, and adoptions from another province are technically considered "international." Also, there are no private agencies in this province, so domestic adoption is a provincial governmental matter. Adopting through the public social services organization, *Association des Centres de Jeuness du Quebec*, tends to be difficult; the wait for a newborn can be as long as eight years. This is a powerful incentive for Quebecois to adopt their children from other countries.

According to Claire-Marie Gagnon, a Quebec adoption specialist and former president of the *Federation des Parents Adoptants du Quebec*, those who do decide to adopt within the province have three classes of adoptions from which to choose: open, closed, and *Banque Mixte*. Open and closed adoptions function similarly in Quebec to how they would in the United States. *Banque Mixte*, the third route, is a somewhat risky method of adopting a child, in that 20 percent of placements are never finalized. In this procedure, a child who *may* become available for adoption through parental abuse or neglect is placed by the department of social services in a home with parents who wish to adopt her. In 80 percent of cases, parental rights are terminated and the adoption goes forward. However, in some instances, reunification takes place between the child and her birth parents. This sometimes happens after the child has been in the hopeful adoptive parents' home for years. The tension and uncertainty involved in a *Banque Mixte* adoption make it a potentially difficult experience, both for the adoptive parents and the child.[7]

International adoption in Quebec is a function of the province, as is domestic, but is perceived by many as being less risky. The Quebecois ministry that has overseen foreign adoptions since 1982 is called the *Secretariat de l'Adoption Internationale*. Any organization that handles international adoptions must be officially recognized by the *Secretariat*. There are sixteen such organizations, called *organismes*. While the *organismes* function somewhat like private agencies, they are, in fact, licensed, nonprofit organizations recognized by the government.

The sixteen *organismes* presently have working relationships with twenty-three countries. These are: Bolivia, Brazil, Bulgaria, Chili, Cambodia, China, Colombia, South Korea, Soviet Georgia, Haiti, Honduras, India, Mexico, Nicaragua, the Philippines, Romania, Russia, Taiwan, Thailand, Vietnam, Guatemala, Belarus, and the Isle Dominique (south of the Dominican Republic). It is noteworthy that several of these countries are among those with which the rest of Canada has either a tenuous adoption relationship or no relationship at all. China is the most frequently adopted-from country, with 600 children placed per year, followed by Haiti, Romania, Russia, and Vietnam.

Resources:

General

Adoption Council of Canada
P.O. Box 8442
Station T
Ottawa, Ontario
K1G 3H8
Attention: Judy Grove
(613) 542-3678

Open Door Society of Canada
(613) 827-3532

Parent Finders
(613) 730-8305

Alberta
Adoptee and Birth Parent
  Reunification
Colleen Elizabeth Clark, MSW, RSW
Alberta Adoption Council
8116 187th St.
Edmonton, Alberta T5T 1K3
(403) 245-5005

Ms. Clark is also the director of
  Imagine
705 1520 4th WW
Calgary, Alberta T2S 0B5
Imagine provides reunification counseling for adoptees and birth parents seeking to find each other.

British Columbia
Adoptive Parents Association of BC
Suite 205
15463 104th Ave.
Surrie, BC V3R 1N9
Attention: Helen Mark
(604) 588-7300
(604) 588-6111

Manitoba
Web site for adoption in Manitoba:
www.concentric.net/~Klinde/

New Brunswick
New Brunswick Dept. of Health and
  Community Services
P.O. Box 5100
Fredericton NB E3B 5G8
(506) 453-2949
Good Web site:
www.toddlersonline.com/old/nb/
index.html

Newfoundland/Labrador
Post Adoption Services
Dept. Social Services
Box 8700 Confederate Building
St. Johns, Newfoundland A1B 4J6
(709) 729-2662

Northwest Territories
Program Officer
Family and Children's Services
Department of Social Services
Box 1320
Government of Northwest Territories
Yellowknife NWT X1A 2L9
(403) 873-7943

Nova Scotia
Nova Scotia Dept. of Community
  Services
P.O. Box 696
Halifax, Nova Scotia B3J 2T7
(902) 424-2755

Ontario
Adoption Council of Ontario
(416) 482-0021
(416) 484-7454 (fax)
Provides workshops for adoptive
  parents

Vanier Institute of the Family
120 Holland Ave., Suite 300
Ottawa, Ontario K1Y 0X6
(613) 722-4007 (fax)
This group publishes a French/English
  newsletter covering many family
  issues, including adoption.

Prince Edward Island
Provincial Adoption Services
Department of Health and Social
  Services
Box 2000
Charlottetown, PEI C1A 7N8
(902) 368-4932

Quebec
Association of Parents (Quebec)
(514) 271-8297
May reach member who speaks only
  French, but other members also
  speak English.

Centre de Protection de l'Enfance et
  de la Jeunesse
Service de l'Adoption
10,001 boul. Maisonneuve est.
  6E etage
Montreal, PQ
H2l 4R5
(514) 896-3200

Claire-Marie Gagnon
4264 Ferncrest Rue
Pierrefonds, Quebec
H9H 2A1
(514) 696-0508

Quebec: International Adoptions
Secretariat de l'Adoption
3700, rue Berre
Montreal, Quebec H2L 4G9
(514) 873-1709 (fax)

Saskatchewan
Provincial Adoption Registry
Ministry of Social Services
207-2240 Albert St.
Regina, SASK S4P 3V7
(306) 787-3655

Yukon Territory
Department of Health and Social
  Services
Government of Yukon
Box 2703 (H-10)
Whitehorse, YT Y1A 2C6
(403) 667-3002

Chapter Fourteen

Adopting a Toddler

WHY TODDLERS ARE AVAILABLE

It is well documented that babies and toddlers who are in institutions or who go from one foster home to another before being adopted do not fare as well as children who are placed into adoptive homes at birth. Yet, in spite of this most children are not placed as infants but as toddlers. Essentially, the only way to adopt a newborn infant is through a domestic adoption conducted by a private agency or attorney. If you adopt a child through social services or internationally, it is nearly impossible to adopt a newborn baby. Infants placed into the care of social services usually go to a foster home first before an adoption plan is made, and usually these babies have been drug-exposed. In 1997, 42 percent of children placed for adoption through public agencies were between one and five years old and only 1 percent were under one year of age.[1]

Primarily toddlers are available through international adoption because laws in many countries require the children to be on registries for a certain period of time before they can leave the country. And even if you are assigned a very young child, bureaucracy can delay the placement, and the very young baby that you saw on a video is ten months old when you receive him.

There are the obvious challenges when adopting an older child. Usually the child is placed after difficult life circumstances at best and after being abused or neglected at worst. Even if the child grew up in an orphanage and received adequate care and food, the child may very likely suffer emotionally from growing up in an institution. A child's physical and psychological development has much to do with how well the infant had his needs met in the first year of life. It is believed that adopting a child over two years old greatly increases the likelihood that the child will have serious emotional problems. But what about the child who is adopted under thirty-six months old, but not as a newborn baby? What issues can the adoptive parents expect to face? This is the question that everyone who is adopting internationally needs to ask. For this reason we give every client a copy of the book, *Toddler Adoption: The Weaver's Craft.* This book is realistic yet optimistic.

So many clients enter into the adoption of an older baby—even though they are often referred to as infants—thinking that as parents all they have missed out on are the first few months of life. However, not only have the parents missed out, but the child probably has also missed out on some very important needs being met during this critical stage of life. Some experts believe that a child learns 50 percent of everything he knows in the first year of life and 75 percent by the end of his second year. This learning includes how he relates to the world and to people, and his ability to control his world. How the child's mother or other primary caretaker meets the child's needs through touch, eye contact, smiles, sound, and food can affect a child's overall attitudes. If his needs were not met, he may feel anger, hopelessness, and distrust because the world is not a safe place.

Also, if a child's needs are not met, she can develop insecure attachments, which makes it difficult for her to attach to you. Those who are adopting even very young babies or toddlers will want to know whether or not a child can attach.

Signs of Attachment Difficulties (Birth–1 year)
- Does not respond with recognition to face of primary caretaker in first six months.
- Hardly coos or babbles or cries
- Delayed creeping, crawling, sitting
- Does not like to be cuddled and will become rigid when held
- Excessive fussiness and irritability
- Passive or withdrawn
- Poor muscle tone—limp

Signs of Attachment Difficulties (Ages 1–5)
- Excessively clingy and whiny
- Persistent, frequent tantrums
- High threshold of pain—does not seem to notice if too cold or too warm; does not feel injury on body
- Unable to occupy self in a positive way without involving others
- Resistant to being held
- Demands affection in a controlling way
- Intolerant of separation from primary caretakers except on the child's terms.
- Indiscriminate display of affection, sometimes to strangers.

- Problems of speech development, problems of motor coordination—considered accident-prone.
- Hyperactivity
- Feeding problems
- By five, may be manipulative, devious, destructive, hurtful to pets, lie frequently.

Of course, some children will display some of these signs and not necessarily have an attachment problem. Also, attachment problems can be on a continuum, so it does not mean that a child will have all of the signs. However, if the child you adopt does not want to be held and snuggled softly but is whiny and clingy and will not let you out of her sight and seems very demanding, this can be indicative of an attachment problem. Also, it is the degree of the problem that may indicate an attachment problem. All two-year-olds can be whiny and clingy, have temper tantrums, be hyperactive, and be picky eaters. The problem is not when the child has these characteristics some of the time. It is when these characteristics tend to dominate the child's personality that there is a problem.

Not only are toddlers who have been in institutions more at risk for emotional problems, but because of the lack of stimulation in an orphanage setting, even young babies in orphanages are not as developmentally advanced as other infants, and usually they are sicklier. An American family who lives in Romania adopted two unrelated babies who were three months old at placement. Now the babies are about six months old, and the parents recently looked at the videos taken of their babies in the orphanage, one week before the children's placement. They said the babies looked very sickly in the video. The parents had forgotten how different their children were just a few months go. Now these babies are alert, healthy, and chubby.

TODDLERS THROUGH PRIVATE ADOPTION

When toddlers are adopted through private channels, usually a birth mother, or more often a grandparent, contacts an attorney or private agency and states that she has a child that needs to be adopted. Grandparents who may be aging sometimes realize that a child needs more attention, and they just do not have the health and energy to raise a toddler to adulthood.

If the child was well cared for by the grandparents, the adjustment goes fairly smoothly. It is best if the child can make the transition gradually from the grandparent to the adoptive family. Or the adoptive family, if appropriate, should allow the grandparents to be in the child's life and be what they were meant to be—grandparents, not caretakers.

Even though the child may not have been abused or neglected, the adjustment to a toddler coming from another home can sometimes be difficult. You do not have the opportunity to "grow" into the job. Toddlers are full of energy and take much time, and sometimes too few naps. As an attorney, the only situation in which I've had clients change their minds was when fourteen-month-old twins were placed directly from a birth mother to a couple who had no other children. The adoptive mother called a few days after the children were with her and said that caring for the children was beyond her ability. Multiple toddlers who are running in two different directions can be overwhelming to someone who has never parented before.

Another family adopted their third child when he was sixteen months old, while the two older children were adopted at birth. At the time the third child was placed with the family, the second child was also about sixteen months old. The mom said she looks back and wonders how she did it. She said that she was never educated about the reality of adopting a child whose birth mother most likely had given the child inconsistent attention at best. When the 16-month-old arrived in the family, the natural inclination was to view the two toddlers as being like twins. But the reality is that they were very different emotionally and developmentally, and these differences went beyond their being two different children. The differences were clearly a result of being in two contrasting environments for the first several months of their lives.

Now the son is doing well and is very sweet. He has attention deficit disorder, which is well controlled with medication. His parents set clear guidelines for him and consistent discipline, and although he sometimes has difficulty following through on directions, he is a happy and delightful child. And most likely, he is very different from the child he would have been if his environment had stayed the same.

PREPARING FOR A TODDLER

Adoptive parents who choose to adopt through the social services system or internationally must accept the fact that they cannot receive a newborn. Accepting does not mean resigning yourself to adopting a toddler, nor does it mean entering into the situation and thinking, "I've only lost a few months with her." You have lost something and so has she. She may have lost being held, being fed on time, and being sung to. You have also lost the opportunity to meet your child's needs during those first few months. Before you adopt a toddler you may find that you need to grieve not having an infant from birth. And once you get your child and are thoroughly delighted with her, you may need to grieve that you were not there to care and nurture her during those first months of life.

Although most families, if given the choice, want to adopt a newborn infant, some families deliberately choose to adopt a toddler because the child will fit into their lifestyle more easily. These families may find that the downside of adopting a child who has been in an institution far outweighs the inconveniences of caring for an infant.

Dr. Mary Hopkins-Best, an educational specialist and the author of *Toddler Adoption*, states that those who deliberately choose to adopt a toddler, after carefully considering such factors as their own ages and the availability of more toddlers than infants, have the most successful experience. These are the people who understand both the positives and negatives of adopting a toddler and are well prepared. The good news is that adopting a toddler is a very viable option because so many are available, and if you are well prepared and realistic, then the transitioning of your child into your home will go much more smoothly.

Being well prepared means knowing what to expect when adopting a toddler who has been in less than an ideal setting. You absolutely cannot compare an eighteen-month-old who has recently arrived in your home with your friend's toddler. For those who already have had birth children, the comparison can be quite pronounced. Your expectations must be realistic. One mother, who had three birth children and then adopted two-year-old twins from an orphanage, said one of the children had difficulty attaching, was not affectionate, and showed little or no preference for her parents. The child saw tenderness and kindness as a weakness. The child also did not want her sister to be content and would try to antagonize her.

Because this mother thought that she and her daughters were going to experience the usual day-to-day toddler fun, the mom had to go through a grieving period when she realized that her toddlers could not be as her three biological children were as toddlers. She had expected her newly adopted children to integrate into the family nearly immediately, but once she realized that it would take time, she accepted the fact there would be a transition period. Now at nearly four years old, the twins are very well integrated into the family and family life with them is enjoyable and pleasant.

Fortunately for this mother, she had been a special-education teacher, and she quickly realized that the usual way of parenting had to be altered. She knew what normal development was as an educator and as a parent. She also knew what was out of the normal developmental range.

Like this mother, you will want to be able to distinguish normal behavior from that which is not typical. For example, if your child has a temper tantrum you will want to know if this "normal." A thirty-month-old kicking and screaming for two minutes is normal; doing this for four hours is not.

Hopkins-Best encourages parents also to be familiar with developmental milestones. For example, the age at which children begin to speak and walk falls within predicable ranges. If your child's development falls far outside these ranges, this can indicate serious physical, cognitive, or emotional problems. [2]

It's not that children have to be scarred for the rest of their lives because they lived in orphanages or had multiple moves early on, or their birth mothers were neglectful. It's just that these children may need extra time and understanding. Also, parents need to be understanding of themselves, and to understand that it would be abnormal for a child coming from a very different environment to suddenly fit into everyday life with a family. Best-Hopkins addresses how if the child is to develop a healthy autonomy, he must first attach to his primary caretaker.

On the other hand, there can be problems if the child is beyond other children his age raised here in the United States. For example, a child reared in an orphanage may know how to dress himself and make his bed at two years old. Or a fourteen-month-old may already be potty-trained. Actually the orphanage staff is trained—to sit the children on little potties at prescribed times until each child goes to the bathroom.

If your child is fourteen months old and is "potty-trained," it probably is best to allow the child to start using diapers again. The same goes for using a bottle. Allow the child to be a baby again, since his babyhood was probably cut short. He needs to experience being held and fed by you. Your pediatrician may not see the importance of this need. In fact, clients have been told by pediatricians that their babies needed to be off bottles as soon as possible. Why, as long as a child does not go to bed with a bottle? These pediatricians did not take into consideration that these children just went from being in a foster home or orphanage in another country, made a trans-Atlantic flight, and are now adjusting to new environments. Why must these babies give up their security?

You will, of course, want to hold and rock your toddler. But some toddlers may be seemingly self-sufficient and not want to be cuddled and held, although this is not typical—most really enjoy being held. If this is an issue, then you will want to read Dr. Martha Welch's book *Holding Time*; this is an excellent guide to getting a child to be held, even though the child may initially resist. Dr. Welch's method encourages the parent to hold the child, even if he strongly resists until he finally relaxes and begins to accept and eventually enjoy being held.

Because living in an institution is not the best environment for a child and can cause emotional and developmental problems, some countries place the child in a foster home. Usually in this situation the child is designated to be adopted, and the child stays in just one home, sometimes straight from the hospital. If the child cannot come home with you immediately after birth, then being in a loving foster home is the next best place for him to be placed at birth. Yet, some adoptive parents actually fear that their baby will bond too much with their foster parents. When they go to receive their child, the parents are sometimes dismayed that the child cries for the foster parents and is not initially smitten with his new adoptive parents. Actually, this is how you want your toddler to respond. If he was receiving love and nurturing from his foster family, and you are strangers, for him to want his foster parents is very normal and healthy. Because he has bonded with one set of parents, he will more easily bond with you. On the other hand, if the child has been in multiple homes he may have difficulty attaching to you because, like his other placements, he thinks you may be temporary.

If the child was in an orphanage, he most likely will be receptive to you. After all, you are probably giving him more and tastier food than he is used to and you are warm and snugly. In Ukraine, clients do not know who their child is until they arrive at the orphanage, where they are permitted to select a child. Once a child is presented to them, and they agree to that child, the child usually warms up to them in a matter of hours. Previously no one person has showered the child with so much individual attention, and the child is usually very pleased to have someone doting on him. As the parents visit the child each day until the court hearing, the child becomes more attached to them, and then may start to fuss if other children from the orphanage are vying for the adoptive parents' attention. The child's response is appropriate given the circumstances from which he came; however, the appropriate response for a child who is attached to his caregivers is to want them over his new adoptive parents. A child most likely will not be well attached to anyone at an orphanage, but he should be attached to his foster parents.

There are challenges in adopting a toddler because his past, even if he cannot remember it, may have been painful. He has first lost his caretakers, and he must make an adjustment to living with you in your home. This does not mean that the child is necessarily scarred for life. But the parents need to be aware of what the child lost during the first months of life, how the baby or toddler may be different from a birth child or a child adopted as newborn, and what steps can be taken so that the child can reach his full emotional and developmental potential.

If your child has come from an orphanage setting, I highly recommend that one parent care for the child for as long as possible. If one parent cannot stay home, make arrangements for one person to care for the child. It does not make sense to place a child who has been in an institution back into a group setting. Being with other children can be delightful for short periods of time. One mother said her son enjoyed being in a nursery school one or two mornings a week. Another mother said that her twins adjusted to the nursery at church very well. However, these are all children whose mothers stay home nearly full-time with them.

LANGUAGE DEVELOPMENT

There can be a delay in the speech development of a toddler because of the environmental influences before he was placed for adoption. If a child came from an orphanage or was in a neglectful home, when he first made sounds at a few months old, chances are that these sounds were not repeated back to him. Also, no one may have spent time talking with him one-on-one. Reading a book and asking a child to point to the man, the ball, and so forth in the pictures is usually not done either. Even a baby who is in a good orphanage or a foster home in another country will most likely not be as stimulated through books, educational toys, and conversation as your child would be in your home.

In addition to your child's language development being delayed, when your child is with you, he will be learning a whole new language. Knowing some simple phrases in your child's native tongue is very helpful, especially those that revolve around food and using the potty. However, children who come to the United States often do not want you to speak in their native tongue. And although they may not be able to speak to you in English (expressive speech), most likely your child will understand you (receptive speech). Also, children love to mimic and may enjoy your pointing to objects, saying the word in English and then repeating what you have said.

Once your child is home, you will want quality one-on-one time with him. Talk slowly and tenderly to your child. Reading simple picture books can also help a child master new language skills. The repeating of the phrases each time you look at the book reinforces the words and allows the child to develop his expressive speech skills.

If a child is having difficulty learning English and appears to be delayed in his speech development, you may want to consider the program Fast ForWord. The program is pricey and a professional administers the program, but it is reported to be very effective. (See resources at the end of this chapter.)

OLDER SIBLINGS AND TODDLERS

Hopkins-Best discusses in *Toddler Adoption* the effect of older siblings on adopted toddlers. As may be expected, the more input that the older sibling has into the adoption, the more comfortable the older child will be with the new arrival. Hopkins-Best further states that children over six years old adjust better than younger siblings. If at all possible, I encourage clients to take their children with them to another country when adopting a child. The logistics and finances do not always make this possible, so if you cannot take your other children, try to make them as much of the process as possible.

PETS AND TODDLERS

Toddlers coming from another country may never have been exposed to cats, dogs, and other animals. In Eastern European countries dogs run wild, so it may be difficult to assess whether your child's encounter with a dog was positive or negative. In one orphanage the dogs that stayed around seemed gentle. The children did not seem to especially like them but nor did they seem afraid of them.

If you have a dog, especially a big one, this animal is probably the size of your child, if not bigger. Unlike an infant who grows up with the animal, the toddler may be terrified of the creature. If the animal is not used to small children, especially a child who may touch its eyes or pull its tail, the pet may, of course, bite the child. For the safety of your child—and your pet—the two may have to be separated unless they are very closely supervised.

If you have more than one animal inside your home, this may be too much for your child. Just as too many people around can feel overwhelming to a toddler who has just entered the family, so can a few pets—especially pets that meet the child at eye level.

Few adoptive parents give their pets away when a child arrives, but a compromise should be taken. If you have animals, try to find one place where they go that the child cannot get to them and the animal cannot get to the child. The child should not feel that an animal is going to come into her space. A child may never have had anything of her own while in foster care or an orphanage, and then to have the dog take her ball or small doll can feel like a great invasion.

ADOPTING MORE THAN ONE TODDLER

What about more than one toddler at a time? Some countries and agencies have a policy that siblings must be adopted together. If you are considering siblings, carefully consider your decision. You must want to adopt more than one child. Making the decision to adopt siblings should *not* be based on your wanting a young child, but being willing to accept his three-year-old sister because they are a package. Each child should be wanted. If the sibling group is made up of three or more children, plan carefully. Adopting more than two children at one time is very difficult unless you have many resources. One family who adopted three siblings said it took them six to nine months to adjust. Although the family is doing very well, caring for three toddlers is an exhausting task.

Many of my clients adopt two unrelated toddlers at the same time. Some believe that it is better to have each child enter the home at separate times, and, in fact, some agencies do not permit families to adopt two unrelated children at a time. However, adopting twice can mean double the expenses and another trip to the country. So because of financial constraints, some families realize that what is best for them is to adopt another child at the same time. Also, some families say that two children entering the home together help in the transition. Just because children are siblings does not mean that they know each other well. Both here in the United States and in other countries, siblings are not necessarily in the same home or orphanage group. A pair of twin toddlers that I know of were in two different orphanage groups and did not know each other until they were with their adoptive families. Of course, they should have been placed together, but their placement was essentially the same as two unrelated toddlers being placed in the same home.

Resources

Speech Development Program
Fast ForWord
Scientific Learning Corporation
1995 University Ave.
Suite 400
Berkeley, CA 94704-1074
(510) 665-9700
(888) 665-9707
(510) 665-1717 (fax)
www.scientificlearning.com

Special Needs
National Resource Center for Special Needs Adoption
Technical assistance and consultation are provided to public and private agency administrators and practitioners regarding policy, practice, and programming in adoption, permanency planning, and cultural competence.
sfs@Spaulding.org
www.spaulding.org/adoption/NRC-adoption.html

National Clearinghouse on Child Abuse and Neglect Information
The National Clearinghouse on Child Abuse and Neglect Information, supported by the Children's Bureau, is a national resource for professionals seeking information on the prevention, identification, and treatment of child abuse and neglect. Their Web site offers information regarding all aspects of child maltreatment, including information, statistics, state statutes, access to databases, and announcements of products and initiatives.
www.calib.com/nccanch

Research and Training Center on Family Support and Children's Mental Health

The Research and Training Center is a service of the National Institute on Disability and Rehabilitation Research (NIDRR), Substance Abuse, and Mental Health Services Administration. The center's activities focus on improving services to families whose children have mental, emotional, or behavioral disorders through a set of related research and training programs. **www.rtc.pdx.edu**

National Child Welfare Resource Center on Organizational Improvement

The National Child Welfare Resource Center strengthens and supports organizations committed to the welfare of children, youth, and families through research, training, technical assistance, and evaluation. Their work improves management and operations, bolsters organizational capacity, and promotes service integration, resulting in improved outcomes for children and families.

www.muskie.usm.maine.edu/helpkids

North American Council of Adoptable Children—National Adoption Assistance Training, Resource, and Information Network (NAATRIN)

NAATRIN offers support and information without charge to adoptive and foster parents, adoption professionals, and other child advocates who have questions about Title IV-E Adoption Assistance. NAATRIN maintains a national database of pertinent state and federal laws and policies, and provides state profile. Typical questions are about eligibility requirements, benefits, how to claim adoption subsidy on tax forms, post-finalization, voluntary relinquishment, Medicaid, and SSI. In addition, NAATRIN staff provides training for adoption workers, parents, and other professionals across the country.

The National Resource Center on Child Sexual Abuse

The National Resource Center on Child Sexual Abuse provides information, resources, and technical assistance to organizations and professionals on child sexual abuse. It publishes the magazine *Round Table*. It also maintains lists of treatment programs for victims in various parts of the country. The center is at 106 Lincoln St., Huntsville, AL 35801, or call (205) 533-KIDS (533-5437).

National Resource Center for Special Needs Adoption

The National Resource Center for Special Needs Adoption is dedicated to improving the effectiveness and quality of adoption and postadoption services for children with special needs nationwide. It does this by providing organizations, states, and professionals with consultation, technical assistance, training, and a variety of written and videotaped materials.

National Resource Center on Legal and Court Issues

The ABA Center on Children and the Law's mission is to improve children's lives through advances in law, justice, knowledge, practice, and public policy. The Center's Web site offers information on the role of state and federal laws and statutes in the lives and welfare of children. This site offers comprehensive information regarding the Adoption and Safe Families Act of 1997.

The National Clearinghouse on Child Abuse and Neglect

The National Clearninghouse on Child Abuse and Neglect collects and disseminates information on child sexual abuse. It will do research upon request on a particular subject at a very low cost. It also has general publications that you can request. Write to the Clearinghouse at P.O. Box 1182, Washington, DC 20013-1182, or call (800) 394-3366.

The C. Henry Kempe National Center for the Prevention and Treatment of Child Abuse and Neglect

The C. Henry Kempe National Center for the Prevention and Treatment of Child Abuse and Neglect provides training, consultation, research and program development on all forms of abuse and neglect. Write to the Center at 1205 Oneida St., Denver, CO 80220, or call (303) 321-3963.

Chapter Fifteen

Special Needs Adoption

Special needs is a general term for children whose characteristics can make them more difficult to place for adoption. Sometimes they are also called "waiting children." This grouping encompasses older children, children of certain ethnic backgrounds, sibling groups, and children who have a disability, medical condition, or psychological problem that either makes them less likely to be adopted or means that their adoptive parents must be equipped to handle the challenge of caring for them. Some special needs children can be adopted through private agencies or independently, and these children as a rule have physical handicaps or are mentally retarded. They are available because their birth mothers make the decision to place them. However, most children with special needs are adopted through state-run public agencies, and most of these children are placed because of parental abuse or neglect.

According to the Department of Health and Human Services, two out of three waiting children have medical, developmental, behavioral, or psychological special needs, and most have more than one condition. About 41 percent of the children are part of a sibling group, making them particularly hard to place.[1]

Often children with special needs also have a complex relationship with their birth parents because of a history of parental abuse or neglect. Usually, the birth parents' rights have been terminated only after considerable disruption and pain in the children's lives. Although the biological parents may be out of the children's lives, their influence on the children can still be very intense. Children with special needs are often older and often remember living with their biological parents as well as with previous foster parents, and, of course, they remember being placed for adoption. Often, indeed, what makes a special needs child "special" is the fact that he has suffered so much.

About one-third of the children who are in the foster-care system and then become eligible for adoption are victims of overt abuse. All neglected and abused children are also emotionally abused. Virtually all children who are removed from their homes must be placed in foster care before their biological parents' rights are terminated. The trauma of being abused and then going to one or more foster homes can have a profound emotional impact on the child. In addition, some children, especially those placed in group homes, become the victims of sexual abuse. The perpetrators are usually older children who themselves were victims of sexual abuse. The child who has gone through one caretaker after another may have deep-seated psychological problems, often expressed in attention deficit disorder, hyperactivity, daytime wetting and soiling, sexual acting out, detachment, and a host of other behavior problems.

Those considering adopting neglected or abused children must go through extensive pre-parenting classes and may also be required to get counseling so that issues they have within their own family systems can be clarified and dealt with before they adopt. Couples who have not had to face family-of-origin issues because they have experienced no real crises may suddenly have to face these issues once a difficult child enters their lives. Adding a child to a family always changes its dynamics; adding a child with psychological scars can change the dynamics in the family dramatically. Being prepared to parent an emotionally abused child and having realistic expectations of yourself and the child are musts. Unlike medical conditions, which tend to fit more or less into textbook models, the emotional problems that these children have can be varied, and the outcome is far less predictable.

TYPES OF SPECIAL NEEDS
Physical and Medical Problems

Physical disabilities can include in utero exposure to drugs and alcohol, sensory disabilities such as blindness and deafness, and diseases such as epilepsy. Although the outcome for certain conditions, especially those related to exposure to drugs and alcohol, is uncertain, most conditions have a predictable course. You may believe you have the background and skills to help a child with a particular kind of physical problem. Of course, if you are considering an older child with a medical condition, you must also recognize that any child who is older will most likely also have some emotional problems. But studies show that those who do adopt such children have a high degree of satisfaction. The placements with the best outcomes are ones in which adoptive mothers are not depressed, have few reservations, are married, have had experience with disabling conditions, and have strong religious beliefs.[2]

Learning Disabilities

There is a much higher than average incidence of attention deficit disorder (ADD), attention deficit hyperactivity disorder (ADHD), and other learning disabilities among adopted children, even among those adopted at birth. Poor parenting, abuse, and neglect can interfere with the child's ability to attach and to learn. Prenatal exposure to drugs and alcohol also increases the likelihood of a child's developing a learning disability.

Emotional and Behavioral Problems

Many children who are removed from their parents as result of abuse or neglect will display a variety of emotional and behavioral problems as a direct result of their traumatic backgrounds. These problems can be further exacerbated by the loss of their biological parents and possibly their foster parents. This means that nearly all adopted children, except those adopted at birth and not exposed to drugs or alcohol, are at risk for emotional problems, although many will not have such problems. Unlike physical conditions, emotional problems are not easily diagnosed and can have uncertain behavioral outcomes. Typical emotional problems for these children include fear, anger, low self-esteem, anxiety, depression, lack of trust, and developmental regression. The problems a child has may be known at the time you plan to adopt her and may subside as a result of her being in your loving and nurturing home environment. On the other hand, a younger preschool child may not have any notable emotional or behavioral problems, but she may develop problems later on.[3]

Many of the behavioral problems children have often resolve themselves after the child feels secure within the adoptive home. Helping a child overcome her emotional problems and the behaviors that accompany them can be very rewarding. It requires a great deal of patience, understanding, and realistic expectations.

Knowing what problems you can and cannot accept is very important. One behavioral problem, even if minor, that one parent can overlook can cause havoc in another family. Also, the child's age can play a role in the parent's attitude. For example, most parents adopting a five year old would accept the fact that she wets the bed; however, some parents cannot cope with bed-wetting in a twelve-year-old. The same is true for lying. A four year old who lies may seem cute; a twelve-year-old with the same behavior is often viewed as cunning and manipulative. As will be discussed later in the chapter, know what you can handle and what you cannot. Also, even though you may be able to accept a wide variety of behavioral problems, this does not mean that you are willing to accept a child with many behavioral problems.

The following description includes the behavioral characteristics often associated with children who have been abused or neglected, or who have moved from one caretaker to another:

- *Delayed development.*
- *Aggression and hyperactivity.*
- *Indiscriminate affection.* These children have not attached to one particular person. Although overly friendly when they are small, as they grow older they may be cold, aloof, demanding, and manipulative.[4]
- *Lack of self-awareness.* The child is not aware of his own needs, including the need to eat or use the bathroom.
- *Control issues.* The child who has had no normal boundaries set for him may try to set his own boundaries.
- *Wetting and soiling clothes.* A child who tries to control his environment may not go to the bathroom and then become constipated or soil or wet his pants during the day.
- *Food hoarding.* A child who has not been able to depend on adults to meet his needs may hide food in his bedroom because he has learned to be self-sufficient.
- *Lying.* The child lies indiscriminately, that is, when the lie is obvious or when telling the truth would not normally lead to punishment.
- *Profound emotional problems, including attachment disorders.*

Attachment Disorders

Nearly everyone who is professionally involved in adoption will be familiar with the term "attachment disorder." Conferences, workshops, and professional meetings have been focusing on this subject for the last few years. If you go to one of these workshops, you may come away wondering, can any adopted child escape an attachment disorder? Certainly yes. However, attachment disorders are a different classification from the usual emotional and behavioral problems a child may have. They are a group of serious, hard-to-treat, and often misdiagnosed conditions. Because they are so difficult to treat, knowing whether a child has an attachment disorder is crucial in making the decision to adopt. And if you do decide to adopt, you need to know how to get help for the child.

Some children who have been grossly neglected or have gone from one caretaker to another without bonding with anyone will probably never bond with anyone without intensive treatment. Such children do not respond to standard therapy because they cannot connect to the therapist. As a general rule, the earlier the abuse and neglect, the more likely the child will have an attachment disorder. This is one of the most difficult emotional disorders to handle, because the child may never respond to your love and affection.

Fortunately, most children who have the risk factors for an attachment disorder—primarily abuse and neglect—will *not* have one. How a child has responded to abuse and neglect is what determines whether she will have an attachment disorder. Children who can learn to gratify themselves when their needs are not met will usually have fewer symptoms, and when placed with proper caretakers, they are more likely to bond with them. The greater the degree of abuse and neglect, by and large, the greater the chance that the child will have an attachment disorder. Yet some children who have more risk factors will have a greater ability to overcome their backgrounds, while other children who were not as severely abused or neglected may display gross behavioral and emotional problems. An issue that is not apparent, for example, is called the "fantasy bond."

> This can occur when children who have no conscious memory of their birth parents continue to have a longing to find their birth parents with the hope, dream, or fantasy that if their birth mother or father knew where they were, they would come for them. Out of this sense of longing, they develop a belief that they must save their love for their "real" momma, the mom who gave birth to them. This tendency of children to withhold their love . . . can increase their chances of continuing to disrupt (fail) in their adoptive or foster placements, exasperating feelings of abandonment and reaffirming their belief that only their birth parents could really love them. Even children who have memories of severe abuse and neglect, when in the care of their birth parents will often, later, deny this experience and fantasize a feeling of close connectedness with their birth parents. . . .They have deeply internalized their experiences of abuse, neglect, and abandonment as being their fault because there was something wrong with them. They fantasize that, if they can go back and act differently, they can then elicit the love from their birth parents that they feel is there for them.[5]

For a diagnosis of attachment and bonding disorders, one or more of the following must have been present:

- *Prenatal exposure to drugs or alcohol.* This causes the most permanent damage.
- *Lack of early bonding with caretaker and lack of love and nurturing.* The child cries for food or for a diaper change. When he is not fed or

changed, he rages. After a cycle of crying and then raging, the child learns self-gratification and to trust only himself.

- *Multiple foster care placements.* When a child has multiple caretakers, he learns not to bond with anyone, knowing that if he does, the pain will be heightened when he leaves that person's home.

- *Other interruptions such as hospitalizations, or going from one relative to another.*

- *Abuse and neglect.* A history of mistreatment, including physical or sexual abuse before adoptive placement, affects the child's level of attachment.[6] The younger the child, the more impact the trauma has on him.

- *Painful medical conditions.* A child who has pain that the parent cannot alleviate may detach.

- *Chaotic family life.* For example, a mother who is on drugs or who suffers from mental illness.

- *Birth mother's emotional state while pregnant.* According to Cathy Helding, coauthor of *Can This Child Be Saved?*, research in prenatal development indicates that bonding takes place before birth; she further states that studies show that errors can occur in the bonding process before and right after birth. Also, a mother who is very stressed while pregnant can actually cause her unborn child to have too many stress hormones; the baby's brain becomes accustomed to this, and when born, the baby is "addicted" to stress. Such an infant can be difficult to comfort and bond with. Helding states this explains why some children adopted immediately after birth can have attachment disorders.

It is important to be aware of the risk factors and symptoms associated with attachment disorder, not only so that a diagnosis can be made but also so that you can decide whether this is the kind of child you want to adopt. If you are adopting a child from another country, you may have a very sketchy background on her, making it difficult to know whether she has been grossly neglected or abused. One way to tell is by looking for the signs associated with an attachment disorder. If she does display the signs, finding resources to help may be very difficult. Also, an internationally adopted child is not eligible for the same subsidies for therapy as a child placed by a state social services agency.

In situations in which parents adopted an international child who has an attachment disorder, most likely they were not given much information during the home study process. Also, the agency placing the child probably minimized any concerns that they may have had and perhaps only provided minimal background information. Also, the doubts that the parents may initially have experienced when they met the child were probably dismissed either by the parents themselves or others involved in the adoption process.

A parent who adopted a child with an attachment disorder said that she knew something was wrong, but she felt that the child would improve once the child was out of the orphanage and settled into home life. Many children's emotional states do improve greatly once they are in a loving home.

Adopting a younger child can minimize the risk of adopting a child with an attachment disorder. Certainly the more time children spend in an orphanage, the more likely they are to have attachment problems. On the other hand, if a child is at least a few months old, then attachment problems that may be caused by prenatal exposure to drugs, alcohol, or other environmental toxins will most likely be apparent.

Because orphanage life can be so detrimental to children, some countries, such as Romania, provide foster care to orphans. Other countries, such as China, have orphanages that are set up more like cottages designed to have more of a family environment. When children are adopted at a young age—usually under twenty-four months, and have been in a good foster home or well-staffed orphanages, then the incidence of attachment disorders decreases.

It is difficult for parents to get a really good sense of a child's emotional well-being when the child is only seen through a video. If you are deciding on adopting a child based on a video, have the child's video and medical records evaluated at a medical center that specializes in assessing international adoptees. Although it is unrealistic to expect these physicians to diagnose an attachment disorder or rule one out, the physician may be able to see signs of problems. If you are considering adopting a child who is older, it may be wise to visit the child before an adoption occurs in the country. The extra money you spend to visit the child is well worth the investment. If the child has an attachment disorder, and this not what your family has the resources or desire to handle, then you can select another child.

Sometimes children who have lived in an orphanage have difficulty adjusting to family life. After all, they probably have no idea what a family is and what it is like to live in one. Of course they like the attention, the food, the warmth, even some of the physical touching—but they may not really be part of the family. In one situation like this, it took a three-year-old child about six months to fully integrate into the family.

Here are some of the symptoms of an attachment disorder:

- *Poor eye contact.* The child may be aloof, make little or no eye contact, and appear to have no conscience. Some people describe such a child's eyes as "hollow." For those who are adopting internationally, this may be the only symptom that can be observed. If the child cannot connect his eyes with yours, he may very well have an attachment disorder.

- *Can be delightful initially.* These children have moved from one household to another and learned to adjust to many different people and situations.
- *Emotional withdrawal.* The child does not respond to affection and will not snuggle with you if you touch her. Or she may display indiscriminate affection with strangers but not be cuddly or affectionate with parents.
- *Overcompetency.* The child may not allow anyone to help him. He may refuse any help with getting dressed or any other activity. This is a very serious problem that is often mistakenly viewed as independence.
- *Aggressive behavior.* A child who is defiant and hyperactive is usually diagnosed with attention deficit disorder. If he improves while taking Ritalin, then the diagnosis is considered to be attention deficit disorder and probably not an attachment disorder.
- *Frequent accidents.*
- *Cruelty to animals, fire-setting, bed-wetting.*
- *Lying.* Crazy lying for no apparent reason; stealing to get caught.
- *Idiosyncratic speech patterns.*
- *Delayed learning;* wanting to act "dumb."
- *Lack of cause-and-effect thinking.*
- *Lack of conscience.*

History of Sexual Abuse

Many children who are removed from their parents have been sexually abused. The factors that led to their removal from their families are the same factors that increase the risk of sexual abuse. For example, lack of parental protection, parental drug use, and parents socializing with other drug users all increase the likelihood of sexual abuse. Also, children who are neglected or abused are often more passive and emotionally vulnerable, making them easier targets for perpetrators.

Adults are not the only perpetrators. Children also abuse other children. This is particularly true in foster or group homes in which younger children are in contact with older children. Some older children, who are usually themselves victims of sexual abuse, abuse younger children. Ironically, a child who has never been sexually abused may be the victim of such abuse once he is removed from his birth family and placed in a foster care setting. The emotional scars from sexual abuse from a child's peers can be just as damaging as those caused by sexual abuse from an adult.

Contrary to popular opinion, sexual abuse is not restricted to males exploiting girls and boys. Children are also abused by women and older girls.

However, when women are the perpetrators, determining sexual abuse is even more difficult to diagnose because of the nature of the abuse and also because boys, especially older boys, may not view the exploitation as offensive.

Overall, diagnosing sexual abuse is difficult because the abuse can be subtle and may never involve actual physical contact with the child. Children can come from homes where there were no emotional boundaries. A mother may share with her son the details of her sexual life. Also, if the child is not the direct victim, but he is aware that his siblings are being abused, he may suffer many of the same effects.

Other examples of covert sexual abuse could be the child who has viewed actual sexual acts or X-rated films and has been the target of inappropriate gestures and comments.

Even if the child was more overtly abused, he may not view it as abuse but as a display of affection and a way of gaining approval. Children often try to normalize such behavior if it is done by a parental figure. If the child does view the abuse as wrong, he may have so much shame that he will not discuss it. Also, children often do not discuss the abuse because their two main fears are that they will not be believed and that nothing will be done. These fears are reinforced if therapy and other interventions do not take place.

Even if no one knows if a child has been sexually abused, the child's behavior may be an indication. Children, even young children, who have been sexually abused are generally more sexually knowledgeable, may act out sexually, and may be sexually provocative around adults as a way of getting attention. Many victims also struggle with such emotional problems as guilt, depression, anger, fear, and inability to trust. Depression in particular appears to be present in nearly all victims.[7]

You may feel that you cannot handle the issues associated with raising a child who has been sexually abused. This is understandable. However, do be aware that *any* child who has been removed from his home may have a history of being sexually abused. Usually the problem behaviors will diminish once the child is in a stable environment in which proper guidelines and trust are established. As with any child who has been abused, the child will require some therapy to deal with her past. Also, adoptive parents who were also the victims of sexual abuse may need to resolve their own issues through therapy before adopting.

The most sensible approach to adopting a child who may sexually act out is to adopt only a very young child or one who is significantly younger than any children already in your family. You certainly would not want an eight year old who may sexually act out if you already have a five year old. This is not to say that every child who has been sexually abused is going to be a perpetrator, but taking such precautions can help the placement of a child in your home go more smoothly.

If you do adopt a child with a history of sexual abuse, remember: A victim may say or do things that are viewed as perverted. Do not regard the child as a deviant but as one whose actions are a result of his background. Helping a child show affection appropriately and express his anger and hurt can assist him or her in healing.

Some experts believe that one in four girls and one in eight boys experience sexual abuse; however, the percentage of sexually abused children in the foster care system is not available. Social workers believe the percentages are much higher for these children.

If a child who has been abused enters your home, and you assume that some type of sexual abuse occurred, certain household habits and routines may need to be changed because what is normal in your household can trigger a sexually-abused child into being angry or withdrawn. For example, one adoptive family said that when their three-year-old adoptive child entered their home, she came as a foster child. At first they were given no information about her background. Then after the child's bath, if the foster father tried to come into her bedroom she would scream and get very upset. So the rule was established that her father would not go into her room without her permission. This gave the child some control, which she had never had. After a few months the child permitted her father to read to her in her bedroom and to tuck into her bed. For many children, the bathroom and the bedroom are two sites where the sexual abuse took place. Therefore, it is best for your sake and the child's that you not be alone with the child and that you allow the child privacy in the bathroom and bedroom. Let the child know that you will not enter these rooms without the child's permission. Of course, you have to be practical about this as well.

No "Secrets." Make it clear that no secret games, particularly with adults, are allowed. Tell the child that if an adult suggests such a game, he or she should tell you immediately.

Being Alone with One Other Person. If your child is behaving seductively, aggressively, or in a sexually acting out manner, these are high risk situations. During those times, it is advisable not to put yourself in the vulnerable position of being accused of abuse. In addition, other children may be in jeopardy of being abused. Therefore, whenever possible during these high risk situations, try not to be alone with your child or allow him/her to be alone with only one other child.

Wrestling and Tickling. As common and normal as these childhood behaviors are, they are often tinged with sexual overtones. They can put the weaker child in an overpowered and uncomfortable or humiliating position. Keep tickling and wrestling to a minimum.

Behaviors and Feelings. Help children differentiate between feelings and behaviors. It is normal to have all kinds of feelings, including sexual feelings. However, everyone does not always act on all the feelings he or she has. Everyone has choices about which feelings he or she acts on, and everyone (except very young children) must take responsibility for his or her own behavior.

The treatment for attachment disorders must usually be intense. Generally the therapy is to help the child rework her negative life experiences and help her reduce anger, resentment, fear, and rage. As she lets go of these negative feelings, the child learns to experience trust and closeness so that she can bond with others. Some children and their adoptive families may be helped through weekly therapy, whereas other children may require an intensive inpatient therapy. Parent participation is crucial to the child's success, so much so that confidentiality between the child and therapist is secondary to having the parents' full understanding and input.[8]

Resources:
For further information about attachment disorders, contact:

Attachment and Bonding Center of Ohio
Dr. Gregory C. Keck, Ph.D.
12608 State Road
Cleveland, OH 44133
(216) 230-1960

Forest Hill
Evergreen, Colorado 80439
(303) 674-6681

The Institute for the Prevention of Child Abuse
www.interlog.com/~ipca/ipca.html
They have a catalog of publications to help adults handle
the needs of abused children.

The National Data Archive on Child Abuse and Neglect
gopher://gopher.ndacan.cornell.edu/
This site mainly contains professional research on child abuse, but
some may be helpful to adoptive parents or foster parents of abused
children.

Sibling Groups

For a sibling group to be considered "special needs," usually there must be three or more children who all need to be placed in the same family. Again, if such children are available, it is usually because they have been removed from their home because of neglect or abuse. These children are also likely to have emotional problems due to their backgrounds.

When abuse or neglect occurs, usually all of the children in the home are removed. These brothers and sisters are often very bonded to each other and may have learned to meet their needs through each other.

Therefore, when adoption is the plan, agencies try to find a family who can adopt all of the children. However, while the children are initially in foster care, they are often separated because it is difficult to find a foster home that can accommodate three or more children. Sometimes one child may become very attached to his foster parents, who may want to adopt him but not his siblings. Such a scenario further complicates the emotional issues these children face as a result of being separated from each other during foster care, being removed from their foster family, and then reunited once again in an adoptive home.

Finding an adoptive home can be difficult for sibling groups if one of the children has a more serious medical condition or behavioral problem. This may mean, for example, that an adoptable four-year-old may wait a long time for a family because she must be placed together with her eight-year-old brother, who has serious emotional problems. However, it can be difficult for social workers to decide when siblings should be separated so that an adoption for at least one of the children is feasible.

The dynamics among the siblings need to be understood before adopting. Often the older child has been the caretaker of the younger children. The older child may have been playing this role for so long that she may find it difficult to relinquish it even after she and her siblings are placed for adoption. If you adopt such children, you will need to help each child learn new family roles. The oldest child will have to learn that her needs and the other children's will be met by you, and that she can be a child again. Although the children must learn new roles, the children's transition to a new home can be eased by the fact that they have a connection with each other.

Initially, the concept of having an instant family of more than one child can seem very attractive. However, be aware that meeting the needs of multiple children requires a great deal of time and commitment. If you already have one or two children, you probably have a more realistic understanding of the responsibility involved in caring for two or more additional children.

In some states, if the number of children in your home is greater than six, then you will need to be licensed as a group home. Once your home is licensed, you will be required to maintain a certain level of fire and safety precautions.

There are funds available for those adopting sibling groups. Generally, these children already qualify for subsidies because they are at risk for emotional problems.

African-American and Racially Mixed Children

Sometimes a child's racial or ethnic background makes it more difficult to find her a home. A child of mixed racial background is usually African-American and Caucasian. Although "Hispanic" is not a race, a child who is both Hispanic and Caucasian may be classified as racially mixed. A child who is two years old, healthy, and seems to be developmentally and emotionally on target may still be considered "special needs" because of her racial background.

Older Children

Defining "older" children is difficult. Some agencies call any child over a year old an "older child." One thing is certain: The older the child, the more emotional problems he is likely to have.

Of the hard-to-place children, 85 percent are over five years old, and 43 percent are over eleven years old. Although most children classified as special needs because of their age are five or older, any child over the age of two who has suffered abuse or neglect, and often younger children too, are going to bear the scars of that trauma in their early lives. If you are considering adopting an older child, you are considering adopting a child who has lost at least one caretaker. The process of going from one caretaker to another can have a great psychological impact on the child. So if you are adopting an older child, you must be prepared to face special emotional problems that may also cause behavioral problems.

In a study of adoptions that were and were not successful, the child's age was the single best predictor of disruption. Older, more troubled children not only entered the foster care system at a later age but remained in foster care longer and waited longer to be freed for adoption and to be placed.

According to statistics, about 42 percent of children placed for adoption through the foster care system were between ages one and five years old, whereas only 28 percent of the children in foster care were in this age category. This represents the largest age category for adoptions. Of course, some the children may have entered a permanent foster home before their first birthday, but the adoptions were not finalized until later. Also, the older children in foster care may be considered adoptable, but getting them adopted is far more difficult.[9]

ADVANTAGES OF SPECIAL NEEDS ADOPTION

As explained, there are often challenges associated with special needs adoption. What are some of the advantages?

1. *Expenses can be minimal.* In many cases, in fact, the child may be eligible for monthly subsidies. Depending on the state you live in, the child's age, and the severity of his problems, you could receive $200 or more per month. These subsidies do not add to your income; they are simply meant to defray the costs of raising a child who requires extra parental care and possibly such specialized services as physical therapy or psychological counseling.

2. *Children are available.* According to the Department of Health and Human Services, in December 1990 there were 69,000 foster children in the United States who needed to have an adoption plan. Today about 30,000 to 50,000 children are legally free to be adopted, and of these, about 15,000 are actively searching for a family. About 50,000 are not legally free for adoption because their parents' rights have not been terminated, but they need a "permanent" home in the meantime.[10]

3. *The wait for a child can be a matter of months.* If you are diligent about getting a home study completed through your social services department, you could have a child in the time it takes to complete a home study and be approved. Sometimes the wait for a child will be directly related to how long it takes for you to complete a series of workshops on adoption, and for the social services department to come to your home to conduct a home study, complete the paperwork, and file all the correct papers.

4. *You can know about the child you are going to adopt.* Unlike most other domestic or international adoptions, you get to meet the child before you adopt him. For some people, the certainty of meeting a child before making the decision to adopt is paramount.

5. *You will have specialized training and workshops as well as pre- and post-adoption support from the agency.* Sometimes the requirements may seem arbitrary or invasive, but most people can benefit from the opportunity to learn more about parenting. Also, once the child is in your home, before and after the adoption is made legal, your agency may provide extensive services to help you meet your child's needs.

6. *You have an opportunity to make a difference in the life of child.* Many people who are able to have biological children also choose to adopt children with special needs because they want to expand their families and make a contribution to the lives of children. Few other achievements can have such an impact on an individual life, or offer you such a reward.

DISADVANTAGES OF SPECIAL NEEDS ADOPTION

What are some of the disadvantages of special needs adoption? For many people, working with the system heads the list. Most children with special needs are adopted through the social services department, and working with a government bureaucracy can be frustrating. The staff may be small and overburdened, and the rules they must follow may seem arbitrary. Having to get supervisor after supervisor to sign off on form after form can slow the process. Take the case of John, who is ten years old. He has been waiting for a home nearly all his life. When he was a toddler, his drug-addicted mother lost her parental rights; his father was unknown. Although John has been legally free for adoption since he was three years old, he has lived in foster and group homes while social workers decide on his best interests and the services that will help him the most. "I'm all wrapped up in programs," this child says. "What I need is a mom."

According to the American Public Welfare Association, the number of children in substitute care is growing thirty-three times faster than America's child population in general. Although the Child Welfare League of America says that more resources are needed, the government is already spending ten billion dollars a year on foster care and adoption services through public agencies. Federal money now accounts for nearly one-third of all foster care funding. According to the ACLU, each child in foster care costs $17,500 per year, including payment made to the foster families. It is clear that the funding system provides incentives to keep adoptable children in state care. It is not clear whether there is sufficient financial incentive to recruit adoptive families.[11] Private adoption agencies are paid to find adoptive families. Public agencies are "paid" for the number of children in the system, not in adoptive families. Caseworkers' hands are often tied, however, because judges are reluctant to terminate parents' rights. More legislation is needed to limit the time allotted to biological parents to get their lives together before their children can return to live with them. Fortunately, special private grants made to state agencies are beginning to speed up the adoption process.

Here are some other disadvantages of special needs adoption:

Special needs children often require special services. This means that you need to live in an area where such services are available. If you live on a large ranch in Wyoming and the closest large city is three hours away, regularly getting your child to a psychologist or an occupational therapist may be very difficult.

Adoptions can disrupt. Those adopting older children with special needs have the highest rate of adoptions not working out. The adoption disruption rate of adolescents can be as high as 25 percent; for older children overall, it is about 10 percent. One study looked at the records of 1,500 children over the age of six. It found that children between the ages of six and eleven years old disrupted at a rate of 10.2 percent during a two-year period, children over eleven at a rate of about 8 percent. The success rate was higher when children were placed with their own siblings. Children who were placed alone but had a sibling living elsewhere disrupted at a rate of 20.6 percent. This could either mean that one or more of the siblings had such profound problems that no family could take on the responsibility of all the children, or that the separation was part of the problem.

Another study found that disruptions were lower in homes where there were biological children already in the home, but still another found that more than 50 percent of the cases of disruption involved serious conflicts between the adopted children and the nonrelated children in the home. A history of previous disruptions is a high indicator for another disruption. The behaviors associated with disruption included cruelty, fighting, and vandalism. Parents who were the most informed about the child, had prepared for the child, and had adoption subsidies were the most likely *not* to disrupt. Psychotherapy also helped families avoid disruption.

A research study lists the following stages of adoption disruption:

1. *Diminishing pleasure.* The joy of taking care of the child becomes outweighed by the burden.
2. *The child is perceived as a major problem.* The parents can't cope with the child. They want change, but the child does not change.
3. *The parents complain to others about the child.* They are urged by friends and family members to vacate the adoption.
4. *The turning point.* A specific event leads the parents to believe they can no longer tolerate the child's behavior. The parents look to life without the child and no longer try to assimilate him into their family.
5. *Deadline.* Either the child is given a "shape-up or ship-out" message, or the parents decide that if the behavior occurs once more, they will vacate the adoption.
6. *Giving up.* The parents give up and return the child to the agency.[12]

The psychological factors can be unpredictable. If the child needs counseling, the costs can be very high. The home study process may also be quite a bit more rigorous. Public agencies and private agencies that place special needs children may be flexible about the size of your home, but they are likely to question you extensively about your attitudes toward marriage, child rearing, adoption, adjustment to stress, and counseling for your children. After all, the caseworker wants to know how you will be able to handle a child with special needs. She may expect you to understand issues related to the separation and loss the child has probably experienced. The home study is not just to see whether your lives are stable but whether you can adjust to having a child who may be very disruptive. If you are choosing to adopt a child with special needs, you are undertaking a responsibility that few social workers would consider. It's risky to take a seven-year-old child and not know how that child is going to be when he hits adolescence. Although the same can be said for nearly every child, the outcome for a child reared in a stable home is much more predicable.

In the book, *Can This Child Be Saved?* Foster Cline honestly addresses how foster and adoptive parents' lives are damaged because of the children that they have in their homes. Often their lives are filled with frustration because teachers, social workers, and even therapists think that the parents are doing something wrong, when in reality the child is extremely manipulative and is not willing to be part of a family. The parents who did something wrong are usually out of the child's life. The foster or adoptive parents are the ones who have to cope with what is happening in the child's life now, and they also receive the blame when things do not go well.

GETTING STARTED

If you are ready to go ahead with a special needs adoption, the first thing to do is join an adoption support group in which a good number of members have adopted children with special needs. Those who have adopted through the Department of Social Services or through a public agency will know what works with the system and what does not. Next, call your local public adoption agency. Find out whether they have upcoming workshops for those who are interested in adopting a child with special needs. These multi-session workshops usually cover the legal issues, the kinds of children available and their special needs, and the relationships these children have with their birth families and foster care parents. Your attitudes about adoption, the kind of child you can accept, emotional problems, and similar issues will also be addressed. Many people "screen" themselves out of the process after going to these workshops.

The next step is to check out local special services in your area. If you want to adopt a certain kind of special needs child, find out what services you'll have access to, what expenses are involved, and whether those expenses are covered by Medicaid. Remember, be realistic about what kinds of children are available and about how much impact you can have on a given child. If you want an essentially healthy but older child, for example, you must recognize that any child who has been removed from his home because of abuse or neglect is likely to have some emotional or developmental or learning problems. If you have successfully raised children through the teenage years, you may feel that you would like an older child. However, the way you measured success in raising your children who came to you at birth or at a very young age will probably not be the standard for success in raising a child from a troubled background. You need to explore how you feel about dealing with a child's emotional problems, the behavior that may accompany the problems, and going with your child to a counselor.

Sit down with your spouse and discuss what you can and cannot accept. Your spouse may be unwilling to care for a child who is mentally retarded but feel very different about adopting a bright child with fairly serious learning disabilities—in other words, one whose problems appear more "correctable." Again, be sure that your expectations are realistic.

Beware of social workers pushing you to accept more than you can handle. Sometimes well-meaning social workers who want children to be placed in a good home will recruit families by showing one set of children on television programs or in special "waiting children" photo-listing books; however, these children may not be available. When the family calls to inquire, they are told they cannot adopt the child they had in mind and are encouraged to adopt one of the other children available instead, often one who is older or part of a sibling group. Or a family who plans to adopt a seven-year-old child may be told there are children available in this age bracket. After going through classes and a home study, the family is then encouraged to adopt a twelve-year-old or a sibling group. Social workers are "stretching" the family expectations, a practice Christine Adamec calls unfair.[13] Most caseworkers who handle adoptions, however, do not take this approach. They want families to be fully informed not only about the child's positive and negative attributes but what may be anticipated down the road. Having realistic expectations is the best insurance against an adoption disruption.

Be especially careful about broadening your level of acceptance because you find a child so attractive. Sometimes a prospective adoptive family will see a child or a picture of the child and fall in love with his cute face and charming personality. At this time the couple may not "hear" what the caseworker is telling them about the emotional, physical, and/or behavioral problems the child has or is at a high risk of having. They see only the adorable four-year-old who, with enough love, will overcome all his problems. One caseworker says that when families change their minds and broaden their level of acceptance, they usually have problems with their adopted child in the specific area they stated on their initial application they would not be able to accept.

Although the overall tone of special needs adoption seems to focus more on what is wrong with the child than what is right, this is done to increase realistic expectations. However, once parents adopt these children, like all parents they also focus in on the children's positive traits and accomplishments. These parents, like most adoptive and biological parents, find the experience rewarding and have felt the same pride in their children.

The Child's Background

The previous list of traits that describes the various types of special needs children is not meant to dissuade you from considering such a child. Rather, it is provided so that you can have a fuller understanding of the issues involved and what you may have to deal with. That is why it is very important to get a child's full social, medical, and psychological history. Of course, it is not always possible to know everything. Ask the caseworker what her "sense" is if the record is not complete. In particular, be sure to ask the following if you feel that the whole background is not presented to you:

- What kind of foster homes was the child in?
- What kinds of emotional, social, or behavioral problems can you expect, based on the child's history?
- What kind of counseling and other medical or special services will the child require?
- Is the agency willing to provide full disclosure of all records prior to adoption finalization?
- What were the circumstances that placed this child in foster care and for adoption?
- What is the history of this child?
- What kind of abuse (physical, emotional, and/or sexual) has this child endured?
- How long has this child been in foster care and what kinds?
- How many times has this child been moved since birth?
- What are the existing or potential problems for this child?
- What postadoption intervention resources are available should problems arise?

To get more ideas about what adoptive parents need to know before adopting a special needs child, read Keck and Kupecky's book *Adopting the Hurt Child*, especially Chapter 6, "Dreams and Realities."

Questions to Ask Yourself

- Do we thoroughly understand the process of attachment or parent-child bonding and the consequences of children experiencing insecure attachment or broken attachments?

- Do we have the necessary commitment to make an investment in parenthood that raising a child requires?
- Do we know what kind of child we would consider bringing into our home?
- Do we have sufficient knowledge to ask the right questions about a child?
- Do we know how to establish resources before we adopt that we may need after the adoption?
- Do we have the patience to participate in pre- and postadoption placement counseling to be prepared for the problems that will arise?
- Do we have the financial resources including adoption subsidies to raise this child?

Choosing the Best Route

If you are pursuing special needs adoption, you may want to try various routes at the same time, especially if you want to adopt an infant or small child. Often there is no application fee to adopt a child with special needs. For example, if you want to adopt a blind infant, you may send letters to attorneys and private agencies telling them of your desire to adopt such a child. You may also want to contact crisis pregnancy centers and let them know that if any woman is carrying a child with a defect, you may be interested in adopting that child. In the meantime, you may want to get your home study done by your public agency. They will usually not charge you for the service.

HOW TO ADOPT A CHILD WITH SPECIAL NEEDS

Most children with special needs are adopted through a public, or state, adoption agency. Some are adopted through private agencies that specialize in placing children with special needs, and others are listed through adoption networks or exchanges. Few are adopted through private means.

Independent Adoption

If you adopt independently you will probably receive an infant, because most independent adoptions involve birth mothers placing their children at birth. The baby you adopt will probably have been designated for another couple originally, and the couple changed their minds because of the child's disability.

If you are interested in adopting a child with special needs, write to every adoption attorney in your area who serves as an intermediary and let them know that you are interested in adopting a child who may be difficult to place. Be specific about the disabilities you are willing to accept—Down's syndrome, cocaine or other drug exposure, cleft palate, etc. Here is an example of such a letter.

Dear Mr. Smith,

My husband and I are interested in adopting an infant or very young child with a physical disability or impediment. These disabilities may include deafness, blindness, cleft palate, or inability to walk.

We know that an opportunity to adopt such a child is limited, so we are sending this letter to several attorneys and private agencies to let them know that in the event that a child with a disability is born, and a couple decides not to adopt the child, we are more than willing to adopt this child.

Enclosed please find copies of our completed home study, including a "sanitized" version you can show to a birth mother. Attached to the home study are two pictures of our family and home.

You can reach us at (800) 123-4567 at any time. Our pager number is (704) 555-1234/PIN 2345 and our e-mail address is 12345@home.com. Please feel free to call us at any time. Thank you.

Sincerely,

Tom and Judy Cook

One person followed this advice and received responses from all over the country. She contacted us to let us know that she had adopted a child with a serious but correctable heart problem. Because in her letter she was not specific about the types of disabilities in a child that she and her husband were prepared to adopt, she received many phone calls. And after her daughter was placed with her, she continued to receive many phone calls. So many, in fact, that she started an outreach of connecting infants and babies with special needs with families who want to adopt these children.

Because this woman's letter was not specific, many families and children have been brought together by her. However, if you do send letters out to attorneys and agencies, be sure to be as specific as possible as to the type of medical or mental problem, or disability in a child that you feel that you have the resources to parent. Also, get a home study done as soon as possible—before you send the letters out—so that if you receive a phone call about a baby that has just been born, you will be ready to travel.

Now that computers can do mail merges for you, getting out letters to hundreds of agencies or attorneys is not difficult. You can even download such lists off the Internet and just send out general letters, and use the names of the downloaded lists for making labels.

Here is another broadcast letter, this one addressed to a birth mother.

Dear Friend:

My husband and I both want very much to adopt a child that perhaps other couples may not want to adopt. We want to give a child with special needs the extra care, time, and attention required. We both are very experienced in dealing with children with disabilities. My husband, Brad, teaches at a school for the deaf and blind. I am a special-education teacher by training and teach part-time. My sister, who is six years younger than I am, has cerebral palsy. In my family I often had the responsibility of taking care of her. Although my sister cannot walk and has limited speech ability, she is a successful accountant for a large corporation.

My husband and I both believe that regardless of a child's physical disability, he or she needs a great deal of love and attention as well as a well-structured environment. We are very committed to our marriage and to loving a child.

We have many resources, including a large extended family that is looking forward to a new addition to the family. Although we are not rich and live in a modest home, my husband's position provides us with excellent medical benefits. This means the child will have access to the best medical care.

We are very open to meeting with you. We would also be glad to share pictures and letters of the child with you so you see how well the baby is growing and developing.

Please feel free to call us so that we can talk further. We know this is a very difficult time for you, and we want to provide the reassurance you need. We can be reached at (800) 555-1234.

Very warmly yours,

Melinda and Brad

With independent adoption, very often the special needs of this child will be a physical or mental disability or problems related to in-utero drug exposure. If you are willing to adopt a child who has been exposed to drugs, you may also end up dealing with the Department of Social Services unless the birth mother places the child immediately after birth. The medical personnel in the hospital usually are required to alert the Department of Social Services if a child or mother tests positive for drug exposure. Because drug exposure is often considered child abuse, the child may be removed from the biological mother and placed in foster care. If this happens, even if the birth mother wants the child to be placed with you, and even if you have an approved home study, DSS may say that you need to become a foster parent first. They may also tell you that other parents are in line waiting for an infant, and that you will just have to wait in line like all other foster-adoptive parents—even if you have been helping to pay for food and housing for the birth mother for the last several months. If, however, the birth mother relinquishes the child to the adoptive family before DSS becomes involved, the placement will usually be allowed. The hospital staff may also be more cooperative about having the child go home with an adoptive family.

By the way, if you adopt privately, you are *not* eligible for federal or state adoption subsidies.

Private Agency Adoption

Many private agencies receive grants to place children with special needs now that more grant monies have become available. These agencies often work in conjunction with the state agency, and the children may still be in the care of the state agency. These private agencies usually screen families, help them prepare for adopting a child, and help the child prepare for being placed in a new family. They also do the postplacement interviews until the child is adopted. The children available through these private agencies are generally eligible for state and federal subsidies. The process involved in adopting a child through a private agency that places such children is very similar to that of a public agency, as explained in the following pages.

Public Agency Adoption

Every state has at least one agency that handles adoptions, usually an extension of the state's social services department. There are over 2,000 such agencies in the United States. In some states there is one agency; in others there is one in every county. Consult your state directory for the name of your state's adoption specialist; this office can direct you to the agency in your county or district.

In the United States at least 50,000 children are searching for a family. These children are in the custody of the state and are often taken from foster home to foster home—even if they are free for adoption. Unlike Baby Jessica or Baby Richard, there are no cameras, no six o'clock news coverage for these children. Yet they hurt deeply because they are caught up in the bureaucracy and have no permanent home.

Contact your state agency to see how to apply. They may send you a preliminary questionnaire and ask that you attend a series of training sessions or workshops. Public agencies conduct workshops not only to educate prospective adoptive parents about issues involved in adopting a child with special needs but also to screen out prospective adoptive parents who are unready to deal with the emotional and behavioral problems of children in the system.

THE HOME STUDY

Next, complete your home study. If your state agency conducts home studies, this is a good place to start because they will usually not charge you if you are interested in public agency adoption. The home study they conduct can also be used to adopt a child through a photolisting service. Remember, a home study conducted by a public agency may be more stringent than a standard study because the social worker is looking for more than good health, a clean record on child abuse, and financial stability. She wants to find out how you cope with setbacks and how you deal with frustration and anger, because these relate to the kind of special needs child you want to adopt. The caseworker will also want to see how flexible you are. If you say you are a childless couple and enjoy traveling all around the world, yet you are willing to adopt a child who is in a wheelchair, the caseworker is going to ask how such a child is going to fit into your vacation routine.

In addition to the basic documents required for a home study (see Chapter 17), a state agency may ask for certain kinds of information. For example, if you have had any kind of counseling, even for infertility, the agency may ask for a letter from your counselor or therapist. They will also have forms for your physician and your references to complete, where a private agency would simply request letters. A standard form can be helpful, actually, because it assures you that most of the information needed will be addressed by completing the forms.

For the most part, the home study for a special needs adoption will be like any other, except that the caseworker may ask you more in-depth questions, especially as certain issues relate to the kind of special needs child you hope to adopt. The questions will have to do with family values, what you learned from your parents that you want to pass on to your children, how you cope, how you and your spouse deal with disagreements, how accepting of the particular child your family and community would be, what support systems you have to care for a child, your attitudes toward the birth parents, how siblings are going to react, and your attitudes toward counseling. Unlike a standard home study, the caseworker may want you to discuss your attitudes toward sex, what you consider sexually age-appropriate behavior in a child, and how you feel about caring for a child and not receiving much appreciation and affection in return. If both of you work, the caseworker will probably go into depth about your child care arrangements. If the child will need special services, the caseworker will also want to know about the availability of these services in your area. One question that may also be asked involves who would care for your child in the event of your death. If you have other children without special needs, and you have appointed legal guardians for them in the event of your death, remember that these same people may not be open to adopting a child with special needs.

Be prepared to explain just what kind of child you want, how much openness with the birth family you are willing to accept, and what legal risk you feel you can handle if the parents' rights have not been terminated. You will probably be asked to fill out a special needs acceptance list, checking off what factors you can accept in a child or in her family background, and to what degree you can accept these characteristics. Before answering this section, you may want to do some basic homework to determine what is meant by such terms as "deformity," "physical disability," or "learning disability." These are broad terms, and you may want to attach a sheet of paper explaining exactly what you can accept. The social worker who comes into your home will also want to explore this with you. For example, if you answer that you can accept no sexual abuse, they may ask you how you will feel if you find out later that the child was sexually abused. Sexual abuse is a very sensitive topic, and the caseworker may want to find out whether there are any underlying reasons why you would not accept this kind of child.

When you have finally attended all the workshops and completed all the paperwork, the agency has a matching system based on the type of child you want. As children become available, you may be selected to adopt a particular one. You will be presented a child or sibling group that the agency thinks matches the kind of child you are willing to accept. You do not have to accept the child. If you feel that the child is not one that you are prepared to parent, tell the agency. You may need to work with them to clarify what kind of child you want. In some cases, of course, parents will say they are willing to accept a child with certain characteristics, but then when they are presented a child who has these characteristics, they are disappointed. It is clear they were secretly hoping to adopt a healthy child with few problems. They should have been honest at the outset.

Assuming you approve the child, however, the next thing that will happen is that she will be placed with you. At this point she may or may not be legally free for adoption. If she is not legally free, and the birth parents are not making any progress, then you must wait until their rights are terminated. (In some cases the parents' rights are terminated at the adoption.) Legal adoption can take between several months and several years to accomplish, although there is now a big drive underway to move adoptions through faster.

THE LEGAL RISKS OF SPECIAL NEEDS ADOPTION

Nearly all adoptions are "legal risks," but ones in which an involuntary termination of parental rights is concerned or ones in which the birth mother may have given false information about the birth father are considered especially risky. Although the media has created much of a sensation regarding this matter, the reality is that a child who has been abused or neglected and cannot go back to his original family is not a high legal risk even if no one can find the child's birth father.

Let's look at three categories of risk: low risk, moderate risk, and high risk.

Low risk. A low-risk adoption means that the consent of the birth mother, the birth father, and any alleged fathers have been given, or their parental rights have been terminated. If there is no consent from the birth father because he cannot be found, then there is documentation to support that efforts were made to find him and tell him of his rights. If the agency says that a child is a low legal risk, ask whether documentation is there to show that both parents' rights have been terminated or that efforts were made to contact the birth father so that he could not contest the adoption if he so chose.

Moderate risk. An example of moderate risk would be a situation in which the birth mother's rights have been terminated, but the birth father cannot be found and there is sketchy documentation regarding the state's effort to find him.

High risk. High-risk adoption is not adoption—it is foster care, called foster-adoptive placements. It means the birth mother's, and probably the father's, rights have not been terminated. Do not necessarily rule out taking a high-risk child initially as a foster-adoptive child; it may be that the birth mom and dad are never going to get their lives together, but that not enough of a paper trail exists to prove that efforts were made to find them and explain their rights. Babies are often high legal risks simply because not enough time has passed to allow their birth parents to do a turnaround. If you find out that no other family member is available to care for the child, and the parents are not making any effort to follow their court-ordered plan, you may want to consider this situation.

OPEN ADOPTION

Openness in a special needs adoption can be very similar to openness in a standard infant adoption, with letters and pictures being exchanged with the birth mother every six months or so. Or it can be quite different. Children with special needs are often old enough to remember their parents or relatives, and, therefore, more openness may be advised. On the other hand, parents who may pose a danger to the child should not have contact with the child.

Where possible, a certain level of openness is now commonly viewed as beneficial to the birth parents, the adoptive parents, and most of all the child. Although the birth parents and the child probably gain the most advantage from openness, adoptive parents and the agency usually have the most control over the matter. Because you will ultimately set the tone for the level of openness that will take place in an adoption, the caseworker will want to know what your comfort level is and also under what circumstances you may or may not be comfortable with openness. Whether or not contact in person or through letters with the biological parents is advised, the caseworker will probably expect that you remain in contact with the child's previous foster parents for at least a few months to make the child's transition easier.

Here are some of the different levels of openness and the times when each kind may be appropriate:

1. *Personal visits with birth parents, extended family members, or foster family members.* No one wants to see a child abruptly removed from his home and placed with a new set of parents, never to see his biological parents or caregivers again. We have all heard about children being taken from the only home they have ever known and sent to live with their biological parents. No matter what we believed was the right legal decision, our hearts ached for the children. Yet every day, 2,000 children in the United States and Canada are separated from their parents and placed in another home.[14] Often they are placed with foster parents with whom they become attached before they move on to be with their adoptive parents. The trauma of separation from parents and other relatives is added to the trauma of neglect and abuse. That is why social service agencies work so hard to reunite children with their parents or to have a relative care for the child if the parent cannot.

   Not all children's parents who have neglected them are malicious. Cocaine and crack have disrupted the lives of many parents who come from seemingly stable family backgrounds. A child of such parents may have aunts and uncles and grandparents who lead normal lives. These extended family members may love the child very much, and although they lack the resources to care for her, may desire to see her at least a few times a year. Since they did not neglect or abuse the child, they may be the ideal people to provide her with the link to her birth family and allow her to feel connected to her original family in a positive way.

Other children have parents who have a mental illness or a level of retardation that makes caring for the children very difficult, causing the parents' rights to be terminated. A child may have parents who truly care about him and wish him no harm, but just cannot provide the day-to-day structure needed. He may well benefit from having contact with his parents, especially if he has strong memories of them and knows that they care about him. Having contact with the birth parents can give him a sense of continuity and connectedness to his biological roots.

Of course, if you adopt an older child—one who can remember phone numbers and make phone calls—openness may not be an option, it may just be a fact. Children can and will make phone calls to relatives.

The child's response to seeing his biological parents or other relatives when they visited him while in foster care should be taken into consideration when deciding whether such visits are appropriate. Depending upon the situation, it is best for such meetings to take place in a public area, such as a restaurant. You probably do not want the family to know exactly where you live.

2. *Letters and pictures.* Sometimes children are placed with adoptive families who live so far away from their birth parents and relatives that personal contact with the birth family is nearly impossible, even if it is appropriate. Sometimes parents' lives are too chaotic or the abuse they inflicted on the child was too severe for visits to take place. In such situations, cards, letters, and pictures may be appropriate. Again, the child's age and history should be taken into consideration. If the child is very young, contact with the birth family is for the birth family's benefit. As the child matures, the contact can be for his benefit.

   If the child's parents' rights were involuntarily terminated, you will probably not want the parents to know your address. All correspondence should go through the agency.

3. *No contact.* Children who were grossly neglected or abused may be traumatized by any contact. The parents can continue to abuse the child psychologically in letters, even if the content of the letters is not overtly abusive. Parents who used code words when they abused the children could still continue to use those terms in a letter. A letter may remind a child of past trauma in a way he is not ready or capable of dealing with; it may even cause flashbacks that may retraumatize the child.

Of course, even if minimal contact with the parent is not appropriate now, some level of contact may be appropriate in the future. If the child is in therapy and needs to confront his abusers on some level, making contact with his parents may be part of his healing process. He may also have to make contact with his biological relatives to understand his genetic background, especially as it evolves over time.

Finally, the child may desire and need to continue contact with the foster parents. Sometimes, however, it is not appropriate for children to have contact with the foster parents if they are trying to sabotage the adoption or are causing the child to have conflicting loyalties.

ADOPTING BY SPECIAL NEEDS CATEGORY

If you are specifically interested in adopting, for example, a blind, deaf, or mentally disabled child, or an orphan child of a parent who died from AIDS, you might begin by contacting support and referral organizations that address the specific concerns of the illness or disability. If you take this approach, getting state and federal adoption subsidies may be difficult, since these children may not be in the foster care system and are probably not receiving foster care subsidies. However, children with profound problems will be eligible for Supplemental Security Income (SSI) and other benefits that are provided to any child with a disability regardless of whether the child is adopted or biological—though she may not receive the benefits if your income is too high. However, if an agency handles the adoption, you very likely could receive subsidies.

Before considering adopting a child with a specific disability or health condition, it is best to find out from those who have children with the condition what issues must be addressed, and what the day-to-day responsibilities will be.

AIDS

Tens of thousands of children will be and are already orphaned as a result of their parents' death from AIDS.[15] (Of course, this may change as better drug therapies delay or possibly even halt the disease's progression.) Programs are now being developed so that prospective adoptive parents can become involved in the lives of children whose moms and possibly dads have AIDS or are HIV-positive. The biological parents care for the child as much as possible, but as their health deteriorates, the prospective adoptive parents take on a more active role. When the parent dies, the child, who then lives with the adoptive parents, has already formed a close-knit relationship with his new family. The adoptive parents can also have the opportunity to know and share in the child's life before placement.

Families adopting HIV-positive children struggle with many problems, including uncertainty and a lack of resources. Social workers can be instrumental in evaluating family needs and in orchestrating and managing resources to fit the legal, foster care, or adoption needs of families with afflicted children. Common issues faced by these children and their families include the need in some cases to keep the child's disease secret.[16]

Resources:

CDC Hotline: (800) 342-AIDS

Children with AIDS Project of America
1414 W. Bethany Home Road, Suite 5
Phoenix, AZ 85019
(800) 866-2437 or (602) 973-4319
jjenkins@indirect.com
www.aidskids.org/index.html

This organization recruits families from all fifty states to adopt HIV children, AIDS orphans, and drug-addicted infants and refers the families to private and public adoption agencies. If you register with them, your name and background will be shared with agencies. The organization maintains a database that includes children, recruited families, and adoptive families. There is no fee for the service.

Down's Syndrome

If you wish to adopt a child with Down's syndrome (DS), it is best to go through a DS support and resource organization, especially if you desire to adopt a newborn or young child. Few very young children with Down's syndrome are available through adoption exchanges.

The Down's Syndrome Center, an organization that provides education and support to families with children who have DS, also provides an informal network to bring together prospective adoptive parents with infants and children who have DS. Some infants become available for adoption because the biological parents discovered at birth that the child has DS. Other times the birth mother is making adoption plans and the initial prospective adoptive parents did not want to adopt a child with DS.

For every child born with DS, at present there are about forty-five families in the United States waiting to adopt him. Because there are more prospective adoptive parents than children available, birth parents can select the family. In general, they want to see a short biography of the adoptive parents, to meet with them, and to maintain a certain level of openness after the child is placed with the couple. Robin Steele, an adoptive mother actively involved with the DS Center, says that couples can expect to wait at least six months before an infant becomes available. Because many couples request a girl, if you have no gender preference, you can adopt sooner.

Steele suggests the following guidelines:

- Gather as much information about DS as possible.
- Get involved in a DS support group and an adoption support group.
- Get your home study completed.
- Send a general letter to as many agencies as possible describing yourselves and expressing your desire to adopt an infant/child with DS. Agencies will often waive their initial fee because they are pleased to keep a list on file of prospective adoptive parents who desire to adopt a child with special needs.
- Contact the DS Center and complete their two-page form. The form asks what agency and caseworker conducted your home study; what age, ethnic background, and gender you desire; and what level of openness you are willing to maintain with the birth family.
- Get an agency involved so that you will be eligible for state funding.

Resources:

Down's Syndrome Association of Greater Cincinnati
Adoption Awareness Committee
(513) 761-5400

Knowledge and Information for Down's Syndrome A-KIDS
(914) 428-1236
This is an adoption exchange program.

ADOPTION NETWORKS OR EXCHANGES

Adoption networks are photolisting services that present children who have not been able to be placed by their own social services department. Such children are usually more difficult to place and therefore need a broader exposure to potential adoptive parents. An adoption exchange is not an agency but a networking system where public and sometimes private agencies can register children who need homes. The exchanges do not have custody of the children; they are merely facilitators in bringing children who are in the custody of an agency or foster care system together with prospective adoptive parents. Exchanges often will try, using a computer, to match prospective adoptive parents with children.

You may be very excited about the number of children available in a photolisting, but remember that many other prospective adoptive parents may be inquiring about the same children and that the children may be in the process of being adopted even as you are beginning plans to find out more about them. As you pore over these books, try not to raise your hopes too high. Prospective adoptive parents have often reported much disappointment.

Rita Laws suggests the following tips for making photolistings work for you:

1. Get a home study completed if you are not already approved. Be sure to use an agency that will give you copies of your study so that you can send them out to the exchanges.
2. As soon as you complete your home study, get a personal subscription to a photolisting, because the children in the updates can be placed very quickly. Call on new listings the day you receive them.
3. Fax or send an overnight copy of your home study as soon as the social worker requests it. Address it to the correct social worker and include a cover letter that tells why you would be the ideal parent for a particular child.
4. Call the exchange the next day to be sure that the correct social worker received your home study. If the home study is being sent out from the agency that conducted it, you will want to be doubly sure that all the paperwork has been sent out.
5. To expedite the process, send out home studies for several children at the same time.
6. Invest in a good medical encyclopedia or computer program. Learn the terminology and what treatments will be necessary. If you have access to medical personnel, review the child's conditions with them. (If the child is available and you are definitely interested in her, you will want your pediatrician to review her medical records.)
7. Keep your photolisting book up-to-date as new pages are sent to you. If most of the children in the new pages are already placed when you call, the listing is not up-to-date. Subscribe to a different listing.
8. Once you have selected a child, ask lots of questions.

The photolisting book is one of the most creative and effective ways available to recruit families for waiting children. Each listing includes the following information:

- The child's first name, month and year of birth, state of residence, ID number, and the date on which he was added to the photolisting book
- The child's likes and dislikes
- A brief medical and social history
- The kind of foster home the child lives in
- The kind of adoptive home that would best suit the child's needs (single woman, married couple with no children, etc.)
- A contact person and number

Because photolistings must present a lot of information in a small space, certain key phrases may suggest much more than they say. Just as "cozy" describes a small home, assume that certain words can be taken literally and that others have deeper meanings. Rita Laws gives some examples:

- "All boy, very active, impulsive, needs a lot of attention, acts out" may mean the child has attention deficit hyperactivity disorder (ADHD).
- "Requires lots of structure, needs constant supervision, manipulative, has experienced several losses, has experienced many moves" may mean the child has emotional and/or behavioral problems, including attachment disorder (AD).
- "Neglected" may mean the child was malnourished, and may also mean attachment disorder.
- "Developmentally delayed, immature, delayed speech" may mean child has mental retardation or even attachment disorder.
- "Has difficulty in school" may indicate that the child has learning disabilities and/or emotional and behavioral problems including attachment disorder.
- "Moody or sad" may mean child has depression and/or other emotional problems.
- "Prenatal exposure to drugs/alcohol" may indicate problems related to cocaine or fetal alcohol syndrome or effects.[17]

Note: A child's history of sexual abuse is not included in photolisting books or other public media; this information will not be provided to you until you become a serious inquirer.

It is best to place yourself on a few adoption exchange lists to increase your opportunities for adopting a child. Different lists cover different geographical territory; some cover a single state, some a region, and some the entire country:

State. It is probably best to begin your search for a child in your own state. First, you are more likely to be selected than an out-of-state parent, because some social workers are opposed to sending a child a long distance away, especially if the child needs a more gradual transition from his foster home to his adoptive home. Second, the adoption process can usually go more smoothly because the Interstate Compact is not involved. Third, it is easier to visit the child before the adoption takes place if you live within a few hours' driving distance.

Regional. A regional exchange lists children in a multistate area. You do not necessarily have to live in the region to adopt a child from this exchange. It is up to the social worker whether to allow the child to go outside the region.

National. A national exchange certainly allows you to select from a greater number of children. Remember, however, that any time you adopt a child from a distance, you must consider the cost of transportation. You will probably be expected to visit the child a few times before making a permanent adoption plan. Traveling can be expensive and time-consuming. Your library, a local adoption agency, or adoption support group in your area may subscribe to these listings. Check to see before you invest in your own copies.

Resources:

North American Council of Adoptable Children
National Adoption Assistance Training, Resource, and Information Network (NAATRIN)

NAATRIN offers support and information without charge to adoptive and foster parents, adoption professionals, and other child advocates who have questions about Title IV-E Adoption Assistance. NAATRIN maintains a national database of pertinent state and federal laws and policies, and provides state profile. Typical questions are about eligibility requirements, benefits, how to claim adoption subsidy on tax forms, post-finalization, voluntary relinquishment, Medicaid, and SSI. In addition, NAATRIN staff provides training for adoption workers, parents, and other professionals across the country.

members.aol.com/nacac/subsidyoverview.html

National and Regional Exchanges

Aid to Adoption of Special Kids (AASK)
657 Mission St.
San Francisco, CA

The Adoption Exchange

The Adoption Exchange provides the connection between families who adopt and children who wait. It is based in the Rocky Mountain region and has offices in Salt Lake City, Albuquerque, and Denver. The Exchange is not an adoption agency. It is, rather, a place for the exchange of resources on behalf of dozens of adoption agencies. When an agency is unable to locate a family for a waiting child, the agency uses the Exchange services to find a family.

www.adoptex.org

The CAP Book, Inc.
700 Exchange St.
Rochester, NY 14608
(716) 232-5110
The CAP Book is a national register that provides a photolisting of
hard-to-place children. Only children who legally can be placed with
out-of-state adoptive parents are included. The book costs $75 per year,
lists hundreds of children, and is updated every other week.

Massachusetts Adoption Resource Exchange
MARE is a private, nonprofit agency whose primary purpose is to link
waiting children with permanent families. MARE focuses on waiting
children who are ages six and older, children of color of all ages, sibling
groups, children with emotional, physical, and intellectual challenges,
and children who are at legal risk. MARE acts as an information and
referral center and recruits potential families for waiting children.
www.mareinc.org

The National Adoption Center
1218 Chestnut St.
Philadelphia, PA 19107
(215) 925-0200
(800) TO-ADOPT
The National Adoption Center operates the National Adoption Exchange,
which also provides a computer matching service for waiting children. You
must contact an adoption caseworker to access the computer system for
you. The center also provides information and training for those adopting.

National Adoption Center—Faces of Adoption
The National Adoption Center is a nonprofit organization whose mission is to expand adoption opportunities throughout the United States
for children with special needs and those from minority cultures.
Founded in 1972, the Center works with social workers and other adoption professionals to bring children and families together through a
computerized photolisting of special needs children and adoption-
related information on the Internet. Check out the National Adoption
Center's Adopt Net, an online support network for adoptive families
with articles and scheduled chat sessions with adoption experts.
www.adopt.org/
www.adoptnet.org

National Resource Center for Special Needs Adoption
16250 Northland Drive
Suite 120
Southfield, MI 48075
(810) 443-7080 x295

North American Council on Adoptable Children (NACAC)
1821 University Ave.
St. Paul, MN 55104
(612) 644-3036
This organization provides materials and videos for a fee and maintains a listing of local adoption support groups. NACAC also maintains an up-to-date listing of adoption professionals and organizations listed on the Internet.

Northwest Adoption Exchange
NWAE facilitates adoptive placements for waiting children in Alaska, Idaho, Nevada, Oregon, Utah, and Washington; helps recruit prospective adoptive parents throughout the United States; gives information and referrals on a wide range of adoption issues; creates public awareness about waiting children and special needs adoption; advocates for and develops projects to expand support services for families throughout the adoption process; and provides consultation, and training and technical assistance to adoption agencies, social workers, and adoptive parent support groups.
www.jetcity.com/~nwae/

Faces of Adoption provides a photolisting of available children with special needs on their Web site, as well as adoption-related information.
www.adopt.org/adopt

The Adoption Exchange Web site links prospective adoptive families with waiting children.
phoenix.uchsc.edu/rmae

The Placenet Web site Adopt America at **www.adopting.org/placenet.html** lists information about waiting families. Adopt America matches about 100 children with families each year. Adopt America only concentrates on children who are more difficult to place. www.adoptamerica.org

FOSTER CARE

Couples often ask whether foster care is a good strategy for those who want to adopt a child. As a rule, the answer is no. Taking a foster child into your home can be a wonderful, challenging opportunity; it is not a means in itself to adopt a child. However, there are opportunities to become a foster parent as a means of adopting. If you are becoming a foster parent as a step toward adopting a child, make this very clear to the state social worker who will be licensing you.

At one time social workers would not allow foster parents to adopt the child they were caring for. The child would be adopted by another family, even if she had been in the foster home from a young age and her foster parents were the only parents she had known. The rationale was that a couple who takes on a foster child in the hope of adopting the child will wish for the termination of his biological parents' rights. Although foster care can be a temporary place for a child whose family is in crisis, it is often a place where a child stays while one or both of his birth parents get their lives together, a process that can take years, if it happens at all. This can be frustrating to the foster parents who love and care for the child as they live in a state of limbo wondering whether the parents are ever going to pull it together. Biological parents may meet marginal requirements, keeping their rights from being terminated, but not meet enough requirements to parent the child fully. Even when one of the biological parents begins to take appropriate actions so that she can resume full responsibility for the child, the foster family can be heartbroken at seeing the child go from a stable situation to a home that is less than stable.

Many foster parents do eventually adopt the children who have been in their home. In some states they are allowed the first opportunity to adopt the children if the children are not going back to their biological families. For the foster parents to qualify, the child must usually have been in the foster home for at least six months.

Foster/Adoption

Foster/adopt does *not* mean becoming foster parents as a way of caring for children who "might" become available for adoption. It means taking a child into your home who will probably become available for adoption. Although 50 to 70 percent of the children in foster care return to their biological families, others will never go back to their biological families and are not being adopted quickly enough. Many could be eligible for adoption, but the legal steps have not been taken to terminate the parents' rights (TPR), or a certain time has not lapsed until the parents' rights can be terminated, so the children are technically not available for adoption. While these children are waiting for a TPR, it is best if their foster home is also their potential adoptive family.

About 60 percent of these children nationwide are already being adopted by their foster parents. In some states, such as Maine and Idaho, about 85 percent of the children are adopted by the foster family. These percentages have increased as social workers recognize the emotional damage that moving from one home to another does to a child and the fact that children tend to see a move as their own fault.

Many children in foster homes are waiting to be adopted by the foster family, but the process can be lengthy and the paperwork extensive. When social workers have limited time and resources and many emergencies to deal with, pushing through the adoption of a child who is in his loving and stable foster/adopt home is not a priority. The actual adoption is important for the child and parents, however. They need to know that this is forever.

Because lawmakers are beginning to recognize what caseworkers already know—it is important for children to be placed in permanent loving homes—there is a trend in the United States to approve more foster/adopt homes. In fact, in some states those becoming foster parents are being prepared as if they could also become adoptive parents. This is sometimes referred to as *dual licensing, flexible family resource, permanency planning foster parents.* The purpose is to screen and prepare a foster family so well that when a child is eligible for adoption, the foster family, who usually has the first right to adopt the child, will be appropriate candidates. It is hard on the both the children and family if they have become attached to each other, but when adoption becomes the plan for the children, they are then moved to an adoptive home.

There are some foster parents who do not want to be adoptive parents and know that they would most likely not be appropriate candidates. For example, some foster moms who are retired love to take care of new babies—usually drug-exposed babies. These babies are either going to go with the birth family or to adoptive homes, and the foster moms have no interest in parenting children into their eighties. On the other hand, a baby should not be placed with a couple who long to be parents, who are licensed foster parents, and who are also approved to adopt the child if she becomes available. This could be devastating to the couple if the child does return to her birth family.

The need for families to take care of babies increases as laws regarding mothers who use drugs during pregnancy are becoming stricter. Either the mom is going to get off drugs or she is not. Now laws are being passed that give these moms a limited time period to become drug free. As the laws become stricter, more adoption plans will be made for babies instead of allowing them to go back and forth to their birth families and into different foster homes.

When a social worker begins to approve a foster family as if they are to become an adoptive home, it usually means that the foster parents are given a more thorough home study and more preparation about adoption.

Also, the foster parents should be treated as if they could become the permanent parents. This would include giving them complete nonidentifying background information on the child before placement. It also means that a child is not suddenly placed with a family. Instead, care goes into matching and transitioning the child into the family.

To become a foster/adopt parent, you must meet requirements both for becoming a foster parent and for becoming an adoptive parent. This process can take a long time, which can be frustrating if you have a particular child in mind. Depending on the requirements of your state for becoming a foster parent, more emphasis may be placed on the safety of your home, compared with adoptive parent requirements. Therefore you will probably need a safety and fire prevention inspection, and any lead paint in your home (common in older homes) may have to be covered or removed.

Resources:

The Foster Parent Home Page contains the most extensive listing of foster parenting resources on the Internet, and provides links to many other foster parenting sites. It is also useful for adoptive parents who have adopted children out of foster care.
www.worldaccess.com/~clg46/

The Usenet newsgroup is dedicated to the exchange of ideas and experiences involved in foster parenting.
alt.support.foster-parents

SPECIAL NEEDS ADOPTION SUBSIDIES
Expenses for adopting a child with special needs can be minimal. In fact, if your employer offers funding for adopting children, the cap on what the employer will pay is often higher for a child with special needs.

Years ago children remained foster children because foster parents who were receiving monthly payments could not afford to lose those benefits if they adopted the children. Other parents interested in adopting a child with complex medical needs, or a sibling group, could not afford to. Now, thanks to the Adoption Assistance and Child Welfare Act of 1980, a whole new pool of parents can consider special needs adoption. This act mandated that all states establish a Title IV-E adoption subsidy program for children previously eligible for funding while in foster care. Title IV-E monies come from both federal and state dollars. Each state also administers other subsidies that come solely from state dollars. (As of this writing, some states are considering limiting or omitting state subsidies.) In 1992 more than $219 million supported over 66,000 children. Unfortunately, many adoptive parents are not even aware of the subsidies—sometimes because social workers neglect to make them aware. In some states adoptive parents may have to go to court to make sure that their state provides them with the funds that are due them. Read on to find out who is eligible for subsidies.

Title IV-E

The first thing to know is that in order to be eligible for subsidies, a child must be under the guardianship of an agency. Children adopted through an attorney are *not* eligible. In about fifteen states, some international adoptees are eligible for one-time reimbursements of up to $2,000.

In general, for a child to receive federal monthly adoption subsidies from Title IV-E, he must have sufficient medical, developmental, or psychological problems or disabilities to be eligible for Supplemental Security Income (SSI), or he must meet the state's criteria for having special needs, and he must come from a birth family or relative's home that was receiving or was eligible to receive Aid to Families with Dependent Children (AFDC). If the child has special needs but does not meet the other criteria, he may be eligible for an equal state subsidy.

Children who are receiving Title IV-E federal foster care maintenance payments are eligible for federal adoption assistance benefits. Many foster children are receiving state and not federal funds, however, so the child may or may not be eligible for federal funding once adopted. Children who are receiving SSI benefits at the time of adoption are financially and categorically eligible for adoption assistance; in fact, even if they have been not receiving SSI benefits, if they meet SSI criteria at the time of adoption, they are eligible for adoption subsidies. With SSI benefits, however, the adoptive parents' income is taken into consideration, which means that most children are not eligible for SSI once adopted.

Even if your income is too high, determining whether a child is eligible for SSI is still a wise idea. First, the child can receive SSI before the adoption is finalized. Second, if she does qualify for SSI, she will qualify for adoption assistance subsidies after finalization, since these are not determined by your income. Remember, prospective adoptive parents cannot receive the maximum amount of federal support from both SSI and the adoption assistance program, even if the child is eligible for both programs.

Following are the general categories of SSI eligibility. This is not a comprehensive list, so be sure to contact your local Social Security office at (800) 772-1213 for more complete information on eligibility criteria and application forms.

- Growth impairment of the musculoskeletal system (e.g., arthritis, disorders of the spine)
- Blindness or hearing impairment
- Respiratory problems (e.g., asthma or cystic fibrosis)
- Cardiovascular problems
- Digestive system disorders
- Malnutrition
- Endocrine system (e.g., thyroid) disorders
- Diabetes
- Blood and lymph disease (e.g., sickle cell disease)
- Cancers
- Multiple body defects
- Down's syndrome
- Immune deficiency
- Neurological problems (e.g., cerebral palsy)
- Mental and emotional problems
- Attention deficit hyperactivity disorder
- Developmental and emotional disorders of newborns and infants
- Genito-urinary problems

If a child is not receiving federal foster care maintenance payments or is not eligible for SSI, two categories must be met in order for her to be eligible for the federal adoption assistance program. The state must determine that the child has special needs, and the child must meet the financial and categorical criteria of AFDC both at the time she was removed from her parents' custody and at the time of adoption.

Each state establishes specific guidelines as to what defines a "special needs" child. In one state a child may have to be six years old to be considered special needs, while in another she must be ten years old. A child who is African-American or of mixed ethnic background will have a lower age requirement than a Caucasian child in order to be considered special needs.

A child is considered to have special needs when she has met these three factors:

1. She cannot or should not be returned to her biological parents. This includes children whose parents have voluntarily released them for adoption.
2. The child has a specific condition, including minority ethnic background, age, being part of a sibling group, or having a medical, mental, or emotional disability or being at risk for one, that would make adoption difficult without a financial incentive.
3. Except where it would be against the best interests of the child to place him, efforts to place the child without offering medical or adoption assistance have been unsuccessful. Federal officials have finally recognized that a focus on "shopping" a child until adoptive parents who do not need the subsidy can be found is contrary not only to sound adoption practice but to the intent of the adoption assistance program.

   If parents cannot or will not adopt without the subsidy, then the requirement is met. Asking parents whether they are willing to adopt without subsidies does not put the placement at risk for them.[18] As a practical matter, however, children with special needs who are easily adoptable, such as a cocaine-exposed Caucasian six-month-old, can easily be placed without subsidies. A few couples will usually be considered for the child, and the one willing to adopt without subsidies will be selected.

Foster parents who have had a child in their home for a significant time do not need to consider whether they are willing to take the child without a subsidy. Because of the emotional ties involved, this requirement is waived.

Aid to Families with Dependent Children

There are two classifications of AFDC requirements: need and deprivation. Deprivation requirements are met if a parent is absent or if parents' rights have been terminated. To qualify for the need category, a child must have been eligible, even if an application was not made, for AFDC, at the following times:

- In the month that a petition was filed with the court for the removal of the child from his home, or six months before
- In the month before the child's parent voluntarily signed an agreement for the child to be placed outside the home, or six months before

In other words, even if the child was not receiving AFDC at the time he was removed from his home, if his biological family qualified for it, he still will meet the AFDC criteria. He must also be eligible when the adoption is petitioned. Children who meet the AFDC requirements at the time they are removed from their parents' custody may or may not meet the criteria when the adoption proceedings are initiated.

Requiring children to be AFDC eligible seems arbitrary, and as of this writing, federal lawmakers are reconsidering the requirement. Meeting the AFDC requirement is not as simple as it may look. More and more children entering foster care who then become eligible for adoption are not coming from welfare homes but from working families. Moreover, even if the child's biological family was AFDC eligible at the time he was removed from his home, his family's work status may change from the time he was removed from the home to the time the adoption petition was put into place. Often the employment status of one of the biological parents does change between the time the child is removed from the home and the time the adoption petition is filed. The biological mother may have gotten a job, making the child ineligible for AFDC status.

Note: A child who is receiving Title IV-E foster care payments at the time the adoption petition is filed meets the AFDC relatedness test.

Resources:

> Information on the **Federal Adoption Assistance Program**, which offers financial assistance in domestic special-needs adoption, can be found on the Children Youth Family Education Research Network (CYFERNet) gopher.
> **gopher://cyfer.esusda.gov:70/00/CYFER-net/funding/faprs/f209**

State Adoption Subsidy Programs

Most states have an adoption subsidy program for children with special needs who do not qualify for federal adoption assistance under Title IV-E—usually because they do not meet the SSI/AFDC requirements. In many states the IV-E adoption assistance and state payment subsidies are administered as the same program, with the same payment rates for families. If a child meets the criteria for special needs but not for the SSI/AFDC requirements, the payments come from state instead of federal funds. Most states have fairly broad standards for defining special needs. Some even say that if a child has been in your home for eighteen months as a foster child, she qualifies as special needs because of the emotional trauma that would be caused if she was removed from your home. Just be aware that as federal and state dollars become tighter, fewer benefits may be offered.

Monthly cash benefits. Once a child is considered to have special needs, she is eligible for monthly assistance, usually in the amount you would receive if you were foster parents. Each state sets up its own fee schedule. As a rule, the higher the cost of living and the older the child, the higher the payments. Some states provide a higher foster care rate for children who require special care. This is called *specialized* or *accelerated care rates.* If the adopted child was eligible for specialized care rates when she was in the foster care system, the rates would stay higher after the adoption.

Medical assistance. Children in the federal adoption assistance program are automatically eligible for Medicaid benefits. Many states also choose to provide Medicaid coverage for children who are receiving benefits from state or local (nonfederal) adoption assistance programs. Although states have broader standards in defining who is a special needs child, the definition for special needs is directly related to having a special medical or psychological need, as opposed to being in a certain age or ethnic background category. A healthy two-year-old African-American child would not necessarily qualify.

Minimum Medicaid benefits for children include inpatient hospital services (except for tuberculosis or mental disease), outpatient hospital services, laboratory and x-ray services, screening and diagnosis, and medical and dental services provided under state law. Children are also entitled to optional services to correct or lessen the effects of physical or mental illnesses or conditions discovered during a health care screening under the Early and Periodic Screening, Diagnosis, and Treatment Program (EPSDT). These services include home health, private duty nursing, clinic services, dental services, physical therapy, prescription drugs, dentures, prosthetic devices, eyeglasses, inpatient psychiatric services, respiratory services, and other medical care.

Even if you have comprehensive health care insurance, you may want the extra security of Medicaid in case your situation changes.

If your child has special mental or physical needs and is to receive Medicaid, try to negotiate as much other assistance as possible. Many physicians will not accept Medicaid, which can be difficult, especially if you have other children who are already going to a particular physician.

Medicaid is especially useful when you are using specialists and not general practitioners and for getting specialized hospital care. You can also request that the state pay for psychological counseling and for one-time medical needs and equipment, such as a wheelchair ramp.[19]

Social Security Block Grants (formerly called Title XX) govern the social services grant, which gives federal money to states to use for helping families maintain self-support, remedying neglect and abuse, and preventing or reducing the need for institutional care by providing these supportive services to adoptive families.

These funds have not been actively promoted by child welfare workers, and the individual states have much latitude in designing the programs. Each state has an outline for services and established activities to be supported and for who will be served. Types of services vary from state to state. Potential services include day care, respite services, in-home support services such as housekeeping and personal care, and counseling.

Unlike the Medicaid program, SSBG is not given automatically to dependent children or children eligible for AFDC. However, the program is designed to make sure that children in the adoption assistance program will not be excluded from services that the state provides children who do receive AFDC. For example, if the state operates a day care program funded by these block grants and gives preference to AFDC children, then a child in the adoption assistance program will have the same preference regardless of the adoptive parents' income.

Other Services and Assistance

The federal law also requires that the adoption assistance agreement include any additional services that are needed for the family or child. Prospective adoptive parents should closely monitor their child's needs and anticipate any future needs. For example, a family may have to change their home to accommodate the physically challenged child now or in the future.

Service subsidies. Many states provide medical, mental health, and other postplacement services that are not covered by the adoptive family's health insurance or by Medicaid. Service subsidies should be established before the adoption is finalized. Some states do provide service subsidies to adoptive families after finalization.

Education. This may include speech and physical therapies.

Reimbursement for nonrecurring adoption expenses. Since 1987 the federal adoption assistance law has required states to pay nonrecurring adoption expenses in the adoption of children with special needs through a state or nonprofit private agency.[20] The cap is usually $2,000 per child. A child need only meet the Federal IV-E definition of a special needs child to qualify for this one-time subsidy; he does not have to meet SSI or AFDC eligibility. You must apply for reimbursement of these expenses in the state where the adoption assistance agreement is signed. If you are not receiving adoption assistance, you must apply in the state where the adoption will be finalized.[21] The subsidy covers:

- Adoptive parents' home study, medical exams, and postplacement supervisions
- Legal and court costs
- Transportation, meals, and lodging
- Adoption fees

Subsidies for International Adoptions

There are a number of states that will consider reimbursing nonrecurring adoption costs for international adoptees.

Adoption Assistance Checklist

Whenever a family receives adoption assistance, a written adoption assistance agreement between the adoptive parents and the state agency will be provided. These agreements vary from state to state, but there is a model adoption assistance agreement available that contains the requirements under Title IV-E, useful for adoptive families who move across state lines. The agreement should state that a commitment is made regardless of where the adoptive parents live and should specify the kinds of care and services that will be provided. It should be specific enough to ensure future enforcement but flexible enough to allow for new provisions if circumstances change. For example, if your child is receiving physical therapy, the agreement should describe the services in detail and state that if the provider can no longer offer services or if you move, equal services will be provided. Services should be described in very specific terms: not just "therapy will be provided" but "individual and family therapy will be provided for at least one hour per week by a licensed child psychologist or social worker." The agreement should also state the date on which each benefit will start and the circumstances under which it can be terminated.

Following is a checklist of questions to refer to when reviewing your adoption assistance agreement:

1. Does the agreement clearly state all the responsibilities of the prospective adoptive parents? Are financial reporting and recertification requirements explicit?
2. Is the agreement signed by someone with proper authority to bind the state agency?
3. Are all necessary agencies parties to the agreement?
4. Does the agreement specify the amount of cash assistance to be provided?
5. Does the agreement state all necessary services to be provided?

6. Does the agreement give the date when each benefit and service will begin?
7. Does the agreement clearly list the conditions under which benefits and services may be terminated?
8. Does the agreement specify the condition under which benefits and services can increase or decrease? Is there any clause that restricts the prospective adoptive parents' authority to negotiate changes in the future?
9. Do the services end when the child turns eighteen or twenty-one?
10. Does the agreement specify what will happen if the adoptive parents die?
11. Does the agreement specify that the agreement itself will still be in effect and that the benefits will remain in effect if the adoptive family moves out of state?
12. Does the agreement provide for Medicaid eligibility?

If you believe your child has special medical or psychological needs that will not be adequately met by the subsidies and services outlined in your agreement, it would be wise to take the child to a specialist of your choosing (orthopedic, neurological, psychiatric) to obtain the clearest prognosis possible so that you can negotiate the best possible agreement for your child. Even if this means taking your child to a specialist who does not accept Medicaid, in the long run it may save you both money and time.

Negotiating an Agreement

Federal policy requires that the child's and the family's circumstances be taken into consideration in establishing an adoption assistance agreement. For example, although there are written state guidelines as to the maximum amount of monthly payments in each age category, the state and the adoptive parents can negotiate the amount. Your goal as adoptive parents should be to provide comprehensive support. Follow these steps:

1. Obtain complete information on the child's family background and medical history, including current health status, psychiatric and psychological evaluations, if necessary, and the current physical, intellectual, and emotional needs of the child. State agencies do not always collect all the essential information about a child, and the information is not always in one place. Nor does the agency always provide prospective adoptive parents all the information available.

Federal law, however, requires that the following be in the child's foster care plan:

- The names and addresses of the child's health and education providers
- The child's grade-level performance
- The child's immunization records
- The child's medical problems
- The child's medications
- Other relevant health and educational information

2. Based on the child's medical needs, and on his social and educational background, a discussion of services may be needed.
3. Give thorough consideration to your resources and ability to meet the child's needs so that he will successfully be incorporated into your family. Take into account not only your income but your other expenses, the number of children in your home, and the circumstances of these children.
4. Compile complete information about the federal and state adoption assistance programs available, including service and medical subsidies.
5. Negotiate a support plan that combines all appropriate programs.
6. Negotiate *specific* guidelines for services to be provided in the event that you move to another state. Although federal law requires federal adoption assistance agreements to state that subsidies remain in effect regardless of where you move, some services may not be specifically addressed in the agreement.[22]

Remember, federal adoption assistance agreements remain in effect regardless of the state in which you live. If you live in South Carolina and your child receives $200 per month in subsidies, and you move to New York City, where the cost of living is much higher, you will still receive only $200 per month.

Enforcement

Most of the disagreements that arise over the negotiation or enforcement of an agreement can be handled on an informal basis. When they cannot, federal law requires that states provide prospective adoptive parents a fair hearing before the appropriate state agency to contest the agreement or petition for its enforcement. Some states have special review panels to hear adoption assistance appeals. A fair hearing can also be helpful if a caseworker is not responsive to the adoptive parents' requests.[23] There are separate fair hearings for Medicaid and Title XX services.

Fair hearings are informal occasions, and the rules of evidence do not strictly apply, so many adoptive and prospective adoptive parents represent themselves instead of hiring an attorney. The fair hearing officers can decide about the fact that is in dispute and order the agency to follow state statutes and agency guidelines. We strongly recommend, however, that you hire an attorney to work with you throughout this process. An attorney can help the family by establishing the eligibility of the child for benefits, by helping plan the negotiation of the adoption assistance agreement and future changes, and by taking legal steps to enforce the agreement if the family does not receive the proper benefits and services. Often additional benefits such as speech therapy, psychological counseling, and equipment for disabilities can be negotiated. Why shortchange yourself or your adopted child? Have an attorney negotiate as much as possible in your favor.

Prospective adoptive parents who are presented with a standard agency form that sets forth the terms should negotiate an individual agreement that meets the child's needs. Except for legal restrictions, there is no requirement that the adoption assistance agreement follow any particular format.

Sometimes foster parents are told that they will not receive adoption assistance if they adopt their foster child, or prospective adoptive parents who want to adopt a particular child are informed that the child will not be eligible for subsidies. In these situations the prospective adoptive parents can request the agency to reconsider the decision, and if necessary can demand a fair hearing. Have your attorney provide the state agency with the information necessary to establish the child's eligibility. If the state criteria are too strict, they may be challenged as not conforming to federal law.

Note: If you adopt a child whose parents signed a voluntary consent, you will need to have a judicial determination that the adoption is in the child's best interests or that remaining with the birth family is contrary to the child's welfare. *This needs to be done within six months of the parents' signing the consent,* because you will not be able to go back later and obtain subsidies should the need arise.[24]

Title IV-E for Child's Blood Relatives

In order for a child who is to be adopted by relatives to meet Title IV-E requirements, the court must usually state that it is against the child's welfare for him to stay in his biological parents' home, or that placement in the adoptive home is in his best interest. There is no need to discuss the manner in which the child came into care. The child must also have been AFDC eligible at the time the adoption petition was filed.

PREPARING FOR YOUR SPECIAL NEEDS CHILD

There are a number of ways to prepare for your special needs child. This section outlines the most important.

Gathering Information

Carol McKelvey and Dr. JoEllen Stevens suggest you compile the following before the adoption placement takes place:

Complete background information, including:
- Full disclosure of the child's social and family background
- Full medical and psychological reports, including those that may result from psychological tests
- Personality and temperament testing of your family, including the Steven Adopt-Match Evaluator
- Disclosure of any problems[25]

Life Books

A life book is a pictorial and descriptive history of a child's life. Like any scrapbook, it can be put together at one time, but it is better if it is made over time. Usually a caseworker assists a child in completing the pages, but a dedicated foster parent may also put in entries.

The older the child, the more important the life book. A child in the foster-care system often has had a fragmented life and may have difficulty knowing where he was and what he was doing at various times. The life book can help put the pieces together. Unlike a regular photo album, the life book provides more than pictures of the child's past; the book can also fill in gaps that even his current social workers may not be able to tell him about. Also, the life book can help a child express his feelings about different points in his life.

Ideally, a child or his caseworker has a regularly updated life book from the time he enters foster care until the time he is adopted. However, this probably will not be the case. First, many children enter foster care with no pictures of themselves, and second, foster parents often do not take pictures. Also, social workers may have limited opportunities to take meaningful pictures of the child, so the pictures may be only of the child's foster home, his church, and his school.

If your child comes with a life book, do treat it as a special object. Go through it with your child so that he can share his past with you. Do this more than once. The child may tell you more and more each time. You will want to add pictures of your child with your family. The life book is the child's personal history, so don't put the book on the coffee table—or in the attic, as one adoptive family did, sending a message to the child that his past was not significant.

Below is a listing of what goes into a life book, but your child's life book may not contain all of these items. You may want to add some of these entries yourself.

- Information about the child's biological family, along with pictures and letters from or about family members
- The child's birth certificate and social security card
- A family tree
- A page about the child's nationality
- A list of relatives, including parents, grandparents, and siblings
- Birth and death dates
- Pictures of your child's family of origin, the homes they lived in, and the pets they had
- The child's health records
- Any family history of diseases
- The child's immunization records
- A record of childhood illnesses and health problems, including injuries
- An education page, including a list of schools the child has attended, photos of teachers, and a list of things the child enjoys
- Pictures of special foster family members and any notes from them you might have
- Illustrated stories by you about funny experiences related to the child
- A letter about why you like and love the child
- A "heart" page where the child describes with words, magazine pictures, etc., how he likes to show feelings and affections and what makes him feel loved
- A "bug" page where you or the child draws or writes down all the things that "bug" him (put a picture of a big bug on this page)
- A page about church/temple and Sunday school experiences, including pictures of a favorite teacher
- Information gleaned from social workers or the child's previous foster family about his day-to-day routine, the foods he likes, his sleeping habits, favorite toys, books, and blankets, and the kinds of clothes he likes.[26]

Telling Others About the Child's Arrival

Share with your close relatives what the child is like and what may be expected. If they live nearby, their assistance could be very important, especially if you have other children in the home.

Finding Professional Assistance

Begin by asking a pediatrician who is very competent in treating children with special needs to review the records. You may also want to ask other appropriate professionals, such as psychologists, to review them. Make it very clear that the review is not to determine whether you want to proceed with the adoption but to get a complete picture of the situation you and the child will be entering. Once you feel you have a clear picture, you can begin to arrange for physicians and other professionals who accept your insurance or Medicaid coverage.

THE CHILD'S ARRIVAL AT YOUR HOME

Depending on the child's age, very likely a child will visit with you a few times and spend a weekend before coming to live with you. It is best if you visit her at least once or twice in her foster home first. You and your spouse may want to go visit the first time; then the second time you may want to take your other children with you, if you have any, and perhaps plan a fun outing all together. The third time you all meet, the child will come to your home, and the fourth visit will probably be a weekend overnight. Again, depending on the child's age, this process should take about two to three weeks.

Before the child arrives at your home, she will have to leave at least one, possibly two, families behind: her immediate foster family and her biological family. Even if she has not lived with her biological family for years, she may still need to "leave" the dream of living with her biological parents. This transition can be very difficult for a child, especially if she has feelings of mixed allegiance to her foster and birth families. If she is older, you or the caseworker may want to arrange a special ceremony in which the birth parents say good-bye to the child. If this is not possible or appropriate, a birth parent will sometimes write a letter wishing the child well in her new home. The child needs to feel that it is all right with her birth parents for her to move on to another home; she may need their "permission." If the birth parents are not available, you may want to arrange a special ceremony. Buy some helium-filled balloons, one representing the child, one for each of her birth parents, one for each of her foster parents, and one for each of you. You can write each person's name on a balloon and then have the "persons" talk to each other. In the end, the child can hold on to the balloons representing herself and you and release the birth and foster parent balloons into the air.

Learning the Child's Routine

The small things in life can go a long way toward making a child's placement successful. If a child needs a lot of structure and routine, that needs to be established before he arrives. If he is very controlling, you will need to decide what is important and what you need to overlook so that everything does not become a power struggle. Often adoptive parents get upset over minor irritants—how much toothpaste is used, food "stealing," eating habits, and so on. A parent who can handle the child's learning disability may get quite upset if the child is clumsy. Issues such as space, sharing, meals, favorite foods, television time, and how to get along should be thought through as much as possible beforehand, and the child's day-to-day activities, preferences, and interests learned. Your caseworker should be able to give you practical tips in dealing with the child.

Depending upon the child's nature and background, you may want to keep things fairly calm the first few days after the child's arrival and not have many people to your home, so that the child does not feel more like a specimen than a new arrival.

Making It Work

Once a child is in your home, the experience can be wonderful. However, after the child arrives—usually about three to six months later, and often even sooner—the relationship with the child may begin to deteriorate. Caseworkers see this as the end of the "honeymoon" period, when the reality of the child's problems begins to hit. Before the child comes to live with the adoptive parents, they may not have fully heard what the caseworker was saying to them about the child's needs and problems.

Although most parents of kids with special needs experience a great deal of joy and personal satisfaction despite the extraordinary demands, many adoptions do disrupt. Planning ahead and having realistic expectations can help reduce the likelihood of an adoption not working out. Here are some suggestions for making the experience as positive as it can be:

Join a support group of parents with special needs kids. If you did not do this before you adopted, do it now. The more information you can gather from others, the more prepared you will be for whatever postadoption issues you will have to face.

Research the special characteristics of your child. Read, read, read. Once you decide on a particular special need you would be comfortable handling, do as much research as possible on the subject. Get to know other parents who have a child with that particular medical, psychological, or disability problem. Visit them at their home, if possible. See how day-to-day family life goes with such a child.

Get a support system in place. No parent can care for a child twenty-four hours a day, seven days a week, and a child who has many needs can be emotionally and physically draining. Get someone to help you and give you a break. If you are reluctant to have yet another person taking care of your child after all the caretakers he has experienced, hire someone to come into the home and help you while you make yourself a cup of tea and go through the mail or read a book.

Studies show that in families in which the father plays a significant role, the parents are able to stay far more committed. Make sure that you have support from friends and family as well. If you are functioning well now, that is a good pre-dictor that you will perform well with an additional child.[27]

Hire an attorney. It is very important for a child to feel that he is in a "for-ever family" and not in legal limbo. If your child's adoption finalization is taking longer, you may need the help of your own adoption attorney. An attorney can review all legal documents and adoption subsidy agreements and can expedite the adoption process, especially if one or both of the birth parents' rights have not been terminated.[28]

TALKING TO YOUR CHILD
ABOUT ADOPTION AND HIS/HER PAST

When you adopt a child with special needs, you are likely to be dealing not just with adoption issues but with issues of why the child's parents could not care for him and perhaps why they abused or neglected him. This kind of abandonment is different from the abandonment that occurs in other countries, in which a child is left in an orphanage. Abandonment in the United States usually involves overt neglect. Similarly, if the child was abused, he will not understand why his parents would do this to him.

Although hearing about the neglect and abuse and why he was placed for adoption is very painful for the child, at some point he will need to know the details surrounding his placement. Children have a right to know their pasts—it helps them understand why they feel what they feel. Without this information, the child may feel like a partly blank slate.

Of course, children do not need to know all this information at an early age or all at the same time. Telling your child the truth is a process that may parallel the discussions you have with him about adoption. Just as you do not explain adoption all at once when the child is four years old, never to bring up the subject again, you would not think of sharing the child's past with him all at the same time. Sharing the past is a process in which information is gradually revealed in ways that the child can understand.

Many adoptive parents feel as if they want to protect the child by with-holding some of the grimmer details of her abuse or neglect. This is understand-able, but they should know that the child may find out elsewhere. It is better if the information comes from you.

As your child asks questions, try to answer her honestly, providing only as much information as she is seeking and as is appropriate for her age. When she asks about her birth parents, try to tell the facts without making a judgment. Do not be overtly condemning of her birth parents. The child may feel she needs to "defend" her biological heritage, and she may become uncomfortable about sharing her feelings or memories if you use those occasions to badmouth her biological parents. Be careful, too, of the way you talk about her biological parents in front of others. Your attitude will come through.

Although it is best, in discussing the child's past, to state the facts without adding a negative interpretation to it, there will be times when a judgment will be needed to let the child know that what was done was wrong. To say, "Your mother was a wonderful woman who drank too much alcohol, and that is why she couldn't keep you" may confuse the child. The child may think, "Why do you think she was so wonderful when I remember going hungry when she was drunk?" or "If she was so wonderful, why didn't she just stop drinking so that I could live with her?" It might be better to say, "Your first mother loved you, but she drank too much alcohol, which made her do bad things like not feed you often enough." The child will understand that he was not necessarily rejected, but that his mother chose not to get help for her alcoholism and therefore was not able to provide for him. Similarly, if a birth mother was a prostitute or the birth father sold crack, you do not want to excuse their lifestyles and diminish the reality of what the child went through. You cannot say that a certain behavior is unacceptable and at the same time that the birth parents were honorable people.

Here are some organizations you may want to contact for referrals for special needs children:

Alliance of Genetic Support Groups
38th and R Streets NW
Washington, DC 20057
(202) 331-0942

Association for Retarded Citizens
2501 Ave. J
Arlington, TX 76006
(817) 588-2000

Cystic Fibrosis Foundation
6931 Arlington Road
Bethesda, MD 20814
(301) 951-4422

Epilepsy Foundation of America
4351 Garden City Drive
Landover, MD 20785
(301) 459-3700

March of Dimes
1275 Mamaroneck Ave.
White Plains, NY 10605
(914) 428-7100

Muscular Dystrophy Association
3561 East Sunrise Drive
Tucson, AZ 85718
(602) 529-2000

National Association for Perinatal Addiction
Research and Education
11 East Hubbard St., Suite 200
Chicago, IL 60611
(312) 329-2512

National Down's Syndrome Adoption Exchange
56 Midchester Ave.
White Plains, NY 10606
(914) 428-1236

National Down's Syndrome Congress
1800 Dempster St.
Park Ridge, IL 60068
(708) 823-7550

Spina Bifida Adoption Referral Program
1955 Florida Drive
Xenia, OH 45385
(513) 372-2040

Spina Bifida Association
1770 Rockville Pike, Suite 540
Rockville, MD 20852
(800) 621-3141

United Cerebral Palsy Association
7 Penn Plaza, Suite 804
New York, NY 10001
(212) 268-6655

Chapter Sixteen

Transracial Adoption

Two years ago on the day before Christmas, we brought home a healthy eight-week-old female puppy. We knew nothing about her background, but she seemed to be part Labrador and part chow. Her breed didn't matter to us; all we wanted was a dog with the temperament to tolerate the poking, pulling, and petting our three- and five-year-old daughters were sure to inflict upon her. If breed could predict the level of a dog's tolerance for small children, we were betting on the most gentle breeds.

When Pepper arrived at our home, we were all instantly taken by her. While I snuggled next to her, I thought about the decision-making process we had gone through in selecting an animal, and how different it was from the process we had entered into when adopting our children.

Like us, most folks select a dog based on its breed's temperament, intelligence, hunting ability, looks, and size. With dogs we can sort and choose. There's even a book that lists the world's dumbest dog breeds. Who on earth wants a dumb dog?

In adopting a child, we may seek certain characteristics, but humans are complex creatures, and we cannot select a child's characteristics based on its ethnic background. You cannot request an Italian infant because Italians are intelligent, obedient, and hardly ever shed, or a German child because Germans are good-looking and quick runners and never grow above 200 pounds. Every child has her own unique characteristics that need to be valued and cultivated. Children will be who they will be, a fact of life that is as true when adopting as when you have a biological child. Yet with adoption you do have some control in the selection process.

One example has to do with the child's race or ethnic background. This does not predict the child's outcome the way breed or species predict behavior in animals, but it may well predict the reactions of others. That is why the first question that comes to mind when you consider adopting a child outside your racial background (a transracial adoption) is often, "What will my family think?" Perhaps you do need to consider the responses of family and friends, especially if you think your family would have difficulty accepting such a child. Often the lack of acceptance, however, has more to do with what your mother's aunt Edna *may* think rather than what your immediate family *will* think. Sometimes people use nonacceptance by family as a way to cover up the fact that they would find it difficult to raise a child who does not look like them or who belongs to a certain race or ethnic group.

If you are truly comfortable with a transracial or international adoption, expecting acceptance from every last relative, including those you see once a year, is unrealistic. If you are concerned that closer family and friends may have difficulty, you may want to discuss some of their concerns with them and let them know that you want to consider their feelings. Your parents may have to go through the stages of grief related to the loss of having biological grandchildren, and from there they may need to come to terms with having grandchildren who do not look like them. It may have taken you months or years to process the decision to adopt transracially; expect your family members to need some time to process their feelings as well.

Remember, though, that grandparents and other close relatives who say they cannot accept a baby of a certain racial or ethnic background will probably be enthralled with him once he arrives. We have heard countless stories of relatives who opposed the adoption of a child outside the family's ethnic background, yet once the child arrived, the grandparents could not wait to care for her. And if they can't accept the child, you may ask yourself, in the words of one adoption attorney, "Do you really want to be around someone who cannot accept a sweet innocent baby because of the color of her skin?"

WHAT TO CONSIDER

If you are Caucasian, for example, and are considering adopting an African-American, biracial, or international child who will look very different from you, here are some questions you may need to ask yourself:

1. How do I feel about raising a child and providing him with a sense of his heritage?
2. How would I handle the comments from others about how my child looks different from me?
3. How would I feel about my child marrying someone of the same racial or ethnic background and having grandchildren of that heritage?

4. How would I feel about my child marrying someone of a different race?
5. Do I have friends or relatives outside of my race or culture?
6. How will I feel if people tell me how lucky my child is to be adopted by an American family?
7. Will my expectations for the child be based on his race or culture?
8. Do I feel differently about adopting a black or Asian girl versus a black or Asian boy?

If you did not answer the questions "correctly," relax. These questions are not designed to trap you; they are there to help you explore your feelings and what biases you may need to overcome.

Some of our biases are sexist as well as racial. For example, there is such a disproportionate number of couples who want to adopt Korean girls that at least one agency will not allow couples to request a girl unless they already have a son. Why the desire for a girl and not a boy? Perhaps it is because we perceive Asian girls and women, who generally are petite, as fitting into our American stereotype of what is feminine, or maybe it is because we have difficulty thinking about having sons, who are supposed to pass on the family name and traits, who do not look like us.

Even if you have worked through any sexist or racial biases you may have, you may believe that because you live in an all-white neighborhood and did not sign up to lead the diversity weekend retreat at work that no agency is going to accept you for a transracial adoption. One Caucasian couple said they considered adopting a biracial or black child but decided against it after an agency sent them a list of questions regarding the racial makeup of their neighborhood, friends, church, employers, and so on. You should not be intimidated by such questionnaires. If you are open-minded, you can change your lifestyle so that an international child of another race or a black child can feel comfortable with your family and friends while retaining a sense of his heritage and culture.

Broadening Your Options

Just as people dream of the ideal biological child, so you may dream about the ideal adopted child. At first this fantasy may be to adopt a child who looks like you and your spouse. Expecting a child to look like you, however, even if you were to find biological parents who resembled you, is unrealistic. Even to expect biological children to look like you is unrealistic. Accept the likelihood that a child will probably *not* look like you—although, when it comes to that, we've seen lots of children who look like their adoptive parents, even those of a different race or ethnic background. Once you arrive at this realization, you may find yourself expanding your ideas about what kind of a child you would be able to accept.

This is not to say that someone who is uncomfortable with adopting a child from outside his or her race is nonaccepting. There are many things to consider when adopting a child, including the child's age, health background, and prenatal exposure to drugs and alcohol. Sometimes, though, looking at what you can accept emotionally, culturally, and financially allows you to move beyond preconceived ideas about what your child will be like and challenges you to consider adopting a child who does not fit into your original, often unrealistic, fantasy.

Regardless of background, every child needs to be loved and accepted for his unique qualities. We do not adopt children to make a social statement, out of pity, or because we feel some kind of social guilt. We adopt because we want children and because children need a loving and supportive home. The positive environment you provide may not compensate for every challenge your child may face, whether she is biological or adopted, but we know that regardless of their backgrounds, children do better in stable, loving homes.

WHAT IS TRANSRACIAL ADOPTION?

Transracial adoption is adopting any child outside of your racial background. Most international adoptions are transracial adoptions, because most of the world's children who are available for adoption are from Asia. Indeed, most transracial adoptions involving Asian children are international, since only 15 percent of Asian births in this country take place out of wedlock. For this reason, this chapter is primarily about Caucasian parents adopting biracial or African-American children. Many of the studies cited and issues discussed, however, could also apply to those adopting Asian and other international children. However, in the U.S. the experience of being an Asian raised by white parents is very different from being black and having white parents. Historically, overall race relations between Asians and Caucasians has been more positive than those between blacks and whites. Asians and whites also tend not to segregate socially as much as whites and blacks. For example, Asians are less likely to live in racially distinct neighborhoods, except in very large cities.

Also, the adoptive couple's extended family members may initially be more accepting of an Asian child than a black child. Perhaps this is because interracial marriages between Asians and Caucasians have been historically more acceptable. In addition, many may feel that only African-Americans should adopt black children, a view regrettably shared by some social workers.

Biracial Adoption

For those who are Caucasian and are considering adopting a biracial child of white and black heritage, there are some considerations that need to be explored.

First, according to Beth Hall of Pact, An Adoption Alliance, Inc., which places children of African, Asian, and Latino heritage, children are identified by the racial background that they most resemble. Most biracial children appear to be black and will therefore be identified by others as black. In our culture, which is very race conscious, to be identified as black is a very different experience from being identified as white.

Hall asks prospective adoptive parents to explore their reasons for wanting to adopt a biracial child, as opposed to one who is fully black. Perhaps, she says, it is because a white couple has difficulty accepting the "blackness" of that child. If a family has difficulty with the "black" part of the child, that message is going to be sent to the child in some form.

Hall's organization does not permit couples to select a birth mother who will deliver a biracial instead of a black child. She believes that to accept a biracial child is to accept his black and white background equally, meaning that parents should feel comfortable adopting either racial background. Some biracial children, after all, look fully black. A white couple needs to be willing to accept the biracial child regardless of what she looks like.[1]

When adopting a biracial child, some adoptive parents plan to wait until after the child is born to determine how dark she is before they proceed with the adoption. Such parents have clearly not accepted the child's black heritage. Yes, some biracial children will look nearly entirely African-American. Biracial siblings with the same two biological parents can, like other siblings, look very different.

Beth Hall is right that prospective adoptive parents need to think through why they want to adopt a biracial child and not a black child. However, it is not necessarily right to say that parents need to be willing to adopt a black child if they plan to adopt a biracial child. Parents have different reasons for wanting to adopt a biracial child. Biracial children are both black and white, and some white parents want the child to match part of their heritage. Other parents are attracted to the "distinct" look that can characterize a biracial child. And what about couples who are multiracial themselves? They may want to adopt a child who resembles them. One African-American couple who describe themselves as being "light-skinned" said that they would prefer to adopt a biracial child so that the child would resemble them.

We believe that to say biracial children are black because they are perceived as black by society detracts from who the child is. Is a child more what he is perceived to be or what he identifies himself to be? Indeed, because biracial children are neither fully black nor fully white, some do have difficulty in how they identify themselves. Biracial children who do not try to be either black or white, but both, tend to have the strongest sense of identity.

THE ADOPTION PROCESS

When you adopt an African-American or biracial child, the same laws and methods apply as with any other adoption. The only difference is the time line for finding a child—about three to six months.

If you want to adopt an infant, it is best to contact several agencies and private attorneys who are permitted to do direct placements. If you have your heart set on a newborn baby, you should plan to wait three to six months, although most couples who are serious about adopting don't wait that long. If you are an African-American or interracial couple, you may not wait long at all before the attorney or agency calls to tell you that a child is ready to be placed.

PRIVATE ADOPTION

If you live in a state where it is legal for an attorney to place a child directly with a couple, the first thing you may wish to do is find a reliable attorney and get yourselves on her waiting list. Some attorneys may waive or lower the retainer fee for placing your name and home study with their office if you are seeking to adopt a black or biracial child. Like many agencies, attorneys like to have couples on hand who are ready to adopt a black or biracial child, because many attorneys have too few prospective adoptive parents to present to a birth mother.

What happens next, as with any independent adoption, is that a birth mother either contacts the attorney directly or calls the office after being referred by adoption clients. These are clients who have placed adoption ads and are seeking to adopt a white child. When a birth mother expecting a biracial child answers an ad, the clients refer her to the attorney's office to find another couple.

In general, our experience is that more biracial babies than African-American babies are available through private adoption. Few African-American birth mothers place their children for adoption through an attorney. The pressure not to is great, not only from her own family but from the birth father's family. We have seen two recent situations where African-American birth mothers chose to raise the child in order to keep the birth fathers' families from taking the children. On the other hand, Caucasian women who are expecting a biracial child will often choose private adoption. They like the control that they can maintain in selecting a couple.

Private adoption expenses are the same regardless of the child's racial background. Sometimes an attorney will reduce her fee when placing an African-American or biracial child, sometimes not. This is not always possible, especially if the adoption is a complicated one.

Advertising

Most advertising is done by Caucasian parents looking to adopt Caucasian children. In fact, years ago a typical ad would read, "Couple looking for healthy white newborn." Most ads today are not so candid, and many couples get calls from birth mothers expecting African-American and biracial children. If you know of someone advertising who wants only a Caucasian child, let that person know that you are interested in phone calls from other birth mothers.

Even if your attorney cannot legally serve as an intermediary, he can tell his clients who are advertising to call you if they receive a call from a birth mother expecting an African-American or biracial child. Joining a local adoption support group or a RESOLVE group can also help you hook up with couples who are advertising.

PRIVATE AGENCY ADOPTION

An agency adoption of an African-American or biracial child will be handled much the same way all other adoptions are handled. However, the agency policy may require you to attend classes so that you can understand some of the issues related to adopting transracially. Also, many agencies have different standards about matters such as age or length of marriage for those adopting transracially.

Private agencies want to place the babies born to birth mothers who come to them. They do not want to send a birth mother away and are usually more than willing to place transracially.

Most private agencies, like all attorneys, permit the birth mother to select the couple. One agency reports that most of their birth mothers expecting biracial children want to place the infant with an interracial couple. Many other birth mothers do not care what ethnic background the parents are. Sometimes a birth mother will specify that she wants to place the child only with an African-American or Caucasian couple. In these agency adoptions, the birth mother's wishes are respected. Sometimes it is difficult, however, to find the match that she desires, since there is often not a large pool of prospective adoptive parents.

Some agencies have a different fee scale for those adopting African-American and biracial children, especially agencies of a religious affiliation that raise support. A private adoption agency without outside support will generally charge you its standard fee plus birth mother living expenses, though it may reduce the application fee to increase the pool of applicants.

There are not as many African-American and biracial newborns available as there are Caucasian newborns, but there are also far fewer couples seeking to adopt these newborns—although the number is growing very quickly. The best way to adopt quickly is to make as many contacts as possible. Join an adoption support group and let people who are in adoption circles know of your desire. It often happens that a couple is sought out suddenly to adopt a new baby, and you could be that couple.

PUBLIC AGENCY ADOPTION

Adopting through your social services department essentially means adopting children in the foster care system. If you are flexible and are willing to adopt a toddler-age child or older, you can have a child fairly quickly. Although dealing with the bureaucracy can sometimes be very frustrating, the fees for the adoption service are minimal, and in some cases the state may provide monthly subsidies if the child is considered to have special needs. In some states, coming from a minority ethnic background is considered in itself to be a special need.

Although no social services department or agency that accepts federal funds can discriminate against you because of your ethnic background if you are seeking to adopt a biracial or black child, many of the public agencies have had policies against transracial adoptions in the past, and because of this, their staffs may make the process more difficult for you. You may be asked numerous questions about your neighborhood and your ability to provide the child with a sense of his culture, as well as the acceptance level by your friends and family. Although yours and other people's attitudes are important to explore, you do not want to be excluded just because you live in an all-white neighborhood. People's acceptance level has more to do with their attitudes than with where they live. Nor does every last relative have to favor your decision. If you live close to parents who will be involved in the child's life, you will certainly want your child to feel as loved and accepted as any other grandchild, and if this seems to be a serious issue, it makes sense to think carefully before insisting on more flexibility than your parents are capable of. But if their hesitation is a normal one of getting used to a new idea, this should not be a serious obstacle.

It is generally difficult to adopt a newborn child through social services, but get your name on their list just in case. This will mean attending a series of classes and having a home study conducted and approved by your social services department.

THE CONTROVERSY OVER TRANSRACIAL ADOPTION

Why was transracial adoption prohibited in the past?

During the 1950s and 1960s, transracial adoption increased sharply as a result of the rise in the number of children in the social service system and the lack of minority homes in which to place minority children. In 1972, however, the National Association of Black Social Workers (NABSW) came out strongly against transracial adoption. Within a year the number of transracial adoptions was cut in half to 1,569, and by 1975 the number was down to 800.[2]

The NABSW policy was and still is that a black child needs to be raised by black parents in order to develop a positive racial identity, and that only black parents can help the child develop skills for coping in a racist society. This view, seconded by many others, has had an unintended side effect: children languishing in foster care because no family of like ethnic background can be found. Until recently, many state agencies simply would not place African-American or biracial children with Caucasian parents.

Waiting Children

Despite this, the NABSW continues to argue that black children in white homes is black cultural genocide. But does this really make sense? Are there really enough transracial adoptions to wipe out black culture? And even supposing there were, shouldn't the child's best interests prevail over a culture's interests? As Peter Hayes observes, "To compromise a child's welfare in the name of culture, especially when the cultural benefit is slight or nonexistent, is inimical to the purpose of child placement and violates the best-interests standard mandated by law."[3]

Consider these statistics. African-Americans and people of color make up 12.3 and 17 percent of the total population, respectively; yet African-American children and children of color make up 34 and 47 percent of the children waiting for homes. According to research by Elizabeth Bartholet, nearly half of the 100,000 children in the United States waiting for homes are children of color. In Massachusetts, for example, about 5 percent of the population is African-American, yet nearly half of the children in need of foster or adoptive homes are. In New York City, 18,000 children are awaiting adoption, of whom 75 percent are black. These children generally wait for two to five years, about twice the average wait for a white child. The numbers alone suggest that even if more recruitment efforts were made to find African-American parents, there would not be enough such parents to fulfill the need.[4]

The number of children in foster care went from 276,000 in 1986 to 450,000 in 1992. This tremendous breakup of families is the result of parental poverty, crime, and substance abuse. These statistics hit minority children the hardest.[5]

Bartholet's research into the practices of adoption agencies responsible for placing African-American children shows that agencies do typically practice racial matching, leading to delays in permanent placement. The costs to the children are great—too great. Six months may be a short time in the life of a bureaucracy, but for a small child it can have significant impact. Racial preferences can also mean that a two-year-old child can be torn from the foster parents who want to adopt him so that he can be placed with parents of the same ethnic background. There are many cases where foster parents have gone to court to contest such disruptions.[6]

It is useful to remember that racial discrimination is against the law. Since the Multiethnic Placement Act, effective as of October 1995, ethnic background can be a consideration for placing a child with a family, but it cannot be the only consideration. Some felt that allowing ethnic background to be a consideration slowed the process of placing African-American and biracial children into families, so this law has been further strengthened. As of January 1, 1997, a child's or adoptive parents' race or ethnicity cannot be a consideration if it delays the placement of that child. The new law is so strict that it appears that transracial adoptions must take place. However, a child's cultural needs will still be considered as a factor in deciding what is in his or her best interests.

In short, the harmful consequences of transracial adoptions remain merely speculative, while the social and economic costs of keeping children in the foster care system are obvious and monumental.

TRANSRACIAL FAMILIES

What can be said in answer to the argument that only same-race placements give a child a positive racial identity? Our response is that it is not necessary for a child to identify with his entire cultural system whether he is black, Asian, Latino, or white. Many white adoptive parents successfully teach their children about their ethnic/racial culture and help foster in them a sense of ethnic pride.

How well white parents do in raising children transracially has been researched for more than twenty-five years. According to Elizabeth Bartholet, however, few of these studies were designed to look at the positive aspects of transracial adoption, and virtually none were set up to assess the negatives associated with same-race placements only. No studies have been done to compare the experience of children placed immediately with white families to those of children held in foster or institutional care while they waited for a same-race home.[7]

In a long research study on transracial adoptions that focused on African-American, international, and Native American children who were placed transracially, adoptees have been found after twenty years to be stable, emotionally healthy, and comfortable with their racial identity and to have positive relationships with their parents.[8] Most of the children in the study were adopted before the age of one.

According to Elizabeth Bartholet, there are no data to demonstrate that transracial adoptions have a harmful effect on children. On the contrary, the evidence is that those who were adopted as babies into transracial homes do as well as those adopted in same-race homes. In an extensive twenty-year study, 90 to 98 percent of transracial adoptees were found to enjoy family life, were well adjusted, and had a strong sense of racial pride. Another longitudinal study also showed positive results. In 1970 the Chicago Child Care Society began a study of the family lives of African-American and biracial children adopted by Caucasian families, and African-American and biracial children adopted by African-American families. The following conclusions are drawn from thirty-five transracial adoptees, twenty intraracial adoptees, and their parents when these adoptees were seventeen years old. It was found that: (1) the children's developmental problems were similar to those found in the general population; (2) most of the adoptees had good self-esteem; and (3) 83 percent of those adopted intraracially said they were black, 33 percent of those adopted by white parents said they were black, and 55 percent said they were of mixed ethnic background.

Some other interesting facts emerged. Among those with white parents, 73 percent lived in primarily white neighborhoods, while 55 percent of those with black parents lived in primarily black neighborhoods. Those with white parents had primarily white friends, while those with black parents had primarily black friends. Of the adolescents with Caucasian parents, the girls were more likely than the boys to date African-Americans. All those adopted transracially knew of their adoption before they were four years old, while 80 percent of those adopted intraracially did not learn about their adoption until after they were four. Finally, 83 percent of those adopted transracially and 53 percent of those adopted intraracially had interest in meeting their biological parents.[9]

PROVIDING YOUR CHILD WITH A POSITIVE ETHNIC IDENTITY
One of the arguments against transracial adoption is that black children need a cultural history. It is logical that a black child should have a positive racial identity; however, it is not necessarily true that black culture is the only route to that positive identity. Several studies have indicated that Caucasian parents of African-American or biracial children usually offer those children a healthy sense of racial identity. Studies conducted by both black and white researchers, proponents and opponents to transracial adoption, show much evidence that adoptees have a strong sense of racial identity while being fully integrated into their families and communities.[10] The studies' positive outcomes also apply to those adopting internationally.

Caucasian parents can support African-American culture and ethnic pride in their children by providing books and music about black culture, encouraging friendships with other African-American children, and participating in African-American cultural events. These activities appear to be associated with being middle class, whether African-American or Caucasian. It is questionable whether a black single parent living in poverty can provide a child with the same positive black cultural background as a white family, though a black middle-class family could probably provide more cultural opportunities and more of the subtle day-to-day experiences distinct to black communities.

What of the argument that only black parents can teach the survival skills needed in a racist society? It is believed that a child's racial identity can affect his ability to cope with the world, and it is true that transracial adoptees are generally less comfortable with African-American children than are intraracial adoptees. However, transracial adoptees associate more comfortably with Caucasian children and do as well as same-race adoptees in interpersonal relationships. African-American children who identify with the dominant cultural values also have higher levels of academic achievement, and transracial adoptees are statistically more likely to get better grades in school than intraracial adoptees.[11]

Children can learn to cope with racism. Caucasian parents who adopt transracially are in general less race conscious than those who adopt intraracially and so are at an advantage to teach children to be less race conscious. The message from the Caucasian parents that all ethnic backgrounds are equal can carry more weight than the same message coming from an African-American parent, who may seem to have more personal interest in protecting her status as a black person.

Professor Joan Mahoney, who has adopted transracially, reports that she and her daughter have African-American friends, that she sends her daughter to integrated schools, and that she provides the child with books and toys that will help her relate to her culture. Mahoney recommends investigating your neighborhood for black role models, for churches and other cultural institutions, and for postadoption counseling.[12]

ADOPTION POLICIES AND PRACTICES

The Adoptive Families of America, like the North American Council on Adoptable Children, believes that a child should be ethnically matched when possible, but that children should not have to wait for long periods of time to find a same-race family. How long is too long is not an exact science. The detriments associated with being in foster care while waiting for a family must be weighed against the advantages of ethnic matching.

Some assert that if immediate placement is given automatic priority over ethnic matching, not enough effort will go into recruiting African-American families to adopt. Others believe that agency standards for adoptive parents are biased in favor of Caucasian parents. If more single parents and those with lower incomes could adopt, they say, then more African-American parents would do so. This may be true, but a child or a sibling group may need the energy of two parents, not just one. Humans are finite, and sibling groups probably need the financial security and time that only two parents can provide.

Still, greater efforts need to be made to recruit African-American families and to build trust in the African-American community so that more African-American families will adopt. Agencies need to provide more thorough training and literature to educate prospective adoptive parents about adopting transracially.[13] In the meantime, Caucasian children are primarily going to Caucasian families, and biracial and African-American children are going to both Caucasian and African-American families. Children are adopted because they need love, and parents adopt because they want to extend their love to the next generation. No child should have to wait for a home because of the color of his skin.

Chapter Seventeen

The Home Study

A lthough each state has its own laws regulating adoption, nearly all require adoptive parents to complete a home study. In a home study a social worker gathers information about you and your spouse and your backgrounds by asking you direct questions about your family, your marriage, and your attitudes about parenting and adoption. Do not confuse a home study with the kind of investigation the FBI conducts when screening applicants for certain jobs. This is a meeting between you and a social worker to discuss the attributes that will make you a good parent.

Historically, a home study was a written investigation conducted by a state's department of social services to ensure that adopting couples were suitable to be parents. Today most states have delegated this responsibility to licensed adoption agencies or to specially authorized social workers. Some agencies perform only this service and do not place children for adoption. Agencies that do place children do not necessarily impose the same restrictions when conducting a home study for an independent adoption, even if the agency itself restricts applications according to age, marital history, etc., of prospective parents who apply for direct placement.

Most states require that a home study be conducted before the baby is placed in your home. If you are adopting a baby from another state, you *must* have the home study conducted beforehand to comply with the Interstate Compact Act. In other states, however, the home study is not required until the baby is placed in your home; then it is called a postplacement investigation or an adoption complaint investigation. This is permitted only in independent adoptions, and only when the baby is born in the same state as the adoptive parents.

Whether you have a preadoption home study or a postadoption investigation, once a child is in your home, all states require postplacement supervisory visits—brief visits with a social worker whose job is to note the child's progress and your family's adjustment. The caseworker will visit with you and your baby at least once, if not more often, until the adoption is finalized. These visits usually take place at your home and are conducted by the same agency that handled your home study.

The home study is designed to protect children from going into the homes of unfit parents, to assess your ability to raise an adopted child and deal with adoption issues, and to introduce you to the caseworker—your advocate and an invaluable adoption resource. A caseworker is there to help you as a couple develop a philosophy of child rearing and to provide you with information so that you can learn more about the issues related to raising an adopted child. Some agencies require that you attend adoption seminars or workshops, some of which may be especially designed for those in the home study process, while others address general adoption issues.

Another of the caseworker's tasks is to obtain information about your adoption process. If you have already found birth parents, for example, or if the child has already been placed with you, the caseworker will ask how you met the birth parents and what expenses you paid for. Usually there are two or three interviews. At least one will take place at your home, and the other may be at the agency's office.

WHEN TO HAVE A HOME STUDY

As a rule it is best to have the home study done just before you begin seeking a birth mother. If an FBI clearance is required, you will need to be fingerprinted; this can take up to a few months to get processed, so start the process as soon as possible. If you are planning to adopt in your own state, however, and the home study is not required until after the baby is placed in your home, you can relax. You do not want to have a home study done too soon, because it is usually valid for only twelve months, after which a small fee is charged for updating it.

Various states have different regulations concerning who needs to undergo a home study and when. Find out which of these apply to your state:

- In some states a home study is not required for those who are adopting independently.
- In some states a home study is not required until after the baby is placed in your home.
- In some states a home study is required before a baby is ever placed in your home.
- In some states you must have a home study conducted before you can advertise in that state.

Remember, if you are adopting a baby from another state, *you must have a home study done before you can take the baby across state lines.*

One reason to start the home study process as soon as you begin looking for a birth mother is that it will help prepare you for meeting one. Many of the questions posed in a home study are the ones you can expect a birth mother to ask. Birth mothers tend to be interested in the same character traits a social worker is looking for in a couple: stability, a good marital relationship, love of children, and strong family values. A birth mother will also be reassured to know that you have met certain state requirements by completing your home study.

Remember, too, that even if you advertise only in your own state, a birth mother from another state may contact you. It is wise to have your home study finished and out of the way in case of the unexpected. Think of it as one fewer hurdle to jump! With your home study complete, you can focus your attention on pursuing an international adoption or on finding a committed birth mother and getting to know her. Otherwise you might find a birth mother and then also have to think about gathering the documents for the home study, instead of focusing on the birth mother and the baby.

If you are considering adopting a child with special needs, a child outside your race, an international child, or a sibling group, be sure that your home study addresses the issues surrounding such an adoption. For example, your home study may approve you for only one child, but you may then have an opportunity to adopt a sibling group of three. You cannot adopt more than one child until you are approved for more. In one situation, a Caucasian couple wanted to adopt a black or biracial child or a sibling group. However, their home study did not address the couple's attitudes about a transracial adoption, and when a sibling group became available through an agency, their home study could not be updated quickly enough to include this information. Another couple ended up adopting the children.

If your home study will be sent out to other agencies, remember that an agency that did not conduct your home study may be reluctant to place a child with you until they have updated information about the type of child you want to adopt and how ready you are to face the issues associated with the adoption.

WHO QUALIFIES TO ADOPT?

Nearly everyone who seeks to adopt is qualified. Not one of our private adoption clients has ever been rejected. Yet many couples worry about supposed skeletons in the closet. When a social worker conducts your home study, she is not looking to disqualify you; she simply wants to know that you are capable of providing a child with a loving and secure environment. Most couples who seek to adopt privately are in their late thirties to early forties and often have accomplished other life goals that lead to being good parents, such as emotional and financial stability. When an agency caseworker writes your home study, she is usually acting as your advocate. As honestly as possible, the caseworker is there to present you in the best light.

If you think something in your past may present a problem, talk with your attorney about the matter and get his advice. Some people worry needlessly about arrests made when they were much younger, such as for shoplifting. Other problems are more serious, such as repeated divorces, a recent recovery from alcoholism, or a criminal history. Your attorney may call an agency, explain your situation, and see how the staff would handle it. For example, if you were treated for alcoholism, an agency may simply require that you have a letter from a counselor explaining your situation and stating that you have not had a drink since your treatment five years ago. If a caseworker believes that a couple may have some emotional or psychological problems, she will usually recommend counseling.

Sometimes couples will ask what they should and should not discuss with a social worker. We suggest that there is no need to bring up issues that serve no purpose. If you had a difficult relationship with your parents during your teen years and, as a result, spent most of your summers with your grandparents, then you can state these facts in positive terms. For example, you might say, "I had wonderful summers at my grandparents' farm milking the cows and tending a large garden. I learned to be very resourceful during these years."

Even a very difficult situation need not be discussed. If a teacher or scout leader sexually abused you when you were young, and you have received therapy for this or have dealt with it through counseling or self-help books, telling the caseworker may not serve any purpose. Some caseworkers may ask you directly, however, if you have ever been emotionally, verbally, physically, or sexually abused. This is usually a question on a home study for a public agency adoption. If you must answer in the positive, explain how you have overcome this abuse. *You are not disqualified for having experienced it*, but you should be able to demonstrate how it may have affected you and how you have dealt with it. The purpose of this question is to make sure that you are emotionally stable in spite of being abused, that you are not going to abuse a child in the same manner, and that a child from a difficult background is not going to "push your buttons" and perhaps trigger problems in your life that you have not sufficiently resolved.

The following "problems" will *not* disqualify you as adoptive parents:

- *You have been married only a short time.* As long as you are married, you have every right to pursue an independent adoption. Some agencies, for direct placement purposes, may require you to have been married a minimum period of time.

- *You are not married.*
- *You are divorced.* If you have been divorced (even more than once), you are still permitted to adopt. A caseworker will ask you about your previous marriage(s), but the agency's main concern is the stability of your current marriage. If someone has gone through multiple marriages because he is unstable, this instability will probably manifest itself in other areas of the person's life as well.
- *You are in therapy.* If one of you has been in therapy individually, or if you have had therapy as a couple, your chances of being approved may not be lessened. In fact, most agency personnel view counseling as a sign of strength. The reasons you give for your counseling are what matter. For example, counseling to deal with issues related to infertility, communication, or family of origin is considered very normal.

  Some agencies may require a letter from your therapist stating why you are in therapy and that you are stable and capable of caring for a child. Some agencies may even require a copy of the therapist's case notes. If they do, you will have to sign a letter of release before the notes can be sent to the agency. You should review all notes before allowing them to be sent to another party.

  Do some research first to find out what the agency's policy is on such matters. A policy of requiring people to submit their case notes can encourage people to be dishonest about their counseling histories. Suppose you have suffered from depression. Instead of revealing that information to the caseworker and letting her know that, thanks to medication and counseling, you are doing well, you may be tempted just to skip the issue and say that you have never sought counseling. You should not have to face this moral dilemma; finding out the agency's policy will prevent you from being placed in this position.
- *You have a history of drug or alcohol abuse.* If you used illicit drugs in the past, do not have a record, and no longer use them, you do not need to reveal this to a social worker. If you have been treated for abusing drugs or alcohol, however, you will need to tell the social worker. Usually, this information will not disqualify you, but the agency will want evidence from a treatment counselor that you have resolved this problem and that the risk that you will become a substance abuser again is minimal. Most agencies will require a letter stating that you are no longer addicted to drugs and alcohol and that you are doing well. Some agencies may want more information—why you entered treatment, what the course of treatment was, and whether you followed the treatment plan.

- *You have a history of psychological problems.* If you have been treated for a psychological disorder such as depression or anorexia, and it has not been a life-dominating problem, then you do not need to mention it. If you are still in treatment, however, and the problem interferes with your life (you are not able to work, say), then you will probably have difficulty being approved by an agency immediately.

- *You have a chronic health condition.* People with physical disabilities should not be disqualified from adopting so long as they can care for a child. Neither should a chronic disease like diabetes disqualify someone, provided it is well controlled. What could disqualify someone is a life-threatening condition like cancer. The purpose of the medical report in the home study is to determine that the parent is expected to have a normal life span and be able to care for a child.

- *You come from a dysfunctional family.* If you have come from a grossly dysfunctional family and have dealt with the issues appropriately, and other facets of your life are in order, then a social worker will minimize your family's past and focus on your life now. If you were physically or emotionally abused as a child and recognize that such behavior is inappropriate, and you can state reasonable measures for disciplining a child, then a caseworker will simply say so in your report.

If you have a criminal history, are grossly dysfunctional, or display other attitudes or behaviors that would make you unfit as a parent, a caseworker cannot recommend you as an adoptive parent. Following are some examples, usually based on law, of factors that can disqualify you. If any pertain to your situation, talk it over with an attorney. He will not reveal what you tell him to an agency, because he is required by law to maintain client confidentiality.

- *You or someone who lives in your home has committed a felony.* If you have been arrested for a crime, even if you were found not guilty, this information may be part of the police department's records. Find out before you begin a home study. Any adult living in your home (including children eighteen years or older) must undergo the same police and FBI screening you do. If your parents live with you, and one of them has a criminal history (at least one conviction, not just an arrest), you may be disqualified because that person is living in the home. Convictions for certain felonies (burglary, forgery, etc.) that occurred over ten years ago are often noted but disregarded if there are no other legal violations.

- *You have been convicted of child abuse.* Even an unfounded investigation for child abuse with no convictions may remain in your record. If you think there may be such a problem, have your attorney contact the police department or other government agency from which you may need clearance to see whether there is any record. Any unfounded investigation should be discussed with a caseworker. Again, anyone living in your home will have to undergo the same child abuse clearance you do. If that person has a history of documented child abuse or neglect (not just allegations), that person will have to move out, or you may be disqualified to adopt.
- *You are still in treatment for substance abuse.*

SELECTING AN AGENCY OR INDEPENDENT INVESTIGATOR

Agencies are required by state law to obtain specific information from couples seeking to adopt. Some agencies, however, require more extensive information than others. Agencies can also vary widely in their fee structures.

Call several agencies before making a decision. Ask specifically about their fees and requirements. Most agencies have forms that you must complete before a caseworker meets with you. Your attorney should advise you about an agency's minimum legal requirements. Some agencies may require more frequent meetings between the couple and the caseworker, or psychological evaluations or participation in parenting classes. Although a more extensive home study may have its merits, the more services an agency provides or requires, the more costly the home study.

Before you select an agency or social worker, you should also ask whether you are permitted to have a copy of your home study, and what the agency's or person's attitude is toward issues like divorce, a limited income, inactive church membership, or a minor criminal history—whatever your concerns are. Try to get a sense of the social worker's background. If she is an adoptive parent, chances are she is more understanding of how you feel than an unmarried twenty-five-year-old who may have little experience with children.

THE HOME STUDY

Relax. The caseworker is not coming in with white gloves, armed for a psychological examination. If possible, talk with her on the telephone before you meet in person to help you feel more comfortable when you do meet.

Prepare for the home visit by making the mood as comfortable as possible. Have some light refreshments such as tea and cookies ready. If you have no children, have your home comfortably clean and tidy. You will be more relaxed. Do not apologize about anything related to your home. If you are in the middle of a move, just say, "We moved here two weeks ago and the boxes in the dining room are waiting to be unpacked."

Turn off all distractions like the TV or radio—perhaps even the telephone. Do not set your appointment so that you are squeezed for time. Put pets outside, or confine them elsewhere. For some caseworkers there is nothing worse than a dog jumping on them or cats crawling around their legs.

If you have children, arrange for them to be there so that the social worker can interview them. If you need to discuss sensitive information, you should also arrange for them to be occupied during that time.

Remember, the caseworker serves as your advocate. Caseworkers have different personalities and styles; you may or may not feel comfortable with someone. Regardless of how well you connect with the caseworker, however, she has specific guidelines to follow and cannot subjectively reject a couple based on personality differences.

A progressive adoption agency will have clear objectives and will focus its questions on your attitudes toward each other and on your parenting style, especially as it relates to an adopted child. The agency will be concerned about adoptive parenting issues and will want to provide you with resources: book titles, the names of adoption support groups, and the names of contact people for play groups once the baby arrives.

Preliminaries

Before you have a home study done, the agency will usually send you an application with questions like the ones the caseworker will pose. Don't be intimidated. Some of the questions may seem invasive or difficult to answer, and you may feel resentful having to answer questions that other parents never have to consider. Such feelings are normal.

When you receive the application, you will also be asked to produce the following documents. It is best (even if not required) to have these ready before you meet the caseworker.

1. *Birth certificates for all members of the household.*
2. *Marriage certificate.*
3. *Divorce decree (if applicable).*
4. *Death certificate (if former spouse died).*
5. *Military discharge (if applicable).*
6. *Photographs of you as a couple or family (if you have children) and pictures of your home.*

7. *Income verification (W-2 or income tax statement).*
8. *Health status statement from physician.* Some agencies may require a complete physical that is no older than one year.
9. *Personal references from friends.* Usually three to five references are required. Some agencies stipulate that one reference must come from a friend, one from a clergy member, one from an employer, and one from a neighbor. (If one partner, particularly the wife, plans to quit working after adopting, using her employer is not wise.) One agency that places 200 to 250 babies a year requires applicants to supply *eight* letters of reference. This is too many. Look for another agency.

   Good references are important in establishing your character. Their purpose is to tell how these people feel about you as potential parents and your readiness to have a child. Of course, every reference is going to be good, because you will select only people who like you. But they will attest that you have the ability to establish solid relationships.

10. *FBI, police, and child abuse clearances indicating no record.* These requirements vary from state to state. In some you must receive a report from your local police department or from the state police. The FBI clearance is done through fingerprints and can hold up the process by up to three months. If you must get FBI clearance, begin this process before or as soon as you start your home study. Once the clearance comes back, have the caseworker finish and date the home study using the date on which the fingerprints were issued, if possible, so that the home study stays current as long as possible.

11. *Statement from each of you declaring that you are not addicted to drugs or alcohol and that you have never been treated for a drug or alcohol addiction.*

As part of the study, you will be asked to provide identifying information such as your name, address, telephone number, and citizenship. You will also be required to answer questions about your history, lifestyle, and attitudes.

Autobiographical Information

Autobiographical information includes a physical description and information about where and how you were raised. Did your parents teach consistent values? Did they emphasize education or sports? Were they very involved in your life; did they encourage independence; were they domineering? Did they abuse alcohol, or were they violent or undisciplined in their lifestyle? How was love demonstrated, and what was the method of discipline? You will be asked to provide background information on your parents, including their names, ages, professions, and work histories, and to say something about your relationship with and attitude toward them, both when you were a child and now.

The names, professions, and ages of any siblings will be requested, along with a description of your relationship with them. Other questions will cover your schooling and education level, your social life as a child and teenager, your interests and hobbies, your profession and work history, your personal strengths and weaknesses, and any history of psychological counseling.

Your Marriage

Considerable attention will be devoted to your marriage. You will be asked about your premarital relationship (how you met, when you were engaged), how you resolve differences, how your relationship has grown and changed over the years, and your spouse's assets and liabilities, including his or her overall emotional stability and maturity as a person and a marriage partner. It is not appropriate for a caseworker to question you about your sex life.

Your Religious Background and Values

Another part of the study will look at your values and religion. You may be asked about your religious tradition, your church, temple, or synagogue attendance, your religious faith as a child, and your current religious beliefs and what impact they have on your life. If you and your spouse practice different faiths, the caseworker will want to know whether this will create a conflict in raising a child. If you do not participate in an organized religion, highlight your strong family values and whatever beliefs provide inner strength and comfort.

Some of the questions in the home study will have to do with character. For example, you may be asked about your goals and how you set and reach them. Discussing your values and their origins is another important aspect of the home study investigation.

Parenting Issues

Be prepared to talk at length about parenting issues. Why do you want to be a parent? Why do you want to adopt? What do you see as an appropriate method of discipline? (Some states require a declaration that you will not use corporal punishment.) Some people feel pressured to say that they will not spank their child, even though they know in their hearts that occasions may arise when they will do so. Nearly every adoptive couple we have talked with believes that at some point a spanking may be appropriate, and most social workers will agree. However, there is no point in discussing with the social worker why you think that a spanking should be given at certain times. If you think it would be false to say that you will never spank your child, tell the caseworker that you will focus on passive forms of discipline and not on corporal punishment. Instead, you would remove the child from the dangerous situation. If the child is unruly, you would remove him, take away a favorite toy, or place him in a "time out" chair.

Other parenting questions will concern the parenting styles of each partner, and how your own styles will be the same or different from your parents'. What attitudes and values do you hope to pass on to your child(ren)? What parenting and child care skills do you already possess, and what is your willingness to acquire new skills? Will one parent be home to care for the child? If not, who will care for the child? How much experience have you had with children? Are you able to give and receive affection? If you have children already, what is their attitude toward the idea of a new sibling?

Infertility Issues

Another area the home study will certainly explore will be your attitudes toward infertility and adoption. You will be questioned about the following:

- Your infertility diagnosis and treatment(s)
- Your infertility resolution
- The impact of infertility on your marriage
- How you came to choose adoption and what resources you used to come to that decision
- What parenting an adopted child means to you (How will this differ from parenting a biological child?)
- What kind of child you seek to adopt (Caucasian newborn, etc.)
- What your attitudes toward birth parents are
- How you feel about the idea of your child seeking his birth parents
- What adoption resources you have access to, including others you know who have adopted

Your Home

The caseworker may ask what you paid for your home and its current value, and what kinds of neighborhood and community resources you have access to—parks, schools, libraries, museums, etc.

Don't go crazy trying to get your home into order. If anything is clearly a potential danger (no cover over the fireplace, frayed wires, clutter that is a fire hazard), take care of it before you have a home study. Have a fire extinguisher and other safety features present in your home. But don't act as if your house is about to be photographed for *Better Homes and Gardens*. The social worker is primarily interested that the home can accommodate a baby or older child. In her report, she will comment on the bedroom or area of the home where the child will sleep.

Don't worry, especially if you already have a child, if your home is not spotlessly clean. Social workers are not looking to see whether Mr. and Mrs. Clean live at your home; they just want to make sure that your home is a safe and healthful environment. If life is getting a little crazy, of course, you could always treat yourself to a housekeeping service before your home study appointment. You will be much more at ease knowing that the cobwebs have been dusted away.

Your Finances

You will be expected to disclose your salaries, savings, and other resources, as well as your debts, health insurance, and life insurance. Your financial status should indicate that you have enough discretionary income each month to meet the needs of a child. However, a large savings account and a substantial stock portfolio are not necessary for you to pass a home study. A social worker will instead look for savings of perhaps two or three months' salary set aside for emergencies, and a general sense that you and your spouse manage your money sensibly.

SAMPLE HOME STUDY

Following is a mock home study to use as a guide. Although it may seem overly perfect, remember: Most home studies are written to show your best assets. This one is very similar to ones used in actual adoptions.

SOCIAL HISTORY

John Smith is a Caucasian American male, born July 4, 1960, in Cape May, New Jersey (verified). Mr. Smith is six feet one inch tall, weighs 190 pounds, and has brown hair and eyes.

John is warm, sincere, and genuine. He openly expresses his desire to adopt a child and raise a family.

John was born and raised in Cape May, New Jersey. In 1978 he graduated from Cape May High School and attended Rutgers University in New Brunswick, New Jersey, where he received a degree in accounting in 1983.

John states that his family was very traditional. His father is vice-president of a bank in Cape May, New Jersey, and his mother is an innkeeper, also in Cape May. Although his father worked hard, he still managed to spend time with John and took him to the shore and on skiing trips. He describes his mother also as hardworking. He vividly describes the fun he and his cousins had living at the shore. Both of his parents are described as people who emphasized values and were fair and consistent.

John and his three siblings hardly presented any discipline problems to their parents. When John had to be disciplined, both of his parents were fair and consistent. Very infrequently did they spank him, but rather talked to him about what he had done wrong.

John has two older sisters and one younger brother. All of his siblings live within the Cape May area. He maintains a warm, close relationship with all three.

Upon graduation from college, John took a job with a real estate firm in Cape May. He worked as an accountant for two years. In 1975 he worked with an accounting firm as an auditor. He took time away from this job to travel through the United States. He states that he was feeling restless and did not want to spend his youth behind a desk working with numbers. He feels that the two and a half years he spent traveling have now helped him to feel more settled. If he had not taken this adventure, he would never have met his wife, Carol.

After traveling, John came back to Cape May and joined an accounting firm in 1990. In 1995 he was named a partner. He says he enjoys his job, but sometimes finds the work tedious and exhausting. He jogs and plays tennis to release his stress.

John and his family are still very close and enjoy activities together. His father has assisted him in business. They still enjoy playing golf together as well as working on home projects. It is clear that his desire to have children is based on his happy childhood as well as his love for his nieces and nephews.

SOCIAL HISTORY

Carol Jones-Smith is a Caucasian American of Irish background who was born on January 16, 1966, in Philadelphia, Pennsylvania (verified). She is five feet five inches tall and weighs 125 pounds. She was reared in the suburbs of Philadelphia, Pennsylvania. Carol's mother stayed at home to rear her children while her father worked as a plumber. Carol's parents and one of her two sisters reside in Pennsylvania. Her other sister lives in California.

Carol is very sociable, warm, and easygoing. Carol desires to be a full-time homemaker and stay-at-home mom until the child is at least two years old.

Carol states that her family is loving. She is close to both parents and believes that they taught her values such as respect and honesty. Although she was never a difficult child, she states that at times she was mischievous. She believes her parents raised her well and disciplined her fairly. Her parents usually took away privileges as a means of discipline.

Carol was very sociable growing up and was involved in Girl Scouts and church activities. She believes that her association with her church instilled many positive character qualities. She enjoyed the many church-related activities as well as camping with the Girl Scouts. Her mother volunteered for the Scouts as well as the PTA and the school library. After high school she went to Pennsylvania State University where she graduated with a degree in elementary education in 1978.

For two years after graduating from college, she substitute-taught, because no full-time teaching positions were available. She and John maintained a long-distance relationship until she could find a job in Cape May.

In the fall of 1991 she took a position as a second-grade teacher. She enjoys teaching and says that second-grade children are old enough to learn, yet young enough not to be a discipline problem.

Carol's hobbies include reading, golf, music, and home projects. She and John enjoy day trips, long walks, and bicycle rides. For special occasions, such as Christmas and baby showers, she enjoys making gifts. She loves having the summers free to focus on such activities.

MARITAL RELATIONSHIP

John and Carol were married on June 10, 1992, in Philadelphia, Pennsylvania (verified). They met in the summer of 1989 while she was visiting her sister in California. He was attracted to her right from the beginning. She was a little bit unsure of a man who was taking such an extended "vacation." After talking to and then maintaining a long-distance relationship with him, she began to understand his commitment to a secure lifestyle while still having a spirit of adventure. In

1990 they became engaged. In the fall of 1991 she took a position as an elementary school teacher in Cape May.

In the initial stages of their relationship, Carol's parents were concerned about the age difference between them (six years) and his job situation. But after he went back to work for a large accounting firm and seemed settled, they soon began to like and trust John. Today they have a comfortable relationship with all four of their parents. John and Carol enjoy spending the holidays with family members. In fact, they say that the more extended-family members present for celebrations, the better. Birthday parties for family members are celebrated by parents and siblings.

The Smiths' good relationships with family are also expressed in their marriage. John and Carol state that they communicate well and often have deep discussions while taking long walks on the beach. They seldom argue, and when they do, they usually compromise until the difference is resolved. They state that their marriage is excellent.

Carol and John appear to be thoughtful of each other's needs. For example, John did not want Carol to continue infertility treatment that would cause her emotional or physical discomfort or to take medications that could have adverse side effects.

VALUES AND RELIGION

Both John and Carol attended church as children and believe it is important for children to receive a solid religious upbringing. As children, John attended a Lutheran church and Carol attended an Episcopalian church. John and Carol are currently visiting churches and believe they will select a Lutheran church in Cape May that is very family oriented and provides special programs for children.

The Smiths both value family life, marriage, and hard work and commitment. They say that they obtained these values from their family and from their friends. John and Carol also have seen the problems in children's lives when parents are not fully committed to the responsibility of parenting or to the marriage.

The Smiths have set several goals that they have reached, including purchasing a home, planting a vegetable garden, and establishing a savings account for a child. Each year they sit down on January 1 or the weekend of the holiday and set individual goals and goals as a couple. This year they decided that they will each read a good book a month. They also want to finish the basement and have already made arrangements with a contractor. Their primary goal is to adopt a child, and they have set aside money to begin the process.

PARENTING ATTITUDES

John and Carol believe they will raise their children according to the positive set of values that helped to shape them. They love children and often care for their siblings' children. This love for family makes them long even more for a child of their own.

In disciplining their children for wrong behavior, they plan to use "time out" or take away a favorite activity or toy.

ATTITUDE TOWARD ADOPTION

John and Carol have undergone about four years of unsuccessful infertility treatment. Carol has endometriosis, and John has a low sperm count. Carol has had surgery and has taken infertility drugs while having intrauterine inseminations done. They decided that more advanced treatment would be too financially and emotionally draining for them. Carol and John both state that the hormonal therapy has not caused any adverse physical or emotional reactions.

They have chosen to end infertility treatment since successful pregnancy is very unlikely. Also, they decided that they were not seeking a pregnancy but wanted a child, and that adoption would provide them with this opportunity. Both John and Carol feel adoption is a very positive alternative to biological children.

The Smiths have read a number of books about the adoption process as well as the raising of an adopted child. They appear to have a good understanding of adoption. For example, they both agree that openly sharing information with a child about her adoption is important. Yet they state that they do not want to overemphasize the difference and perhaps make the child feel out of place. John and Carol are comfortable in communicating with a child's birth parents (i.e., sending photos and letters). Also they recognize that their child may someday seek her birth parents, and understand that this would not be a negative reflection on their relationship with their child.

Carol said that once she adopted, she would want to communicate with other adoptive moms. The Smiths are members of RESOLVE. If they have a child, Mrs. Smith plans to join a play group in which many of the children are adopted.

FINANCE AND THE HOME

John and Carol live in a lovely, well-maintained Victorian house that is within walking distance of the beach. The home has a large eat-in kitchen that John completely renovated. John also renovated a playroom/den. The child's bedroom is spacious and comfortable. In this room there is already a child's toy cradle filled with stuffed animals.

The home is valued at about $160,000, and as John continues to make further improvements, the home may increase in value.

John earns about $60,000 per year, and Carol earns $22,000 per year (verified). The Smiths have no debts except their mortgage payment of nearly $900 per month and property taxes of $300 per month. He has a life insurance policy worth about $150,000, and she, through work, has one valued at $35,000.

TYPE OF CHILD REQUESTED AND FROM WHOM

The Smiths are interested in adopting a healthy Caucasian infant. They have sent letters to friends expressing their desire to adopt. Many people have responded, wishing them well. Next week an advertisement will be placed in a small newspaper in Central New Jersey. An attorney, John Johnson, has been retained by the Smiths.

REFERENCES

Each reference (verified) cites the Smiths as a couple who would provide a loving, moral, stable home for a child. Those who know them say that they are respected by friends and family, are committed to each other, and are energetic, fun-loving people who would provide much happiness to a child.

HEALTH STATUS

Both Carol and John are in good health, according to Dr. Laura Jones, are able to care for a child, and are expected to live a normal life span (verified). Neither person is a smoker.

RECOMMENDATION

John and Carol Smith appear to be open, expressive, and caring individuals who have strong family relationships. It is clear from the love that they express for each other and for their family members that they would offer a truly loving home to a child. They are recommended as adoptive parents.

POSTPLACEMENT SUPERVISORY VISITS

Postplacement supervisory visits are a series of visits made to your home by a caseworker or social worker to ensure that the family is adjusting well to the child and that the child herself is doing well. Supervisory visits are simply a time for you and the caseworker to share how the baby is developing.

Information gathered at a postplacement supervisory visit will begin with the child's medical progress. You should keep a record of his doctor's appointments, illnesses, and routine vaccines. Most people will simply tell the caseworker when the child had his last well-baby checkup and whether he had any reaction to the vaccines.

The caseworker will ask about the child's eating and sleeping patterns, which will change as the child progresses. If the caseworker visits you when the child is two months old, you may share, for example, that he is taking about six four-ounce bottles per day of Similac with iron, and that he generally sleeps from eight P.M. to six A.M., wakes up once in the middle of the night, and during the day has a morning nap, an afternoon nap, and a later afternoon nap. When the caseworker visits you again in two months, you will tell her that the baby is now having apple sauce and rice cereal twice a day, goes to bed around eight P.M. and gets up at six A.M., seldom wakes up in the middle of the night, and generally sleeps for two hours in the morning and an hour and a half in the afternoon.

At each visit you will share with the caseworker the progress your child is making. For example, if the caseworker visits you when the child is two months old, you will probably say that the child smiles and responds to facial expressions. At four months old you will say he can play with his feet and hold an object in his hands. At six months old he may be crawling, sitting up, and cooing.

Some agencies focus on you and your child's appearance as well as the appearance and cleanliness of the home. If you are feeling overwhelmed, hire someone to clean your home before each visit. The investment is well worth the expense, simply because you will feel so much more comfortable during the caseworker's visit.

Finally, the caseworker will want to know how your family is adjusting to the child's arrival. Both of you will be required to be present for at least some of the visits. Sometimes husbands, either because of nervousness or because they do not want to steal the limelight from their wives, do not interact with the child during a caseworker's visits. However, it is very important that the social worker see *both* parents holding and feeding a baby, or attending to the needs of an older child.

The question of how much time the adoptive parents spend with the child will probably come up. The only wrong answer is "none." Social workers are aware that one spouse may work ten- or twelve-hour days, and that both parents may work outside the home. Again, a commonsense approach is all that is required.

Chapter Eighteen

Adoption Expenses

Money is often an emotional issue, and the way you feel about it can affect the way you approach adoption. Most people become involved with adoption after spending years and thousands of dollars on infertility workups and unsuccessful treatments. Often there is a sense of anger about spending more money on another procedure—adoption—that, like infertility treatment, has no guarantee of success.

Paying out thousands of dollars with no tangible return makes a person feel victimized and out of control. Feelings of "Why me?" are natural and common, as are feelings of anger and a sense of futility. The question is, how do we cope with them? Some people cope by developing an unhealthy defensiveness and extreme skepticism toward the idea of adoption. Such attitudes will need to be dealt with and worked through before you take any steps toward adoption. If you do not work through them, they will end up being communicated to the birth mother; you will not be comfortable meeting her, and she will know this. She will feel your angst and your defensiveness. Many adoptive couples have indirectly projected their insecurities and defensiveness onto the birth mother. She will not understand the uneasiness she feels about you as a couple, of course; all she will know is that she has "bad vibes" about you.

Even more self-defeating than this projection of feelings by the adoptive couple is their direct discussion with the birth mother of their fears of losing money or making an emotional investment in an unsuccessful adoption plan. One birth mother let a prospective couple know that she did not want to hear about the adoptive mother's disappointments with unsuccessful infertility treatments and other previous adoption plans. This birth mother felt that she had enough of her own problems; she really did not need to hear the adoptive mother pour her heart out about the lost money and failed attempts.

It may be appropriate and even necessary for the adoptive couple to share their feelings about their emotional and financial investment later in the relationship; however, several birth mothers have experienced this sharing as attempts by adoptive couples to "lay a guilt trip" on them. Remember, a birth mother usually assumes you are middle or upper-middle-class in lifestyle and finances; she assumes your life is structured and in control. It is her life that is out of control, and placing her child for adoption is a way of regaining control. The last thing she wants and needs is to feel that you doubt her honesty or her motives, and that is what will be portrayed if you have not worked through your feelings of victimization.

Adoption author Patricia Johnston writes that finances can be a most uncomfortable issue for everyone involved in the adoption process. Prospective adoptive parents do not like to think about the costs because it reminds them further of how they are different from those who can give birth to a child. Professionals who have to ask clients directly for fees are sometimes uncomfortable charging them, although they rely upon these fees for their livelihood and the functioning of the agency or office. Nor does the issue of fees end when you receive your child. Feelings about the adoption process, including the costs, can color our attitudes for a long time.

Confronting your feelings of victimization helps minimize any anger or bitterness. It is also important to make sure there is clarity between you and the agency or attorney about what fees and expenses are your responsibility. To maintain a good attitude throughout the whole adoption process, you want to make sure not to let misunderstandings get in the way or questions go too long unanswered.

One understanding that needs to be established, of course, is that no matter which route you take, all adoptions, except some public agency adoptions, will involve expenses. If you are pursuing a public agency adoption of a child with special needs, plan to spend from zero to $2,000; for an independent adoption, $5,000 to $25,000; for a domestic agency adoption, $7,000 to $25,000; and for an international adoption, $10,000 to $30,000. Fortunately, there are now adoption tax credits available, and your employer may offer adoption benefits.

Be aware that some attorneys and agencies do overcharge. As Christine Adamec writes in *There ARE Babies to Adopt*, a higher fee does not mean a "better" baby or a better quality of service. She notes that in 1994, one agency was charging about $30,000 per adoption, yet was withholding important birth parent background information.

The expenses you can expect to incur for different types of adoptions follow.

INDEPENDENT ADOPTION

Almost every step of the adoption process requires money. First, a word about birth mother expenses because you most likely will be paying for at least some birth mother-related expenses. Many birth mothers begin interacting with an adoptive couple with no desire or need to accept monies for living expenses. During her pregnancy, however, a birth mother's circumstances will sometimes change, giving rise to a need for assistance. When a birth mother requests help at that point, couples are often quick to feel taken advantage of. They should know that most birth mothers are really reluctant to ask for and accept money and do so only in time of great need. If that need arises shortly after a couple begins working with a birth mother, a couple must be careful not to overreact. Any rapport that exists between the birth mother and the couple could be ruined if the couple suddenly becomes defensive about money.

Then there is the birth mother who asks for money up front, sometimes in large amounts. One birth mother told an adoptive couple that she wanted $12,000 as soon as the baby was born. The couple was speechless, but was able to refer her to their attorney to discuss the amount requested. When asked why she chose $12,000, the birth mother replied that she knew that was the amount adoption agencies were paid, and she assumed she would be paid the same thing, since an agency was not involved. Once it was explained that such an amount was not legal to pay and that only reasonable living expenses were allowed, things were fine. She did place her baby with the couple, and she received reasonable living expenses as allowed by law. We will be saying more about how to handle this kind of situation later in the chapter.

An independent adoption is usually less expensive than an agency adoption. Expenses you are likely to incur include the following (amounts are approximate):

Attorney's fee: $5,000
Advertising costs: $250 to $450 per month
The low figure is the approximate cost of placing an ad in a daily newspaper (usually for a small or average-size town) twice a week. The high figure is the approximate cost of placing an ad in two big-city newspapers twice a week. Sometimes you must hire two attorneys—one in each state or two in the same state so that there is not conflict of interest. Usually the fee is not double.

Telephone installation: $150
You might also consider a distinctive ring option at about $4 per month.

Telephone calls: $50 to $100 per month
The figure depends on the number of calls you receive. Add to this the expense of having an extra line. Once you make contact with a birth mother, she may want to talk with you at length, thus increasing your telephone bill.

The home study: $600 to $1,700

In states like Massachusetts, where independent adoptions are illegal, the home study could be as high as $4,000. A $4,000 home study is not necessarily more comprehensive than a $600 home study. Call around to find out about fees.

Counseling for birth mother: $50 to $100 per hour

Many birth mothers do not ask couples to pay for counseling, but it should be offered by the agency social worker or the attorney representing you. The birth parents often receive counseling if the adoptive couple wants to pursue an identified/agency adoption.

Birth mother's obstetrical and delivery bill: $2,000 to $3,700

Most birth mothers are covered by their own insurance or Medicaid, so you will seldom have to pay this cost. You may need to help her pay her insurance premiums, however.

Birth mother's hospital bill: $3,500 to $7,500

Without complications. Again, most birth mothers are covered.

Infant's hospital nursery bill: $1,000

Many hospitals will not process the infant's bill under the birth mother's coverage (private or Medicaid) once it is disclosed that the baby will be placed for adoption. Your own insurance should pay for this bill. The key language in your medical insurance benefits booklet is the definition of "dependent," which should include the child to be adopted, over whom you have "dominion and control" (meaning coverage should be automatic). Some booklets still specify that coverage begins upon the finalization of the adoption. This simply reflects the drafter's ignorance of the adoption process, since finalization can occur up to one year after placement. Your attorney should provide an explanation to your benefits office or to the insurance company.

Infant's medication, pediatric exam, and circumcision

Again, your insurance should cover this.

Keep close track of all your expenses. You may be eligible for a tax credit (see page 355).

AGENCY ADOPTION

If an agency places a healthy infant directly with you—if, that is, you did not find your own birth mother—their fee may range anywhere from about $7,000 to $35,000. The agency may have a standard fee regardless of what the birth mother's needs are: It may charge you a fee of $12,000 to $15,000 and then add on to that the birth mother's medical, living, and counseling expenses, as well as attorney fees. It is crucial that you understand whether the fees quoted to you by the agency include the birth mother's medical, living, and counseling fees. It would be easy to misconstrue the agency's quoted fee of $12,000, for example, as being your total cost. More than one couple has been surprised when presented with doctor and hospital bills after having already paid the agency fees. If you hire your own attorney to represent you, that will be an additional fee.

In states in which only agencies can legally conduct an adoption, it is not uncommon for agencies to charge an outrageous amount.

IDENTIFIED AND FACILITATED ADOPTION

Some agencies specialize in identified adoptions and even provide workshops on how to find a birth mother. In this kind of adoption, the agency will generally charge a standard identified adoption fee of $4,000 to $12,000, in addition to legal fees and birth mother expenses, usually putting an identified adoption in a higher range than an independent adoption.

HOW TO KEEP YOUR EXPENSES TO A REASONABLE LEVEL

Like any other legal process, adoption requires professional assistance, and adoption specialists deserve to be paid a reasonable fee for their services. There are professionals, however, who prey on the emotions of desperate couples, claiming that if they do not pay a certain amount of money immediately, they will lose this once-in-a-lifetime opportunity to have a baby. Sometimes you need to rely on your instincts to tell you whether an attorney or an adoption agency social worker is pushing too hard or seems overly concerned with money. Here are some guidelines you may find helpful:

1. *View with caution any agency or attorney who asks for more than $1,500 up front without any service being rendered.* Having said that, you should know that there are several reputable agencies that are charging up to $4,000 to initiate your application. These agencies have written refund policies stating that the bulk of the monies will be refunded to you in a year or so if no placement occurs. Have your attorney check the agency's references, and telephone other couples who have obtained placements from the agency to find out whether they were satisfied with their experience.

2. *Make sure that any agency or attorney who charges you gives you an itemized bill.* An attorney may say that her fee is $3,000 for all services. This is fine. But if the bill keeps getting higher as the attorney does more work, or because new expenses keep popping up, make sure you receive an itemized bill.

3. *Find out whether there will be any additional charges for birth father issues.* This is one aspect of adoption procedure that many attorneys and agencies do not make clear. Find out whether there will be an additional fee, for example, if a birth father's rights must be terminated in court by a separate proceeding. Many agencies state that the adoptive couple's attorney must take care of any birth father rights if he does not sign an agency surrender. Again, ask for a written schedule of fees.

PAYING FOR A BIRTH MOTHER'S LIVING EXPENSES

Most states permit an adoptive couple to pay for the birth mother's living expenses. The amount paid may have to be preapproved by a judge, however, to ensure that there is no appearance of "baby buying." Some judges are very particular about this matter. Your attorney should guide you so that you do not pay extensive living expenses. Document all payments. It is best if all monies go through your attorney's escrow account to avoid any appearance of impropriety.

Legal living expenses usually include a few months of average rent (about $400 per month), food ($50 per week), and transportation to the doctor's office. However, what is deemed reasonable depends on the state and even the region of the state. The cost of living in a given place is what determines the appropriateness of expenses. It would be difficult to obtain a decent apartment in southern New Jersey for less than $500 a month, for example, while in northern New Jersey you will pay more like $750. The standard of reasonableness will also change if the birth mother has one or more children to care for.

Birth mothers do have crises—emergency car repairs and other unforeseen expenses. These should be dealt with on a case-by-case basis. Always have your attorney get your permission before advancing money that was not agreed upon beforehand.

Sometimes a birth mother will request money for placing a baby. Perhaps a friend or relative told her that this was a common practice, or perhaps she saw a television program or a magazine article about attorneys and agencies charging $25,000 to $50,000 for an adoption and asked herself, "If the attorney gets that much money, why can't I?" After all, she is the one going through pregnancy, labor, and delivery.

If a birth mother asks you for "placement money" or tells you of another couple who has offered her $10,000 for the baby, tell her that you do not want to jeopardize the baby's welfare. Tell her you would hate to see the baby removed from your home because the authorities discovered that you had paid her monies that are not allowed by law. Emphasize that you are willing to pay what is legal and that you would want to help in her time of need (assuming this is true), but that your attorney must approve everything involving money. You should ask the birth mother to contact your attorney to discuss the money issue further. One couple asked a birth mother who said she had had an offer for $10,000 from another couple, "Would you really want your baby to go to a couple who is willing to pay you $10,000 illegally?" The birth mother placed the child with the honest couple.

Some people can afford to take risks and others cannot. If a birth mother is asking for $1,000 a month in living expenses for herself and her three children, and you make contact with her when she is three months pregnant, these expenses alone will be $6,000—money that you could lose if she changes her mind. Some people can afford to lose this kind of money and move on to another adoption. If you are not among them, you may need to forgo that situation and look for a birth mother who is further along in her pregnancy or has fewer living expenses.

The problem of risk is one of the things that can make international adoption so attractive: You are not dependent upon the birth mother. Unless a country suddenly closes its doors to adoption, if you work with a reputable agency you are virtually guaranteed that your money will pay for what it is intended to. If you have access to $17,000, for example, you can put that money toward an international adoption and be fairly certain that in a matter of six to eight months you will have a baby. In addition, your tax credits can be applied for years to come if the costs of the adoption exceed $5,000—which most likely they will. Also, many international children are considered to have special needs, and you may qualify for an additional $6,000 tax credit each year.

ADOPTION INSURANCE

Some couples purchase adoption insurance to protect them in the event that a birth mother changes her mind. To be eligible, you must be working with an attorney who is using the insurance program. The premium should be low and cover a few thousand dollars in expenses. In the past, the insurance required very high premiums and covered large birth mother expenses, which only served to encourage couples to take on riskier adoptions and pay expenses indiscriminately. You should not be paying $4,000 in insurance premiums to cover $25,000 worth of expenses.

INTERNATIONAL ADOPTION

If you are dealing with an agency, the costs are generally well defined and payments are expected at regular intervals. The fee will vary depending upon the country from which you are adopting. Expect to spend between $7,000 and $30,000 including transportation, lodging, and meals, and having documents authenticated.

When you hire an independent agency, attorney, or facilitator, you should be charged in the range of $4,000 for their services—again, based on the country's fees and the cost of transportation and lodging.

The cost of an international adoption can vary widely, depending on how you go about it. If you have connections to an orphanage in another country, perhaps through a missionary or a religious organization, your only expenses may be $455 to the Immigration and Naturalization Service, the cost of your home study, the child's transportation costs, your transportation and lodging expenses if you travel, a donation to the orphanage, and about $1,500 for legal fees to have the adoption refinalized in the United States. Many times you can file your own papers and refinalize the adoption yourself and eliminate the legal fee. This may total well under $5,000. If you do not know of someone in another country, but you want to facilitate your own adoption instead of hiring an agency or facilitator to help you, you may be able to save $4,000 or more in administrative costs. You may, however, encounter many roadblocks that can add to the cost of the adoption.

By planning ahead, starting with your passport, you can lower many fees that increase when the process is expedited. For example, the country's embassy will usually double fees for the authentication of each dossier document when the papers must be stamped in three days instead of nine days. The fee can increase by several hundreds of dollars if, for example, the fee jumps from $30 per authentication of a document to $60. If you allow plenty of time for documents to be processed at the embassy or consulate, you will not incur the extra fees.

Also, send only important documents via an overnight carrier. There is seldom a need to send easily replaceable documents using Fed Ex or UPS. So instead of spending about $12 to send documents, you can usually send them Priority Mail for $3.20.

Airline rates can vary significantly depending upon when you travel. Usually rates are highest during the summer. Even the specific date you travel on can save you money. For example, leaving on Thanksgiving Day instead of the day before or after can save you several hundred dollars.

When staying in a country, find out if there is a host family with whom you can stay instead of at a hotel. The cost to stay in a home may be incidental, whereas the charge for staying at a Western-style hotel can be $100 to $300 per night.

If you plan to take gifts to the country, start to look for gift items as they come on sale instead of shopping at the last minute.

PUBLIC AGENCY ADOPTIONS

If your funds are very limited, you may want to consider adopting through a public agency. Not only do you pay little to nothing for these adoptions, but you may actually receive subsidies each month to help you support the child.

The fact that you cannot afford another route should not, however, be your primary motivation for selecting a public agency. You must be prepared and have a strong support system to handle the special needs a child adopted through this avenue may have.

If you want to adopt a child from a minority ethnic background, adopting through a public agency will probably be your least expensive route. However, there is no guarantee that you will be chosen when a committee meets to select a family for the child. You may end up waiting a long time.

PAYING FOR YOUR ADOPTION

If you want to adopt privately or internationally, you may not have $20,000 in the bank. Indeed, even a relatively inexpensive adoption will stretch most couples' resources. In her book *There Are Babies to Adopt*, Christine Adamec discusses various techniques for meeting these expenses, from asking relatives for help to taking out a second mortgage. There is nothing shameful about taking out a loan to adopt a baby, but the bank may not approve you because there is no "collateral" except the world's most valuable possession—your baby. You may find yourself thinking along the same lines as your bank, at first—a baby is not a financial investment. But if you consider that an adoption costs less than most new cars, you may gain a different perspective. Why not ride around in your '95 car a few more years instead of spending $25,000 on a new one? Then you can take the payments that you would have used for a car and pay back your "baby loan" for the next five years.

Compare adoption expenses with the costs of infertility treatment. Some infertility treatment is covered by a third party—your insurance company. When another party is paying the bill, the costs do not seem so bad. But many insurance companies do not pay for certain treatments, especially high-tech reproductive procedures such as in vitro fertilization. These kinds of procedures can cost $6,000 to $15,000 per cycle. And, of course, only a certain percentage of couples will achieve a successful pregnancy. Although you cannot choose adoption over having a biological child merely for economic reasons, you need to weigh whether one kind of investment is really more worth it to you than the other. If you were to take the money for two in vitro fertilization cycles, you could easily adopt a child, and probably in less time than it would take you to conceive and carry a child to term.

The truth is, people often decide they cannot afford adoption before they have really explored their options. Even if you have only a few thousand dollars in the bank, you can easily proceed with an adoption. Most attorneys and agencies do not ask for all the adoption fees and expenses up front—and if they do, you should probably not be dealing with them anyway. As you look through the expenses associated with an independent adoption, you will see that you are not required to pay a lot of money up front. You start by advertising, then you may begin helping a birth mother with living expenses, which can be paid monthly, and along the way you may be paying the attorney or agency its fees. If your budget does not allow you to pay an agency or attorney $5,000 to $10,000 up front, then don't. Most agencies charge $1,000 to $4,000 to begin processing your application, then ask for the next installment when a birth mother is matched with you. Even international adoption programs have a fee schedule and monies are paid over time. Adoptions usually take place in stages, allowing a couple time to save money as they go along. Some agencies will even work with you and wait to receive some of the funds after you have received state subsidies or employment benefits.

ADOPTION ASSISTANCE AS AN EMPLOYEE BENEFIT

Just as you must decide when to use limited resources toward an adoption instead of toward infertility treatment, some companies are beginning to see the financial value in providing adoption coverage to their employees. If an employee decides to adopt, that person (or the employee's wife) is probably not going to be accumulating the medical expenses associated with having a baby. For companies that are self-insured (meaning that the company and not a medical insurance company covers its employees' and their families' medical bills), the decision to provide adoption assistance can be even more of a financial incentive. If a self-insured company pays all or part of the costs associated with infertility treatment, as well as the medical costs associated with pregnancy, delivery, and care of a newborn— about $7,000 to $50,000 and up if there are complications—the company may view adoption assistance as a very worthwhile—and less expensive—benefit. Instead of paying what can be at least $20,000 in infertility and birth-related expenses, the company can have a policy of paying, for example, up to $5,000 toward an adoption. In South Carolina, as of this writing, state employees can be reimbursed $5,000 in adoption expenses for a healthy child and $10,000 for a child with special needs. As politicians begin to see the value of adoption, perhaps more states will begin offering their employees such benefits.

For more information about companies that provide adoption assistance, contact the National Adoption Center or Adoptive Families of America. If your company does not offer adoption assistance, you may want to advocate for such a policy. If you talk in terms of what a company can save, those who make such decisions may see the benefit.

Resources:

Adoptive Families of America
3333 Highway 100 North
Minneapolis, MN 55422
(800) 372-3300
(612) 535-4829
adoptivefam.org/

This group is the largest nonprofit organization in the United States providing resources and support to people interested in adoption.

THE ADOPTION TAX CREDIT

The 1996 federal minimum wage bill contains an adoption tax credit for expenses paid and adoptions finalized after January 1, 1997. Qualified expenses include adoption fees, court costs, your attorney's fees, and other adoption-related expenses such as travel. A tax credit is not the same as a tax deduction; a credit is far more generous. If, for example, you paid $15,000 in adoption expenses in 2000, and in 2000 you paid $3,000 in taxes, then you apply the credit and are given back $3,000 on your income tax for 2000. The following year, 2001, you can apply the $2,000 in tax credit and get $2,000 back. If you adopt two children in one year, then you are eligible for a $10,000 tax credit. This carry-over-to-the-next-year credit can be extended for five years and will continue beyond 2001 if your adoption takes place before January 1, 2002.

You can only take the full credit if your family's adjusted gross income is less than $75,000. Partial credits are available for those earning up to $115,000. If you are earning less than $75,000 per year and have adopted two children, chances are that you will not have paid $10,000 in federal taxes. So having this credit extend for five more years can mean that the IRS writes you a check each year for the next couple of years.

You cannot take the credit until the adoption is finalized—whether a domestic or international. If your child is placed with you in 2000, but the adoption is not finalized until the following year, you must wait until you file your 2001 taxes to receive the tax credit. If your internationally adopted child does not meet the IR-3 status, then you must readopt the child in the United States before you are eligible for the tax credit.

The tax credit can include expenses incurred from an unsuccessful adoption. If you incurred $2,000 in adoption expenses in 1999 from a failed adoption and in 2000 you adopted a non-special-needs child, and you incurred $4,000 in adoption expenses, then you can take the $5,000 credit. Although it sounds generous that you get a tax credit for a failed adoption, the truth is that by the time you pay for another adoption, you most likely will have exceeded the $5,000 cap. This credit does not permit you to count each adoption attempt as an adoption.

If in either a domestic or international adoption you make payments after the adoption is finalized (which is seldom done) then you use the tax credit the year of payment.

There is a $6,000 tax credit for a domestic adoption of a child with special needs. Check how your state defines special needs; your child may be eligible even if he was not placed through a social services agency. Because most children who have special needs are placed through social services agencies that have no or few fees, your tax credit can possibly be applied toward expenses for changes made to your home so that you can meet the child's special physical needs. Check with an accountant; your state agency may have to mandate certain changes to your home or articles to be purchased if you are to receive the tax credit.

If your employer provides adoption benefits, these benefits—up to $5,000 for an adoption and up to $6,000 for a special needs adoption—are nontaxable, unless the adoption was not finalized that year. Be careful: Although most employers do not give benefits until the adoption is finalized, if the employer does give benefits before the finalization, then this money from your employer is taxed as income.

Fortunately you can use the tax credit in addition to your employer's benefits if your expenses exceed the employer's benefits. For example, if your adoption costs $15,000, and your employer provides you with $5,000 toward the adoption, you can still take a tax credit for $5,000.

Relative adoptions, except for stepparent adoptions, appear to be covered by this legislation.

This tax credit is in effect only until 2001 but remains permanent for special needs adoptions. However, legislation may permit an extension of the credit indefinitely and increase the tax credit to $10,000 per child as well as increase the maximum family earnings to be eligible to receive the tax credit. As of this writing no new laws are in effect.

Remember you are dealing with the IRS; they have improved their public image considerably, but they are not a social services agency. Because the tax credit has only been available for few years, the IRS agents and your accountant may not be very experienced in the expenses associated with an adoption. The IRS states that fees paid must be reasonable and necessary, so keep a receipt of everything to prove what you spent. Also keep track of the little things: your mileage to your adoption agency, medical expenses you incurred before you even adopted, and every meal eaten out that was related to the adoption.

HOW TO TAKE A CREDIT OR EMPLOYER BENEFIT EXCLUSION

You must file form 8839 with your 1040 or 1040A to take the credit or exclusion. If you are married, you must file a joint return. (There are exceptions for those divorced or separated.) Also, you must provide the child's identifying number on form 8839. If your child does not have a social security number and is not eligible for one, apply for an individual taxpayer identification number on form W-7A. You can also apply, using form W-7A, for an adoption taxpayer identification number for U.S. born children who are in the process of being adopted.

Getting Your Child a Social Security Number

You will want to get your child's social security number as soon as possible. Sometimes there is a problem if a child receives an SSN under one of the birth parents' last names instead of yours. Then you have to reapply. To find out if your child is eligible for an SSN call (800) 772-1213. Most people find getting an SSN to be very simple. Usually you must go to the Social Security Office and apply in person with your child's birth certificate and adoption decree.

NONRECURRING EXPENSES SUBSIDIES

States provide what is called nonrecurring expenses for the adoption of a child with special needs, which are one time subsidies that must be requested *before* the child is adopted. Some states are very strict and require that the child could not have been placed without subsidies and no other home could be found for the child.

Some states are more flexible and allow children adopted internationally and independently to be eligible. Most states provide between $500 and $2,000. In South Carolina, for example, families adopting internationally receive $1,500 per adoption, and nearly all children adopted from another country are considered special needs because they have no or very limited family and medical background reports and usually have been in an orphanage. If your state provides this benefit, and you are adopting from a country such as Ukraine where you do not know who your child will be until you get to the country, and the adoption is then finalized within a few days of meeting your child, you or someone else must send the sub-sidy specialist the name and birth date of your child. The specialist will fax the agreement to you; you then sign the agreement and fax it back. Your adoption agency should take care of this for you if you are overseas, as the government office may not fax documents to another country. However, your subsidy specialist will fax them to your agency, and your agency can then fax them on to you to in the foreign country to sign.

There is no maximum income to be eligible for this subsidy, but the docu-ment given to you does ask "Do you need this subsidy to complete the adoption?" This seems like a trick question since the government does not give you the sub-sidy monies until after the child's adoption is finalized and you have usually paid all of the expenses. If you could not afford the adoption, you would not be doing it. So the clients write in response to this question of need, "Yes, it would help."

One adoptive mother, who is a pediatrician, and her husband, a general practitioner, were about to adopt a child who was born with nerve damage to the inner ear. They applied for the nonrecurring expenses subsidy. The ear problem miraculously corrected without medical intervention. The parents had already received the subsidy. After the child's hearing problem was gone, the mother con-tacted the state and tried to reimburse the money. Forget it; the state does not take money back. Their other child who had been adopted had profound learning delays, even though she had had excellent prenatal care. The mom just thought, "Well, that money can go toward the expenses of the child who truly has special needs." The child with profound learning problems was so healthy at birth that the mom and dad never even considered applying for subsidies.

Summary

Use your imagination when looking for ways to pay for your adoption or receive benefits after adoption. Families come to adoption-information seminars and have no idea that funds are available. Also, when families really are serious about adopting, they often find that family members are very supportive. Also, your church or house of worship, which probably supports many worthwhile pro-jects, may also view your adopting a child as a community endeavor and not just a family matter.

Taking a loan is another way to get the money you need, especially one that you can pay back soon. If you know, for example, that you will receive a tax credit of $5,000 per child, that your state will give you $1,500 in nonrecurring expenses, and that your employer will give you $2,000 toward your adoption once it is final-ized, then you may consider taking out a second mortgage that you will immedi-ately pay back once you receive the $8,500. Of course, $8,500 will not cover the expenses of most international adoptions, but it certainly can make a significant contribution. And if you adopt two children at the same time, and the expenses for the second child are not very high, you may find that once you receive back double the money from these resources that it significantly offsets the cost of the adoption.

One family received $10,000 per child for the adoption of two international children as part of a state employee benefits package; plus they received more funds in nonrecurring adoption subsidies. Because they adopted two children, and the international fee was only $4,000 more for a second adoption, the benefits from the state more than offset the extra expenses incurred. Their adoption expenses were nearly all paid for through the husband's employer and the subsidies.

Also, remember most adoptions do not take place overnight, so there is no need to spend all the money for an adoption in one lump sum. Most agencies do not expect you to pay large amounts of funds at one time. Even if you are spending $20,000 for an adoption, this is usually spread over a six month period of time.

Chapter Nineteen

Healthy Mothers, Healthy Babies

I f you are adopting independently or through a domestic agency, you may be actively involved in the birth mother's prenatal care. The level of medical attention a woman receives while pregnant can greatly influence both her health and the baby's. Not surprisingly, adoptive parents are usually very concerned about the quality of medical care a birth mother receives. Often, indeed, a birth mother has not had any prenatal care before she contacts a couple. Perhaps she did not know she was pregnant at first, and when she found out, she immediately began to make adoption arrangements before doing anything else.

You and your attorney will often make the initial medical arrangements if a birth mother has not already done so. Here is some advice about how to find an obstetrician.

FINDING AN OBSTETRICIAN

First, try to get as much information as possible. It is best to have more than just a list of names from the telephone book. Find out whether the birth mother prefers a male or a female doctor, and do your best to honor that preference. Contact an adoption support group or the RESOLVE chapter closest to where the birth mother is going to deliver her baby, and ask for names of physicians who understand what is involved in an adoption and what special needs a birth mother may have before, during, and after the baby's birth.

A physician should be sensitive and recognize that each birth mother has different needs. Some, for example, may show detachment toward the baby in utero, while others may be very interested. One birth mother may want to see the baby's image on the ultrasound screen, while another may not. Some women want to go to prenatal classes; others do not. After the birth, some birth mothers want to see and care for the baby while in the hospital. Others do not.

If you can't find the right physician through a support group, there are other sources to try. An adoption agency in the birth mother's area may know of some obstetricians who support adoption. Try contacting them. Another person to ask is your gynecologist or infertility specialist. Then there's your attorney, who has handled many adoptions and may even have a list of names on hand.

Some HMOs will pay for a birth mother's expenses if she uses a doctor who is on the adoptive parents' insurance plan. This is not the case with conventional insurance policies. If the HMO pays for the obstetrician's bill, it will pay for the participating hospital's bill as well. Just remember, whether or not you find a doctor who can be paid through your insurance program, the most important criterion for selecting her is that she is supportive of the birth mother's adoption plans.

All this being said, however, most birth mothers will be using Medicaid, which just a few years ago was not the case. Using Medicaid means that you and the birth mother will have much less say in selecting a physician. At a clinic a birth mother may see several different health practitioners, each of whom may have varying views on adoption. Birth mothers are generally very savvy and know how to handle this situation.

Ask the birth mother whether she has any preference about where she receives treatment. The advantage of using a clinic is that they frequently offer prenatal care free or at a minimal cost, based on a sliding scale; also, she and the baby will both be covered in the hospital. Even if your insurance is supposed to cover the expenses of the child, there is sometimes some ambiguity in this area, so it is reassuring to know that in the event of a medical problem, Medicaid will cover the child's medical bills.

To find a prenatal clinic, call the state Medicaid office in the state where the birth mother will deliver and get information from a staff member. In some states a woman who has no medical coverage can go to a prenatal clinic without paying anything under a plan called "presumptive eligibility." The purpose of this plan is to encourage women to seek prenatal care regardless of their financial status. At this first visit the clinic staff will determine, based on the woman's financial resources, what assistance programs she may qualify for. In New York State, for example, if a woman qualifies for Medicaid, the clinic staff can assist her in completing the forms right there instead of at a Medicaid office.

Some states have special prenatal programs like the Healthy Mothers, Healthy Babies program. To find the coordinator in your state, contact:

Healthy Mothers, Healthy Babies
409 12th St., SW
Washington, DC 20024-2188
(202) 863-8444, ext. 2458
(202) 484-5107 (fax)
They will send you a free newsletter.

Contacting the Obstetrician

Before deciding on an obstetrician, you will need to call and ask some questions. For example:

1. *What are your fees?* The physician may want payment up front to protect himself in case the birth mother changes her mind. If she does, she may not be able to pay for the services rendered, and the adoptive parents will not want to. Although the physician's viewpoint is understandable, you certainly do not want to end up paying for a woman's medical bills only to have her change her mind. If a physician does ask for payment up front, and you truly believe that the birth mother is going to place the baby with you, then go ahead and pay. But never pay the doctor more because this is an adoption. That is unethical.

2. *What kind of insurance does the office accept?* When it comes to medical insurance, ask the doctor's office the following questions: (a) Do they accept Medicaid payments? (Most private physicians do not.) (b) Do they expect payment up front before the insurance carrier has reimbursed them? (Some physicians want to be paid up front; the insurance company then reimburses the patient.)

3. *If a woman has no insurance, what is her payment schedule?* If you will be paying for the birth mother's medical expenses, try to set the payment schedule. Try to pay as little as possible before the baby's birth in case the birth mother changes her mind. These medical expenses cannot be recouped. Have the monies put in your attorney's escrow account; if the woman changes her mind about the adoption, the monies will not be sent to the physician.

   The practice of placing the woman's medical expenses in escrow may be deemed illegal in some instances. Some authorities believe the practice should be prohibited when payment is contingent on the birth mother's placing the child for adoption. Never pressure a woman to place her baby for adoption by telling her that her medical bills will not be paid if she does not. Payment arrangements are between you and the doctor.

4. *Will the clinic staff or physician give medical treatment to a woman who will be placing her baby for adoption?* Even before making the first appointment, let the obstetrician know right away of the woman's adoption plans. This is better than finding out later that the obstetrician or the support staff has a negative attitude toward adoption. When you call, you may start by saying, "I am a prospective adoptive mother and am helping a woman find an obstetrician. This woman is planning to place this baby for adoption through private channels with my husband and me. I want to know whether your staff will care for a pregnant woman placing a baby for adoption." If the person answering the phone says that the obstetrician will accept a woman placing her baby for adoption, ask the following questions:

- *Has the obstetrician treated other women who were placing the baby for adoption through private channels?* If the staff says yes, you may want to ask whether everything went well.
- *Does the office have a policy about treating birth mothers?* Most offices will not have a written policy, but by asking the question you let them know that you expect professional protocol to be followed in treating the birth mother.
- *Will the obstetrician permit the adoptive parents to be in the delivery room with the birth mother?* If you and the birth mother are very sure it is in everyone's best interest for you to take her to prenatal visits and to be present in the delivery room, discuss this with the obstetrician right away. Even if you do not have plans to be in the delivery room, this is still a good question to ask. If the obstetrician says yes, this probably signals that she has positive views about adoption.

You might consider having your attorney's staff screen obstetricians before you or the birth mother calls for an appointment. By doing so you can be saved some awkward moments on the telephone. After the attorney's staff has screened various obstetricians' offices, you can then call the office yourself and simply make an appointment for the birth mother.

In the past few years there has been a marked improvement in the attitudes of physicians, nurses, social workers, and others who may be involved in caring for the birth mother, but you could still encounter a lack of understanding and discretion. The obstetrician's staff should be aware of the birth mother's situation, however, in case she wants to make special prenatal arrangements. For instance, she may not want to attend birthing classes that include discussions on baby care. Whether you want to let the health care staff know that you are the prospective adoptive parent is a matter of personal preference. If you will be accompanying the birth mother to her prenatal visits, you will probably want to say who you are, but be prepared for the possibility that although they support the birth mother, they see you as an intruder.

5. *Does the obstetrician have a female midwife or nurse practitioner on staff?* If the obstetrician is male, the birth mother may feel more comfortable being treated by a female nurse practitioner. Nurse practitioners and midwives often have broader views on women's issues, moreover, and may be more supportive of women who choose adoption.

6. *At what hospital(s) does the obstetrician deliver babies?* This is an important question because the social services departments of certain hospitals are known for their negative attitude toward adoption.

Determining the Staff's Attitude Toward Adoption

Based on the responses to your questions, you may have a good idea about the staff's attitude already. If you are still not sure (and this is not unusual), you, the wife, may want to go with the birth mother to her first obstetrical appointment.

If you are dealing with a clinic, there may be counselors who will try to talk her out of her decision to place the baby. Be honest with your birth mother and tell her this. Ask how she would handle this situation.

In all fairness, most obstetricians and their staff have a positive attitude about adoption and will provide a birth mother with proper health care and respect. There are doctors, however, who look on independent adoption as a quasi-legal activity, or at any rate an inappropriate choice for a woman to make.

One doctor told my daughter's birth mother during her first visit that after the baby was born, while she was still in the hospital, the state agency that deals with child abuse cases would visit her to determine why she was not caring for the baby properly. After a few weeks of treating her at our expense, the obstetrician said that he could no longer be her doctor because the adoption was illegal. Needless to say, he lacked even basic knowledge about private adoption.

In another situation an adoptive mother named Linda took her own mother to the doctor's office for an appointment. After her mother was examined, the doctor said hello to Linda and her four-month-old baby. Linda casually mentioned that she had adopted her baby. The doctor responded, "The [birth] parents should be shot."

Some professionals oppose adoption. If the obstetrician you select turns out to be one of them, the earlier you find it out, the better.

PRENATAL CARE

Prenatal health care should be comprehensive and should include the following:

1. *Medical history and complete physical examinations*
2. *Laboratory and diagnostic procedures*, including:

   - Blood pressure
   - Hemoglobin and hematocrit (to test for iron-deficiency anemia)
   - ABO/Rh typing (to determine blood type and Rh factor)
   - Sexually transmitted disease cultures
   - Hepatitis B surface antigen
   - Urinalysis for bacteria in urine

   For high-risk groups:

   - Hemoglobin electrophoresis
   - Rubella antibodies
   - Chlamydia testing
   - HIV testing and counseling

3. *Nutrition assessment and counseling* and, if appropriate, a referral to the government's Woman, Infant, and Children's (WIC) program. Entry into a WIC program is based upon financial and nutritional status. The guidelines are very broad, and a woman who is well above the poverty level may still be eligible. WIC centers have nutritionists and dietitians who counsel women and give them vouchers for specific food items, like milk, cheese, nutritious cereals, and iron-rich foods.
4. *Health education*, including information about fetal development, preventive health care, and preparation for labor and delivery.
5. *Basic psychological assessment.* In particular, anyone suspected of substance abuse should receive special attention and referrals.

   Although the problems associated with alcohol and drug abuse can be profound, do not expect an obstetrician, especially one in private practice, to do a thorough investigation of a birth mother's possible substance abuse. The most the average physician will do along these lines is ask the woman whether she uses alcohol or drugs, and she'll probably just answer no, even if she does. There are ways, however, through careful, appropriate, and tactful questioning, to elicit honest answers from a pregnant woman about her history of drug and alcohol use.

6. *Screening for environmental health hazards* common in the community or work site (pesticides, radiation, parasitic infections, etc.). Many birth defects can be associated with environmental exposures.

THE BABY'S BIRTH AND HOSPITAL STAY

Once you have selected an obstetrician and know the hospital where the baby will be born, either you or your attorney should contact the hospital to find out about its adoption policy. Ask whether you can speak with a social worker. It is likely that a social worker will meet with the birth mother while she is in the hospital.

Here are some questions you will want to ask:

1. *Does the hospital have a policy regarding independent adoption?* If so, is the policy enforced, or do the personnel practice a more flexible policy? (Some hospitals have archaic written policies that are no longer followed.) Based on the way the policy is explained by employees, you will probably discover their attitude toward adoption.

2. *Can adoptive parents be in the delivery room if the birth mother authorizes their presence?* (Ask the obstetrician first.)

3. *Can the adoptive parents visit the baby and birth mother in the hospital?*

4. *If so, can the adoptive parents dress and feed the baby if the birth mother permits?*

5. *If the birth mother does not want to see the baby, what arrangements are made for the baby to be fed, dressed, and bathed?* In one hospital the social workers threatened to call a state agency that deals with child abuse to claim that a birth mother was neglecting the baby. In another case, a nurse forced a birth mother against her will to dress the baby before the woman and child were discharged. Through her tears, this poor woman had to fully dress the infant she did not even want to see.

6. *If the birth mother chooses, can she be placed on a medical/surgical floor after delivery instead of the maternity floor?* Many birth mothers, even those who desire to see the baby, do not want to be on the maternity floor facing questions from other new mothers and nurses.

7. *What hospital personnel are allowed to talk to the birth mother about her decision to adopt, and what are they allowed to say?* Find out whether the

hospital has a policy about the kinds of questions and comments that nurses, social workers, and other hospital personnel are permitted to make to a birth mother about her decision. You will also want to find out whether the hospital has a policy dealing with tactless, unsolicited advice from hospital personnel. Some people feel they have a right to comment about a woman's choice to place a baby for adoption, saying things like, "How can you give away your own baby?" These comments can come from the nurses, social workers, or housekeepers. If you sense that the social worker will not prevent unsolicited advice from hospital staff, then ask how the administrative staff would handle such remarks.

Even more alarming are hospital personnel who know "the perfect couple" to adopt the baby and try to persuade the birth mother to place the baby with a couple other than you. These solicitations can come from anyone, from a physician to the person who delivers meals. Be honest. Warn your birth mother that people may make negative comments or that they may try to get her to place the baby with another couple. Ask her how she would handle such a scenario. Mentally rehearsing her response can help her deal with insensitive people, especially at a time when her emotions are very strong.

8. *Does hospital policy allow direct placement of the baby with the adoptive couple at the hospital?* Some hospitals do not allow anyone except the birth mother or an adoption agency to leave with a baby. Find out whether the adoptive parents and attorney can leave the hospital with the baby if the birth mother has signed the consent forms, or whether the birth mother must leave the hospital with the baby.

If the hospital does not allow you or your attorney to leave with the baby, and if a birth mother does not wish to see the baby, discuss the possibility of having a friend or relative hold the baby and leave with her, or hiring a private-duty nurse to carry the baby out. As the adoptive parents, you can then meet the person carrying the baby outside the hospital.

Financial Arrangements

By law, any woman can walk into a hospital and deliver a baby. She cannot be turned away. Therefore, you are not responsible for paying the hospital bill before the baby's birth. In fact, if the birth mother has no insurance, and she is not able to pay, have the hospital send her the bill. There may be special funds that assist those in a low-income category without insurance, and if you do pay the bill, it will be based on the birth mother's income and not yours. Chances are likely that the hospital bill will be less expensive if it is based on the birth mother's income.

Make all arrangements through your attorney's office. He or she can find out how much the hospital charges for delivery, the mother's care, and the nursery. Make sure he examines all the bills! We have twice caught hospitals charging an adoptive couple $4,000 more than they should have. Apparently, because no insurance carrier was paying the bill (and therefore questioning it), the hospital billing department sought to collect extra revenue. These are *not* isolated examples. *Some hospitals will try to charge extra if an adoptive couple is paying the bill.* When a hospital bill is excessive, your attorney can often negotiate to have it reduced.

What if the hospital bills are excessive because of medical complications? A premature baby with many medical complications can run up a medical bill well over $100,000. Needless to say, even a $20,000 hospital bill can be beyond the means of many couples. (Hospital bills generally run about $1,000 a day for patients.)

How unfortunate that a loving couple with limited means may have to reconsider an adoption if the baby's hospital bill is beyond their financial ability. After all, if the birth mother changed her mind and decided to raise the child, the hospital would have to absorb the bill anyway. If it is impossible for you to pay for the hospital bill, these are some strategies to consider:

First, see whether your health insurance policy will pay for the baby's expenses. Technically, if you are legally bound to pay the bill, then your insurance company is required by law to cover it. This is a gray area, however, and you want to be extra sure. You will probably have to make the decision whether to proceed with the adoption before you get a firm (*and written*) commitment from the insurance company. Some health maintenance organizations (HMOs) will now pay for the infant's medical expenses if the child is born at a participating hospital and is attended by a participating physician.

Second, make sure your insurance company will pay the baby's medical expenses once she is home with you. You are *not* obligated to tell your insurance company (although most ask) whether the child is adopted. Do not allow the insurance company to stall you. Call your state health insurance commissioner. Document all phone calls. Federal legislation now requires insurance companies to pay for the medical expenses of an adopted child at placement.

Third, see whether the birth mother qualifies for Medicaid. Medicaid funds will cover the hospital bill. A birth mother can usually obtain Medicaid coverage retroactively up to ninety days after birth.

If the birth mother cannot take responsibility for the bills, have her claim herself as an indigent. Her hospital bills may then be absorbed by special state funds designated for this purpose.

Never allow the hospital billing department to send you bills directly.

If the birth mother will be "paying" the bills, have your attorney send her the money to send to the hospital. *Carefully document all paperwork. Save all your canceled checks.*

Document every transaction you make and what you have paid, no matter how little or how much you have spent.

The Baby's Delivery

The birth of a baby is one of life's most wonderful events. You and your spouse may want to share in this experience with the birth mother. Of course, there are many factors that can keep you from doing so. But if it is possible to be there, the birth mother may appreciate your support.

Several factors will help determine whether you can be present at the birth, beginning, of course, with the birth mother's preference. She may want the adoptive mother to be there to give support and encouragement, or she may want this to be "her time" with the baby. She may have other support to help her through labor and delivery—the birth father, a family member, or a special friend.

Some hospitals have a policy about nonfamily members being present at the delivery. In others, as soon as hospital staff hear "adoptive parent," red flags start waving and a "policy" is suddenly established that forbids your presence. If you and the birth mother are determined that you will be there, you will have to be the birth mother's "friend" or coach, and simply not reveal your status to hospital personnel. Some hospitals are very cooperative, while others are very uncooperative. If possible, find out what you can expect *before* the baby's birth.

Do take your comfort level into consideration. If you nearly faint when you have blood drawn, then you may not be a good candidate to view a baby's delivery, especially if it turns into a cesarean section birth. If a birth mother really wants you there, perhaps you can compromise and hold her hand and look at her face during delivery.

The Length of the Hospital Stay

A mother who has given birth vaginally will generally stay in the hospital about one to three days. Most newborns are also released after a couple of days. A woman who has had a cesarean section may stay in the hospital a few days longer than the baby. Or if a baby has a medical problem, such as jaundice, he may remain in the hospital after the mother is released.

Usually these circumstances present no problem. If the baby is released after the birth mother is, she must sometimes come back to the hospital so that the hospital staff will permit the baby's release.

The Baby's Medical Records

Once the baby is born, you should receive all relevant hospital records. Like any other parent, you should know your child's health history. This information may be important for future use.

A baby who is released from the hospital is generally a healthy child. However, do not expect the hospital to send any records home with the birth mother or you. You may want to have a pediatrician, whom you should already have selected, contact the hospital to receive all medical records. It is best if you can get the birth mother to sign a release to have all medical records sent to your pediatrician or attorney. Some hospitals will not release the medical information without the birth mother's signature, or will insist on adoption documents before they will release the information.

The Release of the Baby and Birth Mother from the Hospital

For the birth mother, going home from the hospital usually means separation from the baby. This can be an especially emotional time for the birth mother. If you know her address, you may consider sending her flowers or some other small token of caring to her home. If not, have your attorney's office arrange for the delivery of some special small gift and card. Ask your attorney what is an appropriate amount to spend without appearing cheap but remaining within the confines of the law.

The baby will need clothes to wear home from the hospital. You will probably want to bring these to the hospital after the baby is born or send them through your attorney or the birth mother's friend or family member.

We have often encountered the unexpected during our involvement in adoptions over the years—including a wonderful adoptive couple who sent used, stained clothes to the birth mother's attorney. The couple reasoned that there would be no loss in case the birth mother changed her mind. Fortunately, the attorney was sensitive enough to buy new clothes to send to the hospital.

We suggest you purchase a lovely new baby outfit and wash it carefully to protect newborn skin before taking it to the hospital—or borrow an outfit that looks brand-new. If you find shopping for baby clothes too difficult, have a friend shop for you. Also, have a clean, sturdy car seat to take the baby home in. Many hospitals will not allow you to leave without a seat. In fact, it is illegal for a child to ride in a vehicle without an infant restraint system.

Potential Problems at the Hospital

By this time you may well be wondering why some hospital staff seem so hostile toward adoption. In all fairness, hospitals are simply trying to stay out of legal difficulties. Hospital attorneys, social workers, and administrators as a rule know little, if anything, about adoption and the legal process. Each state has very different laws, and sometimes within a state the laws can vary county by county. To expect hospital staff to have a complete grasp of the law may be expecting too much. Hospitals want to maintain a good public image, moreover, and fear that if an adoption situation is handled improperly, they could be sued, or, worse, receive bad publicity. Unfortunately, it often happens that in trying to "keep their hands clean," hospitals end up taking away a birth mother's basic rights.

Of course, these reasons do not explain all the problems at hospitals. Social workers also have their agenda. They have been trained to "preserve" the family unit, meaning that some view adoption as the last option for very desperate women. Some social workers feel they must counsel a birth mother and insist she explain her reasons for wanting to place the baby for adoption. No other patient is required to endure such pressure before she makes a personal, nonmedical decision.

Then there are the nurses and other health care professionals who may not want to deal with a birth mother who will probably not be caring for the infant. In the first place, it may mean more work for the nurses: After all, they, instead of the mother, must feed and change the infant. Second, nurses view the maternity floor as a happy place, and they may not want to see someone leave without her baby. Finally, professionals are accustomed to handling every situation according to a routine, and adoption may mean they have to rethink how they will handle a birth mother and child.

HEALTH RISKS

To cover every possible health problem a child could have would require a whole medical book. Yet as adoptive parents you do want to know the possible genetic and environmental factors that could influence your child's health so that you can make informed decisions. You need this information, first, to assess the medical risks and decide whether you can accept a child with these risk factors. Second, if you proceed with the adoption, your child's medical background may be crucial to his well-being.

It is your attorney's responsibility to do a thorough investigation of the birth parents' medical backgrounds and those of their families. Most birth parents will reveal basic health history information (such as a family history of diabetes or heart disease) to a physician or lawyer. Getting a birth mother to admit her drug and alcohol use during pregnancy is a much more difficult task, and yet obtaining this information is absolutely essential. The consequences of substance or alcohol abuse on the child's development are often profound.

A pregnant woman's use of tobacco, alcohol, or drugs is only one of many risk factors associated with defects in the child. Other risk factors that should be assessed include:

1. *A family history of reproductive problems.*
2. *Multiple previous pregnancies within a short time span.*
3. *Medical problems concurrent with the pregnancy,* such as sexually trans-mitted diseases, diabetes, and health, liver, or kidney disease.
4. *Obesity, poor eating habits, or signs of poor nutrition.*
5. *Poor living conditions and lack of education.*
6. *Excessive stress.*
7. *Inadequate prenatal care.* In 1983 one woman in four had no prenatal visits in the first trimester of pregnancy. It is not unusual for birth mothers to wait until the second or third trimester. Many are not aware of their pregnancy, or are in denial.
8. *Repeated exposure to environmental hazards such as lead, pesticides, or x-rays.*
9. *Being younger than fifteen years old.* Teenage mothers are twice as likely to have low birth weight babies and have a higher incidence of obstetrical complications. Low birth weight infants are forty times more likely to die during the first eight days of life and twenty times more likely to die during the first year of life than other infants. Those who live often have developmental problems. Teenage mothers are also more likely to have sexually transmitted diseases like hepatitis B, because they are more likely to have had multiple sexual partners.

Genetic Diseases

Whether adopted or not, everyone has the right to know his or her genetic background. Indeed, a thorough genetic history may be essential in preventing certain diseases. For example, adult-onset diabetes has a strong genetic compo-nent, yet 80 percent of those who have this kind of diabetes are overweight. If you know that diabetes runs in your family, you can significantly decrease your likeli-hood of getting the disease by keeping your weight in the normal range. Other genetically linked diseases, such as breast and other cancers, should be screened for more frequently if they run in your family.

Simple precautions can prevent the occurrence of other genetic diseases. In one adoption a hospital failed to perform a simple PKU test on an infant. This is a routine test for phenylketonuria, a genetically carried disease. If diagnosed properly, it can easily be treated by altering the child's diet. The child in this case then developed PKU, which led to profound mental retardation. It was extremely unfortunate that the agency social worker involved failed to notice the omission of the test.

Some basic questions should be posed to get a genetic history of the birth parents. The Children's Home Society of Minnesota, with the assistance of geneticist Dr. V. Elving Anderson, University of Minnesota, has developed a comprehensive, twenty-six-page form for gathering birth parents' genetic histories. It covers 138 medical conditions thought to be genetically linked. The form is $3.50 (prepaid—make the check out to the Children's Home Society) and can be ordered from Ann Meagher, CHSM, 2230 Como Ave., St. Paul, MN 55108. The phone number is (651) 646-6393. For further information consider purchasing the book *Genetic Background History*, by Maretta Spener, also from the Children's Home Society of Minnesota.

If possible, have the birth parents, or their parents, describe their traits and those of other family members (parents, grandparents, and siblings), including:

- Physical characteristics
- Educational experience
- Religion
- Nationality and racial background
- Employment history
- Social adjustments (the way they relate to friends, coworkers, community)
- Interests, hobbies, talents, skills, recreational activities
- Intelligence, aptitude, temperament, personality
- Medical history

Hepatitis B

The two sexually transmitted diseases adoptive parents need to be aware of are AIDS (Acquired Immune Deficiency Syndrome) and hepatitis B. Babies are now routinely screened for HIV infection, the virus that causes AIDS, and adoptive parents will be told immediately if the screening is positive. All babies in the United States now also receive hepatitis B immunoglobulin (in case the child has the disease) and HBV vaccine to prevent getting the disease later in life (such as through sexual contact). Studies have shown that immediate treatment beginning two to twelve hours after the baby's birth, with injections of hepatitis B immunoglobulin and hepatitis B vaccine, is 85 to 95 percent effective in preventing hepatitis B virus chronic carrier status in childhood.

HIV and AIDS

An estimated 7,000 infants in 1993 were born to women who carried the AIDS virus. Of these 7,000 infants, between 1,000 and 2,000 are HIV infected, based on a transmission rate of about 15 to 30 percent. If a woman takes zidovudine (ZDV) while pregnant, she can reduce the risk of passing the AIDS virus to the fetus by as much as two-thirds—which means that if all pregnant HIV-positive women took the drug, only about 300 to 600 babies would be born HIV positive.[1]

About 77 percent of the mothers of those 7,000 infants were African-American and Hispanic. The rate of AIDS infection in non-Hispanic Caucasian women was 3.8 per 100,000 population; for non-Hispanic blacks, 62.7, for Hispanics, 26.0, and for Asians, 13.2.

This means that if your birth mother is Caucasian, the chance is less than 1 in 800 that she is HIV positive, and if she is, there is only a 15 to 30 percent chance that the child will contract the disease—5 to 10 percent if she takes ZDV during her pregnancy. Even if a child tests positive at birth, moreover, that does not necessarily mean that she is HIV positive. It could just mean the child carries the HIV antibody. (It is through the presence of the antibody, not the virus, that the diagnosis is made.) These antibodies can remain in the child's blood until he is fifteen months old. Such babies are tested regularly to see whether the antibodies have left the blood. If they do, the child does not have the virus for AIDS.

For further information, contact:

CDC National AIDS Clearinghouse
PO Box 6003
Rockville, MD 20849-6003
(800) 458-5231

CDC National AIDS Hotline
(800) 342-AIDS

Poor Nutrition

Malnutrition is a major cause of low birth weight babies. These babies are ten times more likely to be mentally retarded. A 1972 study found nearly half the children who were underweight at birth had an IQ of 70, well below the normal rating of 100. This is not surprising, considering that the baby's brain develops the most during the last trimester of pregnancy and the first month after birth. A birth mother who is undernourished can cause irreversible neurological and brain underdevelopment. Lack of oxygen, birth injuries, and respiratory distress, moreover, mostly affect babies who weigh less than five and a half pounds.

Most women should gain at least twenty-four pounds during pregnancy. Studies have shown that a thirty-five-pound weight gain produces babies who weigh an average of eight pounds. These larger babies are more active, mentally more alert, and generally healthier than five-pound babies.[2]

Substance Abuse

Certain medical problems can arise if a birth mother uses drugs, alcohol, or tobacco during her pregnancy. Although the problems associated with these substances are not always apparent at birth, they may, for example, develop into a learning disability when the child reaches age five.

And yet a birth mother's use of these substances does not guarantee that the child will have problems. Only 30 percent of babies born to mothers who used crack or cocaine, for example, display health or learning problems. Most birth defects are not attributable to maternal drugs and alcohol use but to genetic or other factors.

If you suspect that a birth mother is using drugs or alcohol during her pregnancy, find out as much as possible about the effects of what she is taking on the unborn child and the problems that may arise as the child matures.

You may be under the impression that middle-class white women do not use drugs to the extent that poor black women do. If so, you are mistaken. A study conducted in 1989 by the National Association of Perinatal Addiction Research and Education (NAPARE) found that pregnant, middle-class Caucasian women in private care used drugs nearly as much as women in public health clinics. The women's urine was screened for cocaine, alcohol, marijuana, and opiates to test who had used drugs in the last forty-eight hours and who had consumed alcohol in the last eight hours. The results were startling: 16 percent of the women in the public health care centers tested positive, as did *13 percent of the women in the private obstetrical offices.* Ethnic background and economics are not necessarily risk factors for drug use.

If a birth mother is Caucasian and middle class, it is very unlikely that she will be screened appropriately for substance abuse. In one study, physicians were asked to report drug use based on the women's urine at the time of delivery, or on the infant's urine. The study found that African-American women were ten times more likely to be tested and reported than Caucasian women. Questioned about this, physicians explained that Caucasian women stop using drugs when pregnant, whereas African-American women do not. As we have seen, this is simply not the case.

Studies show that the typical pattern of drug use among pregnant women is as follows: A woman decreases her drug use immediately after finding out she is pregnant. By the second trimester, her rate of drug use is similar to what it was before she was pregnant. During the third trimester, the rate may be higher than her pre-pregnancy rate because of the stress of pregnancy.

Some believe that adopted children are more likely to have been exposed to drugs than nonadopted children. According to Dr. Ira J. Chasnoff, who heads Northwestern University's Medical School Perinatal Center for Chemical Dependence, adopted children are more likely to be exposed to drugs and alcohol in utero because birth mothers are young and are likely to be risk takers. Often they do not realize that they are pregnant when drinking alcohol or using drugs. Dr. Chasnoff says that drug use peaks in the twenty-five to thirty-five-year-old age group and that alcohol use is very high among college-age women.

What You Need to Know

You will want a detailed list of any over-the-counter and prescription medications or illicit drugs a woman has used during her pregnancy. Certain medications, whether prescribed by a doctor or not, can have a detrimental effect on the fetus.

To find out about a birth mother's possible tobacco, drug, and alcohol use, a doctor, lawyer, or adoption counselor needs to ask the appropriate questions. Unfortunately, although the doctor is certainly the most appropriate person to raise this issue, few doctors know how to ask a pregnant woman about her drug history in a way that elicits an accurate response. Sometimes a woman is simply not honest; other times she just does not know how to answer a direct yet vague question like "Do you use drugs?" Her idea of what constitutes a "drug" or "drug use" may be different from the doctor's.

If you are involved in an identified adoption, the agency, by law, is responsible for investigating and evaluating the medical condition and background of all children to be adopted and to communicate that information to the adoptive parents. It is up to the agency, therefore, to ask appropriate questions. Certainly an adoption counselor, like a physician, is in a better position than you or your attorney to raise these sensitive questions. If you are using an agency, make sure that the counselor investigates all avenues to determine any medical problems or history of drug or alcohol use.

In the case of an independent adoption, however, because you cannot depend upon the birth mother's obstetrician, you may have to ask your attorney to collect this sensitive information as part of the woman's medical background. It may be a little more difficult for an attorney to find an appropriate way to ask a woman about her alcohol and drug use. After all, he is representing the couple, and the birth mother may see these questions as a threat. He must, however, carefully and tactfully pose the questions to elicit a truthful response; it is his legal responsibility to obtain all information important to a child's health and to share this information with the adoptive parents. Make it clear to your attorney that you want this information. If you are working with an agency, that also means he should check to make sure the agency has investigated the drug-use issue thoroughly.

Of course, you may be the person most likely to see the birth mother on a regular basis. However, it is a very delicate matter for adoptive parents to ask questions that relate to substance abuse. You cannot come out and bluntly pose such a question, but through discussion and other leading questions, you may be able to elicit some honest responses.

All of this raises thorny ethical issues. A professional's interest in maintaining a woman's right to confidentiality must be weighed against the unborn child's right to medical intervention if the mother is abusing drugs or alcohol. These issues are further complicated when adoptive parents want to know whether a woman is using drugs and alcohol. For this reason it is not surprising that some health professionals may be more comfortable than others about revealing a woman's drug use, even to prospective adoptive parents.

In asking a woman whether she is using tobacco, alcohol, or drugs, the following techniques can be helpful. The first is to frame questions about substance abuse within the context of another questionnaire. A medical or dietary intake form, for example, can ask, "What do you like to drink: water, milk, juice, beer, soft drinks, wine, iced tea?" That way the woman's drinking history is asked matter-of-factly, minimizing any embarrassment.

Another technique is simply to ask the woman about substance abuse, but to keep your tone casual. Ask whether she ever used illicit drugs in the same sentence, if possible, in which you ask her about prescription and over-the-counter drugs. You might say, "Are you taking any medications or drugs such as aspirin, cold medications, vitamins, or prescription medicines like Phenobarbital; or other drugs such as cocaine, crystal, speed, barbiturates, or heroin?" Notice that this question moves from over-the-counter medications to prescription medications to illicit drugs. Or you could ask whether she has ever used stimulants or tranquilizers. Use the specific brand names of the drugs. For example, ask, "Do you take Valium?"

If she answers yes to any of these questions, then in the same casual tone, ask what her approximate maximum use or consumption is. Try to "normalize" immoderate consumption so that she does not feel ashamed. When a woman answers, for example, that she drinks beer, ask, "How much do you drink—two or three cans or about one or two six-packs a day?" If she sees that you are comfortable discussing these amounts of alcohol consumption, she is more likely to be honest with you. When asking about consumption, it is important to follow up by asking, "Do you ever use more?" The purpose of this question is to determine whether the woman ever binges on alcohol or drugs or both.

If direct questions do not seem appropriate for any reason, asking a woman about how she relaxes, deals with stress, and handles her emotions can be a good way to lead into questions about alcohol and drug use. Ask questions like these:

"How do you usually relax when you are tired or stressed?"

"Do you find that smoking a cigarette helps you to relax?"

"Do you talk with a friend over a drink or take some time out for yourself?"

You can also ask whether she has ever used drugs in the past. A woman who is too embarrassed to tell you that she is using drugs during her pregnancy may be willing to reveal that she has used them just before pregnancy. If so, this is a strong indicator that she is still using them or at least used them before she found out she was pregnant. Many birth mothers do not know they are pregnant until three to four months into their pregnancy. So even if she states truthfully that she did not use drugs or alcohol after she found out she was pregnant, she may still have used them up to her second trimester. If a woman admits that she has used tobacco, alcohol, and drugs in the past, try to get as much detailed information as possible about previous use.

Physicians are in a position to administer questionnaires about drug use and to include a drug screening as part of a routine urine test. The questionnaire may even state, "Your urine will be tested for diabetes and for drug use. Do you know of any drugs that may be in your urine?" Women often provide very accurate answers to such questionnaires. A skilled physician may know how to ask a woman directly about her drug and alcohol use in a way that gets an honest response. He or she might say, for example, "Alcohol and other drugs, even over-the-counter drugs, may make pregnancy more difficult or harm the baby. Because many women drink or use drugs, it is important to know exactly which ones are used. Many women do not fully understand that using alcohol or drugs while pregnant may cause problems. We need complete information from every pregnant patient so we can give you the personal advice you need." The physician should explain that all information is helpful and that all answers are held in strictest confidence, but that under the law, professionals are required to tell adoptive parents about any significant information related to the baby's background and health. He also needs to explain some of the reasons why it is important for adoptive parents to know this information.

Signs of Substance Abuse

Sometimes simple, careful observation of a birth mother can provide information about possible substance abuse. Here are some of the clues and symptoms associated with various substances:

Tobacco
- Dry coughing, yellow stains on fingers and teeth, "tobacco breath."
- Jitteriness. If you meet with her for an extended period of time, you may notice that after an hour or so she has to use the ladies' room or go outside.
- A sibling who smokes. According to our research, the strongest indicator of a teenager's being a smoker is if an older sibling smokes.

Alcohol
- History of low birth weight delivery. If a woman had a previous pregnancy, find out the child's weight and whether the birth mother had any problems in delivery, particularly placental abnormalities.
- The smell of alcohol on her breath.
- A family history of alcohol abuse.
- No prenatal care.

Drugs
- Disease. Diseases that are spread through intravenous use, like hepatitis B, can be one indication that a woman has used drugs.
- Malnourishment. Drug abusers often eat poorly, leading to malnourishment.
- Nasal inflammation, track marks. Evidence of snorting cocaine and drug injection.

Helping Women with Substance Abuse Problems

Physicians, agency caseworkers, and other professionals have an obligation to talk to birth mothers about substance abuse and its consequences for the developing fetus. Many women, when told of the harmful effects that tobacco, alcohol, and drugs can have on the unborn child, will stop using these substances. Such information must be given in a simple and positive manner so that it is clear and well understood. If the risks associated with a certain drug are exaggerated, the birth mother may dismiss the message to quit. For example, it would be inappropriate to insist that a woman stop drinking all caffeinated beverages. Here are examples of positive language:

> If you stop drinking now, you will have a better chance of having a healthier baby.
> You and the baby will feel better if you are sober.

If gentle encouragement is not enough incentive for her to quit smoking, drinking, or using drugs, the woman is addicted and cannot quit without help. She will need to be referred to a treatment center. Making a good referral, however, is not always easy. Some treatment centers will not accept pregnant women. And although women who use one drug often abuse another, treatment centers often focus on only one substance. (Most people in treatment centers are also smokers, yet smoking as an addiction is seldom addressed.)

Ideally, a pregnant woman should receive comprehensive treatment both for her dependency and for her pregnancy. A multidisciplinary approach employing social workers, nurses, doctors, and counselors would best meet a woman's needs.

CONSEQUENCES OF PRENATAL DRUG AND ALCOHOL EXPOSURE

According to Dr. Chasnoff, it is difficult to determine the specific prenatal effects of any one drug apart from alcohol, whose effects have been well documented. Drug abusers tend to use more than one substance. Alcohol and marijuana are the two drugs most commonly used together. The worst combination is that of alcohol and cocaine, which forms byproducts harmful to the child. These are also believed to be the only two drugs that can produce physical abnormalities.[3]

Dr. Chasnoff lists the following essential information in assessing a drug-exposed child:

- Birth weight
- Head circumference
- Physical examination
- Tests for syphilis and HIV
- Neurological and behavioral state[4]

Nicotine

Although most people do not view it as a drug, the nicotine in tobacco is as addictive as heroin. Because tobacco has so many toxins and is so widely used, it is one of the primary causes of infant mortality in the United States. Nicotine is associated with low birth weight babies, and the complications that accompany low birth weight are the leading causes of infant death. Prenatal exposure to nicotine is also strongly associated with sudden infant death syndrome (SIDS), the number one cause of death in infants under the age of one.

Although the problems associated with prenatal tobacco exposure are not always obvious, such exposure often means that the child does not have the same full potential he could have had if not exposed to tobacco. Tobacco use can mean a newborn weighs six pounds at birth instead of, for example, seven pounds. In fact, years ago physicians encouraged pregnant women to smoke and to restrict their diets to produce smaller babies. Tobacco use is also associated with a decrease in a child's academic potential, but this is difficult to evaluate. A bright child could perhaps have been even smarter if his mother had not smoked during pregnancy.

Here are some of the possible effects of nicotine on a newborn infant:

- *Low birth weight.* Low birth weight babies are forty times more likely than normal weight babies to die before they are one month old. Those who do survive may have health problems, including mental retardation, cerebral palsy, and hearing and visual problems.
- *Increased risk of physical abnormalities.*
- *Malformations such as heart defects, cleft palate, and hernias.*
- *Central nervous system defects.*
- *Threefold risk of sudden infant death syndrome (SIDS)*

As the child grows, the following problems may arise:

- *Hyperactivity and lack of self-control*
- *Decreased attention span*
- *Irritability*
- *Decreased language development*
- *Decreased academic ability*

Alcohol

Among the health problems associated with prenatal alcohol use, fetal alcohol syndrome is the most serious. Indeed, prenatal exposure to alcohol is now considered more dangerous to the health of the child than cocaine. Its consequences include:

- Growth retardation (decreased weight, height, and head circumference)
- Specific facial abnormalities (the eyes are almond-shaped, the nose is short and upturned, the upper lip is thin, and the area between the mouth and nose is flattened)
- Decreased intellectual and motor abilities, as well as microencephaly (small head and profound mental retardation)

Long-term problems include such psychosocial problems as poor judgment, short attention span, and inability to pick up social cues and form friendships. These problems are evident into adulthood even in those with normal IQs. They interfere with learning, and most of the children cannot live or work independently. Children who were in foster care or adopted do not do better than those raised by their birth families. *FAS is the third leading cause of mental retardation after Down syndrome and spina bifida in the United States, and the leading cause of mental retardation in the world.* Unlike these disabilities, however, FAS is completely preventable.

It is difficult to recognize FAS in a newborn. Small size and abnormal behavior in the newborn can result from any number of factors, including prenatal exposure to cigarettes or drugs. The typical FAS facial features may not be apparent.[5] In an international adoption the diagnosis may be even more difficult, especially when no maternal history is known, no growth and developmental records are available, and poor growth and development may be attributed to living in an orphanage and poor nutrition.

A physician diagnosing FAS must recognize three problem areas: pre- or postnatal growth deficiency, central nervous system abnormality, and facial signs. When a child has abnormal findings in one or more of these areas with a suspected history of prenatal exposure, the term "fetal alcohol effect" or "subclinical FAS" is often used. Research in animals shows that just one-fifth the amount of alcohol needed to produce the obvious problems associated with FAS can cause learning problems in the offspring. Such problems are not obvious, but the effects can manifest themselves as the child grows.

Heavy drinking is defined as having two or more drinks per day, or fourteen or more per week. A drink is equal to one twelve-ounce beer; one 4-ounce glass of wine; or one 1-ounce glass of distilled spirits such as vodka, whiskey, or scotch.[6] Problems associated with heavy drinking include:

- Classic FAS
- Partial FAS
- Sleep disturbances
- Jitteriness
- Poor muscle tone
- Poor sucking response
- Minimal brain dysfunction
- Slight malformations
- Behavior problems such as hyperactivity, decreased alertness, disrupted sleep patterns, feeding difficulties, and decreased intellectual capability

As the amount and frequency of alcohol consumption increase, so do the likelihood and extent of medical problems. Even two drinks a day can cause growth retardation. Fetal alcohol effects can occur in babies whose mothers have two to four drinks a day about 10 percent of the time during the pregnancy. This means there are potential problems for the baby if a pregnant woman has two drinks, three or four days a month.

Studies demonstrate that pregnant women should not consume any alcohol. The American Council on Science and Health (ACSH) recommends that women avoid alcohol completely throughout their pregnancies.

Alcohol can have different effects at different stages of fetal development. In the beginning stages of pregnancy, about six drinks per week is too much, even if the woman stops drinking after she learns that she is pregnant. Alcohol can impair or halt the delivery of oxygen through the umbilical cord. During the first months of pregnancy, even a few minutes of oxygen deprivation can have negative effects on the fetus's brain. Alcohol can also interfere with the passage of nutrients through the placenta to the fetus.

How does one decide whether to adopt a baby who has been prenatally exposed to alcohol? First, it is important to recognize that the likelihood of a birth mother having consumed some alcohol during pregnancy is very high, especially if she is a young woman enduring an unplanned pregnancy. Working with a birth mother who has taken a few drinks at the beginning of her pregnancy is probably not taking an unnecessary risk. Most of our mothers probably had a few drinks during their pregnancies. (Back in the 1950s and 1960s there was no established correlation between alcohol and birth defects.) With evidence now indicating that the higher the birth mother's level of alcohol intake, the more likely the child may be to develop learning or other medical problems, however, adoptive couples will want to know about a birth mother's drinking patterns during her pregnancy. The more you know, the more informed a decision you can make.

Knowing that a woman drank alcohol during her pregnancy should not necessarily disqualify her as a birth mother for you. Instead, you will want to find out how her habits may have affected the child's health. If you do know that a birth mother has drunk heavily at any point in her pregnancy, especially in the beginning, you will want to decide what disabilities and learning problems you can accept. Even if the likelihood of the child's having fetal alcohol syndrome or its effects is low, you should think carefully beforehand about the possibility. If you feel you cannot accept the risk of problems that may not even manifest themselves until the child is in school, then you should not continue dealing with this birth mother. Perhaps you are willing to accept a child who has been exposed to alcohol, but not if the child has profound problems. In some cases the problems may be apparent at birth. An infant with profound FAS will probably display the facial characteristics associated with the syndrome. If so, you may decide at birth whether or not you want to rear a child who may also be mentally retarded or have a lower-than-average IQ.

Resources:

National Health/Education Consortium
Fetal Alcohol Syndrome: The Impact on Children's Ability to Learn
(202) 822-8405
A summary of knowledge, misconceptions, and strategies in the education of a child with FAS. The National Organization on Fetal Alcohol Syndrome home page at **www.nofas.org** offers information and resources for families affected by FAS. To view pictures of children with FAS and obtain additional resources, visit **www.come-over.to/ fasstar.**

Cocaine

Cocaine can pose a great threat to unborn babies, beginning with its tendency to cause a decrease in the mother's functioning—leading to increasing drug exposure and poor prenatal care.[7] Some of the other effects include:

- Threefold risk of premature birth.
- Increased risk of a stroke (caused by increased fetal blood pressure). This is rare but can cause permanent brain damage.
- Smaller head circumference, which may mean child will have a smaller brain.
- Increased likelihood of low weight at birth. Low birth weight babies are forty times more likely than babies with a normal weight to die before they are one month old. Those that do survive have increased health problems, including mental retardation, cerebral palsy, and hearing and visual problems.
- Tenfold risk of sudden infant death syndrome (SIDS).
- Increased likelihood of genito-urinary defects that can cause life-threatening infections.

A cocaine-exposed infant may display some or all of the following symptoms at birth:

- Decreased scores on motor ability reflexes, attention, and mood control
- Low response to human faces or voices
- Jitteriness and irritability
- Sensitivity to any stimuli, including the slightest touch or sound
- Withdrawal and unresponsiveness
- Avoidance of stimuli by staying in a deep sleep most of the day

As with any drug exposure, the most significant long-term effects of prenatal cocaine exposure are on a child's behavior. About 20 percent of the children studied have had significant behavioral problems, and another 15 percent showed less severe but similar problems.[8] As cocaine-exposed children mature, they are at a much higher risk for incurring developmental and learning problems, according to Dr. Ira J. Chasnoff of the National Association for Perinatal Addiction Research and Education. And Dr. Dan Griffith, developmental psychologist at Northwestern University, says a baby's neurological problems show up later as hyperactivity, learning disabilities, and difficulty focusing.

In one study, foster toddlers who had been prenatally exposed to cocaine were compared to those who had not. Those who had been prenatally exposed to cocaine had more risk factors at birth and experienced more illnesses after; they scored lower on conceptual development but excelled in areas of expression of feelings and peer interaction. They also displayed more physically violent behavior than those not exposed. All scored below normal in most areas of development.

According to Jane Schneider, a physical therapist at Children's Memorial Hospital in Chicago, cocaine-exposed children are forty times more likely to have delayed motor development,[9] including delayed language development. Drug-exposed children often have difficulty expressing language. Although they can understand what they hear, speech production is delayed. In fact, 70 percent of three-year-old cocaine-exposed adopted children are in some kind of speech therapy.[10]

According to Dr. Chasnoff, the question that parents ask is, "Are these children adoptable?" He answers with an emphatic yes. True, they may need a few extras, such as speech therapy and maybe some learning disability classes early on. They may also need a little extra love, because they can test your patience. An infant going through withdrawal from drugs can be difficult, but with the right help, the child has a very bright future. Even with some of the potential problems associated with maternal drug use, cocaine-exposed infants are adoptable. In fact, in a study in which 1,269 adoptive families completed questionnaires, almost all the parents of drug-exposed children were highly satisfied, almost as satisfied as those whose adopted children had not been exposed. Overall, the idea that drug-exposed children are significantly different from non-drug-exposed children and that adopting them is less satisfying received no support.[11]

Most children are unharmed by prenatal cocaine exposure. According to Dr. Chasnoff's research, about 70 percent of the cocaine-exposed children seem to develop normally, while the remaining 30 percent have a range of developmental, behavioral, and attention span problems. Many of these can be minimized through a good environment. As can be expected, for example, drug-exposed infants who are adopted early have significantly higher IQs at age three than those reared by their biological mothers—higher than children who were not exposed but who lived in deprived conditions.

If you are planning to adopt a baby who has been exposed to cocaine, understand that he may need special attention, particularly during the first eight to ten weeks, when he may be extremely sensitive to stimuli. Even eye contact can overload the child's system, causing him to close his eyes. Often the baby is either crying or in a deep sleep, making it difficult to bond with him. Parents may be convinced that the child simply doesn't love them. The problem is not psychological, however, but physiological. With early intervention, says Dr. Chasnoff, children can develop normally and can even be mainstreamed.

Of course, not only are adoptive parents likely to provide a more stimulating environment for these children, they may also be saving many of them from abuse. Experts believe that the rise in cocaine-exposed babies being placed with their cocaine-abusing mothers has probably accounted for a 27 percent increase in child abuse and neglect. It is very difficult for a woman with few support systems to care for even a healthy infant. Complicating the mother's situation is her own drug use, her lack of resources, and an infant who alternates between a shrill cry and a "shutting down" of his system. This can lead to an explosive situation.[12]

Heroin and Opiates

Heroin and opiates belong to a group of drugs called opioids and are natural and synthetic drugs that act primarily on the central nervous system. They include such therapeutic medicines as morphine, opium, codeine, meperidine (Demerol), oxcycodone (Percodan), and methadone (Dolophine), which is used in treating heroin dependency.

Heroin can be taken in different forms, but mostly it is injected. Pregnancy complications for heroin addicts include early separation of the placenta, premature labor, and ruptured membranes. Toxemia during pregnancy affects 10 to 15 percent of addicts, resulting in high blood pressure and even seizures. About half of infants born to heroin-abusing women with no prenatal care were of low birth weight, and 80 percent had serious medical problems. The chaotic lifestyles of addicts also increase their chances of contracting AIDS through sex or needle sharing.[13]

Heroin readily crosses the placenta. If the mother suddenly stops taking the drug while pregnant, the fetus can experience withdrawal and die.[14] Although opioid exposure before birth is not associated with an increased risk for physical malformations, one in four infants born to mothers in a methadone treatment program had strabismus, a visual disorder in which the infant's eyes cannot focus properly. It was unclear whether heroin or other drugs had caused the disorder.

Between 60 and 90 percent of these newborns develop withdrawal symptoms and require special gentle handling and medication. Like the jittery cocaine babies, they are challenging to care for. Withdrawal symptoms can include high-pitched crying, fever, irregular breathing, and seizures within forty-eight to seventy-two hours after birth. Occasionally these symptoms do not begin until two to four weeks after birth. Irritability resulting from overarousal usually ends at about one month but can last up to three months or more.

After these babies are a month old, however, only subtle differences can be observed between them and those not exposed to narcotics in utero. Muscle development may be uneven, and coordination may be impaired. Studies are difficult to conduct, as mothers often drop out of the studies, and the home environments usually make it difficult to distinguish problems associated with drug exposure from those stemming from poor parenting. Like the cocaine-exposed children, physical and psychological development seem to be within normal ranges, but speech development may be impaired.

In another study, heroin-exposed babies at age one tended to be impulsive, were easily upset, and had sleep disturbances and temper tantrums. Between twelve to eighteen months they were hyperactive. At age one the most distinguishing characteristic for these children was an early separation from their biological mothers. Only 8 percent of these three-year-old children had contact with their mothers. Either these mothers could not care for their children, or the children were removed from their homes.[15]

These points are made not because an adopted child will display these tendencies but to show what lives these children may lead when not placed for adoption. Again, the problems associated with any drug exposure are inseparable from parental influence unless studies are conducted with children who have been adopted into stable homes.

PCP

PCP (Phencyclidine) is a synthetic drug with no clinical use. Very little research has been conducted on prenatally exposed infants, because women who take PCPs often take other drugs as well.

Like infants born to mothers who use cocaine or heroin, PCP-exposed newborns were jittery, had poor visual coordination, and were difficult to console. Although these babies alternated between restlessness and calm, they did not have withdrawal symptoms. Animal studies suggest that PCP at very high doses may cause birth defects.[16]

Marijuana

There is limited knowledge about the long-term effects marijuana has on the developing fetus. It is known, however, that its primary component easily crosses the placenta. Marijuana use may be associated with low birth weight and birth defects similar to those with fetal alcohol syndrome and depression of the central nervous system in the newborn.[17]

Sedatives and Tranquilizers

All minor tranquilizers have been associated with increased fetal malformations if used during the first trimester of pregnancy. These birth defects are similar to those of babies with fetal alcohol syndrome. Nearly all the infants are also significantly below normal birth weight.

Valium (diazepam). When taken in the first trimester, Valium increases fourfold the likelihood of a cleft palate, lip anomalies, and malformations of the heart and arteries. This risk increases when Valium is combined with smoking and alcohol. If it is taken within the last two to four months of pregnancy, even in low dosages (ten to fifteen milligrams), the infant may suffer from tremors, lethargy, and other symptoms associated with withdrawal in newborns.[18]

Barbiturates. Barbiturates are commonly used drugs that include sedative hypnotics and antiseizure medications. They are associated with birth defects similar to fetal alcohol syndrome. Infants born to mothers who use barbiturates can suffer from tremors, restlessness, high-pitched crying, and convulsions.[19]

Prescription Drugs

Accutane (isotretinoin). Accutane, an antiacne medication, is associated with major abnormalities such as microencephalus (small head with severe mental retardation) and external ear and cardiovascular defects.[20]

Antibiotics. Some antibiotics, including tetracycline and some sulfanilamides, when taken during the last four to five months of pregnancy may cause permanent discoloration of the child's teeth. For the most part, antibiotics are considered safe.[21]

Anticonvulsants. Anticonvulsants have been associated with an increase in heart defects, cleft lip and palate, microencephaly, mental deficiency, and impaired growth. However, even with this risk, doctors often recommend that the mother continue taking the drug, as withdrawal may cause seizures, resulting in oxygen reduction and threat to the fetus.[22]

WHAT RISKS CAN YOU ACCEPT?

Before you adopt, you and your spouse will want to decide what conditions you can and cannot accept in a child. Your decisions will also influence the kind of adoption that you will choose. For example, you may be able to accept a problem if it is present right at birth (such as cleft palate), and you know the exact treatment that the child will receive (e.g., surgery and speech therapy). However, you may not be able to accept a child who may develop learning problems later on because the birth mother used cocaine occasionally during her pregnancy. Often an agency will ask you what problems you can or cannot accept, and to what degree.

Most doctors do not routinely screen women, and even if the birth mother is screened, the results may not prove anything. Drugs stay in the system for a period of time only and cannot be detected in the mother's blood or the infant's meconium (first stool sample). You may therefore have to assume on some level that a birth mother may have drunk at least some alcohol, taken some over-the-counter medicines, and perhaps even used illicit drugs. You may have to base your decision on your gut feelings and the actual health of the baby at delivery.

With your spouse, list the medical conditions you could accept and those that you could not. In each case, ask yourselves, could you truly accept a child with this disease? Could you live with the condition and all it may entail? Would you constantly be looking for any sign of the disease, to the child's detriment? For example, a professional psychologist and her husband were told of a birth mother who had a three-generation family history of clinical depression. Knowing this, the couple felt they would be watching for signs of depression at all times.

Based on the conditions you agree you can accept, ask yourselves next what resources you have that can enable you to handle each condition appropriately. Include financial resources, time, personal strength and patience, support systems, and access to care.

What if you cannot accept the child's health status?

The choice is yours. Do not feel guilty if you cannot accept certain medical problems. You have the right to choose, just as the birth mother has the right to select you as parents and then to change her mind. Remember, many couples are willing to adopt newborns with physical problems and mental retardation.

One day a birth mother contacted our office and said that she had a one-week-old baby who had a 95 percent chance of developing muscular dystrophy (MD)—a condition in which the child can have profound disabilities and an early death. The child's MD status could not be determined for sure until he was three months old. We contacted a couple that same day, the couple said they were interested, and that day the child went home with his adoptive parents.

Another couple was ready to adopt a baby through private channels. After the baby was born, the birth mother revealed that she had used cocaine during her pregnancy, having previously stated that she was not using drugs. The couple decided that they did not want to take any chances, yet they felt very guilty because they had visited the baby in the hospital and were concerned about her overall future, especially if the birth mother decided to raise the child herself. An agency was contacted and the child was immediately placed in a loving home. Fortunately, the baby is perfectly healthy and at this point shows no adverse effects from drug exposure.

Adoption is a positive choice in our society, although, sad to say, it is not always viewed that way. As a prospective adoptive parent, however, you should not make the decision to adopt based on your concern about the negative environment the child may encounter if you do not. This is not a good reason to adopt a child. Children have the right to be loved for themselves, not because someone felt sorry for them. No adoptive parent should be a martyr, and no child should be considered a burden.

If you decide that you cannot go ahead with an adoption, refer the birth mother to another couple or to an agency with the resources to place the baby with a loving couple. Virtually all babies, no matter how severe their condition, can be placed in an adoptive home.

Genetic Illness

Should you proceed with an adoption if genetic illness is in the family?

When agreeing to commit yourself to a birth mother, even one who does not use alcohol, tobacco, or drugs, you know that the baby has at least the same risk of medical problems as if you yourself had given birth. None of us lives in a risk-free world, even in the best circumstances. Some risks, however, are known and calculated. If a birth mother tells you that a certain kind of genetic illness has been diagnosed in her family, then you must decide whether you can accept a child who may have the genetic potential for it.

If a baby is to be born with a genetic disease like hemophilia, you must first decide whether you can accept a child who has this disease. If you cannot and you know it, be honest with the birth mother and tell her so. You may know of other couples who are interested in adopting a child with this disease. It is comforting to be able to give a birth mother the name of a couple or an adoption agency. If you are uncertain about accepting a particular medical condition, tell the birth mother that your acceptance depends upon how profound the problem is. You could wait until the child is born or ask for amniocentesis, if appropriate, then tell the birth mother whether you are interested in adopting the baby. If you can accept the disease, start to research what help you could provide the child to minimize the impact of the disease.

Mental Illness

In some ways it is harder to accept a child who *may* develop a disease later in childhood. For some the uncertainty is worse than dealing with the disease itself. You may feel as if you are living with a time bomb, particularly if the child has a genetic predisposition to certain mental illnesses.

One couple had agonized over whether to adopt a baby whose family has a history of schizophrenia. They decided that they would find it very difficult to raise a child who might develop the disease in early adolescence. In some ways they wished they had not known, since their knowledge meant that they would always be looking for a sign of mental illness in the child. This watchfulness could cause them to overreact to any emotional problems the child might have. After much discussion, the couple decided not to adopt this baby.

Very often the birth mother's genetic history is known, but not the birth father's. Had it been the birth father who had a family history of schizophrenia, it is likely that no one would ever have known, and the couple would have adopted the baby. Someone with one manic-depressive parent has about a 20 percent chance of inheriting the disease. If the birth father is very young, he may not even have begun to display the behavior associated with manic depression. No one would know that he would someday have the condition or that he is a genetic carrier.

HOW TO ACCEPT A CHILD WITH A MEDICAL CONDITION

Just as people dream of the ideal biological child, those who are infertile resolve to adopt and then begin to fantasize about the ideal adopted child. If a problem does arise, you can go through another stage of resolution and accept the condition. Some people are better suited than others to deal with a child's medical condition or disability. You may not know how strongly you may feel for a child, and you may find yourself willing to rear a child who has limitations.

Get all the information you can. If a problem does arise during pregnancy or right after birth, your attorney should get hold of the birth mother's and child's medical records so that he and you can discuss the possible problems with the attending physicians.

Let your child know that you accept him. A few years down the road, a child who is different will know it. To show your child that you accept him, demonstrate that you accept all kinds of people. This can mean that you participate in intercultural events, that you restrict your comments about other people's habits and characteristics, and that you show an interest in a broad range of subjects and ideas. Accepting a child who has a medical or behavior problem or the potential for one is like accepting any other child—adopted or biological. We accept a child for who he is—not what we want him to become.

Know your financial limitations. A child born with an acute medical condition needs care that may not be covered by your insurance. Hospital bills, for instance, can be tremendous. Have your attorney make arrangements so that if you do proceed with the adoption, you are not responsible for the child's medical bills. One way of doing this is to use an adoption agency, which may then be able to apply for Medicaid to finance the child's hospital costs. Another is to get state funds to support the child. For more about financial assistance for special needs children, read chapter 15, or contact:

North American Council on Adoptable Children
970 Raymond Ave.
Suite 106
St. Paul, MN 55114-1149
(800) 470-6665

You may find, however, that your insurance will cover all the child's medical needs. Adopted children can now have the same medical coverage that biological children have. The Omnibus Budget Reconciliation Act of 1993 mandates that so long as your insurance covers dependents, then adopted children are covered by the same standards as soon as they are placed with you. There cannot be restricted coverage because the child has a pre-existing condition. Only those whose insurance is subject to the Employee Retirement Income Security Act of 1974 (ERISA) are exempt from this new law. Check with your employer if you are not sure.

This new legislation may benefit the child and your pocketbook before the child even comes home. For example, if a newborn baby has surgery while in the hospital, and the birth mother is not permitted to sign a consent terminating her rights until three or more days after birth, your insurance company is probably obligated to pay for the baby's surgery. In fact, it should probably pay for the birth mother's medical expenses as well, if you are legally obligated to pay for them.

If a child is covered by Medicaid and has complications after birth requiring expensive medical intervention, check with your insurance company first to see what it will pay for once the consent for adoption is signed. You may want to delay having the birth mother sign a consent while the child is in the hospital if you are not sure your insurance company will pay all medical expenses. Often Medicaid coverage does not extend to the child once the baby is placed for adoption—even if he is still in the hospital. You do not want to be in a situation where you are morally or legally obligated to pay tens of thousands of dollars because you were in health insurance limbo.

Chapter Twenty

Preparing for a Baby's Homecoming

I n preparing for a new baby or child's homecoming, one of your first tasks will be to select a pediatrician. As an adoptive parent you will probably have special considerations. The first thing you will want to know is, what is the pediatrician's attitude toward adoption? When you interview a pediatrician, explain that you will be adopting and would like to have the child examined. Ask whether the baby's medical records can be sent to her, since most hospitals will not give them to you directly. The doctor's response should give you a good idea of her attitude about adoption. Most pediatricians understand the situation and do not expect you to have the child's or birth parents' complete medical histories. If you are adopting a newborn infant, also ask whether the pediatrician would be willing to call the hospital physician who treated the baby to discuss the baby's overall health, since the records may not arrive for weeks.

If your child is born in another state, you may have to select a pediatrician there for the child's first visit. Call an adoption support group in that area for a recommendation.

Since some hospitals may not give you a full medical history of the infant, you will want to have him examined within a day or two of his release from the hospital, not to determine whether he is healthy enough to proceed with the adoption but simply to reassure you that all is well. If there are any medical problems, they are almost certain to be minor ones, since no infant with a serious illness or condition would be released from the hospital. At this first visit you can begin to establish a rapport with the doctor, who may need to be called from time to time for general information or in case of an emergency.

Most pediatricians will tell you the baby's APGAR scores. This test, which is administered one and five minutes after birth, measures color, pulse rate, muscular tone, respiratory rate, and reflex activity, with a possible score of 0, 1, or 2 in each category. Ten is a perfect score.

INFANT CARE

Like any first-time parent you will want to know how to care for an infant. Most couples get some of this training in childbirth classes, but some hospitals, agencies, and adoption support groups now offer infant care and parenting classes. Call a local chapter of RESOLVE or some other adoption support group for information. Classes usually cost about $25 to $50 for five sessions.

In addition to taking classes, it is a good idea to buy or borrow from the library a general baby care book such as Penelope Leach's *Your Child from Birth to Five Years Old*. Such books can be found in any general bookstore.

Breastfeeding/Bottle Feeding

You may have heard that adoptive mothers can breastfeed their children. This is true. And because there are many advantages for the child in receiving breast milk as opposed to formula, you may want to consider breastfeeding. Approach it realistically, however. Most women who have nursed an adopted infant did so for less than a month. It is difficult and tiring, and even maximum milk production supplies only 25 percent of the milk your child needs. The rest must come from formula. Of course, getting some human milk, with its natural antibodies, is better than formula alone.

If you decide to pursue this option, your doctor may offer to prescribe hormones—prolactin and oxytocin—to cause milk production. Debra Stewart Peterson suggests in *Breastfeeding the Adopted Baby*, however, that you not take these drugs. She says the baby's regular nursing will send the message to the pituitary gland to produce these hormones naturally, stimulating milk production. Also, some women experience fatigue with these medications.

To prepare for nursing an adopted child, Peterson suggests wearing nipple shells to stimulate the hormone oxytocin, instead of pumping your breasts before the baby is placed with you. Once the baby is with you, you can start using a supplemental device called Supplemental Nutrition System or Lact-Aid. These involve tubes that connect a bottle of formula to your nipples. Every time the child is fed, she is nursing at the same time she is getting formula from a bottle. The more relaxed you are, writes Peterson, the easier it is to build up your own milk supply. Of course, you may find it difficult to get the formula warmed up and attach the nursing tubing to your breasts while your infant is crying for milk, especially in the middle of the night.

Even if you know ahead of time that you would like to try nursing your infant, you may not want to pump your breasts, wear nipple shells, or take hormones before the child's birth in case the birth mother changes her mind or the adoption does not proceed as quickly as you had anticipated. And one final note:

Although you can produce breast milk, you cannot produce colostrum, a thin, yellowish fluid that is secreted by a woman in the first days after childbirth and that is present in the milk for weeks afterward. Colostrum is rich in antibodies and minerals and is considered very beneficial to infants. You can get colostrum from other nursing mothers, if you can find someone who is willing to pump; just make sure the woman is someone you know well, because drugs, alcohol, bacteria, and viruses can be passed to the baby through her milk.

Resources:

For further information, contact the **La Leche League**. They publish *Nursing Your Adopted Baby* for $4.95 including shipping and handling. Call (800) LA LECHE.

Debra Stewart Peterson's book *Breastfeeding the Adopted Baby* is published by Corona Publishing Company, San Antonio, TX, 1994. For a copy of that book and supplies such as a breast pump, supplemental feeding system, and breast shells, call (801) 392-9074.

Ross Laboratories, the producers of Similac baby formula, sponsor a **Welcome Addition Club**. Call (800) BABYLINE to register. You can receive a free twelve-can case of ready-to-feed formula, coupons, printed material, and baby gifts. You can also request their Adoptive Gift Package.

Infant Equipment

Of course you will be excited about preparing a nursery. We recommend, however, that you not set up a nursery until you actually have the baby. Just keep the room in reserve, ready for a baby, and if you like, cover the walls in a color scheme that will coordinate with baby decor. We decorated our nursery in yellow wallpaper—just in case we ever had children. When selecting the pattern, we knew we could not stand to look at teddy bears or other baby motifs until we actually had a child.

You may want to ask some friends or family to hold on to a few basic items, such as undershirts and one-piece pajamas, a bassinet or cradle, and a car seat. You might make arrangements with a friend whose child has outgrown his infant gear and clothing to use some of these items until you purchase them yourself or receive them as gifts. As soon as you take the baby home, your friends and family will probably inundate you with gifts. In any case, the only items you will really need to begin with are some warm blankets and a few outfits. The hospital usually sends the child home with formula and diapers, and you will not need a crib until the child is about two or three months old. In fact, if you suddenly get a call to pick up a baby, there's nothing wrong with taking a drawer out of the bureau and lining it with blankets for a cradle.

NAMING THE CHILD

Selecting a name for an adopted child is not very different from selecting a name for a biological child. Sometimes, however, there may be special considerations.

In years past the birth mother selected the child's name, and the adoptive parents called the child by that name. During the last few decades, however, the birth mother has selected a name to go on the original birth certificate, and the adoptive parents have selected another name that goes on the child's permanent birth certificate. Now, as open adoption becomes more acceptable, a birth mother may request that you give the child a name she has selected, or you may request that she put the name you have selected on the original birth certificate. Why? Because when you communicate with the birth parents, it is easier and less awkward for everyone to refer to the child by the same name. You do not want the birth mother referring to the child as Melinda when you named her Catherine. By keeping the names similar or the same, you preserve the child's original identity instead of taking it away. When older adoptees meet their birth mothers, the first two questions they often ask are "What did you name me?" and "Why did you place me for adoption?"

If your birth mother asks you to give the child a name you do not like, consider using it as a middle name. Sometimes, however, you may need to suggest that she reconsider the name she has chosen. If the birth mother tells you that she is giving the child a name she has always loved, or is naming him after a dear cousin who died, or is selecting a name for some other very strong reason, suggest that she not do so. Encourage her to choose a name that she truly loves but to save the special name for later when she is married and prepared to raise a child. If she gives the child a name that has a strong sentimental association, she may identify the adoption with that person or tragic event. For example, she does not need to be reminded of her adoption plans every time she hears her deceased father's name mentioned.

If your child is of a certain nationality, such as Spanish, and clearly looks Spanish, and you and your spouse are of Norwegian extraction, giving your child a very Nordic family name may cause comment: "How did such a dark-haired boy get the name Leif?" Try not to select a name that will make the child feel he must continually explain that he is adopted.

Once you have selected a name, discuss your choice with the birth mother, if you feel it is appropriate to do so. Perhaps together you can agree on a name for the baby.

The names, addresses, and telephone numbers of each state's adoption specialist, state bar association, and Interstate Compact on the Placement of Children Unit are listed, as well as adoption attorneys, private adoption agencies, and adoption support groups. How each can be of assistance to you is briefly discussed below.

THE STATE ADOPTION SPECIALIST

The adoption specialist is usually in the state's social services office (or Office of Children's Protective Services). Sometimes this person also serves in the office of the Interstate Compact on the Placement of Children (see below). This specialist should have a comprehensive view of the state's adoption system and may provide statistical data, the names of licensed agencies, details about adoption statutes, subsidized adoption programs, and other information.

The specialist's staff may also be able to recommend attorneys who are thorough and who submit paperwork in a timely manner.

If you feel that an agency or attorney is not handling your case ethically or properly, you can call the state specialist to question the procedure. Do not report any unethical practices to this office, because complaints of this nature should be directed to the attorneys' ethics office of the state bar association or the state Supreme Court. Complaints concerning agencies should be directed to the adoption agency licensing office in the state's department of social services.

THE STATE BAR ASSOCIATION

Most bar associations will refer you to attorneys who practice family and adoption law. Be aware that an attorney listed as practicing family law most likely handles divorces and not adoptions. If the attorney indicates that he does handle adoptions, make sure he has experience handling your type of adoption, as many attorneys have only handled agency or stepparent adoptions. When you receive a referral, check the attorney's credentials with another source (e.g., a member of an adoption support group or RESOLVE).

The state bar association may also give information about appropriate legal fees.

In discussing your specific adoption with an attorney, do not hesitate to ask the attorney detailed questions, such as whether he will interact directly with a birth mother in a private adoption (and if he has done so in the past), or with the agency social worker in an agency adoption. Also, will the attorney review agency surrender documents or international adoption decrees before an adoption is finalized? Many attorneys who indicate they do adoptions simply mean they will file the court documents at the time you are ready for court. The involvement of these attorneys is quite limited and can be inadequate; for example, we have had many couples tell us that a particular attorney was "an adoption attorney," and yet, the same attorney never assisted with picking the baby up from the hospital nor in interacting with the hospital social worker prior to delivery or the discharge of the birth mother from the hospital.

THE INTERSTATE COMPACT ON THE PLACEMENT OF CHILDREN (ICPC)

Because adoptive couples and birth parents often live in different states, the need to regulate the interstate movement of children was recognized as early as the 1950s. The Interstate Compact on the Placement of Children provides such a mechanism and also outlines the procedure for the orderly transfer of children across state lines. The ICPC states that each state must have an office (or a separate unit of its social services agency) to monitor the individuals, organizations, or other entities involved in the placement of children in other states.

These include:

- The birth mother and birth father
- The adoption agency
- Any other person having custody of the child, including grandparents and other relatives
- Any corporation or association
- A court
- The state or the appropriate agency, or a subdivision of a state agency

The Compact does not involve the placement of a child by a family member into the home of another close relative, unless the child is in the custody of the state social services department. It only covers children placed through the foster care system, court-ordered placements of children, and children placed for adoption into the homes of nonrelatives.

Within the legal language of the Compact, the birth mother of a child to be placed is called the "sending agency," and the state from which the child comes is called the "sending state." (Note: If a birth mother's rights have been terminated and an adoption agency is involved, then the agency is known as the sending agency.) The sending ICPC office or unit retains jurisdiction over the child when he or she crosses a state line to the "receiving state." Keeping jurisdiction means that the ICPC unit receives supervisory reports and other regular reports detailing the child's adjustment to the new home and general progress. (Generally, this information comes from the postplacement supervisory visits, which are similar to a home study.) It also means that if the sending ICPC unit or sending agency (birth mother or adoption agency) believes that the adoptive family is not providing a home in "the best interests" of the child, then the sending ICPC unit or sending agency has the right to petition the court to have the child removed from the home.

The sending ICPC unit must be given the adoptive couple's approved home study before the child is placed with the adoptive parents. Until an adoption is finalized, the sending agency is technically responsible for the legal and financial protection of the child.

States began participating in the Compact beginning in 1960. New Jersey was the last state to join in 1990. All states now participate in the Compact and have enacted similar Compact laws.

While ICPC laws in each state are generally the same, certain guidelines vary. For example, some states require that the home study include a criminal and child-abuse clearance provided by the appropriate state law enforcement agency, while others simply request a letter stating that the couple has no criminal history from the couple's hometown police department.

Connecticut residents are required to use only an "approved" agency in the state in which the child is born. In fact, many states' ICPC guidelines mandate that a couple's home study be completed only by an approved adoption agency, and not by a certified social worker, who is normally allowed to provide home studies for in-state adoptions.

If you are adopting a child from out of state, it is critical that your attorney know the regulations for both the sending and the receiving states. Sometimes the guidelines for each state can appear contradictory. For example, in Virginia the adoptive and birth parents must know each other's names and addresses, while another state may require that all information be kept confidential. Also, sometimes the ICPC guidelines or state laws can change. Therefore, your attorney should talk with the correct personnel in the ICPC units for exact regulations and procedures. He should do this even if you have retained an attorney in the sending state. Unless your attorney has dealt extensively with the attorney in the sending state, he or she should not simply assume the other attorney knows his own state adoption laws and ICPC regulations.

Each state has a compact administrator, as well as one or more deputy administrators, who are responsible for day-to-day tasks. The deputy compact administrator generally handles all telephone calls and correspondence and grants the necessary approval to place a child with an out-of-state couple.

Contacting the right person at the ICPC office and having your attorney(s) quickly submit the correct paperwork is very important when the child you are about to adopt is in another state. Until all the required documents are submitted to and approved by the ICPC offices of both the sending and receiving states, the adoptive couple is not allowed to cross state lines with the child.

For example, if you are from New York and you locate a baby born in Utah, you will most likely go to Utah once the infant is discharged from the hospital. However, you cannot leave the state with the child until the ICPC offices in both Utah and New York give you permission. If the paperwork is not processed properly, you could find yourself living in a hotel for a couple of weeks with your new baby while you wait for approval from the ICPC offices. Of course, you want an attorney who will process all paperwork very quickly so that you can return home as soon as possible.

Do not depend on the ICPC personnel to fully assist you. Many ICPC offices are very helpful and do take the time to provide information; most are particularly helpful in dealing with attorneys who want a list of that state's ICPC requirements. However, many of the units are understaffed, so your lawyer should develop a good relationship with the adoption attorney in the state where the baby is born so that he or she can monitor the flow of paper and any new requests for information put forth by the ICPC offices.

ADOPTION ATTORNEYS

The adoption attorneys listed are either members of the American Academy of Adoption Attorneys or attorneys who have conducted a significant number of adoptions and are well versed in adoption law. In some states in which the population is very low, an attorney may conduct only a few adoptions, but the attorney should still be very knowledgeable. None of the attorneys are endorsed by the authors. Call a local RESOLVE support group or adoption support group members to determine if other people have used the attorney. Also, you can telephone the ICPC office and ask for names of attorneys who practice adoption law regularly in that state.

ADOPTION LAW: QUESTIONS AND ANSWERS

This section is provided to answer some of the most commonly asked questions about adoption law, primarily for those adopting independently or through a private agency. We have not attempted to address the laws and regulations relative to adoptions in which the birth parents' rights have been terminated due to abuse or neglect. However, some of the laws we do discuss can be applied to such situations.

Laws are subject to change, and even within a state, there can be county-by-county differences based on the way a judge interprets the law.

Several guides were considered in addressing the questions, including *Adoption Laws: Answers to the Most-Asked Questions*, published by the National Adoption Information Clearinghouse. In addition, scores of attorneys were interviewed, as well as the state adoption specialists and/or staff at ICPC units in nearly every state to determine how the law is actually practiced there.

Can an attorney serve as an intermediary?

This question asks whether an attorney can "find" a birth mother for an adoptive couple. In most states this is permissible as long as the attorney is not paid for her role as the intermediary. In several other states, an attorney technically is not even supposed to tell an adoptive couple about a birth mother. In many states that permit intermediaries, an attorney cannot directly place the baby with a couple. He may refer the birth mother to the adoptive couple, and the parties must then communicate with each other, either face-to-face or through letters or telephone calls.

In these states, an attorney cannot operate like an agency. The birth mother cannot place the baby first with the attorney and allow him or her to then select the adoptive parents. The attorney also cannot present information about and pictures of several couples to a birth mother and let her choose the couple.

Also, in many states the attorney cannot charge a fee for assisting a couple with finding a birth mother. Some judges will not even allow an attorney to charge an hourly rate for the services involved in finding and making arrangements to match a birth mother with an adoptive couple. Instead, the attorney may only charge a flat rate related to legal services provided, regardless of whether the couple finds a birth mother or not. Sometimes an attorney who does locate birth mothers for couples will have a higher fee than one who does not.

Is advertising permitted?

In most states and Washington, D.C., you can place an adoption advertisement in a newspaper. Some newspapers may have their own restrictions and may require you to have a letter from your attorney verifying that your interest in adoption is legitimate.

The *Gale Directory of Publications and Broadcast Media* provides a state-by-state listing of newspapers and magazines in the United States and Canada. This can be found in your library's reference section.

Who must consent to the adoption?

In almost all states, if a birth mother does not sign a surrender, then she must at least provide a written consent to the adoption. A consent or surrender is not necessary in those situations in which her rights are terminated because of mental illness, child abuse, neglect, etc. State laws vary on the circumstances in which a birth father's consent is required. A small number of states do not even require a birth parent's written consent before placement; the birth parents must, however, receive notice of the hearing that terminates their parental rights. It is a wise practice, however, to have in writing the birth parents' consent to the adoption (at the very least, that of the birth mother's) to avoid any later allegations of wrongdoing or kidnapping.

When a birth parent is under 18 years of age, a parent or court-appointed guardian may also have to consent to the adoption.

Again, after consent is given, the birth parents usually must be notified of the court hearing that will terminate their rights.

What is the difference between a birth mother's consent to adoption and the surrender or relinquishment of her parental rights?

A document that indicates that the birth mother is consenting to the adoption of her child by the adoptive couple is often referred to as the birth mother's consent to adoption. The birth mother's rights are not terminated by her signing this consent document; it is simply a statement by her that she is agreeable to the placement of her child with the adoptive couple, knowing that the couple will start legal proceedings to adopt the child. It is written evidence that the adoptive couple has physical custody of the child with the birth mother's approval.

A document which, if signed by the birth mother, terminates her parental rights, is known as a surrender or relinquishment of parental rights and is often referred to simply as a surrender or relinquishment. Most states allow only an approved adoption agency to "take a surrender" after several hours of counseling with a birth mother and birth father. Obviously, signing such a document is a serious matter and all attempts must be made to ensure that the birth parents really want to place the baby for adoption and understand fully the consequences of their actions. As an aside, the counseling provided must also inform the birth parents of state financial assistance available to them if they decide to keep the child. Some states allow an attorney or certified social worker to take a surrender without involving an adoption agency.

Some states allow the surrender document to be signed in front of a notary or an attorney, but some require that it be signed in court before a judge. Many states specify that the birth parent's rights are terminated immediately upon signing the surrender documents, while other states have a revocation period that allows the birth parents to revoke their surrender of parental rights within a specific amount of time. Such revocation periods are noted where applicable.

Because most of the state laws we reviewed referred to the surrender document as a "consent," the section on surrender of parental rights also uses "consent" to describe the termination of parental rights. Many attorneys and agency social workers also refer to the surrender as the consent. In discussing the termination of parental rights with an attorney or ICPC staff, it is wise to confirm that the consent referred to has the same legal effect as the surrender of parental rights.

What is a notice of an adoption hearing?

Notice of the adoption hearing must be given to the birth parents unless they waive their rights to this notice, which some states allow, or unless, as indicated before, they have already signed surrender documents. The notice document states that the adoptive couple (usually first names only) desires to adopt "Baby Boy Smith" and a hearing will be held on the matter; the time, date, and place of the hearing are also stated. Some states require that the adoption petition or complaint be served on the birth parent by a process server. Most states, except Virginia, allow all confidential information about the adoptive couple to be "whited out." Usually the birth parents must be given notice within a specified time period (usually between twenty to thirty days) prior to the hearing. How this is given varies from state to state. Sometimes notice is given in person (which means that a process server or law enforcement officer personally hands the legal documents to the birth parent), while other states allow the notice to be provided by certified mail. If the birth parent cannot be found or their identity is not known, notice is given by publication in a newspaper. Exactly what is published depends of course on the state; the notice is placed in the legal notes section of a newspaper along with notices of foreclosure actions and local zoning board applications and meetings. The basic contents of such a notice are that a baby was born on a certain date to the birth mother, the birth father is alleged to be the father of the child, and if he desires to assert his parental rights to the baby before the adoption is finalized he must do so within a certain time frame.

Several states, such as North Carolina, allow birth parents twenty-one days after signing a surrender to revoke it. In many states such as New Jersey and South Carolina, the surrender is not revocable unless the birth parents can show they were coerced into signing, or that they did not understand the seriousness of their actions because they were taking medications at the time that affected their judgment.

A small number of states require the birth parents to testify in court that they signed the surrender documents with full knowledge and understanding and that it was their intention to place the baby for adoption; until this is done, the surrenders can be revoked within a certain time period (ten to forty-five days). In lieu of the birth parents' attending a court hearing, some states allow the adoptive couple's attorney to present to the judge the signed surrender documents for the judge's inspection and approval.

Again, if an attorney or ICPC staff member discusses adoption law and practice with terms such as "consent" or "surrender," be sure to ask for definitions. It is important to know whether "consent" as used in that attorney's state means termination of parental rights or simply the birth mother's written statement of approval that the adoptive parents have custody of the baby with the intentions to adopt him or her. Ask whether there is a time period for revocation; also, ask if the birth parents must go to court to finalize the surrender in front of a judge.

What is a petition or complaint for adoption?

To schedule an adoption hearing in court, the attorney for the couple files with the clerk of the court (usually the family court clerk of court) an adoption petition or complaint, usually in the county in which the couple lives. The petition tells the court of the adoptive couple's desire to adopt the baby placed with them. The identities of the birth mother and birth father are disclosed; if the identity of the birth father is not known or the birth mother refuses to name him, then this is stated. The petition for adoption also requests that the judge terminate the birth parents' rights (if they have not already been terminated) and finalize the adoption. The information most often required in a petition is:

- Identifying information about the adoptive parents, including names, ages, and addresses
- The relationship between the adoptive parents and the child
- The legal reason that the birth parents' rights are being terminated
- An explanation of why the adoption is in the child's best interest
- Proof that the adoptive parents are fit to adopt the child

- The name of the guardian appointed for the child, if required, and
- The name of the adoption agency or certified social worker chosen by the court to conduct postplacement supervision and to provide a written report to the court.

Some states require that only one hearing be held to terminate birth parents' rights and to finalize the adoption. Other states have a two-step process. The first hearing, scheduled ten to ninety days after placement, is known as a preliminary hearing, which allows the judge to terminate the rights of the birth parents (assuming they have no objections) and to review the home study report. The final hearing is scheduled months later and simply allows more time for the placement to be reviewed by the court vis-à-vis the post-supervisory visit reports. The preliminary hearing is the critical one; the rights of the birth parents are terminated and the adoptive couple acquire "the legal rights of parents" but not the legal title of parents. The purpose of the final hearing has nothing to do with the birth parents' rights, because these have already been terminated. Rather, it is to allow the state to further evaluate by home visits the fitness of the adoptive couple as the parents of the child to be adopted. It is at the final hearing that the adoptive couple acquire the legal title of parents.

The judgment of adoption or order of adoption is signed by the judge holding the hearing and is the legal document that states the adoptive couple have legally adopted the child. This document allows the birth certificate to be revised showing the adoptive couple as parents as of the date of birth of the adopted child.

When can consent be taken from birth mother (father) and how long after the consent is signed can it be revoked?

In most states, a birth mother cannot sign a surrender form until after the baby's birth. In states in which she can sign it before the birth, it is not valid until after the birth. In many states, the surrender cannot be signed until seventy-two hours or more after the baby's birth.

In some states, a birth mother can also revoke her surrender within a certain time period (such as ten to thirty days after signing). If this happens, the court usually must then determine what is in the child's best interest.

A birth mother's surrender in some states, such as South Carolina, automatically terminates her rights. In other states, a birth mother signs a surrender, but her rights must also be terminated by a judge (e.g., Colorado).

What are the birth father's rights?

See Chapter 8 for more information on this issue.

What fees can the adoptive parents pay?

In most states, adoptive parents are allowed to pay reasonable fees associated with the adoption so that placing a child is not financially burdensome to a birth mother. However, direct payment to the birth mother for placing a child for adoption is illegal in all states. State laws vary as to the penalty for this crime, but in nearly all states, babybuying is grounds for a birth mother to revoke her consent, even after the adoption is finalized.

In all states the adoptive parents can pay for medical fees and their own legal fees, and in most states the adoptive parents can also pay for some living expenses. However, the issue is subject to much interpretation. Often an attorney will, as required by some state laws, have all living expenses preapproved by the judge who will oversee the adoption. Because living expenses for a birth mother can be high (for example, if a birth mother lives at a fancy hotel), most judges place a cap on what is considered "reasonable."

Another rule of thumb for defining reasonable expenses is that after all adoption-related expenses are paid, the birth mother should not have a financial gain. In other words, she should not have extra money in her bank account or a new car in her driveway as a result of placing the baby for adoption.

Where does the final adoption take place?

In most states you and your baby will attend an adoption finalization. This usually takes place at your county courthouse. If your child was born in your state, your attorney may suggest that the adoption proceedings take place in the county where the child was born, depending upon the presiding judge. For example, one judge may define "reasonable" living expenses that can be paid to the birth mother more broadly than another judge. You may want the more lenient judge to finalize your adoption.

If you are finalizing the adoption in another state (usually the state where the baby was born), you will probably go to court in the county where the baby was born. NOTE: In some states you cannot finalize an adoption unless you are a resident.

How are familial and stepparent adoptions different from nonbiological adoptions?

When a relative or stepparent is adopting a child, the laws will often be more lenient and requirements such as the home study may be less stringent or waived altogether. In general, the legal process is much easier unless the adoption is contested.

Can a nonresident finalize an adoption in the state?

If you adopt a child who is born outside of your state, you may have the option of finalizing the adoption in that state. However, many states do not permit you to adopt unless you are a resident.

NOTE: If you plan to advertise in a state where you are not a resident and, because of your state adoption laws, you also need to finalize the adoption there, call an attorney or the ICPC in that state and make sure you are still permitted to finalize there. (For example, if you live in Georgia and you find a birth mother through advertising in another state, you cannot finalize the adoption in Georgia.) To spend the money on advertising only to find out that you cannot finalize in that state is a waste of time and money.

If you just moved to a state, the laws specifying how long you have to live in a state before you can adopt generally do not apply. You can usually proceed with your adoption plans, because by the time the adoption is finalized you will have lived in the state long enough to qualify for residency.

ADOPTION AGENCIES AND SUPPORT GROUPS

In an attempt to make this book a complete adoption resource we have included lists of private adoption agencies and support groups for each state. There are also numerous public adoption agencies, and the adoption specialist's office of each state can forward you a list or refer you to the proper state office for more information about state-operated adoption agencies. Since there was no way for us to confirm the professionalism and competency of all the adoption agencies and support groups listed, check with a local adoption support group for references. Also, you or your attorney can call the state office responsible for licensing adoption agencies for background information on any particular agency. Your attorney can also call the person at your local family court who is responsible for processing adoption cases; this person can probably provide a reference to a particular agency.

ALABAMA

State Adoption Specialist

Office of Adoption, Family
　Services Division
Alabama Department of Human
　Resources
Carole Burton
50 Ripley Street
Montgomery, AL 36130-4000
(334) 242-1374
Fax: (334) 242-0939
www.dhr.state.al.us/acfs/acfs.html
cburton@dhr.state.al.us

State ICPC Administrator

Alabama Department of
　Human Resources
S. Gordon Persons Building, 2nd
　Floor, 50 Ripley Street
Montgomery, AL 36130-1801
(334) 242-9500

State Adoption Exchange/State Photolisting Service

Family Finders
Alabama Department of Human
　Resources, Office of Adoption
1933 Richard Arrington Jr.
　Boulevard South, Suite 102
Birmingham, AL 35209
(205) 271-1703
Fax: (205) 271-1770
Toll Free: (800) 926-8887
www.familyfinders.org

Licensed Private Adoption Agencies

Alabama Baptist Children's Home
　and Family Ministries, Inc.
P.O. Box 862084
Birmingham, AL 35236-2084
(205) 945-0037

Association for Guidance,
　Aid, Placement and Empathy
　(AGAPE) of North Alabama,
　Inc.
P.O. Box 3887
Huntsville, AL 35810
(256) 859-4481

Association for Guidance, Aid,
　Placement and Empathy
　(AGAPE), Inc.
P.O. Box 230472
Montgomery, AL 36123
(334) 272-9466

Association for Guidance,
　Aid, Placement and Empathy
　(AGAPE), Inc.
P.O. Box 850663
Mobile, AL 36685
(334) 343-4875

Catholic Family Services
2164 11th Avenue, South
Birmingham, AL 35205
(205) 324-6561

Catholic Family Services
733 37th Street, East
Tuscaloosa, AL 35405
(205) 533-9045

Catholic Family Services
P.O. Box 745
Huntsville, AL 35804
(256) 536-0041

Catholic Social Services
P.O. Box 759
Mobile, AL 36601
(334) 434-1550

Catholic Social Services
4455 Narrow Ln Rd.
Montgomery, AL 36116-2953
(334) 288-8890

Children of the World
201 Oswalt Street
Fairhope, AL 36562
(334) 990-3550

Children's Aid Society
3600 Eighth Ave South, Suite 300
Birmingham, AL 35222
(205) 251-7148

Family Adoption Services
529 Beacon Parkway West,
　Suite 108
Birmingham, AL 35209
(205) 290-0077

Lifeline Children's Services
2908 Pumphouse Road
Birmingham, AL 35243
(205) 967-0919

Southern Social Works
P.O. Box 8084
Anniston, AL 36207
(256) 831-4005

United Methodist Children's
　Home
P.O. Box 859
Selma, AL 36702
(334) 875-7283

Villa Hope International
　Adoption
6 Office Park Circle, Suite 218
Birmingham, AL 35223
(205) 870-7359
Fax: (205) 871-6629
www.pbwebstuff.com/villahope
villahope@worldnet.att.net

Adoptive Parent Support Groups

Adoption Connection
2620 Charlotte Oaks Drive
Mobile, AL 36695
(334) 661-4682

Alabama Friends of Adoption
145 S. Pointe Drive
Birmingham, AL 35209
(256) 290-0375

Alabama Friends of Adoption
P.O. Box 1453
Huntsville, AL 35807
(205) 535-2531

Greater Birmingham FPA and
　North American Council on
　Adoptable Children
　Representative
925 26th Street
Birmingham, AL 35244
(205) 925-6655
members.aol.com/nacac

North American Council on
　Adoptable Children
　Representative
131 Westbrook Road
Harpersville, AL 35078
(205) 672-2204
members.aol.com/nacac

Parents Adopting Children
　Together
1433 Varner Avenue
Auburn, AL 36830

Parents of International Children
9710 Dortmond Drive
Huntsville, AL 35803
(256) 880-8004

Single Adoptive Parents
　Support Group
Alabama Friends Adopt.
2407 Titonka Rd.
Birmingham, AL 35244
(205) 733-0976
catkins@dhhs.state.nh.us

The Adoption Support Group
Providence Hospital: Moorer
6801 Airport Boulevard,
    Moorer Conference Room
Mobile, AL 36608
(334) 377-7379
triadmember@yahoo.com

Search Support Groups

Adoptee Liberty Movement
    Association (ALMA)

P.O. Box 531262
Birmingham, AL 35253

Adoption Support Group
259 Vanderbilt Drive
Mobile, AL 36608
Benefiting Birthparents
4845 Avenue V, #32
Birmingham, AL 35205
(205) 923-4834

Orphan Voyage
1610 Pinehurst Boulevard
Sheffield, AL 35660
(256) 383-7377

Orphan Voyage
155 Whisperwood Lane
Madison, AL 35758
(205) 461-8679

ALABAMA LAWS RELATED TO ADOPTION: QUESTIONS AND ANSWERS

Can an attorney serve as an intermediary?
Yes, but an attorney can only provide outreach services to birth mothers; he or she cannot directly place a child with the adoptive parents.

Is advertising permitted?
Yes.

Who must consent to the adoption?
1. The birth mother
2. The birth mother's husband, regardless of paternity, if he and the mother were married and the child was born during the marriage or within 300 days after the marriage was terminated; or before the child's birth if he and the mother had attempted to marry in compliance with the law, although the attempted marriage is invalid, and the child was born during the attempted marriage or within 300 days after termination of cohabitation; or after the child's birth if he and the mother were married or attempted to marry and with his knowledge or consent he was named father on the birth certificate, if he is obligated to pay child suport; or if he received the adoptee into his home and openly held out the child as his own
3. The adoption agency that has legal custody of the adoptee, unless the court orders placement without the agency's consent
4. The presumed father, if he is known to the court and if he responds within thirty days to the notice he receives
5. The adoptee, if fourteen years of age or older, unless the adoptee is found not to have the mental capacity to consent

If the parent of the child to be adopted is a minor, a guardian ad litem must be appointed to represent the birth parents' interests of the parent.

When can consent be taken from the birth mother (father), and how long after the consent is signed can it be revoked?
Consent may take place at any time, except that once signed it may be withdrawn in writing within five days after the signing of the consent, whichever comes last. Consent can be withdrawn if the court finds that it is in the child's best interest within fourteen days after the child's birth or after the signing of consent. Consent can also be withdrawn within one year if it was obtained by fraud, duress, mistake, or undue influence.

Generally, independent adoptions are finalized ninety days after birth, and agency adoptions are finalized 180 days after birth.

What are the birth father's rights?
His rights are the same as the birth mother's, but it is essential to consult your attorney, as each case is different. The unwed birth father's consent can be dispensed with if he signs an affidavit saying that he is not the father or indicating that he has no interest in the child. His consent is also not necessary if he has not provided support or communicated with the child for a period of six months; the birth father's rights are considered terminated after this six-month period by reason of abandonment. While it is not clear from case law whether the birth father must receive notice of the adoption hearing if he does abandon his parental rights, it is wise to ensure the receipt of such notice. The birth father's rights are terminated if he does not respond within thirty days after being provided notice of the adoption proceeding. If he cannot be located or if his identity is unknown, then he can be served by publication; that is, a notice of the adoption proceeding is placed in a newspaper in the town or county of his last known whereabouts. If he does not respond to such publication, then his rights are terminated.

A putative father who files notice with the putative father registry within 30 days of the birth of the child is entitled to notice of adoption hearings. If he does not file within this time period, he is presumed to have given irrevocable implied consent to the adoption.

What fees can adoptive parents pay?
Adoptive parents can pay reasonable fees such as medical, living, and legal expenses with court approval.

Where does the adoption hearing take place?
The hearing can take place in the county in which the adoptive parents live, the child lives, or where the agency that has custody of the child is located.

How are familial and stepparent adoptions different from nonbiological adoptions?
Home studies are very seldom required, and there is no requirement as to disclosure of fees and costs. There is a one-year waiting period for a child in the home before the adoption can proceed. In stepparent and relative adoptions, visitation rights for grandparents may be given at the discretion of the court.

Can a nonresident finalize an adoption in this state?
Yes. After the child is placed in the adoptive home, at least one adoptive parent must be able to be at home with the child for at least sixty days.

ALASKA

State Adoption Specialist

Alaska Department of Health
and Social Services
Linda West
P.O. Box 110630, 350 Main
Street, 4th Floor
Juneau, AK 99811-0630
(907) 465-3631
Fax: (907) 465-3190
linda_west@health.state.ak.us

Alaska Department of Health
and Social Services
Suzanne Maxson
P.O. Box 110630,
350 Main Street, 4th Floor
Juneau, AK 99811-0630
(907) 465-3209
Fax: (907) 465-3190
www.hss.state.ak.us/dfys/
Overview.htm
suzanne_maxson@health.state.ak.us

State ICPC Administrator

Division of Family &
Youth Services
Alaska Department of Health
& Social Services
P.O. Box 110630
Juneau, AK 99811-0630
(907) 465-2105
Fax: (907) 465-3397

**State Adoption Exchange/State
Photolisting Service**

Alaska Adoption Exchange
P.O. Box 110630
Juneau, AK 99811-0630
(907) 465-3631

Northwest Adoption Exchange
600 Stewart Street, Suite 1313
Seattle, WA 98101
(206) 441-6822
Fax: (206) 441-7281
Toll Free: (800) 927-9411
www.nwae.org
nwae@nwresource.org

**Regional/District Public
Agencies**

Alaska Division of Family and
Youth Services, Anchorage
550 West Eighth Avenue,
Suite 300
Anchorage, AK 99501
(907) 269-3900

Alaska Division of Family and
Youth Services, Aniak
P.O. Box 149
Aniak, AK 99557
(907) 675-4377

Alaska Division of Family and
Youth Services, Barrow
P.O. Box 1079
Barrow, AK 99723
(907) 852-3397

Alaska Division of Family and
Youth Services, Bethel
P.O. Box 328, State Office
Building
Bethel, AK 99559
(907) 543-3141

Alaska Division of Family and
Youth Services, Cordova
P.O. Box 1688
Cordova, AK 99574
(907) 424-7133

Alaska Division of Family and
Youth Services, Craig
P.O. Box 254
Craig, AK 99921
(907) 826-3266

Alaska Division of Family and
Youth Services, Delta
P.O. Box 686
Delta Junction, AK 99737
(907) 895-4452

Alaska Division of Family and
Youth Services, Dillingham
P.O. Box 1290
Dillingham, AK 99576
(907) 842-2341

Alaska Division of Family and
Youth Services, Fairbanks
751 Old Richardson Highway,
Suite 300
Fairbanks, AK 99701
(907) 451-2650

Alaska Division of Family and
Youth Services, Fort Yukon
P.O. Box 149
Ft. Yukon, AK 99740
(907) 662-2331

Alaska Division of Family and
Youth Services, Galena
P.O. Box 239
Galena, AK 99741
(907) 656-1667

Alaska Division of Family and
Youth Services, Haines
P.O. Box 189
Haines, AK 99827
(907) 766-2608

Alaska Division of Family and
Youth Services, Homer
P.O. Box 1420
Homer, AK 99603-1420
(907) 235-7114

Alaska Division of Family and
Youth Services, Kenai
145 Main Street Loop, Suite 100
Kenai, AK 99611-7768
(907) 283-3136

Alaska Division of Family and
Youth Services, Ketchikan
415 Main Street, State Building,
Room 201
Ketchikan, AK 99901
(907) 225-6611

Alaska Division of Family and
Youth Services, King Salmon
P.O. Box 537
King Salmon, AK 99613
(907) 246-6642

Alaska Division of Family and
Youth Services, Kodiak
316 Mission Road, Suite 215
Kodiak, AK 99615
(907) 486-6174

Alaska Division of Family and
Youth Services, Kotzebue
P.O. Box 370
Kotzebue, AK 99752
(907) 442-3226

Alaska Division of Family and
Youth Services, Mat-su
268 E. Fireweed
Palmer, AK 99645
(907) 745-1701

Alaska Division of Family and
Youth Services, McGrath
P.O. Box 81
McGrath, AK 99627
(907) 524-3848

Alaska Division of Family and
Youth Services, Nome
P.O. Box 910
Nome, AK 99762
(907) 443-5247

Alaska Division of Family and
  Youth Services, Petersburg
P.O. Box 1089
Petersburg, AK 99833
(907) 772-3565

Alaska Division of Family and
  Youth Services, Seward
P.O. Box 148
Seward, AK 99664
(907) 224-5236

Alaska Division of Family and
  Youth Services, Sitka
210A Moller Street
Sitka, AK 99835
(907) 747-8608

Alaska Division of Family and
  Youth Services, St. Mary's
P.O. Box 124
St. Mary's, AK 99658
(907) 438-2138

Alaska Division of Family and
  Youth Services, Unalaska
P.O. Box 490
Unalaska, AK 99685
(907) 581-1236

Alaska Division of Family and
  Youth Services, Valdez
P.O. Box 2740
Valdez, AK 99686
(907) 835-4789

Alaska Division of Family and
  Youth Services, Wrangell
P.O. Box 970

Wrangell, AK 99929
(907) 874-3789

**Licensed Private Adoption
Agencies**

Adoption Advocates
  International
218 Martin Drive
Fairbanks, AK 99712
(907) 457-3832

Alaska International Adoption
  Agency
3605 Arctic Blvd #1177
Anchorage, AK 99503
(907) 276-8018
Fax: (907) 258-5410
aiaa@alaska.net

Catholic Social Services
3710 E. 20th, Suite 1
Anchorage, AK 99508
(907) 276-5590

Fairbanks Counseling
  and Adoption
912 Barnette
Fairbanks, AK 99701
(907) 456-4729
Fax: (907) 456-4623

Kawerak Adoption Agency
P.O. Box 948
Nome, AK 99762
(907) 443-4376

**Adoptive Parent Support
Groups**

Anchorage Adoptive Parents
  Association
550 West Seventh, Suite 1780
Anchorage, AK 99502
(907) 276-1680

North American Council on
  Adoptable Children State
  Representative
1018 26th Avenue
Fairbanks, AK 99701
(907) 452-5397
members.aol.com/nacac

Search Support Groups

Adoptee Liberty Movement
  Association (ALMA)
P.O. Box 585
Douglas, AK 99824
(907) 364-3133

American Adoption Congress
  State Representative
Box 2456
Sitka, AK 99835
(907) 747-5982

Concerned United Birthparents
  (CUB)
7105 Shooreson
Anchorage, AK 99504
(907) 333-2272
www.webnations.com/cub
cub@webnations.com

ALASKA LAWS RELATED TO ADOPTION: QUESTIONS AND ANSWERS

Can an attorney serve as an intermediary?
Yes.

Is advertising permitted?
Yes.

Who must consent to the adoption?
1. The birth mother
2. The birth father, if he was married to the mother at the time of conception, or at any time after conception, or if he is the child's father by adoption, or has otherwise legitmated the child
3. Any person who has custody of the child, or the court if the legal guardian is not empowered to consent
4. The adoptee, if older than 10 years of age, unless the court dispenses with this consent
5. The spouse of the adoptee

Written consent must indicate whether the child or parent is a member of an Indian tribe.

When can consent be taken from the birth mother (father), and how long after the consent is signed can it be revoked?
Consent can be taken at any time after the birth. It can be withdrawn in writing before the entry of the decree of the adoption and within 10 days after consent is given, or after 10 days if the court finds it to be in the child's best interest.

What are the birth father's rights?
The birth father's consent to the adoption is required if he has legitimized the child by marrying the mother. It is doubtful that the requirement of marriage to assert birth father rights would hold up in the state Supreme Court or in the U.S. Supreme Court. If the birth father acknowledged the child as his, maintained contact with the child, and supported him or her monetarily, then marrying the birth mother to assert his rights would not be necessary in view of the Supreme Court cases dealing with birth father rights. If the birth father has not had contact with the child for six months, then it is presumed that he has abandoned his parental rights and his consent is not necessary.

A putative father who files notice with the putative father registry within 30 days of the birth of the child is entitled to notice of adoption hearings. If he does not file within this time period, he is presumed to have given irrevocable implied consent to the adoption.

What fees can adoptive parents pay?
Adoptive parents must submit all expenses to the court. The report should include expenses for the child's birth and placement, the birth mother's medical care, and adoption services (agency adoption).

Where does the adoption hearing take place?
The hearing may take place in the district in which adoptive parents live, the child lives, or where the agency is located.

How are familial and stepparent adoptions different from nonbiological adoptions?
There are few requirements regarding birth parent notice and the home study. No disclosure of fees is required. Grandparents may have visitation rights if a stepparent or other grandparent has adopted the child.

Can a nonresident finalize an adoption in this state?
Yes.

In addition to state laws, rules must be followed that are written in the Alaska Rules of Court. An adoption attorney should have this rule book.

ARIZONA

State Adoption Specialist
Arizona Department of
   Economic Security
Carole Linker
P.O. Box 6123
Phoenix, AZ 85005
(602) 542-2359
Fax: (602) 542-3330

*www.childsworld.org/adoption/
   index.htm*
carole.linker@mail.de.state.az.us

State ICPC Administrator
Arizona Department of
   Economic Security
P. O. Box 6123
Phoenix, AZ 85005-6123
(602) 235-9134
Fax: (602) 351-2271

**State Adoption Exchange/State
   Photolisting Service**

Arizona Adoption Exchange Book
c/o Arizona Families for Children
P.O. Box 17951
Tucson, AZ 85731
(520) 327-3324
www.adopt.org

Regional/District Public Agencies

Department of Economic Security
Administration for Youth and Families
1789 West Jefferson
Phoenix, AZ 85007
(602) 542-3981

Licensed Private Adoption Agencies

Adoption Care Center
8233 Via Paseo Del Norte, Suite E250
Scottsdale, AZ 85258
(480) 820-1121

Aid to Adoption of Special Kids (AASK) of Arizona
501 E. Thomas Rd, Suite 100
Phoenix, AZ 85012
(602) 254-2275
Fax: (602) 212-2564
www.AASK-AZ.org

Arizona Baptist Children's Services
8920 North 23rd Avenue
Tucson, AZ 85021
(602) 943-7760

Arizona Children's Association
2700 S. Eighth Avenue
Tucson, AZ 85725
(520) 622-7611

Arizona Family Adoption Services, Inc.
346 East Palm Lane
Phoenix, AZ 85004-1531
(602) 254-2271
Fax: (602) 254-1587

Birth Hope Adoption Agency
3225 N. Central, Suite 1217
Phoenix, AZ 85012
(602) 277-2860

Black Family and Children Services
2323 N. Third Street, Suite 202
Phoenix, AZ 85004
(602) 256-2948

Casey Family Program/Tucson Division
1600 North Country Club, Suite 150
Tucson, AZ 85716
(520) 323-0886

Catholic Community Services of Western Arizona
1700 First Avenue, Suite 100
Yuma, AZ 85364
(520) 783-3308

Catholic Community Services/Cochise County
P.O. Box 177
Bisbee, AZ 85617
(520) 783-3308

Catholic Social Services of East Valley
430 North Southern Avenue, Suite 101
Mesa, AZ 85201
(480) 964-8771

Catholic Social Services of Flagstaff
201 West University Drive
Flagstaff, AZ 86001-0814
(520) 774-9125

Catholic Social Services of Phoenix
1825 W. Northern Avenue
Phoenix, AZ 85021
(602) 997-6105

Catholic Social Services of Tucson
155 W. Helen
Tucson, AZ 85703-5746
(520) 623-0344

Catholic Social Services of Yavapai
116 N. Summitt
Prescott, AZ 86301
(520) 778-2531

Catholic Social Services/Mohave County
2064 Plaza Drive, Suite F
Bullhead, AZ 86442
(520) 758-4176

Child Hope and Aid International
1645 North Alvernon Way
Tucson, AZ 85712
(520) 881-7474

Christian Family Care Agency
3603 N. Seventh Avenue
Phoenix, AZ 85013-3638
(602) 234-1935

Commonwealth Adoptions International, Inc.
4601 East Ft. Lowell, Suite 200
Tucson, AZ 85712

(520) 327-7574
Fax: (520) 327-8640
Toll Free: (888) 324-4651
www.commonwealthadoption.org
info@commonwealthadoption.org

Dillon Southwest
3014 N. Hayden Road, Suite 101
Scottsdale, AZ 85257
(480) 945-2221
www.dillonsouthwest.org
info@dillonsouthwest.org

Family Service Agency
1530 E. Flower
Phoenix, AZ 85014
(602) 264-9891

Hand in Hand International Adoptions
931 East Southern Avenue, Suite 103
Mesa, AZ 85204
(480) 892-5550
www.hihiadopt.org/
arizona@hihiadopt.org

Home Builders For Children, Inc.
7119 East Shea Boulevard, #109-676
Scottsdale, AZ 85254
(480) 922-1934

LDS Family Services
5049 E. Broadway Boulevard, Suite 126
Tucson, AZ 85711
(520) 745-6459

LDS Family Services
P.O. Box 856
Snowflake, AZ 85937
(520) 536-4117

LDS Social Services
235 S. El Dorado
Mesa, AZ 85202
(480) 968-2995

Lutheran Social Ministry of the Southwest
2020 W. Indian School Road, Suite B-20
Phoenix, AZ 85015
(602) 248-8248

Russian and Eastern European Adoption Center
8260 East Raintree Drive, Suite 111
Scottsdale, AZ 85260
(480) 905-3120
Fax: (602) 998-4366

Adoptive Parent Support Groups

Adopt America Network and North American Council on Adoptable Children
Representative
2911 E. Michigan
Phoenix, AZ 85032
(602) 493-1722
tseptember@aol.com

Advocates for Single Adoptive Parenting
8702 East Malcomb Drive
Scottsdale, AZ 85250
(480) 951-8310

Arizona Families for Children
1011 N. Craycroft, Suite 470
Tucson, AZ 85711
(520) 327-3324

Children With AIDS Project of America
Jim Jenkins
4141 Bethany Home Road
Phoenix, AZ 85019-1863
(602) 973-4319
Toll Free: (800) 866-AIDS
www.aidskids.org/
jljenkins@worldnett.att.net

Family and Adoption Counseling Center
2211 East Highland Avenue

Phoenix, AZ 85016
(602) 224-9757

Family Counseling Center
301 East Bethany Home Road, Suite C-296
Phoenix, AZ 85012
(602) 264-1800

Post Adoption Support Services
109 West Grant Road
Tucson, AZ 85705
(520) 975-6425
Fax: (520) 624-8154
strait@uswest.net

Search Support Groups

Adoptee Liberty Movement Association (ALMA)
P.O. Box 4544
Cave Creek, AZ 85327
(602) 595-2058

Adoption Counseling Home
1038 East Michigan Avenue
Phoenix, AZ 85022
(602) 614-9222
American Adoption Congress State Representative
P.O. Box 1432
Litchfield Park, AZ 85340-1432

Concerned United Birthparents (CUB)
8372 N. Sage Place

Tucson, AZ 85704
(520) 297-4204
www.webnations.com/cub
joypant@aol.com

Flagstaff Adoption Search and Support Group
P.O. Box 1031
Flagstaff, AZ 86002
(520) 779-3817

Scottsdale Adoption Connection
Box 2512
Scottsdale, AZ 85251

Search Triad
Box 10181
Phoenix, AZ 85064
(602) 834-7417

T.R.I.A.D.
7155 E. Freestone Drive
Tucson, AZ 85730
(520) 790-6320

T.R.I.A.D.
Box 12806
Tucson, AZ 85732
(520) 881-8250

Tracers Ltd.
Box 18511
Tucson, AZ 85730
(520) 885-5958

ARIZONA LAWS RELATED TO ADOPTION: QUESTIONS AND ANSWERS

Can an attorney serve as an intermediary?
Yes, attorneys may assist in direct placement adoptions. However, prior to attorney involvement the birth parents must have already selected the adoptive parents, or if after attorney involvement an adoptive couple certified by the court as a couple approved to adopt. Also, the adoptive parents must already have an approved home study filed with the court.

Is advertising permitted?
Yes.

Who must consent to the adoption?
1. The birth mother
2. The agency who has given consent to place the child for adoption
3. The birth father, if he was married to the birth mother at the time of conception or at any time prior to the child's birth, or if a court has established paternity

When can consent be taken from the birth mother (father), and how long after the consent is signed can it be revoked?

Consent cannot be taken until seventy-two hours after the baby's birth, and is irrevocable, unless obtained by fraud, duress or undue influence.

What are the birth father's rights?

The law permits the serving of a "Potential Father Notice" on any man identified by the birth mother. This notice can be served at any time that an adoption plan is being considered. The birth father has thirty days after being served the notice to proceed with paternity proceedings. If he fails to respond within thirty days, his consent is not required.

Arizona law also provides for a registry in which a putative father can file a claim as to his paternity of a child to be born. If he does not file a claim within thirty days after the child's birth, then he may not assert any parental interest in the child (unless he can show that he was unable to file such a claim and that he then did file within thirty days after being able to file). The fact that he was not aware of the birth mother's pregnancy is not a valid excuse for not filing a claim.

If the birth father is married to the birth mother, his rights are the same as hers.

What fees can adoptive parents pay?

Reasonable medical and legal expenses can be paid. Living expenses can be paid with court approval. Expenses are reviewed by the court.

Where does the adoption hearing take place?

The adoption hearing takes place in the court in the county in which the adoptive parents live.

How are familial and stepparent adoptions different from nonbiological adoptions?

No home study is required, and a stepparent adoption can be expedited depending upon how long the stepparent has been married to the parent, and how long the child has been in the home.

Can a nonresident finalize an adoption in this state?

No.

SOURCE: ARIZONA REVISED STATUTES CHAPTER 1, ARTICLE 1, SECTIONS 8-101 TO 8-132 (1998)

ARKANSAS

State Adoption Specialist

Arkansas Department of
   Human Services
Alden Roller
P.O. Box 1437, Slot 808
Little Rock, AR 72203-1437
(501) 682-8462
Fax: (501) 682-8094
Toll Free: (888) 736-2820
*www.state.ar.us/dhs/adoption/
   adoption.html*
alden.roller@mail.state.ar.us

State ICPC Administrator

Division of Children & Family
   Services, Arkansas
   Department of Human
   Services
P. O. Box 1437, Slot 830
Little Rock, AR 72203
(501) 682-8556
Fax: (501) 682-8561

**State Adoption Exchange/State
Photolisting Service**

Arkansas Department of
   Human Services
P.O. Box 1437, Slot 808
Little Rock, AR 72203-1437
(501) 682-8462
*www.state.ar.us/dhs/adoption/
   adoption.html*

State Reunion Registry

Arkansas Department of
  Human Services
Arkansas Mutual Consent
  Voluntary Adoption Registry
P.O. Box 1437, Slot 808
Little Rock, AR 72203-1437
(501) 682-8462

**Licensed Private Adoption
  Agencies**

Adoption Advantage
1014 West 3rd Street
Little Rock, AR 72201
(501) 376-7778

Adoption by Family Therapy of
  the Ozarks, Inc.
3433 S. Campbell, Suite S
Springfield, MO 65807
(417) 882-7700
Fax: (417) 882-5494
Toll Free: (800) 449-2229

Adoption Choices
1616 East 19th Street, Suite 101
Edmond, OK 73013-6674
(405) 715-1991
Fax: (405) 715-2640
Toll Free: (800) 898-6028

Adoption Services, Inc.
2415 North Tyler
Little Rock, AR 72207
(501) 664-0340
Fax: (501) 664-9186

Association for Guidance,
  Aid, Placement and Empathy
  (AGAPE) Child and Family
Services
111 Racine Street
Memphis, TN 38111
(901) 323-3600
Fax: (901) 272-7488

Bethany Christian Services
1100 North University Avenue,
  Suite 66
Little Rock, AR 72207
(501) 664-5729
Fax: (501) 664-5740
Toll Free: (800) 238-4269
www.bethany.org
info@bethany.org

Children's Home, Inc.
Church of Christ
1502 E. Kiehl Avenue, Suite B
Sherwood, AR 72120
(501) 835-1595
Children's Home, Inc. Church
  of Christ
5515 Old Walcott Road
Paragould, AR 72450
(870) 239-4031

Families Are Special
2200 Main Street, P.O. Box 5789
North Little Rock, AR 72119
(501) 758-9184

Gladney Center for Adoption
P.O. Box 94615
North Little Rock, AR 72190-
  4615
(501) 791-3206
www.gladney.org/
info@gladney.org

Highlands Child Placement
  Services
5506 Cambridge Avenue
Kansas City, MO 64130-0198
(816) 924-6565

Integrity, Inc.
P.O. Box 55014
Little Rock, AR 72215
(501) 614-7200

LDS Social Services of
  Oklahoma
4500 S. Garnett, Suite 425
Tulsa, OK 74102
(918) 665-3090

Mississippi Children's Home
  Society and Family Service
  Association
1900 North West Street, P.O.
  Box 1078
Jackson, MS 39215-1078
(601) 352-7784

Searcy Children's Home
  Church of Christ
900 N. Main Street
Searcy, AR 72143
(501) 268-5383

Small Miracles International
107 Mid America Blvd #3
Midwest City, OK 73110
(405) 732-7295
Fax: (405) 732-7297
www.smiint.org
MORR@smiint.org

Southern Christian Home
P.O. Box 556
Morrilton, AR 72110
(501) 354-2428

Volunteers of America of
  North Louisiana
360 Jordan Street
Shreveport, LA 71101
(318) 221-5000

Western Arkansas Youth
  Shelter
P.O. Box 48, Highway 96
Cecil, AR 72930
(501) 667-2946

**Adoptive Parent Support
  Groups**

Adopt America Network and
  North American Council on
  Adoptable Children
Representative
Field Representative
1314 N. Boston Avenue
Russellville, AR 72801
(501) 967-9337

AFACT and North American
  Council on Adoptable
  Children
17 McKee Circle
North Little Rock, AR 72166
(501) 758-7061

River Valley Adoption
  Support Group
1005 W. 18th Terrace
Russellville, AR 72801
(501) 967-1641

Search Support Groups

Orphan Train Heritage Society
  of America, Inc.
4912 Trout Farm Road
Springdale, AR 72764
(501) 756-2780
pda.republic.net/othsa

Orphan Voyage
601 S. Birch
Harrison, AR 72601-5911

ARKANSAS LAWS RELATED TO ADOPTION: QUESTIONS AND ANSWERS

Can an attorney serve as an intermediary?
Yes.

Is advertising permitted?
Yes.

Who must consent to the adoption?
1. The birth mother
2. The birth father, if he was married to the mother at the time the child was conceived or at any time thereafter; if he adopted the child; if he has custody of the child at the time the petition for adoption is filed; or if he has otherwise legitmated the child
3. Any person who has custody of the child, or the court if the legal guardian is not empowered to consent
4. The adoptee, if ten years of age or older, unless the court waives this
5. The spouse of the adoptee

When can consent be taken from the birth mother (father), and how long after the consent is signed can it be revoked?
Consent may take place at any time after the birth of the child and cannot be withdrawn after the entry of the decree of adoption. Consent may be withdrawn before the entry of the decree of adoption, but must be withdrawn within ten calendar days after the consent was given or after the child was born, whichever is later.

What are the birth father's rights?
Adoption law provides that if the birth father is not married to the birth mother his consent is not necessary, and he must file a claim of paternity with the putative father registry located at the Department of Vital Records; a birth father who files such a claim is entitled to notice of any adoption proceedings. The birth father's written consent for the adoption is needed if he was married to the birth mother at the time of conception or any time thereafter, or if he has legitimized the child.

In cases involving a child born to an unmarried mother, a search must be made of possible fathers in the putative father registry. If someone has filed a claim of paternity, he must receive notice of the pending adoption. After being notified, the putative father has a given time, set by the State, to claim an interest in the child.

What fees can adoptive parents pay?
Medical and legal fees can be paid, as well as living expenses. A listing of these expenses must be submitted to the court.

Where does the adoption hearing take place?
The hearing can take place in the county in which the adoptive parents live, the child lives, or where the agency that has custody of child is located.

How are familial and stepparent adoptions different from nonbiological adoptions?
No home study is required. The adoption process is less complicated, and, therefore, less expensive.

Can a nonresident finalize an adoption in this state?
Yes. Nonresidents can usually obtain a final decree of adoption within two weeks after the baby's birth, and, therefore, no Interstate Compact approval is required.

Arkansas requires prospective adoptive parents to have FBI fingerprint clearance before an adoption hearing.

CALIFORNIA

State Adoption Specialist

California Department of Social Services
Adoptions Branch
Wesley Beers
744 P Street, MS 19-69
Sacramento, CA 95814
(916) 445-3146
Fax: (916) 445-9125
Toll Free: (800) 543-7487
TTY: (916) 445-5837
www.dss.cahwnet.gov/getser/ cfsadopt.html
wesbeers@dss.ca.gov

State ICPC Administrator

Adult and Family Services Division
California Department of Social Services
744 P Street, MS 17-18
Sacramento, CA 95814
(916) 657-2614

State Adoption Exchange/State Photolisting Service

California Waiting Children
California Department of Social Services
744 P Street, MS 19-68
Sacramento, CA 95814
(916) 445-9124
Toll Free: (800) 543-7487
www.childsworld.org/

State Reunion Registry

California Department of Social Services
Adoption System Unit
744 P Street, MS 19-31
Sacramento, CA 95814
(916) 322-3778
www.childsworld.org/

Regional/District Public Agencies

California Department of Social Services, Chico
520 Cohasset Road, Suite 11
Chico, CA 95926
(530) 895-6143

California Department of Social Services, Fresno
770 E. Shaw, Suite 109
Fresno, CA 93710-7708
(209) 445-6556

California Department of Social Services, Los Angeles
1000 Corporate Center Drive, Suite 630
Monterey Park, CA 91754
(323) 981-1730

California Department of Social Services, Oakland
1515 Clay Street, Suite 308
Oakland, CA 94621
(510) 622-2650

California Department of Social Services, Rohnert - Eureka Subdistrict Office
231 Second Street
Eureka, CA 95501
(707) 445-6305

California Department of Social Services, Rohnert Park
101 Golf Course Drive, Suite 250
Rohnert Park, CA 94928
(707) 588-5000

California Department of Social Services, Sacramento
2035 Hurley Way, Suite 300-B
Sacramento, CA 95825
(916) 263-2001
Fax: (916) 263-2395

Licensed Private Adoption Agencies

AASK (Adopt A Special Kid)
287 17th Street, Suite 207
Oakland, CA 94612

(510) 451-1748
Fax: (510) 451-2023
Toll Free: (888) 680-7349
www.adoptaspecialkids.org

ACCEPT (An Adoption and Counseling Center)
339 S. San Antonio Road, Suite 1A
Los Altos, CA 94022
(650) 917-8090
www.adopting.org/ ACCEPT@ccnet.com

Across the World Adoptions
399 Taylor Blvd., Suite 102
Pleasant Hill, CA 94523
(925) 356-6260
Fax: (925) 827-9396
Toll Free: (800) 610-5607
www.adopting.com/atwa atwakids@pacbell.net

Adopt International
East Bay Office
5927 College Avenue, Suite A
Oakland, CA 94618
(510) 653-8600
www.adopt-intl.org adoptinter@aol.com

Adopt International
121 Springdale Way
Redwood City, CA 94062
(650) 369-7300
Fax: (650) 369-7400
www.adopt-intl.org/ adoptinter@aol.com

Adoption Connection
Jewish Family and Children Services
3272 California Street
San Francisco, CA 94118
(415) 202-7494
Fax: (415) 351-2707

Adoption Horizons
302 Fourth Street, 2nd Floor
Eureka, CA 95501-0302
(707) 444-9909
Fax: (707) 442-6672
Toll Free: (800) 682-3678

Adoption Options, Inc.
4025 Camino Del Rio South,
Suite 300
San Diego, CA 92108-4108
(619) 542-7772
Fax: (619) 267-7007
Toll Free: (877) 542-7772
www.cx1.com/options/

Adoption Services International
2021 Sperry Avenue, Suite 41
Ventura, CA 93003
(805) 644-3067
Fax: (805) 644-9270
adopting.org/asi.html
asicas@aol.com

Adoptions Unlimited
11800 Central Avenue, Suite 110
Chino, CA 91710
(909) 902-1412
Fax: (909) 902-1414

Alternative Family Services
   Adoption Agency
Suite 201, 25 Division Street
San Francisco, CA 94103
(415) 626-2700
Fax: (415) 626-2760

Angels' Haven Outreach
370 W. Grand, Suite 207
Corona, CA 92882
(909) 735-5400
www.angels-haven.com
info@angels-haven.com

Aspira Foster & Family Services
333 Gellery Bouldevard,
   Suite 203
Daly City, CA 94015
(650) 758-0111

Bal Jagat Children's World, Inc.
9311 Farralone Avenue
Chatsworth, CA 91311
(818) 709-4737
Fax: (818) 772-6377
www.adopt.baljagat.org/
bjcw@earthlink.net

Bay Area Adoption Services, Inc.
465 Fairchild Drive, Suite 215
Mountain View, CA 94043
(650) 964-3800
Fax: (650) 964-6467
www.baas.org/
info@baas.org

Bethany Christian Services -
   North Region
3048 Hahn Drive
Modesto, CA 95350-6503

(209) 522-5121
Fax: (209) 522-1499
Toll Free: (800) 454-0454
www.bethany.org
info@bethany.org

Bethany Christian Services -
   South Region
11929 Woodruff Avenue
Downey, CA 90241
(562) 803-3454
Fax: (562) 803-6674
www.bethany.org
info@bethany.org

Bethany Christian Services, Inc.
14125 Telephone Avenue,
   Suite 12
Chino, CA 91710-5771
(909) 465-0057
Fax: (909) 628-8294
www.bethany.org
info@bethany.org

Better Life Children Services
1337 Howe Avenue, Suite 107
Sacramento, CA 95825
(916) 641-0661

Black Adoption Placement and
   Research Center
Vallejo Office
508 Couch St
Vallejo, CA 94590
(707) 552-3658

Black Adoption Placement and
   Research Center
125 Second Street, 2nd Floor
Oakland, CA 94607
(510) 839-3678
Fax: (510) 839-3765

Catholic Charities Adoption
   Agency
349 Cedar Street
San Diego, CA 92101-3197
(619) 231-2828

Catholic Charities of the
   Archdiocese of San Francisco
814 Mission St., 5th Floor
San Francisco, CA 94103
(415) 844-4781

Children's Bureau of
   Los Angeles
Palmdale Office
1529 E. Palmdale, Suite 210
Palmdale, CA 93550
(805) 272-9996

Children's Bureau of
   Los Angeles
3910 Oakwood Avenue
Los Angeles, CA 90004
(213) 953-7356

Children's Bureau of
   Los Angeles, Inglewood
   District Office
610 N. Eucalyptus
Inglewood, CA 90302
(310) 673-7830

Children's Bureau of
   Los Angeles, Orange
   County Office
50 S. Anaheim Boulevard,
   Suite 241
Anaheim, CA 92805
(714) 517-1900

Christian Adoption
   Family Services
1698 Greenbriar Lane,
   Suite 219
Brea, CA 92821-5919
(714) 529-2949
Fax: (714) 671-7834
www.Nightlight-intl.com
Stoddart@Nightlight-intl.com

Chrysalis House
4025 North Fresno Street,
   Suite 106
Fresno, CA 93726
(559) 229-9862
Fax: (559) 229-9863
www.chrysalishouse.com
contact-us@chrysalishouse.com

East West Adoptions, Inc.
2 Parnassus Road
Berkeley, CA 94708
(510) 644-3996
Fax: (510) 548-0740

Families for Children
3650 Auburn Boulevard,
   Suite C-206
Sacramento, CA 95821
(916) 974-8744
Fax: (916) 487-1494

Families for Children
Benicia Office
560 First Street, Suite 201
Benicia, CA 94510
(707) 748-4150

Families for Children
Modesto Office
1317 Oakdale Road, Suite 1220
Modesto, CA 95355
(209) 548-9953

FamiliesFirst
1909 Galileo Court
Davis, CA 95616
(530) 753-0220

FamiliesFirst
Hercules Office
825 Alfred Nobel Drive, Suite F
Hercules, CA 94547
(510) 741-3100

FamiliesFirst
Sacremento Office
6507 4th Avenue, Suite 400
Sacramento, CA 95817
(916) 641-9595
Toll Free: (800) 495-9559

Family Builders By Adoption
528 Grand Avenue
Oakland, CA 94610
(510) 272-0204
Fax: (510) 272-0277
www.placenet.net/FACES
faces@familybuilders.org

Family Connections Adoptions
Sacramento Office
1832 Trubute Road, Suite 216
Sacramento, CA 95818
(916) 568-5966
Fax: (916) 568-6005

Family Connections Adoptions
Fresno Office
P.O. Box 7680
Fresno, CA 93747
(559) 438-9638
Fax: (559) 438-9485

Family Connections Adoptions
Oceanside Office
2181 S. El Camino Real,
Suite 206
Oceanside, CA 92054-6221
(760) 754-0200
Fax: (760) 754-0201

Family Connections Adoptions
P.O. Box 576035
Modesto, CA 95367-6035
(209) 869-8844
Fax: (209) 869-7334

Future Families, Inc.
South Bay Office
1671 The Alameda
San Jose, CA 95126-2222

(408) 298-8789
www.adopting.org/FutureFamilies.
html
FutureFams@aol.com

Future Families, Inc.
3233 Valencia Avenue,
Suite A-6
Aptos, CA 95003
(831) 662-0202
www.futurefamilies.org
graham@futurefamilies.org

God's Children International
Adoption Agency
19389 Live Oak Canyon Road
Trabuco Canyon, CA 92679
(949) 858-7621
Fax: (949) 858-5431
adopt@godschildrenadoption.org

Hand in Hand Foundation
200 Helen Court
Santa Cruz, CA 95065
(831) 476-1866

Heartsent Adoptions, Inc.
15 Altarinda Road, Suite 100
Orinda, CA 94563
(925) 254-8883
Fax: (925) 254-8866
www.heartsent.org

Holt International
Children's Services
3807 Pasadena Avenue,
Suite 170
Sacramento, CA 95821
(916) 487-4658
Fax: (916) 487-7068
www.holtintl.org
info@holtintl.org

Holy Family Services -
Counseling and Adoption
San Bernardino Office
1441 N. D Street
San Bernardino, CA 92405-4738
(909) 885-4882
www.hfs.org

Holy Family Services -
Counseling and Adoption
402 S. Marengo Avenue
Pasadena, CA 91101-3113
(626) 432-5680
www.hfs.org

Holy Family Services -
Counseling and Adoption
Santa Ana Office
1403 S. Main Street
Santa Ana, CA 92707-1790

(714) 835-5551
www.hfs.org

Independent Adoption Center
Central Office, Headquarters
391 Taylor Boulevard,
Suite 100
Pleasant Hill, CA 94523
(925) 827-2229
Fax: (925) 603-0820
Toll Free: (800) 877-6736
www.adoptionhelp.org
iacorg@earthlink.net

Independent Adoption Center
Sacramento Office
6929 Sunrise Boulevard,
Suite 102-I
Sacramento, CA 95610
(916) 723-6962
www.adoptionhelp.org
iacorg@earthlink.net

Independent Adoption Center
Los Angeles Office
5777 Century Boulevard,
Suite 1240
Los Angeles, CA 90045
(310) 215-3180
Fax: (310) 215-3252
Toll Free: (800) 877-6736
www.adoptionhelp.org
iacorg@earthlink.net

Independent Adoption Center
Laguna Hills Office
23441 South Pointe Drive,
Suite 250
Laguna Hills, CA 92653
(949) 699-2420
Fax: (949) 699-2414
Toll Free: (800) 877-6736
www.adoptionhelp.org
iacorg@earthlink.net

Indian Child and
Family Services
28441 Rancho California Road,
Suite J
Temecula, CA 92590
(909) 676-8832
Fax: (909) 676-3950
Toll Free: (800) 969-4237

Infant of Prague
6059 N. Palm Avenue
Fresno, CA 93704
(559) 447-3333
Fax: (559) 447-3322

Inner Circle Foster Care and
Adoption Services
7120 Hayvenhurst Avenue,
Suite 204
Van Nuys, CA 91406
(818) 988-6300

Institute for Black Parenting
Inland Empire Office
3233 Arlington Avenue,
Suite 202
Riverside, CA 92506
(714) 782-2800

Institute for Black Parenting
9920 La Cienega Boulevard,
Suite 806
Inglewood, CA 90301
(310) 348-1400
Toll Free: (800) 367-8858

International Christian
Adoptions
41745 Rider Way, #2
Temecula, CA 92590
(909) 695-3336
Fax: (909) 308-1753

International Foster Family and
Adoption Agency
460 E. Carson Plaza Drive,
Suite 212
Carson, CA 90746
(310) 715-3100

Kinship Center
Santa Ana Office
1520 Brookhollow Drive,
Suite 41
Santa Ana, CA 92705
(714) 979-2365
Fax: (714) 979-8135
www.kinshipcenter.org/
kinship@redshift.com

Kinship Center
22 Lower Ragsdale Drive, Suite B
Monterey, CA 93940
(831) 649-3033
Fax: (831) 646-4843
www.kinshipcenter.org/
kinship@redshift.com

LDS Family Services
Fountain Valley Office
17350 Mt. Herrmann Circle
Fountain Valley, CA 92708
(714) 444-3463

LDS Family Services
Colton Office
791 N. Pepper Avenue
Colton, CA 92324
(909) 824-0480

LDS Family Services
California North Agency
6060 Sunrise Vista Drive,
Suite 1160
Citrus Heights, CA 95610
(916) 725-5032

LDS Family Services
Concord Office
2120 Diamond Boulevard,
Suite 120
Concord, CA 94520-5704
(510) 685-2941

LDS Family Services
Fresno Office
1425 N. Rabe Avenue,
Suite 101
Fresno, CA 93727
(559) 255-1446

LDS Family Services
San Jose Office
4320 Stevens Creek Boulevard,
Suite 129
San Jose, CA 95129
(408) 243-1688

LDS Family Services
Van Nuys Office
7100 Hayvenhurst Avenue,
Suite 102
Van Nuys, CA 91406
(818) 781-5511

LDS Family Services, California
South Agency
5675 Ruffin Road, Suite 325
San Diego, CA 92123
(619) 467-9170

Life Adoption Services
440 W. Main Street
Tustin, CA 92780
(714) 838-5433
Fax: (714) 838-1160
www.lifeadoption.com
lifeadoption@fea.net

Lilliput Children's Services
130 East Magnolia
Stockton, CA 95202
(209) 943-0530
Fax: (209) 943-6829
Toll Free: (800) 408-2533
www.lcsadopt.org
LCSadopt@aol.com

Lilliput Children's Services
San Leandro Office
525 Estudillo Avenue, Suite D
San Leandro, CA 94577
(510) 483-2030
Fax: (510) 483-2084

Toll Free: (800) 408-2533
www.lcsadopt.org
LCSadopt@aol.com

Lilliput Children's Services
Sacramento Office
1610 Arden Way, Suite 273,
Suite 210
Sacramento, CA 95815
(916) 923-5444
Fax: (916) 923-6829
Toll Free: (800) 408-2533
www.lcsadopt.org
LCSadopt@aol.com

North Bay Adoptions
862 Third Street
Santa Rosa, CA 95404
(707) 570-2940
Fax: (707) 570-2943
www.wco.com/~nbadopt
nbadopt@wco.com

Olive Crest Adoption Services
2130 E. Fourth Street,
Suite 200
Santa Ana, CA 92705
(714) 543-5437, Ext: 164

Optimist Adoption Agency
758 Colorado Boulevard
Los Angeles, CA 90041
(323) 341-5561
Fax: (323) 257-6418
Toll Free: (800) 454-5561

Partners For Adoption
4527 Montgomery Drive,
Suite A
Santa Rosa, CA 95409
(707) 539-9068
www.sonic.net

Sierra Adoption Services
Sacramento Office
8928 Volunteer Lane, Suite 240
Sacramento, CA 95826
(916) 368-5114
www.gv.net/~sas/
sas@gv.net

Sierra Adoption Services
117 New Mohawk Rd., Suite A
Nevada City, CA 95959
(530) 265-6959
Fax: (530) 265-9223
www.gv.net/~sas/
sas@gv.net

Southern California F.F.A.-
Adoption Program
155 N. Occidental Boulevard
Los Angeles, CA 90026
(213) 365-2900

The Family Network, Inc.
307 Webster Street
Monterey, CA 93940
(831) 655-5077
Fax: (831) 655-3811
Toll Free: (800) 888-0242

The Sycamores Adoption Agency
2210 South DeLacey Avenue,
Suite 110
Pasadena, CA 91105-2006
(626) 395-7100

Trinity Children and
Family Services
1111 Howe Avenue, Suite 455
Sacramento, CA 95825
(916) 646-1256

Trinity Children and
Family Services
Long Beach Office
4647 Long Beach Boulevard,
Suite B2
Long Beach, CA 90805
(562) 595-9225

True to Life Children's Services
400 Morris Street, Suite E
Sebastopol, CA 95472
(707) 823-7300

Valley Teen Ranch
2610 W. Shaw, Suite 105
Fresno, CA 93711
(559) 437-1144
Fax: (559) 438-5004

Vista Del Mar Child Care
Services
3200 Motor Avenue
Los Angeles, CA 90034
(310) 836-1223

Westside Children's Center
4600 Lindblade Drive
Culver City, CA 90230
(310) 390-0551

**Adoptive Parent Support
Groups**

ACCEPT
416 Chardonnay Drive
Fremont, CA 94539
(510) 490-4402

Adopt America Network of San
Diego
544 Augusta Drive
San Marcos, CA 92069
(619) 741-5399

Adoption Assistance and
Support Group
16255 Ventura Boulevard,
Suite 704
Encino, CA 91436-2302

Adoption Choice of America
716 N. Ventura Road, Suite 348
Oxnard, CA 93030
(805) 483-2551

Adoption Horizons
302 Fourth Street, 2nd Floor
Eureka, CA 95501
(707) 444-9909

Adoption Information Center
638 9th Street
San Pedro, CA 90731
(310) 732-1023
Fax: (310) 732-1101
iaaic@pactbell.net

Adoption Options
5101 Glen Verde Drive
Bonita, CA 91902-2625
(619) 267-4090

Adoption Support and
Information Group
16255 Ventura Boulevard,
Suite 704
Encino, CA 91436
(818) 501-6800

Adoption Support Center
Stephen S. Wise Temple, 15500
Stephen S. Wise Drive
Los Angeles, CA 90077-1598
(310) 476-8561, Ext: 2209

Adoptive Parent Support
and Referral
12065 Persimmon Terrace
Auburn, CA 95603
(916) 885-1944

Adoptive Parent Support Group
1584 North Ferger Avenue
Fresno, CA 93728
(209) 486-2019

AFTER- Adoptive Family
Therapeutic and Educational
Resources
115 East Gish Road #246
San Jose, CA 95112
(877) 332-3837
www.afteradoption.org

Bal Jagat Children's World, Inc.
9311 Farralone Avenue
Chatsworth, CA 91311

(818) 709-4737
Fax: (818) 722-6377
www.adopt.baljagat.org/
bjcw@earthlink.net

Bay Area Adoption Support
465 Fairchild Drive, Suite 215
Mountain View, CA 94043
(650) 964-3800
Fax: (650) 964-6467

Bay Area Single Adoptive
Parent Group
North
3816 Via Verde
El Sobrante, CA 94803
(510) 758-9431

Bay Area Single Adoptive
Parent Group
South
385 S. 14th Street
San Jose, CA 95112
(408) 292-1638

Building Families Through
Adoption
19150 Gorstrom Lane
Ft. Bragg, CA 95437
(707) 964-3973

California Adoption Advocacy
Network
718 E. Meadow
Palo Alto, CA 94303
(415) 494-3057

Children's Home Society
of California
17050 Chatsworth Street,
Suite 206
Granada Hills, CA 91344-5879
Toll Free: (800) 564-9095

Colombian Adoption Network
23059 Cohasset Street
West Hills, CA 91307
(818) 883-5748

Conejo Adoptive Families
1124 Hendrix Avenue
Thousand Oaks, CA 91360-3647

Cooperative Adoption
Consulting
54 Wellington Avenue
San Anselmo, CA 94960
(415) 453-0902

Faces
2510 Smith Grade Road
Santa Cruz, CA 95060
(831) 423-3870

Families Adopting in Response
(FAIR)
P.O. Box 51436
Palo Alto, CA 94303
(650) 856-3513
Fax: (650) 494-2971
www.fairfamilies.org
info@fairfamilies.org

Families for Russian and
Ukrainian Adoptions
San Francisco and Northern
California Chapter
9 De Anza Court
San Mateo, CA 94402
(650) 341-1596
j.e.lawrence@worldnet.att.net

Families with Children
From China
San Francisco Bay Area
San Francisco, CA
www.fwcc.org/SanFrancisco
amyk@alumni.stanford.org

Families with Children
from China
2265 Via Tempo
Cardiff-by-the-Sea, CA 92007-
1216
(619) 753-1965
RPWhitFam@world.att.net

Family Adoption Network
5869 North Bethel
Clovis, CA 93612
(209) 298-1760

Foothill Adoptive Parent
Support Group
12490 Erin Drive
Auburn, CA 95603
(916) 885-4617

For the Children
13074 Larkhaven Drive
Moreno Valley, CA 92553
(714) 656-4240

Friends of Korea
P.O. Box 5585
El Dorado Hills, CA 95762
(916) 964-0345
KAAN@aol.com

Grandparents Parenting Again
1014 Hopper Avenue, Suite 221
Santa Rosa, CA 95403
(707) 566-8676
Fax: (707) 566-8677

Hand in Hand
P.O. Box 529
Loomis, CA 95650
(916) 660-0229
bowler@foothill.net

Hand in Hand
874 Phillip Court
El Dorado Hills, CA 95762
(916) 933-4562

Heal the Hearts Foundation, Inc.
3385 Somis Drive
Riverside, CA 92507
(909) 788-5966
Fax: (909) 788-5966
www.healtheheart.org
terri@healtheheart.org

Heartline
37680 Green Knolls Road
Winchester, CA 92396
(714) 677-1124

Holt San Diego Support Group
8690 Via Del Luz
El Cajon, CA 92021
(619) 390-1487

Humbolt County Council on
Adoptable Children
P.O. Box 4767
Arcata, CA 95521
(707) 444-2565

Inter Country Adoption
Network
10419 Pearson Place
Sunland, CA 91040
(818) 352-0332

Korean American Adoptee
Adoptive Family Network
P.O. Box 5585
El Dorado Hills, CA 95762
members.aol.com/kaanet
KAANet@aol.com

MICA
1744 N. Damon
Simi Valley, CA 93063

North Coast Adoptive Families
2136 Parrish Drive
Santa Rosa, CA 95404
(707) 575-8663

Open Door Society and North
American Council on
Adoptable Children
Representative
170 E. Highland, Room E
Sierra Madre, CA 91204
(818) 355-5920

Open Door Society of
Los Angeles
12235 Silva Place
Cerritos, CA 90701
(562) 402-3664

Orange County Parents
Association
39 Foxboro
Irvine, CA 92714
(714) 786-6494

OURS Through Adoption
Box 85152-343
San Diego, CA 92138
(619) 282-6164

PACT, an Adoption Alliance
Los Angeles
c/o Vista Del Mar - Community
Services, 3200 Motor Avenue
Los Angeles, CA 90034
(310) 836-1223, Ext: 343
Fax: (510) 482-2089
www.pactadopt.org
info@pactadopt.org

PACT, an Adoption Alliance
1700 Sacramento Street,
Suite 111
San Francisco, CA 94111
(415) 221-6957
Fax: (510) 482-2089
www.pactadopt.org
info@pactadopt.org

Parents and Children Together
638 9th Street
San Pedro, CA 90731
(310) 732-1023
Fax: (310) 732-1019

Parents of Adoptees in Crisis
1664 Springvale Road
Placerville, CA 95667
(916) 626-6891

Parents of Peruvian Adoptees
623 Prospect Avenue, Suite 3
South Pasadena, CA 91030
(818) 403-0512

Patchwork Adoptive Families
P.O. Box 5153
Stockton, CA 95205
(209) 942-2812

Peninsula Adoptive Parents
Group
248 Parks Avenue
San Carlos, CA 94070
(415) 594-9195

Placer Adoption/Attachment
P.O. Box 7155
Auburn, CA 95604
(916) 885-5258

Post Adoption Center for
Education and Research
(PACER)
P.O. Box 743
Corte Madera, CA 94976
(925) 935-6622
Fax: (415) 898-5599
www.mo.com/pacer

Post Adoption Center for
Education and Research
(PACER) of Marin
Box 826
Larkspur, CA 94977
(415) 924-7047

Post Adoption Support Group
3805 Regent Road
Sacramento, CA 95821
(916) 487-7243

Private Adoption-Where to
Begin?
P.O. Box 405
Boulder Creek, CA 95006

Resolve of Northern California
312 Sutter Street, 4th Floor
San Francisco, CA 94108

Single Adoptive Parent Group
4316 G Street
Sacramento, CA 95819
(916) 457-4278

Single Adoptive Parents of
Los Angeles
12720 Burbank Blvd. No. 218
N. Hollywood, CA 91607
(818) 769-3376

Single Adoptive Parents,
North Bay Chapter
1839 Catalina
Berkley, CA 94707
(510) 524-5050

Single Adoptive Parents,
South Bay Chapter
385 South 14th Street
San Jose, CA 95112
(408) 292-1638

Solano County Adoption Group
212 Sunhaven Drive
Fairfield, CA 94533
(707) 429-5447

Stars of David International Inc.
Jewish Family Service -
Orange County Chapter
250 Baker Street East, Suite G
Costa Mesa, CA 92626-4500
(714) 939-1111, Ext: 106
Fax: (714) 939-1772
www.starsofdavid.org
starsdavid@aol.com

Stars of David International Inc.
Jewish Adoption Information
Exchange
7 Admiral
Irvine, CA 92714
(949) 262-3447
www.starsofdavid.org
starsdavid@aol.com

Stars of David International Inc.
Jewish Adoption Information
Exchange
Los Angeles/San Fernando
Valley Chapter
Northridge, CA
(818) 368-0737
www.starsofdavid.org
MyrnaM3@aol.com

Stars of David International Inc.
Los Angeles/San Fernando
Valley Chapter
5924 Nora Lynn Drive
Woodland Hills, CA 91367
(818) 884-7169
www.starsofdavid.org
starsdavid@aol.com

Stars of David International Inc.
South Bay/Sunnyvale Chapter
10156 Camberley Lane
Cupertino, CA 95014-2633
(408) 996-9752
www.starsofdavid.org
RecruitsCA@aol.com

Stars of David International Inc.
Los Angeles/San Fernando
Valley Chapter
12150 Bowmore Avenue
Northridge, CA 91326
(818) 366-7030
www.starsofdavid.org
starsdavid@aol.com

Stars of David International Inc.
South Bay/Sunnyvale Chapter
959 Astoria Drive
Sunnyvale, CA 94087-3006
(408) 739-9419
www.starsofdavid.org
starsdavid@aol.com

Stars of David International Inc.
Jewish Family Service of
San Diego
3715 6th Avenue
San Diego, CA 92103-4316
(619) 291-0473
Fax: (619) 291-2419
www.starsofdavid.org
jfs-sd@msn.com

Stars of David International Inc.
Jewish Adoption Information
Exchange
107 Mandala Court
Walnut Creek, CA 94596
(925) 932-3078
www.starsofdavid.org/
MikeREllen@aol.com

Stephen S. Wise Adoption
Support Center
15500 Stephen S. Wise Drive
Los Angeles, CA 90077
(310) 889-2209
Fax: (310) 472-9395

Together Expecting a Miracle
(TEAM)
1300 Astoria Place
Oxnard, CA 93030
(805) 485-4677

Search Support Groups

Adoptee Liberty Movement
Association (ALMA)
17595 Vierra Canyon Road,
Box 165
Prunedale, CA 93907

Adoptee Liberty Movement
Association (ALMA)
San Francisco Bay
P.O. Box 21554
Concord, CA 94521
(510) 689-5583

Adoptee Liberty Movement
Association (ALMA)
933 E. Sierra Madre
Fresno, CA 93704
(209) 229-8950

Adoptee Liberty Movement
Association (ALMA)
P.O. Box 4572
Lancaster, CA 93539

Adoptee Liberty Movement
Association (ALMA)
P.O. Box 191514
Sacramento, CA 95819
(916) 455-ALMA

Adoptee Liberty Movement
Association (ALMA)
P.O. Box 1233
Simi Valley, CA 93062
(805) 583-0965

Adoptee Liberty Movement
Association (ALMA)
P.O. Box 271
Vina, CA 96092
(530) 824-4790

Adoptee Liberty Movement
Association (ALMA)
P.O. Box 9425
Canoga Park, CA 91309
(626) 441-0858

Adoptees Birthparents
Association
P.O. Box 33
Camarillo, CA 93011
(805) 482-8667

Adoptees Birthparents
Association
2027 Finch Court
Simi Valley, CA 93063
(805) 583-4306

Adoption Reality
2180 Clover Street
Simi Valley, CA 93065
(805) 526-2289

Adoption Reunion Support
Group
1115 Sunset Drive
Vista, CA 92083
(619) 726-1924

Adoption Support Group of
Santa Monica
1452 26th Street, #103
Santa Monica, CA 90404

Adoption Triad Support Group
1755 Diamond Mountain Road
Calistoga, CA 94515
(707) 943-5877

Adoption with Truth
66 Panoramic Way
Berkeley, CA 94704
(415) 704-9349

Adoption/Birth Family Registry
Dept. R, Box 803
Carmichael, CA 94303

American Adoption Congress
State Representative
12702 Ninth Street
Garden Grove, CA 92840

(714) 827-2418
BillBossert@compuserve.com

American Adoption Congress
State Representative
154 Bryant Street
Palo Alto, CA 94301-1102
(650) 328-1125
suhamm@aol.com

American Adoption Congress
State Representative
Box 230643
Encinitas, CA 92023-0643
(760) 753-8288
Fax: (760) 753-8073
choard@worldnet.att.net

Americans for Open Records
P.O. Box 401
Palm Desert, CA 92261

Association of Korean Adoptees
108 N. Branch Boulevard
Glendale, CA 91202
(818) 547-4945

Bay Area Birthmothers
Association
1546 Great Highway, #44
San Francisco, CA 94122

Birthparent
Connection/Adoption
Connection of San Diego
P.O. Box 230643
Encinitas, CA 92023-0643
(619) 753-8288

Central Coast Adoption
Support Group
Box 2483
Goleta, CA 93117
(805) 682-5250

Central Coast Adoption
Support Group
1718 Longbranch
Grover City, CA 93433
(805) 481-4086

Concerned United Birthparents
(CUB)
10997 Road 252
Terra Bella, CA 93270
(209) 535-4084
www.webnations.com/cub
cub@webnations.com

Concerned United Birthparents
(CUB)
7345 Alicante Road, #S
Carlsbad, CA 92009

(619) 930-9322
www.webnations.com/cub
kayleevee@earthlink.net

Equality Nationwide/Unwed
Fathers
4724 Lincoln Boulevard, #334
Marina del Rey, CA 90292
(310) 821-4581

Full Circle
Box 816
Lake Forrest, CA 92630
(714) 951-1689

Hand in Hand
391 Teasdale Street
Thousand Oaks, CA 91360
(714) 951-1689

Independent Search Consultant
P.O. Box 10192
Costa Mesa, CA 92627
home.rmci.net/isc/
isc@rmci.net

Kerr Heritage Institute
P.O. Box 232578
Encinitas, CA 92023-2578
(619) 944-6752

Los Angeles County Adoption
Search Association
P.O. Box 1461
Roseville, CA 95661
(916) 784-2711

May Day Project for
Birthmothers
P.O. Box 8445
Berkeley, CA 94707

Mendo Lake Adoption Triad
620 Walnut Avenue
Ukiah, CA 95482
(707) 468-0648

PURE, Inc.
P.O. Box 638
Westminster, CA 92683
(714) 892-4098

R.O.O.T.S.
P.O. Box 40564
Bakersfield, CA 93384-0564
(805) 832-5549

ReConnections of California
41669 Zinfandel Avenue
Temecula, CA 92591
(909) 695-1152
www.lanz.com/reconnect
lisarick@aol.com

Santa Cruz Birthmother
   Support
Box 1780
Freedom, CA 95019
(831) 728-3876

Search and Find
Box 8765
Riverside, CA 92515

Search Finders of California
P.O. Box 24595
San Jose, CA 95154
(408) 356-6711

Searchers Connection
7709 Skyhill Drive
Los Angeles, CA 90068
(213) 878-0630

Second Abandonment
2323 Eastern Canal
Venice, CA 90291
(805) 379-4186

South Coast Adoption Research
   and Support
P.O. Box 39
Harbor City, CA 90710
(213) 833-5822

Stephen S. Wise Adoption
   Support Center
15500 Stephen S. Wise Drive
Los Angeles, CA 90077
(310) 889-2209
Fax: (310) 472-9395

Triad Research
300 Golden West
Shafter, CA 93262

Triple Hearts Adoption
   Triangle
P.O. Box 51082
Riverside, CA 92517
(909) 797-2367
jam21@webtv.net

Westside Adoption Support
4117 Overland Avenue
Culver City, CA 90230
(310) 470-9065

CALIFORNIA LAWS RELATED TO ADOPTION: QUESTIONS AND ANSWERS

Can an attorney serve as an intermediary?
Yes. In fact, many nonattorneys also serve as intermediaries and operate as independent facilitators.

Is advertising permitted?
No, only a licensed intermediary, attorney, or adoption agency can advertise. Many prospective adoptive parents simply advertise in other states or in national publications.

Who must consent to the adoption?
1. The birth mother
2. The man who is presumed to be the father by marriage or attempted marriage to the mother at the time of birth or within 300 days prior to birth; or had been legitimated as the father by other specified means
3. Department of Social Services or county adoption agency, where parental consent is not necessary
4. An adoptee who is over 12 years of age

When can consent be taken from the birth mother (father), and how long after the consent is signed can it be revoked?
The birth mother must be counseled twice by a state-authorized adoption service provider (there are many in the state). The first advisement can occur before the child's birth; the birth mother must then be readvised at least ten days between the first and second session before she can sign a placement agreement that contains the consent. The maximum fee for being advised is $500; however, travel and counseling time can also be added to the fee.

The consent can be given any time after the baby is born and the mother is discharged from the hospital. In an agency adoption the relinquishment is binding, and in an independent adoption the birth parents can withdraw consent before ninety days or waive those ninety days.

The waiver must be signed in front of a state social worker, but finding such a social worker can sometimes be difficult. If a state social worker is not available because the birth mother lives in a remote area, she can go before a judge—but this very seldom is necessary. There is no charge for the social worker's service.

Because a preplacement home study is not required for an in-state placement, a social worker will not take a waiver until she knows more about the adoptive parents, and usually the social worker will want to meet the parties involved.

If a child is born in another state, the taking of a consent must follow California procedure and there must be ten days in between the advisement of counsel and the second advisement before a consent can be taken. The birth mother's consent and waiver can be taken by an attorney who represents her exclusively in lieu of a state-authorized adoption placement provider and a state social worker.

Regarding independent adoptions, any required consents may be withdrawn, until 90 days have passed, at which time the consent becomes permanent. A parent's relinquishment to an adoption agency, filed with the department, is final. It may be rescinded only upon mutual agreement of the relinquishing parents and adoption agency.

NOTE: Your adoption can become an identified agency adoption in which the agency conducts your home study and takes the birth mother's relinquishment seventy-two hours after the child is born. This process can be done without signing an adoption placement agreement and without involvement of the Department of Social Services.

What are the birth father's rights?
The court shall order that relevant persons and agnecies make efforts to identify the alleged natural father. Any potential natural father who is identified must be given notice of the hearing. After the natural father, or more than one natural father, is notified, he must claim paternity within theirty days and appear at the hearing or parental rights will be terminated. If the natural father does appear in court, the court will determine if he is in fact the father and then determine if it is in the child's best interest for the father to retain his parental rights. If so, the father's consent will be required. If not, the court will terminated the father's parental rights.

What fees can adoptive parents pay?
Adoptive parents can pay medical, legal, and reasonable living expenses, and must file with the court a report of all expenses paid.

Where does the adoption hearing take place?
The hearing takes place in the county where the adoptive parents live. In the case of adult adoptions, the hearing takes place in the county where the adoptive parent resides or where the adult adoptee resides.

How are familial and stepparent adoptions different from nonbiological adoptions?
The home study is more superficial and is conducted by the county. In a stepparent adoption, the parents must be married at least one year.

In a relative adoption, the birth parents' rights can be terminated by a citation hearing as well as by the same methods as an independent adoption. Consents are revocable, by court order, until the final adoption. No accounting report is required and no placement agreement is required. Also, there is no requirement for the birth parent to meet with an adoption service provider.

In a stepparent adoption, there is no statutory time limit in which the adoption must be completed, so the process often takes a long time.

If a child is adopted by a stepparent or grandparent and one of the child's parents is deceased, then the deceased parent's parents may be granted visitation rights if it is in the child's best interest.

Can a nonresident finalize an adoption in this state?
No.

NOTE: There are many facilitators who "find" birth mothers. They market themselves to look like agencies and try to recruit adoptive parents. While doing so, they also find birth mothers, although they cannot advertise to find birth mothers. The facilitators' fees can be very high—as much as $6,000—just to find a birth mother. If a facilitator finds a birth mother, you must also use an attorney and a counselor for the birth mother. Some facilitators do much for the birth mother and their fee includes making many arrangements such as finding an apartment, making health care visits, and so on.

Birth mothers are often contacted through obstetricians. In California, this method of contacting birth mothers is very different from most states. Since physicians can serve as intermediaries; perhaps this is the reason why so many are willing to tell birth mothers and adoptive parents about each other.

COLORADO

State Adoption Specialist

Colorado Department of
  Human Services
Child Welfare Services
Barbara Killmore
1575 Sherman Street, 2nd Floor
Denver, CO 80203-1714
(303) 866-3209
Fax: (303) 866-4629
www.cdhs.state.co.us/cyf/
  cwelfare/cwweb.html
barbara.killmore@state.co.us

State ICPC Administrator

Colorado Department of
  Human Services
1575 Sherman Street, 2nd Floor
Denver, CO 80203
(303) 866-2998
Fax: (303) 866-4629

**State Adoption Exchange/State
  Photolisting Service**

Colorado Adoption Resource
  Registry (CARR)
Colorado Department of
  Human Services Child
  Welfare Services
1575 Sherman Street, 2nd Floor
Denver, CO 80203-1714

(303) 866-3209
www.cdhs.state.co.us/cyf/cwel-
  fare/cwweb.html

The Adoption Exchange
14232 East Evans Avenue
Aurora, CO 80014
(303) 755-4756
Toll Free: (800) 451-5246
www.adoptex.org
kids@adoptex.org

State Reunion Registry

Colorado Voluntary Adoption
  Registry
Colorado Department of Health
4300 Cherry Creek Drive,
  South
Denver, CO 80222-1530
(303) 692-2188

**Licensed Private Adoption
  Agencies**

AAC Adoption for All Children
Adoption and Family Network
735 East Highway 56
Berthoud, CO 80513
(970) 532-3576
Fax: (970) 532-3764
rainbowkids.com/aac.html
aacadopt@frii.com

ABBA Family Services
3428 Colfax, Place A
Denver, CO 80206
(303) 333-8652

Adoption Alliance
3090 S. Jamaica Court, Suite 106
Aurora, CO 80014
(303) 337-1731
Fax: (303) 337-5481
www.adoptall.com
info@adoptall.com

Adoption Choice Center
729 S. Cascade Avenue, Suite 2
Colorado Springs, CO 80903
(719) 444-0198

Adoption Connection
702 S. Nevada Street
Colorado Springs, CO 80903
(719) 442-6880

Adoption Options
2600 South Parker Road, #3-320
Aurora, CO 80014
(303) 695-1601
Fax: (303) 695-1626

Adoption Services, Inc.
1108 N. Star Drive
Colorado Springs, CO 80906
(719) 632-9941

Adoptions: Advocacy &
Alternatives
1115 7th Street
Greeley, CO 80631
(970) 356-3428
www.help-yourself.com/
Adopt/AAA.html

Adoptions: Advocacy &
Alternatives
2500 South College Avenue
Fort Collins, CO 80525
(970) 493-5868
www.help-yourself.com/
Adopt/AAA.html

Adventist Adoption and Family
Services Program
6040 S.E. Belmont Street
Portland, OR 97215
(503) 232-1211
Fax: (503) 232-4756
www.tagnet.org/adventistadoption/
adventistadoption@msn.com

Bethany Christian Services
3700 Galley Road, Suite 210
Colorado Springs, CO 80909-
4446
(719) 591-7595
Fax: (719) 591-0732
Toll Free: (800) 986-4484
www.bethany.org
info@bethany.org

Bethany Christian Services
of Colorado
9185 E. Kenyon Avenue,
Suite 190
Denver, CO 80237-1856
(303) 221-0734
Fax: (303) 221-0960
Toll Free: (800) 986-4484
www.bethany.org
info@bethany.org

Catholic Charities and
Community Services
2525 W. Alameda Avenue
Denver, CO 80219
(303) 742-0828

Catholic Community Services
of Colorado
825 E. Pikes Peak Avenue
Colorado Springs, CO 80903
(719) 578-1222

Catholic Social Services, Inc.
Family Counseling Center
302 Jefferson
Pueblo, CO 81004
(719) 544-4234

Chinese Children Adoption
International
6920 South Holly Circle,
Suite 100
Englewood, CO 80112
(303) 850-9998
Fax: (303) 850-9997
www.chinesechildren.org
info@chinesechildren.org

Christian Family Services
1399 S. Havana Street, Suite 204
Aurora, CO 80012
(303) 337-6747

Christian Home for Children, Inc.
1880 S. Cascade Avenue
Colorado Springs, CO 80906-
2590
(719) 632-4661

Colorado Adoption Center
1136 E. Stuart Street, Suite 2040
Fort Collins, CO 80525
(970) 493-8816

Colorado Christian Home
2950 Tennyson Street
Denver, CO 80212
(303) 433-2541

Colorado Christian Services
4796 S. Broadway, Suite 110
Englewood, CO 80110
(303) 761-7236

Creative Adoptions
2329 W. Main Street, Suite 220
Littleton, CO 80120
(303) 730-7791
www.creativeadoptions.com/
Krac010@aol.com

Designated Adoption Services
of Colorado, Inc.
1420 Vance Street, Suite 202
Lakewood, CO 80215
(303) 232-0234

Family Extension
525 Third Avenue
Longmont, CO 80502
(303) 776-1224
Fax: (303) 776-4766

Family Ties Adoption Agency
7257 Rogers Street
Arvada, CO 80403
(303) 420-3660

Friends of Children of Various
Nations
1562 Pearl Street
Denver, CO 80203

(303) 837-9438
Fax: (303) 837-9848
fcvn@WebAccess.Net

Hand in Hand International
Adoptions
453 East Wonderview Avenue,
PMB #333
Estes Park, CO 80517
(970) 586-6866
Fax: (970) 577-9452
www.hihiadopt.org/
colorado@hihiadopt.org

Hope's Promise
309 Jerry Street, Suite 202
Castle Rock, CO 80104
(303) 660-0277
www.hopespromise.com/
hopes@henge.com

Innovative Adoptive Solutions
1395 Bellaire Street
Denver, CO 80220
(303) 355-2107

LDS Family Services
3263 Fraser Street, Suite 3
Aurora, CO 80011
(303) 371-1000

Littlest Angels International
2191-2225 Drive #1
Cedaredge, CO 81413-9690
(970) 856-6177
Fax: (970) 472-0462
Toll Free: (800) 875-4253
www.co-biz.com/
angelsinternational
angels@rof.net

Loving Homes
4760 Oakland Street, Suite 700
Denver, CO 80239-1022
(303) 371-9185
Fax: (303) 371-1193
www.lovinghomes.org/
lhomes@aol.com

Loving Homes
212 West 13th
Pueblo, CO 81003
(719) 545-6181
www.lovinghomes.org/
lhomes@aol.com

Lutheran Family Services of
Colorado
Southern Area Office
108 East Saint Vrain, Suite 21
Colorado Springs, CO 80903
(719) 227-7571
Fax: (719) 227-7581
www.lfsco.org/index.htm
Newhomess@lfsco.org

*Lutheran Family Services
of Colorado
Northern Area Office
3800 Automation Way,
Suite 200
Ft. Collins, CO 80525
(970) 266-1788
Fax: (970) 266-1799
www.lfsco.org/index.htm
Newhomesn@lfsco.org

Lutheran Family Services
of Colorado, Inc.
Central Area Office Family
Services Central Area Office
Central Area
363 S. Harlan Street
Denver, CO 80226
(303) 922-3433
Fax: (303) 922-7335
www.lfsco.org/index.htm
Newhomesc@lfsco.org

MAPS Colorado
P.O. Box 42
Silverthorne, CO 80498
(970) 262-2998
Fax: (970) 262-2998
www.mapsadopt.org
phage@lynx.csn.net

Parent Resource Center
7025 Tall Oak Drive
Colorado Springs, CO 80919
(719) 599-7772

Professional Adoption Services
1210 S. Parker Road, Suite 104
Denver, CO 80231
(303) 755-4797

Rainbow House International
547 Humboldt Street
Denver, CO 80218
(303) 830-2108
www.rhi.org
rainbow@rhi.org

Small Miracles
5555 Denver Tech Center
Parkway, Suite B-2100
Englewood, CO 80111
(303) 220-7611
Fax: (303) 694-2622
smallmir@aol.com

Top of the Trail
406 S. 2nd Street
Montrose, CO 81401
(970) 249-4131
Fax: (970) 249-4218

Whole Family
1675 Carr Street 210N
Lakewood, CO 80215-3176
(303) 232-3377

**Adoptive Parent Support
Groups**

Adoptive Families of Boulder
P.O. Box 2118
Boulder, CO 80306
(303) 939-8375

Adoptive Families of Colorado
Springs
2625 Tuckerman Court
Colorado Springs, CO 80918
(719) 590-7126

Adoptive Families of Denver
and North American Council
on Adoptable Children
Representative
6660 South Race Circle West
Littleton, CO 80121
(303) 795-2890
members.aol.com/nacac

Adoptive Parent Support Group
for Developmentally Disabled
3635 W. 77th
Westminster, CO 80234
(303) 428-4266

Advocates for Black Adoption
4715 Crystal Street
Denver, CO 80239
(303) 375-1531

Attachment Center at
Evergreen
27618 Fireweed
Evergreen, CO 80439
(303) 674-1910
www.attachmentcenter.org/

Attachment Disorder Network
P.O. Box 18475
Boulder, CO 80308
(303) 443-1446

Colorado Heritage Camps Inc.
2052 Elm Street
Denver, CO 80207
(303) 388-3930

Colorado Parents for All
Children
7872 Lakeshore Court
Parker, CO 80134
(303) 841-0875

Colorado Parents for All
Children
P.O. Box 2850
Frisco, CO 80443
(719) 668-3780

Denver Adoptive Mothers Club
1881 S. Meade
Denver, CO 80219
(303) 935-3847

Evergreen Consultants in
Human Behavior
28000 Meadow Drive, Suite 206
Evergreen, CO 80439
(303) 674-5503

Families for Russian and
Ukrainian Adoptions
763 E. Long Avenue
Englewood, CO 80112
(303) 770-1444
JWondra@aol.com

Family Attachment Institute
P.O. Box 1731
Evergreen, CO 80437
(303) 674-0547

HCC Adoption Link
9495 E. Florida Avenue
Denver, CO 80231
(303) 369-8514

Helping Hands
6267 S. Jamaica Court
Englewood, CO 80111
(303) 773-3627

Innovative Adoption Solutions,
Inc.
1395 Bellaire Street
Denver, CO 80220

International Concerns for
Children, Inc.
911 Cypress Drive
Boulder, CO 80303
(303) 494-8333
www.iccadopt.org
ICC@Boulder.net

Jewish Children's Adoption
Network
P.O. Box 16544
Denver, CO 80216-0544
(303) 573-8113

Loving Bonds
1221 Lindenwood Drive
Fort Collins, CO 80524
(970) 491-3001

Loving Homes and North
American Council on
Adoptable Children
Representative
4760 Oakland, Suite 700
Denver, CO 80239
(303) 371-9185
Fax: (303) 371-1193
www.lovinghomes.org
Lhomes@aol.com

Multi-Racial Family Support
Resources
11804 Stallion Drive
Pine, CO 80470
(303) 838-0127

Parenting Center in Boulder
585 Juniper Avenue
Boulder, CO 80304

Parents of East Indian Children
13715 W. Alaska Place
Lakewood, CO 80228

South Suburban Mothers Club
CO
(303) 972-1471

Stars of David
100 Julian Street
Denver, CO 80219
(303) 922-3037

www.starsofdavid.org/
starsdavid@aol.com

The Adoption Exchange -
Project WINGS
14232 E. Evans Avenue
Aurora, CO 80014
(303) 333-0845

Search Support Groups

Adoptees and Birthparents
Together
708 Garfield
Ft. Collins, CO 80524
(970) 226-2956

Adoptees in Search
P.O. Box 24556
Denver, CO 80224
(303) 232-6302

American Adoption Congress
State Representative
112 Bonfoy, Apt. 10
Colorado Springs, CO 80909
(719) 630-7130
bbetzen@aol.com

American Adoption Congress
State Representative
728 Meadow Station Circle
Parker, CO 80134
(303) 841-4586

Birthparents Group
Box 16512
Colorado Springs, CO 80935

Concerned United Birthparents
(CUB)
1337 S. Tejon St.
Denver, CO 80223
(303) 935-6408
www.webnations.com/cub
cub@webnations.com

Concerned United Birthparents
(CUB)
460 Arapahoe Avenue
Boulder, CO 80302
(303) 447-2756
www.webnations.com/cub
cub@webnations.com

Re-Unite
P.O. Box 7945
Aspen, CO 81612
(970) 927-2400

Search and Support of Denver
805 S. Ogden
Denver, CO 80209
(303) 778-8612

COLORADO LAWS RELATED TO ADOPTION: QUESTIONS AND ANSWERS

Whether independent adoption is legal or not in Colorado is debatable, as the statute is unclear. However, an attorney has outlined a uniform code for family court judges to follow when interpreting the statute. In addition, an independent adoption must become a "designated" adoption, which is essentially an identified agency adoption. A birth mother and adoptive parents can meet without the assistance of an agency, but an agency must become involved by providing counseling to the birth mother, conducting a home study for the prospective adoptive couple, and completing certain forms.

In Colorado, adoptive parents can seek a birth mother through an intermediary such as an attorney, physician, or member of the clergy, and can also advertise. (Intermediaries cannot be reimbursed for that specific service.)

If an out-of-state couple finds a birth mother in Colorado, the couple must have their home study comply with Colorado Interstate Compact regulations.

Can an attorney serve as an intermediary?
Yes, although the attorney is not licensed to place children with adoptive parents and cannot charge for such a service.

Is advertising permitted?
Yes.

Who must consent to the adoption?

Both birth parents must consent, unless the birth father has abandoned the child and/or birth mother by lack of support or contact.

When can consent be taken from the birth mother (father), and how long after the consent is signed can it be revoked?

Consents cannot be given until after the child is born and a personal court appearance is required.

What are the birth father's rights?

He must have notice of the adoption proceedings if he has not consented to the adoption.

What fees can adoptive parents pay?

Attorney fees and other fees are permitted if approved by the court. Adoptive couples who have made direct contact with the birth mother may pay limited reasonable living expenses in addition to reasonable telephone and maternity clothing expenses. Only an adoption agency can receive payment in locating or identifying a child for adoption. A statement of all fees must be submitted to the court.

Where does the adoption hearing take place?

The hearing takes place in the county where the adoptive parents live or where the child placement adoption agency is located.

How are familial and stepparent adoptions different from nonbiological adoptions?

No agency involvement is required. The adoption process for a stepparent adoption is very simple. In a familial adoption, the adoptive parents can be named as guardians at the time of placement.

Can a nonresident finalize an adoption in this state?

Yes, if they comply with Colorado law. The birth parents' rights must be terminated through a court hearing. This usually occurs about 30 days after the child is born.

SOURCE: COLORADO REVISED STATUTES, SECTIONS 19-5-20 TO 19-5-304 (1998)

CONNECTICUT

State Adoption Specialist

Connecticut Department of
  Children and Families
Office of Foster & Adoption
  Services
Elizabeth Johnson-Tyson
505 Hudson Street
Hartford, CT 06106
(860) 550-6463
Fax: (860) 566-6726
Toll Free: (800) 842-6385
www.state.ct.us/dcf/foster.htm

Connecticut Department of
  Children and Families
Office of Foster and Adoption
  Services
Gretchen Closs
505 Hudson Street
Hartford, CT 06106
(860) 550-6578
Fax: (860) 566-6726
Toll Free: (800) 842-6385
www.state.ct.us/dcf/foster.htm

State ICPC Administrator

Connecticut Department of
  Children & Families
505 Hudson Street
Hartford, CT 06106
(860) 242-1160

**State Adoption Exchange/State
Photolisting Service**

Office of Foster and Adoption
  Services
505 Hudson Street
Hartford, CT 06106
(860) 550-6469
Fax: (860) 566-6726
www.state.ct.us/dcf

State Reunion Registry

Connecticut Department of
  Children and Families
Office of Foster and Adoption
  Services
505 Hudson Street
Hartford, CT 06106
(860) 550-6463

Fax: (860) 550-3453
www.state.ct.us/dcf/
foster.htm#search

**Regional/District Public
Agencies**

Connecticut Department of
Children and Families
Children's Protective Services,
Eastern
2 Courthouse Square
Norwich, CT 06360
(860) 886-2641

Connecticut Department of
Children and Families
Children's Protective Services,
South Central
1 Long Wharf
New Haven, CT 06511
(203) 786-0600

Connecticut Department of
Children and Families
Children's Protective Services,
North Central
250 Hamilton Street
Hartford, CT 06105
(860) 418-8000

Connecticut Department of
Children and Families
Children's Protective Services,
North West
395 W. Main Street
Waterbury, CT 06702
(203) 759-7000

Connecticut Department of
Children and Families
Children's Protective Services,
South West
3885 Main Street
Bridgeport, CT 06604
(203) 365-6200

**Licensed Private Adoption
Agencies**

A Child Among Us
The Center for Adoption Inc.
2410 New London Turnpike
South Glastonbury, CT 06073
(860) 657-2467
Fax: (860) 659-5786
Toll Free: (800) 360-2220
www.achildamongus.org
information@achildamongus.org

Casey Family Program East,
Bridgeport Division
2400 Main Street
Bridgeport, CT 06606
(203) 334-6991

Casey Family Program East,
Hartford Division
43 Woodland Street
Hartford, CT 06105
(860) 727-1030

Casey Family Services East
1 Corporate Drive, Suite 515
Shelton, CT 06484
(203) 929-3837
Toll Free: (800) 332-6991

Catholic Charities of
Fairfield County
238 Jewett Avenue
Bridgeport, CT 06606
(203) 372-4301
www.cathcharitiesffldcty.com
info@cathcharitiesffldcty.com

Catholic Charities of the
Diocese of Norwich
11 Bath Street
Norwich, CT 06360
(860) 889-8346

Catholic Charities, Catholic
Family Services Archdiocese
of Hartford
467 Bloomfield Avenue
Bloomfield, CT 06002
(860) 242-9577

Catholic Charities, Hartford
District Office
896 Asylum Avenue
Hartford, CT 06105-1991
(860) 522-8241

Catholic Charities, New Haven
District Office
478 Orange Street
New Haven, CT 06502
(203) 787-2207

Catholic Charities, Waterbury
District Office
56 Church Street
Waterbury, CT 06702
(203) 755-1196

Child Adoption Resource
Association, Inc.
P.O. Box 1846
New London, CT 06320
(860) 442-2797

Children's Center
1400 Whitney Avenue
Hamden, CT 06514
(203) 248-2116

Downeyside
829 Wethersfield Avenue
Hartford, CT 06114
(860) 296-3310

Family and Children's
Agency, Inc.
9 Mott Avenue
Norwalk, CT 06850
(203) 855-8765
Fax: (203) 838-3325
www.townline.com/FCAdopt
FCAdoption@aol.com

Family Services, Inc.
92 Vine Street
New Britain, CT 06052
(860) 223-9291

Franciscan Family Care Center,
Inc.
271 Finch Avenue
Meriden, CT 06450
(860) 237-8084

Friends in Adoption
44 South Street, P.O. Box 1228
Middletown Springs, VT 05757-
1228
(802) 235-2373
www.capital.net/com/fia
fia@vermontel.com

Highland Heights
St. Francis Home for Children,
Inc.
651 Prospect Street, Box 1224
New Haven, CT 06505
(203) 777-5513

International Alliance for
Children, Inc.
2 Ledge Lane
New Milford, CT 06776
(860) 354-3417

Jewish Family Service of
New Haven
1440 Whalley Ave
New Haven, CT 06515
(203) 389-5599
Fax: (203) 389-5904

Jewish Family Services, Inc.
2370 Park Avenue
Bridgeport, CT 06604
(203) 366-5438

Jewish Family Services
Infertility Center
740 North Main Street
West Hartford, CT 06117
(860) 236-1927

LDS Family Services
1000 Mountain Road
Bloomfield, CT 06002
Toll Free: (800) 735-0149

LDS Social Services
547 Amherst Street, Suite 404
Nashua, NH 03063-4000
(603) 889-0148
Fax: (603) 889-4358
Toll Free: (800) 735-0419

Lutheran Social Services of
New England
2139 Silas Deane Hwy, #201
Rocky Hill, CT 06067
(860) 257-9889
Fax: (860) 257-0340
Toll Free: (800) 286-9889
www.adoptlss.org
LSSadoptct@aol.com

MAPS International
400 Commonwealth Avenue
Boston, MA 02115
(617) 267-2222
Fax: (617) 267-3331
www.mapsadopt.org/

New Life Adoption Agency
Suite 301, 430 E. Genesee Street
Syracuse, NY 13202-2155
(315) 422-7300
Fax: (315) 475-7727
www.newlifeadoption.org
newlife@newlifeadoption.org

Nine Months Adoptions
8676 West 69th Street, Suite 200
Overland Park, KS 66212
Toll Free: (800) 768-7009
www.ninemonths.org
adoptions@ninemonths.org

Professional Counseling Center
1 Eliot Place
Fairfield, CT 06430
(203) 259-5300

Quinebaug Valley Youth and
Family Services
303 Putnam Road
Wauregan, CT 06387
(860) 564-6100
Toll Free: (800) 953-0295

The Village for Families and
Children, Inc.
1680 Albany Avenue
Hartford, CT 06105
(860) 236-4511

*Thursday's Child, Inc.
227 Tunxis Avenue
Bloomfield, CT 06002
(860) 242-5941
Fax: (860) 243-9898

Wheeler Clinic, Inc.
91 Northwest Drive
Plainville, CT 06062
(860) 527-1644

Wide Horizons for Children
34 Connecticut Boulevard,
Suite 7
East Hartford, CT 06108
(860) 291-8610

**Adoptive Parent Support
Groups**

Adoption Connection
3 Hampden Circle
Simsbury, CT 06070

Adoptive Families Exchange
Support Group
6 Putnam Park Road
Bethel, CT 06801
(203) 743-9283

Attachment Disorder Parents
Network of Connecticut
85 Westwood Avenue
Plainville, CT 06062
(860) 669-2750

Birthparent Support Network
55 Old Willamack Road
Columbia, CT 06237
(860) 228-0076

Casey Family Services
789 Reservoir Avenue
Bridgeport, CT 06606
(203) 372-3722
Fax: (203) 372-3558
Toll Free: (800) 332-6991

Casey Family Services
789 Reservoir Avenue
Bridgeport, CT 06606
(203) 372-3722
Fax: (203) 372-3558
Toll Free: (800) 332-6991

Casey Family Services Gothic
Park
43 Woodland Street
Hartford, CT 06105
(860) 727-1030
Toll Free: (800) 732-6921

Christian Family, Inc.
224 Todd Road
Wolcott, CT 06716
(203) 879-9545

Connecticut Center for
Post-Adoption Services
81 South Main Street
West Hartford, CT 06107
(860) 561-1530

Connecticut Children's
Medical Center
282 Washington Street
Hartford, CT 06106
(860) 545-9021

Connecticut Friends of
Adopted Children
P.O. Box 3246
Waterbury, CT 06705

Connecticut Parents of Indian
Children
136 Cold Springs Street
New Haven, CT 06511
(203) 624-2243

Department of Children and
Families
2 Courthouse Square
Norwich, CT 06360
(860) 886-2641

FAITH
60 Wells Avenue
Shelton, CT 06484

Families with Children
From China
P.O. Box 101
Thompson, CT 06277
robyn1@neca.com

International Adoptive Families
433 Quarry Brook Drive
South Windsor, CT 06074
(203) 644-0600

International Adoptive Families
of Connecticut
266 Thistle Lane
Southington, CT 06489
ourworld.compuserve.com/
homepages/S_Ford3/
74741.1365@compuserve.com

Latin America Parents
Association of Connecticut,
Inc.
P.O. Box 523
Unionville, CT 06085-0523
(203) 270-1424
www.lapa.com
joet@highcaliber.com

Latin American Parents
  Association
55 Jeremiah Road
Sandy Hook, CT 06482
(203) 270-1424

Lutheran Social Services and
  North American Council on
  Adoptable Children
Representative
2139 Silas Deane Highway
Rocky Hill, CT 06067
(860) 257-9899
Fax: (860) 257-0340
lssadoptct@aol.com

National Adoption Foundation
100 Mill Plain Road
Danbury, CT 06811
(203) 791-3811

North American Council on
  Adoptable Children
  Representative
506 Taylor Road
Enfield, CT 06082
(203) 749-9123

Open Door Society of
  Connecticut
P.O. Box 478
Hartford, CT 06101
(860) 248-9937

Single Adoptive Parent
  Support Group
228 Barlow Mountain Road
Ridgefield, CT 06877
(203) 431-6652

Single Parents for the Adoption
  of Children Everywhere
52 Back Lane
Wethersfield, CT 06109
(860) 257-9331

Stars of David International Inc.
Southern Connecticut Chapter
1060 Johnson Road
Woodbridge, CT 06525
(203) 389-5400
www.starsofdavid.org
debkasa@aol.com or
  joelsac10@aol.com

Stars of David International Inc.
Bridgeport Area Chapter
Jewish Family Service, 2370
  Park Avenue
Bridgeport, CT 06604
(203) 366-5438
Fax: (203) 366-1580
www.starsofdavid.org
jfs18@concentric.net

Thursday's Child
227 Tunxis Avenue
Bloomfield, CT 06002
(860) 242-5941
Fax: (860) 243-9898

Village for Families and
  Children
1680 Albany Avenue
Hartford, CT 06105
(860) 236-4511

Search Support Groups

Adoptees Search Connection
1203 Hill Street
Suffield, CT 06078
(203) 668-1042

Adoption Answers Support
  Kinship (AASK)
8 Homestead Drive
So. Glastonbury, CT 06073-
  2804
(860) 657-4005

Adoption Crossroads
956 Broad Street
Stratford, CT 06497

Adoption Healing
F2 Hadik Parkway
South Norwalk, CT 06854
(203) 866-6475

Ties That Bind
P.O. Box 3119
Milford, CT 06460
(203) 874-2023

CONNECTICUT LAWS RELATED TO ADOPTION: QUESTIONS AND ANSWERS

Can an attorney serve as an intermediary?
No.

Is advertising permitted?
Yes.

Who must consent to the adoption?
1. Birth parents
2. The adoptive parents

When can consent be taken from the birth mother (father), and how long after the consent is signed can it be revoked?
A consent can be taken forty-eight hours after the child's birth and is revocable until the court hearing (about thirty days later).

Because most birth mothers and adoptive parents do not want the baby in foster care, some agencies place the baby directly in the adoptive couple's home before the first court hearing. This is considered a "legal risk placement" (i.e., the birth mother can change her mind after the baby is in the adoptive parents' home).

What are the birth father's rights?
If he has been named or claims to be the birth father, he must be notified of the adoption proceedings. He must assert his rights or his rights will be terminated.

What fees can adoptive parents pay?
This issue is not addressed in the existing laws, but a couple can pay all reasonable living and medical expenses through an agency.

Where does the adoption hearing take place?
The hearing takes place in the county where the adoptive parents live or where the child placement adoption agency is located.

How are familial and stepparent adoptions different from nonbiological adoptions?
No agency involvement is required. If all necessary persons have consented, the court will waive the investigation and report by the Children and Youth Services.

Can a nonresident finalize an adoption in this state?
Yes.

DELAWARE

State Adoption Specialist

Delaware Department of
  Services for Children, Youth
  and Their Families
Frank Perfinski
1825 Faulkland Road
Wilmington, DE 19805
(302) 633-2655
Fax: (302) 633-2652
www.state.de.us/kids/adoption.htm
Fperfinski@state.de.us

State ICPC Administrator

Delaware Department of
  Services for Children, Youth
  and Their Families
1825 Faulkland Road,
  2nd Floor
Wilmington, DE 19805
(302) 633-2698
Fax: (302) 633-2652

**Licensed Private Adoption
  Agencies**

Adoption House
3411 Silverside Road
Wilmington, DE 19810
(302) 477-0944

Adoptions From The Heart
18-A Trolley Square
Wilmington, DE 19806

(302) 658-8883
www.adoptionsfromtheheart.org/
adoption@adoptionsfromtheheart.org

Bethany Christian Services
550 Pinetown Road, Suite 100
Fort Washington, PA 19034-2606
(215) 628-0202
Fax: (215) 628-2944
Toll Free: (800) 215-0702
www.bethany.org
info@bethany.org

Catholic Charities
442 S. New Street
Dover, DE 19901
(302) 674-1600

Catholic Charities
2601 West 4th Street
Wilmington, DE 19805
(302) 655-9624

Child and Home Study
  Associates
101 Stone Crop Road
Wilmington, DE 19810
(302) 475-5433

Children and Families First
Milford Professional Plaza, 771
  Masten Suite 111
Milford, DE 19963
(302) 658-5177

Children's Choice of Delaware
910 B Walker Road
Dover, DE 19901-2759
(302) 678-0404

LDS Family Services
502 West Chestnut Hill
Newark, DE 19711
(302) 456-3782

Madison Adoption Agency
1009 Woodstream Drive
Wilmington, DE 19810
(302) 475-8977

Tressler Center of Delaware
2 Centerville Road
Wilmington, DE 19808
(302) 995-2294
Fax: (302) 995-2323
www.tressler.org
TLSAdopt@tressler.org

Trialog Children's Bureau
2005 Baynard Boulevard
Wilmington, DE 19802
(302) 658-5177

Welcome House, Inc.
P.O. Box 485
Wilmington, DE 19807
(302) 654-7683

DELAWARE LAWS RELATED TO ADOPTION: QUESTIONS AND ANSWERS

Independent adoption is illegal in Delaware. Identified adoptions are permitted, however, and most agencies are willing to conduct them.

If the fees for an agency are too high, it is suggested that a Delaware couple contact an attorney, then advertise and finalize an adoption in one of the following nearby states: New York, New Jersey, Pennsylvania, Maryland, Washington, D.C., Virginia, or South Carolina. (In New Jersey, Maryland, and D.C. an agency must be involved if an out-of-state couple finalizes there.) However, a Delaware agency must conduct your home study.

Can an attorney serve as an intermediary?
No.

Is advertising permitted?
No.

Who must consent to the adoption?
1. Both birth parents
2. A licensed agency or the Department of Services for Children, Youth and Their Families

When can consent be taken from the birth mother (father), and how long after the consent is signed can it be revoked?
Consent cannot be given by the birth mother until the child is born, but can be given by the birth father before the child's birth. The birth parents or agency can request the court to revoke the consent within sixty days after filing the adoption petition. The court will then decide what is in the best interest of the child.

What are the birth father's rights?
The presumed father's consent is required unless he has abandoned the child.

What fees can adoptive parents pay?
The agency can only charge for services rendered, court costs, and legal fees.

Where does the adoption hearing take place?
The hearing can take place in the county where the adoptive parents reside or where the child placement agency is located.

How are familial and stepparent adoptions different from nonbiological adoptions?
An agency adoption is not required, but a home study is required, and the child must be in the home for at least one year.

Can a nonresident finalize an adoption in this state?
No. You must be a resident. However, no specific length of time is required to establish residency.

DISTRICT OF COLUMBIA

State Adoption Specialist

District of Columbia Child and
Family Services Agency
J. Toni Oliver
609 H Street, N.E.
Washington, DC 20002
(202) 698-6402
Fax: (202) 546-1253
toliver@609-hdom.org

State ICPC Administrator

Department of Human Services
District of Columbia Child and
Family Services Agency
District of Columbia Child
and Family Services Agency
609 H Street N.E., 5th Floor
Washington, DC 20002
(202) 698-4637
Fax: (202) 727-6881

**Regional/District Public
Agencies**

District of Columbia
Department of Human
Services
625 H Street, N.E.
Washington, DC 20002
(202) 727-3161

**Licensed Private Adoption
Agencies**

Adoption Center of
Washington
Suite 1101, 1726 M Street,
N.W.
Washington, DC 20036
(202) 452-8278
Fax: (202) 452-8280
Toll Free: (800) 452-3878
www.adoptioncenter.com
info@adoptioncenter.com

*Adoption Service Information
Agency (ASIA)
7720 Alaska Avenue, N.W.
Washington, DC 20012
(202) 726-7193
Fax: (202) 722-4928
www.asia-adopt.org
info@asia-adopt.org

Barker Foundation
4400 MacArthur Boulevard,
N.W., Suite 200
Washington, DC 20007
(202) 363-7751
Fax: (301) 229-0074
Toll Free: (800) 673-8489
www.barkerfoundation.org
bfinfo@atlantech.net

Catholic Charities Archdiocese
of Washington
Satellite Office
4914 Ayres Place S.E.
Washington, DC 20019
(202) 581-3630

Catholic Charities Archdiocese
of Washington
1438 Rhode Island Avenue, N.E.
Washington, DC 20018
(202) 526-4100

Datz Foundation
311 Maple Avenue West, Suite E
Vienna, VA 22180
(703) 242-8800
Fax: (703) 242-8804
www.datzfound.com
datz@patriot.net

Family and Child Services of
Washington, D.C.
400 6th Street, S.W.
Washington, DC 20024
(202) 671-5683
Fax: (202) 371-0863

International Children's
Alliance
1101 17th Street, N.W.,
Suite 1002
Washington, DC 20036

(202) 463-6874
Fax: (202) 463-6880
www.adoptica.org
adoptionop@aol.com

International Families, Inc.
5 Thomas Circle, N.W.
Washington, DC 20005
(202) 667-5779

Lutheran Social Services of the
National Capital Area
4406 Georgia Avenue, N.W.
Washington, DC 20011
(202) 723-3000
Fax: (202) 723-3303

Progressive Life Center
1123 11th Street, N.W.
Washington, DC 20001
(202) 842-2016

**Adoptive Parent Support
Groups**

Adoption Resource Exchange
for Single Parents (ARESP)
8605 Cameron Street #220
Silver Spring, MD 20910
(301) 585-5836
Fax: (301) 585-4864
www.aresp.org
arespinc@aol.com

Adoption Support Institute
1319 Geranium Street, N.W.
Washington, DC 20012
(202) 291-2290

ASIA Family and Friends
7720 Alaska Avenue, N.W.
Washington, DC 20012
(202) 726-7193

Association for Single Adoptive
Parents
P.O. Box 3618
Merrifield, VA 22116-9998
(703) 521-0632

Barker Foundation Parents of
Adopted Adolescents Group
7945 MacArthur Boulevard,
Suite 206
Cabin John, MD 20818
(301) 229-8300

Center for Adoption Support
and Education, Inc. (C.A.S.E.)
11120 New Hampshire Avenue,
Suite 205
Silver Spring, MD 20904
(301) 593-9200
www.adoptionsupport.org
caseadopt@erols.com

D.C. One Church, One Child
7600 Georgia Avenue, N.W.,
Suite 100 N
Washington, DC 20012
(202) 726-4248

Families Adopting Children
Everywhere and North
American Council on
Adoptable Children
Representative
P.O. Box 28058
Baltimore, MD 21239
(410) 488-2656

Families for Private Adoption
P.O. Box 6375
Washington, DC 20015-0375
(202) 722-0338
www.ffpa.org

Families Like Ours
Washington, DC
(202) 488-3967

Interracial Family Circle
P.O. Box 53290
Washington, DC 20009
(202) 393-7866
Toll Free: (800) 500-9040
www.geocities.com/Heartland/
Estates/4496
ifcweb@yahoo.com

Korean Focus for Adoptive
Families
1906 Sword Lane
Alexandria, VA 22308
(703) 799-4945
www.helping.com/family/pa/kfaf.htm
koreanfocus@hotmail.com

Latin America Parents
Association of the National
Capital Region
P.O. Box 4403
Silver Spring, MD 20904-4403
(301) 431-3407
www.lapa.com
joet@highcaliber.com

National Council for Single
Adoptive Parents
P.O. Box 15084
Chevy Chase, MD 20825
(202) 966-6367
www.adopting.org/ncsap.html
singladopt@aol.com

Open Adoption Discussion
Group
22310 Old Hundred Road
Barnesville, MD 20838
(301) 972-8579
msaasta@hotmail.com

RESOLVE of Washington
Metropolitian Area, Inc.
P.O. Box 39221
Washington, DC 20016
(202) 362-5555

Stars of David International
Inc.
Metro DC Chapter
c/o The Datz Foundation, 311
Maple Avenue West
Vienna, VA 22180
(703) 242-8800
Fax: (703) 242-8804
Toll Free: (800) 829-5683
www.starsofdavid.org
datz@patriot.net

Search Support Groups

Adoptee-Birthparent Support
Network (ABSN)
P.O. Box 8273
McLean, VA 22106-8273
(202) 628-4111
www.geocities.com/Heartland/
Flats/3666/ABSN.html
absnmail@aol.com

Adoptees in Search
P.O. Box 41016
Bethesda, MD 20014
(301) 656-8555
Fax: (301) 652-2106
AIS20824@aol.com

American Adoption Congress
1025 Connecticut Ave., N.W.,
Suite 1012
Washington, DC 20036
(202) 483-3399
www.american-adoption-cong.org

Barker Foundation Adult
Adoptee Support Group
7945 MacArthur Boulevard,
Suite 206
Cabin John, MD 20818
(301) 229-8300

Barker Foundation Birthparent
Support Group
7945 MacArthur Boulevard,
Suite 206
Cabin John, MD 20818
(301) 229-8300

Concerned United Birthparents
(CUB)
DC Metro Branch
P.O. Box 15258
Chevy Chase, MD 20815
(202) 966-1640
www.webnations.com/cub
LEC9@aol.com

D. C. LAWS RELATED TO ADOPTION: QUESTIONS AND ANSWERS

Can an attorney serve as an intermediary?
No.

Is advertising permitted?
Yes.

Who must consent to the adoption?
1. Both birth parents
2. The child placement adoption agency, if involved

When can consent be taken from the birth mother (father), and how long after the consent is signed can it be revoked?

A relinquishment is given in an agency adoption and a consent is given in an independent adoption. These can both be signed seventy-two hours after the child's birth. A relinquishment can be revoked up to ten days after signing. A consent is irrevocable.

What are the birth father's rights?

As long the birth father has been given notice and it can be shown during a hearing that he has abandoned the child or has not provided support to the child for at least six months, his consent is not required. Also, his consent is not required if the court determines after a hearing that consent is withheld contrary to the best interests of the child. If the birth father cannot be located, the court will waive his consent after a detailed search is conducted.

What fees can adoptive parents pay?

There are no laws regarding permissible fees; however, medical and legal fees can be paid.

Where does the adoption hearing take place?

The Superior Court of D.C. has jurisdiction if the adoptive couple is a legal resident of D.C. or has lived there for one year, or if the child is in the legal custody of an agency licensed by D.C.

How are familial and stepparent adoptions different from nonbiological adoptions?

In a stepparent adoption, the court may waive the home study if the noncustodial parent consents to the adoption.

Can a nonresident finalize an adoption in D.C.?

Yes. However, the adoption must be an agency placement.

SOURCE: DISTRICT OF COLUMBIA CODE, CHAPTER 3, SECTIONS 16-301 TO 16-315 (1997)

FLORIDA

State Adoption Specialist

Florida Department of Children
and Families
Carol Hutcheson
1317 Winewood Boulevard
Tallahassee, FL 32399-0700
(850) 487-2383
Fax: (850) 488-0751
www.state.fl.us/cf_web/adopt
carol_hutcheson@dcf.state.fl.us

State ICPC Administrator

Childen, Youth & Family
Services
Florida Department of Children
and Families
1317 Winewood Boulevard
Tallahassee, FL 32399-0700

(850) 487-2760
Fax: (850) 487-4337

State Adoption Exchange/State Photolisting Service

Adoption Information Center
Daniel Memorial, Inc.
134 East Church Street
Jacksonville, FL 32202
(904) 353-0679
Fax: (904) 353-3472
Toll Free: (800) 962-3678
www.state.fl.us/cf_web/adopt/

Florida's Adoption Exchange
Florida Department of Children
and Families
1317 Winewood Boulevard,
Building 7 Room 208
Tallahassee, FL 32399-0700
(850) 487-2383
Fax: (850) 488-0751

State Reunion Registry

Florida Adoption Reunion
Registry (FARR)
Florida Department of Health
and Rehabilitation Services
2811-E Industrial Plaza Drive
Tallahassee, FL 32301
(850) 353-0679
Toll Free: (800) 962-3678

Regional/District Public Agencies

Florida Department of Children
and Families, District Eight
P.O. Box 60085, 2295 Victoria
Avenue
Fort Myers, FL 33901
(941) 338-1454
Fax: (941) 338-1443
TTY: (941) 338-1432

Florida Department of Children
and Families, District Eleven
401 N.W. Second Avenue,
Room 1007, NorthTower
Miami, FL 33128
(305) 377-5006

Florida Department of Children
and Families, District Fifteen
Ft. Pierce Regional Service
Center, 337 N. 4th Street,
Suite A
Ft. Pierce, FL 34950-4206
(561) 467-4177
Fax: (561) 467-4169
TTY: (800) 467-3138

Florida Department of Children
and Families, District Five
Mary Grizzle State Office Building,
11351 Ulmerton Road
Largo, FL 33778
(727) 588-7055

Florida Department of Children
and Families, District Four
P.O. Box 2417,
5920 Arlington Expressway
Jacksonville, FL 32231-0083
(904) 723-2050
Fax: (904) 723-5389
TTY: (904) 724-8606

Florida Department of Children
and Families, District Fourteen
4720 Old Highway 37
Lakeland, FL 33813-2030
(941) 648-3336
Fax: (941) 648-3336
TTY: (800) 955-8771

Florida Department of Children
and Families, District Nine
111 S. Sapodilla Ave
West Palm Beach, FL 33401
(561) 837-5595
Fax: (561) 837-5106
TTY: (800) 226-1347

Florida Department of Children
and Families, District One
160 Governmental Center, P.O.
Box 8420
Pensacola, FL 32576
(850) 595-8211
Fax: (850) 595-8064
TTY: (850) 595-8215

Florida Department of Children
and Families, District Seven
400 West Robinson Street,
Suite 1129, South Tower
Orlando, FL 32801

(407) 245-0400
Fax: (407) 245-0575

Florida Department of Children
and Families, District Six
4000 Martin Luther King, Jr.
Boulevard
Tampa, FL 33614
(813) 871-1068

Florida Department of Children
and Families, District Ten
201 W. Broward Boulevard,
Suite 406
Fort Lauderdale, FL 33301
(954) 467-4298
Fax: (954) 467-4623

Florida Department of Children
and Families, District
Thirteen
1601 W. Gulf-Atlantic Highway
Wildwood, FL 34785
(352) 330-1374
Fax: (352) 330-1374
TTY: (800) 955-8771

Florida Department of Children
and Families, District Three
1000 N.E. 16 Ave Box 3
Gainesville, FL 32601
(352) 955-5163
Fax: (352) 955-5010
TTY: (800) 342-9004

Florida Department of Children
and Families, District Twelve
210 N. Palmetto Avenue,
Suite 430
Daytona Beach, FL 32114
(904) 238-4750
Fax: (904) 238-4905
TTY: (904) 238-4648

Florida Department of Children
and Families, District Two
2639 N. Monroe Street,
Suite 200-A
Tallahassee, FL 32399
(850) 488-0567
Fax: (850) 488-6513
TTY: (800) 226-6223

**Licensed Private Adoption
Agencies**

A Bond of Love Adoption
Agency, Inc.
1800 Siesta Drive
Sarasota, FL 34239
(941) 957-0064
Fax: (941) 957-0064

Adoption Advisory Associates
299 Camino Gardens
Boulevard, Suite 205
Boca Raton, FL 33432
(561) 362-5222

Adoption Advocates, Inc.
11407 Seminole Boulevard,
Suite D
Largo, FL 33778
(727) 391-8096
www.quickweb.net:80/adoption/
about.htm
adoption@quickweb.net

Adoption Agency of
Central Florida
1681 Maitland Avenue
Maitland, FL 32751
(407) 831-2154

Adoption By Choice
St. Andrew's Square, 4102 W.
Linebaugh Avenue, Suite 200
Tampa, FL 33624
(813) 960-2229
Fax: (813) 969-2339
Toll Free: (800) 421-2229

Adoption Placement, Inc.
2734 E. Oakland Park
Boulevard, Suite 104
Ft. Lauderdale, FL 33306
(954) 564-2950
Fax: (954) 564-0694
www.adoptionplacement.com
api@adoptionplacement.com

Adoption Resources of Florida
2753 State Road 580, Suite 206
Clearwater, FL 34629
(727) 726-3555
Fax: (727) 726-3601
Toll Free: (888) 726-3555
www.adoptionfl.com
adoptionfl@aol.com

Adoption Source, Inc.
2295 Corporate Boulevard,
N.W., Suite 230
Boca Raton, FL 33431
(561) 912-9229
Fax: (561) 912-9912
adoptionsource@att.net

Advocates for Children and
Families
16831 N.E. 6th Avenue
North Miami, FL 33162
(305) 653-2474
Fax: (305) 653-2746

*All About Adoptions, Inc.
505 East New Haven Avenue
Melbourne, FL 32901
(407) 723-0088
Fax: (407) 952-9813
grassadopt@aol.com

All About Adoptions, Inc.
1164 B. Normandy Drive
Miami Beach, FL 33141
(305) 940-9227

An Angel's Answer Adoption
Agency
98 S.E. 6th Avenue, #3
Del Ray, FL 33483
(561) 276-0660

Catholic Charities
1505 N.E. 26th Street
Wilton Manors, FL 33305
(954) 630-9404

Catholic Charities
803 East Palmetto Street
Lakeland, FL 33801
(941) 686-7153

Catholic Charities
P.O. Box 8246
West Palm Beach, FL 33407
(561) 842-2406

Catholic Charities
1111 South Federal Highway,
Suite 119
Stuart, FL 34995
(561) 283-0541

Catholic Charities
6533 9th Avenue N,
Suite 1 - East
St. Petersburg, FL 33710
(727) 893-1313

Catholic Charities Bureau
134 E. Church Street, Suite 2
Jacksonville, FL 32202-3130
(904) 354-3416

Catholic Charities Bureau
225 West King Street
St. Augustine, FL 32095
(904) 829-6300

Catholic Charities Bureau
1717 N.E. 9th Street
Gainesville, FL 32609
(352) 372-0294

Catholic Charities of
Tallahassee
855 W. Carolina Street
Tallahassee, FL 32309
(850) 222-2180

Catholic Charities of the
Diocese of Venice, Inc.
1900 Main Street, Suite 204
Sarasota, FL 34236
(941) 484-9543

Catholic Social Service of
Bay County
3128 E. 11th Street
Panama City, FL 32404
(850) 785-8935

Catholic Social Services
771 A. Briarwood Drive
Daytona Beach, FL 32114
(904) 255-6521

Catholic Social Services
1771 N. Semoran Boulevard
Orlando, FL 32807
(407) 658-1818

Catholic Social Services
817 Dixon Blvd, #16
Cocoa, FL 32922
(407) 636-6144

Catholic Social Services
11 First Street S.E.
Ft. Walton Beach, FL 32548
(850) 244-2825

Catholic Social Services of
Pensacola
222 E. Government Street
Pensacola, FL 32501
(850) 436-6410

Children of the Nations
International Program
P.O. Box 1735
New Port Richey, FL 34656-1735
(727) 859-0365

Children's Home Society of
Florida
800 N.W. 15th Street
Miami, FL 33136-1495
(305) 324-1262
Fax: (305) 326-7430
www.chsfl.org
rjohnson@chsfl.org

Children's Home Society of
Florida
1495 Maple Drive
Fort Myers, FL 33907

(941) 277-0096
Fax: (941) 277-0662
www.chsfl.org
rjohnson@chsfl.org

Children's Home Society of
Florida
300 S.E. First, Suite C
Ocala, FL 34471
(352) 620-3471
Fax: (352) 629-3545
www.chsfl.org
rjohnson@chsfl.org

Children's Home Society of
Florida
303 Magnolia Avenue
Panama City, FL 32401
(850) 872-4726
www.chsfl.org
rjohnson@chsfl.org

Children's Home Society of
Florida
605 N.E. 1st Street, Suite H
Gainesville, FL 32607
(352) 376-5186
www.chsfl.org
rjohnson@chsfl.org

Children's Home Society of
Florida
401 N.E. 4th Street
Ft. Lauderdale, FL 33301
(954) 763-6573
Fax: (954) 764-6458
www.chsfl.org
rjohnson@chsfl.org

Children's Home Society of
Florida
3535 Lawton Road, Suite 260
Orlando, FL 32803
(407) 895-5800
Fax: (407) 895-5801
www.chsfl.org
rjohnson@chsfl.org

Children's Home Society of
Florida
2100 45th Street
West Palm Beach, FL 33407
(561) 844-9785
Fax: (561) 848-0195
Toll Free: (800) 433-0010
www.chsfl.org
rjohnson@chsfl.org

Children's Home Society of
Florida
820 E. Park Avenue, Building E,
Suite 100
Tallahassee, FL 32301

(850) 921-0772
Fax: (850) 921-0726
www.chsfl.org
rjohnson@chsfl.org

Children's Home Society of
  Florida
314 South Missouri Avenue,
  Suite 101
Clearwater, FL 33756
(727) 298-2600
Fax: (727) 298-2610
www.chsfl.org
rjohnson@chsfl.org

Children's Home Society of
  Florida
5375 N. 9th Avenue, Box 19136
Pensacola, FL 32523
(850) 494-5990
Fax: (850) 494-5981
Toll Free: (800) 235-2229
www.chsfl.org
rjohnson@chsfl.org

Children's Home Society of
  Florida
3027 San Diego Road,
  P.O. Box 10097
Jacksonville, FL 32247-0097
(904) 348-2811
Fax: (904) 348-2818
www.chsfl.org
rjohnson@chsfl.org

Children's Home Society of
  Florida
415 Avenue A, Suite 101
Fort Pierce, FL 34950
(561) 489-5601
Fax: (561) 489-5604
www.chsfl.org
rjohnson@chsfl.org

Children's Home Society of
  Florida
3270 Suntree Boulevard,
  Suite 100
Melbourne, FL 32940
(407) 752-3170
Fax: (407) 752-3179
www.chsfl.org
rjohnson@chsfl.org

Children's Home Society of
  Florida
2400 Ridgewood Avenue,
  Suite 32
Daytona Beach, FL 32114-6185
(904) 304-7600
Fax: (904) 304-7620
www.chsfl.org
rjohnson@chsfl.org

Children's Home, Inc.
10909 Memorial Highway
Tampa, FL 33615
(813) 855-4435

Christian Family Services
2720 S.W. 2nd Avenue
Gainesville, FL 32607
(352) 378-6202

Everyday Blessings
13129 St. Francis Lane
Thonotosassa, FL 33592
(813) 982-9226

First Coast Adoption
  Professionals
3601 Cardinal Point Drive
Jacksonville, FL 32257
(904) 448-1933

Florida Baptist Children's Home
6220 Keating Road
Pensacola, FL 32504
(850) 494-9530

Florida Baptist Children's Home
8415 Buck Lake Road
Tallahassee, FL 32311-9522
(850) 878-1458

Florida Baptist Children's Home
7748 S.W. 95th Terrace
Miami, FL 33156
(305) 271-4121

Florida Baptist Family
  Ministries
1015 Sikes Boulevard
Lakeland, FL 33815
(941) 687-8811

Gift of Life, Inc.
136 4th Street, N.
St. Petersburg, FL 33701
(727) 549-1416

Given in Love Adoptions
151 Mary Esther Blvd., Suite 305
Mary Esther, FL 32569
(850) 243-3576

Gorman Family Life Center, Inc.
dba Life for Kids
315 N. Wymore Road
Winter Park, FL 32789
(407) 628-5433

International Adoption Services
7203 13 Avenue West
Bradenton, FL 32409
(954) 255-7212

International Children's
  Foundation
8620 N.E. Second Avenue,
  Suite 207
Miami, FL 33138
(305) 751-9600

Jewish Adoption and Foster Care
10001 West Oakland Park
  Blvd, Suite 101
Sunrise, FL 33324
(954) 749-7230

Jewish Family Services
2719 Hollywood Blvd
Hollywood, FL 33020
(954) 370-2140

Jewish Family Services
300 41st Street, Suite 216
Miami Beach, FL 33145
(305) 672-8080

Jewish Family Services, Inc., of
  Broward County
100 S. Pine Island Boulevard,
  Suite 130
Plantation, FL 33324
(954) 370-2140

Lake County Boys Ranch
P.O. Box 129
Altoona, FL 32702
(352) 669-3252

LDS Family Services
950 N. Orlando Avenue,
  Suite 360
Winter Park, FL 32789
(407) 628-8899

Lifelink Child and Family
  Services Corporation
1031 S. Euclid Street
Sarasota, FL 34237
(941) 957-1614
www.lifelink.org
lifelink@flash.net

Nine Months Adoptions
3001 N. Rocky Point
Tampa, FL 33607
(813) 383-9775
Toll Free: (800) 768-7009
www.ninemonths.org
adoptions@ninemonths.org

One World Adoption Services,
  Inc.
1030 South Federal Highway,
  Suite 100
Hollywood, FL 33019

(954) 922-8400
Fax: (954) 922-4575
adoptbaby@aol.com

Open Door Adoption Agency
220 Alba Avenue
Quincy, FL 32327
(850) 627-1420
www.opendooradoption.com
opendoor@rose.net

Shepherd Care Ministries
dba Christian Adoption
Services
5935 Taft Street
Hollywood, FL 33021
(954) 981-2060

Shepherd Care Ministries
1221 Lee Road, #202
Orlando, FL 32810
(407) 290-3286

St. Vincent Adoption Center
18601 S.W. 97th Avenue
Miami, FL 33157
(305) 445-5714

Suncoast International
Adoptions, Inc.
12651 Walsingham Road, Suite C
Largo, FL 33774
(727) 596-3135
Fax: (727) 593-0106
www.letmesee.com/adoptions
siai@flanet.com

Tedi Bear Adoptions Inc.
415 North Pablo Road, Suite 100
Jacksonville Beach, FL 32250
(904) 242-4995
Fax: (904) 242-8951
www.tedibearadoptions.org
TediBearH@aol.com

The Southwest Florida
Children's Home
4551 Camino Real Way
Miami, FL 33156-7599
(941) 275-7151

Universal Aid for Children
3450 East Fletcher Avenue
Tampa, FL 33613
(813) 978-8542

Universal Aid for Children
1435 South Miami Avenue
Miami, FL 33130
(305) 577-8977

*Universal Aid for Children
Cypress Village East, 167 S.W.
6th Street
Pompano Beach, FL 33060
(954) 785-0033
Fax: (954) 785-7003
uacadopt@aol.com

Adoptive Parent Support Groups

Adoption Support Network
15183 Normandy Boulevard
Jacksonville, FL 32234
(904) 289-7579

AdoptNet
130 N.W. 28th Street
Gainesville, FL 32607-2511
(352) 377-6455
*www.geocities.com/Heartland/
Ranch/2641*

Bay Area Adoptive Families
305 Orangewood Lane
Largo, FL 34640
(727) 581-6010

Cherish
5735 S.W. 130 Street
Miami, FL 33156
(305) 547-0666

Daniel Memorial Adoption
Infor-mation Center and
North American Council on
Adoptable Children
Representative
134 East Church Street
Jacksonville, FL 32202
(904) 353-0679
Fax: (904) 353-3472
Toll Free: (800) 962-3678

FACT
191 S.E. Fallon Drive
Port St. Lucie, FL 34983
(407) 879-4356

Families for Russian and
Ukrainian Adoptions
FL
Loro123@aol.com

Families of Adopted Children
Together
234 S.E. Grove Avenue
Lucie, FL 34983
(561) 879-0668

Families Through Adoption
Box 420085
Naples, FL 33942
(813) 591-4403

Gainesville Adoption
Information Network
130 N.W. 28th Street
Gainesville, FL 32607

Hope: Share-N-Care
4062 Greenwillow Lane, East
Jacksonville, FL 32211
(904) 743-9024

North American Council on
Adoptable Children
Representative
11421 Old Lakeland Highway
Dade City, FL 33525
(352) 523-1276
dfredric@innet.com

Parents Adoption Lifeline, Inc.
18 Cayman Place
Palm Beach Gardens, FL 33418
(561) 775-3092

People Adopting Children
Everywhere
P.O. Box 560293
Rockledge, FL 32956-0293
(407) 639-8895

Rainbow Families
9661 49th Way
Pinellas Park, FL 34666
(813) 541-7084

Rainbow Families
11578 Tradewinds Boulevard
Largo, FL 34643
(727) 585-6010

Sarasota County Adoption
Support Group
2570 Loma Linda Street
Sarasota, FL 34239
(941) 953-3426

SNAP and North American
Council on Adoptable
Children Representative
15913 Layton Court
Tampa, FL 33647
(813) 971-4752

Stars of David International Inc.
Jewish Adoption Information
Exchange
9101-15 N.W. 57th Street
Tamarac, FL 33351
(305) 721-7660
www.starsofdavid.org/
Rabbigold@aol.com

Stars of David International Inc.
Jewish Adoption Information
  Exchange
16002 Langhorne Court
Tampa, FL 33647
(813) 971-3983
www.starsofdavid.org
starsdavid@aol.com

Stars of David International Inc.
Jewish Adoption Information
  Exchange
21300 Ruth and Baron
  Coleman Boulevard
Boca Raton, FL 33428
(561) 852-3380
Fax: (561) 852-3332
www.starsofdavid.org
starsdavid@aol.com

Stressed Out Adoptive Parents
1403 N.W. 40th Avenue
Lauderhill, FL 33313
(954) 797-8368

Tapestry
3862 Marquise Lane
Mulberry, FL 33860
(941) 425-4112

Search Support Groups

Active Voices in Adoption
Box 24-9052
Coral Gables, FL 33124
(305) 667-0387

Adoptee Liberty Movement
  Association (ALMA)
P.O. Box 4358
Fort Lauderdale, FL 33338
(954) 462-0958

Adoption Connection
5524F Lakewood Circle
Margate, FL 33063
(954) 979-9351

Adoption Connection of Florida
3100 Hunter Road
Ft. Lauderdale, FL 33331
(954) 384-8909

Adoption Search and Support
  of Tallahassee
P.O. Box 3504
Tallahassee, FL 32315
(850) 893-0004

Adoption Support and
  Knowledge
11646 N.W. 19th Drive
Coral Springs, FL 33071
(954) 753-3878

Adoption Triangle
1301 N.W. 2nd Avenue
Delray Beach, FL 33444
(561) 276-5737

American Adoption Congress
  State Representative
761 N.W. 7th Avenue
Plantation, FL 33324
(954) 236-3856
SSH359@aol.com

American Adoption Congress
  State Representative
3100 Hunter Road
Ft. Lauderdale, FL 33331
(954) 384-8909
Fax: (954) 384-8602
kathy3100@aol.com

Birthmothers Support Group of
  Tallahassee
1522 Doolittle Avenue
Tallahassee, FL 32310
(850) 574-2787

Birthparent Support Group
176 Harris Street, N.E.
Ft. Walton Beach, FL 32547
(850) 863-5877

Christian Adoptees Support
  Exchange
2354 Willard Street
Ft. Myers, FL 33901

Circle of Hope
1125 N.W. 18th Avenue
Delray Beach, FL 33445
(561) 272-2930

Forever Families
130 N.W. 28th Street
Gainesville, FL 32607
(352) 377-6455

Mid-Florida Adoption Reunions
P.O. Box 3475
Belleview, FL 34421
(352) 237-1955

Mother and Child Reunion
2219 S.W. Mt. Vernon Street
Port St. Lucie, FL 34953
(561) 878-9101

O.A.S.I.S.
P.O. Box 530761
Miami Shores, FL 33153
(305) 948-8933

Orphan Voyage-at-St.
  Augustine (Florida)
P.O. Box 5495
St. Augustine, FL 32085
(904) 810-5596

People Searching News
Adoption Search National
  Hotline & Reunion Registry
  Adoptee-Birthparent
Connection
P.O. Box 100444
Palm Bay, FL 32910-0444
(407) 768-2222

Search Light
1032 Veronica Street
Pt. Charlotte, FL 33952

Searches International
1600 W. 64th Street
Hialeah, FL 33012-6106

Tallahassee Adoption Support
  Group
275 John Knox Road, #F104
Tallahassee, FL 32303
(850) 385-8703

Triad Search and Support
  Group
3408 Neptune Drive
Orlando, FL 32804
(407) 843-2760

Triad-Central Florida
2359 Summerfield
Winter Park, FL 32792
(561) 877-8711

FLORIDA LAWS RELATED TO ADOPTION: QUESTIONS AND ANSWERS

Can an attorney serve as an intermediary?
Yes. According to ICPC guidelines, an attorney or physician licensed in Florida can place children within the state. It is unlawful for an intermediary to accept a fee of more than $1,000 without obtaining prior court approval.

Attorneys and agencies outside of Florida may place children in the state if they adhere to ICPC guidelines and the Florida Adoption Act. Birth parents who wish to place a child outside of the state must surrender the child to a licensed agency, which can then place the child with the out-of-state couple designated by the birth mother as the adoptive parents.

Is advertising permitted?
Yes. Technically only attorneys and agencies and obstetricians may advertise, but advertising is a well-accepted practice. The law requires that a license number be shown on all adoption-related advertisements in the state. However, in practice a couple can place an ad without an attorney. Many newspapers will require a letter from your attorney.

Who must consent to the adoption?
1. The birth mother
2. The birth father, if he has acknowledged in writing that he is the child's father or was married to the mother when the child was conceived or born, or if he has supported the child

When can consent be given by the birth mother (father), and how long after the consent is signed can it be revoked?
Consent cannot be given until the child is born. Once the consent is signed, it is irrevocable.

Unless excused by the court, the law requires an independent, licensed psychologist or social worker to interview the birth parents to ensure that consent was given on a voluntary basis. The same social worker would also conduct the adoptive couple's resident home study before the baby is placed in their home.

What are the birth father's rights?
The birth father may only challenge the adoption if he has provided meaningful emotional and financial support. The court must either excuse his consent or it must be obtained. The birth father's consent is not needed if he does not respond in writing to a request for his consent within sixty days.

What fees can adoptive parents pay?
All fees for an attorney or physician intermediary or out-of-state adoption agency must be submitted to the court for prior approval. Payment of living expenses is permitted up to six weeks after the baby's birth. Any fees over $1,000, except for medical, hospital, or court costs, must be preapproved by the court. A final report of all fees associated with the adoption must be reported to the court.

Where does the adoption hearing take place?

The adoption hearing takes place in the county where the adoptive parents reside, or where the child placement agency is located.

How are familial and stepparent adoptions different from nonbiological adoptions?

No home study is required unless requested by the court. If the grandparents have visitation rights, their rights continue if a relative or stepparent adopts the child.

Can a nonresident finalize an adoption in this state?

No. Only those whose primary residence and place of employment is Florida may adopt, unless a special-needs child is involved.

SOURCE: FLORIDA STATUTES, SECTIONS 63.012 TO 63.301 (1997)

GEORGIA

State Adoption Specialist
Anne Jewett
Georgia Department
of Human Resources
Two Peachtree Street, N.E. 13th
Floor, Suite 317
Atlanta, GA 30303
(404) 657-3550

Compact Administrator
Douglas Greenwell, Director
Division of Family and Children
Services
Georgia Department
of Human Resources
Atlanta, GA 30303-3180

Deputy Compact Administrator
Janese Pullen, Acting Director
Social Services
Department Of Human Resources
Atlanta, GA 30303-3180

Independent Placements
Edith Horne, Adoption
Consultant
Division of Family
and Children Services
Georgia Department
of Human Resources
2 Peachtree Street, N.W., 12th
Floor, Room 100
Atlanta, GA 30303-3180
(404) 894-3706
fax (404) 894-4672

Adoption Assistance
Gail Merlinger, Adoption
Consultant
(404) 894-4469
Office hours:
Monday-Friday
8:00 A.M.-5:00 P.M.
Eastern Time Zone

State Adoption Exchange
Georgia State Adoption Exchange
Department of Human Resources
Two Peachtree Street N.W., 13th
Floor, Suite 400
Atlanta, GA 30303
(404) 657-3550

State Photo Listing
My Turn Now
Two Peachtree Street, 12th Floor,
Suite 204
Atlanta, GA 30303
(404) 657-3479

Private Adoption Agencies
Adoption Care
1447 Peachtree Street, Suite 511
Atlanta, GA 30309
(404) 897-1766

Adoption Planning, Inc.
17 Executive Park Drive,
Suite 480
Atlanta, GA 30329
(404) 248-9105

Adoption Services, Inc.
P.O. Box 155
Pavo, GA 31778
(912) 859-2654

Bethany Christian Services
1867 Independence Square,
Suite 201
Atlanta, GA 30338
(404) 396-7700

Bethany Christian Services
of Tennessee, Inc.
4719 Brainerd Road, Suite D
Chattanooga, TN 37411
(615) 622-7360

Catholic Social Services, Inc.
Adoption Program
680 West Peachtree Street, N.W.
Atlanta, GA 30308
(404) 881-6571

Covenant Care Services, Inc.
363 Pierce Avenue, Suite 202
Macon, GA 31204
(912) 741-9829

Edgewood Baptist Church, Inc.
New Beginning Adoption
and Counseling Agency
1316 Wynnton Court, Suite A
Columbus, GA 31906
(706) 571-3346

Families First
1105 West Peachtree Street
Atlanta, GA 30309
(404) 853-2800

Family Counseling
Center/CSRA, Inc.
603 Ellis Street
Augusta, GA 30901
(706) 722-6512

Family Partners Worldwide, Inc.
1776 Peachtree Street N.W.,
Suite 210 North
Atlanta, GA 30309
(404) 872-6787

Friends of Children, Inc.
5064 Roswell Road, N.E.,
Suite B-201
Atlanta, GA 30342
(404) 256-2121

Georgia Association for Guidance,
Aid, Placement and Empathy
(AGAPE), Inc.
3094 Mercer University Drive,
Suite 200
Atlanta, GA 30341
(404) 452-9995

Georgia Baptist Children's Home
and Family Ministries
North Area (Palmetto)
Route 2, Box 4
Palmetto, GA 30268
(404) 463-3344

Greater Chattanooga
Christian Services
400 Vine Street
Chattanooga, TN 37403
(615) 756-0281

Hope for Children, Inc.
1511 Johnson Ferry Road,
Suite 100
Marietta, GA 30062
(404) 977-0813

Jewish Family Services, Inc.
Cradle of Love Adoption
Counseling and Services
1605 Peachtree Street, N.E.
Atlanta, GA 30309
(404) 873-2277

LDS Social Services
4832 North Royal Atlanta Drive
Tucker, GA 30084
(404) 939-2121

Lutheran Ministries of Georgia
726 West Peachtree Street, N.W.
Atlanta, GA 30308
(404) 607-7126

Open Door Adoption
Agency, Inc.
403B N. Broad Street
P.O. Box 4
Thomasville, GA 31792
(912) 228-6339

Parent and Child
Development Services
21 East Broad Street
Savannah, GA 31401
(912) 232-2390

Partners in Adoption, Inc.
1050 Little River Lane
Alpharetta, GA 30201
(404) 740-1371

ROOTS
5532G Old National Highway,
Suite 250
College Park, GA 30349
(404) 209-8311

**Adoptive Parent Support Groups
and Postadoption Services**

Adopted Kids and Parent Support
Group (AKAPS)
Attn.: Marsha Kennedy
4137 Bellflower Court
Roswell, GA 30075
(404) 640-0031

Adoption Center
Atlanta Area
(404) 321-6900

Adoption Information Services
Attn.: Marsha Barker
Atlanta, GA
(404) 339-7236

Adoption Resource Exchange
Attn.: Norman Race
P.O. Box 6692
Americus, GA 31709
(912) 937-2591

Adoption Resource Exchange
of Columbus
Attn.: Ivy Mallisham
P.O. Box 9304
Columbus, GA 31908-9304
(706) 569-9199

Adoption Services, Inc.
Parents Support Group
Attn.: Roxanne Walker
P.O. Box 155
Pavo, GA 31778
(912) 859-2654

Adoptive Families
of Gwinnett County
Attn.: Marjorie Thomaston
3980 Rocmar Drive
Lithonia, GA 30058
(404) 827-6114

Adoptive Families Support Group
Attn.: Nancy Sanderson
(706) 689-5562

Adoptive Parents Association
Attn.: Karen Turner
911 Moss Drive
Savannah, GA 31410
(912) 897-6840

All God's Children
Attn.: Garry Seitz
3621 Mars Hill Road
Watkinsville, GA 30677
(404) 725-7658

Alliance of Single
Adoptive Parents
Attn.: Sharyn Hilley
687 Kennolia Drive, S.W.
Atlanta, GA 30314
(404) 755-3280

American-Romanian Connection
Attn.: Mary Springer
(404) 978-0019

Augusta Adoption
League/Home Base
Attn.: Rick Derby
4245 Match Point Drive
Augusta, GA 30907-2712
(404) 863-0583

Augusta Adoption Agency
Special Needs Group
Attn.: Brenda Brown
(706) 541-1640

Bartow/Paulding Adoptive
Families
Attn.: Sylvia Baldwin
(404) 387-1008 or 387-3710

Cherokee County Adoptive
Parent Support Group
Attn.: Pam Collins
3075 Batesville Road
Woodstock, GA 30188
(404) 475-7410

Clarke County Adoption
Resource Exchange
Attn.: Susan Jones
P.O. Box 6311
Athens, GA 30604
(706) 353-8539
(706) 542-9800
(Special Needs Group)

Clayton County Adoptive
Parent Support Group
Attn.: Drive Sherry Ramey
(404) 996-7622

Coffee County Adoption
Support Group
Attn.: Cheryl Cleveland
P.O. Box 422
Douglas, GA 31533

Decatur County Adoptive
Parents Support Group
Attn.: Brenda Reddick
(912) 248-2420

Douglas Region Adoptive
Families Together (DRAFT)
Attn.: Carol E. Jones
(404) 489-2239

Early Tri-County
Adoption Support Group
Attn.: Nancy Mock
(912) 723-4331

Emanuel County
Adoptive Parents Group
Attn.: Billie Scott
(912) 237-6494

Families Adopting Across Racial
Lines Support Group
Bethany Christian Services
Attn.: Karen Sievert
(404) 924-8645

Families By Choice
Attn.: Connie Sealy
(912) 474-8952

Families First Adoptive
Parent Support Group
1105 West Peachtree Street
Atlanta, GA 30309
(404) 853-2800

Families Forever
Post Adoption Project
Attn.: Noreen Horrigan
Two Peachtree Street, 13th Floor,
Suite 400
Atlanta, GA 30303
(404) 657-3556

Flint River Adoptive
Parent Support Group
Attn.: Jill Holder or Marsha Raleigh
(404) 954-2354 or 954-2014

Fulton County Adoptive
Parent Support Group
Attn.: Drive McClellon Cox
3653 Rainbow Drive
Decatur, GA 30335
(404) 220-0210

Georgia Adoptive Parents
Attn.: Peggy Bethea
178 Sams Street
Decatur, GA 30030
(404) 658-7327 or 508-0081

Georgia Council
on Adoptable Children
Attn.: Linda Price
(404) 986-0760

Glynn County Adoptive Parents
Attn.: Mary Cira
(912) 638-8556

Gwinnett County Adoptive
Parents Support Group
Attn.: Barbara Sorenson
530 Northdale Road
Lawrenceville, GA 30245
(404) 995-2100

Houston County Adoptive
Parent Support Group
Attn.: Nancy McDowell
202 William John Lane
Bonaire, GA 31005
(912) 922-9699

Interracial Family Alliance
Attn.: Mark Lockhart
P.O. Box 20290
Atlanta, GA 30324
(404) 924-8453

Jenkins County
Adoptive Parents Group
Attn.: Billie Scott
(912) 237-6494

Lowndes Area
Adoption Support Group
Attn.: Claudia Benson
P.O. Box 3674
Valdosta, GA 31604
(912) 244-2852

Lutheran Ministries
Parent Support Group
Attn.: Joyce Hayes
(404) 607-7126

Lutheran Ministries
Parent Support Group
Attn.: Kari Manning
955 Ridgedale Drive
Lawrenceville, GA 30243
(404) 962-7370

Mid-Town
Adoptive Parent Group
Attn.: Susan Zoukis
(404) 892-0587

North American Council
on Adoptable Children
State Representative
Attn.: Kathryn Karp
P.O. Box 7727
Atlanta, GA 30357
(404) 657-3479

North Georgia OURS
Attn.: Barbara Gale
One Legion Drive
Lindale, GA 30147
(404) 232-2128

One Church,
One Child Program, Inc.
General L.M. Smoot
P.O. Box 115238
Atlanta, GA 30310
(404) 766-0383
(800) 662-3651

Prospective Adoptive Parent
and Adoptive Parent Group
of Marietta
Attn.: Kasey and Kimberly
Summer
225 Hamilton Court
Marietta, GA 30068

Screven County
Adoptive Parents Group
Attn.: Billie Scott
(912) 237-6494

Single Women
Adopting Children
Attn.: Lauri Lanning
(404) 730-4593

Soweta Six
Adoptive Parents Group
Attn.: Brenda Riddick
(912) 248-2420

Stars of David
Attn.: Jill Glass
3300 Arborwood Drive
Alpharetta, GA 30202

Statesboro Adoptive Families:
Action, Reassurance and Ideas
(SAFARI)
Attn.: Laurie Bradford
(912) 764-8130

Terrell Tri-County Adoption
Support Group
Attn.: Nancy Mock
(912) 723-4331

Warren, McDuffie, and Glascock
Counties Adoption Support
Group
Attn.: Brenda Brown
(706) 541-1640

White County Adoption Support
Group
Attn.: Kay Clinard
(706) 896-3524

Wilkes, Taliaferro, and Lincoln
  Counties Adoption Support
  Group
Attn.: Eloise Wood
(706) 678-2814

**Adopted Person and Birth
  Relative Support Groups**

Adoptee Birthparent Connection
4565 Pond Lane
Marietta, GA 30062
(404) 642-9063

Adoptee Liberty Movement
  Association (ALMA)
1344 Surrey Lane
Marietta, GA 30060

Adoptee's Search Network
3317 Spring Creek Drive
Conyers, GA 30208

Adoption Beginnings
P.O. Box 440121
Kennesaw, GA 30144
(404) 971-5263

Bridges in Adoption
665 Peach Creek Terr.
Alpharetta, GA 30302-4350
(404) 351-6779

Families First
1105 West Peachtree Street, N.E.
Atlanta, GA 30305
(404) 853-2800

State Bar of Georgia
800 The Hurt Building
50 Hurt Plaza
Atlanta, GA 30303
(404) 527-8700
(706) 456-2339

Adoption Attorneys

Adoption Planning, Inc.
Rhonda Fishbein*
17 Executive Park, Suite 480
Atlanta, GA 30329
(404) 248-9205
fax (404) 248-0419

> Ms. Fishbein has conducted
> about sixty independent
> adoptions, 175 agency
> adoptions, and twenty-five
> international adoptions.

Adoption Information Services,
  Inc.*
558 Dovie Place
Lawrenceville, GA
(770) 339-7236

* Provides education and makes
  referrals to domestic and
  international adoption
  programs.

Jerrold W. Hester
3941 Holcomb Bridge Road,
  #200
Norcross, GA 30092
(404) 446-3645

Richard A. Horder
1100 Peachtree Street, #2800
Atlanta, GA 30309-4530
(404) 815-6538

Irene A. Steffas
4187 Kindlewood Court
Roswell, GA 30075-2686
(404) 642-6075

Allan J. Tanenbaum
359 E. Paces Ferry Road, #400
Atlanta, GA 30305
(404) 266-2930

GEORGIA LAWS RELATED TO ADOPTION: QUESTIONS AND ANSWERS

Can an attorney serve as an intermediary?
No.

Is advertising permitted?
No, and you may not post flyers either. Networking in Georgia is limited to those you know.
We recommend getting out your school yearbook, and professional, church denomination,
and volunteer membership directories and send letters to as many people as possible.

   Georgia residents who advertise in another state cannot finalize the adoption in
Georgia; they must finalize in the state where they advertised. Therefore, make sure nonresidents can finalize in that state before you advertise.

Who must consent to the adoption?
1. The birth mother
2. The child placement agency, if involved
3. The birth father, unless he has abandoned the child, cannot be found, or has failed to
    support or communicate with the child or mother for longer than one year, or if he
    failed to support or communicate with the mother during her pregnancy

When can consent be taken from the birth mother (father), and how long after the consent is signed can it be revoked?

Consent cannot be obtained until twenty-four hours after the child's birth. In both an agency and independent adoption, the birth parents have ten days after signing the consent to withdraw consent.

What are the birth father's rights?

Georgia law requires that a known or unknown birth father whose consent is not required has a right to a notice. The birth father of a child born out of wedlock must be served with notice of the hearing. If he does not respond within thirty days to notice of adoption, his parental rights will be terminated, and he cannot legally object to the adoption. If his location is not known, a petition will be filed with the court to terminate his rights and allow the adoption to occur. The court will then make a decision to proceed with the adoption based on whether the birth father has established a familial bond with the child or if reasonable efforts were made to locate him. Publication for the unknown birth father must be done.

Judges very seldom permit a birth mother to not name the birth father. In one scenario, an adoption took more than a year to finalize because the birth mother would not name a birth father who had threatened her life.

Parental rights can also be terminated because of a felony and imprisonment that has a negative effect on the parent-child relationship.

A birth father who has registered with the putative father registry is entitled to notice of adoption proceedings.

What fees can adoptive parents pay?

Only medical and legal expenses for the birth mother and child are permitted. Any other payment is considered an inducement. Only in an agency adoption can living expenses be paid. A report of payments must be filed with the court. Every attorney must also file a report of all fees paid or promised to the attorney for all services rendered.

Where does the adoption hearing take place?

The hearing takes place in the court in the county where the adoptive parents reside.

How are familial and stepparent adoptions different from nonbiological adoptions?

Some courts do not require a home study. The child's biological parents must give written permission for a relative or stepparent to adopt the child.

If the grandparents have court-ordered visitation rights previous to an adoption, they may file an objection to an adoption by another blood relative. The court will then decide if the child should be adopted by the other relative. If the court approves the adoption, the grandparent's visitation rights remain.

Can a nonresident finalize an adoption in this state?

No. You must be a resident of Georgia for at least six months before filing to adopt.

HAWAII

State Adoption Specialist

Hawaii Department of Human
Services
Lynn Mirikidani
810 Richards Street, Suite 400
Honolulu, HI 96813
(808) 586-5698
Fax: (808) 586-4806
www.state.hi.us/dhs/index.html
lmirikidani@dhs.state.hi.us

State ICPC Administrator

Hawaii Department of Human
Services
810 Richards Street, Suite 400
Honolulu, HI 96813
(808) 586-5701
Fax: (808) 586-4806

State Adoption Exchange/State Photolisting Service

Central Adoption Exchange
of Hawaii
810 Richards Street, Suite 400
Honolulu, HI 96813
(808) 586-5698
Fax: (808) 586-4806

State Reunion Registry

Family Court Central Registry
Court Management Service
777 Punchbowl Street
Honolulu, HI 96811

Regional/District Public Agencies

Department of Human Services
Social Service Division, Kauai
3060 Eiwa Street, Room 104
Lihue, HI 96766-1890
(808) 274-3300

Department of Human Services
Social Service Division, East
Hawaii
75 Aupuni Street, Suite 112
Hilo, HI 96720
(808) 933-0689

Department of Human Services
Social Service Division, Maui
1955 Main Street, Suite 300
Wailuku, HI 96793
(808) 243-5256

Department of Human Services
Social Service Division, Oahu
420 Waiakamilo Road,
Suite 300B
Honolulu, HI 96817-4941
(808) 832-5451

Department of Human Services
Social Service Division,
West Hawaii
Captain Cook State Civic
Center, P.O. Box 230
Captain Cook, HI 96704
(808) 323-4581

Licensed Private Adoption Agencies

Adopt International
900 Fort Street Mall, Pioneer
Plaza, Suite 1700
Honolulu, HI 96813
(808) 523-1400
Fax: (808) 969-6665
www.adopt-intl.org/
adoptinter@aol.com

Casey Family Program
1848 Nuuanu Avenue
Honolulu, HI 96817
(808) 521-9531

Catholic Services to Families
200 N. Vineyard Boulevard,
3rd Floor
Honolulu, HI 96817
(808) 537-6321

Child and Family Services
200 N. Vineyard Boulevard,
Suite 20
Honolulu, HI 96817
(808) 521-2377

Crown Child Placement
International, Inc.
P.O. Box 3990
Mililani, HI 96789
(808) 626-9292

Hawaii International Child
Placement and Family
Services, Inc.
P.O. Box 240486
Honolulu, HI 96824
(808) 377-0881
Fax: (808) 373-5095
www.h-i-c.org
info@h-i-c.org

LDS Family Services Hawaii
Honolulu Agency
1500 S. Beretonia Street,
Suite 403
Honolulu, HI 96826
(808) 945-3690

Queen Liliuokalani Children's
Center
1300 Halona Street
Honolulu, HI 96817
(808) 847-1302

Adoptive Parent Support Groups

Forever Families
7719 Waikapu Loop
Honolulu, HI 96825
(808) 396-9130

Resolve of HI-Kafuai Site
3721-A Omao Road
Koloa, HI 96756
(808) 742-8885

Stars of David International Inc.
Shaloha Chapter
P.O. Box 61595
Honolulu, HI 96839
(808) 988-1989
Fax: (808) 988-1989
www.starsofdavid.org
wolffwrite@aol.com

Search Support Groups

Access Hawaii and Concerned
United Birthparents
Box 1120
Hilo, HI 96721
(808) 965-7185

Adoption Circle of Hawaii
P.O. Box 61723
Honolulu, HI 96839-1723

Committee on Adoption
Reform and Education
55 Niuiki Circle
Honolulu, HI 96821
(808) 377-2345

HAWAII LAWS RELATED TO ADOPTION: QUESTIONS AND ANSWERS

Can an attorney serve as an intermediary?
Yes.

Is advertising permitted?
No. Only attorneys can advertise.

Who must consent to the adoption?
1. The birth mother
2. The presumed birth father

When can consent be taken from the birth mother (father), and how long after the consent is signed can it be revoked?
Consent can be taken at any time after the sixth month of pregnancy and is considered irrevocable once the child is placed, unless placement is not in the child's best interest.

The birth parents may have to appear in court unless the consent is taken before the court hearing and is accepted by the court without a personal appearance.

What are the birth father's rights?
The birth father's consent is required if he was married to the birth mother (or attempted to marry her) at the time of child's birth or if the child was born within 300 days after their marriage ended; or if he has received the child in his home as his own child or acknowledges paternity in writing or agreed to his name being placed on the child's birth certificate; or, if by court order or written promise, he agrees to support the child.

Also, a birth father's consent is required if he is not a "legal," "court approved," or a "presumed" father but is a father who has shown interest in the child's welfare within the first thirty days of the child's life, or before the birth mother consented to the adoption; or before the placement of the child with the adoptive parents (whichever time period is greater).

A birth father's consent is not required if he was not married to the birth mother at time of conception or birth and has not met the preceding requirements. Nor is his consent required if the court determines he is not fit or able to provide the child with a proper home and education However, a birth father must still receive notice of an adoption proceeding.

What fees can adoptive parents pay?
The law does not address this matter.

Where does the adoption hearing take place?
The hearing may take place in the family court where the adoptive parents live, where the child was born, or where the child placement agency is located.

How are familial and stepparent adoptions different from nonbiological adoptions?
The law does not address this issue.

Can a nonresident finalize an adoption in this state?
Yes.

IDAHO

State Adoption Specialist

Idaho Department of Health
and Welfare
Meri Brennan
5th Floor, P.O. Box 83720
Boise, ID 83720-0036
(208) 334-5700
Fax: (208) 334-6664
*www.state.id.us/dhw/hwgd_www/
famcomsv/fcs/96adopt.pdf*
Brennanm@dhw.state.id.us

State ICPC Administrator

Idaho Department of Health
and Welfare
Division of Family &
Community Services
P.O. Box 83720, 5th Floor
Boise, ID 83720
(208) 334-5700
Fax: (208) 334-6699

State Central Register

Illinois Department of Children
& Family Services
406 East Monroe
Springfield, ID 62701-1498
(217) 785-2680
Fax: (217) 785-2459

State Adoption Exchange/State
Photolisting Service

Idaho Department of Health
and Welfare
P.O. Box 83720
Boise, ID 83720-0036
(208) 334-5700
www.nwae.org

Northwest Adoption Exchange
600 Stewart Street, Suite 1313
Seattle, WA 98101
(206) 441-6822
Fax: (206) 441-7281
Toll Free: (800) 927-9411
www.nwae.org
nwae@nwresource.org

State Reunion Registry

Voluntary Adoption Registry,
Vital Records Section
Center for Vital Statistics and
Health Policy
450 W. State Street
Boise, ID 83720-0036
(208) 334-5990
*www.state.id.us/dhw/hwgd_www/
famcomsv/fcs/96adopt4.html*

Regional/District Public Agencies

Idaho Department of Health
and Welfare
Division of Family & Children's
Services, Caldwell
3402 Franklin Road, Box 1219
Caldwell, ID 83605
(208) 454-0421

Idaho Department of Health
and Welfare
Division of Family & Children's
Services, Boise
1720 Westgate Drive, Suite A
Boise, ID 83704
(208) 334-6800

Idaho Department of Health
and Welfare
Division of Family & Children's
Services, Coeur D'Alene
1250 Ironwood Street, Suite 204
Coeur D'Alene, ID 83814
(208) 769-1515

Idaho Department of Health
and Welfare
Division of Family & Children's
Services, Lewiston
P.O. Drawer B
Lewiston, ID 83501
(208) 799-3360

Idaho Department of Health
and Welfare
Division of Family & Children's
Services, Idaho Falls
150 Shoup Avenue
Idaho Falls, ID 83401
(208) 520-5905

Idaho Department of Health
and Welfare
Division of Family & Children's
Services, Pocatello
P.O. Box 4166
Pocatello, ID 83205
(208) 235-2940

Idaho Department of Health
and Welfare
Division of Family & Children's
Services, Twin Falls
601 Poleline Road, Suite 6
Twin Falls, ID 83301
(208) 736-3020

Licensed Private Adoption
Agencies

Casey Family Program
6441 Emerald
Boise, ID 83704
(208) 377-1771

*Children's Adoption Services,
Inc.
2308 North Cole
Boise, ID 83704
(208) 376-0558
Fax: (208) 376-1931
Toll Free: (800) 376-0558
www.adoptcasi.org
info@adoptcasi.org

Family Wellness Center
420 W. Bannock
Boise, ID 83701
(208) 344-0094

Idaho Youth Ranch Adoption
Services
P.O. Box 8538
Boise, ID 83707
(208) 377-2613

LDS Family Services
255 N. Overland Avenue
Burley, ID 83318
(208) 678-8200

LDS Family Services
1169 Call Creek Place, Suite B
Pocatello, ID 83201
(208) 232-7780

LDS Family Services
1420 E. 17th, Suite B
Idaho Falls, ID 83404
(208) 529-5276

LDS Family Services
10740 Fairview, Suite 100
Boise, ID 83704
(208) 376-0191

New Hope Child & Family
Agency
510 East 17th Street, Suite 210
Idaho Falls, ID 83404
(208) 522-7000
Toll Free: (800) 574-7705
www.newhopekids.org
info@newhopekids.org

Northwest Services
112 S. Kimball Avenue, #140
Caldwell, ID 83605
(208) 459-6772

Adoptive Parent Support
Groups

A Special N.E.S.T. Inc.
2389 Jerome
Pocatello, ID 83201
(208) 237-1267

Adopted Child
P.O. Box 9362
Moscow, ID 83843
(208) 882-1794
*www.moscow.com/Resources/Ado
ption/Adoption.html*

Families of MAC (Multicultural
Adopted Children)
2820 Shamrock Ave
Nampa, ID 83686
(208) 463-4040
www.familiesofmac.com
kym@familiesofmac.com

Magic Valley Adoptive Parent
Support Group
Department of Health and
Welfare
601 Poleline Road, Suite 6
Twin Falls, ID 83301
(208) 734-4000

North American Council on
Adoptable Children
1301 Spokane Street
Post Falls, ID 83854
(208) 773-5629
members.aol.com/nacac

Special Needs Adoptive Parents
(SNAP) and North American
Council on Adoptable
Children Representative
10809 Hinsdale
Boise, ID 83713
(208) 377-5635

Special Needs Adoptive Parents
(SNAP) Lutheran Social
Services
420 W. Bannock
Boise, ID 83701
(208) 344-0094

Search Support Groups

Adoptee Liberty Movement
Association (ALMA)
P.O. Box 190655
Boise, ID 83719
(208) 362-2364

Adoption Support Group
Box 2316
Ketchum, ID 83340
(208) 726-8543

American Adoption Congress
State Representative
4348 Maverick Way
Boise, ID 83709
(208) 362-2281
MTYMO@aol.com

Helping Hands
Box 249
Pinehurst, ID 83850
(208) 682-4280

Search Finders of Idaho
P.O. Box 7941
Boise, ID 83707
(208) 375-9803

Search Light
Box 5341
Coeur d'Alene, ID 83814
(208) 689-3255

IDAHO LAWS RELATED TO ADOPTION: QUESTIONS AND ANSWERS

Can an attorney serve as an intermediary?
Yes.

Is advertising permitted?
No.

Who must consent to the adoption?
The birth parents

**When can consent be taken from the birth mother (father), and how long after the
consent is signed can it be revoked?**
The birth mother cannot give consent until forty-eight hours after the child's birth, and
the consent is irrevocable.

What are the birth father's rights?
The birth father may claim rights if he registers with the Registry of Vital Statistics of the
Department of Health and Welfare. This claim must occur before the child is placed with
an adoption agency. If he fails to file, he can never try to establish paternity, and his
parental rights may be terminated. The Department of Health and Welfare, the adoption
agency, or the adoption attorney must notify him of his need to register so that if he
desires, he can give his intent to support the child and exercise his rights. If the birth

father cannot be located, an attempt must be made to notify him through publication at least ten days before parental rights are terminated or the child is placed with an agency.

What fees can adoptive parents pay?
Payment of medical, legal, and some living expenses is permitted.

Where does the adoption hearing take place?
The hearing usually takes place in the District Court in the county where the adoptive parents reside.

How are familial and stepparent adoptions different from nonbiological adoptions?
A home study may be required if requested by the court. There is no state residency requirement.

Can a nonresident finalize an adoption in this state?
No. You must live in the state for at least six consecutive months.

SOURCE: IDAHO CODE, SECTIONS 16-1501 TO 16-1513 (1997)

ILLINOIS

State Adoption Specialist

Illinois Department of Children
and Family Services
Division of Foster Care and
Permanency Services
Jane Elmore
406 E. Monroe Street,
Station #225
Springfield, IL 62701
(217) 524-2422
Fax: (217) 524-3966
cfs9je@jesi.state.il.us

Illinois Department of Children
and Family Services
Division of Foster Care and
Permanency Services
June Dorn
100 W. Randolph, Suite 6-100
Chicago, IL 60601
(312) 814-6858
Fax: (312) 814-3064
www.state.il.us/dcfs/
adoptmain1.htm
jdorn@idcfs.state.il.us

**State Adoption Exchange/State
Photolisting Service**

Adoption Information Center of
Illinois (AICI)
188 W. Randolph, Suite 600
Chicago, IL 60606
(312) 346-1516
Fax: (312) 346-0004

Toll Free: (800) 572-2390
www.adoptinfo-il.org
aici@adoptinfo-il.org

State Reunion Registry

Illinois Department of Public
Health
Office of Vital Records
Adoption Registry
605 West Jefferson
Springfield, IL 62702
(217) 782-6553

**Regional/District Public
Agencies**

Illinois Department of Children
and Family Services
200 S. Wyman Street,
2nd Floor
Rockford, IL 61101-1232
(815) 987-7200

Illinois Department of Children
and Family Services
2309 W. Main Street
Marion, IL 62959
(618) 993-7100

Illinois Department of Children
and Family Services
10251 Lincoln Trail
Fairview Heights, IL 62208
(618) 394-2100

Illinois Department of Children
and Family Services
4500 S. Sixth Street Road
Springfield, IL 62703-5192
(217) 786-6830

Illinois Department of Children
and Family Services
2125 S. First Street
Champaign, IL 61820
(217) 333-1037

Illinois Department of Children
and Family Services
2301 N.E. Adams
Peoria, IL 61603
(309) 686-8700

Illinois Department of Children
and Family Services
8 E. Galena Boulevard, 4th
Floor
Aurora, IL 60506
(630) 801-3400

Illinois Department of Children
and Family Services
Adoptive Family Development
1911 S. Indiana Ave, Suite 9
Chicago, IL 60616-1310
(312) 814-6036

**Licensed Private Adoption
Agencies**

Adoption-Link, Inc.
Suite 104, 1145 Westgate
Oak Park, IL 60301

(708) 524-1433
Fax: (708) 524-9691
maxsite.com/adoption/
alink@theramp.net

Aunt Martha's Youth Services
4343 Lincoln Highway, #340
Matteson, IL 60443
(708) 747-2701

Aurora Catholic Social Services
1700 N. Farnsworth Avenue
Aurora, IL 60505
(708) 892-4366

Baby Fold
210 Landmark, Suite A
Normal, IL 61761
(309) 454-1770

Bethany Christian Services
9718 South Halsted Street
Chicago, IL 60628-1007
(773) 233-7600
Fax: (773) 233-7617
www.bethany.org
info@bethany.org

Bethany Home Family Services
1606 Brady Street, Suite 309
Davenport, IA 52803-4708
(319) 324-9169

Catholic Charities,
  Chicago Archdiocese
126 North DesPlaines
Chicago, IL 60661
(312) 655-7000

Catholic Charities,
  Joliet Diocese
203 N. Ottawa Street, 2nd
  Floor, Suite A
Joliet, IL 60432
(815) 723-3053

Catholic Charities,
  Springfield Diocese
120 S. 11th Street
Springfield, IL 62703
(217) 525-0500

Catholic Social Services,
  Belleville Diocese
8601 W. Main Street, Suite 201
Belleville, IL 62220
(618) 394-5900

Catholic Social Services, Peoria
  Diocese
413 N.E. Monroe
Peoria, IL 61603
(309) 671-5720

Catholic Social Services,
  Rockford Diocese
921 W. State Street
Rockford, IL 61102
(815) 965-0623

Center for Family Building, Inc.
1740 Ridge Avenue, Suite 208
Evanston, IL 60201
(847) 869-1518
Fax: (847) 869-4108
http;//www.centerforfamily.com
info@centerforfamily.com

Central Baptist Family Services
2100 S. Indiana, Suite 360
Chicago, IL 60616
(312) 326-7430

Chicago Child Care Society
5467 S. University Avenue
Chicago, IL 60615
(773) 643-0452

Chicago Youth Centers
10 W. 35th Street
Chicago, IL 60616
(312) 225-8200

Children's Home and Aid
  Society of Illinois
217 N. Jefferson, 5th Floor
Chicago, IL 60661-1111
(312) 831-1133

Children's Home and Aid
  Society of Illinois
1819 S. Neil, Suite D
Champaign, IL 61820
(217) 359-8815

Children's Home and Aid
  Society of Illinois
910 Second Street
Rockford, IL 61104
(815) 962-1043
Fax: (815) 962-1272

Counseling and Family Service
330 S.W. Washington
Peoria, IL 61602
(309) 676-2400

Cradle Society
2049 Ridge Avenue
Evanston, IL 60201
(847) 475-5800
Fax: (847) 475-5871
www.cradle.org
cradle@cradle.org

*Evangelical Child and
  Family Agency
1530 N. Main
Wheaton, IL 60187
(630) 653-6400

Family Counseling Clinic, Inc.
19300 W. Highway 120
Grayslake, IL 60030
(847) 223-8107

Family Resource Center
5828 North Clark Street
Chicago, IL 60660
(773) 334-2300
Fax: (773) 334-8228
Toll Free: (800) 676-2229
www.f-r-c.org
km@rmsbus.com

Family Service Agency of
  Adams County
915 Vermont Street
Quincy, IL 62301
(217) 222-8254

Family Service Center of
  Sangamon County
1308 S. Seventh Street
Springfield, IL 62703
(217) 528-8406

Glenkirk
2501 N. Chestnut
Arlington Heights, IL 60004
(847) 394-2171

Hobby Horse House
208 S. Mauvaisterre Street
Jacksonville, IL 62651
(217) 243-7708

Hope for the Children
1530 Fairway Drive
Rantoul, IL 61866
(217) 893-4673
www.hope4children.org
h4tc@soltec.net

Illinois Baptist Children's Home
4243 Lincolnshire Drive
Mt. Vernon, IL 62864
(618) 242-4944

Illinois Children's Christian
  Home
P.O. Box 200
St. Joseph, IL 61873
(217) 469-7566

Jewish Children's Bureau
1 S. Franklin Street
Chicago, IL 60606
(312) 346-6700

Lifelink/Bensenville Home
 Society
331 S. York Road
Bensenville, IL 60106
(630) 766-5800
www.lifelink.org
jwdil@ix.netcom.com

Lutheran Child and Family
 Services
2408 Lebanon Avenue
Belleville, IL 62221
(618) 234-8904

Lutheran Child and Family
 Services
120 S. Marion
Oak Park, IL 60302
(708) 763-0700

Lutheran Child and Family
 Services
800 S. 45th Street, Wells Bypass
Mt. Vernon, IL 62864
(618) 242-3284

Lutheran Child and Family
 Services
431 S. Grand Avenue, West
Springfield, IL 62704
(217) 544-4631

Lutheran Social Services
 of Illinois
701 Devonshire, Suite 204,
 Box C-9
Champaign, IL 61820
(217) 398-3011

Lutheran Social Services
 of Illinois
1144 Lake Street, 3rd Floor
Oak Park, IL 60301-1043
(708) 445-8341

Lutheran Social Services
 of Illinois
610 Abington
Peoria, IL 61603
(309) 671-0300

Lutheran Social Services of
 Illinois, Chicago South Office
11740 S. Western
Chicago, IL 60643
(773) 239-3700

New Life Social Services
6316 N. Lincoln Ave
Chicago, IL 60659
(773) 478-4773
Fax: (773) 478-7646
nlss2@aol.com

PSI Services, Inc.
111 E. Wacker Drive,
 Suite 2500
Chicago, IL 60601
(312) 946-0740

Saint Mary's Services
717 W. Kirchoff Road
Arlington Heights, IL 60005
(847) 870-8181

Sunny Ridge Family Center, Inc
2 South 426 Orchard Road
Wheaton, IL 60187
(630) 668-5117
Fax: (630) 668-5144
www.sunnyridge.org
info@sunnyridge.org

Uniting Families Foundation
P.O. Box 755
Lake Villa, IL 60046
(847) 356-1452
Fax: (847) 356-1584
members.aol.com/UnitingFam/
 index.html
UnitingFam@aol.com

Volunteers of America
 of Illinois
4700 State Street
East St. Louis, IL 62205
(618) 271-9833

Volunteers of America
 of Illinois
224 N. Desplaines, Suite 500
Chicago, IL 60661
(312) 707-9477

**Adoptive Parent Support
 Groups**

Adoptees, Birth and Adoptive
 Parents Together
729 Zaininger Avenue
Naperville, IL 60563
(630) 778-0636
adoption@kwom.com

Adoption Preservation Parent
 Support
610 Abington
Peoria, IL 61603

Adoption Seminar
1212 South Naper Boulevard,
 Box 119
Naperville, IL 60540
(630) 961-2229

Adoption Support Group of
 Northeastern Illinois
2764 Lauretta Place
Highland Park, IL 60035
(847) 433-3184

Adoptive Families of
 DeKalb Area
303 N. Second Street
DeKalb, IL 60115-3236
(815) 758-4307

Adoptive Families of
 Northern Illinois
P.O. Box 15332
Rockford, IL 61132
(815) 389-1030

Adoptive Families Today
P.O. Box 1726
Barrington, IL 60011-1726
(847) 382-0858
Fax: (847) 382-0831
www.adoptivefamiliestoday.org
ADOPTAFT@aol.com

Adoptive Family Support Group
RR#2, Box 295F
Camp Point, IL 62320
(309) 828-2353

Adoptive Parents Together
309 Pleasant Ridge Road
Fairview Heights, IL 62208
(618) 394-0139

All-Dopt Support Group
727 Ramona Place
Godfrey, IL 62035
(618) 466-8926

BHS International Reachout
470 Glen Echo Road
Naperville, IL 60565
(630) 416-7604

Central Illinois Adoptive
 Families
2206 Oakwood Avenue
Bloomington, IL 61704
(309) 662-3349

Chicago Area Families
 for Adoption
1212 S. Naper Boulevard,
 Suite 119
Naperville, IL 60540
(630) 653-1797

Child International
4121 Crestwood Drive
Northbrook, IL 60062
(847) 272-2511

Children Remembered, Inc.
P.O. Box 234
Northbrook, IL 60062
(847) 291-3572

Christian Adoption Ministries
327 N. High
Carlinville, IL 62626
(217) 854-8871

Families with Heart
307 S. Webster
Robinson, IL 62454
(618) 544-7195

Foster Another Child
   This Season
OS628 Kirk
Elmhurst, IL 60126
(630) 941-7793

Fox Valley Adoption Group
3106 Royal Fox Drive
St. Charles, IL 60174
(630) 513-1370

Hands Around the World
1417 E. Miner
Arlington Heights, IL 60004
(847) 255-8309

Heart of Illinois Adoptive
   Families
730 High Point Lane
East Peoria, IL 61611
(309) 698-6011

Illiana Adoptive Parents
P.O. Box 412
Flossmoor, IL 60422
(708) 799-7844

Illinois Coalition for TRUTH
   in Adoption
P.O. Box 4638
Skokie, IL 60076-4638
(217) 664-3342
www.prairienet.org/icta
ICTA97@aol.com

Illinois Council on
   Adoptable Children
809 Laurel Avenue
Des Plaines, IL 60016
(847) 698-3668

Illinois Parents for Black
   Adoptions and North
   American Council on
   Adoptable
Children
7930 S. Colfax Avenue
Chicago, IL 60617
(312) 734-2305

International Families
3296 Knox Drive
Freeport, IL 61032
(815) 232-7547

Keeping the Promise -
   Champaign County
210 Landmark, Suite A
Normal, IL 61761
(309) 452-1170

Keeping the Promise -
   McLean County
210 Landmark, Suite A
Normal, IL 61671
(309) 452-1170

Midwest Adoption Center
3158 Des Plaines River Road,
   Suite 120
Des Plaines, IL 60016
(847) 298-9096
Fax: (847) 298-9097
www.macadopt.org
macadopt@aol.com

North American Council
   on Adoptable Children
   Representative
487 Bradford Place
Bolingbrook, IL 60440
(312) 633-3425
members.aol.com/nacac

North American Council
   on Adoptable Children
   Representative
2426 Austin Drive
Springfield, IL 62704
(217) 787-7367
Fax: (217) 524-3966
members.aol.com/nacac

OURS for a United Response
   of Northern Illinois
P.O. Box 15332
Rockford, IL 61132
(815) 389-1030

OURS of East Central Illinois
209 W. Nevada
Urbana, IL 61801
(217) 328-7352

Ours Through Adoption and
   North American Council on
   Adoptable Children
Representative
2618 Arlington Avenue
Davenport, IA 52803
(319) 322-6469

Parents Adopting Children
   Together
4413 Chelsea
Lisle, IL 60532
(630) 963-4121

Resolve of Illinois
318 Half Day Road, #300
Buffalo Grove, IL 60089
(773) 743-1623

Saint Paul's Adoption
   Support Group
1508 Karin Drive
Belleville, IL 62220
(618) 277-6422

Single Adoptive Parent
   Support Group
P.O. Box 578478
Chicago, IL 60657
(847) 604-1974

Special Needs Adoption
   Support Group
   Lifelink/Bensenville Home
   Society
331 York Road
Bensenville, IL 60106
(630) 766-5800, Ext: 282

Special Needs Adoption
   Support Group
   Lifelink/Bensenville
   Home Society
Avalon Community Church
8100 S. Dante Avenue
Chicago, IL 60619
(630) 766-5800

Stars of David International, Inc.
Chicago Area Chapter
3175 Commercial Avenue,
   Suite 100
Northbrook, IL 60062-1915
(847) 509-9929
Fax: (847) 509-9545
Toll Free: (800) 782-7349
www.starsofdavid.org/
StarsDavid@aol.com

Search Support Groups

Adoptee Liberty Movement
   Association (ALMA)
P.O. Box 74
Lebanon, IL 62254
(618) 537-2198

Adoptee Liberty Movement
Association (ALMA)
North and West Suburban
Chapter
P.O. Box 1802
Skokie, IL 60076
(312) 409-0273

Adoptee Liberty Movement
Association (ALMA)
P.O. Box 2043
Palatine, IL 60078
(312) 631-5816

Adoptee Liberty Movement
Association (ALMA)
P.O. Box 23255
Belleville, IL 62223
(618) 538-5599

Adoptees, Birthparents &
Adoptive Parents Together
Faith Evangelical Covenant
Church, 2 S. 571 Lakeview
Drive
Wheaton, IL 60187
(630) 778-0636
adoption@kwom.com

Adoption Search and
Support Group
638 S. Randolph
Macomb, IL 61455
(309) 837-9174

Adoption Triangle
Department of Children and
Family Services
Suite 200, 200 S. Wyman
Rockford, IL 61101-1232
(815) 987-7117

Adoption Triangle
c/o Children's Home and Aid
Society
1819 S. Neil, Suite D
Champaign, IL 61820
(217) 359-8815

Adoption Triangle
Box 384
Park Forest, IL 60466
(219) 365-0574

Adoption Triangle
512 Oneida Street
Joliet, IL 60435
(815) 722-4999

Adoption Triangle Rockford
318 Church Street
Rockford, IL 61101

American Adoption Congress
1201 South First Street
Springfield, IL 62704
(217) 789-0796
www.american-adoption-cong.org

American Adoption Congress
222 E. Pearson, Suite 602
Chicago, IL 60611
(312) 642-3617
www.american-adoption-cong.org
sgante@monticello.net

American Adoption Congress
State Representative
222 East Pearson #602
Chicago, IL 60611
(312) 642-3617
Fax: (312) 255-8408
Bspinazze@aol.com

Concerned United Birthparents
(CUB)
702 E. Algonqiuin Rd.,
Apt. K111
Arlington Heights, IL 60005
(847) 439-7644
Fax: (847) 439-8799
www.webnations.com/cub
Bonniebis@aol.com

Concerned United Birthparents
(CUB)
1701 Riverview Drive
Macomb, IL 61455
(309) 836-3809
sbkreapp@macomb.com

Concerned United Birthparents
(CUB)
1701 Riverview Drive
Macomb, IL 61455
(309) 836-3809
www.webnations.com/cub
cub@webnations.com

Concerned United Birthparents
(CUB)
1401 E. 55th St. Apt. 704
Chicago, IL 60615
(773) 363-5252
www.webnations.com
cub@webnations.com

Concerned United Birthparents
(CUB)
734 Noyes Street, Suite M3
Evanston, IL 60201
(847) 869-2978
www.webnations.com/cub
cub@webnations.com

Family Tree
P.O. Box 233
Libertyville, IL 60048
(847) 362-3721

Folk Finders
P.O. Box H
Neoga, IL 62447
Toll Free: (800) 277-3318

Healing Hearts
P.O. Box 606
Normal, IL 61761
(309) 452-9849

Healing Hearts Inc.
P.O. Box 136
Stanford, IL 61774
(309) 379-5401

Heritage Finders
1337 Park Drive
Montgomery, IL 60538
(630) 801-1554
ifind4u@aol.com

Heritage Finders
20955 S. Canterbury
Shorewood, IL 60436
(815) 725-8960

Hidden Birthright
100 Cumberland
Rochester, IL 62563-9238

Informed Choice for
Birthparents
Route 1, Box 5
DeLand, IL 61839
(217) 664-3342

Lost Connection
2661 N. Illinois Street,
Suite 147
Belleville, IL 62221
(618) 235-9409

Missing Pieces
P.O. Box 7541
Springfield, IL 62791-7541
(217) 787-8450

People Searching for People
P.O. Box 5442
Rock Island, IL 61204-5442

Reflections
606 Shipley Street
Carmi, IL 62821
(618) 382-3142

Search Connection
P.O. Box 2425
Brideview, IL 60455
(708) 430-9133

Truth Seekers in Adoption
P.O. Box 366
Prospect Heights, IL 60070-
0366
(847) 342-8742

ILLINOIS LAWS RELATED TO ADOPTION: QUESTIONS AND ANSWERS

Can an attorney serve as an intermediary?
Many attorneys do, but technically they should not.

Is advertising permitted?
Technically it is not permitted, but it is done extensively.

Who must consent to the adoption?
1. The birth mother
2. The birth father, if married to the birth mother, or if the child was born out of wedlock and he has lived with the child for six months and has openly stated that he is the child's father, or has maintained substantial and continuous contact with the child during a six-month period of the prior year; if the child is placed less than 6 months after birth and the birth father has held himself out as the birth father within 30 days of birth and has likely paid or made good faith effort to pay for the expenses of birth and further financial support of the child within 30 days of birth; if he has registered with the putative father registry and commenced a paternity action within 30 days of birth or within 10 days of it being possible to register in cases where the birth father can show that he could not register through no fault of his own

When can consent be taken from the birth mother (father), and how long after the consent is signed can it be revoked?
Consent cannot be given until seventy-two hours after the child's birth. However, the birth father's consent can be given before the birth, and he can revoke his consent within seventy-two hours of the birth if he notifies the representative to whom he had given consent. Rights are terminated via written consents taken in the presence of a notary public or, preferably, in the presence of a judge. Consent is irrevocable.

What are the birth father's rights?
Illinois has a putative father registry, and a birth father (generally) must register within thirty days of birth and initiate a parentage action. He can also establish his rights by marrying the birth mother, holding himself out as the birth father and by having substantial contact with the birth mother, and by paying for expenses and support.

What fees can adoptive parents pay?
Any fees or expenses paid that exceed $3,500 must be filed with the court. If all costs are less than $3,500, an affidavit must be submitted stating this. No fees can be paid for placing a child.

Where does the adoption hearing take place?
The hearing may take place in the county where the adoptive parents reside, where the birth parents reside, where the baby was born, or where the child placement agency is located.

How are familial and stepparent adoptions different from nonbiological adoptions?
The process is faster (four to six weeks), and the home study and criminal check are not mandatory. If a home study is conducted, there is minimal investigation. Grandparents have visitation rights if the adoption is by close relatives and occurs after the death of both parents.

Can a nonresident finalize an adoption in this state?
Yes, but only if the child is placed by an agency; otherwise, adoptive parents must have lived in the state for six months.

SOURCE: ILLINOIS REVISED STATUTES, SCTIONS 750-50-.01 TO 750-5-24 (1998)

INDIANA

State Adoption Specialist

Indiana Division of Family
& Children
Family Protection/Preservation
Jody Pearce
402 West Washington Street,
W-364
Indianapolis, IN 46204
(317) 233-1743
Fax: (317) 232-4436
Toll Free: (888) 204-7466
www.state.in.us/fssa/adoption
jppearce@fssa.state.in.us

State ICPC Administrator

Indiana Division of Family &
Children
402 Washington Street, Room
W-364
Indianapolis, IN 46204-2739
(317) 232-4769
Fax: (317) 232-4436

State Adoption Exchange/State Photolisting Service

Indiana Adoption Resource
Exchange
Indiana Division of Family
and Children
402 W. Washington Street,
Third Floor, W-364
Indianapolis, IN 46204-2739
(317) 233-1743
www.state.in.us/fssa/adoption/

State Reunion Registry

Indiana Adoption History
Registry
Attn: Registrar, Vital Records
Division
P.O. Box 1964
Indianapolis, IN 46206-1964
(317) 233-7253

Licensed Private Adoption Agencies

AD-IN, Inc.
8801 N. Meridian Street,
Suite 105
Indianapolis, IN 46260
(317) 573-0149

Adoption Network Domestic
and International, Inc.
4334 Miami
South Bend, IN 46614
(219) 299-9583

Adoption Resources Services,
Inc.
810 W. Bristol, Suite R
Elkhart, IN 46514
(219) 262-2499

Adoption Services, Inc.
3050 N. Meridian Street
Indianapolis, IN 46208
(317) 926-6338

Adoption Support Center
6331 N. Carrolton Avenue
Indianapolis, IN 46220
(317) 255-5916
Toll Free: (800) 274-1084

www.adoptionsupport.com
jcraft@adoptionsupport.com

Adoptions Alternatives
116 South Taylor Street
South Bend, IN 46617
(219) 232-5881
Fax: (219) 232-5844

Americans for African
Adoptions, Inc.
8910 Timberwood Drive
Indianapolis, IN 46234
(317) 271-4567
Fax: (317) 271-8739
www.cyberspacepr.com/
outreach2.html
amfaa@aol.com

Baptist Children's Home
354 West Street
Valparaiso, IN 46383
(219) 462-4111

Bethany Christian Services
830 Cedar Parkway
Schererville, IN 46375-1200
(219) 864-0800
Fax: (219) 864-1865
www.bethany.org
info@bethany.org

Bethany Christian Services
6144 N. Hillside Avenue,
Suite 10
Indianapolis, IN 46220
(317) 254-8479
Fax: (317) 254-8480
www.bethany.org
info@bethany.org

Catholic Charities
315 E. Washington
Fort Wayne, IN 46802
(219) 439-0242

Catholic Charities
120 S. Taylor Street
South Bend, IN 46601
(219) 234-3111
Fax: (219) 289-1034
Toll Free: (800) 686-3112

Catholic Charities Bureau
123 N.W. Fourth Street,
Suite 603
Evansville, IN 47708
(812) 423-5456

Catholic Family Services
973 W. Sixth Avenue
Gary, IN 46402
(219) 882-2723

Catholic Family Services of
Michigan City
1501 Franklin Street
Michigan City, IN 46360-3709
(219) 879-9312

Center for Family Building, Inc.
450 St. John Road, Suite 301-12
Michigan City, IN 46360
(847) 869-1518
Fax: (847) 869-4108
www.centerforfamily.com
info@centerforfamily.com

Childplace, Inc.
2420 Highway 62
Jeffersonville, IN 47130
(812) 282-8248
Fax: (812) 282-3291
Toll Free: (800) 787-9084
www.adoption.com/childplace/
childplac@aol.com

Children Are the Future
504 Broadway, Suite 725
Gary, IN 46402
(219) 881-0750

Children's Bureau of
Indianapolis
English Foundation Building,
615 N. Alabama Street,
Suite 426
Indianapolis, IN 46204
(317) 264-2700

Coleman Adoption Agency
419 English Foundation
Building, 615 N. Alabama
Street, Suite 119
Indianapolis, IN 46204
(317) 638-0965

*Compassionate Care
Route 3, Box 12B
Oakland City, IN 47660
(812) 749-4152
Toll Free: (800) 749-4153

Families Thru International
Adoption
991 South Kenmore Drive
Evansville, IN 47714-7514
(812) 479-9900
Fax: (812) 479-9901
Toll Free: (888) 797-9900
www.ftia.org
adopt@ftia.org

Family and Children's Services
655 S. Hebron
Evansville, IN 47414
(812) 471-1776

Family Resource Place
46th Street
Indianapolis, IN 46205
(317) 545-5281

G.L.A.D.
P.O. Box 9105
Evansville, IN 47724
(812) 424-4523

Hand In Hand International
Adoptions
201A North Orange Street
Albion, IN 46701
(219) 636-3566
Fax: (219) 636-2554
www.hihiadopt.org/
indiana@hihiadopt.org

Independent Adoption Center,
Inc.
537 Turtle Creek Drive, South,
Suite 23
Indianapolis, IN 46227
(317) 788-1039
Fax: (317) 788-1094
Toll Free: (800) 877-6736
www.adoptionhelp.org
iacorg@earthlink.net

Indiana One Church, One
Child Program, Inc.
850 North Meridian Street
Indianapolis, IN 46204
Toll Free: (800) 323-1660

Indiana Youth Advocate
Program
2626 E. 46th Street, Suite 140
Indianapolis, IN 46268
(317) 471-8081

Jeremiah Agency
P.O. Box 864
Greenwood, IN 46142-0864
(765) 887-2434

LDS Family Services
Indiana Agency
3333 Founders Road, Suite 200
Indianapolis, IN 46268-1397
(317) 872-1749
Toll Free: (877) 872-1749
well-fs-indiana@ldschurch.org

Loving Option
206 S. Main Street
Bluffton, IN 46714
(219) 824-9077

Lutheran Child and Family
Services
1525 N. Ritter Avenue
Indianapolis, IN 46219
(317) 359-5467

Lutheran Social Services
330 Madison Avenue
Fort Wayne, IN 46857-1329
(219) 426-3347

Lutheran Social Services,
Northwest Regional Office
1400 N. Broad Street
Griffith, IN 46319
(219) 838-0996
Fax: (219) 838-0999

Open Arms Christian Homes
Highway 54 E
Switz City, IN 47465
(812) 659-3564

Paralegal on Call, Inc
P.O. Box 652
Greenwood, IN 46142
(317) 888-6707
paroncall@aol.com

SAFY
2000 N. Wells Street,
Building #1
Ft. Wayne, IN 46808
(219) 422-3672

St. Elizabeth's
2500 Churchman Avenue
Indianapolis, IN 46203
(317) 787-3412

St. Elizabeth's of Southern
Indiana
601 E. Market
New Albany, IN 47150
(812) 949-7305

*Sunny Ridge Family Center, Inc
2 South 426 Orchard Road
Wheaton, IL 60187
(630) 668-5117
Fax: (630) 668-5144
www.sunnyridge.org
info@sunnyridge.org

The Villages, Inc.
652 N. Girl's School Road,
Suite 240
Indianapolis, IN 46214-3662
Toll Free: (800) 874-6880

Valley Children's Services
One Professional Center, 1801
N. Sixth Street, Suite 600
Terre Haute, IN 47804
(812) 234-0181

Adoptive Parent Support Groups

Adopt America Network
P.O. Box 402
Cicero, IN 46304-0402
www.aask.org/

Adopt America Network
Support Group
2500 Old Orchard Place
Vincennes, IN 47591

Adoptive and Foster Parent
Support Group of Delaware
County
RR 1, Box 60A
Daleville, IN 46334

Adoptive Parents Together and
North American Council on
Adoptable Children State
Representative
756 Woodruff Place
Indianapolis, IN 46201
(317) 638-0965

Association for the Rights
of Children
1017 Foster Avenue
South Bend, IN 46617

Black Adoptive Parents
Together
3131 E. 38th Street
Indianapolis, IN 46218
(317) 875-7066

Council on Adoptable Children
1021 Holly Drive
Lafayette, IN 47906

Council on Adoptable Children
of Grant County
503 E. Washington Street
Fairmont, IN 46928

Council on Adoptable
Children/Association for the
Rights of Children
10414 E. 25th Street
Indianapolis, IN 46229

Delaware County Foster Parent
Association
227 S. Mississinewa
Albany, IN 47319

Families Adopting Children
Today
819 N. Rensselaer
Griffith, IN 46319

Families Adopting Children
Together
29746 CR 118
Elkhart, IN 46517

Families Adopting Children
Together
RR 1, Box 151
Gentryville, IN 47537
(812) 925-3341

Families for Russian and
Ukrainian Adoptions
Central Indiana
10236 Bent Tree Lane
Fishers, IN 46038
(317) 598-9566
rick@nerdsoncall.com

Families for Russian and
Ukrainian Adoptions
Northern Indiana
IN
(219) 982-7390
mpater@boilermakers.net

Indiana Foster Care and
Adoption Association
3901 N. Meridian Street,
Suite 24
Indianapolis, IN 46208
(317) 925-1320
Toll Free: (800) 468-4228

Indiana Foster Care Association
Route 1, Box 102
Waveland, IN 47989

Indiana One Church One Child
Program, Inc.
850 N. Meridian Street
Indianapolis, IN 46204
(317) 684-2181

OURS by Adoption
4614 Morning Wind Place
Fort Wayne, IN 46806
(219) 436-3268

Rainbow Families of OURS
3003 S. Main Street
Goshen, IN 46526

Search Support Groups

Adoptee Identity
Doorway/Reunion Registry of
Indiana
P.O. Box 361
South Bend, IN 46624
(219) 272-3520

Adoptees Birthparents and
Siblings Enlightenment
Network of Thorntown
(A.B.S.E.N.T.)
711 W. Plum Street
Thorntown, IN 46071-1249
(765) 436-7257

Adoption Searching with Love
Spaeth Road
Mariah Hill, IN 47556
(812) 937-2485

Adoption Support Connection
21518 Burtzelbach Road
Guilford, IN 47022
(812) 487-2108

Adoption Triangle NW Indiana
7361 Wilson Place
Merrillville, IN 46410
(219) 736-5515

American Adoption Congress
State Representative
11678 N. McCulloch Road
Syracuse, IN 46567
(219) 856-2352
crisdehart@usa.net

Common Bond
Box 833
Kendallville, IN 46755
(219) 636-2404

Connected by Adoption
1817 Woodland Drive
Elkhart, IN 46514
(219) 262-0210

Coping with Adoption
61 Country Farm Road
Peru, IN 46970
(765) 472-7425

Double Heritage
332 Briner Road
Marion, IN 46953
(765) 664-2116

Indiana Adoption
  Coalition/Support of Search
P.O. Box 1292
Kokomo, IN 46901
(765) 453-4427

Lafayette Adoption
  Search/Support Organization
5936 Lookout Drive
West Lafayette, IN 47906
(765) 567-4139

Past and Present Association
3548 Revere Court
Lake Station, IN 46405

Reflections
7401 Washington Avenue
Evansville, IN 47715-4513

Search Committee
Madison County Historical
  Society
P.O. Box 523
Anderson, IN 46016
(765) 641-2442
HWLeedom@aol.com

Search for Tomorrow
P.O. Box 441
New Haven, IN 46774
(219) 749-4392

INDIANA LAWS RELATED TO ADOPTION: QUESTIONS AND ANSWERS

Can an attorney serve as an intermediary?
Yes, intermediaries are permitted to place children for adoption.

Is advertising permitted?
Yes.

Who must consent to the adoption?
1. The birth mother
2. The birth father, if married to the birth mother, or if the birth father's paternity is established by the court
3. The parents of a birth parent who is under eighteen years old, if the court decides that it is in the adoptee's best interest to get their consent

When can consent be taken from the birth mother (father), and how long after the consent is signed can it be revoked?
Consent can be given twenty-four hours after the child's birth. It can be revoked up to the time the adoption is finalized if the court determines it is in the child's best interest (which is very difficult to prove). The adoption usually takes place three to four months after the consent is signed, but it can take up to a year. Every county is different.

What are the birth father's rights?
Birth fathers are entitled to receive a notice of the adoption, either before or after the birth. If the birth mother identifies the birth father and provides his address, he will receive the notice. If the birth mother does not name him or provide his address, he must file with the putative father registry any time during the pregnancy or up to thirty days after the child's birth or the filing of the adoption petition in order to assert his rights. A birth father's or putative father's consent is irrevocably implied without any court action if 30 days after receiving actual notice he fails to file a paternity action or in the case where he files he fails to establish paternity within a reasonable time frame.

What fees can adoptive parents pay?
Reasonable expenses are permitted for the birth mother's medical needs and legal fees. Reasonable costs for housing for the birth mother during her pregnancy and up to six

weeks later can also be paid. Some other living expenses can be paid if approved by the court; however, what is permitted can vary depending upon the judge.

Where does the adoption hearing take place?
The hearing may take place in the county where the adoptive parents reside, where the adoptee lives, or where the child placement agency is located.

How are familial and stepparent adoptions different from nonbiological adoptions?
These adoptions are handled the same way as nonrelative adoptions, except that written approval of an adoption agency or the Department of Public Welfare is not necessary. Grandparents may be given visitation rights when adopted by a stepparent.

Can a nonresident finalize an adoption in this state?
No, unless they are adopting a special-needs child.

SOURCE: INDIANA CODE, SECTIONS 31-19-1-1 TO 31-19-25-14 (1998)

IOWA

State Adoption Specialist

Iowa Department of Human
  Services
Adult, Children and Family
  Services
Charlcie Y. Carey
Hoover State Office Building,
  5th Floor
Des Moines, IA 50319-0114
(515) 281-5358
Fax: (515) 281-4597
www.iakids.org
ccarey@dhs.state.ia.us

State ICPC Administrator

Iowa Deparment of Human
  Services
Adult, Children and Family
  Services
Hoover State Office Building,
  5th Floor
Des Moines, IA 50319-0114
(515) 281-5730
Fax: (515) 281-4597

**State Adoption Exchange/State
  Photolisting Service**

Iowa Adoption Resource
  Exchange
Adult, Children, and Family
  Services
Hoover State Office Building,
  5th Floor
Des Moines, IA 50319
(515) 281-5358
www.adopt.org

**Licensed Private Adoption
  Agencies**

Adoption International, Inc.
900 55th Street
West Des Moines, IA 50266
(515) 224-0500

American Home Finding
  Association
217 E. Fifth Street
Ottumwa, IA 52501
(515) 682-3449

Baptist Children's Home and
  Family Ministries
224 1/2 N.W. Abilene Road
Ankeny, IA 50021
(515) 964-0986

Bethany Christian Services
P.O. Box 143
Orange City, IA 51041-0143
(712) 737-4831
Fax: (712) 737-3238
www.bethany.org
info@bethany.org

Bethany Christian Services
8525 Douglas Avenue, Suite 34
Des Moines, IA 50322-3300
(515) 270-0824
Fax: (515) 270-0605
www.bethany.org
info@bethany.org

Bethany Christian Services
617 Franklin Street, Suite 201
Pella, IA 50219-1522
(515) 628-3247
Fax: (515) 628-1579

www.bethany.org
info@bethany.org

Bethany Home Family Services
1606 Brady Street, Suite 309
Davenport, IA 52803-4708
(319) 324-9169

Catholic Charities of Sioux City
1601 Military Road
Sioux City, IA 51103
(712) 252-4547

Catholic Charities of the
  Archdiocese of Dubuque
1229 Mt. Loretta
Dubuque, IA 52004-1309
(319) 588-0558
Toll Free: (800) 772-2758

Children and Families of Iowa
1111 University Avenue
Des Moines, IA 50314
(515) 288-1981

Children's Square U.S.A.
  Child Connect
541 Sixth Avenue, Box 8-C
Council Bluffs, IA 51502-3008
(712) 322-3700

Coleman Counseling
1105 28th Street
Sioux City, IA 51104
(712) 855-4321

Families of N.E. Iowa
108 W. Maple
Maquoketa, IA 52060
(319) 652-4958

*Family Resources, Inc.
115 W. Sixth Street
Davenport, IA 52803
(319) 323-1853

First Resources Corporation
109 C East Marion, P.O. Box 107
Sigourney, IA 52591
(515) 622-2543

Four Oaks, Inc.
5400 Kirkwood Boulevard, S.W.
Cedar Rapids, IA 52406-5216
(319) 364-0259

Gift of Love International
  Adoptions, Inc.
5750 Columbine Drive
Johnston, IA 50131
(515) 276-9277
Fax: (515) 276-6615
www.giftoflove.org
cannadopt@aol.com

Healing the Children
412 E. Church Street
Marshalltown, IA 50158
(515) 753-7544

Holt International Children's
  Services, Midwest Office
430 South 35th Street, Suite 2
Council Bluffs, IA 51501
(712) 328-1224
Fax: (712) 328-1198
www.holtintl.org
info@holtintl.org

Integrative Health Services, Inc.
118 S. Main
N. English, IA 52316
(319) 664-3278

Keys to Living
463 Northland Avenue, N.E.
Cedar Rapids, IA 52402-6237
(319) 377-2161

Lutheran Family Service
230 Ninth Avenue, North
Fort Dodge, IA 50501
(515) 573-3138

Lutheran Social Service
  of Iowa
3116 University Avenue
Des Moines, IA 50311
(515) 277-4476

Ralston Adoption Agency
2208 S. Fifth Avenue
Marshalltown, IA 50158-4515
Toll Free: (800) 304-0219

Tanager Place
2309 C Street, S.W.
Cedar Rapids, IA 52601
(319) 365-9164

The Crittenton Center
1105 28th Street
Sioux City, IA 51104
(712) 855-4321

Young House, Inc.
724 N. Third
Burlington, IA 52601
(319) 752-4000

**Adoptive Parent Support
Groups**

Family Connections and North
  American Council on
  Adoptable Children
Representative
66684 110th Street
McCallsburg, IA 50154
(515) 487-7833
Fax: (515) 487-7833
members.aol.com/nacac
mcbritco@netins.net

Iowa Foster & Adoptive Parents
  Association (IFAPA)
6864 N.E. 14th Street, Suite 5
Ankeny, IA 50021
(515) 289-4567
Fax: (515) 289-2080

Iowa Parents of (East) Indian
  Children
420 First Ave, W.
Newton, IA 50208
(515) 792-7843

Iowa Parents of (East) Indian
  Children
1805 11th Street
Eldora, IA 50627
(515) 858-5072

Iowans for International
  Adoption
31496 Iron Bridge Road
Spragueville, IA 52074
(319) 672-3273

KidSake Adoption Project
Coalition for Family and
  Children's Services in Iowa
1111 Ninth Street, Suite 200
Des Moines, IA 50314
(515) 244-0074
Fax: (515) 244-0075

Lifeline for Children
611 N.W. 45th Avenue
Coconut Creek, IA 33066
(954) 972-2735

North Iowa Adoption Group
408 28th, S.W.
Mason City, IA 50401
(515) 423-4224

Ours Through Adoption and
  North American Council on
  Adoptable Children
Representative
2618 Arlington Avenue
Davenport, IA 52803
(319) 322-6469

Search Support Groups

Adoptee Liberty Movement
  Association (ALMA)
P.O. Box 2071
Waterloo, IA 50704

Adoptees Quest
1513 Buresh Avenue
Iowa City, IA 52245

Adoption Experience
1105 Fremont
Des Moines, IA 50316

Adoption Experience
Route 5, Box 22
Osceola, IA 50213
(515) 342-4803

Concerned United Birthparents
  (CUB)
P.O. Box 8151
Des Moines, IA 50301
(515) 282-7549

Concerned United Birthparents
  (CUB)
National Headquarters
2000 Walker Street
Des Moines, IA 50317
(515) 263-9558
Toll Free: (800) 822-2777
www.webnations.com/cub
cub@webnations.com

Concerned United Birthparents
  (CUB)
790 Lilly Lane
Boone, IA 50036
(515) 432-9356
www.webnations.com/cub
cub@webnations.com

Concerned United Birthparents
(CUB)
2415 Lincoln Road
Bettendorf, IA 52722
(319) 359-4068
www.webnations.com
cuc@webnations.com

Concerned United Birthparents
(CUB)
308 S. Johnston Street
Iowa City, IA 52240
(319) 339-4357
www.webnations.com/cub
cub@webnations.com

Heritage Finders
1330 Prodehl
Lockport, IA 50441
(815) 838-5801

Iowa Reunion Registry
P.O. Box 8
Blairsburg, IA 50034-0008

Origins
4300 Ashby Avenue
Des Moines, IA 50310-3540
(515) 277-7700

IOWA LAWS RELATED TO ADOPTION: QUESTIONS AND ANSWERS

Can an attorney serve as an intermediary?
Yes, attorneys can place children in adoptive homes.

Is advertising permitted?
Yes.

Who must consent to the adoption?
The birth parents must consent.

When can consent be taken from the birth mother (father), and how long after the consent is signed can it be revoked?
The consent cannot be taken until seventy-two hours after the child's birth. The birth parent can revoke consent within ninety-six hours after signing. This means the child must be at least eight days old before the consent is irrevocable.

At least three hours of counseling must be made available to birth parents who request it.

What are the birth father's rights?
If a birth father cannot be located or refuses to give consent, the court will determine if the adoption is in the child's best interest without such a consent.

Iowa has a putative father registry, and a man seeking birth father rights must register before or after the child's birth.

What fees can adoptive parents pay?
The adoptive parents must file with the court a statement of all money paid.

Where does the adoption hearing take place?
The hearing takes place in the county where the adoptive parents reside.

How are familial and stepparent adoptions different from nonbiological adoptions?
Family relations may be distant and the adoption can still be considered a relative adoption. The child does not necessarily have to live in the home for at least six months, as is the case with other adoptions, in order for the adoption to be finalized.

Grandparents may be given visitation rights when a grandchild is adopted by a stepparent, as long as the grandparents already have a substantial relationship with the child and it is in the child's best interest.

Can a nonresident finalize an adoption in this state?
No.

SOURCE: IOWA CODE SECTIONS 600.1 TO 600.24. 24 (1997).

KANSAS

State Adoption Specialist

Kansas Department of Social
and Rehabilitation Services
Children and Family Policy
Division
Lois Mitchell
Docking State Office Building,
915 S.W. Harrison,
5th Floor South
Topeka, KS 66612
(785) 296-0918
Fax: (785) 368-8159
loxm@srskansas.org

State ICPC Administrator

Commission of Chidlren &
Family Services
Kansas Department of Social
and Rehabilitation Services
915 S.W. Harrison,
5th Floor South
Topeka, KS 66612
(785) 296-4648

**State Adoption Exchange/State
Photolisting Service**

Lutheran Social Services
Kansas Families for Kids (KFFK)
603 S. Topeka Boulevard,
Suite 206
Topeka, KS 66603
(785) 354-4663
Fax: (785) 354-4684
Toll Free: (800) 210-5387
www.kffk.org
patricial@kffk.org

**Regional/District Public
Agencies**

Lutheran Social Services of
Kansas - Concordia Offfice
P.O. Box 308, 213 W. 6th Street
Concordia, KS 66901
(785) 243-7971
Fax: (785) 243-7975

Lutheran Social Services of
Kansas - Great Bend Office
2701 24th Street
Great Bend, KS 67530
(316) 793-5734

Lutheran Social Services of
Kansas - Hays Office
2002 Main
Hays, KS 67601
(785) 625-4673
Fax: (785) 625-2441

Lutheran Social Services of
Kansas - Kansas City Office
4600 W. 51st, Suite 301
Roeland Park, KS 66205
(913) 432-4445
Fax: (816) 531-4114

Lutheran Social Services of
Kansas - Topeka Office
2942 S.W. Wanamaker Drive,
Building B, Suite 1C
Topeka, KS 66614
(785) 272-7883
Fax: (785) 228-9405

Lutheran Social Services of
Kansas - Wichita Office
1855 N. Hillside
Wichita, KS 67214
(316) 686-6645
Fax: (316) 686-0453

**Licensed Private Adoption
Agencies**

A Child's Dream
413 South 10th Street
Atchison, KS 66002
amadoption@aol.com

A.C.T. (Adoption,
Consultation and Training
Services, Inc)
4717 McCormick Court
Lawrence, KS 66047
(913) 727-2288

Adoption and Counseling
Services for Families
10045 Hemlock
Overland Park, KS 66212
(913) 383-8448
Fax: (913) 383-8448

Adoption Centre of Kansas
1831 Woodrow
Wichita, KS 67203
(316) 265-5289

Adoption Option
7211 W. 98th Terrace, #100
Overland Park, KS 66212
(913) 642-7900

Adoption Works, Inc.
400 N. Woodlawn, Suite 24
Wichita, KS 67208
(316) 687-4393

Catholic Charities, Diocese of
Dodge City
2546 20th Street
Great Bend, KS 67530
(316) 792-1393

Catholic Charities, Diocese of
Salina
428 West Iron Road
Salina, KS 67402
(785) 825-0208

Catholic Community Services
2220 Central Avenue
Kansas City, KS 66102
(913) 621-1504

Catholic Social Service
425 N. Topeka
Wichita, KS 67202
(316) 264-8344

Christian Family Services of the
Midwest, Inc.
10550 Barkley, Suite 100
Overland Park, KS 66212
(913) 383-3337

Family Life Services of Southern
Kansas
305 S. Summit
Arkansas City, KS 67005-2848
(316) 442-1688

Hagar Associates
115 S.W. 7th Street
Topeka, KS 66614
(913) 271-6045

Heart of America Adoption
Center
108 E. Poplar
Olathe, KS 66061
(913) 342-1110

Heartland International
  Adoptions
1831 Woodrow Avenue
Wichita, KS 67203-2932
(316) 265-5289

Helping Hand, Inc.
Executive Centre III
10901 Lowell Avenue, Suite 120
Overland Park, KS 66210
(913) 345-8855
Fax: (913) 451-1626

Inserco, Inc.
5120 E. Central, #A
Wichita, KS 67208
(316) 681-3840

Kansas Children's Service
  League
1365 N. Custer Street
Wichita, KS 67201
(316) 942-4261

Kansas Children's Service
  League
Black Adoptions Project
630 B Minnesota Street,
  Suite 310
Kansas City, KS 66117
(913) 621-2016

Kaw Valley Center
4300 Brenner Road
Kansas City, KS 66104
(913) 334-0294

Lighthouse of Kansas
6900 College Boulevard,
  Suite 860
Overland Park, KS 66211
(913) 361-2233

Lutheran Social Services
1855 North Hillside
Wichita, KS 67214-2317
(316) 686-6645

Lutheran Social Services
  of Kansas
2942 S.W. Wanamaker Drive
Topeka, KS 66614
(785) 272-7883
Fax: (785) 228-9405
Toll Free: (800) 210-5387
bkarstensen@lss.org

Nine Months Adoptions
8676 West 69th Street, Suite 200
Overland Park, KS 66212
Toll Free: (800) 768-7009
www.ninemonths.org
adoptions@ninemonths.org

*Special Additions
10985 W. 175th Street
Olathe, KS 66062
(913) 681-9604

St. Francis Academy, Inc.
10985 W. 175th Street
Olathe, KS 66062
(913) 681-9604

Sunflower Family Services
1503 Vine, Suite E
Hays, KS 67601-8384
(913) 625-4600
Toll Free: (800) 555-4614

The Villages, Inc.
2209 S.W. 29th Street
Topeka, KS 66611
(785) 267-5900

**Adoptive Parent Support
Groups**

Adoption with Wisdom and
  Honesty and North American
  Council on Adoptable
  Children State Representative
15153 W. 132nd Street
Olathe, KS 66062
(913) 768-6456
members.aol.com/nacac

Families for Russian and
  Ukrainian Adoptions
Kansas City Area FRUA
  Chapter
38209 Bethel Church Road
Osawatomie, KS 66064
ed@micoks.net

From China with Love
1308 N. Cardington
Witchita, KS 67212
kufford@aol.com

International Families of Mid
  America
6708 Granada Road
Prairie Village, KS 66208
(913) 722-5697

Ours Through Adoption
c/o Humana Hospital Education
  Department
10500 Quivira
Overland Park, KS 66215
(913) 384-0459

Salina Adoptive Parents Group
  Hope Center
First Presbyterian Church
308 S. Eighth
Salina, KS 67401

Special Needs Adoption Project
University of Kansas Medical
  Center Children's
  Rehabilitation Unit
3901 Rainbow Boulevard, #5017
Kansas City, KS 66103
(913) 588-5745

Search Support Groups

Adoption Concerns Triangle
411 S.W. Greenwood Avenue
Topeka, KS 66606
(785) 235-6122

Adoption Support Group
1425 New York Street
Lawrence, KS 66044

Adoption With Wisdom and
  Honesty
1333 Ranch Road
McPherson, KS 67460
(316) 241-6116

American Adoption Congress
  State Representative
1918 S.W. Sieben Court
Topeka, KS 66611
(785) 234-0130
Fax: (785) 862-1066

American Adoption Congress
  State Representative
411 S.W. Greenwood
Topeka, KS 66606-1231
(785) 235-6122
waugh5@aol.com

Reunions, Ltd.
2611 E. 25th Street
Topeka, KS 66608

Tri-Adoption Search and
  Support Group
2546 20th Street
Great Bend, KS 67530
(316) 792-1393

Wichita Adult Adoptees
4551 S. Osage Street
Wichita, KS 67217-4743
(316) 522-8772
www.feist.com/~lpsp1024/
  index.html
lpsp1024@feist.com

KANSAS LAW RELATED TO ADOPTION: QUESTIONS AND ANSWERS

Can an attorney serve as an intermediary?
Yes.

Is advertising permitted?
Possibly. Even though the existing statute forbids it, there has been some allowance of advertising. People are advertising in Kansas newspapers.

By law, only adoption agencies can advertise in newspapers; however, attorneys can place ads in the yellow pages.

Who must consent to the adoption?
Both birth parents.

When can consent be taken from the birth mother (father), and how long after the consent is signed can it be revoked?
Consents (for independent adoptions) and relinquishments (for agency adoptions) cannot be obtained until twelve hours after the baby's birth and are irrevocable. Consents must be acknowledged before a judge. The birth parents' rights in an independent adoption are terminated at a court hearing that takes place thirty to sixty days after the adoption petition is filed. The birth father can sign a consent or relinquishment before the birth.

What are the birth father's rights?
The birth father's consent is not necessary if he is not a "presumed" father, if his relationship has not been established by the court, or if he is not married to the birth mother. If he voluntarily agrees to place the child for adoption, the birth mother must file a petition to terminate his parental rights. A birth father's parental rights may be involuntarily terminated for failure to support the birth mother during the last six months of pregnancy, unfitness, abandonment of the child, abandonment of the mother despite knowledge of her pregnancy, rape, or nonsupport of the child for at least two years. (The proceeding terms, as appropriate, also apply to birth mothers.)

The court must make efforts to determine who the father is based on certain factors (e.g., if he has provided for the child or was married to the mother at time of conception). If these factors cannot be found, and he does not claim his rights to the child, his rights can be terminated.

What fees can adoptive parents pay?
Legal, medical, living expenses, and counseling fees associated with the adoption can be paid, and these fees must be approved by the court.

Health insurers are required to offer adoptive parents the option to purchase coverage for the birth mother's delivery expenses.

Where does the adoption hearing take place?
The hearing can take place in the county where the adoptive parents live, the child lives, or where the adoption agency is located.

How are familial and stepparent adoptions different from nonbiological adoptions?
Home studies are not necessary in stepparent adoptions, and the court may waive the
need for one when grandparents are adopting. All other issues remain the same.

Can a nonresident finalize an adoption in this state?
Yes.

KENTUCKY

State Adoption Specialist

Cabinet for Families and
 Children
Judy Johnson
275 East Main Street
Frankfort, KY 40621
(502) 564-2147
Fax: (502) 564-3096
cfc-chs.chr.state.ky.us/dcbs.htm

Cabinet for Families and
 Children
Annettee Bruce
275 East Main Street
Frankfort, KY 40621
(502) 564-2147
Fax: (502) 564-3096
cfc-chs.chr.state.ky.us/dcbs.htm

Cabinet for Families and
 Children
Betty Sweeny
275 East Main Street
Frankfort, KY 40621
(502) 564-2147
Fax: (502) 564-3096
cfc-chs.chr.state.ky.us/dcbs.htm

Cabinet for Families and
 Children
Jenny Smith
275 East Main Street
Frankfort, KY 40621
(502) 564-2147
Fax: (502) 564-3096
cfc-chs.chr.state.ky.us/dcbs.htm

State ICPC Administrator

Kentucky Cabinet For Families
 and Children
275 East Main Street, 4th Floor
Frankfort, KY 40621
(502) 564-4826

**State Adoption Exchange/State
 Photolisting Service**

Kentucky Adoption Resource
 Exchange
Department of Social Services
275 E. Main Street, 6th Floor,
 West
Frankfort, KY 40621
(502) 564-2147

Special Needs Adoption
 Program
Cabinet For Family and
 Children, Department for
 Community Based Services
908 W. Broadway, 8W
Louisville, KY 40203
(502) 595-4303

Special Needs Adoption Project
 (SNAP)
Department for Social Services
710 W. High Street
Lexington, KY 40508
(606) 252-1728
*cfc-chs.chr.state.ky.us/CFC/DSS/
 SNAP/snap.htm*

State Reunion Registry

Program Specialist
Department for Social Services
275 East Main Street, Sixth
 Floor, West
Frankfort, KY 40621
(502) 564-2147

**Regional/District Public
 Agencies**

Kentucky Department for
 Social Services, Barren River
P.O. Box 10177
Bowling Green, KY 42102
(502) 746-7447

Kentucky Department for
 Social Services, Bluegrass
710 W. High Street
Lexington, KY 40508-2499
(606) 246-2263

Kentucky Department for
 Social Services, Bluegrass
 West and Bluegrass East
627 W. Fourth Street
Lexington, KY 40508-9990
(606) 246-2310

Kentucky Department for
 Social Services, Buffalo Trace
 and Gateway
P.O. Box 1036
Moorehead, KY 40351-5036
(606) 784-6687

Kentucky Department for
 Social Services, Cumberland
 Valley
Regional State Office Bldg.,
 Room 211
London, KY 40741-9011
(606) 864-8779

Kentucky Department for
 Social Services, Fivco and
 Big Sandy
P.O. Box 1507
Ashland, KY 41105-1507
(606) 920-2007

Kentucky Department for
 Social Services, Green River
311 W. Second Street
Owensboro, KY 42301-0734
(502) 687-7491

Kentucky Department for
 Social Services, Jefferson
908 W. Broadway, 8W
Louisville, KY 40203-2015
(502) 595-4021

Kentucky Department for Social
 Services, Kentucky River
113 Lovern St., 2nd Floor
Hazard, KY 41701-1700
(606) 435-6052

Kentucky Department for
 Social Services, Lake
 Cumberland
P.O. Box 888
Jamestown, KY 42606
(502) 343-3512

Kentucky Department for
Social Services, Lincoln Trail
P.O. Box 39
Elizabethtown, KY 42702-0039
(502) 766-5099

Kentucky Department for
Social Services, Northern
Kentucky
624 Madison Ave.
Covington, KY 41011-2592
(606) 292-6340

Kentucky Department for
Social Services, Pennyrile
115 Hammond Plaza
Hopkinsville, KY 42241-4929
(502) 889-6570

Kentucky Department for
Social Services, Purchase
P.O. Box 1007
Mayfield, KY 42066-1007
(502) 247-2900

Kentucky Department for
Social Services, Salt River
11 Village Plaza
Shelbyville, KY 40065-1749
(502) 633-1892

**Licensed Private Adoption
Agencies**

A Helping Hand Adoption
Agency
P.O. Box 8336
Lexington, KY 40533
(606) 223-0112
Fax: (606) 296-2937
www.serve.com/ahh

Adopt! Inc.
135 Lackawana Rd.
Lexington, KY 40503
(606) 276-6249
www.iglou.com/kac/adopt!.htm
ADOPTinc@aol.com

Adoption Assistance
510 Maple Avenue
Danville, KY 40422
(606) 236-2761

Adoptions of Kentucky
One Riverfront Plaza, Suite 1708
Louisville, KY 40202
(502) 585-3005

Bluegrass Christian Adoption
Services
1309 S. Limestone
Lexington, KY 40503
(606) 276-2222

Catholic Charities
2911 S. Fourth Street
Louisville, KY 40208
(502) 637-9786
Fax: (502) 637-9780
www.iglou.com/kac/ccas.htm

Catholic Social Service Bureau
1310 W. Main Street
Lexington, KY 40508
(606) 253-1993

Catholic Social Services of
Northern Kentucky
3629 Church Street
Covington, KY 41015
(606) 581-8974

Childplace
4500 Westport Road
Louisville, KY 40207
(502) 363-1633
Toll Free: (800) 787-9084
www.adoption.com/childplace/
childplac@aol.com

Children of the Americas
1890 Lyda Avenue
Bowling Green, KY 42104
(502) 843-0300

Children's Home of Northern
Kentucky
200 Home Road
Covington, KY 41011-1942
(606) 261-8768
Fax: (606) 291-2431
www.iglou.com/kac/chnk.htm
shamilton.cinoh@juno.com

Children's Sanctuary
200 High Rise, Suite 155
Louisville, KY 40213
(502) 969-4005

Chosen Children Adoption
Services, Inc.
5427 Bardstown Road, Suite
One
Louisville, KY 40291
(502) 231-1336
Fax: (502) 231-4098
www.iglou.com/kac/chosen.htm

Cumberland River Region
MH-MR Board
1203 American Greeting Road
Corbin, KY 40702
(606) 528-7010

Holston United Methodist
Home for Children
503 Maple Street
Murray, KY 42071
(270) 759-5007

Home of the Innocents
10936 Dixie Highway
Louisville, KY 40272
(502) 561-6600

Hope Hill Children's Home
10230 Hope-Means Road
Hope, KY 40334
(606) 498-5230

Jewish Family and Vocational
Service
3640 Dutchmans Lane
Louisville, KY 40205
(502) 452-6341
Fax: (502) 452-6718
www.jfvs.com
jfvs@jfvs.com

Kentucky Adoption Services
9 Highland Avenue
Ft. Thomas, KY 41075
(606) 442-9888

Kentucky Baptist Homes for
Children
809 E. Chestnut
Louisville, KY 40204-1014
(502) 568-9115

Kentucky One Church One
Child Adoption Agency
1730 West Chestnut Street
Louisville, KY 40203
(502) 561-6827

LDS Social Services
1000 Hurstbourne Lane
Louisville, KY 40224
(502) 429-0077

Mary Kendall Campus
193 Phillips Court
Owensboro, KY 42301
(502) 683-6481

Pathways Child Placement
Services, Inc.
1579 Bardstown Road
Louisville, KY 40205
(502) 459-2320

Shoemakers Christian Homes
for Children and Adolescents
1939 Goldsmith Lane, Suite 136
Louisville, KY 40218
(502) 485-0722

Specialized Alternatives for
Families and Youth of
America
145 Burt Road, Suite 7
Lexington, KY 40503
(606) 278-6333

St. Elizabeth's Regional
Maternity Center
10503 Timberwood Circle,
Suite 204
Louisville, KY 40223
(502) 412-0990

St. Joseph's Children's Home
2823 Frankfort Avenue
Louisville, KY 40206
(502) 893-0241

The Villages
4021 Preston Highway
Louisville, KY 40213
(502) 361-7010

The Villages
109 North Main Street
Henderson, KY 42420
(502) 827-9090

Treatment Foster Care and
Adoption Services
116 Buckhorn Lane
Buckhorn, KY 41721
(606) 398-7245

**Adoptive Parent Support
Groups**

Adoptive Parents Guild
1888 Douglass Boulevard
Louisville, KY 40205
(502) 452-6578

APAK and North American
Council on Adoptable
Children
400 Chippewa Drive
Frankfort, KY 40601
(502) 695-5104

Bluegrass Adoptive Parents
Support Group
3319 Ridgecane Road
Lexington, KY 40513-1127
(606) 271-3299

Families and Adoptive Children
Together
150 Ridgemont Road
Paducah, KY 42003
(502) 554-0203

Kentuckiana Families for
Adoption
10417 Scarlet Oak Court
Louisville, KY 40241
(502) 339-8412

Northern Kentucky for
International Adoption
728 Mill Valley Drive
Taylor Mill, KY 41015
(606) 431-3020

Parents & Adoptive Children of
Kentucky
139 Highland Drive
Madisonville, KY 42431
(502) 825-2158

Resolve of Kentucky Adoptive
Parents Support Group
1401 Elkin Station Road
Winchester, KY 40391
(606) 745-4319

SNAP and North American
Council on Adoptable
Children State
Representative
710 W. High Street
Lexington, KY 40508

(606) 252-1728
members.aol.com/nacac

Search Support Groups

Adoptee Awareness
P.O. Box 23019
Anchorage, KY 40223
(502) 241-6358

Adoption Reunion
Registry/Adoption Education
of Lexington
P.O. Box 1218
Nicholasville, KY 40340
(606) 885-1777
Toll Free: (800) 755-7954

American Adoption Congress
State Representative
P.O. Box 1218
Nicholasville, KY 40340
(606) 885-6634
Fax: (606) 885-1778
Lcecil@aol.com

Binding Together
4500 Westport Road
Louisville, KY 40207
(502) 961-0512
STIV10@gte.net

Concerned United Birthparents
(CUB)
9803 Encino Court
Louisville, KY 40252
(502) 423-1438
www.webnations.com/cub
LVLT10A@prodigy.com

KENTUCKY LAWS RELATED TO ADOPTION: QUESTIONS AND ANSWERS

Can an attorney serve as an intermediary?
Yes, in a stepparent or relative adoption, and only upon written approval of the Secretary
of Human Resources as to private adoption

Is advertising permitted?
No. Prospective adoptive parents cannot advertise in newspapers or other publications,
but they can post flyers and distribute business cards.

Who must consent to the adoption?
1. The birth mother
2. The birth father, if he is married to and lives with the birth mother; or if not married
   to the birth mother but his paternity has been determined by a court order, or if an
   affidavit of paternity if filed

When can consent be given by birth mother (father), and how long after the consent is signed can it be revoked?
Consent cannot be given until seventy-two hours after birth. The consent can be only be revoked if done within twenty days after the adoptive parents have been appproved by the Cabinet for Human Resources. If a relinquishment is given, the birth parents' rights can be terminated within ten days by going to court with an aggressive attorney.

What are the birth father's rights?
The birth father's consent is needed if paternity has been determined by the court, or an affidavit of paternity is filed with the court. He generally must assert his paternity within sixty days after birth. The birth father will lose his parental rights if he has abandoned the child for 90 days or has not cared for or protected the child for at least 6 months

What fees can adoptive parents pay?
Adoptive parents can pay for medical, legal, counseling, and living expenses, subject to court review and approval. An adoption agency is permitted to charge reasonable fees.

Where does the adoption hearing take place?
The hearing takes place in the county where the adoptive parents live.

How are familial and stepparent adoptions different from nonbiological adoptions?
Home studies may not be necessary in a stepparent or close relative adoption. The law does not specifically address these types of adoptions.

Can a nonresident finalize an adoption in this state?
No. Only residents and nonresidents who have lived in Kentucky for at least one year can adopt.

SOURCE: KENTUCKY REVISED STATUTES ANNOTATED, SECTIONS 199.470 TO 199.590 (1997)

LOUISIANA

State Adoption Specialist

Louisiana Department of Social Services
Office of Community Services
Ada K. White
P.O. Box 3318
Baton Rouge, LA 70821
(225) 342-4086
Fax: (225) 342-9087
www.dss.state.la.us/offocs/index.htm
fcada@ocs.dss.state.la.us

State ICPC Administrator

Office of Community Services
Louisiana Department of Social Services
P. O. Box 3318
Baton Rouge, LA 70821
(225) 342-2297

State Adoption Exchange/State Photolisting Service

Louisiana Adoption Resource Exchange (LARE) Louisiana Department of Social Services, Office of Community
P.O. Box 3318
Baton Rouge, LA 70821
(225) 342-4040
Toll Free: (800) 259-3428
www.adopt.org/la/

State Reunion Registry

Louisiana Adoption Registry
P.O. Box 3318
Baton Rouge, LA 70821
(225) 342-6837
Toll Free: (800) 259-2456
www.dss.state.la.us/html/
registry.html

Regional/District Public Agencies

Louisiana Office of Community Services, Alexandria
900 Murray Street
Alexandria, LA 71301
(318) 487-5212

Louisiana Office of Community Services, Baton Rouge
1967 North Street
Baton Rouge, LA 70821
(225) 342-0494

Louisiana Office of Community Services, Covington
351 Holiday Boulevard
Covington, LA 70433
(504) 893-6363

Louisiana Office of Community
Services, Jefferson
800 W. Commerce, Suite 500
Harahan, LA 70123
(504) 736-7151

Louisiana Office of Community
Services, Lafayette
825 Kaliste Saloom Road,
Brandwine I, Room 218
Lafayette, LA 70508
(337) 262-5970

Louisiana Office of Community
Services, Lake Charles
4016 Avenue F, 1st Floor
Lake Charles, LA 70615
(337) 491-2189

Louisiana Office of Community
Services, Monroe
122 St. John Street, Room 450
Monroe, LA 71201-7384
(318) 362-3362

Louisiana Office of Community
Services, New Orleans
1001 Howard Avenue,
17th Floor
New Orleans, LA 70113
(504) 568-7413

Louisiana Office of Community
Services, Shreveport
1525 Fairfield Avenue,
Room 850
Shreveport, LA 71101-4388
(318) 676-7100

Louisiana Office of Community
Services, Thibodaux
1416 Tiger Drive
Thibodaux, LA 70301-4337
(504) 447-0945

**Licensed Private Adoption
Agencies**

Acorn Adoption, Inc.
118 Ridgelake Drive
Metairie, LA 70001
(504) 838-0080

Adoption Options of LA Inc.
aka Global Adoptions Inc.
1724 N. Burnside, Suite 7
Gonzales, LA 70737
(225) 644-1033

Beacon House Adoption
Services, Inc
750 Louisiana Avenue, Suite C
Port Allen, LA 70767
(504) 387-6365
www.adopting.com/BeaconHouse

Catholic Charities Archdiocese
of New Orleans
1000 Howard Avenue,
Suite 1200
New Orleans, LA 70113-1916
(504) 523-3755

Catholic Community Services
Counseling, Maternity, and
Adoption Department
4884 Constitution Avenue,
Suite 1-B
Baton Rouge, LA 70808
(225) 927-4930

Catholic Social Services of
Houma - Thibodaux
1220 Aycock Street
Houma, LA 70360
(504) 876-0490

Catholic Social Services of
Lafayette
1408 Carmel Avenue,
2nd Floor
Lafayette, LA 70501
(337) 261-5654

Children's Bureau of New
Orleans
210 Baronne Street, Suite 722
New Orleans, LA 70112
(504) 525-2366

Family Christian Services of
Louisiana
8786 Goodwood Boulevard,
Suite 108
Baton Rouge, LA 70806-7917
(225) 927-3235
Fax: (225) 927-3274
www.bethany.org
info@bethany.org

Gladney Center for Adoption
2300 Hemphill Street
Fort Worth, TX 76110
(817) 922-6088
Fax: (817) 922-6040
Toll Free: (800) 452-3639
www.gladney.org
info@gladney.org

Holy Cross Child Placement
Agency, Inc.
910 Pierremont Road, Suite 356
Shreveport, LA 71106
(318) 865-3199

Jewish Children's Regional
Service of Jewish Children's
Home
5342 St. Charles Avenue, Suite
202, P.O. Box 15225
New Orleans, LA 70115
(504) 899-1595

Jewish Family Service of
Greater New Orleans
3330 W. Esplanade Ave. S.,
Suite 600
Metairie, LA 70002-3454
(504) 831-8475

LDS Social Services
2000 Old Spanish Trail, Pratt
Center, Suite 115
Slidell, LA 70458
(504) 649-2774

Louisiana Baptist Children's
Home
7200 DeSiard Road
Monroe, LA 71203
(318) 343-2244

Mercy Ministries of America
P.O. Box 3028, 804 Spell Street
West Monroe, LA 71210
(318) 388-2040

St. Elizabeth Foundation
8054 Summa Avenue, Suite A
Baton Rouge, LA 70809
(225) 769-8888
*www.rouge.net/business/steliz/
agency.html*
stlezfd@rouge.net

St. Gerard's Adoption Network,
Inc.
100 S. Vivian Street
Eunice, LA 70535
(318) 457-1111

Sunnybrook Children's Home,
Inc.
2101 Forsythe Avenue
Monroe, LA 71201
(318) 329-8161

Volunteers of America
Greater Baton Rouge at Lake
Charles
340 Kirby Street
Lake Charles, LA 70601
(318) 497-0034

Volunteers of America -
Maternity/Adoption Services
3939 North Causeway
Boulevard, Suite 203
Metairie, LA 70002
(504) 835-3005

Volunteers of America of North
Louisiana
360 Jordan Street
Shreveport, LA 71101
(318) 221-5000

**Adoptive Parent Support
Groups**

Adopt Older Kids
818 Briarwood Drive
New Iberia, LA 70560

Families for Russian and
Ukrainian Adoptions
1420 Rue Bayonne
Mandeville, LA 70471
(504) 674-2273
bradleyb@neosoft.com

Korean-American Resource
Exchange
4107 St. Elizabeth Drive
Kenner, LA 70065-1644

LEEAF- Louisiana Eastern
European Adoptive Families
1420 Rue Bayonne
Mandeville, LA 70471
(504) 727-1074
www.LEEAF.homestead.com
bradleyb@neosoft.com

Louisiana Adoption Advisory
Board (LAAB), Inc.
P.O. Box 3318
Baton Rouge, LA 70821
(225) 342-4086

North American Council on
Adoptable Children
3528 Vincennes Place
New Orleans, LA 70125
(504) 866-4449
members.aol.com/nacac

North American Council on
Adoptable Children
10139 Seawood Street
New Orleans, LA 70127
(504) 241-1534
members.aol.com/nacac

Search Support Groups

Adoptees' Birthrights
Committee
Box 9442
Metairie, LA 70005
(504) 835-4284

Adoption Connection of LA
7301 W. Judge Perez, #311
Arabi, LA 70032
(504) 277-0030

Adoption Triad Network
Box 324
Swartz, LA 71281

Adoption Triad Network
511 Blue Bell
Port Allen, LA 70605

Adoption Triad Network, Inc.
120 Thibodaux Drive
Lafayette, LA 70503
(318) 984-3682

Adult Adoptee Search and
Support Group
195 Arthur Street
Shreveport, LA 71105
(318) 865-7784

Lost and Found
18343 Weatherwood Drive
Baton Rouge, LA 70817
(225) 769-2456

Volunteers of America Birth
Mother Support Group
360 Jordan Street
Shreveport, LA 71106
(318) 865-7784

LOUISIANA LAWS RELATED TO ADOPTION: QUESTIONS AND ANSWERS

Can an attorney serve as an intermediary?
Yes.

Is advertising permitted?
Yes.

Who must consent to the adoption?
1. The birth mother
2. The birth father
3. The parents or guardian of any birth parents who are under the age of eighteen at the time of surrender (applies to independent adoptions only)

When can consent be taken from the birth mother (father), and how long after the consent is signed can it be revoked?
In both agency and private adoptions a consent cannot be given by a birth mother until the child is five days old. Consent is essentially irrevocable. A birth parent can attempt to

withdraw consent within thirty days of signing; however, the adoption will proceed if it is in the child's best interest.

Birth parents' rights are terminated at a court hearing, but the birth parents' appearance is not required.

What are the birth father's rights?

The birth father of a child born out of wedlock must consent to the adoption before the mother's termination or relinquishment, unless he has signed a valid surrender. In Louisiana, legal fathers, or fathers who have formally acknowledged or legitimized the child (even if they are not the biological father), or fathers who register with the putative father registry must provide a Consent or Surrender of Parental Rights, except in cases in which the birth father has failed to support the child or has failed to communicate with or visit the child for two years.

What fees can adoptive parents pay?

Medical, hospital, and legal fees can be paid. A statement of fees paid must be included in the adoption petition.

Where does the adoption hearing take place?

The hearing may take place in the county where the adoptive parents reside.

How are familial and stepparent adoptions different from nonbiological adoptions?

No home study is required. The adoption can be finalized quickly and no written termination of parental rights is necessarily required. In stepparent adoptions in which the former spouse has died, the grandparents may be granted limited visitation rights.

Can a nonresident finalize an adoption in this state?

Yes

SOURCE: LOUSIANA REVISED STATUTES ANNOTATED SECTIONS 9:400, CH. C. TITLE XII AND 40:74 TO 40.79 (1997)

MAINE

State Adoption Specialist

Maine Department of Human Services
John Levesque
221 State Street, State House, Station 11
Augusta, ME 04333
(207) 287-5011
Fax: (207) 287-5282
www.adoptorg.me
john.levesque@state.me.us

State ICPC Administrator

Bureau of Child & Family Services
Maine Department of Human Services
221 State Street, State House, Station 11
Augusta, ME 04333
(207) 287-5060
Fax: (207) 287-5282

State Adoption Exchange/State Photolisting Service

Northern New England Adoption Exchange
Department of Human Services
221 State Street, State House
Augusta, ME 04333
(207) 287-5060

State Reunion Registry

Maine State Adoption Reunion Registry
Office of Vital Records
221 State Street
Augusta, ME 04330-0011
(207) 287-3181

Regional/District Public Agencies

Maine Department of Human Services - Augusta District 4 Office
35 Anthony Avenue, SHS #11
Augusta, ME 04333
(207) 624-8222

Maine Department of Human
Services - Bangor District 6
Office
396 Griffin Road
Bangor, ME 04401
(207) 561-4220

Maine Department of Human
Services - Biddeford District 1
Office
208 Graham Street
Biddeford, ME 04005
(207) 286-2508

Maine Department of Human
Services - Caribou District 7
Office
Route 2, Box 8700
Caribou, ME 04736
(207) 493-4140

Maine Department of Human
Services - Ellsworth District 6
Office
17 Eastward Lane
Ellsworth, ME 04605
(207) 667-1600

Maine Department of Human
Services - Fort Kent District 8
Office
92 Market St.
Fort Kent, ME 04743
(207) 834-7720

Maine Department of Human
Services - Houlton District 8
Office
11 High St.
Houlton, ME 04730
(207) 532-5106

Maine Department of Human
Services - Lewiston District 3
Office
200 Main Street
Lewiston, ME 04240
(207) 795-4620

Maine Department of Human
Services - Machias District 8
Office
13 Prescott Drive
Machias, ME 04654
(207) 255-2024

Maine Department of Human
Services - Portland District 2
Office
509 Forest Avenue
Portland, ME 04101
(207) 822-2231

Maine Department of Human
Services - Rockland District 5
Office
360 Old Country Road
Rockland, ME 04841
(207) 596-4262

Maine Department of Human
Services - Skowhegan District
5 Office
140 North Avenue
Skowhegan, ME 04976
(207) 474-4850

**Licensed Private Adoption
Agencies**

C.A.R.E. Development
P.O. Box 2356
Bangor, ME 04401
(207) 945-4240

Families & Children Together
(F.A.C.T)
16 Penn Plaza, Suite 23
Bangor, ME 04401
(207) 941-2347

Good Samaritan Agency
100 Ridgewood Drive
Bangor, ME 04401
(207) 942-7211

International Adoption Services
Centre
432 Water Street, P.O. Box 56
Gardiner, ME 04345
(207) 582-8842
Fax: (207) 582-9027
105342.2617@compuserve.com

Maine Adoption Placement
Service (MAPS)
International Office
277 Congress Street Portland,
ME 04101
(207) 775-4101
Fax: (207) 775-1019
www.mapsadopt.org
maps@mapsadopt.org

Maine Adoption Placement
Service (MAPS)
58 Pleasant Street, P.O. Box 772
Houlton, ME 04730
(207) 532-9358
Fax: (207) 532-4122
www.mapsadopt.org/
mapsinfo@mapsadopt.org

*Maine Adoption Placement
Service (MAPS)
306 Congress Street
Portland, ME 04101
(207) 772-3678
Fax: (207) 773-6776
www.mapsadopt.org/
maps@mapsadopt.org

Maine Adoption Placement
Service (MAPS)
Bangor Office
181 State Street
Bangor, ME 04402
(207) 941-9500
Fax: (207) 941-8942
www.mapsadopt.org/
mapz@bangornews.infi.net

Maine Children's Home for
Little Wanderers
34 Gilman Street
Waterville, ME 04901
(207) 873-4253

Sharing in Adoption
366 US Route 1
Falmouth, ME 04105
(207) 781-3092

SMART
P.O. Box 547
Windham, ME 04062
(207) 893-0386

St. Andre Home, Inc.
283 Elm Street
Biddeford, ME 04005
(207) 282-3351

**Adoptive Parent Support
Groups**

Adoptive and Foster Families of
Maine
351 Center Street
Old Town, ME 04468
(207) 827-2331
Fax: (207) 827-1974
Toll Free: (800) 833-9786
AFFM@aol.com

Adoptive Families of Maine
P.O. Box 350
Portage, ME 04708
(207) 435-8018

Adoptive Families of Maine and
North American Council on
Adoptable Children
156 Essex Street
Bangor, ME 04401
(207) 941-9500

Central Maine Area Adoption
Group
7 Noyer Street
Waterville, ME 04901
(207) 873-6020

Coastal Adoption Support
Group
c/o International Adoption
Service Center
P.O. Box 56
Gardiner, ME 04345
(207) 586-5058

Maine Families with Children
from Asia
280 Blanchard Road
Cumberland, ME 04021
(207) 883-1133
ckukka@deepriver.com

Maine Foster Parent
Association
15 College Avenue
Waterville, ME 04901
(207) 872-2265

Search Support Groups

Adoption Support of Penobscot
Bay
Taylor's Point
Tenant's Harbor, ME 04860

Mina Bicknell Adoption
Resource Center
P.O. Box 2793
S. Portland, ME 04106
(207) 842-6622

MAINE LAWS RELATED TO ADOPTION: QUESTIONS AND ANSWERS

Can an attorney serve as an intermediary?
Yes.

Is advertising permitted?
Yes.

Who must consent to the adoption?
The birth mother and the birth father (if married to the birth mother)

When can consent be taken from the birth mother (father), and how long after the consent is signed can it be revoked?
The law is not clear, but it appears consent can be given any time after the child's birth. Parental consent in an independent adoption is executed before a probate judge. A birth mother has until the first hearing (about ninety days after consent is given) to revoke her consent and the court may permit her to do so up until the final adoption if it is in the child's best interest. In an agency adoption, consents are not given until seventy-two hours after birth and are irrevocable.

What are the birth father's rights?
The birth father must provide a consent if his name is on the birth certificate, if his whereabouts are known, and he is involved in the child's life. Otherwise, his consent is not needed. If the birth father has been given notice of the adoption, he has twenty days to petition the court to establish his paternity. The judge will then decide whether to give the birth father parental rights, based on the birth father's ability and willingness to support the child.

What fees can adoptive parents pay?
Only reasonable fees for services can be charged by an agency or intermediary.

Where does the adoption hearing take place?
The hearing can take place in the county where the adoptive parents live, where the child lives, or where the adoption agency is located.

How are familial and stepparent adoptions different from nonbiological adoptions?
When a blood relative is adopting, no home study is required.

Can a nonresident finalize an adoption in this state?
Yes.

SOURCE: MAINE REVIDED STATUTES ANNOTATED TITLE 19, SECTIONS 1101 TO 1144 TITLE 22, 2706-A TO 2766, 4171 TO 4176, AND 8201 TO 8204 (1997)

MARYLAND

State Adoption Specialist

Maryland Department of
   Human Resources
Social Services Administration
Stephanie Johnson-Pettaway
311 W. Saratoga Street
Baltimore, MD 21201
(410) 767-7506
Fax: (410) 333-0127
www.dhr.state.md.us/adopt.htm
spettaway@mail.dhr.state.md.us

State ICPC Administrator

Social Services Administration
Maryland Department of
   Human Resources
311 West Saratoga Street
Baltimore, MD 21201
(410) 767-7249
Fax: (410) 333-0127

State Adoption Exchange/State Photolisting Service

Maryland Adoption Resource
   Exchange (MARE)
Social Services Administration
311 W. Saratoga Street
Baltimore, MD 21201
(410) 767-7359
www.dhr.state.md.us/adpt_pg1.htm

State Reunion Registry

Maryland Mutual Consent
   Voluntary Adoption Registry
Social Services Administration
311 West Saratoga
Baltimore, MD 21201
(410) 767-7423
www.dhr.state.md.us/voladopr.htm

Licensed Private Adoption Agencies

Adoption Resource Center, Inc.
6630 Baltimore National Pike,
   Suite 205-A
Baltimore, MD 21228
(410) 744-6393
Fax: (410) 744-1533
members.aol.com/AdoptRC/
ADOPTRC@aol.com

Adoption Service Information
   Agency (ASIA)
7720 Alaska Avenue, N.W.
Washington, DC 20012
(202) 726-7193
Fax: (202) 722-4928
www.asia-adopt.org
info@asia-adopt.org

Adoption Service Information
   Agency, Inc. (ASIA)
8555 16th Street, Suite 200
Silver Spring, MD 20910
(301) 587-7068
Fax: (301) 587-3869
www.asia-adopt.org
info@asia-adopt.org

Adoptions Forever
5830 Hubbard Drive
Rockville, MD 20852
(301) 468-1818
Fax: (301) 881-7871

Adoptions Together Inc.
10230 New Hampshire Avenue,
   Suite 200
Silver Spring, MD 20903
(301) 439-2900
Fax: (301) 439-9334
www.adoptionstogether.com
adoptintl@aol.com

Adoptions Together, Inc.
5740 Executive Drive, #108
Baltimore, MD 21228
(410) 869-0620
Fax: (410) 869-8419
www.adoptionstogether.com
adoptintl@aol.com

*Associated Catholic Charities
Archdiocese of Baltimore
19 West Franklin Street, 3rd
   Floor
Baltimore, MD 21201
(410) 659-4031
Fax: (410) 659-4060

Barker Foundation
7945 MacArthur Boulevard
Cabin John, MD 20818
(301) 229-8300
Fax: (301) 229-0074
Toll Free: (800) 673-8489
www.barkerfoundation.org
bfinfo@atlantech.net

Bethany Christian Services
1641 State Route #3
   Northbound, Suite 205
Crofton, MD 21114
(410) 721-2835
Fax: (410) 721-5523
TTY: (410) 267-5590
www.bethany.org
info@bethany.org

Board of Child Care
3300 Gaither Road
Baltimore, MD 21244
(410) 922-2100
Fax: (410) 922-7830

Burlington United Methodist
   Family Services, Inc.
St. Pauls United Methodist
   Church, 18 East Oak Street,
   P.O. Box 477
Oakland, MD 21550-1504
(301) 334-1285
Fax: (301) 334-6352

Catholic Charities Archdiocese
   of Washington
1438 Rhode Island Avenue,
   N.E.
Washington, DC 20018
(202) 526-4100

Catholic Charities Archdiocese
of Washington D.C.
1504 St. Camillus Drive
Silver Spring, MD 20903
(301) 434-2550
Fax: (301) 434-5982

Catholic Charities, Inc.,
Diocese of Wilmington,
Delaware
1405 Wesley Drive
Salisbury, MD 21801
(410) 749-1121
Fax: (410) 543-0510
ccsal@ce.net

Children's Choice
301 N. Charles Street, Suite 400
Baltimore, MD 21201
(410) 576-9225
Fax: (410) 576-0520

Children's Choice
City Center Plaza, Suite 304,
213 W. Main Street
Salisbury, MD 21801
(410) 546-6106
Fax: (410) 219-2640

Children's Choice
Scott Plaza Two, Suite 325
Philadelphia, PA 19113
(610) 521-6270
Fax: (610) 521-6266

Cradle of Hope Adoption
Center, Inc.
8630 Fenton Street, Suite 310
Silver Spring, MD 20910
(301) 587-4400
Fax: (301) 588-3091
www.cradlehope.org/
cradle@cradlehope.org

Creative Adoptions, Inc.
10750 Hickory Ridge Road,
Suite 109
Columbia, MD 21044
(301) 596-1521
Fax: (301) 596-0346
www.creativeadoptions.org/
cai@creativeadoptions.org

Datz Foundation
16220 Frederick Road
Gaithersburg, MD 20877
(301) 258-0629
Fax: (301) 921-6689
www.datzfound.com
datz@patriot.net

Family and Child Services of
Washington, DC, Inc.
5301 76th Avenue
Landover Hills, MD 20784
(301) 459-4121, Ext: 334
Fax: (202) 371-0863

Family and Children's Services
of Central Maryland, Inc.
Baltimore Family Center
204 W. Lanvale Street
Baltimore, MD 21217
(410) 366-1980
Fax: (410) 728-2972
TTY: (410) 669-0770

Family Building Center
The Mercantile-Towson
Building, 409 Washington
Avenue, Suite 920
Towson, MD 21204-4903
(410) 494-8112

For the Love of a Child
Adoption Agency, Inc.
2 East Church Street
Frederick, MD 21701
(301) 682-5025
Fax: (301) 682-5026

Holy Cross Child Placement
Agency, Inc.
St. John's Episcopal Church,
6701 Wisconsin Avenue
Chevy Chase, MD 20815
(301) 907-6887
Fax: (202) 237-2846

International Children's
Alliance
9810 Farmington Court
Ellicott City, MD 21042
(202) 463-6874

International Families, Inc.
613 Hawkesburg Lane
Silver Spring, MD 20904
(301) 622-2406

Jewish Family Services -
Adoption Alliances
6 Park Center Court, Suite 211
Owings Mills, MD 21117
(410) 581-1031
Fax: (410) 356-0103
www.jfs.org
adoption@jfs.org

Jewish Social Services Agency
of Metropolitan Washington
6123 Montrose Road
Rockville, MD 20852-4880
(301) 881-3700
Fax: (301) 881-6156
TTY: (301) 984-5662

Latter Day Saints Social
Services-East Coast
198 Thomas Johnson Drive,
Suite 13
Frederick, MD 21702
(301) 694-5896
Fax: (301) 662-8737
Toll Free: (800) 477-6177

Lutheran Social Services of the
National Capital Area
4406 Georgia Avenue, N.W.
Washington, DC 20011
(202) 723-3000
Fax: (202) 723-3303

Lutheran Social Services of the
National Capital Area
Zion Evangelical Lutheran
Church, 7410 New
Hampshire Avenue
Takoma Park, MD 20017
(301) 434-0080
Fax: (202) 723-3303

New Family Foundation
5537 Twin Knolls Road,
Suite 440
Columbia, MD 21045
(410) 715-4828

New Life Adoption Agency
9051 Baltimore National Pike,
Building 1, Suite 1-D
Ellicott City, MD 21042
(410) 480-0652
Fax: (410) 480-0653

The Kennedy Krieger Institute
2901 East Biddle Street
Baltimore, MD 21213
(410) 559-9411
Fax: (410) 559-9344
TTY: (410) 550-9806

Tressler Lutheran Services of
Maryland
c/o The Lutheran Center
700 Light Street
Baltimore, MD 21230
(410) 230-2700
www.tressler.org
TLSAdopt@tressler.org

World Child
9300 Colombia Boulevard
Silver Spring, MD 20910
(301) 588-3000
Fax: (301) 585-7879
www.worldchild.org/
Info@worldchild.org

*World Child - Frank Adoption
and Assistance, Inc.
207 Brooks Avenue
Gaithersburg, MD 20877
(301) 977-8339
Fax: (301) 608-2425
www.worldchild.org/
Info@worldchild.org

Adoptive Parent Support
Groups

Adoption Resource Exchange
for Single Parents (ARESP)
8605 Cameron Street #220
Silver Spring, MD 20910
(301) 585-5836
Fax: (301) 585-4864
www.aresp.org
arespinc@aol.com

Adoptive Families and Friends
12087 Boxwood Lane
Union Bridge, MD 21791

Adoptive Families and Friends
1815 Beaver Creek Lane
Frederick, MD 21702
(301) 695-2633
www.members.aol.com/
Dwasserba/info.html
Dwasserba@aol.com

Adoptive Families Network, Inc.
P.O. Box 7
Columbia, MD 21045
(410) 379-0891
Fax: (301) 984-6133
www.erols.com/giconklin

Association for Single Adoptive
Parents
P.O. Box 3618
Merrifield, VA 22116-9998
(703) 521-0632

Barker Foundation Parents of
Adopted Adolescents Group
7945 MacArthur Boulevard,
Suite 206
Cabin John, MD 20818
(301) 229-8300

Birthbonds
St.Pius X Catholic Church
3300 Moreland Avenue, Route
450
Bowie, MD 20715
(202) 581-3632

Catholic Charities
19 West Franklin Street
Baltimore, MD 21201
(410) 659-4050

Center for Adoption Support
and Education, Inc.
(C.A.S.E.)
11120 New Hampshire Avenue,
Suite 205
Silver Spring, MD 20904
(301) 593-9200
www.adoptionsupport.org
caseadopt@erols.com

Center for Adoptive Families
10230 New Hampshire Avenue,
Suite 200
Silver Spring, MD 20903
(301) 439-2900
Fax: (301) 439-9334
www.thomtech.com/~ati/caf.htm

Families Adopting Children
Everywhere and North
American Council on
Adoptable
Children Representative
P.O. Box 28058
Baltimore, MD 21239
(410) 488-2656

Families for Private Adoption
P. O. Box 6375
Washington, DC 20015-0375
(202) 722-0338
www.ffpa.org

Families Like Ours
Washington, DC
(202) 488-3967

Families with Children
from China
4215 Crest Heights Road
Baltimore, MD 21215
(410) 358-1170
fccbalt.med.jhmi.edu
emmali@erols.com

Interracial Family Circle
P.O. Box 53290
Washington, DC 20009
(202) 393-7866
Toll Free: (800) 500-9040
www.geocities.com/Heartland/
Estates/4496
ifcweb@yahoo.com

Joint Council on International
Children's Services
7 Cheverly Circle
Cheverly, MD 20785-3040
(301) 322-1906
Fax: (301) 322-3425
www.jcics.org

Latin America Parents
Association of the National
Capital Region
P.O. Box 4403
Silver Spring, MD 20904-4403
(301) 431-3407
www.lapa.com
joet@highcaliber.com

National Council for Single
Adoptive Parents
P.O. Box 15084
Chevy Chase, MD 20825
(202) 966-6367
www.adopting.org/ncsap.html
singladopt@aol.com

Open Adoption Discussion
Group
22310 Old Hundred Road
Barnesville, MD 20838
(301) 972-8579
msaasta@hotmail.com

Our Special Family
6 Autumn Wind Court
Reisterstown, MD 21136
(410) 561-1250

Resolve of Maryland
P.O. Box 19049
Baltimore, MD 21284-9049

Stars of David International Inc.
Metro DC Chapter
c/o The Datz Foundation, 311
Maple Avenue West
Vienna, VA 22180
(703) 242-8800
Fax: (703) 242-8804
Toll Free: (800) 829-5683
www.starsofdavid.org
datz@patriot.net

Stars of David International Inc.
Jewish Family Services
6 Park Center Court, Suite 211
Owings Mills, MD 21117
Toll Free: (800) 803-0710
www.starsofdavid.org or
www.jfs.org
adoption@jfs.org

Stars of David International Inc.
Jewish Family Services
5750 Park Heights Avenue
Baltimore, MD 21215
(410) 466-9200
Fax: (410) 664-0551
www.starsofdavid.org/ or
www.jfs.org
jfs@jfs.org

Search Support Groups

Adoptee Birthfamily
  Connection
P.O. Box 115
Rocky Ridge, MD 21778
(301) 271-3037

Adoptee-Birthparent Support
  Network (ABSN)
P.O. Box 8273
McLean, VA 22106-8273
(202) 628-4111
*www.geocities.com/Heartland/
  Flats/3666/ABSN.html*
absnmail@aol.com

Adoptees in Search
P.O. Box 41016
Bethesda, MD 20014
(301) 656-8555
Fax: (301) 652-2106
AIS20824@aol.com

Adoption Connection
  Exchange
204 W. Lanvale Street
Baltimore, MD 21217
(410) 669-9000

Adoptions Together, Inc.
  Birthparent Support Group
10230 New Hampshire, Suite
  200
Silver Spring, MD 20903
(301) 439-2900
Fax: (301) 439-9334
www.adoptionstogether.com
adoptintl@aol.com

American Adoption Congress
  State Representative
327 Dogwood Road
Millersville, MD 21108
(410) 544-0083
MargyMc@aol.com

Barker Foundation Adult
  Adoptee Support Group
7945 MacArthur Boulevard,
  Suite 206
Cabin John, MD 20818
(301) 229-8300

Barker Foundation Birthparent
  Support Group
7945 MacArthur Boulevard,
  Suite 206
Cabin John, MD 20818
(301) 229-8300

Concerned United Birthparents
  (CUB)
DC Metro Branch
P.O. Box 15258
Chevy Chase, MD 20815
(202) 966-1640
www.webnations.com/cub
LEC9@aol.com

Concerned United
  Birthparents, Baltimore Area
327 Dogwood Road
Millersville, MD 21108
(410) 544-0083
www.webnations.com/cub
cub@webnations.com

ENCORE
RD 8, Box 419
York, PA 17403
(410) 466-0222

MARYLAND LAWS RELATED TO ADOPTION: QUESTIONS AND ANSWERS

Can an attorney serve as an intermediary?
No.

Is advertising permitted?
Yes.

Who must consent to the adoption?
Birth mother
Birth father who is married to the birth mother; is named on the birth certificate; is identified by the birth mother or birth father; or who has held himself out as the birth father and the birth mother agrees.
Adopting agency which placed child

When can consent be taken from the birth mother (father), and how long after the consent is signed can it be revoked?
Consent cannot be taken until the child's birth. The birth parents can revoke their consent up to thirty days after signing or until the final adoption decree is entered, whichever occurs first. A final adoption decree can be challenged up to six months after finalization for reasons of fraud or duress.

What are the birth father's rights?

His consent is not required in cases in which the child is abandoned by the birth father or the adoption is in the best interest of the child; provided, however, the child has not been in the birth father's custody for at least one year; the child has been in the adoptive couple's custody for six months; the adoptive couple has bonded with the child; the birth father has no contact with the child or has not supported or cared for the child.

What fees can adoptive parents pay?

Payments for reasonable medical, hospital, and legal services are permitted. In an independent adoption, the birth parents will be advised of their right to receive legal counsel and adoption counseling; the court may order the adoptive parents to pay all or some of these costs. A description of all fees paid must be filed with the court.

Where does the adoption hearing take place?

The law does not address this issue. According to ICPC, the petition for adoption is filed in the county where the adoptive parents live.

How are familial and stepparent adoptions different from nonbiological adoptions?

Familial adoptions are treated just like an independent adoption, including a home study.

Can a nonresident finalize an adoption in this state?

Yes, but only if an agency receives consent from the birth parents.

SOURCE: MARYLAND CODES ANNOTATED FAMILY LAW SECTIONS 5-301 TO 5-330 AND 5-4A-01 TO 5-4A-07 (1998).

MASSACHUSETTS

State Adoption Specialist

Massachusetts Department of
   Social Services
Mary Gambon
24 Farnsworth Street
Boston, MA 02210
(617) 748-2248
Fax: (617) 261-7437
TTY: (617) 261-7440
www.state.ma.us/dss/adoption/
   adoption.htm
mgambon@state.ma.us

State ICPC Administrator

Massachusetts Department of
   Social Services
24 Farnsworth Street
Boston, MA 02110
(617) 748-2374
Fax: (617) 261-7438

**State Adoption Exchange/State
Photolisting Service**

Massachusetts Adoption
   Resource Exchange, Inc.
   (MARE)
45 Franklin Street, 5th Floor
Boston, MA 02110-1301
(617) 542-3678
Fax: (617) 542-1006
Toll Free: (800) 882-1176
www.mareinc.org

Open Door Society of
   Massachusetts, Inc.
1750 Washington Street
Holliston, MA 01746-2234
(508) 429-4260
Fax: (508) 429-2261
Toll Free: (800) 932-3678
www/odsma.org
odsma@odsma.org

State Reunion Registry

Adoption Search Coordinator
Massachusetts Department of
   Social Service
24 Farnsworth Street
Boston, MA 02210
(617) 727-0900

**Regional/District Public
Agencies**

Massachusetts Department of
   Social Services, Boston Unit
38 Wareham Street
Boston, MA 02118
(617) 574-8575

Massachusetts Department of
   Social Services, Central Unit
340 Main Street, Suite 570
Worcester, MA 01608
(508) 929-2150

Massachusetts Department of
   Social Services, Metro Unit
30 Mystic Street
Arlington, MA 02174-1155
(781) 641-8275

Massachusetts Department of
   Social Services, Northeast
   Unit
15 Union Street
Lawrence, MA 01840
(978) 557-2725
Toll Free: (800) 432-1824

Massachusetts Department of
Social Services, Southeast Unit
141 Main Street
Brockton, MA 02401
(508) 894-3830
Toll Free: (800) 432-6240

Massachusetts Department of
Social Services, West Unit
1537 Main Street, 2nd floor
Springfield, MA 01103
(413) 452-3350

**Licensed Private Adoption
Agencies**

Act of Love Adoptions
734 Massachusetts Avenue
Boston, MA 02476
Toll Free: (800) 277-5387

Adoption Center, Inc.
1105 Washington Street
West Newton, MA 02165
(617) 527-6171

Adoption Program of Parents'
and Children's Services
1105 Washington Street
West Newton, MA 02165
(617) 964-9300

Adoption Resource Associates
124 Mt. Auburn St., Suite 200
Cambridge, MA 02138
(617) 492-8888

Adoption Resource Center at
Brightside
2112 Riverdale Street
West Springfield, MA 01089-
1099
(413) 827-4258
Fax: (413) 747-0182

Adoption Resources
1340 Centre Street
Newton Centre, MA 02159
(617) 332-2218

Adoptions With Love, Inc.
188 Needham Street, Suite 250
Newton, MA 02164
(617) 965-2496
Toll Free: (800) 722-7731

Alliance for Children, Inc.
Suite G80, 40 William Street
Wellesley, MA 02481-3902
(781) 431-7148
Fax: (781) 431-7474
www.allforchildren.org
info@allforchildren.org

*Beacon Adoption Center, Inc.
66 Lake Buel Road
Great Barrington, MA 01230
(413) 528-2749
Fax: (413) 528-4311

Berkshire Center for Families
and Children
480 West Street
Pittsfield, MA 01201
(413) 448-8281

Bethany Christian Services
1538 Turnpike Street
North Andover, MA 01845
(978) 794-9800
Fax: (978) 683-5676
Toll Free: (800) 941-4865
www.bethany.org
info@bethany.org

Boston Adoption Bureau, Inc.
14 Beacon Street, Suite 620
Boston, MA 02108
(617) 277-1336
Toll Free: (800) 338-2224

Cambridge Family and
Children's Services
929 Massachusetts Avenue
Cambridge, MA 02139
(617) 876-4210
*www.tiac.net/users/marisol/cacain
c/cacaone.htm*
CACAINC@maceast.com

Catholic Charities Center of the
Old Colony Area
686 N. Main Street
Brockton, MA 02301
(508) 587-0815

Catholic Charities of Cambridge
and Somerville
270 Washington Street
Somerville, MA 02143
(617) 625-1920

Catholic Charities of the
Diocese of Worcester
10 Hammond Street
Worcester, MA 01610-1513
(508) 798-0191
Fax: (508) 797-5659

Catholic Charities of the
Diocese of Worcester, Inc.
53 Highland Avenue
Fitchburg, MA 01420
(978) 343-4879

Catholic Charities,
Merrimack Valley
454 N. Canal Street
Lawrence, MA 01840
(978) 685-5930
Fax: (978) 685-0329

Catholic Social Services of
Fall River, Inc.
783 Slade Street, P.O. Box M
South Station
Fall River, MA 02720
(508) 674-4681
Fax: (508) 675-2224

Children's Aid and Family
Services of Hampshire
County, Inc.
8 Trumbull Road
Northampton, MA 01060
(413) 584-5690
Fax: (413) 586-9436

Children's Friend
21 Cedar Street
Worcester, MA 01609
(508) 753-5425
Fax: (508) 757-7659

Children's International
Adoption Project
10 Langford Road
Plymouth, MA 02360
(508) 747-3331
Fax: (508) 746-6847
home.att.net/~childrensproject/
ChildrensProject@worldnet.att.net

Children's Services
of Roxbury, Inc.
504 Dudley Street
Roxbury, MA 02119
(617) 542-2366
Fax: (617) 542-2369

China Adoption With
Love, Inc
251 Harvard Street, Suite 17
Brookline, MA 02446
(617) 731-0798
Fax: (617) 232-8088
Toll Free: (800) 888-9812

Concord Family Service
Society, Inc.
111 Old Road to Nine Acre
Cor., Suite 2002
Concord, MA 01742-4174
(978) 369-4909
Fax: (978) 371-1463

DARE Family Services
2 Electronics Avenue, Suite 7
Danvers, MA 01923
(978) 750-0751
Fax: (978) 750-0749

DARE Family Services
17 Poplar Street
Roslindale, MA 02131
(617) 469-2311
Fax: (617) 469-3007

Family and Children's Services
of Catholic Charities
53 Highland Avenue
Fitchburg, MA 01420
(978) 343-4879

Florence Crittenton League
119 Hall Street
Lowell, MA 01854-3612
(978) 452-9671
Fax: (978) 970-0070
www.fcleague.org/
info@fcleague.org

Full Circle Adoptions
39 Main Street
Northampton, MA 01060
(413) 587-0007

Gift of Love Adoption Services,
Inc.
1087 Newman Avenue
Seekonk, MA 02771
(508) 761-5661

Hope Adoptions, Inc.
21 Cedar Street
Worcester, MA 01609
(508) 753-5425

Interfaith Social Services
776 Hancock Street
Quincy, MA 02170
(617) 773-6203
Fax: (617) 472-4987
www.interfaithsocialserv.org
ISS@interfaithsocialserv.org

Jewish Family and Children's
Services Adoption Resources
1340 Centre Street
Newton, MA 02159
(617) 332-2218

Jewish Family Service of
Metrowest
14 Vernon Street, #104
Framingham, MA 01701-4783
(508) 875-3100
Fax: (508) 875-4373
Toll Free: (800) 872-5232

*Jewish Family Services of
Greater Springfield, Inc.
15 Lenox Street
Springfield, MA 01108
(413) 737-2601

Jewish Family Services of
Worcester
646 Salisbury Street
Worcester, MA 01609
(508) 755-3101

LDS Social Services of
Massachusetts, Inc.
150 Brown Street
Weston, MA 02493
(781) 235-2164

Love the Children of
Massachusetts
2 Perry Drive
Duxbury, MA 02332
(781) 934-0063

Lutheran Social Services of
New England
26 Harvard Street
Worcester, MA 01609-2833
(508) 791-4488
Fax: (508) 753-8051
www.adoptlss.org/
LSSadoptma@aol.com
  LSSadoptma@aol.com

MAPS International
400 Commonwealth Avenue
Boston, MA 02115
(617) 267-2222
Fax: (617) 267-3331
www.mapsadopt.org/

Merrimack Valley Catholic
Charities
70 Lawrence Street
Lowell, MA 01852
(978) 452-1421

Merrimack Valley Catholic
Charities
454 North Canal Street
Lawrence, MA 01840
(978) 685-5930

New Bedford Child and Family
Services
682 Purchase Street
New Bedford, MA 02740
(508) 990-0894
Fax: (508) 990-0298

Special Adoption Family
Services
A Program of Communities
for People
418 Commonwealth Avenue
Boston, MA 02215
(617) 572-3678
Fax: (617) 572-3611

The Home for Little Wanderers
271 Huntington Avenue
Boston, MA 02110
(617) 267-3700
Fax: (617) 267-8142

The Home for Little Wanderers
68 Fargo Street
Boston, MA 02210
(617) 428-0440
Fax: (617) 428-0441

United Homes for Children
90 Cushing Avenue
Dorchester, MA 02125
(617) 825-3300

United Homes for Children
1147 Main Street,
  Suite 209-210
Tewksbury, MA 01876
(978) 640-0089
Fax: (978) 640-9652

Wide Horizons For Children
Main Office
38 Edge Hill Road
Waltham, MA 02451
(781) 894-5330
Fax: (781) 899-2769
www.whfc.org/
info@whfc.org

**Adoptive Parent Support
Groups**

Adoption Connection
11 Peabody Square, Room 6
Peabody, MA 01960
(978) 532-1261

Adoption Resource Center
20 Sacramento Street
Cambridge, MA 02138
(617) 547-0909

Berkshire Center for Families
and Children
480 West Street
Pittsfield, MA 01201
(413) 448-8281

Berkshire Learning Center
P.O. Box 1267
Pittsfield, MA 01202
(413) 442-5531

Boston Single Mothers By
 Choice
P.O. Box 600027
Newtonville, MA 02160-0001
(617) 964-9949

Downtown Crossing
105 Chauncy Street, 8th Floor
Boston, MA 02111
(617) 542-2366

Families for Russian and
 Ukrainian Adoptions
New England Area
MA
(508) 650-3674
Jay1956@aol.com

Families with Children
 from China
31 Central Street
Acton, MA 01720
(978) 635-1982
www.ultranet.com/~emd92/
 fcc_ne.html
susanA@ultranet.com

Families with Children
 From China
P.O. Box 101
Thompson, CT 06277
robyn1@neca.com

Family Center Pre and Post
 Adoption Consulting Team
385 Highland Avenue
Somerville, MA 02144
(617) 628-8815

International Concerns
 Committee for Children
130 Temple Street
West Newton, MA 02165
(617) 969-7025

Latin American Adoptive
 Families
211 Turner Road
Falmouth, MA 02536
(508) 457-4525

Nazarene Association for Foster
 Care & Adoption
167 Amesbury Road
Haverhill, MA 01830

Open Door Society of
 Massachusetts
Berkshire County
14 Merriam Street
Dalton, MA 01226
(413) 684-4580

Open Door Society of
 Massachusetts
Berkshire County
121 Bridges Road
Williamstown, MA 01267
(413) 458-3452

Open Door Society of
 Massachusetts
Neponset
10 Standish Drive
Canton, MA 02021
(781) 821-4692

Open Door Society of
 Massachusetts
North Central
119 Bayberry Hill Road
West Townsend, MA 01474
(508) 597-8046

Open Door Society of
 Massachusetts
North Shore
637 Essex Avenue
Gloucester, MA 01930
(978) 281-3981

Open Door Society of
 Massachusetts
Cambridge to Lexington
28 Gorham Street, Suite 2
Cambridge, MA 02138
(617) 491-4265

Open Door Society of
 Massachusetts
Wrentham/Attleboro
15 Summer Street
Wrentham, MA 02093
(508) 883-4790

Open Door Society of
 Massachusetts
Lower Cape Cod
57 Quail Hollow Road
Brewster, MA 02631
(508) 896-5226

Open Door Society of
 Massachusetts
Hampshire/Franklin
247 Park Hill Road
Northhampton, MA 01062
(413) 585-8871

Open Door Society of
 Massachusetts
Upper Cape Cod
P.O. Box 714
Woods Hole, MA 02543
(508) 289-2645

Open Door Society of
 Massachusetts
Westboro Area
109 Stony Hill Road
Shrewsbury, MA 01545
(508) 845-6794

Open Door Society of
 Massachusetts
Westboro Area
29 Long Drive
Westborough, MA 01581
(508) 898-9501

Open Door Society of
 Massachusetts
South Shore
15 Birch Bottom Circle
Rockland, MA 02370
(781) 878-6657

Open Door Society of
 Massachusetts
New Bedford
80 B Nemasket Place
New Bedford, MA 02740
(508) 996-2353

Open Door Society of
 Massachusetts
Downtown Crossing
105 Chauncey Street, 8th Floor
Boston, MA 02111
(617) 542-2366

Open Door Society of
 Massachusetts
Neponset
78 Spruce Road
Norwood, MA 02062-1338
(781) 769-3638

Open Door Society of
 Massachusetts
Framingham
9 Nonesuch Drive
Natick, MA 01760
(508) 655-1402

Open Door Society of
 Massachusetts
Harvard University
Two Brattle Square
Cambridge, MA 02138
(617) 495-4950

Open Door Society of
  Massachusetts
Merrimack Valley
36 Orchard Street
Merrimac, MA 01860
(978) 346-4582

Open Door Society of
  Massachusetts
Metrowest North
242 Old Marlboro Road
Concord, MA 01742
(978) 287-0503

Open Door Society of
  Massachusetts
Cambridge to Lexington
41 Vassal Lane, Suite 3
Cambridge, MA 02138
(617) 492-1944

Open Door Society of
  Massachusetts
Neponset
10 Standish Drive
Canton, MA 02021
(781) 821-4692

Open Door Society of
  Massachusetts
Framingham
25 Goodnow Lane
Marlboro, MA 01752
(508) 624-0783

Open Door Society of
  Massachusetts
Milford
14 Jionzo Road
Milford, MA 01757
(508) 478-5423

Open Door Society of
  Massachusetts
Framingham
One Steven Circle
Natick, MA 01760
(508) 650-0946

Open Door Society of
  Massachusetts
Mid-Cape Cod
141 Bridle Path
Marstons Mills, MA 02648
(508) 428-4390

Open Door Society of
  Massachusetts and North
  American Council on
  Adoptable
Children State Representative
43 King Street
Groveland, MA 01834
(987) 521-6205
Toll Free: (800) 93A-DOPT

Pioneer Valley Open Door
40 Peabody Lane
Greenfield, MA 01301
(413) 773-5025

Single Parents Adopting
  Children Everywhere
40 Smith Street
Arlington, MA 02174
(781) 641-9816

Single Parents for the Adoption
  of Children Everywhere
6 Sunshine Avenue
Natick, MA 01760
(508) 655-5426

Stars of David International Inc.
Jewish Family Service of
  Greater Springfield Inc.
15 Lenox Street
Springfield, MA 01108
(413) 737-2601
www.starsofdavid.org
starsdavid@aol.com

Search Support Groups

Adoptee Liberty Movement
  Association (ALMA)
P.O. Box 204
West Groton, MA 01472
(508) 448-6886

Adoptee Liberty Movement
  Association (ALMA)
P.O. Box 115
Townsend, MA 01469

Adoption Connection
11 Peabody Square, #6
Peabody, MA 01960
(978) 532-1261
Fax: (978) 532-0427
www.adoptionconnection.qpg.com/
s_darke@hotmail.com

Adoption Support
118 Union Avenue
Framingham, MA 01701
(508) 875-6603

Adoption Triad Seeking
  Support
10 W. Hollow Lane
Webster, MA 01570
(508) 949-1919

American Adoption Congress
  State Representative
112 Mt. Vernon Street
Boston, MA 02108

(617) 624-4364
Fax: (617) 624-9606
debspr@aol.com

American Adoption Congress
  State Representative
101 Richardson Drive
Fitchburg, MA 01420
(508) 342-8196

Boston Adoptees
112 Mt. Vernon St.
Boston, MA 02108
(617) 624-4364
debspr@aol.com

C.A.R.E.S.
20 Blanchard Street
Harvard, MA 01451
(508) 772-2699

Cape Cod Adoption
  Connection
P.O. Box 336
Brewster, MA 02631
(508) 896-7332

Center for Family Connections
Box 383246
Cambridge, MA 02238-3246
(617) 547-0909

Concerned United Birthparents
  (CUB)
Harvard Square, P.O. Box 396
Cambridge, MA 02238
(508) 443-3770
www.webnations.com/cub
cub@webnations.com

Family Connections
1770 Massachusetts Avenue,
  #211
Cambridge, MA 02140
(617) 498-9660

Family Ties Support Group
11 Alvanos Drive
Haverhill, MA 01830
(978) 373-7446

Love the Children
1 Burnham Lane
Danvers, MA 01923
(978) 373-7446

TRY Resource Center
P.O. Box 989
Northampton, MA 01061-0989
(413) 584-6599
www.try.org
try@try.org

MASSACHUSETTS LAWS RELATED TO ADOPTION: QUESTIONS AND ANSWERS

Independent adoption is illegal in Massachusetts; however an agency-identified adoption is permissible. Adoptive parents may participate in independent adoptions in other states. The other state's laws and guidelines would then govern the process.

Can an attorney serve as an intermediary?
An attorney can serve as intermediary provided the adoptive family has a home study done by a Massachusetts agency, and the child is surrendered to an agency.

Is advertising permitted?
No.

Who must consent to the adoption?
The birth mother and the child placement agency; birth father if he is married to the birth mother.

When can consent be taken from the birth mother (father), and how long after the consent is signed can it be revoked?
Consent cannot be taken until four days after the child is born and is irrevocable.

What are the birth father's rights?
Notice must be sent to the birth father who files a declaration of paternity with the Department of Social Services. Consent of the birth father is not necessary if notice of the adoption preoceedings is served on him and he does not object within a certain period of time or if the court finds that it is in the child's best interest not to require the consent in view of the birth father's lack of ability, capacity, fitness, and readiness to take parental responsibility or if the child has been in an adoption agency's custody at least one year.

What fees can adoptive parents pay?
Payments for reasonable living, medical, hospital, and legal services are permitted.

Where does the adoption hearing take place?
The hearing takes place in the county where the child or the adoptive parents live.

How are familial and stepparent adoptions different from nonbiological adoptions?
No home study or agency involvement is required, thereby saving time and expenses.

Can a nonresident finalize an adoption in this state?
Yes, but only if an agency receives consent from the birth parents.

SOURCE: MASSACHUSETTS GENERAL LAWS CHAPTER 210, SECTION I TO 11 A (1998)

MICHIGAN

State Adoption Specialist

Family Independence Agency
Jean Hoffman
P.O. Box 30037
Lansing, MI 48909
(517) 373-3513
Fax: (517) 335-4019
www.mfia.state.mi.us/Adoption/
Adopt.htm
hoffmanj2@state.mi.us

State ICPC Administrator

Office of Children's Services
Michigan Family Independence
  Agency
P.O. Box 30037
Lansing, MI 48909
(517) 335-6158
Fax: (517) 373-6177

State Adoption Exchange/State Photolisting Service

Kinship/Family Adoption
  Registry
30215 Southfield Road
Southfield, MI 48076
(248) 443-0306
Toll Free: (800) 267-7144
www.mare.org/

Michigan Adoption Resource
  Exchange
P.O. Box 6128
Jackson, MI 49201
(517) 783-6273
Fax: (517) 783-5904
Toll Free: (800) 589-6273
www.mare.org
njennings@voyager.net

State Reunion Registry

Central Adoption Registry
Michigan Family Independence
  Agency
P.O. Box 30037, 235 South
  Grand
Lansing, MI 48909
(517) 373-3513
Fax: (517) 335-4019
www.mfia.st.mi.us/adoption

Licensed Private Adoption Agencies

Adoptees Help Adopt
  International
5955 N. Wayne Road
Westland, MI 48185
(734) 467-6222
Fax: (734) 467-8020

Adoption Alternatives
61 N. St. Joseph Street
Niles, MI 49120
(616) 684-3350

Adoption Associates, Inc
13535 State Road
Grand Ledge, MI 48837-9626
(517) 627-0805
www.adoptassoc.com
adopt@adoptassoc.com

Adoption Associates, Inc.
1338 Baldwin Street
Jenison, MI 49428
(616) 667-0677
Fax: (616) 667-0920
www.adoptassoc.com
adopt@adoptassoc.com

Adoption Associates, Inc.
3609 Country Club Drive
St. Clair Shores, MI 48082-
  2952
(810) 294-1990
Fax: (616) 667-0920
www.adoptassoc.com
adopt@adoptassoc.com

Adoption Consultants
22749 Michigan Avenue
Dearborn, MI 48124
(313) 271-8805
Fax: (313) 824-0066
www.aciadoption.com
aciadopt@customnet.net

Adoption Cradle
554 Capital Avenue, S.W.
Battle Creek, MI 49015
(616) 963-0794
Fax: (616) 963-7140
ajhacker@voyager.net

Adoption Services International
725 S. Adams, Suite 270
Birmingham, MI 48009
(248) 646-9318

Adoptions of the Heart
4295 Summerwind Avenue, N.E.
Grand Rapids, MI 49525
(616) 365-3166
Fax: (616) 365-2955

Alternatives for Children and
  Families
644 Harrison
Flint, MI 48502
(810) 235-0683
Fax: (810) 235-4619

Americans for International Aid
  & Adoption
2151 Livernois
Troy, MI 48083
(248) 362-1207
Fax: (248) 645-2288
www.rainbowkids.com/aiaa.html
aiaateri@aol.com

Anishnabek Community Family
  Services
2864 Ashmun Street
Sault Ste. Marie, MI 49783
(906) 632-5250
Fax: (906) 632-5266

Bethany Christian Services
1435 E. 12-Mile Road
Madison Heights, MI 48701
(248) 414-4080
Fax: (248) 414-4085
www.bethany.org
info@bethany.org

Bethany Christian Services
6995 W. 48th Street, P.O. Box
  173
Fremont, MI 49412-0173
(231) 924-3390
Fax: (231) 924-2848
www.bethany.org
info@bethany.org

Bethany Christian Services
12048 James Street
Holland, MI 49424-9556
(616) 396-0623
Fax: (616) 396-2315
www.bethany.org
br330@bethany.org

Bethany Christian Services
4225 West Main Street, Suite M
Kalamazoo, MI 49006
(616) 384-0202
Fax: (616) 384-2001
www.bethany.org
branch_942kalamazoo@bethany
  .org

Bethany Christian Services
901 Eastern Avenue N.E.
Grand Rapids, MI 49501-0294
(616) 224-7618
Fax: (616) 224-7619
www.bethany.org
info@bethany.org

*Bethany Christian Services
2041 30th Street
Allegan, MI 49010-9514
(616) 686-0157
Fax: (616) 686-8133
www.bethany.org
info@bethany.org

Bethany Christian Services
919 East Michigan Avenue,
  P.O. Box 155
Paw Paw, MI 49079-0155
(616) 657-7096
Fax: (616) 657-4642
www.bethany.org
info@bethany.org

Bethany Christian Services
5030 North Wind Drive,
  Suite 108 E
East Lansing, MI 48823
(517) 336-0191
Fax: (517) 336-0101
www.bethany.org

Binogii Placement Agency
2864 Ashmun Street,
  Third Floor
Sault Ste. Marie, MI 49783
(906) 632-5250
Fax: (906) 632-5266

Catholic Family Services
1819 Gull Road
Kalamazoo, MI 49001
(616) 381-9800
Fax: (616) 381-2932

Catholic Family Services of the
  Diocese of Saginaw
915 Columbus Avenue
Bay City, MI 48708
(517) 892-2504
Fax: (517) 892-1923

Catholic Family Services of the
  Diocese of Saginaw
220 W. Main
Midland, MI 48640
(517) 631-4711
Fax: (517) 832-5525

Catholic Family Services of the
  Diocese of Saginaw
710 N. Michigan Avenue
Saginaw, MI 48602
(517) 753-8446
Fax: (517) 753-2582

Catholic Human Services
1000 Hastings Street
Traverse City, MI 49686
(231) 947-8110
Fax: (231) 947-3522

Catholic Human Services
154 S. Ripley Boulevard
Alpena, MI 49707
(517) 356-6385

Catholic Human Services
111 S. Michigan
Gaylord, MI 49735
(517) 732-6761

Catholic Social Services of Flint
901 Chippewa Street
Flint, MI 48503
(810) 232-9950
Fax: (810) 232-7599
ccsflint@gfn.org

Catholic Social Services of Kent
  County
1152 Scribner N.W.
Grand Rapids, MI 49504
(616) 456-1443
Fax: (616) 732-6391

Catholic Social Services of
  Macomb County
15980 Nineteen Mile Road
Clinton Township, MI 48038
(810) 416-2311
Fax: (810) 416-2311
Toll Free: (888) 422-2938
csmacomb@teleweb.net

Catholic Social Services of
  Marquette, Upper Penisula
347 Rock Street
Marquette, MI 49855
(906) 228-8630
Fax: (906) 228-2469
lkearney@dioceseofmarquette.org

Catholic Social Services of
  Monroe County
16 E. Fifth Street
Monroe, MI 48161
(734) 242-3800
Fax: (734) 242-6203

Catholic Social Services of
  Monroe County
8330 Lewis Avenue
Temperance, MI 48182
(734) 847-1523

Catholic Social Services of
  Muskegon
1095 Third Street, Suite 125
Muskegon, MI 49441
(231) 726-4735
Fax: (231) 722-0789
cssmusk@aol.com

Catholic Social Services of
  Oakland County
50 Wayne Street
Pontiac, MI 48342
(248) 333-3700
Fax: (248) 333-3718

Catholic Social Services
  of St. Clair
2601 13th Street
Port Huron, MI 48060
(810) 987-9100
Fax: (810) 987-9105

Catholic Social Services of
  Upper Michigan
500 S. Stephenson Avenue,
  Suite 400
Iron Mountain, MI 49801
(906) 774-3323

Catholic Social Services of
  Washtenaw
4925 Packard
Ann Arbor, MI 48108-1521
(734) 971-9781
Fax: (734) 971-2730
loisplant@aol.com

Catholic Social Services of
  Wayne County
9851 Hamilton Avenue
Detroit, MI 48202
(313) 883-2100
Fax: (313) 883-3957

Catholic Social Services, St.
  Vincent Home
2800 W. Willow Street
Lansing, MI 48917
(517) 323-4734
Fax: (517) 323-0257

Child and Family Services
1352 Terrance Street
Muskegon, MI 49442
(616) 726-3582

Child and Family Services of
  Michigan, State Office
2157 University Park Drive
Okemos, MI 48805
(517) 349-6226
Fax: (517) 349-0969
Toll Free: (800) 878-6587

Child and Family Services of
  Northeast Michigan
P.O. Box 516
Alpena, MI 49707
(517) 356-4567
Fax: (517) 354-6100
Toll Free: (800) 779-0396
www.cfsm.org
alpena@cfsm.org

Child and Family Services of
  Northwestern Michigan
820 Arlington
Petosky, MI 49770
(231) 347-4463
www.cfsm.org/
traversecity@cfsm.org

Child and Family Services of
  Northwestern Michigan
3785 Veterans Drive
Traverse City, MI 49684
(231) 946-8975
Fax: (231) 946-0451
TTY: (231) 946-2186
www.cfsm.org/
traversecity@cfsm.org

Child and Family Services of
  Saginaw County
2806 Davenport
Saginaw, MI 48602-3734
(517) 790-7500
Fax: (517) 790-8037
www.cfsm.org
cfsm@cfsm.org

Child and Family Services of
  Southwestern Michigan
2000 South State Street
St. Joseph, MI 49085
(616) 983-5545
Fax: (616) 983-4920
Toll Free: (888) 237-1891
www.cfsm.org/
stjoseph@cfsm.org

Child and Family Services of
  the Upper Peninsula
1440 W. Ridge Street
Marquette, MI 49855
(906) 226-2516
Fax: (906) 226-2297
www.cfsm.org
cfsm@cfsm.org

Child and Family Services of
  the Upper Peninsula, Inc.
Houghton Field Office
705 W. Sharon Avenue, Suite 2
Houghton, MI 49931
(906) 482-4488
Fax: (906) 482-4401
www.cfsm.org
cfsm@cfsm.org

Child and Family Services of
  Western Michigan
321 South Beechtree Street
Grand Haven, MI 49417
(616) 846-5880
www.cfsm.org/
holland@cfsm.org

Child and Family Services of
  Western Michigan
Holland Office
412 Century Lane
Holland, MI 49423
(616) 396-2301
Fax: (616) 396-8070
www.cfsm.org/
holland@cfsm.org

Child and Family Services,
  Capital Area
4801 Willoughby Road, Suite 2
Holt, MI 48842
(517) 699-1600
Fax: (517) 699-2749
www.childandfamily.org
info@childandfamily.org

Child and Family Services,
  SW Michigan
2000 S. State Street
St. Joseph, MI 49085
(616) 983-5545

Child and Parent Services
30600 Telegraph, Suite 2215
Bingham Farms, MI 48025
(248) 646-7790
Fax: (248) 646-4544
Toll Free: (800) 248-0106

Children's Center of
  Wayne County
100 W. Alexandrine
Detroit, MI 48201
(313) 831-5520
Fax: (313) 831-5520

Children's Hope Adoption
  Services
7823 S. Whiteville Road
Shepherd, MI 48883
(517) 828-5842
Fax: (517) 828-5799

Christ Child House
15751 Joy Road
Detroit, MI 48228
(313) 584-6077
Fax: (313) 584-1148

Christian Care Maternity
  Ministries
Baptist Children's Home
214 N. Mill Street
St. Louis, MI 48880
(517) 681-2172

Christian Cradle
535 N. Clippert, Suite 2
Lansing, MI 48912
(517) 351-7500
Fax: (517) 351-4810

Christian Family Services
17105 W. 12 Mile Road
Southfield, MI 48076
(248) 557-8390
Fax: (248) 557-6427

D.A. Blodgett Services
805 Leonard, N.E.
Grand Rapids, MI 49503
(616) 451-2021
Fax: (616) 451-8936
www.dablodgett.org/
dab@iserv.net

Developmental Disabilities
420 W. 5th Avenue
Flint, MI 48503
(810) 257-3714

Eagle Village Family Living
  Program
4507 170th Avenue
Hersey, MI 49639
(231) 832-2234
Fax: (231) 832-2470
Toll Free: (800) 748-0061
www.eaglevillage.org
family@eaglevillage.org

Eastern European Adoption
  Services
INC 22233 Genesis
Woodhaven, MI 48183
(313) 479-2348
Fax: (313) 479-6330
www.adoptalways.com
eeas@adoptalways.com

Eastern European Adoption
  Services
177 Biddle
Wyandotte, MI 48192
(734) 246-9802
Fax: (734) 246-9802

Ennis Center for Children
91 S. Telegraph Road
Pontiac, MI 48341
(248) 333-2520
Fax: (248) 333-3410

Ennis Center for Children
2051 Rosa Parks Boulevard
Detroit, MI 48216
(313) 963-7400
Fax: (313) 963-7424

Ennis Center for Children
129 E. Third Street
Flint, MI 48502
(810) 233-4031
Fax: (810) 233-0008

Ennis Center for Children
20100 Greenfield Road
Detroit, MI 48235
(313) 342-2699
Fax: (313) 342-2180

Evergreen Children's Services
10421 W. Seven Mile Road
Detroit, MI 48221
(313) 862-1000
Fax: (313) 862-6464
ecsnew@aol.com

Family Adoption Consultants
45100 Sterritt, Suite 204
Utica, MI 48317
(810) 726-2988
Fax: (810) 726-2599
www.facadopt.org
Mpara@sprynet.com

Family Adoption Consultants
421 West Crosstown Pkwy,
   P.O. Box 50489
Kalamazoo, MI 49005
(616) 343-3316
Fax: (616) 343-3359
www.facadopt.org
melissa@facadopt.org

Family and Children's Service
   of Calhoun
632 North Avenue
Battle Creek, MI 49017
(616) 965-3247
Fax: (616) 966-4135
www.cfsm.org/
battlecreek@csfm.org

Family and Children's Service
   of Calhoun and Barry
   Counties
450 Meadow Run
Hastings, MI 49058
(616) 948-8465
www.cfsm.org/
battlecreek@csfm.org

Family and Children's Service
   of Midland
1714 Eastman Avenue
Midland, MI 48640
(517) 631-5390
Fax: (517) 631-0488
www.cfsm.org/
midland@csfm.org

Family and Children's Service
   of the Kalamazoo Area
1608 Lake Street
Kalamazoo, MI 49001
(616) 373-0248
Fax: (616) 344-0285
www.cfsm.org/
kalamazoo@csfm.org

Family Counseling and
   Children's Service of
   Lenawee County
213 Toledo Street
Adrian, MI 49221
(517) 265-5352
Fax: (517) 263-6090
www.cfsm.org/
adrian@cfsm.org

Family MatchMakers
2544 Martin, S.E.
Grand Rapids, MI 49507
(616) 243-1803
fammatch@iserv.net

Family Services and Child Aid,
   Jackson
330 W. Michigan Avenue
Jackson, MI 49204
(517) 787-2738

Forever Families Inc.
42705 Grand River Avenue,
   Suite 201
Novi, MI 48375
(248) 344-9606
Fax: (248) 344-9604
foreverfamilies@ameritech.net

Hands Across the Water
2300 Washtenaw, Suite 103B
Ann Arbor, MI 48104
(734) 913-0831
Fax: (734) 429-4823
www.hatw.org
info@hatw.org

HelpSource
118 S. Washington Street
Ypsilanti, MI 48197
(734) 480-1800
Fax: (734) 480-1200

HelpSource
27676 Cherry Hill Road
Garden City, MI 48135
(734) 422-5401
Fax: (734) 422-7893

Homes for Black Children
511 E. Larned Street
Detroit, MI 48226
(313) 961-4777
Fax: (313) 961-2994

Interact Family Services
1260 Woodkrest Drive
Flint, MI 48532

International Adoption
   Association
517 Baldwin Street
Jenison, MI 49428
(616) 457-6537

Fax: (616) 457-1260
Toll Free: (888) 546-4046
www.adoptionpros.com
IAAInc@aol.com

International Adoption
   Consultants
4064 7th Street
Wyandotte, MI 48192
(313) 281-4488
Fax: (313) 281-2919

Jewish Family Service Alliance
   for Adoption
24123 Greenfield Road
Southfield, MI 48075
(248) 559-1500
Fax: (248) 559-9858

Judson Center
23077 Greenfield, Suite 107
Southfield, MI 48075
(248) 443-5000
Fax: (248) 204-1375

Judson Center/Washtenaw
   County
4925 Packard Road, Suite 200
Ann Arbor, MI 48108
(734) 528-1720
Fax: (734) 528-1695

Keane Center for Adoption
930 Mason
Dearborn, MI 48124
(313) 277-4664
Fax: (313) 278-1767
cbrail@provide.net

LDS Social Services
37634 Enterprise Court
Farmington Hills, MI 48331
(248) 553-0902
Fax: (248) 553-2632

Lula Belle Stewart Center
11000 W. McNichols, Suite 116
Detroit, MI 48221
(313) 862-4600
Fax: (313) 864-2233

Lutheran Adoption Service
21700 Northwestern Highway,
   Suite 1490
Southfield, MI 48075-4901
(248) 423-2770
Fax: (248) 423-2783
www.voyager.net/lutheran

Lutheran Adoption Service
Grandville Branch
2976 Ivanrest, Suite 140
Grandville, MI 49418-1440
(616) 532-8286
Fax: (616) 532-8919

Lutheran Adoption Service
Bay City Branch
6019 W. Saginaw Road
Bay City, MI 48707
(517) 686-3170
Fax: (517) 686-7683
www.voyager.net/lutheran/

Lutheran Adoption Service
Lansing Branch
801 S. Waverly, Suite 103
Lansing, MI 48917
(517) 886-1380
Fax: (517) 886-1586
www.voyager.net/lutheran/

Lutheran Social Service of
Wisconsin and Upper
Michigan
1009 West Ridge Street
Marquette, MI 49855
(906) 226-7410
Fax: (906) 226-9800
www.lsswis.org

Methodist Children's Home
Society
26645 W. 6 Mile Road
Detroit, MI 48240
(313) 531-3140
Fax: (313) 531-1040

Michigan Indian Child Welfare
Agency
Baraga Office Tribal Center
Route #1
Baraga, MI 49908
(906) 353-6178
Fax: (906) 353-7540

Michigan Indian Child Welfare
Agency
6425 S. Pennsylvania Avenue,
Suite 3
Lansing, MI 48911
(517) 393-3256
Fax: (517) 393-0838

Michigan Indian Child Welfare
Agency
1345 Monroe Avenue N.W.,
Suite 220
Grand Rapids, MI 49505
(616) 454-9221
Fax: (616) 454-3142

Michigan Indian Child Welfare
Agency
Hannaville Office Tribal Center
N14911 B1 Road
Wilson, MI 49896
(906) 466-9221

Michigan Indian Child Welfare
Agency
405 E. Easterday Avenue
Sault Ste. Marie, MI 49783
(906) 632-8062
Fax: (906) 632-1810
Toll Free: (800) 562-4957

Morning Star Adoption
Resource, Inc.
26711 Woodward Street,
Suite 209
Huntington Woods, MI 48070
(248) 399-2740

Oakland Family Services
114 Orchard Lake Road
Pontiac, MI 48341
(248) 858-7766
Fax: (248) 858-8227
ofs@ofsfamily.org

Orchards Children's Services
42140 Van Dyke Road,
Suite 206
Sterling Heights, MI 48314
(810) 997-3886
Fax: (810) 997-0629

Orchards Children's Services
30215 Southfield Road
Southfield, MI 48076
(248) 433-8653
Fax: (248) 258-0487

Orchards Children's Services
163 Madison Avenue, 3rd Floor
Detroit, MI 48226
(313) 223-1800
Fax: (313) 223-1820

Sault Tribe Binogii Placement
Agency
2864 Ashmun Street
Sault St. Marie, MI 49783
(906) 632-5250

Spaulding for Children
16250 Northland Drive,
Suite 120
Southfield, MI 48075
(248) 443-0300
Fax: (248) 443-2845
www.spauldingforchildren.org

Spectrum Human Services
23077 Greenfield Road,
Suite 500
Southfield, MI 48075
(248) 552-8020
Fax: (248) 552-1135

Spectrum Human Services
28303 Joy Road
Westland, MI 48185
(734) 458-8736
Fax: (734) 458-8836

St. Francis Family Services
17500 W. 8 Mile Road
Southfield, MI 48075
(248) 552-0750
Fax: (248) 552-9019

St. Vincent-Sarah Fisher Center
27400 W. 12 Mile Road
Farmington Hills, MI 48334
(248) 626-7527
Fax: (248) 539-3584
www.home-sweet-home.org
svs@aol.com

Starfish Family Services
30000 Hivley Road
Inkster, MI 48141
(734) 728-3400
Fax: (734) 728-3500
www.sfish.org
ocash@sfish.org

Teen Ranch - Port Huron
3815 Lapeer Road
Port Huron, MI 48060
(810) 987-6111
Fax: (810) 987-6116
www.netonecom.net/~christal/
ranch/
teenranch@centuryinter.net

Teen Ranch Family Services
2861 Main Street
Marlette, MI 48453
(517) 635-7511
Fax: (517) 635-3324
www.centuryinter.net/
teenranch.m/

Teen Ranch Family Services
15565 Northland Drive, Suite
300, East
Southfield, MI 48075
(248) 443-2900
Fax: (248) 443-1695
www.netonecom.net/~christal/
ranch/
teenranch@centuryinter.net

The Adoption Team
26211 Central Park Boulevard,
Suite 500
Southfield, MI 48076
(248) 352-7400

Whaley Children's Center
1201 N. Grand Traverse
Flint, MI 48503
(810) 234-3603
Fax: (810) 232-3416

**Adoptive Parent Support
Groups**

A.D.O.P.T.
6939 Shields Court
Saginaw, MI 48603
(517) 781-2089

Adopt America Network and
North American Council on
Adoptable Children
3051 Siebert Road
Midland, MI 48640
(517) 832-8117

Adoptive Families of
Southwestern Michigan
51558 Indian Lake Road
Dowagiac, MI 49047
(616) 424-3531

Building Families Through
Adoption
4874 Meyer Street
Cadillac, MI 49601
(231) 775-6202

Children's Charter of the
Courts of Michigan
324 N. Pine Street
Lansing, MI 48933
(517) 482-7533
Fax: (517) 482-2626

Community of Hope
544 Graafschap
Holland, MI 49423
(616) 396-1863

Concerned Citizens for
International Adoption
Box 1083
Portage, MI 49082-1083

European Adoptive Families of
S.W. Michigan
47540 Saltz Road
Canton, MI 48187
(734) 981-6534

Families for International
Children
6475 28th Street, S.E., #124
Grand Rapids, MI 49546
(616) 676-2044

Families of Latin Kids
Box 15537
Ann Arbor, MI 48106
(734) 429-4312

Families on the Move and
North American Council on
Adoptable Children
18727 Avon
Detriot, MI 48219
(313) 532-0012
Fax: (313) 532-1345

Families on the Move and
North American Council on
Adoptable Children
Representative
38250 Santa Anna
Clinton, MI 48036
(810) 468-9827
dfredric@innet.com

FIAA of Ann Arbor
1503 Linwood
Ann Arbor, MI 48103
(734) 761-8265

Genesee County Community
Mental Health Board
Developmental Disabilities
420 W. Fifth Avenue
Flint, MI 48503
(810) 257-3714

Greater Jackson Families For
Adoption
6243 Mountie Way
Jackson, MI 49201
(517) 782-9023

Greater Lansing OURS
by Adoption
P.O. Box 25161
Lansing, MI 48909

International Families Through
Adoption
1507 Marlboro
Muskegon, MI 49441
(231) 755-1484

Jewish Family Services of the
Jewish Federation of
Washtenew County
2939 Birch Hollow
Ann Arbor, MI 48108
(734) 971-3280
Fax: (734) 677-0109

Kinship
P.O. Box 62
Bay City, MI 48707
(517) 894-1068

Latin American Families
Through Adoption
608 Marcelletti Avenue
Paw Paw, MI 49079
(616) 657-6498

Marquette Adoption Group
1702 Gray Street
Marquette, MI 49855
(906) 226-6208

Michigan Association for
Openness in Adoption
P.O. Box 5117
Traverse City, MI 49684
(231) 929-4545

Michigan Association of Single
Adoptive Parents
7412 Coolidge
Centerline, MI 48015
(810) 758-6909

Michigan Association of Single
Adoptive Parents
10085 Kingston
Huntington Woods, MI 48070
(248) 547-8893

Michigan Foster and Adoptive
Parent Association
2450 Delhi Commerce Drive,
Suite 13
Holt, MI 48842
(517) 694-1056
Fax: (517) 694-3092
Toll Free: (800) 632-4180

National Coalition to End
Racism in America's Child
Care System
22075 Koths
Taylor, MI 48180
(313) 295-0257

National Resource Center for
Special Needs Adoption
16250 Northland Drive,
Suite 120
Southfield, MI 48075
(248) 443-7080
Fax: (248) 443-7099
*www.spaulding.org/adoption/
NRC-adoption.html*
sfc@spaulding.org

North American Council on
Adoptable Children
Representative
23891 Bedford Road
Battle Creek, MI 49017
(616) 660-0448.

O.C.A.P.
13660 Sherwood
Oak Park, MI 48237
(248) 546-8113

Orchards Adoptive Parent
Support Group
30215 Southfield Road,
Suite 100
Southfield, MI 48076
(248) 258-1278

OURS by Adoption
4330 Van Vleet
Swartz Creek, MI 48473

People Adopting Children
Everywhere
2948 160th Avenue
Holland, MI 49424
(616) 399-4096

Post Adoption Resources
21700 Northwestern Highway,
Suite 1490
Southfield, MI 48075-4901
(248) 423-2770

Post-Adoption Support Services
N. 1194 W. Tie Lake Road
Wetmore, MI 49895
(906) 573-2817

Psychotherapy Center for
Adoptive Families
17500 Northland Park Court
Southfield, MI 48075
(248) 531-9659

Singles Adopting from
Everywhere
2645 Knightsbridge Street
Grand Rapids, MI 49546
(616) 285-9979

Singles for Adoption
619 Norton Drive
Kalamazoo, MI 49001
(616) 381-2581

Stars of David International
Inc.
Metro Detroit Chapter
7423 Westbury
West Bloomfield, MI 48322
(248) 661-3978
www.starsofdavid.org/
fingyroll@juno.com

Support for Parents and Older
Adopted Kids
3666 Boulder
Troy, MI 48084
(248) 649-3469

The Family Tree Support Group
27821 Santa Barbara
Lathrup Village, MI 48076
(248) 557-3501

West Michigan Friends
of Adoption
7635 Yorktown Street
Richland, MI 49083-9637
(616) 629-9037

Yellin and Associates Adoption
Consultants
27600 Farmington Road,
Suite 107
Farmington Hills, MI 48334
(248) 489-9570

Search Support Groups

A.P.A.R.T. (Adoptees and
Parents Alone Rejoicing
Together)
11175 Roberts Road
Stockbridge, MI 49285
(517) 851-7129

Adoptee, Birthparent, Adoptive
Parent Support Groups
21700 N.W. Highway,
Suite 1490
Southfield, MI 48075
(248) 423-2770

Adoptee's Search for
Knowledge
P.O. Box 762
East Lansing, MI 48826-0762
(517) 321-7291

Adoption Connections
Box 293
Cloverdale, MI 49035-0293
(616) 623-8060

Adoption Identity Movement
(AIM)
Southeast Michigan Area
P.O. Box 812
Hazel Park, MI 48030
(248) 548-6291
DGeorgeW@aol.com

Adoption Identity Movement
(AIM) of Grand Rapids
P.O. Box 9783
Grand Rapids, MI 49509
(616) 531-1380
Fax: (616) 532-5589

Adoption Identity Movement
(AIM) of Northern Michigan
P.O. Box 5414
Traverse City, MI 49696-5414

(231) 922-1986
aimofnorthernmi@hotmail.com

Adoption Insight
P.O. Box 171
Portage, MI 49081
(616) 327-1999

Adoption Support Group
2008 Katherine Street
Port Huron, MI 48060
(810) 982-9774

Alliance for Adoption
7423 Westbury
West Bloomfield, MI 48322
(248) 661-3978
Fax: (248) 559-9858

Birth Parent, Adoptee and
Search Support Groups
4925 Packard Road
Ann Arbor, MI 48108
(734) 971-9781
Fax: (734) 971-2370

Bonding by Blood, Unlimited
4710 Cottrell Road
Vassar, MI 48768
(517) 823-8248

Concerned United Birthparents
(CUB)
524 Westchester Drive
Saginaw, MI 48603
(517) 792-5876
www.webnations.com/cub
cub@webnations.com

Family Tree Support Group
27821 Santa Barbara Drive
Lathrup Village, MI 48076
(248) 557-3501

Kalamazoo Birthparent Support
Group
P.O. Box 2183
Portage, MI 49081
(616) 324-9987
ggrayadopt@aol.com

Michigan Association for
Openness in Adoption
P.O. Box 5117
Traverse City, MI 49684
(231) 275-6221

Post Adoption Support Services
N. 1194 W. Tie Lake Road
Wetmore, MI 49895
(906) 573-2817

Roots and Reunions
210 Barbeau Street
Sault St. Marie, MI 49783-2402
(906) 635-5922

Search In Michigan
P.O. Box 5027
North Muskegon, MI 49445

(231) 744-2413
SearchinMI@aol.com

Truth in the Adoption Triad
1815 Sunrise Drive
Caro, MI 48723
(517) 672-2054

West Michigan Birth Mother
  Group
2215 44th S.W.
Wyoming, MI 49509
(616) 532-0757

MICHIGAN LAWS RELATED TO ADOPTION: QUESTIONS AND ANSWERS

Can an attorney serve as an intermediary?
Yes, but the attorney cannot be reimbursed for this service.

Is advertising permitted?
Yes. Some newspapers may accept classified ads with a letter from an attorney or agency.

Who must consent to the adoption?
1. Both birth parents must consent unless they have released the child to an adoption agency, or the birth father's consent is not required for the reason(s) outlined below.
2. If an agency has custody of the child, the agency must consent.

When can consent be taken from birth mother (father), and how long after the consent is signed can it be revoked?
A consent is not needed if the child is released to an adoption agency and the rights of the birth parents are thereafter terminated by court proceedings, notice of which they must receive. Consent must be given within a reasonable time frame; if this is not done, the court may determine if the withholding of consent is "arbitrary and capricious." If the birth parents select the adoptive parents, then approval must be granted by the probate court as to the placement.

What are the birth father's rights?
If the alleged birth father's consent cannot be obtained, the adoption cannot take place until his rights are terminated. The birth mother can terminate her own parental rights while waiting for him to do so. The birth father's rights can be terminated if these requirements are met:
- he does not respond to notice of the adoption
- he denies interest in custody of the child
- he fails to appear at the adoption hearing and denies interest in the child
- his identity or location are unknown and reasonable efforts have been made to find him, and he has not provided for or cared for the child for at least ninety days
- If the birth father requests custody, the court shall determine his ability to care for the child if it is in the child's best interest.

What fees can adoptive parents pay?
Adoptive parents can pay for the birth mother's medical expenses, counseling, legal fees, travel, and reasonable living expenses. Fees and charges must be approved by the court.

Where does the adoption hearing take place?

The hearing can take place in the court of the county where the adoptive parents live or where the child lives.

How are familial and stepparent adoptions different from nonbiological adoptions?

There are no specific provisions in the law for relative adoptions. In a stepparent adoption, a parent who does not have legal custody of the child but whose rights have not been terminated must consent to the adoption.

Can a nonresident finalize an adoption in this state?

Yes.

MINNESOTA

State Adoption Specialist

Minnesota Department of
Human Services
Family & Children's Services
Robert DeNardo
444 Lafayette Road, Human
Services Building
St. Paul, MN 55055-3832
(651) 296-3740
Fax: (651) 297-1949
*www.dhs.state.mn.us/childint/
fostercare/default.htm*
bob.denardo@state.mn.us

State ICPC Administrator

Minnesota Deparment of
Human Services
Family & Children's Services
444 Lafayette Road
St. Paul, MN 55155-3815
(651) 296-3740
Fax: (612) 297-1949

State Adoption Exchange/State Photolisting Service

Minnesota Adoption Resource
Network
2409 West 66th St.
Minneapolis, MN 55423
(612) 861-7115
Fax: (612) 861-7112
www.mnadopt.org/
MNadopt@aol.com

State Reunion Registry

Minnesota Department of
Human Services
Adoption/Guardianship Section
444 Lafayette Road
St. Paul, MN 55155-3831
(651) 296-2795

Licensed Private Adoption Agencies

African American Adoption
and Permanency Planning
Agency (AAAPPA)
1821 University Avenue, Suite
N-263, P.O. Box 40039
St. Paul, MN 55104
(651) 659-0460, Ext: 106
Fax: (651) 644-5306
Toll Free: (888) 840-4084
www.aaappa.org
kiddforkid@aol.com

Bethany Christian Services
3025 Harbor Lane, Suite 223
Plymouth, MN 55447-5138
(612) 553-0344
Fax: (612) 553-0117
www.bethany.org
info@bethany.org

Caritas Family Services
Suite 100, 305 North Seventh
Avenue
St. Cloud, MN 56303
(320) 252-4121

Catholic Charities of the
Archdiocese of Minneapolis-
St. Paul
1276 University Avenue
St. Paul, MN 55104-4101
(651) 641-1180

Catholic Charities of the
Archdiocese of Winona
111 Market Street, P.O. Box 3
Winona, MN 55987-0374
(507) 454-2270

Child Link International
6508 Stevens Ave. S.
Richfield, MN 55423
(612) 861-9048
Fax: (612) 869-2004
www.child-link.com
ChildLink1@aol.com

*Children's Home Society of
Minnesota
2230 Como Avenue
St. Paul, MN 55108
(651) 646-6393
Fax: (651) 646-0436
Toll Free: (800) 952-9302
www.chsm.com
info@chsm.com

Christian Family Life Services
203 South 8th Street
Fargo, ND 58103-1824
(701) 237-4473
Fax: (701) 280-9062

Crossroads Adoption Services
4620 W. 77th Street, Suite 105
Minneapolis, MN 55435
(612) 831-5707
Fax: (612) 831-5129
www.crossroadsadoption.com
kids@crossroadsadoption.com

Downey Side
400 Sibley Street, Suite 560
St. Paul, MN 55101
(651) 228-0117

European Children's Adoption
Services
6925 Empire Lane
Maple Lane, MN 55311
(612) 420-6632

Family Resources
11311 Dayton River Road,
Raintree Plaza
Dayton, MN 55327
(612) 323-8050

Forever Families International
Adoption Agency
2004 Highway 37
Eveleth, MN 55734
(218) 744-4734

Hope International Adoption
and Family Services, Inc.
421 S. Main Street
Stillwater, MN 55082
(651) 439-2446
Fax: (651) 439-2071

International Adoption Services
Suite 338, 4940 Viking Drive
Minneapolis, MN 55435
(612) 893-1343
Fax: (612) 893-9193

Love Basket
3902 Minnesota
Duluth, MN 55802
(218) 720-3097
lovebskt@theriver.net

Lutheran Social Services
of Minnesota
2414 Park Avenue, South
Minneapolis, MN 55404
(612) 879-5230
Toll Free: (888) 205-3769

New Horizon Adoption Agency
P.O. Box 623
Frost, MN 56033
(507) 878-3200
Fax: (507) 878-3200

New Horizons Adoption
Agency, Inc.
Frost Benco Building,
Highway 254
P.O. Box 623
Frost, MN 56033
(507) 878-3200

New Life Family Services
1515 E. 66th Street
Minneapolis, MN 55423-2674
(612) 866-7643

North Homes Inc.
924 City Home Road
Grand Rapids, MN 55744
(218) 327-3055

PATH (Professional
Association of Treatment
Homes)
2324 University Avenue,
Suite 101
St. Paul, MN 55114
(651) 646-3221

*Reaching Arms International,
Inc.
904 Main Street, Suite 330
Hopkins, MN 55343
(612) 932-9331
Fax: (612) 932-4215
www.raiadopt.org
raiadopt@raiadopt.org

Summit Adoption Home
Studies, Inc.
1389 Summit Avenue
St. Paul, MN 55105
(651) 645-6657
Fax: (651) 645-6713
www.summitadoption.com
summitadopt@uswest.net

The Village Family Service
Center
715 11th Street, Suite 302
Moorhead, MN 56560
(218) 233-6158

Upper Midwest American
Indian Center
1035 W. Broadway
Minneapolis, MN 55411
(612) 522-4436

Wellspring Adoption Agency
1219 University Avenue, S.E.
Minneapolis, MN 55414
(612) 379-0980

**Adoptive Parent Support
Groups**

Adopcion, Inc.
1901 Cape Cod Place
Minneapolis, MN 55305
(612) 545-7409

Adoptive Families of America
2309 Como Avenue
St. Paul, MN 55108
(651) 645-9955
Toll Free: (800) 372-3300
www.AdoptiveFam.org/
info@AdoptiveFam.org

Adoptive Families Together
Route 1, Box 248
Pierz, MN 56364
(612) 468-6032

Adoptive Families Together
RR 3, Box 189
Sebeka, MN 56477
(218) 837-5145

Adoptive Family Counseling
Center
3338 18th Avenue, South
Minneapolis, MN 55407
(612) 722-5362

Adoptive Parent Support Group
90 Riverside Drive, S.E.
St. Cloud, MN 56304
(612) 252-1625

Adoptive Parent Support Group
Box 367, Route 1
Richville, MN 56576
(218) 495-3239

Children of Korean Heritage
2230 Como Avenue
St. Paul, MN 55108
(651) 646-6393

Children's Home Society
Wright County, MN
(612) 682-7484

Children's Home Society
Sherburne County, MN
(612) 241-2656
Toll Free: (800) 433-5239

Children's Home Society Single
Parent Support Group
Anoka County, MN
(651) 646-4414, Ext: 224

Diversity Resource Network
P.O. Box 19671
Minneapolis, MN 55419

Eden Prairie Psychological
Resources
Anoka, MN
(612) 939-0167, Ext: 3116

Families for Russian and
Ukrainian Adoptions
2475 Bridle Creek Trail
Chanhassen, MN 55317-9369
wallestadN@aol.com

Families Helping Families in
Adoption
Anoka County, MN
(612) 767-9076

Families of Mixed Race
Adoptions
10 Woodview Drive
Mankato, MN 56001
(507) 345-1850

Families Under Severe Stress
2230 Como Avenue
St. Paul, MN 55108
(651) 646-6393

Love Has No Boundaries
911 Albion Avenue
Fairmont, MN 56031
(507) 235-8748

Minnesota Adoption Support
  and Preservation
2409 West 66th Street, P.O.
  Box 39722
Minneapolis, MN 55439
(612) 861-7115
Fax: (612) 861-7112
www.mnasap.org/
MNadopt@aol.com

Minnesota Council for Children
  in Adoption and Foster Care
15700 Lac Lavon Drive
Burnsville, MN 55306
(612) 831-5707

Minnesota Kinship Caregivers
  Association
501 East 45th Street
Minneapolis, MN 55409

Ninos de Paraguay
7801 Bush Lake Drive
Bloomington, MN 55438
(612) 829-0938

North American Council on
  Adoptable Children
970 Raymond Avenue, Suite
  106
St. Paul, MN 55114-1149

(651) 644-3036
Fax: (651) 644-9848
members.aol.com/nacac
nacac@aol.com

North Suburban Ours for a
  United Response
2723 Crown Hill Court
White Bear Lake, MN 55110
(651) 429-0357

Northwest Minnesota Families
  Through Adoption
Box 135
Crookston, MN 56716

Parents of (Asian) Indian
  Children
1395 Simpson Street
St. Paul, MN 55108
(651) 645-9068

Parents of Latin American
  Children
16665 Argon Street, N.W.
Anoka, MN 55304
(612) 427-6277

Peruvian Adoptive Families
2717 Cedar Lane
Burnsvile, MN 55337
(612) 890-8430

Support Adoptions
5500 Lincoln Drive Suite 130
Minneapolis, MN 55436-9273

West Central Minnesota
  Adoptive Families
918 N.Third Street
Montevideo, MN 56265
(612) 269-8620

Search Support Groups

Adoptee Liberty Movement
  Association (ALMA)
P.O. Box 613
Excelsior, MN 55331
(612) 470-9544

American Adoption Congress
  State Representative
15511 Afton Hills Drive South
Afton, MN 55001
(612) 436-2015
Fax: (612) 436-3151
amy_silberberg@fourthgen.com

Concerned United Birthparents
  (CUB)
6429 Mendelsohn Lane
Edina, MN 55343
(612) 938-5866
www.webnations.com/cub
cub@webnations.com

Minnesota Reunion
  Registry/Liberal Education for
  Adoptive Families
23247 Lofton Court, North
N. Scandia, MN 55073-9752
(612) 436-2215

Orphan Voyage
6901 W. 84th, #311
Bloomington, MN 55438
(612) 943-9037

MINNESOTA LAWS RELATED TO ADOPTION: QUESTIONS AND ANSWERS

Can an attorney serve as an intermediary?
No.

Is advertising permitted?
Yes.

Who must consent to the adoption?
1. The birth parents
2. If a birth parent is a minor, consent of the minor's parent or guardian is also required.

When can consent be taken from birth mother (father), and how long after the consent is signed can it be revoked?
Consent cannot be signed until seventy-two hours after birth. The consent can be revoked up to ten working days afterward. After that time frame, it is irrevocable. A consent must be signed before an agency or a judge. If a birth mother refuses counseling by an agency, she must sign the consent in front of a judge.

What are the birth father's rights?
A birth father is the presumed father if his name is on the birth certifcate, he has substantially supported the child, or has been identified as the father. The presumed birth father must have his rights terminated through a consent or in court after providing him notice of the hearing and showing that he has abandoned the child over a certain period of time. If a nonpresumed birth father wants to retain his rights, he must file an affidavit within sixty days after the child is placed or ninety days after the child's birth, whichever is sooner.

The unwed birth father must be served a notice of the adoption placement and hearing, but this can be waived if the child was conceived as a result of rape or incest, or if locating him might cause physical or severe emotional harm to the birth mother or child.

What fees can adoptive parents pay?
Adoptive parents can pay for legal, medical, counseling, and reasonable living expenses.

Where does the adoption hearing take place?
The hearing takes place in the court of the county where the adoptive parents live.

How are familial and stepparent adoptions different from nonbiological adoptions?
Familial adoptions are not different from nonfamilial adoptions. In stepparent adoptions the court can waive the home study requirement. Also, the consent requires just two witnesses and a notary public; no agency or judge is required to take the consent. In a stepparent adoption, the residence requirement of living in Minnesota for one year may also be waived.

Can a nonresident finalize an adoption in this state?
No. The adoptive parents must have lived in Minnesota for at least one year and with the child for three months. The court can waive this requirement.

SPECIAL NOTE: If the biological parents request that the child be placed with an adoptive family of the same or similar religious or ethnic background, the agency shall do so if a family is available.

SOURCE: MINNESOTA CODE ANNOTATED SECTIONS 259:10 TO 259:49 (1996)

MISSISSIPPI

State Adoption Specialist

Adoption Unit Mississippi
Department of Human Services
 (LMSW)
Delores Harris
750 N. State Street
Jackson, MS 39202
(601) 359-4981
Fax: (601) 359-2525
www.mdhs.state.ms.us/
 fcs_adopt.html

State ICPC Administrator

Mississippi Department of
 Human Services
P.O. Box 352
Jackson, MS 39205
(601) 359-4998
Fax: (601) 359-4978

State Adoption Exchange/State Photolisting Service

Mississippi Adoption Resource
 Exchange
P.O. Box 352
Jackson, MS 39205
(601) 359-4407
Toll Free: (800) 821-9157
www.mdhs.state.ms.us/
 fcs_adopt.html

Regional/District Public Agencies

Mississippi Department of
 Human Services, Region I
P.O. Box 728
Booneville, MS 38829
(601) 728-8020
Toll Free: (800) 821-9157

Mississippi Department of
 Human Services, Region II
P.O. Box 1638
Grenada, MS 38901
(601) 226-1351
Toll Free: (800) 821-9157

Mississippi Department of
 Human Services, Region III
P.O. Box 1829
Vicksburg, MS 39181
(601) 636-1597
Toll Free: (800) 821-9157

Mississippi Department of
 Human Services, Region IV
P.O. Box 910
Meridian, MS 39302
(601) 486-2992
Toll Free: (800) 821-9157

Mississippi Department of
 Human Services, Region V
P.O. Box 470
McComb, MS 39648
(601) 684-0195
Toll Free: (800) 821-9157

Mississippi Department of
 Human Services, Region VI
P.O. Box 247
Pass Christian, MS 39571
(601) 452-2465
Toll Free: (800) 821-9157

Licensed Private Adoption Agencies

Acorn Adoptions, Inc.
113 South Beach Boulevard
Bay St. Louis, MS 39520
Toll Free: (888) 221-1370

Adoption Ministries of
 Missisipy, Inc.
P.O. Box 20346
Jackson, MS 39289-0346
(601) 352-7888

Association for Guidance, Aid,
 Placement and Empathy
 (AGAPE) Child and Family
 Services
P.O. Box 11411
Memphis, TN 38111
(901) 272-7339

Bethany Christian Services
7 Professional Parkway, #103
Hattiesburg, MS 38402-2637
(601) 264-4984
Fax: (601) 264-2648
Toll Free: (800) 331-5876
www.bethany.org
info@bethany.org

Bethany Christian Services
2618 Southerland Street
Jackson, MS 39216-4825
(601) 366-4282
Fax: (601) 366-4287
Toll Free: (800) 331-5876
www.bethany.org
info@bethany.org

*Bethany Christian Services
116 Lawrence Drive, #3
Columbus, MS 39702-5319
(601) 327-6740
Fax: (601) 327-6533
Toll Free: (800) 331-5876
www.bethany.org
info@bethany.org

Catholic Charities, Inc.
Jackson, MS 39226-2248
(601) 355-8634

Catholic Social and Community
 Services
P.O. Box 1457
Biloxi, MS 39533-1457
(228) 374-8316

Harden House Adoption
 Agency
110 North Gaither Street
Fulton, MS 38843
(601) 862-7318

Jewish Family Services, Inc.
6560 Poplar Avenue
Memphis, TN 38138
(901) 767-8511
Fax: (901) 763-2348

LDS Social Services
2000 Old Spanish Trail, Pratt
 Center, Suite 115
Slidell, LA 70458
(504) 649-2774

Lutheran Ministries of Georgia
 Inc.
756 W. Peachtree Street, N.W.
Atlanta, GA 30308
(404) 875-0201
Fax: (404) 875-9258

Mississippi Children's Home
 Society and Family Service
 Association
1900 North West Street, P.O.
 Box 1078
Jackson, MS 39215-1078
(601) 352-7784

New Beginnings of Tupelo
1445 East Main Street
Tupelo, MS 38804
(662) 842-6752

Southern Adoptions Inc.
1251 Marty Stuart Drive
Philadelphia, MS 39350
(601) 656-3933

*World Child, Inc.
338 Lake Harbor Drive
Ridgeland, MS 39157

**Adoptive Parent Support
  Groups**

Adoption Foster Friends
  Support Group of Warren
  County
MS, and North American
  Council on Adoptable
  Children State
  Representative
209 Henry Road
Vicksburg, MS 39180
(601) 636-3962

Adoption Support Group of
  Coastal Mississippi
Box 247
Pass Christian, MS 39571
(601) 452-2465

F.A.C.E. Adoption Support
  Group for North Mississippi
Box 728
Booneville, MS 38829

Ministers For Adoption
P.O. Box 1078
Jackson, MS 39205
(601) 352-7784

Mississippi Adoption Foster
  Parents Group and North
  American Council on
  Adoptable Children
  Representative
P.O. Box 173, 369 Gore Road
Sand Hill, MS 39161
(601) 829-1095

North American Council on
  Adoptable Children
  Representative
5722 Michelle Ray Street
Jackson, MS 39209
(601) 922-3989

Northwest Mississippi Adoption
  Support Group
P.O. Box 1638
Grenada, MS 38902
(601) 226-1351

Southwest Mississippi Adoption
  Support Group
P.O. Box 470
McComb, MS 39648
(601) 684-0195

Search Support Groups

Adoption Information Network
P.O. Box 4154
Meridian, MS 39304
(601) 482-7556

American Adoption Congress
  State Representative
5917 Fifth Street
Meridian, MS 39307
(601) 482-7556

MISSISSIPPI LAWS RELATED TO ADOPTION: QUESTIONS AND ANSWERS

Can an attorney serve as an intermediary?
Yes.

Is advertising permitted?
Yes.

Who must consent to the adoption?
Both birth parents must consent if married to each other. Consent is not necessary if it can be shown that the parent has abandoned or deserted the child to be adopted. Also, no consent is needed if it can be established that the parent is mentally, morally, or otherwise unfit to raise the child.

**When can consent be taken from birth mother (father), and how long after the con-
  sent is signed can it be revoked?**
Consent cannot be given until child is three days old and is irrevocable.

What are the birth father's rights?
If the birth father is not married to the birth mother, he is not considered a parent.

What fees can adoptive parents pay?
Reasonable fees approved by the court may be charged for the preadoption investigation. Also, medical, legal, and, in some instances, living expenses can be paid.

Where does the adoption hearing take place?
The hearing takes place in the court of the county where the adoptive parents live or where the child lives.

How are familial and stepparent adoptions different from nonbiological adoptions?
The residency requirement is waived.

Can a nonresident finalize an adoption in this state?
No. Adoptive parents must have resided in the state for ninety days before filing the adoption petition.

SOURCE: MISSISSIPPI CODE ANNOTATED SECTIONS 93-17-1 TO 93-17-223 (1998)

MISSOURI

State Adoption Specialist

Missouri Department of Social Services
Division of Family Services
Jerrie Jacobs-Kenner
615 Howerton Court,
P.O. Box 88
Jefferson City, MO 65103-0088
(573) 526-8579
Fax: (573) 526-3971
www.dss.state.mo.us/dfs/adopt.htm
jjacobs@mail.state.mo.us

Missouri Department of Social Services
Division of Family Services
Christine White
615 Howerton Court,
P.O. Box 88
Jefferson City, MO 65103-0088
(573) 751-6529
Fax: (573) 526-3971
www.dss.state.mo.us/dfs/adopt.htm

State ICPC Administrator

Missouri Department of Social Services
Division of Family Services
615 Howerton Court,
P.O. Box 88
Jefferson City, MO 65109
(573) 751-4247

State Adoption Exchange/State Photolisting Service

Missouri Adoption Exchange
Missouri Division of Family Services
615 Howerton Court,
P.O. Box 88
Jefferson City, MO 65103-0088

(573) 751-2981
Fax: (573) 522-2199
www.dss.state.mo.us/dfs/adopt/

State Reunion Registry

Missouri Division of Family Services
Adoption Information Registry
P.O. Box 88
Jefferson City, MO 65103
(573) 751-3171
Toll Free: (800) 554-2222
www.state.mo.us/dss/dfs/adoir.htm

Licensed Private Adoption Agencies

Action for Adoption
1015 Locust Street, Suite 1100
St. Louis, MO 63101
Toll Free: (800) 769-2394

Adoption Advocates
3100 Broadway, Suite 218
Kansas City, MO 64111
(816) 753-1711

Adoption and Beyond, Inc.
401 West 89th Street
Kansas City, MO 64114
(816) 822-2800

Adoption and Counseling Services for Families
10045 Hemlock
Overland Park, KS 66212
(913) 383-8448
Fax: (913) 383-8448

Adoption and Fertility Resources
144 Westwoods Drive
Liberty, MO 64068
(816) 781-8550

*Adoption by Family Therapy of the Ozarks, Inc.
3433 S. Campbell, Suite S
Springfield, MO 65807
(417) 882-7700
Fax: (417) 882-5494
Toll Free: (800) 449-2229

Adoption By Gentle Shepherd
114 West Gregory
Kansas City, MO 64114
Toll Free: (800) 610-2221

Adoption Counseling, Inc.
1420 W. Lexington Avenue
Independence, MO 64052
(816) 507-0822

Adoption of Babies and Children
4330 Bellview
Kansas City, MO 64111
(816) 561-2223

Adoption Option
1124 Main
Blue Springs, MO 64015
(816) 224-1525

American Adoption
100 S. Grand Avenue, Suite 410
Kansas City, MO 64106
Toll Free: (800) 875-2229
www.americanadoptions.com/
adoptions@americanadoptions.com

Annie Malone Children & Family Service Center
2612 Annie Malone Drive
St. Louis, MO 63113
(314) 531-0120

Bethany Christian Services
500 Northwest Plaza, Suite 1016
St. Ann, MO 63074-2225
(314) 209-0909
Fax: (314) 209-0443
www.bethany.org
info@bethany.org

*Catholic Charities
  of Kansas City
1112 Broadway
Kansas City, MO 64111
(816) 221-4377

Catholic Services for Children
  and Youth
4140 Lindell Boulevard
St. Louis, MO 63108
(314) 371-4980

Central Baptist Family Services
1015 Locust Street, Suite 900
St. Loius, MO 63101
(314) 241-4345
Fax: (314) 241-4330

Children's Home Society of
  Missouri
9445 Litzsinger Road
Brentwood, MO 63144
(314) 968-2350

Children's Hope International
aka China's Children
9229 Lackland Road
St. Louis, MO 63114-5412
(314) 890-0086
Fax: (314) 427-4288
www.ChildrensHope.com
adoption@childrenshopeint.org

Christian Family Life Center
125 N. Main Street, Suite 208
St. Charles, MO 63301
(319) 946-1700
Fax: (314) 946-7247

Christian Family Services of the
  Midwest, Inc.
5703 North Flora
Gladstone, MO 64118
(816) 452-2077

Christian Family Services, Inc.
8039 Watson Road, Suite 120
Webster Groves, MO 63119
(314) 968-2216

Christian Salvation Services
4390 Lindell Boulevard
St. Louis, MO 63108
(314) 535-5919

Clayton Counseling Associates,
  Inc.
7700 Clayton Road, Suite 309
St. Louis, MO 63117
(314) 781-9181

*Creative Families, Inc.
9378 Olive Street Road,
  Suite 320
St. Louis, MO 63122
(314) 567-0707

Dillon International, Inc.
The Pines Court Office Center,
  #4E
St. Louis, MO 63141
(314) 514-0077
Fax: (314) 453-9975
www.dillonadopt.com
dillonkids@aol.com

Downey Side Families for Youth
6500 Chippewa, Suite 324
St. Louis, MO 63109
(314) 457-1358

Faith House
5355 Page
St. Louis, MO 63112
(314) 367-5400

Family Builders, Inc.
410 West 8th Street
Kansas City, MO 64105
(816) 822-2169

Foster Family Ministries
3210 Michigan
Kansas City, MO 64113
(816) 923-1256

Friends of African-American
  Families and Children
  Service Center
3920 Lindell Boulevard,
  Suite 102
St. Louis, MO 63108
(314) 535-2453

Future Inc.
643 Wynn Place
St. Louis, MO 63021
(314) 394-9312

General Protestants Children's
  Home
12685 Olive Street
Creve Coeur, MO 63141
(314) 434-5858

Heart of America Adoption
  Center, Inc.
903 Fox Trail Drive
Lake St. Louis, MO 63367
(636) 561-1788

*Heart of America Family
  Services
3100 N.E. 83rd Street,
  Suite 1401
Kansas City, MO 64119
(816) 436-0486

Highlands Child Placement
  Services
5506 Cambridge Avenue
Kansas City, MO 64130-0198
(816) 924-6565

Hope N. Heller Ph. D.
  Adoption Services, Inc.
425 North New Ballas,
  Suite 181
St. Louis, MO 63141
(314) 567-7500

James A. Roberts Agency
3100 Broadway, Penn Tower
  Building, Suite 64111
Kansas City, MO 61104
(816) 753-3333, Ext: 5

Kansas Children's Service
  League
3200 Wayne, W-104
Kansas City, MO 64109
(816) 921-0654

Kaw Valley Center
3210 Lee's Summit Road
Independence, MO 64055
(816) 350-1901

LDS Social Services
517 Walnut Street, Suite 2
Independence, MO 64050
(816) 461-5512

Love Basket, Inc.
10306 State Highway 21
Hillsboro, MO 63050
(314) 797-4100
Fax: (314) 789-4978

Lutheran Family and Children's
  Services
4201 Lindell Blvd., Suite 400
St. Louis, MO 63108
(314) 534-1515
Fax: (314) 534-1588

Missouri Baptist Children's
  Home
11300 St. Charles Rock Road
Bridgeton, MO 63044
(314) 739-6811
Fax: (314) 739-6325

*New Family Connection
201 North Kingshighway
St. Charles, MO 63301
(636) 949-0577

Presbyterian Children's Services
608 Pine
Farmington, MO 63640
(573) 756-6744

Respond, Inc.
4411 N. Newstead Avenue
St. Louis, MO 63115
(314) 383-4243

Safe Cradle Adoption Agency
11715 Administration Drive,
    Suite 101
Creve Coeur, MO 63146
(314) 991-2580

Salvation Army Hope Center
3740 Marine Avenue
St. Louis, MO 63118
(314) 773-0980

Seek International
5427 Telegraph Road
St. Louis, MO 63129
(314) 416-9723

Small World Adoption
    Foundation, Inc.
15480 Clayton Road, #101
Ballwin, MO 63011
(314) 207-9229
Fax: (314) 207-9055
www.swaf.com
staff@swaf.com

Special Additions, Inc.
119 Walnut Street
Kansas City, MO 64106
(816) 421-3737

The Light House
1409 E. Meyer Blvd
Kansas City, MO 64131
(816) 361-2233

Universal Adoption Services
124 E. High Street
Jefferson City, MO 64101
(573) 634-3733

**Adoptive Parent Support
  Groups**

Adoption Today
5350 Casa Royale Drive
St. Louis, MO 63129-3007
(314) 894-4586

Adoptive Family Support Group
Route 1, Box 84
Millersville, MO 63701
(573) 266-3609

Adoptive Parents of Southwest
    Missouri
4925 Royal Drive
Springfield, MO 65804
(417) 887-5788

AMCH
2612 Annie Malone
St. Louis, MO 63113
(314) 531-1907

Citizens for Missouri's Children
    and North American Council
    on Adoptable
Children Representative
701 S. Skinner Boulevard,
    Apt. 303
St. Louis, MO 63105-3326
(314) 962-6397
Fax: (314) 434-3936

Families Blessed with the
    World's Children
An International Adoption
    Support Group
716 Gleed Terrace
Kansas City, MO 64109
(831) 531-6598
woolhead@ix.netcom.com

Families Through Adoption
1350 Summit Drive
Fenton, MO 63026
(573) 343-7658

International Families, Inc.
P.O. Box 4142
Chesterfield, MO 63006
(314) 781-7651
Toll Free: (800) 423-6788
nicabol@aol.com

Missouri Foster Care &
    Adoption Association
303 Country Road 433
Rocheport, MO 65279
(573) 698-2052

Open Door Society of Missouri
9417 Pine
St. Louis, MO 63144
(314) 968-5239

Parents Association of the
    Children's Home Society
    of Missouri
3511 Brookwood Circle
St. Charles, MO 63301
(314) 968-2350

Respond Black Adoption and
    Foster Care Citizen Support
    Group
4411 N. Newstead Avenue
St. Louis, MO 63115
(314) 727-3687

Single Adoptive Parents
    Support Group
1800 Fairview Road
Columbia, MO 65202
(573) 445-1262

Stars of David International Inc.
St. Louis Chapter
1608 Stone Hollow Road
Wildwood, MO 63038-2417
(314) 207-6682
www.starsofdavid.org
starsdavid@aol.com

The Adoption Exchange
100 N. Euclid Avenue, #910
St. Louis, MO 63108
(314) 367-3343
Fax: (314) 367-3363
Toll Free: (877) 723-6781

World Children's Fund
1015 Barberry Lane
Kirkwood, MO 63122
(573) 822-3361

Search Support Groups

Adoptee Searches, Inc.
P.O. Box 803
Chesterfield, MO 63006-0803
Toll Free: (800) 434-0020

Adoption Connection
842 Country Stone Drive
St. Louis, MO 63021

American Adoption Congress
    State Representative
P.O. Box 803
Chesterfield, MO 63006-0803
Fax: (314) 561-5005
Toll Free: (800) 434-0020
vlong38@yahoo.com

Birthparent Connection
121 Weiss Avenue
St. Louis, MO 63125

Birthright
6309 Walnut
Kansas City, MO 64801

Donors' Offspring
P.O. Box 37
Sarcoxie, MO 64862
(417) 548-3679

Kansas City Adult Adoptees
P.O. Box 11828
Kansas City, MO 64138
(816) 229-4075

National Adoption Registry, Inc.
6800 Elmwood Avenue
Kansas City, MO 64132-9963
(816) 361-1627
Toll Free: (800) 875-4347

Search for Life
Route 2, Box 93
Birchtree, MO 65438

Searcher's Forum
830 Marshall Avenue
Webster Grove, MO 63119-
2003

Support Open Adoption
Records Search & Support
Group
4589 Hopewell Road
Wentzville, MO 63385
(314) 828-5726

MISSOURI LAWS RELATED TO ADOPTION: QUESTIONS AND ANSWERS

Can an attorney serve as an intermediary?
Yes.

Is advertising permitted?
Yes.

Who must consent to the adoption?
The birth parents and the court must consent.

When can consent be taken from birth mother (father), and how long after the consent is signed can it be revoked?
Written consent can be given either before or after birth, but is only valid when the consent is filed with the court. The consent should be filed immediately after it is signed. Judges will consider a birth parent who wants to revoke consent up to the first court hearing, which usually takes place about one to two weeks after the consent is filed.

Some judges require the child to be placed in foster care before being placed with the adoptive couple and before the parental rights are terminated. Because many birth mothers and adoptive parents are opposed to this, a court must be selected that will permit direct placement of the child into the couple's home. It appears that using an experienced attorney to resolve this situation is critical.

What are the birth father's rights?
If the birth father's identity is unknown or cannot be determined, then his consent is not needed. Either birth mother or birth father can waive in writing the need to provide consent. Also, no consent is required if either birth parent willfully abandoned the child or neglected to provide the child with care and protection for a period of sixty days (if the child is under one year of age) or for a period of six months (if the child is over one year of age). In addition, consent from either parent is not rquired if that parent is served with the adoption complaint and either does not file an answer with the court or does not appear at the court hearing.

What fees can adoptive parents pay?
Legal, medical, and reasonable living expenses can be paid. All statements of payment must be submitted to the court. The court may refuse to allow the adoption if payments were unreasonable or if adoptive parent did not report all expenses paid.

Where does the adoption hearing take place?
It can take place in the juvenile court in the county where the adoptive parents live or the child lives.

How are familial and stepparent adoptions different from nonbiological adoptions?
The court may waive the home study requirement in a stepparent adoption.

Can a nonresident finalize an adoption in this state?
Yes. If you are not from Missouri but adopt a child there, however, a Missouri adoption agency must review your home study (conducted in your state) and the court must verify the home study. The cost for a Missouri agency to review your home study is usually about $2,000.

SOURCE: MISSOURI REVISED STATUTES, CHAPTER 453, SECTIONS 453.005 TO 453.503 (1997)

MONTANA

State Adoption Specialist

Montana Department of Public
   Health and Human Services
Lynda Korth
P.O. Box 8005
Helena, MT 59604
(406) 444-5919
Fax: (406) 444-5956
www.dphhs.state.mt.us/whowhat/
   cafs.htm
lkorth@mt.gov

State ICPC Administrator

Montana Department of Public
   Health and Human Services
Child and Family Services
   Division
P.O. Box 8005
Helena, MT 59604
(406) 444-5917
Fax: (406) 444-5956

State Adoption Exchange/State
   Photolisting Service

Treasure Book Photo Listing
Helena, MT
Toll Free: (888) 937-5437

Regional/District Public
   Agencies

Montana Department of Public
   Health and Human Services,
   Billings
1211 Grand Avenue
Billings, MT 59230
(406) 252-5601

Montana Department of Public
   Health and Human Services,
   Bozeman
220 W. Lamme, Suite 2E
Bozeman, MT 59715
(406) 585-9984

Montana Department of Public
   Health and Human Services,
   Butte
700 Casey, Suite A
Butte, MT 59701
(406) 496-4950

Montana Department of Public
   Health and Human Services,
   Cut Bank
1210 E. Main, Courthouse
   Annex
Cut Bank, MT 59427
(406) 873-5534

Montana Department of Public
   Health and Human Services,
   Glasgow
501 Court Square, Box 9
Glasgow, MT 59230
(406) 228-8221

Montana Department of Public
   Health and Human Services,
   Great Falls
2300 12th Avenue, South,
   Suite 106
Great Falls, MT 59405
(406) 727-7746

Montana Department of Public
   Health and Human Services,
   Hamilton
210 N. Second
Hamilton, MT 59840
(406) 363-1961

Montana Department of Public
   Health and Human Services,
   Havre
314 Fourth Avenue
Havre, MT 59501
(406) 265-1233

Montana Department of Public
   Health and Human Services,
   Helena
316 N. Park
Helena, MT 59620
(406) 444-2030

Montana Department of Public
   Health and Human Services,
   Kalispell
Drawer 310
Kalispell, MT 59901
(406) 751-5950

Montana Department of Public
   Health and Human Services,
   Lewistown
300 First Avenue, North, Suite
   201
Lewistown, MT 59457
(406) 538-7731

Montana Department of Public
   Health and Human Services,
   Miles City
708 Palmer
Miles City, MT 59301
(406) 232-1385

Montana Department of Public
   Health and Human Services,
   Missoula
610 Woody
Missoula, MT 59802
(406) 523-4100

Montana Department of Public
Health and Human Services,
Polson
P.O. Box 268
Polson, MT 59860-0268
(406) 883-3828

Montana Department of Public
Health and Human Services,
Sidney
221 Fifth Street, S.W.
Sidney, MT 59270
(406) 482-1903

Montana Department of Public
Health and Human Services,
Thompson Falls
Box 519
Thompson Falls, MT 59837
(406) 827-4317

**Licensed Private Adoption
Agencies**

Catholic Social Services
25 S. Ewing
Helena, MT 59624
(406) 442-4130

Catholic Social Services for
Montana
Box 907, 25 South Ewing
Helena, MT 59624
(406) 442-4130
Fax: (406) 442-4192

Catholic Social Services for
Montana
1222 N. 27th St., Suite 101
Billings, MT 59101

LDS Social Services
2001 11th Avenue
Helena, MT 59601
(406) 443-1660

Lutheran Social Services
P.O. Box 1345
Great Falls, MT 59403
(406) 761-4341

**Adoptive Parent Support
Groups**

Adoptive Families of Montana
1499 Cobb Hill Road
Bozeman, MT 59715
(406) 586-9788

Family Support in Adoption
Association and North
American Council on
Adoptable
Children Representative
7049 Fox Lane
Darby, MT 59829
(406) 349-2872

G.I.F.T.
6111 Birdseye
Helena, MT 59601
(406) 443-5099

Montana Adoption Resource
Center, Post Adoption
Center
P.O. Box 634
Helena, MT 59624
(406) 449-3266

Montana State Foster and
Adoptive Parents Association
P.O. Box 8135
Kalispell, MT 59904

Northwest Montana Adoptive
Parent Group
629 Fifth Avenue, East
Kalispell, MT 59102
(406) 257-8221

MONTANA LAWS RELATED TO ADOPTION: QUESTIONS AND ANSWERS

Can an attorney serve as an intermediary?
No.

Is advertising permitted?
No. Nor is any public solicitation permitted, such as posting fliers or sending letters,
except to people that you know.

Who must consent to the adoption?
1. Both birth parents
2. The executive head of an agency (if an agency adoption)

**When can consent be taken from birth mother (father), and how long after the con-
sent is signed can it be revoked?**
Consent cannot be given until seventy-two hours after the child's birth and is irrevocable.
If the birth mother changes her mind, the court will consider the best interests of the child
up until the time the adoption is finalized.

What are the birth father's rights?
If he is named on the birth certificate with his consent or if he is otherwise named, his
consent is required. If he acknowledges paternity in a writing filed with the Department of

Health and Environmental Sciences in the district court in his home county then his consent is also required. If he contests the adoption, he must present his case to the court. A birth father's rights may be terminated without his consent if he is served with a notice thirty days before the child's expected date of delivery and he fails to file a notice of intent to claim paternity before the child's birth. If the birth father's whereabouts are not known, then his rights can be terminated if he has not provided support for the mother or shown any interest in the child or otherwise provided for the child's care during a time period of ninety days before the adoption hearing. If the birth father's identity is unknown, then his rights can be terminated if he has not supported the birth mother during her pregnancy or provided support for the child after the birth.

What fees can adoptive parents pay?
Legal, medical, and other reasonable expenses can be paid. In an independent adoption, all fees and expenses must be submitted in an itemized statement to the court.

Where does the adoption hearing take place?
The adoption hearing takes place in the District Court in the county where the adoptive parents reside.

How are familial and stepparent adoptions different from nonbiological adoptions?
The home study report may be waived by the court. In relative adoptions the preadoption investivation and report that is required of all adoptions may be waived.

Can a nonresident finalize an adoption in this state?
No. You must be residing in the state at the time of petition.

SOURCE: MONTANA CODE ANNOTATED TITLE SECTIONS 42-2-101 TO 42-2-503 (1997)

NEBRASKA

State Adoption Specialist

Division of Protection & Safety
Nebraska Department of Health
  & Human Services
Mary Dyer
P.O. Box 95044
Lincoln, NE 68509-5044
(402) 471-9331
Fax: (402) 471-9034
www.hhs.state.ne.us/chs/chsindex.
  htm
mary.dyer@hhss.state.ne.us

State ICPC Administrator

Division of Protection & Safety
Nebraska Department of Health
  & Human Services
P.O. Box 95044
Lincoln, NE 68509-5044
(402) 471-9331
Fax: (402) 471-9034

State Adoption Exchange/State Photolisting Service

Nebraska Adoption Resource
  Exchange
Division of Protection & Safety,
  Nebraska Department of
  Health & Human Services
P.O. Box 95044
Lincoln, NE 68509
(402) 471-9331
www.hhs.state.ne.us/adp/
  adpxchan.htm

State Reunion Registry

Division of Protection & Safety
Nebraska Health & Human
  Services
P.O. Box 95044
Lincoln, NE 68509
(402) 471-9254
www.hhs.state.ne.us/chs/chsindex.
  htm

Regional/District Public Agencies

Nebraska Department of Health
  and Human Services,
Dakota City
1601 Broadway, Courthouse
Dakota City, NE 68731
(402) 987-3445

Nebraska Department of Health
  and Human Services, Alliance
523 Niobrara
Alliance, NE 69301
(308) 762-6300

Nebraska Department of Health
  and Human Services,
  Broken Bow
P.O. Box 486
Broken Bow, NE 68822-0486
(308) 872-2491

Nebraska Department of Health
and Human Services, Fairbury
P.O. Box 556
Fairbury, NE 68352
(402) 729-6168

Nebraska Department of Health
and Human Services, Fremont
P.O. Box 770
Fremont, NE 68025
(402) 721-7010

Nebraska Department of Health
and Human Services, Gering
1030 N Street
Gering, NE 69341-2897
(308) 436-6500

Nebraska Department of Health
and Human Services, Grand
Island
116 South Pine
Grand Island, NE 68802
(308) 385-6100

Nebraska Department of Health
and Human Services, Hastings
P.O. Box 2005
Hastings, NE 68901
(402) 462-1800

Nebraska Department of Health
and Human Services, Imperial
839 Douglas Street
Imperial, NE 69033
(308) 882-4791

Nebraska Department of Health
and Human Services, Kearney
P.O. Box 218
Kearney, NE 68848
(308) 865-5592

Nebraska Department of Health
and Human Services,
Lexington
7100 N. Washington Street
Lexington, NE 68850
(308) 324-6633

Nebraska Department of Health
and Human Services, Lincoln
1050 N Street
Lincoln, NE 68508-3649
(402) 471-7000

Nebraska Department of Health
and Human Services, McCook
502 Norris Avenue, Courthouse
McCook, NE 69001
(308) 345-3892

Nebraska Department of Health
and Human Services,
Nebraska City
1102 Third Avenue
Nebraska City, NE 68410
(402) 873-6671

Nebraska Department of Health
and Human Services, Norfolk
P.O. Box 339
Norfolk, NE 68701-0339
(402) 644-3120

Nebraska Department of Health
and Human Services,
North Platte
200 S. Silber
North Platte, NE 69101-3995
(308) 532-8200

Nebraska Department of Health
and Human Services, Omaha
1313 Farnam-on-the-Mall, State
Office Building
Omaha, NE 68102-1870
(402) 595-2850

Nebraska Department of Health
and Human Services, O'Neill
P.O. Box 669
O'Neill, NE 68763
(402) 336-2750

Nebraska Department of Health
and Human Services, Pierce
111 W. Court, Courthouse
Pierce, NE 68767
(402) 329-6675

Nebraska Department of Health
and Human Services, Seward
P.O. Box 283
Seward, NE 68434
(402) 643-6614

Nebraska Department of Health
and Human Services, Sidney
P.O. Box 357
Sidney, NE 69162
(308) 254-5891

**Licensed Private Adoption
Agencies**

Adoption Links Worldwide
6901 Dodge Street, Suite 101
Omaha, NE 68132
(402) 556-2367
Fax: (402) 556-2401

*Bethany Christian Services
P.O. Box 143
Orange City, IA 51041-0143
(712) 737-4831
Fax: (712) 737-3238
www.bethany.org
info@bethany.org

Catholic Charities
3300 N. 60th Street
Omaha, NE 68104
(402) 554-0520

Catholic Social Service
301 South 70th Street, Suite 300
Lincoln, NE 68510
(402) 489-1834

Child Saving Institute
115 South 46th Street
Omaha, NE 68132
(402) 553-6000

Holt International Children's
Services, Midwest Office
430 South 35th Street, Suite 2
Council Bluffs, IA 51501
(712) 328-1224
Fax: (712) 328-1198
www.holtintl.org
info@holtintl.org

Jewish Family Services
333 South 132nd Street
Omaha, NE 68154
(402) 330-2024

LDS Social Services
517 Walnut Street, Suite 2
Independence, MO 64050
(816) 461-5512

Lutheran Family Services
120 South 24th Street
Omaha, NE 68102
(402) 342-7007

Nebraska Children's Home
Society
3549 Fontenelle Boulevard
Omaha, NE 68104
(402) 451-0787

Nebraska Christian Services, Inc.
2600 South 124th Street
Omaha, NE 68144
(402) 334-3278

Nine Months Adoptions
8676 West 69th Street, Suite 200
Overland Park, KS 66212
Toll Free: (800) 768-7009
www.ninemonths.org
adoptions@ninemonths.org

Adoptive Parent Support Groups

Families Through Adoption
1619 Coventry Lane
Grand Island, NE 68801-7025
(308) 381-8743

Forever Families
1115 N. 130th Street
Omaha, NE 68154

Intercultural Families
2312 S. 88th
Omaha, NE 68124
(402) 390-0278

Kearney Area Adoption
  Association
14960 W. Cedarview Road
Wood River, NE 68883-9320
(308) 583-2402

North American Council on
  Adoptable Children
  Representative
708 W. Koenig Street
Grand Island, NE 68801
(308) 382-4495
Fax: (308) 385-0407

Open Hearts Adoption Support
  Group
4023 S. 81st Street
Lincoln, NE 68506
(402) 483-7634

Stars of David International Inc.
Jewish Family Services - Omaha
  Chapter
333 South 132nd Street
Omaha, NE 68154
(402) 330-2024
Fax: (402) 333-5497
www.starsofdavid.org
starsdavid@aol.com

Voices for Children in Nebraska
7521 Main Street
Omaha, NE 68127
(402) 597-3100

Search Support Groups

Adoptee Liberty Movement
  Association (ALMA)
P.O. Box 5782
Lincoln, NE 68505

Adoption Identity Desire
1808 W. F Street
North Platte, NE 69101-4972

Concerned United Birthparents
  (CUB)
4075 West Airport Road
Grand Island, NE 68803
(308) 384-2112
www.webnations.com/cub
cub@webnations.com

Concerned United Birthparents
  (CUB)
9621 Parker Street
Omaha, NE 68114
(402) 397-6394
www.webnations.com/cub
cub@webnations.com

Midwest Adoption Triad
P.O. Box 37273
Omaha, NE 68137
(402) 895-3706

Kim Lane
9740 Mainwaring Road
Molt, MT 59057
(406) 669-3189
kimlane@3rivers.net

Reunion Registry
4104 Barbara Lane
Missoula, MT 59803
(406) 251-4158

NEBRASKA LAWS RELATED TO ADOPTION: QUESTIONS AND ANSWERS

Can an attorney serve as an intermediary?
This is open to interpretation; the attorney general opinion states that an attorney can legally assist birth parents and adoptive parents in meeting each other. Also, although it is unlawful for anyone to place a child for adoption without a license, this does not prevent an attorney from assisting a birth parent in selecting an adoptive couple.

Is advertising permitted?
No.

Who must consent to the adoption?
1. Both birth parents must consent if married to each other.
2. The birth mother must consent if the child was born out of wedlock.

When can consent be taken from birth mother (father), and how long after the consent is signed can it be revoked?
Consent in a private placement must be done in front of the birth mother's attorney and at least one other witness. The consent is irrevocable when signed; however, until the final adoption, the birth mother can revoke her consent, which then forces a judge to consider whether remaining with the adoptive couple or being returned to the birth mother is in the best interests of the child. Relinquishment to an agency is irrevocable after the agency accepts full responsibility for the child.

What are the birth father's rights?
The unmarried father's rights are not recognized unless he files a notice to claim paternity within five days after the baby's birth. If he wants custody of the child, the court will determine if he can properly care for the child and if it would be in the child's best interest. If it can be shown that the birth father has abandoned the child for at least six months, then his rights can also be terminated.

What fees can adoptive parents pay?
There are no special provisions in the law, but adoptive parents can pay for living, medical, counseling, and one-time legal expenses.

Where does the adoption hearing take place?
The hearing takes place in the court of the county where the adoptive parents live.

How are familial and stepparent adoptions different from nonbiological adoptions?
In stepparent adoptions the home study is sometimes waived.

Can a nonresident finalize an adoption in this state?
No.

Source: Nebraska Revised Statutes Sections 43-101 to 43-160 (1997)

NEVADA

State Adoption Specialist

Division of Child and Family
  Services
Wanda Scott
6171 W. Charleston Boulevard,
  Building 15
Las Vegas, NV 89102
(702) 486-7650
Fax: (702) 486-7626
www.state.nv.us/hr/dcfs/page4.html
wscott@gov.mail.state.nv.us

State ICPC Administrator

Nevada Division of Child and
  Family Services Family Services
Department of Human Resources
711 East Fifth Street
Carson City, NV 89701-5092
(702) 687-4979
Fax: (702) 687-1074

**State Adoption Exchange/State
  Photolisting Service**

Nevada Adoption Exchange
Division of Child and Family
  Services
610 Belrose Street
Las Vegas, NV 89107
(702) 486-7800
www.adopt.org/adopt/photo.html

Northwest Adoption Exchange
600 Stewart Street, Suite 1313
Seattle, WA 98101
(206) 441-6822
Fax: (206) 441-7281
Toll Free: (800) 927-9411
www.nwae.org
nwae@nwresource.org

State Reunion Registry

Division of Child and Family
  Services
Adoption Registry
711 E. Fifth Street, Capitol
  Complex
Carson City, NV 89710-1002
(702) 684-4415

**Regional/District Public
  Agencies**

Nevada Division of Child and
  Family Services, Battle
  Mountain
145 E. 2nd Street
Battle Mountain, NV 89820
(775) 635-5237

Nevada Division of Child and
  Family Services, Carson
1572 E. College Parkway,
  Suite 161
Carson City, NV 89710
(775) 687-4943

Nevada Division of Child and
  Family Services, Elko
3920 E. Idaho
Elko, NV 89801
(775) 738-2534

Nevada Division of Child and
  Family Services, Ely
725 Avenue K
Ely, NV 89301
(775) 289-1640

Nevada Division of Child and
  Family Services, Fallon
1735 Kaiser Street
Fallon, NV 89406
(775) 423-8566

Nevada Division of Child and
  Family Services, Hawthorne
1000 C Street, P.O. Box 1508
Hawthorne, NV 89415
(775) 945-3602

Nevada Division of Child and
  Family Services, Henderson
145 Panama Street
Henderson, NV 89014
(702) 486-6770

Nevada Division of Child and
  Family Services, Las Vegas
  Adoption Unit
610 Belrose Street
Las Vegas, NV 89107
(702) 486-7800

Nevada Division of Child and
Family Services, Lovelock
535 Western Street
Lovelock, NV 89419
(775) 273-7157

Nevada Division of Child and
Family Services, Reno
Adoption Unit
2655 Enterprise Road, Building 3
Reno, NV 89512
(775) 688-2367

Nevada Division of Child and
Family Services, Tonopah
565 N. Main Street
Tonopah, NV 89049-1491
(775) 482-6626

Nevada Division of Child and
Family Services, Winnemucca
475 W. Haskell, #7
Winnemucca, NV 89446
(775) 623-6555

Nevada Division of Child and
Family Services, Yerington
14 Pacific Street
Yerington, NV 89447
(775) 463-3151

**Licensed Private Adoption
Agencies**

Catholic Charities of Southern
Nevada
531 N. 30th Street
Las Vegas, NV 89101
(702) 385-3351

Catholic Community Services of
Northern Nevada
500 East 4th Street, P.O. Box
5099
Reno, NV 89512
(775) 322-4491

Jewish Family Service Agency
3909 S. Maryland Parkway,
Suite 205
Las Vegas, NV 89119
(702) 732-0304

LDS Social Services
513 S. Ninth Street
Las Vegas, NV 89101
(702) 385-1072

New Hope Child and Family
1515 E. Tropicana, Suite 570
Las Vegas, NV 89119
(702) 734-9665
www.newhopekids.org
info@newhopekids.org

New Hope Child and Family
440 Ridge Street
Reno, NV 89502
(775) 323-0122
www.newhopekids.org
info@newhopekids.org

New Hope Child and Family
Agency
2611 N.E. 125th St.
Seattle, WA 98125
(206) 363-1800
Fax: (206) 363-0318
www.newhopekids.org
info@newhopekids.org

**Adoptive Parent Support
Groups**

Families for Adoption
1858 Citation
Las Vegas, NV 89118

Families for Russian and
Ukrainian Adoptions
1700 County Road, Suite C
Minden, NV 89423
(702) 782-9192
kbaggett@STBaggett.com

North American Council on
Adoptable Children
Representative
4125 Wendy Lane
Las Vegas, NV 89115
(702) 643-7574

Southern Nevada Adoption
Association and North
American Council on
Adoptable
Children Representative
1316 Saylor Way
Las Vegas, NV 89108
(702) 385-5331

Southern Nevada Adoption
Association and North
American Council on
Adoptable
Children Representative
2300 Theresa Avenue
North Las Vegas, NV 89030
(702) 649-8464

The Adoption Exchange -
Nevada Office
3930 East Patrick Lane, Suite 120
Las Vegas, NV 89120
(702) 436-6335
Fax: (702) 436-6304

Search Support Groups

Adoptee Liberty Movement
Association (ALMA)
P.O. Box 40644
Reno, NV 89504

Adoptee Liberty Movement
Association (ALMA)
P.O. Box 34211
Las Vegas, NV 89133

International Soundex Reunion
Registry
P.O. Box 2312
Carson City, NV 89702
(775) 882-7755
www.plumsite.com/isrr/

NEVADA LAWS RELATED TO ADOPTION: QUESTIONS AND ANSWERS

If you live in Nevada but adopt in another state, or if you live in another state and adopt a child from Nevada, you must pay the ICPC fee of $1,000.

Can an attorney serve as an intermediary?
Yes, but no fee can be charged for the service.

Is advertising permitted?
No.

Who must consent to the adoption?
1. Both birth parents
2. An agency, if involved

When can consent be taken from birth mother (father), and how long after the consent is signed can it be revoked?
The birth father can sign a consent before the child's birth if he is not married to the birth mother. The birth mother's consent cannot be given until seventy-two hours after birth. Consent cannot be revoked, and consents must be taken in front of a licensed social worker, preferably a Department of Child and Family Services caseworker.

What are the birth father's rights?
His consent is required. If he wants to parent the child and comes forward in a timely fashion, he has the right to parent unless it can be shown that it would not be in the child's best interests.

What fees can adoptive parents pay?
Reasonable living expenses can be paid, and an affidavit of all medical fees and other expenses paid must be submitted to the court.

Unlike other states, Nevada has a law that makes it illegal for the birth parent to receive money for medical expenses or other necessary expenses from an adoptive parent if she has no true intention of placing the child for adoption. Certainly every birth mother has the right to change her mind; she just cannot use adoption plans as a means of having her bills paid for by an adoptive couple.

Where does the adoption hearing take place?
The hearing takes place in the district court where the adoptive parents live or where the child lives.

How are familial and stepparent adoptions different from nonbiological adoptions?
The court may waive the home study requirement.

Can a nonresident finalize an adoption in this state?
No. You must have resided in Nevada for six months before the adoption.

SOURCE: NEVADA REVISED STATUTES: VOL. 11, SECTIONS 127.005 TO 127.420 (1997)

NEW HAMPSHIRE

State Adoption Specialist

New Hampshire Division for
   Children, Youth and Families
Department of Health and
   Human Services
Catherine Atkins

129 Pleasant Street, Brown
   Building
Concord, NH 03301
(603) 271-4707
Fax: (603) 271-4729
catkins@dhhs.state.nh.us

State ICPC Administrator

New Hampshire Department of
   Health & Human Services
Division for Children, Youth, &
   Families
129 Pleasant Street
Concord, NH 03301
(603) 271-4708
Fax: (603) 271-4729

State Adoption Exchange/State Photolisting Service

New Hampshire Division for
  Children, Youth and Families
Department of Health and
  Human Services
129 Pleasant Street, Brown
  Building
Concord, NH 03301
(603) 271-4707
Fax: (603) 271-4729
www.adopt.org
catkins@dhhs.state.nh.us

Licensed Private Adoption Agencies

Adoptive Families for Children
26 Fairview Street
Keene, NH 03431
(603) 357-4456
Fax: (603) 352-8543

Bethany Christian Services
P.O. Box 320, 183 High Street
Candia, NH 03034-0320
(603) 483-2886
www.bethany.org
info@bethany.org

Boston Adoption Bureau, Inc.
14 Beacon Street, Suite 620
Boston, MA 02108
(617) 277-1336
Toll Free: (800) 338-2224

Casey Family Services
Building 2, 105 Loudon Rd
Concord, NH 03301
(603) 224-8909

Child and Family Services of New
  Hampshire
99 Hanover Street
Manchester, NH 03105-0448
(603) 668-1920
Fax: (603) 668-6260
Toll Free: (800) 640-6486

Creative Advocates for Children
  and Families
817 Lincoln Street #209
Manchester, NH 03103
(603) 623-5006

LDS Social Services
547 Amherst Street, Suite 404
Nashua, NH 03063-4000
(603) 889-0148
Fax: (603) 889-4358
Toll Free: (800) 735-0419

Lutheran Social Services of New
  England
261 Sheep Davis Road, Suite A-1
Concord, NH 03301
(603) 224-8111
Fax: (603) 224-5473
www.adoptlss.org/
Intladopt@aol.com

New Hampshire Catholic
  Charities, Inc.
215 Myrtle Street
Manchester, NH 03105-0686
(603) 669-3030
Fax: (603) 626-1252
Toll Free: (800) 562-5249

New Hope Christian Services
210 Silk Farm Road
Concord, NH 03301
(603) 225-0992
Fax: (603) 225-7400
NewhopeAd@aol.com

Vermont Children's Aid Society
79 Weaver Street, P.O. Box 127
Winooski, VT 05404-0127
(802) 655-0006
Fax: (802) 655-0073
www.vermontchildrensaid.org/
  children/adoption.htm

Vermont Children's Aid Society
128 Merchants Row, Room 501
Rutland, VT 05701
(802) 773-8555
www.vermontchildrensaid.org/chil
  dren/adoption.htm

Wide Horizons for Children
11 Powers Street, P.O. Box 176
Milford, NH 03053
(603) 672-3000
Fax: (603) 672-7182
www.whfc.org
info@whfc.org

Adoptive Parent Support Groups

Casey Family Services
105 Loudon Road, Building 2
Concord, NH 03301
(603) 224-8909

Families with Children from
  China
5 Burnett Street
Nashua, NH 03060-4931
sunny@pop.taic.net

Manchester Concern for
  Adoption
11 Davis Road
Merrimack, NH 03054
(603) 429-2751

New Hampshire Division for
  Children, Youth and Families
40 Terrill Park
Concord, NH 03301
(603) 271-6202

New Hampshire Foster and
  Adoptive Parent Association
  and North American Council
  on Adoptable Children
  Representative
9 Webster Street
Nashua, NH 03060
(603) 594-4112
MJMacKay@email.msn.com

Open Door Society of New
  Hampshire, Inc.
P.O. Box 792
Derry, NH 03038
(603) 679-1099

Ours for a United Response of
  New England
347 Candia Road
Chester, NH 03036
(617) 967-4648

Vermont Children's Aid Society
  Lifetime Adoption Project
P.O. Box 127
Winooski, VT 05404-0127
(802) 655-0006
Toll Free: (800) 479-0015

Search Support Groups

Casey Family Services
105 Loudon Road, Building 2
Concord, NH 03301
(603) 224-8909

Circle of Hope
P.O. Box 127
Somersworth, NH 03878
(603) 692-5917

Living in Search of Answers
Box 215
Gilsum, NH 03448-0215
(603) 357-3762

Pieces of Yesterday
P.O. Box 1703
Manchester, NH 03105

NEW HAMPSHIRE LAWS RELATED TO ADOPTION: QUESTIONS AND
    ANSWERS

Can an attorney serve as an intermediary?
Yes.

Is advertising permitted?
Yes.

Who must consent to the adoption?
1. Both birth parents must consent if married to each other.
2. The involved agency must consent.
3. If the birth mother is under eighteen years old, then her parents may be required to
sign a consent.

**When can consent be taken from birth mother (father), and how long after the con-
sent is signed can it be revoked?**
Consent cannot be taken until seventy-two hours after the child's birth. Consent can be
withdrawn until the final decree if the court finds that it is in the best interests of the child
not to remain with the adoptive couple but to be returned to the birth parent.

What are the birth father's rights?
A birth father has the right to a hearing to prove paternity if he is named by the birth
mother, has filed a notice with the Office of Child Support and Enforcement that he is the
father, or if he is living with the birth mother or child and providing support. He must
request such a hearing within thirty days after receiving notice of the adoption proceeding,
and if he does not do so then he forfeits all parental right to the child.

    If the birth father is not married to the birth mother and has not met the above pater-
nity requirements, then his consent is not required.

What fees can adoptive parents pay?
The adoptive parents must file a statement with the court listing all legal fees and medical
expenses paid, as well as living expenses paid for the birth parents.

Where does the adoption hearing take place?
The hearing takes place in the Probate Court where the adoptive parents or adoptee lives.

How are familial and stepparent adoptions different from nonbiological adoptions?
The court may waive the home study requirement.

Can a nonresident finalize an adoption in this state?
No. There is a six-month residency requirement for the adoptive parent or the child,
unless the child is in the legal care of a licensed adoption agency in New Hampshire. If
that is the case, then the adoption can be finalized in the county in which the agency
maintains its main office.

SOURCE: NEW HAMPSHIRE REVISED STATUTES SECTIONS 170-B: 1 TO 170- B: 26 (1998)

NEW JERSEY

State Adoption Specialist

New Jersey Division of Youth and
Family Services
Office of Adoption Operations
Eileen Crummy
50 East State Street, 5th Floor
Trenton, NJ 08625-0717
(609) 984-2380
Fax: (609) 984-5449
*www.state.nj.us/humanservices/
adoption/adopt.html*
ecrummy@dhs.state.nj.us

State ICPC Administrator

New Jersey Division of Youth &
Family Services
Interstate Services Unit
Capital Center, 7th Floor SE, 50
East State Street
Trenton, NJ 08625
(609) 292-0010
Fax: (609) 633-6931

State Adoption Exchange/State Photolisting Service

Division of Youth and Family
Services Adoption Exchange
Adoption Operations
50 E. State Street, P.O. Box 717
Trenton, NJ 08625
(609) 984-5453
*www.state.nj.us/humanservices/
adoption/childsplash.htm*

State Reunion Registry

Division of Youth and Family
Services
Adoption Registry Unit 966
50 E. State St., PO Box 717
Trenton, NJ 08625
(609) 292-9139
*www.state.nj.us/humanservices/
adoption_registry.html*

Regional/District Public Agencies

New Jersey Division of Youth and
Family Services - Adoption
Resource Center -
Central
3131 Princeton Pike, Suite 202
Lawrenceville, NJ 08648
(609) 219-6565
Toll Free: (800) 392-2735

New Jersey Division of Youth and
Family Services - Adoption
Resource Center -
Essex
153 Halsey Street, 3rd Floor
Newark, NJ 07102
(973) 648-7490
Toll Free: (800) 392-2843

New Jersey Division of Youth and
Family Services - Adoption
Resource Center -
Metropolitan
100 Metroplex Drive, Suite 106
Edison, NJ 08817-2683
(732) 819-7272

New Jersey Division of Youth and
Family Services - Adoption
Resource Center -
Northern
22 Mill Street, 1st Floor
Paterson, NJ 07501
(973) 742-0063

New Jersey Division of Youth and
Family Services - Adoption
Resource Center -
Southern
2 Echelon Plaza, 2nd Floor, Suite
210
Voorhees, NJ 08043
(609) 770-5400
Toll Free: (800) 982-7395

Licensed Private Adoption Agencies

Adoption ARC, Inc.
4701 Pine Street, J-7
Philadelphia, PA 19143
(215) 844-1082
Fax: (215) 842-9881
Toll Free: (800) 884-4004
www.adoptionarc.com
taralaw@aol.com

Adoption Services Associates
5370 Prue Road
San Antonio, TX 78240
(210) 699-6094
Toll Free: (800) 648-1807
www.childadopt.com
adopt@connecti.com or
index@childadopt.com

Adoptions From the Heart
451 Woodland Avenue
Cherry Hill, NJ 08002
(856) 665-5655
www.adoptionsfromtheheart.org
*adoption@adoptionsfromthe-
heart.org*

*Adoptions International Inc.
601 S. 10th Street
Philadelphia, PA 19147
(215) 238-9057
Fax: (215) 238-9071
*www.rainbowkids.com/
adoptionsinternational72.html*
HWall334@aol.com

American Adoption
100 S. Grand Avenue, Suite 410
Kansas City, MO 64106
Toll Free: (800) 875-2229
*www.americanadoptions.com/
adoptions@americanadoptions.com*

Bethanna
Branch Office
348 E. Walnut Lane
Philadelphia, PA 19144
(215) 849-8815

Bethanna
1030 Second Street Pike
South Hampton, PA 18966
(215) 355-6500

Bethany Christian Services
550 Pinetown Road, Suite 100
Fort Washington, PA 19034-2606
(215) 628-0202
Fax: (215) 628-2944
Toll Free: (800) 215-0702
www.bethany.org
info@bethany.org

Bethany Christian Services
1120 Goffle Road
Hawthorne, NJ 07506-2024
(973) 427-2566
Fax: (973) 427-9204
www.bethany.org
info@bethany.org

Bethany Christian Services
739 South White Horse Pike,
Suite 5
Audobon, NJ 08106-1659
(856) 672-9780
Fax: (856) 672-9782
www.bethany.org
info@bethany.org

Better Living Services
560 Springfield Avenue, Suite C,
P.O. Box 2969
Westfield, NJ 07090-2969
(908) 654-0277

Brookwood Child Care
25 Washington Street
Brooklyn, NY 11201
(718) 596-5555

Catholic Charities, Diocese of
Metuchen
Maternity and Adoption Program
319 Maple Street
Perth Amboy, NJ 08861
(732) 324-8200

Catholic Charities, Diocese of
Trenton
115 W. Pearl Street
Burlington, NJ 08016
(609) 386-6221

Catholic Community Services of
Newark
499 Belgrove Drive, Suite 2
Kearny, NJ 07032
(201) 991-3770

Catholic Family and Community
Services
476 17th Avenue
Paterson, NJ 07501
(973) 523-9595

Catholic Guardian Society of
New York
1011 First Avenue
New York, NY 10022
(212) 371-1000

Catholic Home Bureau for
Dependent Children
1011 First Avenue
New York, NY 10022
(212) 371-1000

Catholic Social Services
227 North Eighteenth Street
Philadelphia, PA 19103
(215) 854-7055

Catholic Social Services of the
Diocese of Camden
810 Montrose Street
Vineland, NJ 08360
(609) 691-1841

Child and Home Study Associates
1029 Providence Road
Media, PA 19063
(610) 565-1544

Children of the World
685 Bloomfield Avenue, Suite 201
Verona, NJ 07044
(973) 239-0100
Fax: (973) 239-3443

*Children's Aid and Family
Services, Inc.
200 Robin Road
Paramus, NJ 07652
(201) 261-2800
Fax: (201) 487-1913
www.cafsnj.org
info@cafsnj.org

Children's Aid and Family
Services, Inc.
185 Ridgedale Avenue
Cedar Knolls, NJ 07927
(973) 285-0165
Fax: (973) 285-1679
www.cafsnj.org
info@cafsnj.org

Children's Aid and Family
Services, Inc.
60 Evergreen Place
East Orange, NJ 07019
(973) 673-6454
www.cafsnj.org
info@cafsnj.org

Children's Aid Society
Adoption and Foster Home
Division
150 E. 45th Street
New York, NY 10017
(212) 949-4961

Children's Choice, Inc.
151 Fries Mill Road,
Suite 205-206
Turnersville, NJ 08012
(609) 228-5223

Children's Home Society of
New Jersey
51 Main Street
Clinton, NJ 08809
(908) 852-5825

Children's Home Society of New
Jersey
635 South Clinton Avenue
Trenton, NJ 08611
(609) 695-6274

Chosen Children Adoption
Services, Inc.
5427 Bardstown Road, Suite One
Louisville, KY 40291
(502) 231-1336
Fax: (502) 231-4098
www.iglou.com/kac/chosen.htm

Christian Homes for Children
275 State Street
Hackensack, NJ 07601
(201) 342-4235

Downey Side Families for Youth
146 U.S. Route 130
Bordentown, NJ 08505
(609) 291-2784

Family and Children's Service
1900 Route 35
Oakhurst, NJ 07755
(732) 531-9111

Family and Children's Services
40 North Avenue
Elizabeth, NJ 07207
(908) 352-7474

Family Focus Adoption Services
54-40 Little Neck Parkway, Suite 4
Little Neck, NY 11362
(718) 224-1919
Fax: (718) 225-8360

Family Options
P.O. Box 447
Lincroft, NJ 07738
(732) 946-0880

Friends in Adoption
44 South Street, P.O. Box 1228
Middletown Springs, VT 05757-
1228
(802) 235-2373
www.capital.net/com/fia
fia@vermontel.com

Gladney Center for Adoption
2300 Hemphill Street
Fort Worth, TX 76110
(817) 922-6088
Fax: (817) 922-6040
Toll Free: (800) 452-3639
www.gladney.org
info@gladney.org

Golden Cradle
1050 N. Kings Highway,
Suite 201
Cherry Hill, NJ 08034
(856) 667-2229
Fax: (856) 667-2229
www.goldencradle.org
adoptions@goldencradle.org

Graham-Windham Child Care
33 Irving Place
New York, NY 10003
(212) 529-6445, Ext: 384

Growing Families
178 South Street
Freehold, NJ 07728
(732) 431-4330
Fax: (908) 431-3884

Harlem-Dowling Children
 Services
2090 Adam Clayton Powell, Jr.,
 Boulevard (7th Avenue)
New York, NY 10027
(212) 749-3656

Holt International Children's
 Services
340 Scotch Road, 2nd Floor
Trenton, NJ 08628
(609) 882-4972
www.holtintl.org
info@holtintl.org

Homestudies and Adoption
 Placement Services (HAPS), Inc.
668 American Legion Drive
Teaneck, NJ 07666
(201) 836-5554
Fax: (201) 836-0204
www.haps.org
marie@haps.org

Jewish Child Care Association of
 New York
120 Wall Street
New York, NY 10005
(212) 425-3333

Jewish Family and Children's
 Service of Philadelphia Inc.
10125 Verree Road, #200
Philadelphia, PA 19116
(215) 698-9950
Fax: (215) 698-2148
www.voicenet.com/~adoption
adoption@voicenet.com

Jewish Family and Children's
 Services
1301 Springdale Road, Suite 150
Cherry Hill, NJ 08003-2729
(609) 424-1333
www.voicenet.com/~adoption
adoption@voicenet.com

Jewish Family Services of Central
 New Jersey
655 Westfield Avenue
Elizabeth, NJ 07208
(908) 352-8375

Jewish Family Services of Metro
 West
256 Columbia Turnpike,
 Suite 105
Florham Park, NJ 07932-0825
(973) 674-4210

Jewish Family Services of
 Monmouth County
705 Summerfield Avenue
Asbury Park, NJ 07712
(732) 774-6886

Juvenile Justice Center of
 Philadelphia
100 West Coulter Street
Philadelphia, PA 19144
(215) 849-2112

LDS Social Services
22 IBM Road, Suite 205-B
Poughkeepsie, NY 12601
(914) 462-1288

Lutheran Social Ministries of New
 Jersey
120 Route 156
Yardville, NJ 08620
(609) 585-0303

Marian Adoption Services
600 N. Bethlehem Pike
Ambler, PA 19002
(215) 283-8522
Toll Free: (800) 585-9944
MASAdopt@aol.com

New Beginnings Family and
 Children's Services, Inc.
141 Willis Avenue
Mineola, NY 11501
(516) 747-2204
Fax: (516) 747-2505
www.new-beginnings.org
newbeginn@aol.com

Reaching Out Thru International
 Adoption
312 South Lincoln Avenue
Cherry Hill, NJ 08002
(609) 321-0777

Seedlings, Inc.
1 Tall Timber Drive
Morristown, NJ 07960
(973) 605-1188
Fax: (973) 538-7987
Seedadopt@aol.com

Small World Adoption Programs,
 Inc.
401 Bonna Spring Drive
Hermitage, TN 37076
(615) 883-4372
Fax: (615) 885-7582
Toll Free: (800) 544-5083

Small World Agency
New Jersey Branch Office
257 West Broad Street
Palmyra, NJ 08065-1463
(609) 829-2769

Spence-Chapin Services to
 Families and Children
Branch Office
57 Union Place
Summit, NJ 07901
(908) 522-0043

Tabor Children's Services
601 New Britain Road
Doylestown, PA 18901-4248
(215) 842-4800

The New York Foundling
 Hospital
590 Avenue of the Americas
New York, NY 10011
(212) 727-6810

United Family and Children's
 Society
305 W. Seventh Street
Plainfield, NJ 07060
(908) 755-4848

Voice for International
 Development and Adoption
 (VIDA)
354 Allen Street
Hudson, NY 12534
(518) 828-4527
Fax: (518) 828-0688
members.aol.com/vidaadopt/
 vida.html
vidaadopt@aol.com

Welcome House of the Pearl S.
 Buck Foundation
P.O. Box 181, Green Hills Farm
Perkasie, PA 18944
(215) 249-1516
Fax: (215) 249-9657
Toll Free: (800) 220-2825
www.pearl-s-buck.org
rrosenth@pearl-s-buck.org

Wide Horizons For Children
Main Office
38 Edge Hill Road
Waltham, MA 02451
(781) 894-5330
Fax: (781) 899-2769
www.whfc.org/
info@whfc.org

Women's Christian Alliance
1610-16 North Broad Street
Philadelphia, PA 19121
(215) 236-9911

World Child
P.O. Box 629
Roosevelt, NJ 08555
(609) 426-8136

Youth Consultation Services
284 Broadway
Newark, NJ 07104
(973) 482-8411

Adoptive Parent Support Groups

Adoption Information Service, Inc.
12 Roberts Street
Rockaway, NJ 07866
(973) 586-1552

Adoptive Mothers of
 Essex County
40 Burnett Terrace
Maplewood, NJ 07040
(973) 763-9220

Adoptive Parents Committee
 of New Jersey
P.O. Box 725
Ridgewood, NJ 07451
(201) 689-0995

Adoptive Parents for Open
 Records
625 St. Marks Avenue
Westfield, NJ 07090
(908) 233-2768

Adoptive Single Parents
 of New Jersey
163 Hunter Ave
Sanwood, NJ 07023
(732) 906-3276

Adoptive Single Parents
 of New Jersey
79 Old Army Road
Bernardsville, NJ 07924
(908) 766-6281

Adoptive Single Parents
 of New Jersey
73 Tristan Road
Clifton, NJ 07013
(201) 742-9441

Camden County FACES
130 S. Mansfield Boulevard
Cherry Hill, NJ 08034
(609) 784-1081

Camp Se Jong
79 South Street
Demarest, NJ 07627
(973) 784-1081

Central New Jersey Singles
 Network of Adoptive Parents
P.O. Box 1012
Flemington, NJ 08822
(908) 782-5500

Comprehensive Mental Health
 Services
2480 Pennington Road
Pennington, NJ 08534
(609) 737-7797

Concerned Parents for Adoption
 and North American Council
 on Adoptable Children
State Representative
12 Reed Drive North
Princeton Junction, NJ 08550
(609) 799-3269
lebfrom nj@aol.com

Families for Russian and
 Ukrainian Adoptions
904 Cain Court
Belle Meade, NJ 08502
(908) 431-0318
community.nj.com/cc/Adoption
rucci_m@ix.netcom.com

Families United by Adoption
245 Prospect Drive
Brick, NJ 08724
(908) 840-2277

Jersey Shore Families by Adoption
507 Laurelwood Drive
Lanoka Harbor, NJ 08734
(609) 693-4387

LAPA Northern New Jersey, Inc.
P.O. Box 2666
Fairlawn, NJ 07410
(201) 438-9214
www.lapa-nnj.com

Latin America Parents
 Association
Northern New Jersey Inc.
P.O. Box 77
Emerson, NJ 07630

Latin American Adoptive
 Families NJ/PA
P.O. Box 573
Woodbury, NJ 08096
(609) 384-2764
laaf-nj/pa@aol.com

Links
91 Carlton Avenue
Washington, NJ 07882
(908) 689-5932

Morristown Adoption
 Support Group
3 Harding Terrace at Fenwick
Morristown, NJ 07690-3252
(973) 267-8698

New Jersey Adoptive Parents
 Support Group
20 Jonathan Drive
Sewell, NJ 08080
(609) 863-1166

New Jersey Friends of Holt
43 Fairfield Road
Princeton, NJ 08540

New Jersey Friends Through
 Adoption
30 Endicott Drive
Great Meadows, NJ 07838
(908) 637-8828

Rainbow Families
670 Oakley Place
Oradell, NJ 07649
(201) 261-1148

Roots & Wings
P.O. Box 577
Hackettstown, NJ 07840
(908) 813-8252
www.adopt-usa.com/
rootsandwings
adoption@interactive.net

Singles Network of Adoptive
 Parents
8 N. Whittesbog Road
Browns Mills, NJ 08015
(609) 893-7875

Stars of David International Inc.
Chaverim Chapter
205 Meadow Lane
Woodbury, NJ 08096-1839
(609) 384-2764
www.starsofdavid.org
snjstars@aol.com

Stars of David International Inc.
Central New Jersey Chapter
P.O. Box 471
Holmdel, NJ 07733
(908) 706-9424
www.starsofdavid.org/
starsdavid@aol.com

Stars of David International Inc.
Brunswick Area Chapter
61 David Court
Dayton, NJ 08810
(732) 445-2269
Fax: (732) 445-3571
www.starsofdavid.org
willige@rci.rutgers.edu

Stars of David International Inc.
North Jersey Chapter
54 Joyce Lane
Wayne, NJ 07470
(201) 694-7229
www.starsofdavid.org
starsdavid@aol.com

Stars of David of the Delaware
Valley
135 Forest Hills Drive
Voorhees, NJ 08043
www.starsofdavid.org/
starsdavid@aol.com

Today's Adoptive Families
30 Manchester Way
Burlington, NJ 08016
(609) 386-7237

Search Support Groups

Adoptee Liberty Movement
Association (ALMA)
P.O. Box 1825
West Caldwell, NJ 07007
(973) 243-0101

Adoption Crossroads
85 Paramus Road
Paramus, NJ 07652
(201) 843-9898

Adoption Reunion Coalition of
New Jersey
15 Fir Place
Hazlet, NJ 07730
(201) 843-9898

Adoption Reunion Coalition of
the Jersey Shore
3047 Governors Crossing
Wall, NJ 07719
(732) 739-9365

Adoption Support Group of
Central New Jersey
P.O. Box 362
Belle Mead, NJ 08502
(908) 874-8983

Adoption Support Group of
Southern New Jersey
32 Trotters Lane
Smithville, NJ 08201
(609) 748-8126

Adoption Support Network
505 W. Hamilton Avenue, #207
Linwood, NJ 08221
(609) 653-4242

American Adoption Congress
State Representative
133 N. Burgee Drive
Little Egg Harbor, NJ 08087
(609) 296-7258
Fax: (609) 296-1838
SHEHANS@worldnet.att.net

American Adoption Congress
State Representative
3 Harding Terrace at Fenwick
Morristown, NJ 07960-3252
(973) 267-8698
Fax: (973) 267-3356
JaneNast@compuserve.com

Angles and Extensions
Box 7247
Sussex, NJ 07461
(973) 875-9869

New Jersey Coalition for
Openness in Adoption
29 Hill Street
Morristown, NJ 07960
(973) 292-2440

New Jersey Coalition for
Openness in Adoption
55 High Oaks Drive
Watchung, NJ 07060

New Jersey Coalition for
Openness in Adoption
206 Laurel Place
Laurel Springs, NJ 08021
(609) 784-7532

Origins
289 E. Halsey Road
Parsippany, NJ 07054
(973) 884-1695
DLeMasson@prodigy.net

Origins
P.O. Box 556
Whippany, NJ 07981
(973) 428-9683

Sharing Hope
55 Highland Drive
Barnegat, NJ 08005
(609) 698-7121

NEW JERSEY LAWS RELATED TO ADOPTION: QUESTIONS AND ANSWERS

Can an attorney serve as an intermediary?
Yes, but he or she cannot be paid for such services.

Is advertising permitted?
Yes.

Who must consent to the adoption?
Both birth parents must consent.

When can consent be taken from birth mother (father), and how long after the consent is signed can it be revoked?
In an agency adoption, a surrender of parental rights can be taken seventy-two hours after the child's birth and is irrevocable. In a nonagency independent adoption, the birth

mother can appear before a judge and have her rights terminated. If she does not do that, then her parental rights are not terminated until the first court hearing, which is usually held sixty to ninety days after the adoption petition is filed. Each birth parent must receive notice of this first hearing. During this time the birth parents can revoke their consent and have the child returned to them. New Jersey, unlike other states, does not consider whether it would be in the child's best interests to remain with the adoptive couple unless the parental rights have been terminated.

What are the birth father's rights?
If the birth father cannot be determined or if the birth mother refuses to name him, and the court is unable to determine who he is, his consent is not needed and his parental rights are terminated at the first hearing held two to three months after the adoption is filed. In an independent adoption, notice must be sent by certified mail to a known birth father of the adoption hearing. Some judges want the birth father served with the notice by a process server. If the known birth father does not respond within thirty days and does not appear at the first hearing, then his rights are terminated. The adoption is finalized approximately seven months after the first hearing.

In an agency adoption, the adoption complaint is filed six months after placement and a final hearing is held within thirty days after filing of the complaint. If the birth father has not signed an agency surrender, then his rights can be terminated at the final hearing if he has received notice of the hearing and not responded. An agency can terminate his rights sooner by scheduling a termination hearing at any time after the birth and providing him notice of the hearing. As long as he does not object in writing or appear at the hearing, his rights are terminated.

In both an agency or private adoption, a birth parent's rights can be terminated by the court if it can be established that the birth parent has abandoned his or her rights to the child. This can be established by showing that the birth parent had no contact with or provided no emotional or monetary support for the child during the six-month period prior to placement.

What fees can adoptive parents pay?
Legal, medical, counseling, and living expenses can be paid. However, all expenses must be submitted to the court before the final adoption. In an independent adoption, judges only permit limited expenses to be paid, and may not approve certain items.

Where does the adoption hearing take place?
The hearing take place in the court of the county where the adoptive parents or birth parents reside, or where the agency is located.

How are familial and stepparent adoptions different from nonbiological adoptions?
The court can waive a home study if the child has resided with the adoptive parent for a period of at least six months.

Can a nonresident finalize an adoption in this state?
Yes, but only through an agency.

SOURCE: NEW JERSEY REVISED STATUTES SECTIONS 9:3-38 TO 9 3-54 (1997)

NEW MEXICO

State Adoption Specialist

Central Adoption Unit
New Mexico Children, Youth and
  Families Department
Steve Archuleta
P.O. Drawer 5160, PERA
  Building, Room 254
Santa Fe, NM 87502-5160
(505) 827-8456
Fax: (505) 827-8480
cyf_abq.state.nm.us/adopt/
ninos.html

State ICPC Administrator

New Mexico Children, Youth,
  and Families Department
Protective Services Division
P.O. Drawer 5160
Santa Fe, NM 87502-5160
(505) 827-8457
Fax: (505) 827-8480

State Adoption Exchange/State
  Photolisting Service

New Mexico Adoption Exchange
New Mexico Children, Youth and
  Families Department
P.O. Drawer 5160
Santa Fe, NM 87502
(505) 827-8422
cyf_abq.state.nm.us/adopt/
ninos.html
clgarcia@cyf_abq.state.nm.us

Licensed Private Adoption
  Agencies

A.M.O.R. Adoptions, Inc.
3700 Coors Boulevard, N.W.,
  Suite F
Albuquerque, NM 87120
(505) 831-0888
Fax: (505) 831-2800
Toll Free: (877) 712-2667
www.AMORADoptions.com
info@AMORADoptions.com

Adoption Assistance Agency
10609 San Antonio, N.E.
Albuquerque, NM 87122
(505) 821-7779
Fax: (501) 821-4111
Toll Free: (888) 422-3678
www.flash.net/~adoptast
adoptast@flash.net

Adoptions Plus
6022 Constitution Avenue, N.E.,
  Suite 5
Albuquerque, NM 87110
(505) 262-0446

Catholic Social Services, Inc.
4985 Airport Road
Santa Fe, NM 87505-0443
(505) 424-9789

Chaparral Maternity and
  Adoptions
1503 University Boulevard, N.E.
Albuquerque, NM 87102
(505) 243-2586
Fax: (505) 243-0446

Child Rite/AASK
4801 Indian School Road,
  Suite 204
Albuquerque, NM 87106
(505) 797-4191

Child-Rite/AASK
126 Cavalry Road
Taos, NM 87571
(505) 758-0343

Child-Rite/AASK
2008 Rosina Street
Santa Fe, NM 87505
(505) 988-5177

Christian Child Placement
  Services
1356 NM 236
Portales, NM 88130
(505) 356-4232

Families for Children
6209 Hendrix N.E.
Albuquerque, NM 87110
(505) 881-4200

La Familia Placement Services
Suite 103, 707 Broadway N.E.
Albuquerque, NM 87102
(505) 766-9361

LDS Social Services
925 Cannery Court
Farmington, NM 87401
(505) 327-6123

LDS Social Services
3811 Atrisco Drive, N.W., Suite A
Albuquerque, NM 87120
(505) 836-5947

*Rainbow House International
19676 Highway 85
Belen, NM 87002
(505) 861-1234
Fax: (505) 864-8420
www.rhi.org
rainbow@rhi.org

Triad Adoption Services, Inc.
2811 Indian School Road, N.E.
Albuquerque, NM 87106
(505) 266-0456

Adoptive Parent Support
  Groups

Adoptive Families of Resolve
P.O. Box 13194
Albuquerque, NM 87192
(505) 242-4420

Las Cruces Adoptive Parents
1733 Imperial Ridge
Las Cruces, NM 88001
(505) 522-6543

New Mexico Foster Parent
  Association
1516 Sanford Dr., N.E.
Albuquerque, NM 87106
(505) 266-7548

North American Council on
  Adoptable Children
  Representative
88 Manzano Spring Road
Tijeras, NM 87059
(505) 281-6537
members.aol.com/nacac

Parents of Intercultural Adoption
P.O. Box 91175
Albuquerque, NM 87199
(505) 296-6782

Santa Fe Rainbow Families
Route 9, #58A
Santa Fe, NM 87505
(505) 983-2073

Special Needs Adoptive Parents
  (SNAP)
9800 Academy Hills Dr., N.E.
Albuquerque, NM 87109
(505) 822-0921

Triad Service League
Martha Rode
631 Tulane Place, N.E.
Albuquerque, NM 87108
(505) 266-6384

Search Support Groups

Adoptee Liberty Movement
　Association (ALMA)
P.O. Box 1346
Aztec, NM 87410
(505) 334-2654

Concerned United Birthparents
　(CUB)
358 Joya Loop
Los Alamos, NM 87544
(505) 672-3976
www.webnations.com/cub
cub@webnations.com

Operation Identity
13101 Blackstone, N.E.
Albuquerque, NM 87111
(505) 293-3144

NEW MEXICO LAWS RELATED TO ADOPTION: QUESTIONS AND ANSWERS

A home study must be conducted thirty days before a child can be placed in your home in an interstate independent adoption. If you plan to advertise outside of the state, be sure to have a home study very near completion before placing an ad. Also, your attorney must obtain a court order that permits a child from another state to come into your home.

Can an attorney serve as an intermediary?
No.

Is advertising permitted?
Yes.

Who must consent to the adoption?
1. The birth mother
2. The birth father if he is married to or attempted to marry the birth mother, or if the child was born within 300 days after the marriage ended, or if he has stated he is the father and established a personal and financial relationship with the child.
3. The adoption agency involved, if applicable. Consent is not required if either birth parent has left the child with a third party (the adoptive couple, for example) and has not supported the child or communicated with her for a period of three months if the child is under the age of six years. If the child is over the age of six years then the time period is six months.

When can consent be taken from birth mother (father), and how long after the consent is signed can it be revoked?
Consent cannot be given until forty-eight hours after child's birth and must be taken in front of a judge. Consent cannot be withdrawn unless it was obtained by fraud.

What are the birth father's rights?
His rights are limited, as described above. If he has not registered with a putative father registry within ninety days of the child's birth, then his consent is not needed. In addition, consent is not rquired of a parent who has left the child to be adopted unidentified for a period of 14 days.

What fees can adoptive parents pay?
Medical, legal, and living expenses can be paid. All expenses paid must be filed by the adoptive parents with the court.

Where does the adoption hearing take place?
The hearing takes place in the court of the county where the adoptive parents live, where the child lives, or where the agency is located.

How are familial and stepparent adoptions different from nonbiological adoptions?
If the child has lived with a relative (up to the fifth degree of relation) for at least one year, then the home study can be waived. Grandparent visitation rights apply to adoption by a stepparent or relative, a person designated in the deceased parent's will, or a person who served as a godparent.

Can a nonresident finalize an adoption in this state?
Yes, if the child to be adopted is a resident of New Mexico or has been born in New Mexico and is less than six months old and placed by an adoption agency.

NEW YORK

State Adoption Specialist

New York State Office of
  Children and Family Services
New York State Adoption
  Services
Stephanie Woodard
40 North Pearl Street, Riverview
  Center, 6th Floor
Albany, NY 12243
(518) 474-9603
Fax: (518) 486-6326
www.dfa.state.ny.us/adopt/
an7440@dfa.state.ny.us

State ICPC Administrator

Division of Family & Children's
  Services
New York State Department of
  Social Services
40 North Pearl Street
Albany, NY 12243
(518) 474-9506
anne.furman@dfa.state.ny.us

State Adoption Exchange/State
  Photolisting Service

New York State Adoption Service
Office of Children and Family
  Services
Riverview Center 6th Floor, 40
  North Pearl Street
Albany, NY 12243
Toll Free: (800) 345-KIDS
www.dfa.state.ny.us/adopt

State Reunion Registry

Adoption and Medical
  Information Registry
Department of Health, Public
  Health Representative
Corning Tower, Room 208
Albany, NY 12237
(518) 474-9600

Regional/District Public
  Agencies

New York State Office of
  Children & Family Services
Rochester Regional Office
259 Monroe Avenue, Monroe
  Square
Rochester, NY 14607
(716) 238-8201

New York State Office of
  Children & Family Services
New York City Regional Office
80 Maiden Lane, 6th Floor
New York, NY 10038
(212) 383-1805

New York State Office of
  Children & Family Services
Syracuse Regional Office
351 South Warren Street
Syracuse, NY 13203
(315) 423-1199

New York State Office of
  Children & Family Services
Yonkers Regional Office
525 Nepperhan Avenue
Yonkers, NY 10703
(914) 377-2079

New York State Office of
  Children & Family Services
Albany Regional Office
155 Washington Avenue, 3rd
  Floor
Albany, NY 12210
(518) 473-9684

New York State Office of
  Children & Family Services
Buffalo Regional Office
838 Ellicott Square,
  295 Main Street
Buffalo, NY 14203
(716) 847-3743

Licensed Private Adoption
  Agencies

Abbott House
100 North Broadway
Irvington, NY 10533
(914) 591-3200, Ext: 224

Adoption and Counseling
  Services, Inc.
1 Fayette Park
Syracuse, NY 13202
(315) 471-0109

Adoptions From The Heart
30-31 Hampstead Circle
Wynnewood, PA 19096
(610) 642-7200
Fax: (610) 642-7938
www.adoptionsfromtheheart.org
adoption@adoptionsfromthe-
  heart.org

*Americans for International Aid
and Adoption
P.O. Box 290
Plainville, NY 13137-0290
(315) 638-9449
www.rainbowkids.com/aiaa.html
aiaateri@aol.com

Angel Guardian Home
6301 12th Avenue
Brooklyn, NY 11219
(718) 232-1500

Association to Benefit Children -
Variety House
404 E. 91st Street
New York, NY 10128
(212) 369-2010

Astor Home for Children
P.O. Box 5005
Rhinebeck, NY 12572
(914) 876-4081

Baker Victory Services
790 Ridge Road
Lackawanna, NY 14218
(716) 828-9510

Bethany Christian Services
Warwick Reformed Church,
16 Maple Avenue
Warwick, NY 10990
(914) 987-1453
www.bethany.org
info@bethany.org

Bethany Christian Services
1120 Goffle Road
Hawthorne, NJ 07506-2024
(973) 427-2566
Fax: (973) 427-9204
www.bethany.org
info@bethany.org

Brookwood Child Care
25 Washington Street
Brooklyn, NY 11201
(718) 596-5555

Cardinal McCloskey School
and Home
2 Holland Avenue
White Plains, NY 10603
(914) 997-8000

Catholic Charities
380 Arlington Street
Watertown, NY 13601
(315) 788-4330

*Catholic Charities
105 W. Main Street, Box 385
Malone, NY 12953
(518) 483-1460

Catholic Charities of Buffalo
525 Washington Street
Buffalo, NY 14203
(716) 856-4494

Catholic Charities of Cortland
33-35 Central Avenue
Cortland, NY 13045
(607) 756-5992

Catholic Charities of Ogdensburg
P.O. Box 296, 716 Caroline Street
Ogdensburg, NY 13669-0296
(315) 393-2660

Catholic Charities of Rome
212 W. Liberty Street
Rome, NY 13440
(315) 337-8600

Catholic Charities of Syracuse
1654 W. Onondaga Street
Syracuse, NY 13204
(315) 424-1871

Catholic Family Center
25 Franklin Street
Rochester, NY 14604
(716) 262-7134

Catholic Guardian Society
of New York
1011 First Avenue
New York, NY 10022
(212) 371-1000

Catholic Home Bureau for
Dependent Children
1011 First Avenue
New York, NY 10022
(212) 371-1000

Catholic Social Services of
Broome County
232 Main Street
Binghamton, NY 13905
(607) 729-9166

Catholic Social Services of
Utica/Syracuse
1408 Genesee Street
Utica, NY 13502
(315) 724-2158

Central Brooklyn Coordinating
Council
1958 Fulton Street, 4th Floor
Brooklyn, NY 11233
(718) 778-1400

Child and Family Services of Erie
844 Delaware Avenue
Buffalo, NY 14209
(716) 882-0555
Fax: (716) 882-1451

Child Development Support
Corporation
352-358 Classon Avenue
Brooklyn, NY 11238
(718) 230-0056

Children At Heart Adoption
Services, Inc.
145 N. Main Street
Mechanicville, NY 12118
(518) 664-5988
Fax: (518) 664-1220
www.childrenatheart.com
info@childrenatheart.com

Children's Aid Society
Adoption and Foster Home
Division
150 E. 45th Street
New York, NY 10017
(212) 949-4961

Children's Home of Poughkeepsie
91 Fulton Street
Poughkeepsie, NY 12601
(914) 452-1420

Children's Village
Echo Hills
Dobbs Ferry, NY 10522
(914) 693-0600, Ext: 1223

Coalition for Hispanic Family
Services
315 Wyckoff Avenue, 4th Floor
Brooklyn, NY 11237
(718) 497-6090

Community Maternity Services
27 N. Main Avenue
Albany, NY 12203
(518) 482-8836
Fax: (518) 482-5805

Downey Side Families for Youth
Southgate Tower, Hudson Room,
371 Seventh Avenue
New York, NY 10001-3484
(212) 629-8599

Edwin Gould Services for
Children
41 E. 11th Street
New York, NY 10003
(212) 598-0051

Episcopal Mission Society
18 W. 18th Street
New York, NY 10011-4607
(212) 675-1000

Family and Children's Services of
Broome County
257 Main Street
Binghamton, NY 13905
(607) 729-6206

Family and Children's Services
of Ithaca
204 N. Cayuga Street
Ithaca, NY 14850
(607) 273-7494

Family and Children's Services
of Schenectady
246 Union Street
Schenectady, NY 12305
(518) 393-1369

Family Connections
156 Port Watson Street
Cortland, NY 13045
(607) 756-6574

Family Focus Adoption Services
54-40 Little Neck Parkway,
Suite 4
Little Neck, NY 11362
(718) 224-1919
Fax: (718) 225-8360

Family Service of Utica
Suite 201, 401 Columbia Street
Utica, NY 13502
(315) 735-2236

Family Service of Westchester
1 Summit Avenue
White Plains, NY 10606
(914) 948-8004

Family Support Systems
Unlimited
2530 Grand Concourse
Bronx, NY 10458
(718) 220-5400

Family Tree Adoption Agency
1743 Route 9
Clifton Park, NY 12065
(518) 371-1336
Fax: (518) 371-4262
FamTreAdop@aol.com

Forestdale, Inc.
67-35 112 Street
Forest Hills, NY 11375
(718) 263-0740

Friends in Adoption
44 South Street, P.O. Box 1228
Middletown Springs, VT 05757-
1228
(802) 235-2373
www.capital.net/com/fia
fia@vermontel.com

Gateway-Longview
605 Niagara Street
Buffalo, NY 14201
(716) 882-8468, Ext: 3884

Graham-Windham Child Care
33 Irving Place
New York, NY 10003
(212) 529-6445, Ext: 384

Green Chimneys
Caller Box 719,
Putnam Lake Road
Brewster, NY 10509-0719
(914) 279-2996

Harlem-Dowling Children
Services
2090 Adam Clayton Powell, Jr.,
Boulevard (7th Avenue)
New York, NY 10027
(212) 749-3656

Heartshare Human Services
191 Joralemon Street
Brooklyn, NY 11201
(718) 422-4219

Hillside Children's Center
1337 E. Main Street
Rochester, NY 14609
(716) 654-4529

Ibero American Action League Inc.
817 East Main Street
Rochester, NY 14609
(716) 256-8900

Jewish Board of Family and
Children Services
120 W. 57th Street
New York, NY 10019
(212) 582-9100

Jewish Child Care Association of
New York
120 Wall Street
New York, NY 10005
(212) 425-3333

Jewish Family Services
of Erie County
70 Barker Street
Buffalo, NY 14209
(716) 883-1914

Jewish Family Services
of Rochester
441 E. Avenue
Rochester, NY 14607
(716) 461-0110

Lakeside Family and Children's
Services
185 Montague Street
Brooklyn, NY 11201
(718) 237-9700

LDS Social Services
22 IBM Road, Suite 205-B
Poughkeepsie, NY 12601
(914) 462-1288

Leake and Watts Children's
Home
463 Hawthorne Avenue
Yonkers, NY 10705
(914) 963-5220

Little Flower Children's Services
186 Joralemon Street
Brooklyn, NY 11201
(718) 875-3500

Lutheran Service Society
of New York
234 Minnesota Avenue
Buffalo, NY 14226
(716) 831-9188

Lutheran Social Services, Inc.
83 Christopher Street
New York, NY 10014
(212) 366-6330

MAPS New York
P.O. Box 26920
Rochester, NY 14626
(716) 723-8773
Fax: (716) 723-8302
www.ainop.com/maps/

McMahon Services for Children
305 Seventh Avenue
New York, NY 10001
(212) 243-7070, Ext: 259

Mercy Home for Children
310 Prospect Park, West
Brooklyn, NY 11216
(718) 483-3000

Miracle Makers, Inc.
510 Gates Avenue
Brooklyn, NY 11216
(718) 483-3000

Mission of the Immaculate Virgin
6581 Hylan Boulevard
Staten Island, NY 10309
(718) 317-2627

New Alternatives for Children
37 W. 26th Street
New York, NY 10010
(212) 696-1550

New Beginnings Family and
  Children's Services, Inc.
141 Willis Avenue
Mineola, NY 11501
(516) 747-2204
Fax: (516) 747-2505
www.new-beginnings.org
newbeginn@aol.com

New Hope Family Services
3519 James Street
Syracuse, NY 13206
(315) 437-8300

New Life Adoption Agency
Suite 301, 430 E. Genesee Street
Syracuse, NY 13202-2155
(315) 422-7300
Fax: (315) 475-7727
www.newlifeadoption.org
newlife@newlifeadoption.org

Ohel Children's Home and Family
  Services
4510 16th Avenue, 4th Floor
Brooklyn, NY 11204
(718) 851-6300

Open Arms Adoption and Family
  Center
P.O. Box 4386
Sarasota Springs, NY 12866
(518) 580-1709

Parsons Child and Family Center
60 Academy Road
Albany, NY 12208
(518) 426-2600

Pius XII Youth/Family Services
188 W. 230 Street
Bronx, NY 10463
(718) 562-7855

PRACA Child Care
853 Broadway
New York, NY 10003
(212) 673-7320

Salvation Army Foster Home
132 W. 14th Street
New York, NY 10011
(212) 807-6100

Sheltering Arms Children's
  Services
122 East 29th Street
New York, NY 10016
(212) 679-4242

Spence-Chapin Services to
  Families and Children
6 East 94th Street
New York, NY 10128
(212) 369-0300
www.spence-chapin.org
info@spence-chapin.org

St. Augustine Center
1600 Filmore Avenue
Buffalo, NY 14211
(716) 897-4110

St. Cabrini
Rt. 9 W
West Park, NY 12493

St. Christopher Ottilie
Third Avenue and Eighth Street,
  P.O. Box Y
Brentwood, NY 11717
(516) 273-2733

St. Christopher Ottilie
570 Fulton Street
Brooklyn, NY 11217
(718) 935-9466

St. Christopher Ottilie
90-04 161st Street
Jamaica, NY 11432
(718) 526-7533

St. Christopher Ottilie
12 Main Avenue
Sea Cliff, NY 11579
(516) 759-1844

St. Christopher's Office of
  Placement and Permanency
881 Gerard Avenue
Bronx, NY 10452

St. Christopher's/Jennie Clarkson
71 S. Broadway
Dobbs Ferry, NY 10522
(914) 693-3030, Ext: 209

St. Dominics
343 E. 137th Street
Bronx, NY 10454
(718) 993-5765

St. Joseph's Children's Services
540 Atlantic Avenue
Brooklyn, NY 11217-1982
(718) 858-8700

St. Mary's Child and Family
  Services
525 Convent Road
Syosset, NY 11791
(516) 921-0808

St. Vincent's Services
66 Boerum Place, P.O. Box 174
Brooklyn, NY 11202
(718) 522-3700, Ext: 251

Talbot-Perkins Children Services
116 W. 32nd Street, 12th Floor
New York, NY 10001
(212) 736-2510

The New York Foundling
  Hospital
590 Avenue of the Americas
New York, NY 10011
(212) 727-6810

Urban League of Rochester,
  Minority Adoption Program
265 North Clinton Ave
Rochester, NY 14605
(716) 325-6530

Vermont Children's Aid Society
79 Weaver Street, P.O. Box 127
Winooski, VT 05404-0127
(802) 655-0006
Fax: (802) 655-0073
www.vermontchildrensaid.org/
  children/adoption.htm

Vermont Children's Aid Society
128 Merchants Row, Room 501
Rutland, VT 05701
(802) 773-8555
www.vermontchildrensaid.org/
  children/adoption.htm

Voice for International
  Development and Adoption
  (VIDA)
354 Allen Street
Hudson, NY 12534
(518) 828-4527
Fax: (518) 828-0688
members.aol.com/vidaadopt/
  vida.html
vidaadopt@aol.com

*Wide Horizons For Children
Main Office
38 Edge Hill Road
Waltham, MA 02451
(781) 894-5330
Fax: (781) 899-2769
www.whfc.org/
info@whfc.org

Adoptive Parent Support Groups

A K.I.D.S. Exchange (Adoption,
Knowledge and Information on
Down Syndrome)
27 Eagle Court
White Plains, NY 10606
(914) 428-1236

A.D.O.P.T.
RR 1, Box 430
Jeffersonville, NY 12748
(914) 482-5339

A.N.G.E.L.S. (Adoption Network
to Gain Equal Love and
Support)
3219 St. Paul Boulevard
Rochester, NY 14617
(716) 234-1864

Adoption Group of Orange
County
P.O. Box 156
Chester, NY 10918
(914) 427-2757

Adoption Resource Network, Inc.
P.O. Box 178
Pittsford, NY 14534
(716) 924-5295
www.arni.org
info@arni.org

Adoptive and Foster Families of
Long Island
831 Montauk Avenue
Islip Terrace, NY 11752
(516) 277-7149

Adoptive Families Association of
Tompkins County
P.O. Box 219
Ithaca, NY 14851
(607) 387-9207
dih1@cornell.edu

Adoptive Families Coalition
P.O. Box 603
Glenmont, NY 12077
(518) 448-5295
rdolfi@ibm.net

Adoptive Families of
Chemung County
750 State Route 414
Beaver Dams, NY 14812
(607) 936-4706

Adoptive Families of
Older Children, Inc
149-32A Union Turnpike
Flushing, NY 11367
(718) 380-7234

Adoptive Families of Westchester
11 Bristol Place
Yonkers, NY 10710
(914) 779-1509

Adoptive Family Network of
Central New York
503 Maple Drive
Fayetteville, NY 13066-1735
(315) 446-5607
sferrara@hotmail.com

Adoptive Parents Committee,
Hudson Region
P.O. Box 625
White Plains, NY 10530
(914) 997-7859

Adoptive Parents Committee,
Long Island
Box 71
Bellmore, NY 11710
(516) 326-8621

Adoptive Parents Committee,
New York City
P.O. Box 3525
Church Street Station, NY 10008
(212) 304-8479
SamAPC@aol.com

Adoptive Parents Committee,
New York State
1762 64th Street
New York, NY 11204
(718) 259-7921
FelixAPC@aol.com

Albany County Foster and
Adoptive Parents Association
RR1 Box 5 Elm Lane
Greenville, NY 12083
(518) 966-8649

Allegany County Foster Parent
Association
90 Friendship Street
Bolivar, NY 14715
(716) 928-2119

Angel Guardian Home Foster and
Adoptive Parents Association
241 Greene Avenue
Brooklyn, NY 11238-1304
(718) 398-4301

Brookwood Child Care Foster and
Adoptive Parents Association
131-51 226th Street
Laurelton, NY 11413
(718) 978-0978

Camillus West Support Group
117 Clark Lane
Camillus, NY 13031
(315) 487-0484

Camp Mu Ji Gae, Inc
3 E Bayberry Road
Glenmont, NY 12077
(518) 475-0824

Capital District Foster and
Adoptive Parents Support
Group
4 Arden Road
Scotia, NY 12302
(518) 370-0589

Capitol District - Albany, Troy,
Schenectady, Saratoga Upstate
NY Single
Adoptive Parents
38 Shaker Drive Blvd
Loudonville, NY 12211
(518) 489-4322

Catholic Adoptive Parents
Association
74-07 Kessel Street
Forest Hills, NY 11375-1488
(718) 793-6276

Catholic Home Bureau Foster and
Adoptive Parents Association
P.O. Box 117
Yonkers, NY 10704
(914) 375-3746

Center Kids: The Family Project
of the Lesbian and Gay
Community Services Center
of NY
1171 Fr. Capodanno Boulevard
Staten Island, NY 10306
(212) 620-7310
Fax: (212) 924-2657

Central New York Friends of Love
the Children
P.O. Box 6797
Syracuse, NY 13217
(315) 656-8015

Champlain Valley Adoptive
Families, Inc.
6 Grace Avenue
Plattsburgh, NY 12901
(518) 563-5224
mward@mum.nenc.org

Columbia County Foster Parent
Support Group
668 Breezy Hill Road
Hillsdale, NY 12529
(518) 325-3084

Committed Parents for Black
Adoption
Building 1B, #8A, 900 Baychester
Bronx, NY 10475
(718) 671-6772

Concerned Foster and Adoptive
Parents Support Group
1256 Ocean Avenue
Brooklyn, NY 11230
(718) 421-3247

Cortland County Foster and
Adoptive Parents
RD 2, Box 120
Marathon, NY 13803
(607) 849-6145

Council of Adoptive Parents, Inc.
(COAP)
1724 Five Mile Line Road
Penfield, NY 14526
(716) 383-0947
coap@aol.com

Dare to Care
Foster Parent Association of
Broome County
2 Pease Road
Harpursville, NY 13787
(607) 693-1790

Delaware County Foster and
Adoptive Parents
RD 2 Box 198
Walton, NY 13856
(607) 865-4107

DFCS Foster and Adoptive
Parents Association
413 Clermont Avenue
Brooklyn, NY 11238
(718) 636-1829

Episcopal Social Services Parent
Group
710 Tinton Avenue #5E
Bronx, NY 10455
(718) 585-2137

Erie County Foster and Adoptive
Parents Support Group
75 North Brier Road
Amherst, NY 14228
(716) 691-4872

Families Adopting Need Support
(FANS)
1060 Niagara Falls Boulevard,
Suite 3
Tonawanda, NY 14150
(716) 626-9975
Fax: (716) 636-9106

Families and Children Together
for Support (FACTS)
4104 Allendale Parkway
Blasdell, NY 14219
(716) 648-7960

Families for Russian and
Ukrainian Adoption (FRUA)
5 Avon Road
Larchmont, NY 10538
(914) 560-6184
www.frua.org

Families for the
Children/Adirondack Region
303 Coy Road
Greenfield Center, NY 12833
(518) 893-7699

Families for the Future, Inc
66 Harmon Road
Scotia, NY 12302
(518) 399-8676

Families Interested in Adoption
Support Group of Long Island
3 Brenda Lane
Manorville, NY 11949
(516) 878-6511

Families Interested in Adoption,
Inc. (FIA)
P.O. Box 604
Williamsville, NY 14231
(716) 741-3364

Families Interested in Multi-
Cultural Adoption, Inc.
(FIMA)
56 Southampton Street
Buffalo, NY 14208
(716) 883-5053
EAYM28A@prodigy.com

Families Through Adoption
301 Middle Road
Oneida, NY 13421
(315) 363-4634

Families With Children
From China
P.O. Box 865
Ansonia Station, NY 10023
www.catalog.com/fwcfc
jkelly@inch.com

Families with Children From
China - Rochester
1 Feathery Circle
Penfield, NY 14526
(716) 248-8592

Finger Lakes Adoption Group
(FLAG)
14 Rose Street
Geneva, NY 14456
(315) 789-4560

Forestdale Foster Parents
Assocation
67-35 112th Street
Forest Hills, NY 11375

Foster & Adoptive Parents
Association of Cattaraugus
County
115 S. 12th Street
Olean, NY 14760
(716) 372-3965

Foster & Adoptive Parents
Association of Oneida County,
Inc.
P.O. Box 98
Whitesboro, NY 13492
(315) 736-3909
www.fapaoc.org/contact.html
dac2547@aol.com

Foster and Adoptive Parents
Advisory Committee of Edwin
Gould Services for Children
15-19 West 110th Street #33
New York, NY 10026
(212) 426-5150

Foster and Adoptive Parents
Association of the Society for
Children and Families
P.O. Box 402
Staten Island, NY 10310-0402
(718) 720-5907

Foster and Adoptive Parents
Group of Brookwood Children
Care
131-51 226th Street
Laurelton, NY 11413
(718) 978-0978

Foster and Adoptive Parents
  Organization of New York
536 E. 37th Street, #7
Brooklyn, NY 11203
(718) 282-7413

Foster and Parent Association of
  Angel Guardian Home
134-39 224th Street
Laurelton, NY 11413
(718) 712-6990

Foster Parents Advisory Council
  of Suffolk County (F-PAC)
91 Tree Road
Centereach, NY 11720
(516) 471-3689
FPACPREZ@aol.com

Foster Parents Association of
  Oswego County
4193 S. Railroad Street
Parish, NY 13131
(315) 625-7107

Foster Parents Organization of
  Madison County
South Main Street, Box 242
Munnsville, NY 13409
(315) 495-6556

Friends in Adoption Post
  Placement Group
16 Willey Street
Albany, NY 12203
(518) 452-0271

Friends in Adoption
  Support Group
14 Tioga Terrace
Albany, NY 12208
(518) 437-1604

Friends of Children Everywhere
23 Snowbird Lane
Levittown, NY 11756
(516) 579-8719

Gateway-Longview Foster Parents
202 N. Barry Street
Olean, NY 14760
(716) 373-0139

Gathering International Families
  Together (GIFT)
2229 Walnut Avenue
Ronkonoma, NY 11779
(212) 978-9524

Genesee County Foster and
  Adoptive Parents Association
9374 S. Street Road
LeRoy, NY 14482
(716) 768-7464

Good Sheperd/McMahon
  Assocation for Foster and
  Adoptive Parents
144 Sutter Avenue
Brooklyn, NY 11212
(718) 498-9857

Graham Windham Foster Parent
  Association
4144 Gunther Avenue
Bronx, NY 10466
(719) 325-9154

Grandparents Reaching Out
141 Glen Summer Road
Holbrook, NY 11741
(516) 472-9728

Greater Rochester Committee for
  Single Adoptive Parents
176 Middlesex Road
Rochester, NY 14610
(716) 288-1321

Guarani, New York
61 Jane Street #10D
New York, NY 10014
(212) 243-2067

Harlem Dowling West Center
  Foster and Adoptive Parent
  Council
Apartment 12H,
  100-12 Alcott Place
Bronx, NY 10475-4117
(718) 379-2038

Helping Hands Memorial Fund
256 St. Lawerence Street
Sayville, NY 11782
(516) 567-2890

Hillside Emergency Foster
  Parents Group
40 Pacer Drive
Henrietta, NY 14467
(716) 359-1038

Holt Families Unlimited
Box 25
Candor, NY 13743
(607) 659-7540

International Adoptive Families,
  Inc.
P.O. Box 7249
Albany, NY 12224
(518) 783-6786

Jewish Child Care Association
  Foster Parents
3170 Broadway #11B
New York, NY 10027
(212) 316-1762

Latin America Parents
  Association (LAPA)
P. O. Box 339
Brooklyn, NY 11234
(718) 236-8689
www.lapa.com
joet@highcaliber.com

Latin American Families
104 Cooper Road
Rochester, NY 14617
(716) 342-4247

Livingston County Foster and
  Adoptive Parent
5149 Blank Road
Hemlock, NY 14466
(716) 346-6102

Louise Wise Foster and Adoptive
  Parents Association
116-32 220th Street
Cambria Heights, NY 11411
(718) 712-0702

Love the Children of
  Rochester, Inc.
28 Foxboro Lane
Fairport, NY 14450
(716) 425-7609
Fax: (716) 425-7609

Love the Children of Western
  New York
64 Stillwell Avenue
Kenmore, NY 14217
(716) 875-9505

Minority Foster & Adoptive
  Parents Support Group of
  Monroe County
141 Columbia Avenue
Rochester, NY 14608
(716) 328-6756

Miracle Makers Foster and
  Adoptive Parents Association
510 Gates Avenue
Brooklyn, NY 11216
(718) 483-3000

Monroe County Foster and
  Adoptive Parents Association
P.O. Box 625
Hilton, NY 14468
(716) 392-5026

Montgomery County Foster &
  Adoptive Parents Association
12 Prospect Street
Fultonville, NY 12072
(518) 853-4477

Nassau County Foster and
Adoptive Parents Association
3373 Weidner Avenue
Oceanside, NY 11572
(516) 763-2745

New Alternatives for Children
Foster/Adoptive Parents
Association (NAC FAPA)
405 Westminister Road #RC6
Brooklyn, NY 11218
(718) 469-8802

New Beginnings Parent Group
3379 Weidner Avenue
Oceanside, NY 11572
(516) 536-4229

New Beginnings Single Parent
Support Group
11 Lynn Place
Bethpage, NY 11714
(516) 938-7252

New Life for Black Children
P.O. Box 11164
Rochester, NY 14611
(716) 436-6075

New York Council on Adoptable
Children
Suite 820, 666 Broadway
New York, NY 10012
(212) 475-0222
www.coac.org
coac@erols.com

New York Singles Adopting
Children
P.O. Box 472
Glen Oaks, NY 11004
(212) 289-1705

New York Singles Adopting
Children
220 E. 94th Street, 2B
New York, NY 10128
(212) 289-1705

New York Singles Adopting
Children-Long Island
60-41 251 Street
Little Neck, NY 11362-2433
(718) 229-7240

New York State Citizens'
Coalition for Children and
North American Council on
Adoptable Children
Representative
614 W. State Street, 2nd Floor
Ithaca, NY 14850

(607) 272-0034
Fax: (607) 272-0035
www.nysccc.org
office@nysccc.org

New York State Foster and
Adoptive Parents Association
200-31 Linden Blvd.
St. Albans, NY 11412
(718) 949-4832

Niagara County Foster Parents
881 Sweeney Street
N. Tonawanda, NY 14120
(716) 693-0210

North Chautauqua County Foster
Parents Association
5695 E. Main Road
Brocton, NY 14716-9737
(716) 792-9001

Open Door Society of Long Island
40 Pennsylvania Avenue
Medford, NY 11763
(516) 758-5571

Organization of Foster Families
for Equality & Reform
(OFFER)
88 Plymouth Drive, North
Glen Head, NY 11545
(516) 224-1919

Orleans County Foster and
Adoptive Parents Association
178 Gulf Street
Medina, NY 14103
(716) 798-0722

Otsego Adopt Inc
P.O. Box 323
Springfield Center, NY 13468
(315) 858-0304

Otsego County Special Needs
Adoption Information &
Referral
Box 26
Morris, NY 13808
(607) 263-5093

Ours Through Adoption
51 Ketchum Place
Buffalo, NY 14213
(716) 886-1837

Parents and Children Together,
Columbia County
304 Bushnell Road
Chatham, NY 12037
(518) 392-5848
kstumph@aol.com

Parents Helping Parents
54 Meyers Road
Kingston, NY 12401
thecodfather@mail.msn.com

Parents of Dunbar
P.O. Box 89
Syracuse, NY 13205
(315) 425-1406

Pius XII Foster and Adoptive
Parents Association
66 Judith Drive
Stormville, NY 12582
(914) 221-0753

Positively Kids, Inc
17 Prospect Drive
Queensbury, NY 12804
(518) 798-0915

Private Adoption Support
Group/Western New York
142 Brush Creek Road
Williamsburg, NY 14221
(716) 689-8991

Proud Parents, Inc.
P.O. Box 325, Alden Manor
Branch
Elmont, NY 11003
(914) 223-7663

Putnam County Foster Parent
Association
43 Marie Road
Carmel, NY 10512
(914) 225-5708

Rensselaer County Foster Parents
Wyomanock Road
RR1 Box 116A Wyomanock Road
Stephentown, NY 12168
(518) 733-6393

Richmond Adoptive Parents
P.O. Box 020665
Staten Island, NY 10302
(718) 273-4490

Rochester African-American
Adoption Group
P.O. Box 520
Henrietta, NY 14467
(716) 334-9699

Rochester Attachment Network
227 Aldine Street
Rochester, NY 14619-1204
(716) 527-0514

Rockland County Foster &
  Adoptive Parents Association
1 Jacqueline Road
Chestnut Ridge, NY 10952
(914) 356-0922

Saratoga County Foster Parents
  Support Group
Box 91
Victory Mills, NY 12884
(518) 695-4174

Seneca County Foster and
  Adoptive Parent Group
1 DiPronio Drive
Waterloo, NY 13165-0690
(315) 539-5609

Single Mothers By Choice
P.O. Box 1642,
  Gracie Square Station
New York, NY 10028
(212) 988-0993
mattes@pipeline.com

Single Parents for Adoption
73 Cleveland Avenue
Buffalo, NY 14223
(716) 873-4173

Skaneateles Foster Parent Group
3110 Fall Road
Marcellus, NY 13108
(315) 673-2890

Southern Chautauqua County
  Foster Parents Association
5290 Spooner Road
Ashville, NY 14710
(716) 782-4280

Southern Tier Adoptive Families
  (STAF)
509 Colgate Street
Vestal, NY 13850
(607) 797-3188
lorie@stny.lrun.com

St. Augustine Parent Group
34 Kerns Avenue
Buffalo, NY 14211
(716) 891-5545

St. Catherine's Foster Parents
  Support Group
38 Keir Road
Ravena, NY 12143
(518) 756-3958

St. Christopher - Ottilie Foster
  and Adoptive Parent Group
110-14 173rd Street
St. Albans, NY 11433
(718) 526-2391

St. Christopher - Ottilie Foster
  and Adoptive Parent
  Group/Suffolk
18 South 27 Street
Wyandach, NY 11798
(516) 491-4574

St. Christopher - Ottilie Foster
  and Adoptive Parents Group/
  Kings
230 Osborn Street, #2C
Brooklyn, NY 11213
(718) 922-3508

St. Christopher - Ottilie Foster
  and Adoptive Parents Group/
  Nassau
188-40A 71st Crescent #3C
Fresh Meadows, NY 11365
(718) 454-6316

St. Christopher Jennie Clarkson
  Foster and Adoptive Parents
  Association, Inc.
4 Dennison Street
White Plains, NY 10606
(914) 328-0848

St. Joseph's Foster and Adoptive
  Parents Association
131 Beach 59 Street
Arverne, NY 11692
(718) 634-3730

St. Lawrence County Helping
  Hands Foseter Parent Support
  Group
RD 2, Box 194
Governor, NY 13642
(315) 287-3826

St. Vincent's Foster and Adoptive
  Parents Association
237 E. 93rd Street
Brooklyn, NY 11212
(718) 346-3615

STAF/ Tioga County
226 W. Hill Road
Spencer, NY 14883
(607) 589-4905

Stars of David International Inc.
Jewish Family Service of Rockland
  County
900 Route 45, Suite 2
New City, NY 10956-1140
(914) 354-2121
Fax: (914) 354-2928
www.starsofdavid.org
staff@jfsrockland.org

Stars of David International Inc.
FEGS - Long Island Division
6900 Jericho Turnpike, Suite 306
Syosset, NY 11791
(516) 364-8040, Ext: 139
Fax: (516) 496-9156
www.starsofdavid.org
starsdavid@aol.com

Stars of David International Inc.
Rochester Chapter
1 Terrain Drive
Rochester, NY 14618
(716) 473-2035
www.starsofdavid.org/
mrudnick@frontiernet.net

Stars of David International Inc.
Jewish Child Care Association
  of NY
120 Wall Street
New York, NY 10005
(212) 425-3333
Fax: (212) 371-1275
JCCANAP@aol.com

Stars of David International Inc.
Jewish Family Service of Buffalo
  & Erie County
70 Barker Street
Buffalo, NY 14209-2013
(716) 883-1914
Fax: (716) 883-7637
www.starsofdavid.org
starsdavid@aol.com

Stars of David International Inc.
Long Island Chapter
19 Tiffany Road
Oyster Bay, NY 11771
(516) 922-9481
www.starsofdavid.org
Hjtd@aol.com

Steuben County Foster and
  Adoptive Parents
59 Ellicott Street
Corning, NY 14830
(607) 936-9006
Taustin278@aol.com

Sullivan County Foster and
  Adoptive Parents Association
1181 Horseshoe Lake Road
Swan Lake, NY 12783
(914) 583-5037

Talbot Perkins Children's Services
  Foster Parents Association
147-06 120th Avenue
Jamaica, NY 11436
(718) 529-3299

Tioga County Foster
  Parents Group
40 Elmer Hill Road
Newark Valley, NY 13811
(607) 755-8824
chitchco@us.ibm.com

Tompkins County Foster and
  Adoptive Parents Association
108 Homestead Road
Ithaca, NY 14850
(607) 272-5746

Tri County Families of Korean
  Children
54 Benneywater Road
Port Jervis, NY 12771
(914) 355-3711

United Metropolitan Foster &
  Adoptive Parents Association
151 Main Street
Staten Island, NY 10307
(718) 317-8761

Upstate Adoptive Parents
  Community Support Group
4356 Buckingham Drive
Schenectady, NY 12304
(518) 372-2874

Upstate New York Single
  Adoptive Parent Group
21 Conifer Drive
Saratoga Springs, NY 12866
(518) 581-0891

Washington County Resource
  Parents
RD 2 Box 2159
Fort Ann, NY 12827
(518) 632-5496

Wayne County Foster Parents
2953 Marion Wallworth Road
Marion, NY 14505
(315) 926-1518

We Care Foster and Adoptive
  Parents Association, Inc.
45 Storey Lane
Yonkers, NY 10710
(914) 963-8469
Awilda39@aol.com

Westchester Foster and Adoptive
  Parents Association
1900 Lexington Avenue #4C
New York, NY 10035
(212) 722-8795

Western New York Foster
  Parents Association
2190 Main Street
Buffalo, NY 14214
(716) 835-6851

Search Support Groups

Adoptee Liberty Movement
  Association (ALMA)
485 Magee Street
Southampton, NY 11968

Adoptee Liberty Movement
  Association (ALMA)
P.O. Box 727, Radio City Station
New York, NY 10101-0727
(212) 581-1568

Adoptees in Reunion
11 Janet Lane
Glen Cove, NY 11542
(516) 759-9054

Adoptees Information Service, Inc.
19 Marion Avenue
Mount Vernon, NY 10552

Adoptees Political Action
  Coalition
P.O. Box 2807
Glenville, NY 12302

Adoption Crossroads
P.O. Box 9025
Schenectady, NY 12309
(518) 377-5936

Adoption Crossroads
Box 311
Shenorock, NY 10587
(914) 248-6644

Adoption Crossroads/Council for
  Equal Rights in Adoption
356 E. 74th Street
New York, NY 10021-3925
(212) 988-0110
www.adoptioncrossroads.org/
cera@idt.net

Adoption Kinship
817 Taylor Drive
Vestal, NY 13850
(607) 772-6793

Adoption Support Group
57 Little Neck Road
Centerport, NY 11721

Adoption Support Network of
  Long Island
194 Old Country Road
Mineola, NY 11501
(516) 248-1929

Also Known As, Inc.
P.O. Box 6037, FDR Station
New York, NY 10150
(212) 386-9201
www.akaworld.org
akabulletin@hotmail.com

Always Support for
  Adopted People
12 Sunset Avenue, South
Farmingdale, NY 11735
(516) 694-4289

American Adoption Congress
  State Representative
817 Taylor Drive
Vestal, NY 13850
(607) 772-6793
Fax: (607) 723-4472
jeanvh@spectra.net

American Adoption Congress
  State Representative
469B Allenhurst Road
Amherst, NY 14226
(716) 837-0787
kblake@adelphia.net

American Adoption Congress
  State Representative
188 Vliet Boulevard
Cohoes, NY 12047-1816
(518) 238-2811
Fax: (518) 869-4368

Angels Support Network, Inc.
P.O. Box 67789
Rochester, NY 14617
(716) 234-1864
angelsr5@aol.com

Birth Mothers of Minors
  (B.M.O.M.S.)
P.O. Box 40
New York, NY 10010
(212) 532-7059

Birthmothers, Adoptees,
  Adoptive Parents United in
  Support
P.O. Box 299
Victor, NY 14564
(716) 924-0410

Birthparent Support Network
P.O. Box 120
North White Plains, NY 10603
(914) 682-2250

Birthparent Support Network
93 Main Street
Queensbury, NY 12804
(518) 370-5392

Birthparent Support Network
P.O. Box 34
Old Bethpage, NY 11804
(516) 785-0886

Birthparents and Kids in
   Desperate Search (B.K.I.D.S.)
P.O. Box 43
Erin, NY 14838
(607) 739-2957

Birthparents/Adoptees in Support
39 Tidd Avenue
Farmington, NY 14425

Candid Adoption Talk
175A Fawnhill Road
Tuxedo, NY 10987
(914) 351-3306

Center for Reuniting Families
51 Burke Drive
Buffalo, NY 14215

Concerned United Birthparents
   (CUB)
16 Gillett Lane
Cazenovia, NY 13035
(315) 655-9137
www.webnations.com/cub
SANDY21751@aol.com

Foster and Adoptive
   Parent Network
392 Shirley Avenue
Staten Island, NY 10312

Help Us Regain the Children
235 Dover Street
Brooklyn, NY 11235
(718) 332-0860

Independent Search Counselor
116 Pinehurst Avenue, #C62
New York, NY 10033
(212) 280-2878

Jamestown Adoption Triad
Box 95
Falconer, NY 14733

KinQuest, Inc.
89 Massachusetts Avenue
Massapequa, NY 11758
(516) 541-7383

Long Island Adoption Triad
114 Montgomery Avenue
Mastic, NY 11950
(631) 395-5181
Aorciarra@aol.com

Missing Connection
P.O. Box 712
Brownville, NY 13615
(315) 782-6245

Missing Pieces
P.O. Box 8041
Masena, NY 13662

Origins
216 Carroll Street
Brooklyn, NY 11231

Post Adoption Center for
   Education and Support of
   WNY (P.A.C.E.S.)
P.O. Box 1223
Amherst, NY 14226-7223
(716) 824-3967
kblake@adelphia.net

Springer Registry
4426 Murphy Road
Binghamton, NY 13903
(607) 772-9514

W.A.I.F.
201 E. 28th Street
New York, NY 10016-8538

NEW YORK LAWS RELATED TO ADOPTION: QUESTIONS AND ANSWERS

In New York a birth mother must have separate representation from the adoptive parents; therefore, she must have her own attorney whose fees are paid by the adoptive parents.

Can an attorney serve as an intermediary?
No. Generally, this practice is considered an illegal placement under Social Services Law. It does not matter if the attorney located the birth mother in or out of state.

Is advertising permitted?
Yes.

Who must consent to the adoption?
1. The birth mother
2. The birth father, if the child is born or conceived in wedlock

When can consent be taken from birth mother (father), and how long after the consent is signed can it be revoked?
Consent cannot be signed until the child is born. Generally, in a private placement in which the consent is not taken in court, a birth parent has up to forty-five days to revoke a

consent. The parent must attempt to revoke the consent by notification to the court where the adoption proceeding takes place. If the attempt is timely, then it will open the door legally for the court to conduct a "best interests" hearing to determine whether the child should remain with the adoptive couple or return to the objecting birth parent. If consents are taken by an agency the birth parents have up to thirty days to revoke a consent. However, in an independent adoption, if a judge receives consent from the birth parents, their rights are terminated at that point and are irrevocable even if it is only a few days after placement.

The birth father can also sign an irrevocable consent before the birth.

What are the birth father's rights?
If the child is born in wedlock, the birth father has the same rights as the birth mother. If a child is born out of wedlock, and the birth father has maintained substantial and continuous contact with the child and has financially supported the child, then his consent is needed. If the birth father was not involved during the six months before placement and is named by the birth mother, he must receive a notice. In addition, if a birth father files an acknowledgment of paternity with the putative father registry, then he shall be entitited to notice of the adoption. He is then entitled to a "best interests" hearing if he contests the adoption. In New York the best interestsof the child are paramount, and if the birth father has not shown the prerequisite concern for the child, he may not upset the adoption placement. It is not sufficient for him to suggest that he was not aware of the pregnancy or birth of the child.

What fees can adoptive parents pay?
In a private adoption, the adoptive parents must give the court a statement of all fees and expenses paid. (New York judges usually permit the adoptive parents to pay more living expenses than is generally permitted in other states.) The attorney must also give an affidavit of all fees received.

The adoptive parents' health insurer must cover the baby's medical expenses as soon as he is born.

Where does the adoption hearing take place?
The hearing takes place in the Family Court or Surrogate Court in the county where the adoptive parents reside or where the placement agency is located.

How are familial and stepparent adoptions different from nonbiological adoptions?
Legally, they are handled in the same way. In a stepparent adoption, if the noncustodial birth parent is unwilling to consent, then you need to be able to prove that they abandoned the child for at least six months before the adoption can proceed.

Can a nonresident finalize an adoption in this state?
Yes, if the child is born in the state and the adoptive parents are certified as approved parents by the court.

NEW YORK DOMESTIC RELATIONS LAW, SECTIONS 109 TO 117 AND NEW YORK SOCIAL SERVICES LAW 372 TO 373 (1997)

NORTH CAROLINA

State Adoption Specialist

State of North Carolina,
Department of Health and
Human Services
Division of Social Services,
Children's Services Section
Gwen Horton
325 N. Salisbury Street,
2411 Mail Service Center
Raleigh, NC 27699-2411
(919) 733-4622
Fax: (919) 715-6396
www.dhhs.state.nc.us/dss/adopt
gwen.horton@ncmail.net

State of North Carolina,
Department of Health and
Human Services
Division of Social Services,
Children's Services Section
Esther T. High
325 N. Salisbury Street,
2411 Mail Service Center
Raleigh, NC 27699-2411
(919) 733-4622
Fax: (919) 715-6396
www.dhhs.state.nc.us/dss/adopt
esther.high@ncmail.net

State ICPC Administrator

Division of Social Services
Interstate Compact
325 N. Salisbury Street
Raleigh, NC 27603-5905
(919) 733-9464

State Adoption Exchange/State Photolisting Service

NC Kids
University of North Carolina at
Greensboro
Center for Study of Social Issues,
P.O. Box 26170
Greensboro, NC 27402-6170
(877) 625-4371

North Carolina Adoption
Resource Exchange
Division of Social Services
325 N. Salisbury Street
Raleigh, NC 27603-5905
(919) 733-3801
www.dhhs.state.nc.us/dss/adopt

Licensed Private Adoption Agencies

Another Choice for Black
Children
3028 Beatties Ford Road
Charlotte, NC 28216
(704) 394-1124
Toll Free: (800) 774-3534

Association for Guidance, Aid,
Placement and Empathy
(AGAPE)
302 College Road
Greensboro, NC 27410
(336) 855-7107

Bethany Christian Services
P.O. Box 470036
Charlotte, NC 28247-0036
(704) 541-1833
Fax: (704) 541-1833
www.bethany.org
info@bethany.org

Bethany Christian Services
4008 Barrett Drive, Suite 206
Raleigh, NC 27609-6621
(919) 510-9511
Fax: (919) 510-9512
www.bethany.org
info@bethany.org

Bethany Christian Services, Inc.
25 Reed Street, P.O. Box 15569
Asheville, NC 28813-0569
(828) 274-7146
Fax: (828) 274-3608
www.bethany.org
info@bethany.org

Caring for Children
P.O. Box 19113
Asheville, NC 28815
(704) 236-2877

Carolina Adoption Services, Inc.
1000 N. Elm Street
Greensboro, NC 27401
(336) 275-9660
Fax: (336) 273-9804
carolinaadoption.org
cas1000@aol.com

Catholic Social Ministries of the
Diocese of Raleigh, Inc.
400 Oberlin Road, Suite 350
Raleigh, NC 27605
(919) 832-0225

*Catholic Social Services of the
Diocese of Charlotte, Inc.
1524 E. Morehead Street
Charlotte, NC 28236
(704) 343-9954

Children's Home Society of North
Carolina, Inc.
604 Meadow Street
Greensboro, NC 27405
(336) 274-1538
chsnc@greensboro.com

Christian Adoption Services
624 Matthews-Mint Road,
Suite 134
Matthews, NC 28105
(704) 847-0038
www.perigee.net/~cas
cas@perigee.net

Datz Foundation of
North Carolina
875 Walnut Street, Suite 275
Cary, NC 27511
(919) 319-6635

Family Services, Inc.
610 Coliseum Drive
Winston-Salem, NC 27106-5393
(336) 722-8173

Frank Adoption Center
2840 Plaza Place, Suite 325
Raleigh, NC 27612
(919) 510-9135
Fax: (919) 510-9137
Toll Free: (800) 597-9135
IAS@mindsprings.com

Gladney Center For Adoption
1811 Sardis Road, North,
Suite 207
Charlotte, NC 28270
(704) 845-6106
www.gladney.org
info@gladney.org

Independent Adoption Center
3725 National Drive, Suite 219
Raleigh, NC 27612
(919) 789-0707
Fax: (919) 789-0708
Toll Free: (800) 877-6736
www.adoptionhelp.org
iacorg@earthlink.net

LDS Social Services
5624 Executive Center Drive,
Suite 109
Charlotte, NC 28212-8832
(704) 535-2436

*Lutheran Family Services in the
  Carolinas, Inc.
P.O. Box 12287
Raleigh, NC 27605
(919) 832-2620

**Adoptive Parent Support
Groups**

Adoptive Families Heart to Heart
456 NC Highway 62, East
Greensboro, NC 27406
(336) 674-5024

Adoptive Families of Piedmont
4125 Sewanee Drive
Winston-Salem, NC 27106
(336) 924-0074

Adoptive Parents Together
107 Glenwood Trail
Southern Pines, NC 28387

Capital Area Families for
  Adoption
24616 Thendara Way
Raleigh, NC 27612
(919) 571-8330

Coastal Hearts of Adoption
6002 McClean Drive
Emerald Isle, NC 28549
(910) 354-5826

Families for Russian and
  Ukrainian Adoptions
East North Carolina
Raleigh, NC
mcumm315@aol.com

Family Resources
348 Lake Point Lane
Bellews Creek, NC 27009-9207
(910) 644-1664
Fax: (336) 641-1664

Iredell County Adoptive Families
327 Shoreline Loop
Mooresville, NC 28115
(704) 664-6026

Link
P.O. Box 103
Concord, NC 28026
Toll Free: (888) 272-BABY

Mountain Area Adoptive Parent
  Group
109 Robin Lane
Waynesville, NC 28786

North Carolina Friends
  of Black Children
P.O. Box 494
Sanford, NC 27330
Toll Free: (800) 774-3534

Piedmont Families thru
  International Adoption
29 Carrisbrooke Lane
Winston-Salem, NC 27104
(336) 765-9064
MaMiska@aol.com

Rowan/Cabarrus Adoption
  Support Group
405 Arcadia Road
China Grove, NC 28023
(704) 855-1282

Single Adoptive Parent Support
  Groups
102 South 26th Street
Morehead City, NC 28557
(919) 247-7071

Southern Piedmont Adoptive
  Families of America
P.O. Box 221946
Charlotte, NC 28222
(704) 541-3614

Special Needs Adoption Parents
  Support Group
1220 Onslow Drive
Greensboro, NC 27408
(336) 855-8006

SPICE & TIKA
604 Rollingwood Drive
Greensboro, NC 27410
(336) 295-5385

Stars of David International Inc.
Jewish Family Service
8210 Creedmoor Road, Suite 104
Raleigh, NC 27613
(919) 676-2200
www.starsofdavid.org
starsdavid@aol.com

Stars of David International Inc. -
  Triangle Chapter
Jewish Family Service
3700 Lyckan Parkway, Suite B
Durham, NC 27707
(919) 489-5335
Fax: (919) 489-5788
www.starsofdavid.org
jfeddch@mindspring.com

Triad Adoptive Parent Support
  Group and North American
  Council on Adoptable
Children
133 Penny Road
High Point, NC 27260
(910) 886-8230

Triangle Area Ours for a
  United Response
6609 Chantilly Place
Bahama, NC 27503
(919) 471-9693

Search Support Groups

Adoptee Liberty Movement
  Association (ALMA)
P.O. Box 20351
Greenville, NC 27858
(252) 756-5777

Adoption Information Exchange
8539 Monroe Road
Charlotte, NC 28212
(704) 532-6827

Adoption Information Exchange
  (AIE)
P.O. Box 1917
Matthews, NC 28106
(704) 537-5919
MzChrisLee@aol.com

Adoption Issues and Education
P.O. Box 768
Vanceboro, NC 28586
(252) 975-1510

Adoption Issues and Education
P.O. Box 8314
Greenville, NC 27835

Kinsolving Investigations
P.O. Box 471921
Charlotte, NC 28247
(704) 537-5919
Fax: (704) 846-5123
MzChrisLee@aol.com

National Adoption Awareness
  Convention
P.O. Box 2823
Chapel Hill, NC 27515-2823
(919) 967-5010

North Carolina Adoption
  Connections
P.O. Box 4153
Chapel Hill, NC 27515
(919) 967-5010

NORTH CAROLINA LAWS RELATED TO ADOPTION: QUESTIONS AND ANSWERS

Can an attorney serve as an intermediary?
In a direct placement, a parent must personally select the prospective adoptive parent, but the parent may obtain assistance from another person or entity or an adoption facilitator in locating or evaluating a prospective adoptive parent. Information about the adoptive parent must be given to the birth parent by the adoptive parent or the adoptive parent's attorney. This information must include the home study, and may include additional information if requested by the birth parent. An intermediary is allowed as long as that person is not compensated for services.

Is advertising permitted?
No. You may not post fliers either. Networking is limited to those you know.

Who must consent to the adoption?
1. The birth mother
2. The birth father, if he is married to the birth mother or has established paternity

When can consent be taken from birth mother (father), and how long after the consent is signed can it be revoked?
A consent to adopt an unborn child or one who is less than three months old may be revoked within twenty-one days. A consent to the adoption of an older child may be revoked within seven days.

What are the birth father's rights?
If named, the birth father must consent to the adoption. If the birth father has not consented to the adoption and fails to respond to a notice of adoption proceedings within thirty days after being notified, his consent is not required.

If the birth father wants to contest the adoption of a child born out of wedlock, he must establish paternity by filing a petition for legitimization. Paternity can also be established if he has provided substantial financial support or consistent care to the child and mother.

What fees can adoptive parents pay?
Adoptive parents can pay for medical, traveling, and counseling services that are directly related to the adoption, as well as ordinary living expenses (for no longer than six weeks after delivery) and legal expenses during the pregnancy. An affidavit of all moneys paid in connection with the adoption must be presented to the court.

Where does the adoption hearing take place?
The adoption hearing takes place in the court of the county where the adoptive parents live, where the child lives, or where the child placement agency is located.

How are familial and stepparent adoptions different from nonbiological adoptions?
The child must have resided primarily with the stepparent and the legal parent for at least six months. The state residency and probationary period are waived in stepparent and

grandparent adoptions. Grandparents' visitation rights are still in effect after the adoption. Grandparents may also seek visitation rights if it is in the child's best interest.

Can a nonresident finalize an adoption in this state?
No. Only those who have lived in North Carolina for at least six months can adopt.

SOURCE: GENERAL STATUTES OF NORTH CAROLINA. SECTIONS 48-1 TO 48-38 (1997)

NORTH DAKOTA

State Adoption Specialist

North Dakota Department of
Human Services
Julie Hoffman
600 E. Boulevard Avenue, State
Capitol Building
Bismarck, ND 58505
(701) 328-4805
Fax: (701) 328-2359
sohofj@state.nd.us

State Licensing Specialist

North Dakota Department of
Human Services
Julie Hoffman
600 E. Boulevard Avenue, State
Capitol Building
Bismarck, ND 58505
(701) 328-4805
Fax: (701) 328-3538
sohofj@state.nd.us

State ICPC Administrator

North Dakota Department of
Human Services
State Capitol, Judicial Wing, 600
E. Boulevard Avenue,
Department 325
Bismarck, ND 58505
(701) 328-4152
Fax: (701) 328-2359

State Adoption Exchange/State
Photolisting Service

Department of Human Services
Children and Family Services
600 E. Boulevard Avenue, State
Capitol Building
Bismarck, ND 58505
(701) 328-2316
www.adopt.org

State Reunion Registry

North Dakota Department of
Human Services
Adoption Search/Disclosure
600 E. Boulevard Avenue, State
Capitol Building
Bismarck, ND 58505
(701) 328-4805

Licensed Private Adoption
Agencies

AASK (Adults Adopting
Special Kids)
Lutheran Social Services
P.O. Box 389, 1325 South 11th
Street
Fargo, ND 58107-0389
(701) 271-3265
Fax: (701) 235-7359

AASK (Adults Adopting
Special Kids)
The Village Family
Service Center
411 4th Street, North, Suite 10
Grand Forks, ND 58501
(701) 255-1165
Fax: (701) 255-7647

AASK (Adults Adopting
Special Kids)
Village Family Service Center
308 2nd Avenue, S.W.
Minot, ND 58701
(701) 852-3328
Fax: (701) 838-2521

AASK (Adults Adopting
Special Kids)
Lutheran Social Services
412 Demers Avenue
Grand Forks, ND 58201
(701) 787-7726
Fax: (701) 772-5001

AASK (Adults Adopting
Special Kids)
Child Welfare Office
P.O. Box 900
Belcourt, ND 58316
(701) 477-5688
Fax: (701) 477-5797

AASK (Adults Adopting
Special Kids)
Lutheran Social Services
P.O. Box 389
Fargo, ND 58107-0389
(701) 271-3216
Fax: (701) 235-7359

Catholic Family Service
1223 South 12th Street
Bismarck, ND 58504-6633
(701) 255-1793

Catholic Family Service
2537 South University
Fargo, ND 58103
(701) 235-4457
Fax: (701) 239-8266

Catholic Family Service
311 South Fourth Street
Grand Forks, ND 58201
(701) 775-4196

Catholic Family Service
400 22nd Avenue, N.W.
Minot, ND 58701
(701) 852-2854

Christian Family Life Services
203 South 8th Street
Fargo, ND 58103-1824
(701) 237-4473
Fax: (701) 280-9062

LDS Social Services
P.O. Box 3100
Bismarck, ND 58502-3100
(612) 560-0900

New Horizons Foreign Adoption
Services
2823 Woodland Place
Bismarck, ND 58504
(701) 258-8650
Fax: (701) 250-1844

The Adoption Option
1616 Capitol Way
Bismarck, ND 58501
(701) 223-1510

The Adoption Option
308 2nd Avenue, S.W.
Minot, ND 58701
(701) 852-3328

The Adoption Option
511 1/2 2nd Street, North
Williston, ND 58801
(701) 774-0749

The Adoption Option
P.O. Box 389
Fargo, ND 58107-0389
(701) 235-7341

The Adoption Option
1201 25th Street South,
  P.O. Box 9859
Fargo, ND 58106-9859
(701) 235-6433
Fax: (701) 235-9693

The Adoption Option
412 Demers Avenue
Grand Forks, ND 58201
(701) 772-7577

**Adoptive Parent Support
  Groups**

(AASK) Adults Adopt Special
  Kids
1325 South 11th Street
Fargo, ND 58107
(701) 235-7341

Adopt America Network - VFSC
  and North American Council
  on Adoptable Children
Representative
P.O. Box 9859
Fargo, ND 58103
(701) 235-6433

LSS of North Dakota and North
  American Council on
  Adoptable Children
Representative
P.O. Box 389
Fargo, ND 58107
(701) 271-3265
Fax: (701) 235-7359
iohnsief@ortel.com

Search Support Groups

Lutheran Social Services of North
  Dakota
P.O. Box 389
Fargo, ND 58107-0389
(701) 235-7341

NORTH DAKOTA LAWS RELATED TO ADOPTION: QUESTIONS AND ANSWERS

In general, if you adopt a child in a state in which independent adoption is legal, to finalize the adoption there you must use an agency in that state to meet North Dakota's ICPC regulations. However, check with an attorney to confirm this information, as North Dakota does use The Uniform Adoption Act, which does not require the use of an agency, as its adoption statute.

Can an attorney serve as an intermediary?
No.

Is advertising permitted?
No.

Who must consent to the adoption?
Both birth parents.

When can consent be taken from birth mother (father), and how long after the consent is signed can it be revoked?
Consent can be withdrawn before the adoption decree is final if it is in the child's best interests.

What are the birth father's rights?
He must give consent if he receives the child into his home and claims the child as his biological child, or if he acknowledges paternity in a document filed with the Division of Vital Statistics. Consent is not needed from either birth parent if it can be shown that the child to be adopted has been abandoned by a birth parent, or that a birth parent has not communicated with or supported the child for at least one year. Also, consent is not necessary if the birth parent is unavailable, absent with no explanation, incapable, or has failed to establish a substantial relationship with the child. A court that finds these conditions will terminate the birth parent's parental rights.

What fees can adoptive parents pay?
A full accounting must be given to the court of all fees paid for medical care (both pre- and postnatal care of the birth mother and child) as well as placement and agency fees.

Where does the adoption hearing take place?
The adoption hearing takes place in the court of the county where the adoptive parents live or the child lives, or where the child placement agency is located.

How are familial and stepparent adoptions different from nonbiological adoptions?
In a stepparent adoption, the court does not need an accounting of expenses.

Can a nonresident finalize an adoption in this state?
Yes.

SOURCE: NORTH DAKOTA CENTURY CODE. SECTIONS 14-15-10 TO 14-15-23 (1997)

OHIO

State Adoption Specialist

Bureau of Child and Adult
  Protection
Ohio Department of Human
  Services
Kathy Bartlett
65 E. State Street, 5th Floor
Columbus, OH 43266-0423
(614) 466-9274
Fax: (614) 728-2604
www.state.oh.us/odhs/

State ICPC Administrator

Ohio Department of Human
  Services
65 E. State Street, 5th Floor
Columbus, OH 43215
(614) 466-8520
Fax: (614) 728-6803

State Adoption Exchange/State Photolisting Service

Ohio Adoption Photo Listing
  (OAPL)
Bureau of Child and Adult
  Protection
65 E. State Street, 5th Floor
Columbus, OH 43215
(614) 466-9274
*www.state.oh.us/scripts/odhs/oapl/
  query.asp*

Southwest Ohio Adoption
  Exchange
Department of Human Services
628 Sycamore Street
Cincinnati, OH 45202
(513) 632-6366

State Reunion Registry

Ohio Department of Health
Vital Statistics
P.O. Box 15098
Columbus, OH 43215-0098
(614) 644-5635

Licensed Private Adoption Agencies

A Place to Call Home, Inc
4864 Whisper Cove Court
Gahanna, OH 43230
(614) 476-0850
Fax: (614) 476-0770

A.C.T.I.O.N. Adopting Children
  Today
1927 N. Main Street
Dayton, OH 45405
(937) 277-6101
Fax: (937) 277-2062

Adopt America Network
1025 N. Reynolds Road
Toledo, OH 43615-4753
(419) 534-3350
Fax: (419) 534-2995
www.adoptamerica.org
adoptamer@aol.com

Adoption at Adoption Circle
2500 E. Main Street, Suite 103
Columbus, OH 43209
(614) 237-7222
Fax: (614) 237-8484
Toll Free: (800) 927-7222
www.erinet.com/adoption/
adoption@erinet.com

Adoption by Gentle Care
17 Brickel Street
Columbus, OH 43215-1501
(614) 469-0007
Fax: (614) 621-2229

Adriel School, Inc
914 North Detroit Street, P.O.
  Box 188
West Liberty, OH 43357
(937) 465-0010
Fax: (937) 465-8690

Agape for Youth, Inc.
8067 McEwen
Dayton, OH 45458
(937) 439-4406
Fax: (937) 439-2908

American International Adoption
  Agency
7045 County Line Road
Williamsfield, OH 44093
(330) 876-5656
Fax: (330) 876-8003

Applewood Centers, Inc.
2525 E. 22nd Street
Cleveland, OH 44115
(216) 741-2241
Fax: (216) 459-9821

Baptist Children's Home and
  Family Ministries, Inc.
1934 S. Limestone Street
Springfield, OH 45505
(937) 322-0006
Fax: (937) 322-0049

Beech Acres
6881 Beechmont Avenue
Cincinnati, OH 45230
(513) 231-6630
Fax: (513) 624-0134

Bellefaire Jewish Children's
Bureau
22001 Fairmount Boulevard
Shaker Heights, OH 44118
(216) 932-2800

Berea Children's Home and
Family Services
202 E. Bagley Road
Berea, OH 44017
(440) 234-7501
Fax: (440) 234-7452

Building Blocks Adoption Service,
Inc.
4387 Remsen Road
Medina, OH 44256
(330) 725-5521
Fax: (330) 725-7389
Toll Free: (877) 587-9251
www.buildingblocksadoption.com
dhubbard@ohio.net

Catholic Charities Diocese
of Toledo
1933 Spielbusch Avenue
Toledo, OH 43624
(419) 244-6711
Fax: (419) 244-4781

Catholic Charities Services of
Lorain County
2136 N. Ridge Road
Elyria, OH 44035
(440) 324-2614
Fax: (440) 324-2985

Catholic Community Services
1175 Laird Avenue, 3rd Floor,
P.O. Box 1740
Warren, OH 44482-5224
(330) 393-4254
Fax: (330) 393-4050

Catholic Community Services of
Stark County, Inc
625 Cleveland Avenue, N.W.
Canton, OH 44702
(330) 455-0374
Fax: (330) 455-2101

Catholic Service League
4200 Park Avenue, 3rd Floor
Ashtabula, OH 44004
(440) 992-2121
Fax: (440) 992-5974

Catholic Social Service of
Cuyahoga County
7800 Detroit Avenue
Cleveland, OH 44102-2814
(216) 631-3499
Fax: (216) 631-3654

Catholic Social Services of
Lake County
2806 Euclid Avenue
Wickliffe, OH 44080
(440) 946-7264
Fax: (440) 585-8469

Catholic Social Services of
Southwestern Ohio
100 E. Eighth Street
Cincinnati, OH 45202
(513) 241-7745
Fax: (513) 241-4333

Catholic Social Services of the
Miami Valley
922 Riverview Avenue
Dayton, OH 45407
(937) 223-7217
Fax: (937) 222-6750

Catholic Social Services, Inc.
197 E. Gay Street
Columbus, OH 43215
(614) 221-5891
Fax: (614) 228-1125

Children's Home of Cincinnati,
Ohio
5050 Madison Road
Cincinnati, OH 45227
(513) 272-2800
Fax: (513) 272-2807

Christian Children's Home of
Ohio
2685 Armstrong Road
Wooster, OH 44691
(330) 345-7949
Fax: (330) 345-5218

Crittenton Family Services, Inc
1414 E. Broad Street
Columbus, OH 43205
(614) 251-0193
Fax: (614) 251-1177

Diversion
101 E. Sandusky Street
Findlay, OH 45840
(419) 422-4770
Fax: (419) 422-8117

European Adoption Consultants
9800 Boston Road
North Royalton, OH 44133
(440) 237-3554
Fax: (440) 237-6910
www.eaci.com
EACADOPT@aol.com

*Family Adoption Consultants
8536 Crow Drive, Macedonia
Professional Building #230
Macedonia, OH 44056
(330) 468-0673
Fax: (330) 468-0678
www.facadopt.org
facohio@acclink.com

Family Service Association
P.O. Box 1027 Steubenville, OH
43952
(740) 283-4763
Fax: (740) 283-2929

Family Services of Summit
County
212 E. Exchange Street
Akron, OH 44304
(330) 376-9494
Fax: (330) 376-4525

Focus on Youth, Inc
2718 East Kemper Road
Cincinnati, OH 45241
(513) 771-4710
Fax: (513) 771-4768

Hannah's Hope Adoption By
Cathedral Ministries
5225 Alexis Road
Sylvania, OH 43560
(419) 882-8463
Fax: (419) 885-2296

Harambee, Services for Black
Families
11811 Shaker Boulevard, Suite 420
Cleveland, OH 44120
(216) 791-2229

Harambee: Services to Children
and Families
11811 Shaker Boulevard, Suite
420
Cleveland, OH 44120
(216) 791-2229
Fax: (216) 791-8210

Harbor House Maternity Home
119 E. Fayette Street,
P.O. Box 357
Celina, OH 45822
(419) 586-5941
Fax: (419) 586-8961

Inner Peace Homes
P.O. Box 895
Bowling Green, OH 43402
(419) 354-6525
Fax: (419) 354-6016

Jewish Family and Children's
Services
517 Gypsy Lane
Youngstown, OH 44504
(330) 746-7929
Fax: (330) 746-7939

Jewish Family Service
4501 Denlinger Road
Dayton, OH 45426
(937) 854-2944
Fax: (937) 854-2850

Jewish Family Service
6525 Sylvania Avenue
Sylvania, OH 43560
(419) 885-2561
Fax: (419) 885-7427

Jewish Family Service
83 N. Miller Road
Akron, OH 44313
(330) 867-3388
Fax: (330) 867-3396

Jewish Family Services/Adoption
Connection
11223 Cornell Park Drive
Cincinnati, OH 45242
(513) 489-1616
Fax: (513) 489-4213

KARE, Inc. (Kids Are Really
Essential)
P.O. Box 328
Dayton, OH 45406
(937) 275-5715
Fax: (937) 275-3510

LDS Social Services
4431 Marketing Place,
P.O. Box 367
Groveport, OH 43125
(614) 836-2466
Fax: (614) 836-1865

Lutheran Children's Aid and
Family Services
4100 Franklin Boulevard
Cleveland, OH 44113-2895
(216) 281-2500
Fax: (216) 281-2506

Lutheran Social Services of
Central Ohio
750 East Broad Street
Columbus, OH 43205-1000
(614) 228-5200
Fax: (614) 228-3059

Lutheran Social Services of
Northwestern Ohio, Inc.
2149 Collingwood Boulevard
Toledo, OH 43620
(419) 243-9178
Fax: (419) 243-4450

Lutheran Social Services of the
Miami Valley
P.O. Box 292680
Dayton, OH 45429-0680
(937) 643-0020
Fax: (937) 643-9970

Marycrest
8010 Brookside Road
Independence, OH 44131
(216) 524-5280
Fax: (216) 524-2127

Mathis Care
1191 Galbraith Road
Cincinnati, OH 45231
(513) 522-7390
Fax: (513) 522-9844

Mid-Western Children's Home
4581 Long Spurling, P.O. Box 48
Pleasant Plain, OH 45162
(513) 877-2141
Fax: (513) 877-2145

New Hope Adoptions
International
101 W. Sandusky Street
Findlay, OH 45840
(419) 423-0760
Fax: (419) 423-8977

Newstart Foundation, Inc
119 Main Street
Chardon, OH 44024
(330) 286-1155
Fax: (330) 286-1712

Northeast Ohio Adoption
Services
5000 East Market Street, Suite 26
Warren, OH 44484
(330) 856-5582
Fax: (330) 856-5586

Ohio Youth Advocate Program,
Inc.
3780 Ridge Mill Drive, #100
Hilliard, OH 43026
(614) 777-8777
Fax: (614) 777-8840

Options for Families and Youth
P.O. Box 798
Brook Park, OH 44042
(440) 234-3147
Fax: (440) 267-7075

Private Adoption Services
3411 Michigan Avenue
Cincinnati, OH 45208
(513) 871-5777
Fax: (513) 871-8582

Spaulding Adoption Program
Beech Brook
3737 Lander Road
Pepper Pike, OH 44124
(216) 831-2255
Fax: (216) 831-1442

Specialized Alternatives for
Families and Youth
10100 Elida Road
Delphos, OH 45833
(419) 695-8010
Fax: (419) 695-0004
Toll Free: (800) 532-7239

St. Aloysius Orphanage
4721 Reading Road
Cincinnati, OH 45237
(513) 242-7600
Fax: (513) 242-2845

St. Joseph Children's Treatment
Center
650 St. Paul Avenue
Dayton, OH 45410
(937) 254-3562
Fax: (937) 254-6777

The Adoption Center, Inc.
12151 Ellsworth Road
North Jackson, OH 44451
(330) 547-8255
Fax: (330) 547-3327

V. Beacon Agency
743 South Bryne Road
Toledo, OH 43609
(419) 382-3572
Fax: (419) 389-0328

Westark Family Services, Inc
325 Third Street, S.E.
Massillon, OH 46646
(330) 832-5043
Fax: (330) 830-2537

World Family Adoption Studies,
Inc.
669 Edgecliff Drive
Worthington, OH 43235
(614) 841-1808

Youth Engaged for Success
3930 Salem Avenue
Dayton, OH 45406
(937) 275-0762
Fax: (937) 275-8431

Youth Services Network of
  Southwest Ohio
3817 Wilmington Pike
Kettering, OH 45429
(937) 256-9113
Fax: (937) 294-7440

**Adoptive Parent Support
  Groups**

ACT Group, Advocates for
  Children Today
3965 Ganyard
Brunswick, OH 44212
(330) 225-1088

Adopt America Network of Ohio
340 Bank Street
Painesville, OH 44077
(440) 352-3780

Adoption Awareness Alliance
11370 Springfield Pike, Suite 200
Cincinnati, OH 45246
(513) 771-3515

Adoption Support Group
4012 Venice Road, #77
Sandusky, OH 44870
(419) 626-0360

Adoptive and Foster Parents
  Together Scheaffer
190 Jeanne Drive
Springboro, OH 45066
(513) 748-9299

Adoptive Families and Friends
6891 Cherry Blossom Drive
Mentor, OH 44060-8430
(216) 257-7746

Adoptive Families of Greater
  Cincinnati
4686 Yankee Road
Cincinnati, OH 45044
(513) 539-9787

Adoptive Families Together
7314 Parkdale Avenue
Cincinnati, OH 45237
(513) 245-9773

Adoptive Family Support
  Association
P.O. Box 91247
Cleveland, OH 44101-3247
(216) 491-4638

Adoptive Parent Support Group
2272 Harrisburg Pike
Grove City, OH 43123
(614) 871-1164

Adoptive Parenting Support
2612 San Rae Drive
Kettering, OH 45419
(513) 299-2110

Adoptive Parents Support
  Organization
2638 Ridgecliffe Avenue
Cincinnati, OH 45212-1324
(513) 631-2883

Adoptive Parents Together
3955 Euclid Avenue
Cleveland, OH 45419
(216) 431-4500, Ext: 2729

Adoptive Parents Together
P.O. Box 112
Sandyville, OH 44671

Athens County Children Foster
  Parent Group
14 Stoneybrook Drive
Athens, OH 45701
(740) 592-3061

Attachment and Bonding Center
  of Ohio
12608 State Road
Cleveland, OH 44133
(440) 230-1960

Attachment Disorders Parents
  Network
P.O. Box 176
Cortland, OH 44410

Black Adoption Recruitment
  Committee
1882 Nason Avenue
Columbus, OH 43208

Catholic Charities, Diocese of
  Toledo
1933 Spielbusch Avenue
Toledo, OH 43697-0985
(419) 244-6711
Fax: (494) 244-4781

Celebrate Adoption
OH
(513) 351-5412

Central Ohio Families with
  Children from China (COFCC)
P.O. Box 554
Hillard, OH 43026-0554
(513) 351-5412

Charting the Course
Parenthesis Family Advocates
3915 Patricia Drive
Columbus, OH 43220
(614) 459-2833

Clearcreek Valley of Ohio
  Adoptive Parent Group
P.O. Box 338
Amanda, OH 43102-0338
(740) 969-4475

Compagnons
P.O. Box 21668
South Euclid, OH 44121
(216) 691-9216

Comprehensive Psychological and
  Psychiatric Services
1555 Bethel
Columbus, OH 43220
(614) 442-0664

Concern for Children, Inc.
6425 Somerset Drive
North Olmstead, OH 44070
(216) 734-7580

Connections
c/o Jewish Family Services
6525 Sylvania Avenue
Toledo, OH 43560
(419) 885-2561

Dayton Area Minority Adoptive
  Parents, Inc. and North
  American Council on
Adoptable Children State
  Representative
191 Coddington Avenue
Xenia, OH 45385
(513) 372-5700

Down Syndrome Association
  of Cincinnati
9666 Rexford Drive
Cincinnati, OH 45241
(513) 542-3286

FACT (Families for Acceptable
  Care and Treatment)
565 Children Drive, West
Columbus, OH 43230
(614) 228-5523

Families Blessed by Adoption,
  Ross County
74 Clinton Road
Chillicothe, OH 45601
(740) 775-6784

Families for Russian and
  Ukrainian Adoptions
Greater Cincinnati
704 Tweed Avenue
Cincinnati, OH 45226
(513) 871-5969

Families Forever
15903 Road 133
Cecil, OH 45821
(419) 399-2134

Families Through Adoption
426 Goosepond Road
Newark, OH 43055
(740) 364-0797
repyke@akron.infi.net

Families Thru Adoption
3423 Bluerock Road
Cincinnati, OH 45239
(513) 741-0929

Families thru World Adoption
2933 Lower Bellbrook Road
Spring Valley, OH 45370

Families United by Adoption
2112 Sherwood Forest Drive
Miamisburg, OH 45342
(937) 866-1337

Families with Children
from China
1855 Finderberg Road
New Carlisle, OH 45344
(513) 769-7733
bgambill-1@cinergy.com

Family Defense Fund
702 S. Main Street
Ada, OH 45810
(419) 825-1308

Family Outings
310 Haynes St.
Dayton, OH 45410
(937) 256-0127

Foreign Adoptive Children-
Eastern Suburbs
11875 Laurel Road
Chesterland, OH 44026
(440) 729-2535

Foster Parent Association
8729 Peter Hoover Road
New Albany, OH 43054
(614) 855-9785

Geauga County Adoptive Family
Group
303 N. Hambden
Chardon, OH 44024
(440) 285-9141
Fax: (440) 350-4399

Good Samaritan Hospital School
of Nursing
375 Dixmyth Avenue
Cincinnati, OH 45220-2489
(513) 872-3727
dee_daniels@trihealth.com

Group of Black Adoptive Parents
1055 Grayview Court
Cincinnati, OH 45224
(513) 541-4166

Jewish Community Center,
Adoptive Parent Support
Group
26001 South Woodland Road
Beachwood, OH 44122
(216) 831-0700

Korean Family Connection
OH
(513) 321-4097

Lake County Catholic Services
8 N. State Street, Suite 455
Painesville, OH 44077
(440) 946-7264

Latin American Families
3568 Stoneboat Court
Maineville, OH 45039
(513) 677-1732

Life RAFFT (Raising Adoptive &
Foster Families Together)
207 Hilltop Drive
Chardon, OH 44024
(440) 632-5933

Miami Valley Adoption
Coalition, Inc.
4631 Cantura Drive
Dayton, OH 45415
(937) 854-2944

New Roots
P.O. Box 14953
Columbus, OH 43214
(614) 470-0846

North American Council on
Adoptable Children
Representative
1371 Virginia Avenue
Columbus, OH 43212
(614) 299-0177
TimOHanlon@aol.com

Ohio Council on Adoption
132 Aspen Court
Delaware, OH 43015

Ohio Family Care Association
2931 Indianola Avenue
Columbus, OH 43202
(614) 299-9261

Open Adoption Support Group
541 Brandywynne Court
Dayton, OH 45406
(513) 275-9628

Our Children Of Stark County
1223 11th Street, N.W.
Canton, OH 44703
(330) 454-7715

Parents Supporting Parents
19306 Boerger Road
Marysville, OH 43040
(937) 349-7105

Pathway
Caring For Children
4949 Fulton Drive
Canton, OH 44718-2383
(330) 493-0083
Fax: (330) 493-3689
pathway@nci2000.net

Project Orphans Abroad
P.O. Box 29337
Parma, OH 44129
(216) 526-3618

Rainbow Connection
1065 CR 1600 Route 7
Ashland, OH 44805
(419) 281-3837

Rainbow Families of Toledo
1920 S. Shore Boulevard
Oregon, OH 43618
(419) 693-9259

RESOLVE of Ohio
P.O. Box 141277
Columbus, OH 43214-6277
(216) 468-2365
Toll Free: (800) 414-6446

Single Adoptive Parents
1185 Franklin Avenue
Columbus, OH 43205
(614) 253-4318

Single Parent by Adoption
Support System
2547 Talbott Avenue
Cincinnati, OH 45211
(513) 661-5170

Southeast Ohio Adoptive Family
   Support Group
P.O. Box 75
Athens, OH 45701
(740) 448-6119

Stark County Family Council
   Adoption Support Group
1205 Grove Street, N.E.
North Canton, OH 44721
(330) 494-2327

Stars of David International Inc.
Jewish Family Service of Toledo
6525 Sylvania Avenue
Sylvania, OH 43560
(419) 885-2561
Fax: (419) 885-7427
www.starsofdavid.org
starsdavid@aol.com

Stars of David International Inc.
Jewish Family Services
2831 East Main Street
Columbus, OH 43209
(614) 421-7709
Fax: (614) 231-4978
www.starsofdavid.org
starsdavid@aol.com

Trumbull County Foster
   Parent Association
2282 Reeves Road, N.E.
Warren, OH 44483
(216) 372-2010

Western Reserve Adoptive
   Parents
2787 Citadel, N.E.
Warren, OH 44483
(330) 372-2060

Search Support Groups

Adoption Connection
P.O. Box 2482
Youngstown, OH 44509
(330) 792-3546

Adoption Network Cleveland
291 East 222nd Street
Cleveland, OH 44123-1751
(216) 261-1511
www.AdoptionNetwork.org
info@adoptionnetwork.org

Adoption Option
P.O. Box 429327
Cincinnati, OH 45242
(513) 793-7268

Adoption Station
12164 Unity Road
New Springfield, OH 44443
(330) 542-2367

Adoption Triad Support
980 Main Street
Wellsville, OH 43968
(330) 532-4990

Adoption Triad Support Center
5900 S.O.M. Center Road, #273
Cleveland, OH 44094
(216) 943-2118

Adoption Triangle Unity
4144 Packard Road
Toledo, OH 43613-1938
(419) 244-7072

Aftermath
P.O. Box 201
New Carlisle, OH 45344
(513) 845-9980

Akron Adoption Support Group
7385 Herrick Park Drive
Hudson, OH 44236
(216) 656-4153

American Adoption Congress
   State Representative
291 E. 222nd Street
Cleveland, OH 44123
(216) 481-4171
bln2@po.cwru.edu

Birthmother Support Group
1575 Cleveland Avenue
East Liverpool, OH 43920

Birthparent Support
3423 Bluerock Road
Cincinnati, OH 45239
(513) 741-0929

Birthright
6779 Manchester Road
Clinton, OH 44216

Birthright of Columbus, Inc
22 East Gay Street, Suite 881
Columbus, OH 43215
(614) 221-0844

Chosen Children
311 Springbrook Boulevard
Dayton, OH 45405
(937) 274-8017

Circle of Love
409 W. Mechanic Street
Wapakoneta, OH 45895-1050
(419) 738-8862

Immigrant Children
18460 Bishop Lane
Strongsville, OH 44136
(440) 238-1004

Mum's the Word
381 Bartley Avenue
Mansfield, OH 44903
(419) 524-0564

Ohio Adoptee Searches
P.O. Box 856
Waynesville, OH 45068
(513) 897-2120
Fax: (513) 897-1423
Ohio.Adoptee@Winning.Com

Pieces of Yesterday
856 Pine Needles Drive
Centerville, OH 45458
(937) 436-0593

Reconnections
2468 N. Knoll Drive
Beavercreek, OH 45431
(937) 426-0646

Reunite
P.O. Box 694
Reynoldsburg, OH 43068
(614) 861-2584

Southeastern Ohio Searchers
   (S.O.S.)
4 Cook Drive
Athens, OH 45701
(740) 592-1070

Sunshine Reunions
1175 Virginia Avenue
Akron, OH 44306
(330) 773-4691

Support for Birthparents
1983 Sitterly Road
Canal Winchester, OH 43110
(614) 833-1647

Swirls
132 E. South Street
Fostoria, OH 44830
(419) 435-0325

Twelve Step Adoption Healing
   Group
2120 Pershing Blvd.
Dayton, OH 45420
(937) 252-9560

OHIO LAWS RELATED TO ADOPTION: QUESTIONS AND ANSWERS

Can an attorney serve as an intermediary?
Yes.

Is advertising permitted?
No. If a prospective adoptive parent does advertise, the Department of Human Services will contact you and ask you not to do so, although they will not prosecute. It is recommended that you advertise instead in newspapers along the Pennsylvania and West Virginia borders, as these publications are often available in Ohio.

Who must consent to the adoption?
1. The birth mother
2. The birth father if child was conceived or born while he was married to the birth mother, or if he claims to be the father and establishes a relationship with the child before placement, or if he has acknowledged the child in writing before placement, signed the birth certificate, or filed an objection to the adoption before the placement

When can consent be taken from birth mother (father), and how long after the consent is signed can it be revoked?
Consent can be taken seventy-two hours after the child's birth and is irrevocable unless the birth parents attempt to withdraw before the final adoption decree; any such withdrawal will be successful only if the court finds it is in the child's best interest. An adoption cannot be finalized until the child has lived in the adoptive parents' home for at least six months.

What are the birth father's rights?
If the birth father has abandoned the birth mother during the pregnancy or if he has failed to provide for the child, his consent is not required. If after thirty days of the child's placement, he does not file a paternity case or an objection to the adoption, his parental rights are terminated. As with all birth fathers, he must receive notice of the adoption proceedings.

What fees can adoptive parents pay?
Only medical and legal expenses and agency fees are permitted. The adoptive parents must submit a statement to the court of all fees and expenses paid.

Where does the adoption hearing take place?
The adoption hearing takes place in the court of the county where the adoptive parents live, where the child was born, where the birth parents live, or where the placement agency is located.

How are familial and stepparent adoptions different from nonbiological adoptions?
If a child is adopted by a stepparent, this does not curtail the court's power to award visitation rights to grandparents. A home study is not required in a stepparent or grandparent adoption.

Can a nonresident finalize an adoption in this state?
Yes.

Source: Ohio Revised Code Annotated Sections 3101.01 to 3107.44 (1998)

OKLAHOMA

State Adoption Specialist

Oklahoma Department of
  Human Services
Permanency Planning Section
Deborah Goodman
P.O. Box 25352
Oklahoma City, OK 73125
(405) 521-2475
Fax: (405) 521-4373
*www.okdhs.org/programs/
  programs.htm*
deborah.goodman@okdhs.org

State ICPC Administrator

Oklahoma Department of
  Human Services
P. O. Box 25352
Oklahoma City, OK 73125
(405) 521-2475
Fax: (405) 521-4488

State Reunion Registry

Voluntary Adoption Reunion
  Registry
Oklahoma Department of Human
  Services
P.O. Box 25352
Oklahoma City, OK 73125
(405) 521-4373

**Licensed Private Adoption
  Agencies**

Adoption Affiliates
6136 E. 32nd Place
Tulsa, OK 74135
(918) 664-2275
Toll Free: (800) 253-6307

Adoption Center of Northeastern
  Oklahoma
6202 South Lewis, Suite Q
Tulsa, OK 74136
(918) 748-9200
Fax: (918) 748-0369

Adoption Choices
1616 East 19th Street, Suite 101
Edmond, OK 73013-6674
(405) 715-1991
Fax: (405) 715-2640
Toll Free: (800) 898-6028

Associated Catholic Charities
1501 N. Classen Boulevard,
  Suite 200
Oklahoma City, OK 73106
(405) 523-3000
Fax: (405) 523-3030

Baptist Children's Home
16301 S. Western
Oklahoma City, OK 73170
(405) 691-7781

Bethany Adoption Service
3940 North College
Bethany, OK 73008
(405) 789-5423
Fax: (405) 787-6913

Bless This Child, Inc.
Route 4, Box 1005
Checotah, OK 74426
(918) 473-7045

Catholic Social Services
P.O. Box 6429
Tulsa, OK 74148
(918) 585-8167

Chosen Child Adoption Agency
P.O. Box 55424
Tulsa, OK 74155-5424
(918) 298-0082
Fax: (218) 749-8784

Christian Homes of Abilene
802 N. 10th
Duncan, OK 73533
(405) 252-5131
www.christianhomes.com
christianhomes@abilene.com

Cradle of Lawton
902 N.W. Kingswood Road
Lawton, OK 73505
(580) 536-2478
*members.delphi.com/cradle2/
  index.html*
jan.howenstine@juno.com

Crisis Pregnancy Outreach
11604 East 58th Street
Tulsa, OK 74146
(918) 296-3377

Deaconess Home Pregnancy and
  Adoption Services
5300 North Meridian Avenue,
  Suite 9
Oklahoma City, OK 73112
(405) 949-4200

Dillon International, Inc.
3530 East 31st Street, Suite 102
Tulsa, OK 74135-1519
(918) 749-4600
Fax: (918) 749-7144
*www.dillonadopt.com/
  dillonintl@dillonadopt.com*

Eagle Ridge
601 N.E. 63rd
Oklahoma City, OK 73105
(405) 840-1359

Gladney Center for Adoption
P.O. Box 33054
Tulsa, OK 74153-1054
(918) 627-3467
Toll Free: (888) 883-7492
*www.gladney.org/
info@gladney.org*

Hannah's Prayer Adoption
  Agency
8621 S. Memorial
Tulsa, OK 74133
(918) 254-0189
Fax: (918) 461-1593

Heritage Family Services
5200 S. Yale #300
Tulsa, OK 74135
(918) 491-6767

LDS Social Services of Oklahoma
4500 S. Garnett, Suite 425
Tulsa, OK 74102
(918) 665-3090

Lutheran Social Services
3000 United Founders Boulevard,
  Suite 141
Oklahoma City, OK 73112-4279
(405) 848-1733

McAlester Counseling Center
319 South 6th
McAlester, OK 74501
(918) 423-1998

Natasha's Story, Inc.
1554 S. Yorktown Place
Tulsa, OK 74104
(918) 747-3617

Project Adopt
1901 N. Classen
Oklahoma City, OK 73106
(405) 521-0495

SAFY of America
1217 Sovereign Row
Oklahoma City, OK 73108
(405) 942-5570

Small Miracles International
107 Mid-America Blvd #3
Midwest City, OK 73110
(405) 732-7295
Fax: (405) 732-7297
*www.smiint.org
MORR@smiint.org*

The Elizaveta Foundation
6517 S. Barnes
Oklahoma City, OK 73159
(405) 681-2722

Women Care
P.O. Box 188
Edmond, OK 73083-0188
(405) 330-4700

**Adoptive Parent Support
  Groups**

Adopt America Network
Oklahoma Field Representative
448 Claremont
Norman, OK 73068
(405) 364-4956

Adopt America Network
of Oklahoma
5150 N. Harrah Road
Harrah, OK 73045
(405) 454-2913

Adopt America Network
Oklahoma
3517 N.W. 66th
Oklahoma City, OK 73116

Adoptive Families Support
Organization
2009 W. Dena Drive
Edmond, OK 73034
(405) 359-0812

Adoptive Parents of
Central Oklahoma
1237 Mountain Brook Drive
Norman, OK 73072-3446
(405) 364-8488

Adoptive Parents of Northeast
Oklahoma
2939 S. 95th East Avenue
Tulsa, OK 74129
(918) 665-7778

Adoptive Parents Support Group
Meadowlake Hospital
Enid, OK 73703
Toll Free: (800) 522-1366

Attachment Network
P.O. Box 532
Broken Arrow, OK 74013
(918) 251-7781

Babb Enterprises and North
American Council on
Adoptable Children
Representative
488 Claremont
Norman, OK 73069
(405) 329-9294
annebabb@homes4kids.org

Chickasha Support Group
217 N. Third
Chickasha, OK 73018
(405) 224-2733

Citizen Band Potawatomi Tribe
1901 S. Gordon Cooper Drive
Shawnee, OK 74801
(405) 275-3121

Concerned Families
Reaching Out
615 E. First Street
Watonga, OK 73772
(580) 623-8622

Cradle of Lawton
902 N.W. Kingswood Road
Lawton, OK 73505
(580) 536-2478

Evangelistic Baptist Church
3129 N. Martin Luther King Ave.
Oklahoma City, OK 73111-4212
(405) 424-1714

Families and Friends of
Southeast Oklahoma
P.O. Box 188
Broken Bow, OK 74728
(580) 536-2478

Families by Choice
P.O. Box 879
Apache, OK 73006
(580) 588-3348

Families Helping Families
Route 1, Box 58
Mead, OK 73449
(580) 920-0188

Lake County Adoptive Families
614 Q Street, S.W.
Ardmore, OK 73401
(580) 223-1037

North American Council on
Adoptable Children
Representative
P.O. Box 25
Harrah, OK 73045

(405) 454-1179
Fax: (405) 454-1179
rlaws@homes4kids.org

North Central Oklahoma New
Beginnings in Adoption
Route 5, Box 740
Ponca City, OK 74601
(580) 762-7213

Northwest Aware
Route 1, Box 325
Sharon, OK 73857
(580) 256-8741

Oklahoma Adoption Support
Association
5721 S. Cedar
Broken Arrow, OK 74011
(918) 455-7771

Oklahoma Council on Adoptable
Children and North American
Council on Adaptable
Children
2609 N.W. 38th Street
Oklahoma City, OK 73112
(405) 942-0810

Parents of Unattached Kids
Tulsa, OK
(918) 272-6250

Siblings Support Group
1615 Rosedale
Ardmore, OK 73401
(580) 226-1838

Southeast Oklahoma Adoptive
Parent Society Johnson
Route 1, Box 815
Antlers, OK 74523
(580) 298-3995

Search Support Groups

Adoptee Liberty Movement
Association (ALMA)
P.O. Box 1421
Edmond, OK 73083-1421

Adoption Tree of Support
3703 S. Nogales Avenue
Tulsa, OK 74107
(918) 445-1493

ALARM Network
909 Bell Avenue
Lawton, OK 73507
(580) 355-5535

American Adoption Congress
State Representative
P.O. Box 187
Perkins, OK 74059
(405) 707-0010
Fax: (405) 707-0020
imssomeone@aol.com

AR Adoption Connections
Route 1, Box 54
Roland, OK 74954
(918) 427-0453

Oklahoma Adoption Triad
Box 471008
Tulsa, OK 74147
(918) 254-1014

Shared Heartbeats
P.O. Box 12125
Oklahoma City, OK 73157
(405) 943-4500

Shepherds Heart
2401 Slagle Road
Newalla, OK 74857
(405) 391-4308

OKLAHOMA LAWS RELATED TO ADOPTION: QUESTIONS AND ANSWERS

Can an attorney serve as an intermediary?
Yes.

Is advertising permitted?
Yes.

Who must consent to the adoption?
1. Both birth parents, if sixteen years or older
2. If the birth mother or father is younger than sixteen, then a guardian or parent must also give written consent
3. The child placement agency, if it has custody of the child

When can consent be taken from birth mother (father), and how long after the consent is signed can it be revoked?
The birth parents can appear before the judge and consent in writing to the adoption and a termination of their parental rights seventy-two hours after the birth of the child. The consent can be withdrawn up to thirty days after signing if the court finds it is in the child's best interest. An agency surrender can be signed in front of the agency caseworker and the birth parent need not go to court. The surrender is irrevocable at the time of signing.

What are the birth father's rights?
The birth father's consent is not required if he fails to acknowledge his paternity and does not support the mother during pregnancy; or if he fails to prove that he is the father or fails to exercise parental duties toward the child within ninety days of the birth; or if he waives his right to notice of the adoption hearing; or if he does not appear at the adoption hearing after receiving notice.

Consent is also not necessary from a birth parent who willfully fails to communicate and maintain a significant relationship with or who fails or refuses to support a child for twelve months.

What fees can adoptive parents pay?
Medical and legal expenses are permitted. Living expenses can be paid in a private adoption with court preapproval.

Where does the adoption hearing take place?
The hearing can take place in the court of the county where the adoptive parents live, where the birth parents live, or where the placing agency is located.

How are familial and stepparent adoptions different from nonbiological adoptions?
Generally, in a stepparent adoption no home study is required. A stepparent adoption can be finalized in about three to four weeks. Grandparent visitation rights are permitted in stepparent adoptions or relative adoptions only if at least one of the biological parents is deceased and it is in the child's best interest. In a relative adoption, a home study is required and the steps for a nonbiological adoption are followed.

Can a nonresident finalize an adoption in this state?
Yes, but only if the child is a resident of Oklahoma.

OREGON

State Adoption Specialist

Oregon State Office for Services
to Children and Families
Kathy Ledesma
HSB 2nd Floor South, 500
Summer Street, N.E.
Salem, OR 97310
(503) 945-5677
Fax: (503) 945-6969
www.scf.hr.state.or.us/adopting.htm
Kathy.ledesma@state.or.us

State ICPC Administrator

State Office, Services to Children
& Families
Oregon Division of Human
Resources
500 Summer Street, N.E.
Salem, OR 97310-1017
(503) 945-7019
Fax: (503) 947-5072

**State Adoption Exchange/State
Photolisting Service**

Northwest Adoption Exchange
600 Stewart Street, Suite 1313
Seattle, WA 98101
(206) 441-6822
Fax: (206) 441-7281
Toll Free: (800) 927-9411
www.nwae.org
nwae@nwresource.org

The Boys and Girls Aid Society
of Oregon
18 S.W. Boundary Court
Portland, OR 97201
(503) 222-9661
adoptions.scf.hr.state.or.us/
adopt.htm

State Reunion Registry

Oregon State Office for Services
to Children and Families
Assisted Search and Registry
Program, Permanency and
Adoption Services Unit
HRB 2nd Floor South, 500
Summer Street, N.E.
Salem, OR 97310-1017
(503) 945-5677
www.scf.hr.state.or.us/adoptreg.htm

**Regional/District Public
Agencies**

Oregon State Office for Services
to Children and Families, Baker
3080 Pocahontas Rd.
Baker, OR 97814
(541) 523-6423
Fax: (541) 523-7048
Toll Free: (800) 646-5430

Oregon State Office for Services
to Children and Families,
Benton
555 N.W. Fifth Street
Corvallis, OR 97330
(541) 757-4121
Fax: (541) 757-4214

Oregon State Office for Services
to Children and Families,
Clackamas
P.O. Box 5329
Oregon City, OR 97045
(503) 657-2112
Fax: (503) 657-6810
Toll Free: (800) 628-7876

Oregon State Office for Services
to Children and Families,
Clatsop
450 Marine Drive, Suite 210
Astoria, OR 97103
(503) 325-9179
Fax: (503) 325-0972
Toll Free: (800) 643-4606

Oregon State Office for Services
to Children and Families,
Columbia
500 N. Highway 30, Suite 220
St. Helens, OR 97051
(503) 397-3292
Fax: (503) 397-1092
Toll Free: (800) 428-1546

Oregon State Office for Services
to Children and Families, Coos
P.O. Box 467
Northbend, OR 97459
(541) 756-5500
Fax: (541) 756-4200
Toll Free: (800) 500-2730

Oregon State Office for Services
to Children and Families,
Crook
1495 N.E. Third Street, Suite B
Prineville, OR 97754
(541) 447-6207
Fax: (541) 447-7213

Oregon State Office for Services
to Children and Families, Curry
P.O. Box 887
Gold Beach, OR 97444
(541) 247-5437
Fax: (541) 247-6999
Toll Free: (800) 510-0000

Oregon State Office for Services
to Children and Families,
Deschutes
1001 S.W. Emkay Drive, Suite E
Bend, OR 97702
(541) 388-6161
Fax: (541) 388-6401

Oregon State Office for Services
to Children and Families,
Douglas
1937 W. Harvard Boulevard
Roseburg, OR 97470
(541) 440-3373
Fax: (541) 440-3448
Toll Free: (800) 305-2903

Oregon State Office for Services
to Children and Families,
Eastern Region
20310 Empire Boulevard,
Suite A-100
Bend, OR 97701-5723
(541) 388-6414
Fax: (541) 388-6017

Oregon State Office for Services
to Children and Families,
Gilliam-Wheeler
425 Washington
Condon, OR 97823
(541) 384-4252
Fax: (541) 384-4262

Oregon State Office for Services
to Children and Families, Grant
725 W. Main Street, Suite C
John Day, OR 97845
(541) 575-0728
Fax: (541) 575-0656

Oregon State Office for Services
to Children and Families,
Harney
809 W. Jackson, Suite 200
Burns, OR 97720
(541) 573-2086
Fax: (541) 573-1538

Oregon State Office for Services
to Children and Families,
Hermiston
950 S.E. Columbia Drive, Suite C
Hermiston, OR 97838
(541) 567-7611

Oregon State Office for Services
to Children and Families,
Hood River
910 Pacific Avenue, Suite 500
Hood River, OR 97031
(541) 386-2962
Fax: (541) 386-7066

Oregon State Office for Services
to Children and Families,
Jackson
P.O. Box 1549
Medford, OR 97501
(541) 776-6120
Fax: (541) 776-6063

Oregon State Office for Services
to Children and Families,
Jefferson
678 N.E. Highway 97, Suite C
Madras, OR 97741
(541) 475-2292
Fax: (541) 475-6830

Oregon State Office for Services
to Children and Families,
Josephine
P.O. Box 189
Grants Pass, OR 97526
(541) 474-3120
Fax: (541) 471-2873
Toll Free: (800) 930-4364

Oregon State Office for Services
to Children and Families,
Klamath
700 Klamath Avenue, Suite 500
Klamath Falls, OR 97601
(541) 883-5570
Fax: (541) 883-5570

Oregon State Office for Services
to Children and Families, Lake
108 N. E Street, Suite 201
Lakeview, OR 97630
(541) 947-2273
Fax: (541) 947-2373
Toll Free: (800) 811-4201

Oregon State Office for Services
to Children and Families, Lane
1899 Willamette
Eugene, OR 97401
(541) 686-7555
Fax: (541) 485-8566

Oregon State Office for Services
to Children and Families,
Lincoln
119 N.E. Fourth Avenue, Room 5
Newport, OR 97365
(541) 265-8557
Fax: (541) 265-3237
Toll Free: (800) 305-2850

Oregon State Office for Services
to Children and Families, Linn
118 S.E. Second Avenue, Suite D
Albany, OR 97321
(541) 967-2060
Fax: (541) 967-2127
Toll Free: (800) 358-2208

Oregon State Office for Services
to Children and Families,
Malheur
702 Sunset Drive, Suite 300
Ontario, OR 97914
(541) 889-9194
Fax: (541) 889-9588
Toll Free: (800) 445-4273

Oregon State Office for Services
to Children and Families,
Marion
2045 Silverton Road, N.E., Suite A
Salem, OR 97303-3122
(503) 378-6800
Fax: (503) 378-3061
Toll Free: (800) 854-3508

Oregon State Office for Services
to Children and Families,
Metro Region
827 N.E. Oregon, Suite 250
Portland, OR 97232-2108
(503) 731-3000
Fax: (503) 731-3410

Oregon State Office for Services
to Children and Families,
Morrow
P.O. Box 498
Boardman, OR 97818
(541) 481-9482
Fax: (541) 481-2960

Oregon State Office for Services
to Children and Families,
Multnomah East
3618 S.E. 122nd Avenue
Portland, OR 97236-3403
(503) 731-4293
Fax: (503) 257-4403

Oregon State Office for Services
to Children and Families,
Multnomah Midtown
1425 N.E. Irving, Lloyd Plaza,
Building 400
Portland, OR 97232-4204
(503) 731-3147
Fax: (503) 731-3151

Oregon State Office for Services
to Children and Families,
Multnomah
North/Northeast
30 N. Webster, Suite D
Portland, OR 97217-2766
(503) 280-6993
Fax: (503) 280-6638

Oregon State Office for Services
to Children and Families,
Multnomah St. Johns
7825 N. Lombard Street
Portland, OR 97203-3125
(503) 731-4400
Fax: (503) 731-3363

Oregon State Office for Services
to Children and Families,
Multnomah, Gresham
355 N.W. Division Street
Gresham, OR 97030-5523
(503) 674-3610
Fax: (503) 674-3620

Oregon State Office for Services
to Children and Families,
Pendleton
700 S.E. Emigrant Street, State
Office Building, Suite 200
Pendleton, OR 97801
(541) 276-9220
Fax: (541) 276-9349
Toll Free: (800) 547-3897

Oregon State Office for Services
to Children and Families, Polk
P.O. Box 198
Dallas, OR 97338
(503) 623-8118
Fax: (503) 623-5426

Oregon State Office for Services
to Children and Families,
Reedsport
2630 Frontage Road
Reedsport, OR 97467
(541) 271-4851
Fax: (541) 271-5162

Oregon State Office for Services
to Children and Families,
Tillamook
3600 E. Third Street
Tillamook, OR 97141
(503) 842-5571
Fax: (503) 842-5028

Oregon State Office for Services
to Children and Families,
Union
1901 Adams Avenue
LaGrande, OR 97850
(541) 963-8571
Fax: (541) 963-2906

Oregon State Office for Services
to Children and Families,
Wallowa
P.O. Box A
Enterprise, OR 97828
(541) 426-4558
Fax: (541) 426-4092

Oregon State Office for Services
to Children and Families,
Wasco-Sherman
700 Union Street, Room 230
The Dalles, OR 97058
(541) 298-5136
Fax: (541) 296-8722

Oregon State Office for Services
to Children and Families,
Washington
5920 N.E. Ray Circle, Suite 200
Hillsboro, OR 97124
(503) 648-8951
Fax: (503) 640-1108
Toll Free: (800) 275-8952

Oregon State Office for Services
to Children and Families,
Western Region
15875 S.W. 72nd Avenue
Tigard, OR 97224
(503) 431-2078

Oregon State Office for Services
to Children and Families,
Woodburn
1235 Mt. Hood Avenue
Woodburn, OR 97071
(503) 981-3071
Fax: (503) 982-5917
Toll Free: (800) 358-2571

Oregon State Office for Services
to Children and Families,
Yamhill
P.O. Box 478
McMinnville, OR 97128
(503) 472-4634
Fax: (503) 472-3815
Toll Free: (800) 822-3903

Licensed Private Adoption Agencies

Adventist Adoption and Family
Services Program
6040 S.E. Belmont Street
Portland, OR 97215
(503) 232-1211
Fax: (503) 232-4756
www.tagnet.org/adventistadoption/
adventistadoption@msn.com

Albertina Kerr Center for
Children
722 N.E. 162nd
Portland, OR 97232
(503) 255-4205
Fax: (503) 255-5095
marciah@albertinakerr.or

All God's Children International
4114 N.E. Fremont Street
Portland, OR 97212
(503) 282-7652
Fax: (503) 282-2582
agi@usa.net

Associated Services for
International Adoption (ASIA)
5935 Willow Lane
Lake Oswego, OR 97035-5344
(503) 697-6863
Fax: (503) 697-6957
www.asiadopt.org
info@asiadopt.org

Bethany Christian Services
149 E. 3rd Avenue, Suite 200
Hillsboro, OR 97123-4080
(503) 693-6873
Fax: (503) 846-1203
www.bethany.org
bcswashor@aol.com

Bridges Adoption and Family
Services, Inc.
1130 S.W. Maple Crest Drive
Portland, OR 97219
(503) 246-2445
Fax: (503) 246-5998
www.pcez.com/Bridges/
bridges@pcez.com

Caring Connections
5439 S.E. Bantam Court
Milwaukie, OR 97267
(503) 282-3663
l.schwalb@juno.com

*Cascade International Children's
   Services, Inc.
153 East Historical Columbia
   River Highway
Troutdale, OR 97060
(503) 665-1589
Fax: (503) 665-7865
cascade-int@juno.com

Casey Family Program
3910 S.E. Stark Street
Portland, OR 97214
(503) 239-9977
Fax: (503) 232-3851
www.casey.org/
hgilge@casey.org

Catholic Charities, Inc.
231 S.E. 12th Avenue
Portland, OR 97214
(503) 231-4866
Fax: (503) 231-4327

China Adoption Services
P.O. Box 19699
Portland, OR 97280
(503) 245-0976
Fax: (503) 246-2973
info@chinadopt.org

Columbia Counseling, Inc.
1445 Rosemont Road
West Linn, OR 97068
(503) 655-9470
Fax: (503) 557-8134
cci@ipns.com

Dove Adoptions International,
   Inc.
3735 S.E. Martins
Portland, OR 97202
(503) 774-7210
Fax: (503) 771-7893
www.adoptions.net
dovadopt@cnnw.net

Families Are Forever
4114 N.E. Fremont Street
Portland, OR 97212
(503) 282-7652
Fax: (503) 282-2582
agci@usa.net

Give Us This Day, Inc.
P.O. Box 11611
Portland, OR 97211
(503) 282-1123
Kmitchell@msn.com

Heritage Adoptions
516 S.E. Morrison Street, Suite 800
Portland, OR 97214
(503) 233-1099
Fax: (503) 223-0587
HeritageOR@aol.com

*Holt International Children's
   Services
P.O. Box 2880, 1195 City View
Eugene, OR 97402
(541) 687-2202
Fax: (541) 683-6175
www.holtintl.org
info@holtintl.org

Journeys of the Heart Adoption
   Services
P.O. Box 39
Hillsboro, OR 97123
(503) 681-3075
Journeys_Heart@msn.com

LDS Family Services
530 Center Street, Suite 706
Salem, OR 97301
(503) 581-7483
Fax: (503) 581-7484
lloydcampbell@desertonlin

Lutheran Family Services
605 S.E. 39th Avenue
Portland, OR 97214
(503) 231-7480
Fax: (503) 236-8815
lss@Teleport.com

Medina Children's Services, Black
   Child Adoption Program
123 16th Avenue
Seattle, WA 98122-0638
(206) 461-4520
Fax: (204) 461-8372
www.medinachild.org/
medina@medinachild.org

New Hope Child & Family
   Agency
4370 N.E. Halsey St., Suite 215
Portland, OR 97213
(503) 282-6726
Toll Free: (800) 228-3150

New Hope Child and Family
   Agency
2611 N.E. 125th St.
Seattle, WA 98125
(206) 363-1800
Fax: (206) 363-0318
www.newhopekids.org
info@newhopekids.org

Northwest Adoptions and Family
   Services
2695 Spring Valley Lane, N.W.
Salem, OR 97304
(503) 581-6652
Fax: (503) 370-9822
pinkerton@eathlink.net

Open Adoption & Family
   Services, Inc.
5200 S.W. Macadam, Suite 250
Portland, OR 97201
(503) 226-4870
Fax: (503) 226-4890
adoptopen@aol.com

Orphans Overseas
14986 N.W. Cornell Raod
Portland, OR 97229
(503) 297-2006
Fax: (503) 292-1258
orphans@teleport.com

Plan Loving Adoptions Now
   (PLAN) International
   Adoption Services
203 East 3rd Street, 2nd Floor,
   P.O. Box 667
McMinnville, OR 97128
(503) 472-8452
Fax: (503) 472-0665
cs.georgefox.edu/PLAN/
ascott@macnet.com

The Boys & Girls Aid Society
   of Oregon
18 S.W. Boundary Court
Portland, OR 97201
(503) 222-9661
Fax: (503) 224-5960
Toll Free: (800) 342-6488
portland.citysearch.com/E/V/PDX
   OR/0002/63/45/
orbagas@aol.com

Tree of Life Adoption Center
9498 S.W. Barbur Boulevard,
   Suite 304
Portland, OR 97219
(503) 244-7374
www.toladopt.org
info@toladopt.org

**Adoptive Parent Support
   Groups**

Adoptive Families Unlimited
Box 40752
Eugene, OR 97404
(541) 688-1654
stevenseahl@juno.com

Coos County Adoptive Parents
c/o SCF Coos County
P.O. Box 467
North Bend, OR 97459
(541) 756-1242

North American Council on
Adoptable Children
Representative
357 Alta Street
Ashland, OR 97520
(541) 482-7288
Fax: (541) 482-3850
members.aol.com/nacac
linsday@wave.net

Northwest Adoptive Families
Association and North
American Council on
Adoptable
Children Representative
5737 S.W. Pendleton
Portland, OR 97122-1762
(503) 244-2440, Ext: 109
Fax: (503) 245-2498
members.aol.com/nacac
kgstocker@aol.com

Oregon Post Adoption
Resource Center
621 S.W. Morrison St., Suite 1225
Portland, OR 97205
(503) 241-0799
Fax: (503) 241-0925
Toll Free: (800) 764-8357
www.orparc.org
orparc@nwresource.org

Rogue Valley Adoptive Families
1156 Conestoga Drive
Grants Pass, OR 97527
(541) 471-3608
turnbull@chatlink.com

Single Adoptive Parents
Support Group
5621 S.E. Oak Street
Portland, OR 97215
(503) 234-7042

Stars of David International Inc.
Jewish Family and Child Services
1130 S.W. Morrison, #316
Portland, OR 97205
(503) 226-7079
Fax: (503) 226-1130
www.starsofdavid.org
starsdavid@aol.com

Search Support Groups

Adoptee Birthfamily Connection
Box 50122
Eugene, OR 97405
(541) 345-6710
DL_MAY@prodigy.net

ALARM Network
11505 S.W. Dutchess
Beaverton, OR 97005

American Adoption Congress
State Representative
10031 S.E. Witchita Avenue
Milwaukie, OR 97222
(503) 794-0915
Spitty@teleport.com

American Adoption Congress
State Representative
15170 S.W. Emerald Street
Beaverton, OR 97007
(503) 916-8511
Fax: (503) 590-9717
Dteller962@aol.com

Oregon Adoptive Rights
Association
P.O. Box 882
Portland, OR 97202
(503) 235-3669
www.oara.org

The Circle
1090 Ellendale Sp. 14
Medford, OR 97504
(541) 773-4554

The Circle
635 Elkader
Ashland, OR 97520
(541) 482-5554
pjflorin@jeffnet.org

OREGON LAWS RELATED TO ADOPTION: QUESTIONS AND ANSWERS

Can an attorney serve as an intermediary?
Yes.

Is advertising permitted?
Yes, if the adoptive parents have an Oregon-approved home study.

Who must consent to the adoption?
The birth parents.

When can consent be taken from birth mother (father), and how long after the consent is signed can it be revoked?
A birth mother can sign the consent after birth when she has recovered from the effects of delivery. The consent is irrevocable once a certificate of irrevocability has been filed with the court.

What are the birth father's rights?
Unless the birth father has supported the birth mother and the child (by monetary means or\and emotional relationship) or he files with the putative father registry indicating that he is the father, he is not entitled to notice of any adoption proceedings and cannot contest the adoption. The birth father's rights can also be terminated if it can be established that he has not maintained a relationship with the child for a certain period of time.

What fees can adoptive parents pay?

Medical, legal, and reasonable living expenses can be paid. The adoptive parents must submit to the court an itemized list stating all fees and expenses paid.

No fees can be paid or accepted for finding a child or an adoptive parent, unless it is the reasonable fee of a licensed adoption agency. The Children's Services Division may charge up to $750 for a home study.

Where does the adoption hearing take place?

The adoption hearing can take place in the court of the county where the adoptive parents live, where the child's birth parents live, or where the agency is located.

How are familial and stepparent adoptions different from nonbiological adoptions?

No home study is required in a stepparent adoption or a relative adoption if the child has resided with the stepparent or relative for six months before filing the petition.

Can a nonresident finalize an adoption in this state?

Yes, if the birth mother is a resident. The adoptive parent, birth parent, or child must reside in Oregon continuously for six months prior to the date of the adoption petition.

SOURCE: OREGON REVISED STATUTES SECTION 109.305 TO 109.500 AND 432.405 YO 432.430 (1997)

PENNSYLVANIA

State Adoption Specialist

Pennsylvania Department of
Public Welfare
Eileen West
Health and Welfare Annex, P.O.
Box 2675
Harrisburg, PA 17105-2675
(717) 783-7376
Fax: (717) 705-0364
*www.dpw.state.pa.us/ocyf/
ocyfas.asp*
ewest@dpw.state.pa.us

State ICPC Administrator

Pennsylvania Department
of Public Welfare
Office of Children, Youth, &
Families
Health & Welfare Building,
Room 131, P.O. Box 2675
Harrisburg, PA 17105-2675
(717) 772-7016
Fax: (717) 772-6857

**State Adoption Exchange/State
Photolisting Service**

Pennsylvania Adoption Exchange
Office of Children, Youth and
Families
P.O. Box 2675
Harrisburg, PA 17105

(717) 772-7015
Toll Free: (800) 227-0225
www.dpw.state.pa.us/adoptpakids
JewellM@dpw.state.pa.us

Statewide Adoption Network
Pennsylvania Office of Children,
Youth and Families
P.O. Box 2675
Harrisburg, PA 17105
(717) 772-7040
Fax: (717) 772-6857
Toll Free: (800) 585-7926
sandyg@dpw.state.pa.us

Statewide Adoption Network's
Prime Contractor
Common Sense Adoption
Services
5021 E. Trindle Road
Mechanicsburg, PA 17055
(717) 766-6449
Fax: (717) 766-8015
Toll Free: (800) 445-2444
www.csas-swan.org/frame.htm

State Reunion Registry

Adoption Medical History
Registry
Hillcrest, Second Floor, P.O. Box
2675
Harrisburg, PA 17105-2675
(717) 772-7015
Toll Free: (800) 227-0225
*www.dpw.state.pa.us/adoptpakids/
paemedicalhist.asp*
JewellM@dpw.state.pa.us

**Licensed Private Adoption
Agencies**

A Second Chance
204 North Highland Avenue
Pittsburgh, PA 15206
(412) 665-2300

Adopt-A-Child
6315 Forbes Avenue, Suite L-111
Pittsburgh, PA 15217
(412) 421-1911
Fax: (412) 421-9303
Toll Free: (800) 246-4848
www.adopt-a-child.org/

Adoption ARC, Inc.
4701 Pine Street, J-7
Philadelphia, PA 19143
(215) 844-1082
Fax: (215) 842-9881
Toll Free: (800) 884-4004
www.adoptionarc.com
taralaw@aol.com

Adoption by Choice
2312 West 15th Street
Erie, PA 16505
(814) 459-4050

Adoption Connection The
709 Third Avenue
New Brighton, PA 15066
(724) 846-2615

Adoption Home Study Associates
of Chester County
1014 Centre School Way
West Chester, PA 19382
(215) 431-7862

Adoption Horizons
899 Petersburg Road
Carlisle, PA 17103
(717) 249-8850

Adoption Services, Inc.
28 Central Boulevard
Camp Hill, PA 17011
(717) 737-3960
Fax: (717) 731-0517
www.adoptionservices.org/
mail@adoptionservices.org

Adoption Unlimited
2770 Weston Road
Lancaster, PA 17603
(717) 872-1340

Adoption World, Inc.
3246 Birch Road
Philadelphia, PA 19154
(215) 271-1361
adoptionworld.org
adoption@adoptionworld.org

Adoptions Abroad
67 Old Clairton Road
Pittsburgh, PA 15236
(412) 653-5302
adoption@icubed.com

Adoptions From The Heart
800 Main Street, Suite 101
Hellertown, PA 18055
www.adoptionsfromtheheart.org
adoption
    @adoptionsfromtheheart.org

Adoptions From The Heart
9 Claremont Drive
Greensburg, PA 15601
(724) 853-6533
www.adoptionsfromtheheart.org/
adoption
    @adoptionsfromtheheart.org

Adoptions From The Heart
Suite 501, 1525 Oregon Pike
Lancaster, PA 17601
(717) 399-7766
www.adoptionsfromtheheart.org/
adoption
    @adoptionsfromtheheart.org

*Adoptions From The Heart
P.O. Box 5158
Pleasant Gap, PA 16823
(814) 383-0125
www.adoptionsfromtheheart.org
adoption
    @adoptionsfromtheheart.org

Adoptions From The Heart
3117 Lehigh Street, Suite 202
Allentown, PA 18103
(610) 709-8800
www.adoptionsfromtheheart.org

Adoptions From The Heart
P.O. Box 60093
Harrisburg, PA 17106
(717) 691-9686
www.adoptionsfromtheheart.org
adoption
    @adoptionsfromtheheart.org

Adoptions From The Heart
30-31 Hampstead Circle
Wynnewood, PA 19096
(610) 642-7200
Fax: (610) 642-7938
www.adoptionsfromtheheart.org
adoption
    @adoptionsfromtheheart.org

Adoptions International Inc.
601 S. 10th Street
Philadelphia, PA 19147
(215) 238-9057
Fax: (215) 238-9071
www.rainbowkids.com/
    adoptionsinternational72.html
HWall334@aol.com

Alliance Adoption Agency
341 Park Road
Ambridge, PA 15003
(724) 266-3600

American Friends of Children
619 Gawain Road
Plymouth Meeting, PA 19464
(610) 828-8166

Asociacion Puertorriquenos
en Marcha
445-47 Luray Street
Philadelphia, PA 19122
(215) 235-6788

Baby Adoption International
2473 Napfle Street
Philadelphia, PA 19152
(215) 677-2808

Bennett and Simpson Enrichment
Services Adoption
4300 Monument Road
Philadelphia, PA 19131
(215) 877-1925

Best Nest
325 Market Street
Williamsport, PA 17701
(717) 321-1969

Best Nest
1335-37 Pine Street
Philadelphia, PA 19107
(215) 546-8060

Bethanna
Branch Office
348 E. Walnut Lane
Philadelphia, PA 19144
(215) 849-8815

Bethanna
1030 Second Street Pike
South Hampton, PA 18966
(215) 355-6500

Bethanna
301 N. Duke Street
Lancaster, PA 17602
(717) 299-1926

Bethany Christian Services
550 Pinetown Road, Suite 100
Fort Washington, PA 19034-2606
(215) 628-0202
Fax: (215) 628-2944
Toll Free: (800) 215-0702
www.bethany.org
info@bethany.org

Bethany Christian Services
694 Lincoln Avenue
Pittsburgh, PA 15202-3421
(412) 734-2662
Fax: (412) 734-2110
www.bethany.org
info@bethany.org

Bethany Christian Services
1681 Crown Avenue, Suite 203
Lancaster, PA 17601-6303
(717) 399-3213
Fax: (717) 399-3543
www.bethany.org
info@bethany.org

Bethany Christian Services
7152 Germantown Avenue,
    2nd Floor
Philadelphia, PA 19119-1843
(215) 247-5473
Fax: (215) 247-5497
www.bethany.org
info@bethany.org

Capital Area Adoption Services
514 Landsvale Street
Marysville, PA 17053
(717) 957-2513

Catholic Charities Counseling
and Adoption Services
90 Beaver Drive, Suite 111B
Dubois, PA 15801-2424
(814) 371-4717

Catholic Charities Counseling
and Adoption Services
786 E. State Street
Sharon, PA 16146
(412) 346-4142

Catholic Charities Counseling
and Adoption Services
329 W. Tenth Street
Erie, PA 16502
(814) 456-2091

Catholic Charities of the Diocese
of Harrisburg
4800 Union Deposit Road
Harrisburg, PA 17105
(717) 657-4804

Catholic Charities of the Diocese
of Pittsburgh, Inc.
212 Ninth Street
Pittsburgh, PA 15222-3507
(412) 471-1120

Catholic Social Agency
928 Union Boulevard
Allentown, PA 18103
(610) 435-1541

Catholic Social Agency
2147 Perkiomen Avenue
Reading, PA 19606
(610) 370-3378

Catholic Social Services
227 North Eighteenth Street
Philadelphia, PA 19103
(215) 854-7055

Catholic Social Services
81 South Church Street
Hazleton, PA 18201
(717) 485-1521

Catholic Social Services
102 Warren Street
Tunkhannock, PA 18657

Catholic Social Services
411 Main Street
Stroudsburg, PA 18360
(717) 476-6460

Catholic Social Services of
Luzerne County
33 E. Northhampton Street
Wilkes-Barre, PA 18701-2406
(717) 822-7118

Catholic Social Services of
Lycoming County
1015 Washington Boulevard
Williamsport, PA 17701
(717) 322-4220

Catholic Social Services of the
Archdiocese of Philadelphia
222 N. 17th Street
Philadelphia, PA 19103
(215) 587-3900

Catholic Social Services of the
Diocese of Altoona-Johnstown
1300 12th Avenue
Altoona, PA 16603
(814) 944-9388

Catholic Social Services of the
Diocese of Scranton
400 Wyoming Avenue
Scranton, PA 18503
(717) 346-8936

CATY Services
415 Gettysburg Street
Pittsburgh, PA 15206
(412) 362-3600

Child and Home Study Associates
1029 Providence Road
Media, PA 19063
(610) 565-1544

Children's Aid Home Programs of
Somerset County
574 E. Main Street
Somerset, PA 15501
(814) 445-2009

Children's Aid Society in
Clearfield County
1004 S. Second Street
Clearfield, PA 16830
(814) 765-2685

Children's Aid Society of Franklin
County
225 Miller Street
Chambersburg, PA 17201-0353
(717) 263-4159

Children's Aid Society of Mercer
County
350 W. Market Street
Mercer, PA 16137
(724) 662-4730

Children's Aid Society of
Montgomery County
1314 DeKalb Street
Norristown, PA 19401
(215) 279-2755

Children's Choice
5 Courtyard Offices
Selinsgrove, PA 17870
(717) 743-0505

Children's Choice
415 E. 22nd Street
Chester, PA 19013-5501
(610) 872-6200

Children's Choice
4814 Joneston Road
Harrisburg, PA 17109
(717) 541-9809

Children's Choice
Scott Plaza Two, Suite 325
Philadelphia, PA 19113
(610) 521-6270
Fax: (610) 521-6266

Children's Home of Pittsburgh
5618 Kentucky Avenue
Pittsburgh, PA 15232
(412) 441-4884
www.adopt-infant.org
ryave@netservices.com

Children's Services
1315 Walnut Street
Philadelphia, PA 19107
(215) 546-3503

Chinese Adoption Services
322 Sue Drive
Hummelstown, PA 17036
(717) 564-7478

Church of the Brethren Youth
Services
1417 Oregon Road
Leola, PA 17540
(717) 656-6580

Common Sense Adoption
Services
5021 E. Trindle Road
Mechanicsburg, PA 17055
(717) 766-6449
Toll Free: (800) 445-2444
www.csas-swan.org

Community Adoption Services of
Heavenly Vision Ministries
6513 Meadow Street
Pittsburgh, PA 15206
(412) 661-4774

Concern
550 Pinetown Road, Suite 150
Fort Washington, PA 19034
(215) 654-1963

Concern
1 W. Main Street
Fleetwood, PA 19522
(610) 944-0445

Council of Spanish Speaking
Organization
705-709 North Franklin Street
Philadelphia, PA 19123
(215) 627-3100

Covenant Family Resources
743 Roy Road
King of Prussia, PA 19406
(610) 354-0555

Eckels Adoption Agency
915 Fifth Avenue
Williamsport, PA 17701
(717) 323-2520

Every Child, Inc.
6401 Penn Avenue, Third Floor
Pittsburgh, PA 15206
(412) 665-0600
Fax: (412) 665-0755
everych98@aol.com

Families Across Boundaries
5208 Library Road
Bethel Park, PA 15102
(412) 854-0330

Families Caring for Children
96 Front Street
Nanticoke, PA 18634
(717) 735-9082

Families Caring for Children
Mercy Medical Arts
8 Church Street
Wilkes-Barre, PA 18702
(717) 823-9823

Families International
Adoption Agency
1205 Farragut Street
Pittsburgh, PA 15217
(412) 681-7189

Families United Network
54 South Brown Street
Elizabethtown, PA 17022
(717) 367-9798

Family Adoption Center
960 Penn Avenue, Suite 600
Pittsburgh, PA 15222
(412) 288-2138

Family Health Council, Inc.
Suite 600, 960 Penn Avenue
Pittsburgh, PA 15222
(412) 288-2130
Fax: (412) 288-9036

Family Service
630 Janet Avenue
Lancaster, PA 17601
(717) 397-5241

Family Services and Children's
Aid Society of Venango County
716 E. Second Street
Oil City, PA 16301
(814) 677-4005

Family Services of Northwestern
Pennsylvania
5100 Peach Street
Erie, PA 16509
(814) 864-0605

FIMEL-Family Institute for More
Effective Living
3605 Geryville Pike
Greenlane, PA 18054
(215) 679-5609

Friends Association for the Care
and Protection of Children
206 N. Church Street
West Chester, PA 19381
(215) 431-3598

Genesis of Pittsburgh
185 Dakota Street
Pittsburgh, PA 15202
(412) 766-2693

Infant and Youth Care
6801-17 North 16th Street
Philadelphia, PA 19126
(215) 424-1144

Infant and Youth Care
54 South Brown Street
Elizabethtown, PA 17022
(717) 367-9798

Institute for Human Resources
and Services
Suite 301, 250 Pierce Street
Kingston, PA 18704
(717) 288-9386

International Assistance Group
21 Brilliant Avenue
Pittsburgh, PA 15215
(412) 781-6470

International Families
Adoption Agency
518 South 12th Street
Philadelphia, PA 19147
(215) 735-7171
Fax: (215) 545-3563

Jewish Family and Children's
Service
5743 Barlett Street
Pittsburgh, PA 15217
(412) 683-4900

Jewish Family and Children's
Service of Philadelphia Inc.
10125 Verree Road, #200
Philadelphia, PA 19116
(215) 698-9950
Fax: (215) 698-2148
www.voicenet.com/~adoption
adoption@voicenet.com

Jewish Family Service
3333 N. Front Street
Harrisburg, PA 17110
(717) 233-1681

Juvenile Justice Center of
Philadelphia
100 West Coulter Street
Philadelphia, PA 19144
(215) 849-2112

Kaleidoscope of Family
Servies, Inc.
355 Lancaster Avenue
Haverford, PA 19041
(215) 473-3991
www.netreach.net/people/
kaleidoscope/
kaleidoscope@netreach.net

Kidspeace National Centers for
Kids in Crisis
1650 Broadway
Bethlehem, PA 18015
(215) 867-5051

*La Vida Adoption Agency
150 South Warner Road,
Suite 144
King of Prussia, PA 19344
(610) 688-8008
Fax: (610) 688-8028
www.lavida.org/
info@lavida.org

LDS Social Services
46 School Street
Greentree, PA 15205
(412) 921-8303

Living Hope Adoption Agency
3205 Meetinghouse Road
Telford, PA 18969
(215) 672-7471

Love the Children
221 West Broad Street
Quakertown, PA 18951
(215) 536-4180
Fax: (215) 536-2582
www.members.bellatlantic.net/
~LTCHome
LTCHome@bellatlantic.net

Lutheran Children & Family
Service of Eastern Pennsylvania
1256 Easton Road
Roslyn, PA 19001
(215) 951-6850

Lutheran Home at Topton
1 S. Home Avenue
Topton, PA 19562
(610) 682-1504

Madison Adoption Associates
619 Gawain Road
Plymouth Meeting, PA 19462
(215) 459-0454

Marian Adoption Services
600 North Bethlehem Pike
Ambler, PA 19002-2601
(610) 941-0910
Fax: (610) 941-9946

Marian Adoption Services
600 N. Bethlehem Pike
Ambler, PA 19002
(215) 283-8522
Toll Free: (800) 585-9944
MASAdopt@aol.com

New Beginnings Family and
Children's Services
8 Pennsylvania Avenaue
Matamoras, PA 18336
(516) 747-2204

PAACT
703 N. Market Street
Liverpool, PA 17045
(717) 444-3629

Pinebrook Services for Children
& Youth
1033 Sumner Avenue
Whitehall, PA 18052
(610) 432-3919

Plan-It For Kids, PC
501 Main Street
Berlin, PA 15530
(814) 267-3182
Fax: (814) 267-4340
cadopt@shol.com

Presbyterian Children's Village
452 S. Roberts Road
Rosemont, PA 19010
(610) 525-5400

Pressley Ridge Youth
Development Extension
Program
801 Beaver Street
Sewickley, PA 15143
(412) 740-1310

Project STAR of Permanency
Planning Advocates of Western
Pennsylvania
6301 Northumberland Street
Pittsburgh, PA 15217
(412) 521-9000

PSI Services
Suite 1700, 714 Market Street
#233
Philadelphia, PA 19163-2326
(215) 569-1206

Rainbow Project
200 Charles Street
Pittsburgh, PA 15238
(412) 782-4457

Rehabilitation Auditing and
Placement Services (RAP)
100 West Mall Plaza, 2nd Floor
Carnegie, PA 15106
(412) 278-8550

St. Joseph's Center
2010 Adams Avenue
Scranton, PA 18509
(717) 342-8379

Tabor Children's Services
601 New Britain Road
Doylestown, PA 18901-4248
(215) 842-4800

Tabor Children's Services, Inc.
4700 Wissahickon Ave
Philadelphia, PA 19144
(215) 842-4800
Fax: (215) 842-4809

The Children's Home of
Pittsburgh
5618 Kentucky Ave
Pittsburgh, PA 15232
(412) 441-4884
Fax: (412) 441-0167

The Children's Home Society of
New Jersey
771 North Pennsylvania Avenue
Morrisville, PA 19067
(215) 736-8550

The Eckels Adoption Agency
340 Harding Ave
Williamsport, PA 17701
(717) 323-2520
Fax: (717) 323-2520

Three Rivers Adoption
Council/Black Adoption
Services
307 4th Avenue, Suite 710
Pittsburgh, PA 15222
(412) 471-8722

Tressler Lutheran Services
836 S. George Street
York, PA 17403
(717) 845-9113
Fax: (717) 852-8439
www.tressler.org/ccfstext.htm
TLSAdopt@tressler.org

Tressler Lutheran Services
1139 Chester Street
Williamsport, PA 17701
(717) 327-9195
www.tressler.org
TLSAdopt@tressler.org

Tressler Lutheran Services
960 Century Drive, P.O. Box
2001
Mechanicsburg, PA 17055-0707
(717) 795-0300
www.tressler.org/ccfstext.htm
TLSAdopt@tressler.org

Welcome House of the Pearl S.
Buck Foundation
P.O. Box 181, Green Hills Farm
Perkasie, PA 18944
(215) 249-1516
Fax: (215) 249-9657
Toll Free: (800) 220-2825
www.pearl-s-buck.org
rrosenth@pearl-s-buck.org

Women's Christian Alliance
1610-16 North Broad Street
Philadelphia, PA 19121
(215) 236-9911

Your Adoption Agency
R.D. 2, Germantown Road
Susquehanna, PA 18847
(717) 853-2022

**Adoptive Parent Support
Groups**

Adoption Center of the
Delaware Valley
1500 Walnut Street, Suite 701
Philadelphia, PA 19102
(215) 735-9988

Adoption Connection, Inc.
P.O. Box 28030
Philadelphia, PA 19131
(215) 927-5144

Adoption Forum
P.O. Box 12502
Philadelphia, PA 19151
(215) 238-1116
Fax: (215) 862-3087
www.adoptionforum.org
alovett215@aol.com

Adoption Information Services
901B E. Willow Grove Avenue
Wyndmoor, PA 19118
(215) 233-1380

Adoption Support Group State
College
146 Meadow Lane
State College, PA 16801
(814) 237-5568

Adoption World
3246 Birch Road
Philadelphia, PA 19154
(215) 632-4479

Adoptive Families Together
712 Herman Road
Butler, PA 16001
(724) 285-1594

Adoptive Families Together
2510 Elkridge Drive
Wexford, PA 15090
(412) 935-9607

Adoptive Family Rights Council
239 Fourth Avenue, Suite 1403
Pittsburgh, PA 15222
(412) 232-0955

Adoptive Parents Group of
Delaware Valley
1147 Myrtlewood Avenue
Upper Darby, PA 19082
(610) 853-1042

Adoptive Parents of
Delaware County
5129 Palmers Mill Road
Clifton Heights, PA 19018
(610) 622-3890

After Adoption and Parenting
Services for Families
5500 Wissahickon Avenue,
Alden Park Manor, A-202
Philadelphia, PA 19144
(215) 844-1312

Common Sense Associates
5021 E. Trindle Road
Mechanicsburg, PA 17055
(717) 766-6449

Concerned Adoptive Parents
2803 E. Kings Highway
Coatesville, PA 19320
(610) 383-4260

Council on Adoptable
Children of Allegheny County
807 Sleepy Hollow Road
Pittsburgh, PA 15234
(412) 561-1603

Council on Adoptable Children of
Southwestern Pennsylvania and
North American
Council on Adoptable Children
State Representative
224 S. Aiken Avenue
Pittsburgh, PA 15206
(412) 471-8722

Elizabeth S. Cole Associates
286 Thompson Mill Road
New Hope, PA 18938
(215) 598-0414

Families for Russian and
Ukrainian Adoptions
Philadelphia, PA
(610) 525-0185

Families of Children from Various
Nations/Open Door Society
1835 Troxell Street
Allentown, PA 18103
(610) 865-1882

Families Together
Apollo Lane
Rochester, PA 15074
(724) 772-7260

Families with Attachment
Disordered Children
1733 Locust Road
Sewickley, PA 15143
(412) 366-7113
Fax: (209) 797-5416
marleenk@icubed.com

Families with Children from Asia
3111 North Second Street
Harrisburg, PA 17110-1302
(717) 233-0755
rsteele@epix.net

Foreign Adoption Network
286 Levan Street
Reading, PA 19606
(215) 779-O727

International Adoptive Families
402 Pebblecreek Drive
Cranberry Township, PA 16066
(814) 772-5787

International Families of Somerset
County
875 Hemlock Road
Warmister, PA 18974-4122

Korean Konnection
2390 Deep Hollow Road
Dover, PA 17315-2512
(717) 292-4983

Lehigh Valley Adoptive
Parents Group
1710 Monroe Street
Bethlehem, PA 18017-6439
(215) 896-1549

Love the Children Support Group
384 Tampa
Pittsburgh, PA 15228
(412) 563-4931

National Adoption Center
1500 Walnut Street, Suite 701
Philadelphia, PA 19102
(215) 735-9988
www.adopt.org/adopt/nac/nac.html
nac@adopt.org

Our Children
1305 Joan Drive
Southampton, PA 18966
(215) 364-7675

Parent Network for the Post-
Institutionalized Child
Box 613
Meadow Lands, PA 15347
(724) 222-1766

Parents and Adopted Children's
Organization of Lawrence
County
RD 4, Box 397
New Castle, PA 16101

Parents and Adopted Children's
Organization of Mercer County
105 Wasser Road
Greenville, PA 16125
(724) 962-1039

Parents and Adopted Children's
Organization of the Midwest
330 Winters Road
Butler, PA 16001
(724) 586-9316

Parents and Adopted Children's
Organization of Washington
County
551 McCrea Avenue
Donora, PA 15033
(724) 379-5716

Parents and Adopted Children's
Organization of Westmoreland
3550 Meadowgate Drive
Murrysville, PA 15668
(724) 327-4798

Parents of Adopted African
Americans
544 W. 31st Street
Erie, PA 16508-1743
(814) 455-2149

Pittsburgh Adoption Support
Group
105 Church Lane
Pittsburgh, PA 15238
(412) 767-4250
pghadoptsuprtgr@webtv.net

Post Adoption Support System
1256 Easton Road
Roslyn, PA 19001
(215) 881-6800, Ext: 229
judyw@lcfsinpa.org

Pre and Post Adoption
Consultation and Education
47 Marchwood Road, Suite 1E
Exton, PA 19341
(610) 524-9060

Single Adoptive Parents of
Delaware Valley
2239 Strahle Street, 2nd Floor
Philadelphia, PA 19152
(215) 745-2855

Stars of David International Inc.
Central Pennsylvania Chapter
Jewish Family Service of
Harrisburg,
3333 North Front Street
Harrisburg, PA 17110
(717) 233-1681
Fax: (717) 234-8258
www.starsofdavid.org/
starsdavid@aol.com

Taplink and North American
Council on Adoptable Children
Representative
478 Moyers Road
Harleysville, PA 19438-2302
(215) 256-0669
Fax: (215) 256-0669
www.taplink.org/
pjs@taplink.org

Tremitiere, Ward and Associates
122 W. Springettsbury
York, PA 17403
(717) 845-9113

Welcome House Adoptive
Parents Group
604 Hasting Street
Pittsburgh, PA 15206
(412) 665-1458

Welcome House Adoptive
Parents Group
275 Glen Riddle Road,
Apartment C-1
Media, PA 19063
(215) 358-3894

Search Support Groups

Adoption Forum
P.O. Box 582
New Hope, PA 18938
(215) 862-2695
Fax: (215) 862-3087

Adoption Forum (Harrisburg)
100 North Front Street
Wormleysburg, PA 17043-1328

Adoption Healing, Family
Services of Western
Pennsylvania
46th and Hatfield Streets
Pittsburgh, PA 15201
(412) 687-0100

Adoption Lifeline of Altoona
414 28th Avenue
Altoona, PA 16601

American Adoption Congress
State Representative
P.O. Box 582
New Hope, PA 18938
(215) 862-2695
Fax: (215) 862-9002
alovett215@aol.com

American Adoption Congress
State Representative
955 Saw Creek Estates
Bushkill, PA 18324
(717) 588-1706
Fax: (717) 588-1716
annwalk20@aol.com

Berks County Branch of Adoption
Forum
21 Northridge Drive
Mohnton, PA 19540-1239
(610) 777-9742
cotton@epix.net

Bucks County Chapter of
Adoption Forum and PACFOA
(Pennsylvania Coalition for
Openness in Adoption)
20 Runnemede V2
New Hope, PA 18938
(215) 862-2695

ENCORE
RD 8, Box 419
York, PA 17403
(410) 466-0222

Lansdale Adoption Connection
1167 Hill Drive
Lansdale, PA 19446-2125
(215) 361-9679

Lost Loved Ones
621 W. Crawford Street
Edensberg, PA 15931

NW Pennsylvania Adoption
Connection
115 Willow Road
St. Mary's, PA 15857
(814) 781-7312

Open Line Adoption Connection
817 East Third Street
Oil City, PA 16301
(814) 677-7850

Origins
Box 1032, Hemlock Farms
Hawley, PA 18428
(717) 775-9729

Parents/Adoptees Support
Together (PAST)
8130 Hawthorne Drive
Erie, PA 16509
(814) 899-1493

Pittsburgh Adoption Connection
37 Edgecliff Road
Carnegie, PA 15106-1006
(412) 279-2511
Gshay@aol.com

Searching
P.O. Box 7446
Harrisburg, PA 17113-0446
(717) 939-0138

Pennsylvania Adoption Reunion
Registry (PARR)
201 Jay Street, Apt. I108
Stowe, PA 19464

Pittsburgh Adoption Lifeline
P.O. Box 52
Gibsonia, PA 15044
(724) 443-3370

PENNSYLVANIA LAWS RELATED TO ADOPTION: QUESTIONS AND ANSWERS

Can an attorney serve as an intermediary?
Yes. However, he or she cannot accept any fees or charge on an hourly basis for this service.

Is advertising permitted?
Yes.

Who must consent to the adoption?
1. The birth parents
2. The birth mother's husband, if he was married to her at any time within one year before the child's birth, unless he proves not to be the child's biological father

When can consent be taken from birth mother (father), and how long after the consent is signed can it be revoked?
Consents can be given seventy-two hours after the child's birth. All consents must be confirmed by a court hearing, which occurs at least fifty days after the consents are taken. The consents are filed with the court at least forty days after they are signed; the court then schedules a hearing to confirm consents at least ten days later. The birth parents must receive notice of this hearing, and they can revoke their consents up until the court hearing. Generally, this hearing occurs two to four months after the baby's birth, making Pennsylvania a "legal risk" state.

Birth fathers can sign consents, even before birth.

What are the birth father's rights?
He can sign a consent before or after birth, and his rights essentially end when the birth mother's rights are terminated, at the termination hearing. In general, if the birth father does not sign a consent, his rights can be terminated as a "putative father" as long as he is not married to the birth mother and has failed to acknowledge paternity, and does not appear in court to oppose the adoption.

What fees can adoptive parents pay?
No living expenses can be paid in an agency or independent adoption. In an independent adoption, only medical and hospital expenses are permitted. In an agency adoption, reasonable administrative costs and counseling fees are permitted.

The court may also require the adoptive parents to pay for the birth parents' legal fees and the child's guardian. An itemized statement of all money paid must be made in the adoption report.

Where does the adoption hearing take place?

The hearing can take place in the court of the county where the adoptive parents live, where the birth parents live, or where the placement agency is located.

How are familial and stepparent adoptions different from nonbiological adoptions?

They are handled the same way other adoptions are conducted, except that a home study may be waived in a stepparent adoption. The attorney can request that the hearing to confirm the consent also be the final hearing, instead of waiting for the final hearing to be held at a later date.

Can a nonresident finalize an adoption in this state?

Yes. For nonresidents to finalize in Pennsylvania, they must have proof that they have no history of child abuse or child-related crimes.

SOURCE: PENNSYLVANIA CONSOLIDATED STATUTES TITLE 23, SECTIONS 2101 AND TITLE 55, SECTIONS 33501. 1 TO 3350.14 (1997)

RHODE ISLAND

State Adoption Specialist

Rhode Island Department for
Children, Youth and Family
Services
Paula Fontaine
530 Wood Street
Bristol, RI 02805
(401) 254-7076
Fax: (401) 254-7099
www.adoptionri.org
paula_f@dcyf.state.ri.us

State ICPC Administrator

Rhode Island Department for
Children and Their Families
530 Wood Street
Bristol, RI 02809
(401) 254-7077
Fax: (401) 254-7099

State Adoption Exchange/State Photolisting Service

Adoption Rhode Island
500 Prospect Street
Pawtucket, RI 02860
(401) 724-1910
Fax: (401) 724-1910
www.adoptionri.org/
adoptionri@ids.net

State Reunion Registry

State of Rhode Island and
Providence Plantations
Family Court, Juvenile Division
One Dorrance Plaza
Providence, RI 02903
(401) 277-3352

Licensed Private Adoption Agencies

Adoption Network, Ltd.
P.O. Box 1233
East Greenwich, RI 02818
Toll Free: (800) 285-0450

Adoption Options
229 Waterman Street
Providence, RI 02906
(401) 331-1244

Alliance for Children
500 Prospect Street
Pawtucket, RI 02860
(401) 725-9555
www.allforchildren.org
info@allforchildren.org

Alliance for Children, Inc.
Suite G80, 40 William Street
Wellesley, MA 02481-3902
(781) 431-7148
Fax: (781) 431-7474
www.allforchildren.org
info@allforchildren.org

Bethany Christian Service
P.O. Box 2292
Pawtucket, RI 02861-2292
(401) 467-1395

Catholic Social Services
Reaching Out Adoption
& Foster Care
311 Hooper Street
Tiverton, RI 02878
(401) 624-9270

Children's Friend & Service
153 Summer Street
Providence, RI 02903
(401) 331-2900

Friends in Adoption
44 South Street, P.O. Box 1228
Middletown Springs, VT 05757-
1228
(802) 235-2373
www.capital.net/com/fia
fia@vermontel.com

Friends in Adoption
224 5th St.
Providence, RI 02906
(401) 831-1120
Toll Free: (800) 982-3678
www.capital.net/com/fia
fia@vermont.com

Gift of Life Adoption Services
1053 Park Ave
Cranston, RI 02910
(401) 943-6484
Fax: (401) 943-6806
75317.1056@compuserve.com

International Adoptions, Inc.
726 Front Street
Woonsocket, RI 02895
(401) 767-2300

Jewish Family Services/ Adoption
Options
229 Waterman Avenue
Providence, RI 02906
(401) 331-5437

*Little Treasures Adoption
  Services
P.O. Box 20555
Cranston, RI 02920
(401) 828-7747
ltltreasur@aol.com

Lutheran Social Services
  of New England
Rhode Island Adoption Program
116 Rolfe Street
Cranston, RI 02910
(401) 785-0015
Fax: (401) 785-0599
www.adoptlss.org/about.htm
LSSRIAdopt@aol.com

Urban League of Rhode Island, Inc.
Minority Recruitment and Child
  Placement Program
246 Prairie Avenue
Providence, RI 02905
(401) 351-5000

Wide Horizons for Children
116 Andre Avenue
Wakefield, RI 02879
(401) 783-4537

Wide Horizons for Children
117 Eddie Dowling Hwy., Suite 7
North Smithfield, RI 02896
(401) 766-9197

**Adoptive Parent Support
  Groups**

Adoption Rhode Island and
  North American Council on
  Adoptable Children
Representative
500 Prospect Street
Pawtucket, RI 02860

(401) 724-1910
Fax: (401) 724-1910
www.adoptionri.org
adoptionri@ids.net

AGAND USA
621 Wakefield Street
W. Warwick, RI 02893
(401) 821-2220

Children's Friends and Service -
  ASAP Program
153 Summer Street
Providence, RI 02903
(401) 331-2900
Fax: (401) 331-3285

Families with Children
  From China
P.O. Box 101
Thompson, CT 06277
robyn1@neca.com

Getting
  International/Transcultural
  Families Together (GIFT)
11 Baneberry Drive
Cranston, RI 02921
(401) 944-6517

GIFT
c/o Lynn Sheridan
144 Old North Road
Kingston, RI 02881

GIFT of Rhode Island
9 Shippee School House Road
Foster, RI 02825
(401) 647-2021

Jewish Family Services Adoptive
  Parent Support Group
229 Waterman Avenue
Providence, RI 02906
(401) 331-1244

Minority Adoptive Support
  Group, Inc.
246 Prairie Avenue
Providence, RI 02905
(401) 351-5000

Stars of David International Inc.
Providence Chapter
33 Edward Avenue
Rumford, RI 02916-3304
(401) 431-0728
www.starsofdavid.org
starsdavid@aol.com

Search Support Groups

Jewish Child & Family
  Services/Adoption Options
  Birth Parent Support Group
229 Waterman Aveman
Providence, RI 02906
(401) 331-1244

PALM
Box 15144
E. Providence, RI 02915
(401) 433-4692

PALM (Parents and Adoptees
  Liberty Movement)
861 Mitchell's Lane
Middletown, RI 02840

Yesterday's Children
77 Homer Street
Providence, RI 02903

RHODE ISLAND LAWS RELATED TO ADOPTION: QUESTIONS AND ANSWERS

In an independent adoption, even if the child is brought into the state, the Department of Children and Their Families must be notified within fifteen days. Failure to notify could result in the court ordering the child to be removed from the adoptive parents' home.

A home study must be conducted within fifteen days of a child's placement. If you plan to advertise in another state, you may not have to have a home study completed at time of placement; however, the state in which the child is born will require a completed home study, as well as Interstate Compact approval, before the child is permitted to leave the state.

The religious preference of the biological parents is honored, as much as is practically possible, when placing a child.

Can an attorney serve as an intermediary?
Yes.

Is advertising permitted?
Technically not, but ads are placed.

Who must consent to the adoption?
1. The birth parents
2. The birth parents' guardian or court-appointed guardian if the birth parent is a minor

When can consent be taken from birth mother (father), and how long after the consent is signed can it be revoked?
Consent cannot be given sooner than fifteen days after the child's birth. No law discusses revocation, but case law suggests it is only possible due to fraud, duress, or misrepresentation.

What are the birth father's rights?
Unless the birth father has neglected to provide care for the child for at least one year, is excessively using drugs or alcohol, is unfit based on conduct or mental illness, or has abandoned or deserted the child, his consent is required.

What fees can adoptive parents pay?
The law does not address this issue. However, paying legal, medical, and reasonable living expenses is permitted.

Where does the adoption hearing take place?
The law does not address where the adoption hearing takes place, but it is usually conducted in the county where the adoptive parents live.

How are familial and stepparent adoptions different from nonbiological adoptions?
A specific statute deals with stepparent adoption. Relative adoptions are not significantly different from nonbiological adoptions.

Can a nonresident finalize an adoption in this state?
Yes, but only in an agency adoption.

SOURCE: GENERAL LAWS OF RHODE ISLAND SECTIONS 15-7-2 TO 15-7-22 (1997)

SOUTH CAROLINA

State Adoption Specialist

South Carolina Department of
  Social Services
Division of Adoption and Birth
  Parent Services
Carolyn Orf
P.O. Box 1520
Columbia, SC 29202-1520
(803) 898-7707
Fax: (803) 898-7561
Toll Free: (800) 922-2504
www.state.sc.us/dss/adoption
corf@dss.gov.sc

State ICPC Administrator

South Carolina Department of
  Social Services
P.O. Box 1520
Columbia, SC 29202-1520
(803) 898-7523

**State Adoption Exchange/State
  Photolisting Service**

South Carolina Seedlings
2627 Millwood Avenue, Suite AA
Columbia, SC 29205

(803) 783-2226
Toll Free: (888) 515-2622
www.sc-adopt.org/
sccoac@thestate.infi.net

State Reunion Registry

South Carolina Department of
  Social Services
Adoption Reunion Register
P.O. Box 1520
Columbia, SC 29202-1520
(803) 898-7570
Toll Free: (800) 922-2504

Regional/District Public Agencies

South Carolina Department
of Social Services
Division of Adoption and Birth
Parent Services
P.O. Box 1520
Columbia, SC 29202-1520
(803) 898-7561
Fax: (803) 898-7641

South Carolina Department of
Social Services - Region I
454 South Anderson Road
Rock Hill, SC 29730
(803) 329-9626
Fax: (803) 324-7956
Toll Free: (800) 922-1537

South Carolina Department of
Social Services - Region II
Century Plaza, Suite 101-A, 211
Century Drive
Greenville, SC 29607
(864) 241-1070
Fax: (864) 241-1021
Toll Free: (800) 868-6595

South Carolina Department of
Social Services - Region III,
Aiken DSS Office
P.O. Drawer 1268
Aiken, SC 29802-1268
(803) 502-1826
Fax: (803) 502-1837

South Carolina Department of
Social Services - Region III,
Calhoun County DSS
P.O. Box 467
St. Matthews, SC 29135-0467
(803) 655-5568
Fax: (803) 655-5541

South Carolina Department of
Social Services - Region III,
Orangeburg DSS Office
P.O. Box 1087
Orangeburg, SC 29167-1087
(803) 515-1846
Fax: (803) 531-2045

South Carolina Department of
Social Services - Region V
1905 Sunset Blvd.
West Columbia, SC 29169
(803) 936-9542
Fax: (803) 936-9554

South Carolina Department of
Social Services - Region VI
3346 Rivers Avenue - Suite F
North Charleston, SC 29405
(843) 740-0750
Fax: (803) 740-6145
Toll Free: (800) 922-1518

South Carolina Department of
Social Services - Region VII
Children's Center of South
Carolina, 2638 Two Knotch
Road, Suite 200
Columbia, SC 29204
(803) 929-2555
Fax: (803) 253-7660
Toll Free: (888) 711-7095

South Carolina Department of
Social Services -Region IV
181 E. Evans Street, Suite 112
Florence, SC 29501
(803) 661-2495
Fax: (803) 317-1599
Toll Free: (800) 763-6637

Licensed Private Adoption Agencies

A Loving Choice Adoption
Agency
233 E. Blackstock Road, #F
Spartanburg, SC 29301-2652
(864) 576-7033
alcadopt@aol.com

A Loving Choice Adoption
Agency
1535 Sam Rittenburg Boulevard
Charleston, SC 29407
(803) 556-3391

Adoption Center of South
Carolina
2740 Divine Street, Suite 5
Columbia, SC 29202
(803) 771-2272

Bethany Christian Services
550 Forestbrook Road #300
Myrtle Beach, SC 29579-7912
(843) 236-5433
Fax: (843) 903-2629
Toll Free: (800) 922-0682
www.bethany.org
info@bethany.org

Bethany Christian Services
620 E. Washington Street
Greenville, SC 29601-2995
(864) 235-2273
Fax: (864) 233-6641
Toll Free: (800) 922-0682
www.bethany.org
info@bethany.org

Bethany Christian Services
1411 Barnwell Street
Columbia, SC 29201-2300
(803) 779-0541
Fax: (803) 799-9799
Toll Free: (800) 922-0682
www.bethany.org
info@bethany.org

Bethany Christian Services
817-C Second Loop Road,
P.O. Box 6044
Florence, SC 29502-6044
(843) 629-1177
Fax: (843) 629-1177
Toll Free: (800) 922-0682
www.bethany.org
info@bethany.org

Carolina Hope Christian
Adoption, Inc.
307 Sassafras Drive
Taylors, SC 29687
(864) 268-0570

Catholic Charities of Charleston
1662 Ingram Road
Charleston, SC 29407
(843) 769-4466

Child of the Heart
741 Johnnie Dodds Boulevard,
Suite 207
Mt. Pleasant, SC 29407
(843) 881-2973
Fax: (843) 971-7901

Children First
P.O. Box 11907
Columbia, SC 29211
(803) 771-0534

Children Unlimited, Inc.
The Attachment Center of South
Carolina
1825 Gadsden Street
Columbia, SC 29211
(803) 799-8311
Fax: (803) 765-0284
Toll Free: (800) 822-0877
www.midnet.sc.edu/children/
child1.htm
cuadop@scsn.net

Christian Family Services
2166 Gold Hill Drive
Ft. Mill, SC 29715
(843) 548-6030

Christian Family Servies
5072 Tara Tea Drive
Tega Cay, SC 29715
(803) 548-6030

*Christian World Adoption, Inc.
669 N. Marina Drive
Wando, SC 29492
(843) 856-0305
Fax: (803) 856-0350
www.cwa.org/
cwa@cwa.org

Epworth Children's Home
2900 Millwood Avenue
Columbia, SC 29250
(803) 256-7394

LDS Social Services
5624 Executive Center Drive,
Suite 109
Charlotte, NC 28212-8832
(704) 535-2436

Lutheran Family Services
652 Bush River Plaza
Columbia, SC 29210
(803) 750-9917
Fax: (803) 731-1263

Reid House
P.O. Box 22132
Charleston, SC 29413
(843) 723-7138
Fax: (843) 722-8797

Southeastern Children's
Home, Inc.
155 Children's Home
Duncan, SC 29334
(864) 439-0259

World Wide Adoptions
202 Overland Drive
Spartanburg, SC 29304
(864) 583-6981

**Adoptive Parent Support
Groups**

Center for Child and Family
Studies
Post-Legal Adoption Education
and Training
University of South Carolina
Columbia, SC 29208
(803) 777-9408

Single Adoptive Parents
of South Carolina
P.O. Box 417
Norway, SC 29113-0417
(803) 263-4502

South Carolina Council on
Adoptable Children/South
Carolina Seedlings and North
American Council on Adoptable
Children Representative
2627 Millwood Avenue, Suite AA
Columbia, SC 29205
(803) 783-2226
Toll Free: (888) 515-2622
sccoac@thestate.infi.net

Search Support Groups

Adoptees & Birthparents in
Search (ABIS)
P.O. Box 13
Lexington, SC 29071
(803) 356-0059

Adoption Reunion Connection
(A.R.C.)
263 Lemonade Road
Pacolet, SC 29372
(864) 474-3479

Adoption Search for Life
303 Brighton Road
Anderson, SC 29621
(864) 224-8020

Bits and Pieces
P.O. Box 85
Liberty, SC 29657-0085
(864) 843-9307
www.innova.net/~goob

D.E. Ward Research
P.O. Box 402
Moncks Corner, SC 29461
(803) 899-4007
Fax: (803) 899-3130

Ever Check Where
P.O. Box 849
Roebuck, SC 29376-0849
(864) 576-7593
Fax: (864) 587-7235

Triad, Inc.
1725 Atascadero Drive
Columbia, SC 29206
(803) 787-3778

SOUTH CAROLINA LAWS RELATED TO ADOPTION: QUESTIONS AND ANSWERS

If you advertise in South Carolina and are not a state resident, you must petition the South Carolina Family Court to take a child out of state.

Nonresidents may adopt a child who has special needs or in cases where there has been pubic notoriety concerning the child or the child's family. They may also adopt if they are a relative; or if one of the adoptive parents is in the military in South Carolina; or there are unusual or exceptional circumstances making adoption by a nonresident in the child's best interest. If you personally meet with a birth mother and she selects you as the adoptive parent, then the courts will usually permit adoption under the "unusual or exceptional circumstances" clause. (See discussion below.)

Can an attorney serve as an intermediary?
Yes. A person who facilitates an adoption is not required to be licensed.

Is advertising permitted?
Yes.

Who must consent to the adoption?
1. The birth mother
2. The birth father, if he is married to the birth mother, or if he states that he is the biological parent and has either lived with the birth mother for six months or more before the child was born or has paid medical and other expenses during the mother's pregnancy

When can consent be taken from birth mother (father), and how long after the consent is signed can it be revoked?
Consent cannot be given until the child is born and the birth mother has basically recovered from the effects of delivery; once given, it cannot be withdrawn unless it was given involuntarily or obtained under duress or through coercion. The final adoption decree makes the consent irrevocable.

What are the birth father's rights?
Essentially, the birth father must have supported the birth mother during her pregnancy if his consent is to be required. If he has not done so for at least the last six months during her pregnancy, or if he has not supported the child during the last six months before placement, he must only be given notice of the adoption; his surrender is not required.

What fees can adoptive parents pay?
The following expenses can be paid: medical expenses, reasonable living expenses for a limited period of time, fees for investigation and report, fees for those required to take the surrender, reasonable attorney fees and the fee of the guardian appointed by the court, and reasonable fees to a child-placing agency.

Where does the adoption hearing take place?
The adoption hearing may take place in the court of the county where the adoptive parents live, where the child was born, or where the child placement agency is located.

How are familial and stepparent adoptions different from nonbiological adoptions?
A home study is not required.

Can a nonresident finalize an adoption in this state?
The law states that only a resident of South Carolina can adopt a child. Yet, according to Interstate Compact on the Placement of Children guidelines, nonresidents may adopt at the discretion of the court in state.

SPECIAL NOTE:
South Carolina was known for years as the "adoption capital" of the nation; its laws were not highly structured or restrictive. It was not until Time Magazine put South Carolina on its front cover and intimated that it was the country's baby market that the South Carolina legislature enacted the "special needs" requirement. Now, South Carolina law states that a child cannot be placed with an out-of-state adoptive parent unless there are unusual or exceptional circumstances. However, what has developed since the 1989

enactment of the law is a flexible approach in allowing out-of-state couples to adopt children born or residing in South Carolina.

The ambiguous nature of the law in South Carolina is an example that demonstrates the need for an experienced adoption attorney.

SOURCE: SOUTH CODE OF LAWS. SECTIONS 20-7-1650 TO 20-7-1895 (1997)

SOUTH DAKOTA

State Adoption Specialist

South Dakota Department of
Social Services
DiAnn Kleinsasser
700 Governor's Drive, Richard F.
Kneip Building
Pierre, SD 57501-2291
(605) 773-3227
Fax: (605) 773-6834
*www.state.sd.us/social/CPS/
index.htm*
diann.kleinsasser@state.sd.us

State ICPC Administrator

South Dakota Department
of Social Services
Child Protection Services
Richard F. Kneip Building, 700
Governors Drive
Pierre, SD 57501-2291
(605) 773-3227
Fax: (605) 773-6834

State Reunion Registry

South Dakota Voluntary Registry
700 Governor's Drive, Richard F.
Kneip Building
Pierre, SD 57501-2291
(605) 773-3227
Fax: (605) 773-6834
diann.kleinsasser@state.sd.us

Regional/District Public Agencies

South Dakota Department of
Social Services, Aberdeen
P.O. Box 1300
Aberdeen, SD 57402-1300
(605) 626-2388

South Dakota Department of
Social Services, Brookings
1310 Main Avenue, South,
Suite 100
Brookings, SD 57006-0708
(605) 688-4334

South Dakota Department of
Social Services, Chamberlain
P.O. Box 430
Chamberlain, SD 57325-0430
(605) 734-6581

South Dakota Department of
Social Services, Huron
P.O. Box 1408
Huron, SD 57350-1408
(605) 353-7105

South Dakota Department of
Social Services, Mission
P.O. Box 818
Mission, SD 57555-0818
(605) 856-4431

South Dakota Department of
Social Services, Mitchell
P.O. Box 310
Mitchell, SD 57301-0310
(605) 995-8000

South Dakota Department of
Social Services, Mobridge
P.O. Box 160
Mobridge, SD 57601-0160
(605) 845-2922

South Dakota Department of
Social Services, Pierre
912 E. Sioux
Pierre, SD 57501-5070
(605) 773-3521

South Dakota Department of
Social Services, Pine Ridge
P.O. Box 279
Pine Ridge, SD 57770-0279
(605) 867-5865

South Dakota Department of
Social Services, Rapid City
P.O. Box 2440
Rapid City, SD 57709-2440
(605) 394-2434

South Dakota Department of
Social Services, Sioux Falls
300 E. Sixth Street
Sioux Falls, SD 57103-7020
(605) 367-5460

South Dakota Department of
Social Services, Watertown
100 S. Maple Street,
P.O. Box 670
Watertown, SD 57201-0670
(605) 882-5050

South Dakota Department of
Social Services, Winner
649 W. Second Street
Winner, SD 57580-1598
(605) 842-0400

South Dakota Department of
Social Services, Yankton
3113 N. Spruce Street, Suite 200
Yankton, SD 57078-5320
(605) 668-3030

Licensed Private Adoption Agencies

Bethany Christian Services
1719 West Main Street
Rapid City, SD 57702-2564
(605) 343-7196
Fax: (605) 394-5738
www.bethany.org
info@bethany.org

Bethany Christian Services
231 South Phillips Avenue,
Suite 255
Sioux Falls, SD 57104-6326
(605) 336-6999
Fax: (605) 330-0820
www.bethany.org
info@bethany.org

Catholic Family Services
Catholic Diocese of Sioux Falls
523 N. Duluth Ave.
Sioux Falls, SD 57104-2714
(605) 988-3775

Catholic Social Services
918 Fifth Street
Rapid City, SD 57701-3798
(605) 348-6086

Child Protection Program
Sisseton Wahpeton Dakota
Nation
P.O. Box 509
Agency Village, SD 57262-9802
(605) 698-3992

Children's Home Society
801 N. Sycamore Avenue
Sioux Falls, SD 57101-1749
(605) 334-3431

LDS Social Services
2525 West Main Street, #310
Rapid City, SD 57702-2443
(605) 342-3500

Lutheran Social Services
600 W. 12th Street
Sioux Falls, SD 57104-6048
(605) 336-3347

New Horizons Adoption Agency
27213 473rd Avenue
Sioux Falls, SD 57106
(605) 332-0310

Yankton Sioux Tribal
Social Services
P.O. Box 248
Marty, SD 57361-0248
(605) 384-3804

**Adoptive Parent Support
Groups**

Adoptive Families of Black Hills
3737 Corral Dr.
Rapid City, SD 57702

Families Through Adoption
Box 851
Sioux Falls, SD 57101
(605) 371-1404

North American Council on
Adoptable Children State
Representative
c/o Native American Child and
Family Resource Center
29758 202nd Street
Pierre, SD 57501
(605) 224-9045
members.aol.com/nacac

Tiwahe Olota Adoption and
Foster Care Support Group
Box 565
Reliance, SD 57569
(605) 476-5610

Search Support Groups

Adoptee Liberty Movement
Association (ALMA)
1325 S. Bahnason
Sioux Falls, SD 57103

Concerned United Birthparents
(CUB)
41004 259 Street
Mitchell, SD 57301
(605) 966-6691
www.webnations.com/cub
cub@webnations.com

SOUTH DAKOTA LAWS RELATED TO ADOPTION: QUESTIONS AND ANSWERS

Can an attorney serve as an intermediary?
No.

Is advertising permitted?
Yes.

Who must consent to the adoption?
1. The birth mother
2. The birth father, if he married to the birth mother, or if he states the child is his and asserts paternity within sixty days after the birth

When can consent be taken from birth mother (father), and how long after the consent is signed can it be revoked?
Consent can be taken any time before or after the child's birth but is not valid until after birth. Birth parents can revoke consent up until termination of their parental rights. This occurs about five days later when the birth mother goes to court. The birth father does not have to go to court but can have his rights terminated by power of attorney.

What are the birth father's rights?
If he is known and identified by the birth mother, his consent is required. If he is unknown, newspaper notices must be placed in an effort to locate him as a "John Doe" birth father. If a known birth father has abandoned the child for a period of one year, then his rights can be terminated without his consent.

What fees can adoptive parents pay?

Only fees and expenses approved by the court and fees charged by a child placement agency are permitted. If any other adoption-related moneys are paid without approval from the court, you could be charged with a felony.

Where does the adoption hearing take place?

The adoption hearing takes place in the court of the county where the adoptive parents live or where the child lives.

How are familial and stepparent adoptions different from nonbiological adoptions?

In a stepparent adoption, a judge may, but is not compelled to, order a home study.

Can a nonresident finalize an adoption in this state?

Yes.

TENNESSEE

State Adoption Specialist

Tennessee Department of
  Children's Services
Jane Chittick
436 Sixth Avenue North, Cordell
  Hull Building, 8th Floor
Nashville, TN 37243-1290
(615) 532-5637
Fax: (615) 532-6495
*www.state.tn.us/youth/adoption/
  index.htm*
jchittick@mail.state.tn.us

State ICPC Administrator

Tennessee Department
  of Human Services
Citizens Plaza, 400 Deaderick
  Street, 8th Floor
Nashville, TN 37243-1290
(615) 532-1130
Fax: (615) 532-5618

State Adoption Exchange/State
  Photolisting Service

Resource Exchange for Adoptable
  Children in Tennessee
201 23rd Avenue, North
Nashville, TN 37203-9000
(615) 321-3867
*www.state.tn.us/youth/
  adoption/react.htm*

Licensed Private Adoption
  Agencies

Adoption Consultants of
  Tennessee, Inc.
8921 Shallowford Road
Knoxville, TN 37923
(423) 769-9441
Fax: (423) 769-9442

Adoption Counseling Services
2185 Wickersham Lane
Germantown, TN 38139
(901) 753-9089

Adoption Home Studies and
  Social Services
909 Oak Street
Chattanooga, TN 37403
(423) 756-3134
Fax: (423) 756-2530

Adoption Place, Inc.
505 Oak Forest Circle
Antioch, TN 37013
(615) 399-2841

Adoption Resource Center
8529 Timberwalk Cove
Cordova, TN 38018
(901) 754-7902
Fax: (901) 752-8489

American Family Institute
1314 Chamberlain
Chattanooga, TN 37404
(423) 266-6939
Fax: (423) 267-8276

*Associated Catholic Charities of
  East Tennessee
119 Dameron Avenue
Knoxville, TN 37917
(423) 971-3560
Fax: (423) 971-3575

Associated Catholic Charities of
  the Diocese of Memphis
St. Peter's Home
3060 Baskin Street
Memphis, TN 38127-7799
(901) 354-6300
Fax: (901) 354-6343

Association for Guidance, Aid,
  Placement and Empathy
  (AGAPE)
4555 Trousdale Drive
Nashville, TN 37204
(615) 781-3000

Association for Guidance, Aid,
  Placement and Empathy
  (AGAPE) Child and Family
Services
P.O. Box 11411
Memphis, TN 38111
(901) 272-7339

Association for Guidance, Aid,
  Placement and Empathy
  (AGAPE) Child and Family
Services
111 Racine Street
Memphis, TN 38111
(901) 323-3600
Fax: (901) 272-7488

*Bethany Christian Services
1200 Division Street, Suite 206
Nashville, TN 37203-4000
(615) 242-0909
Fax: (615) 242-9440
Toll Free: (800) 765-7335
www.bethany.org
info@bethany.org

Bethany Christian Services
Mid-South Christian Services
920 Estate Drive, Suite 5
Memphis, TN 38119-3608
(901) 818-9996
Fax: (901) 761-9350
Toll Free: (800) 972-8887
www.bethany.org
info@bethany.org

Bethany Christian Services
4719 Brainerd Road, Suite D
Chattanooga, TN 37411-3842
(423) 622-7360
Fax: (423) 622-9085
Toll Free: (800) 765-7335
www.bethany.org
info@bethany.org

Bethany Christian Services
P.O. Box 1912
Bristol, TN 37621-1912
(423) 844-0380
Fax: (423) 844-0383

Bethany Christian Services
5816 Kingston Pike
Knoxville, TN 37919-6341
(865) 588-5283
Fax: (865) 588-3647
Toll Free: (800) 765-7335
www.bethany.org
info@bethany.org

Camelot Care Center
183 Fiddler's Lane
Kingston, TN 37763
(423) 376-2296
Fax: (423) 376-1850

Catholic Charities of
Tennessee, Inc.
30 White Bridge Road
Nashville, TN 37205
(615) 352-3087
Fax: (615) 352-8591
Toll Free: (800) 227-3002

Centerstone - Dede Wallace
Residential Treatment Facility
315 Hospital Drive
Madison, TN 37115
(615) 460-4260
Fax: (615) 460-4262

*Child and Family Services of
Knox County
901 E. Summit Hill Drive
Knoxville, TN 37915
(423) 524-7483
Fax: (423) 524-4790

Chosen Children
5020 University Drive, Suite 10
Collegedale, TN 37315
(423) 396-4770
Fax: (423) 396-4771

Church of God Home
for Children
449 McCarn Circle
Sevierville, TN 37864
(423) 453-4644
Fax: (423) 453-8812

Crisis Pregnancy Support Center
1810 Hayes Street
Nashville, TN 37203
(615) 321-0005
Fax: (615) 321-5863

East Tennessee Christian
Services, Inc.
4638 Chambliss Avenue
Knoxville, TN 37919
(423) 584-0841
Fax: (423) 588-6560

ENCMA
105 South Parkway West
Memphis, TN 38109
(901) 947-9700
Fax: (901) 947-9707

Family and Children's Services-
Center for Adoption
1210 Foster Avenue
Nashville, TN 37211
(615) 253-3289
Fax: (615) 253-3326

Family and Children's Services of
Chattanooga, Inc.
300 East 8th Street
Chattanooga, TN 37403
(423) 755-2800
Fax: (423) 755-2758

Frayser Family Center
21500 Whitney Avenue
Memphis, TN 38127
(901) 354-7365
Fax: (901) 354-7390

Free Will Baptist Family
Ministries
90 Stanley Lane
Greeneville, TN 37743
(423) 693-9449
Fax: (423) 693-9449

Frontier Health/TRACES
2001 Stonebrook Place
Kingsport, TN 37660
(423) 232-2679
Fax: (423) 224-1023

Goodwill Homes Community
Services, Inc.
4590 Goodwill Road
Memphis, TN 38109
(901) 785-6790
Fax: (901) 789-8351

Greater Chattanooga Christian
Services & Children's Home
744 McCallie Avenue, Suite 329,
Doctor's Building
Chattanooga, TN 37403
(423) 756-0281
Fax: (423) 265-7326

Guardian Angel International
Adoption Agency
116 Pulaski
Lawrenceburg, TN 38464
(931) 766-5277
Fax: (931) 766-1503

Happy Haven Homes, Inc.
2311 Wakefield Drive
Cookeville, TN 38501
(931) 526-2052
Fax: (931) 372-8837

Harmony Adoptions of Tennessee
2412 North Park Boulevard
Knoxville, TN 37917
(423) 522-0704
Fax: (423) 525-2975

Heaven Sent Children, Inc.
316 West Lytle Street, Suite 110
Murfreesboro, TN 37130
(615) 898-0803
Fax: (615) 898-1990

Helen Ross McNab
Center/TRACES
320 Arthur Street
Knoxville, TN 37921-6319
(423) 523-8695
Fax: (423) 523-6827

Holston United Methodist Home
for Children, Inc.
Holston Drive, P.O. Box 188
Greeneville, TN 37743
(423) 638-4171
Fax: (423) 638-7171
Toll Free: (800) 628-2986
holston@usit.net

*Jewish Family Services, Inc.
6560 Poplar Avenue
Memphis, TN 38138
(901) 767-8511
Fax: (901) 763-2348

John Tarleton Home for Children
2455 Sutherland Avenue
Knoxville, TN 37919
(423) 870-9033
Fax: (423) 870-4170

Life Care for Youth
15354 Old Hickory Boulevard
Nashville, TN 37211
(615) 834-6171
Fax: (615) 834-4463

Life Choices, Inc.
2235 Covington Pike, Suite 14
Memphis, TN 38128
(901) 388-1172
Fax: (901) 388-1225

Lutheran Services in
   Tennessee, Inc.
2636 Maryville Pike
Knoxville, TN 37920
(423) 577-8925
Fax: (423) 577-3929

Madison Children's Home
616 N. Dupont Avenue
Madison, TN 37116
(615) 860-4461
Fax: (615) 860-6817

Mercy Ministries, Inc.
15328 Old Hickory Boulevard
Nashville, TN 37211-6210
(615) 831-6987
Fax: (615) 315-9749

Mid-Cumberland Children's
   Services, Inc.
106 N. Mountain Street
Smithville, TN 37166
(615) 597-7134

Mid-South Christian Services
920 Estate Drive, Suite 5
Memphis, TN 38119-3608
(901) 818-9996
Fax: (901) 761-9350

Monroe Harding Children's Home
1120 Glendale Lane
Nashville, TN 37204
(615) 298-5573
Fax: (615) 298-1281

Mur-Ci Homes, Inc.
PO Box 735,
   2984 Baby Ruth Lane
Antioch, TN 37013
(615) 641-6446
Fax: (615) 641-2416

New Life Homes for Boys, Inc.
4220 Dayton Blvd., Suite J
Chattanooga, TN 37415
(423) 877-7897
Fax: (423) 877-7224

Oasis Center, Inc.
1216 17th Avenue South
Nashville, TN 37212
(615) 320-0026
Fax: (615) 329-1444

Omni Visions
101 Lea Avenue
Nashville, TN 37210
(615) 726-3603
Fax: (615) 726-0393

Pathways of Tennessee
   Youth Center
650 Nuckolls Road
Bolivar, TN 38008
(901) 935-8200
Fax: (901) 935-8327

Porter-Leath Children's Center
868 N. Manassas Street
Memphis, TN 38107-2516
(901) 577-2500
Fax: (901) 577-2506

Residential Services, Inc.
1451 Elm Hill Pike, Suite 161
Nashville, TN 37210-4523
(615) 367-4333
Fax: (615) 360-3894

Second Chance, Inc.
3505 Houston Levee Road
Memphis, TN 38138
(901) 368-5683
Fax: (901) 854-9059

Senior Services, Inc.
   Stepping Stones
4700 Poplar Avenue
Memphis, TN 38117
(901) 766-0600
Fax: (901) 766-0699

Small World Adoption
   Programs, Inc.
401 Bonna Spring Drive
Hermitage, TN 37076
(615) 883-4372
Fax: (615) 885-7582
Toll Free: (800) 544-5083

Tennessee Baptist
   Children's Home
6896 Highway 70
Memphis, TN 38134
(901) 386-3961
Fax: (901) 382-9754

Tennessee Baptist
   Children's Home
6623 Lee Highway
Chattanooga, TN 37421
(423) 892-2722
Fax: (423) 855-1304

Tennessee Baptist Children's
   Home, Inc. - Northeast Region
215 University Parkway
Johnson City, TN 37601
(423) 929-2157
Fax: (423) 929-9134

Tennessee Baptist Children's
   Homes, Inc.
1310 Franklin Road
Brentwood, TN 37027
(615) 377-6551
Fax: (615) 377-6973

Tennessee Children's Home
1312 Campbell
Jackson, TN 38301
(901) 989-7335
Fax: (901) 989-7288

Tennessee Children's Home
P.O. Box 10, Main Street
Spring Hill, TN 37174
(931) 486-2274
Fax: (931) 486-1231

The Guidance Center:
   Connections Program
1338 West College
Murfreesboro, TN 37129
(615) 849-8939
Fax: (615) 849-2346

Therapeutic Interventions, Inc.
176 Thompson Lane, Suite 103
Nashville, TN 37210
(615) 385-5188
Fax: (615) 385-5521

United Family Services
3320 Dodd Avenue
Chattanooga, TN 37407
(423) 698-4724
Fax: (423) 629-5230

*Williams International
  Adoptions, Inc
5100 Stage Road, Suite A
Memphis, TN 38134
(901) 373-6003
Fax: (901) 373-0130
www.williamsinternational.org
wiai@usit.net

Youth Emergency Services of
  Middle Tennessee
553 Victor Avenue
Lebanon, TN 37087
(615) 443-7222
Fax: (615) 444-5430

Youth Town of Tennessee
Route 2, Highway 45
Pinson, TN 38366
(901) 988-5251
Fax: (901) 427-5605

Youth Villages
Serendipity House
100 Oaks Office Tower, 719
  Thompson Lane, Suite 600
Nashville, TN 37204
(615) 383-2232
Fax: (615) 250-7280

Youth Villages, Inc.
5515 Shelby Oaks
Memphis, TN 38134
(901) 252-7610

Zambo Counseling and
  Consulting Services
20795 E. Main Street
Huntingdon, TN 38344
(901) 986-2001
Fax: (901) 986-4889

**Adoptive Parent Support
  Groups**

BRAG
1104 Hunter's Trail
Franklin, TN 37901
(615) 370-5846

Council on Adoptable Children
  and North American Council
  on Adoptable Children
State Representative
7630 Luscomb Drive
Knoxville, TN 37919
(423) 693-8001

Families for Russian and
  Ukrainian Adoptions
Nashville, TN
(615) 781-2356

Forever Families
6151 Ashley Road
Arlington, TN 38002
(901) 377-8867

Mid-South Families Through
  Adoption
3559 Oak Limb Cove
Memphis, TN 38135
(901) 388-2095

Mountain Region Adoption
  Support Group
4428 Fieldstone Drive
Kingsport, TN 37664
(423) 523-7206

North American Council on
  Adoptable Children
  Representative
27 Windhaven Lane
Oak Ridge, TN 37830
(423) 482-5264

Ours of Middle Tennessee
3557 Bethlehem Road
Springfield, TN 37172
(615) 643-3426

Pappoos
7856 Harpeth View Drive
Nashville, TN 37221
(615) 646-8144

Parents of International Children
  (PIC)
615 Tidesbridge Court
Murfreesboro, TN 37128
(615) 848-5278
www.parentsofintchildren.com

West Tennessee AGAPE Parents
  Group
P.O. Box 11411
Memphis, TN 38111
(901) 272-7339

Search Support Groups

Adoptee Liberty Movement
  Association (ALMA)
P.O. Box 15064
Chattanooga, TN 37415

Adoptees and Birth
  Parents in Search
P.O. Box 901
Cleveland, TN 37364

Adoption Support and Education
921 Belvoir Hills Drive
East Ridge, TN 37412
(931) 622-5341

American Adoption Congress
  State Representative
5182 Oak Meadow
Memphis, TN 38134
(901) 386-2197
dglad@bellsouth.net

Birthparents Search for Answers
2750 Ward Road
Millington, TN 38053

Concerned United Birthparents
  (CUB)
21 Vaughns Cap J163
Nashville, TN 37205-4303
(615) 353-9754

Group for Openness in Adoption
518 General George Patton Road
Nashville, TN 37221
(615) 646-8116

R.O.O.T.S.
P.O. Box 9662
Knoxville, TN 37940
(423) 573-1344

Tennessee Department
  of Human Services
400 Deaderick Street
Nashville, TN 37248-9000
(615) 741-5935

Tennessee Searches for Truth
7721 White Creek Pike
Joelton, TN 37080

Tennessee's Right to Know
P.O. Box 34334
Memphis, TN 38134
(901) 373-7049

TENNESSEE LAWS RELATED TO ADOPTION: QUESTIONS AND ANSWERS

Can an attorney serve as an intermediary?
Yes, but no fee can be charged.

Is advertising permitted?
Yes.

Who must consent to the adoption?
1. The birth mother
2. The birth father, if he is married to the birth mother, or if he listed on the birth certificate or named by the birth mother and has claimed paternity

When can consent be taken from birth mother (father), and how long after the consent is signed can it be revoked?
A surrentder can be taken anytime after birth and if a petition to adoption has not been filed a birth mother has 15 days to revoke the consent.

In cases of conflict, the courts are instructed to favor (not merely consider) the child's best interest.

What are the birth father's rights?
If the birth father is named by the birth mother and his whereabouts are unknown, a diligent search must be made to find him and notify him of the adoption. If he cannot be found, then he must be informed of the adoption through public notice (usually placed in a newspaper).

The court is allowed to exclude the birth father if the child is born out of wedlock and the birth father has failed to register with the putative father registry within thirty days of the child's birth and to file change of address information within ten days of any such change. If he is registered, this will subject him to court-ordered child support and medical payments. If he fails to register, his rights can be terminated. After receiving notice of the birth, the birth father must file a legitimation complaint and if he does not, then his rights can be terminated.

The birth father is also required to pay pregnancy-related expenses and child support as soon as he is informed of the birth mother's pregnancy or the child's birth. If he does not do so, then his rights can be terminated.

What fees can adoptive parents pay?
Only an adoption agency can receive fees for serving as an intermediary. Reasonable medical and legal fees and living expenses can be paid. The adoptive parents must give the court a statement of any fees paid or received.

Where does the adoption hearing take place?
The adoption hearing takes place in the court of the county where the adoptive parents live, where the adoptee lives, or where the child placement agency is located.

How are familial and stepparent adoptions different from nonbiological adoptions?
The home study and the six-month waiting period before finalization are waived.

Can a nonresident finalize an adoption in this state?

No. You must have lived in Tennessee for at least one year before filing the petition to adopt. This requirement is waived for those serving in the military who were residents of Tennessee for one year before entering the military.

The birth parents must be given notice of the availability of counseling. If the birth parent cannot afford counseling, the adoptive couple must pay for the counseling.

SOURCE: TENNESSEE CODE ANNOTATED SECTIONS 36-1-102 TO 36-1-206 (1997)

TEXAS

State Adoption Specialist

Texas Department of Protective
and Regulatory Services
Susan Klickman
P.O. Box 149030
Austin, TX 78717-9030
(512) 438-4986
Fax: (512) 438-3782
www.tdprs.state.tx.us
klickms@tdprs.state.tx.us

Texas Department of Protective
and Regulatory Services
Chris Johnson
P.O. Box 149030, M.C. E-557
Austin, TX 78714-9030
(512) 438-4982
Fax: (512) 438-3782
www.tdprs.state.tx.us
johnsocm@tdprs.state.tx.us

State ICPC Administrator

Texas Department of Protective
and Regulatory Services
P.O. Box 149030, Y-942
Austin, TX 78714-9030
(512) 834-4474
Fax: (512) 834-4476

State Adoption Exchange/State Photolisting Service

Texas Adoption Resource
Exchange
Texas Department of Protective
and Regulatory Services
P.O. Box 149030, M.C. E-557
Austin, TX 78714-9030
Toll Free: (800) 233-3405
*www.tdprs.state.tx.us/adoption/
tare.html*
TARE@tdprs.state.tx.us

State Reunion Registry

Central Adoption Registry
Bureau of Vital Statistics
P.O. Box 140123
Austin, TX 78714-0123
(512) 458-7388
*www.tdh.state.tx.us/bvs/car/
car.htm*

Regional/District Public Agencies

Texas Department of Protective
and Regulatory Services,
Region 1
P.O. Box 10528
Lubbock, TX 79408
(806) 762-2680
Toll Free: (800) 233-3405
www.tdprs.state.tx.us

Texas Department of Protective
and Regulatory Services,
Region 1
6200 I-40 West
Amarillo, TX 79116-3700
(806) 358-6211
Toll Free: (800) 233-3405
www.tdprs.state.tx.us

Texas Department of Protective
and Regulatory Services,
Region 10
119 N. Stanton
El Paso, TX 79901
(915) 542-4535
Toll Free: (800) 233-3405
www.tdprs.state.tx.us

Texas Department of Protective
and Regulatory Services,
Region 11
4201 Greenwood Drive
Corpus Christi, TX 78416
(361) 854-2011
Toll Free: (800) 233-3405
www.tdprs.state.tx.us

Texas Department of Protective
and Regulatory Services,
Region 11
2520 South I Road
Edinburg, TX 78539-7016
(956) 381-5791
Toll Free: (800) 233-3405
www.tdprs.state.tx.us

Texas Department of Protective
and Regulatory Services,
Region 2
P.O. Box 6635
Abilene, TX 79602
(915) 691-8100
Toll Free: (800) 233-3405
www.tdprs.state.tx.us

Texas Department of Protective
and Regulatory Services,
Region 3
1351 E. Bardin Road
Arlington, TX 76018-2134
(817) 264-4000
Toll Free: (800) 233-3405
www.tdprs.state.tx.us

Texas Department of Protective
and Regulatory Services,
Region 4
302 E. Rieck Road
Tyler, TX 75703
(903) 561-5359
Toll Free: (800) 233-3405
www.tdprs.state.tx.us

Texas Department of Protective
and Regulatory Services,
Region 5
285 Liberty, 19th Floor
Beaumont, TX 77701
(409) 981-5920
Toll Free: (800) 233-3405
www.tdprs.state.tx.us

Texas Department of Protective
and Regulatory Services,
Region 5
2027 N. Stallings Drive
Nacogdoches, TX 75964
(409) 569-5317
Toll Free: (800) 233-3405
www.tdprs.state.tx.us

Texas Department of Protective
and Regulatory Services,
Region 6
2525 Murworth
Houston, TX 77701
(713) 394-4000, Ext: 5550
Toll Free: (800) 233-3405
www.tdprs.state.tx.us

Texas Department of Protective
and Regulatory Services,
Region 7
P.O. Box 15995
Austin, TX 78761
(512) 834-3195
Toll Free: (800) 233-3405
www.tdprs.state.tx.us

Texas Department of Protective
and Regulatory Services,
Region 8
3635 S.E. Military Drive
San Antonio, TX 78223-0990
(210) 337-3344
Toll Free: (800) 233-3405
www.tdprs.state.tx.us

Texas Department of Protective
and Regulatory Services,
Region 9
901 West Wall
Midland, TX 79701
(915) 686-2273
Toll Free: (800) 233-3405
www.tdprs.state.tx.us

**Licensed Private Adoption
Agencies**

A Cradle of Hope
311 N. Market Street, Suite 300
Dallas, TX 75202
(214) 747-4500

AAA-Alamo Adoption Agency
10615 Perrin Beitel, Suite 803
San Antonio, TX 78217
(210) 967-5337

AAI - Adoptions and Aid
International
1036 High Ridge Drive
Duncanville, TX 75137

(972) 709-3954
Fax: (972) 298-7224
www.adoptionsandaid.com
info@adoptionsandaid.com

AASK of Texas
1060 W. Pipeline Road, Suite 106
Hurst, TX 76053
(817) 595-0497
Fax: (817) 595-0490

ABC Adoption Agency, Inc.
417 San Pedro Avenue
San Antonio, TX 78212
(210) 227-7820
Fax: (210) 227-7820

About Life, Inc.
4131 N. Central, Suite 675
Dallas, TX 75204
(214) 522-5433

Abrazo Adoption Associates
10010 San Pedro, Suite 540
San Antonio, TX 78216
(210) 342-5683
Toll Free: (800) 454-5683

Adoption Access
8340 Meadow Road, Suite 231
Dallas, TX 75231
(214) 750-4847

Adoption Advisory, Inc.
3607 Fairmount
Dallas, TX 75219
(214) 520-0004
www.adopt-ad.com
AAI@adopt-ad.com

Adoption Advocates, Inc.
328 West Mistletoe Avenue
San Antonio, TX 78212
(210) 734-4470
Fax: (210) 734-5966

Adoption Affiliates, Inc.
215 W. Olmos Drive
San Antonio, TX 78212
(210) 824-9939

Adoption Alliance
7303 Blanco Road
San Antonio, TX 78216
(210) 349-3991

Adoption As An Option
12611 Kingsride Lane
Houston, TX 77024
(713) 468-1053

Adoption Family Services
13140 Coit Road, Suite 400
Dallas, TX 75240
(972) 437-9950

Adoption Information and
Counseling
2020 Southwest Freeway,
Suite 326
Houston, TX 77098
(713) 529-5125

Adoption Resource Consultants
P.O. Box 1224
Richardson, TX 75083
(972) 517-4119
Fax: (972) 423-1297

Adoption Services Associates
5370 Prue Road
San Antonio, TX 78240
(210) 699-6094
Toll Free: (800) 648-1807
www.childadopt.com
adopt@connecti.com or
  index@childadopt.com

Adoption Services, Inc.
3500 Overton Park, West
Fort Worth, TX 76109
(817) 921-0718

Adoption-A Gift of Love
P.O. Box 50384
Denton, TX 76206
(817) 387-9311

Adoptions and Aid International
1306 High Ridge Drive
Duncanville, TX 75137
(972) 709-3954

All-Church Home for Children
1424 Summit Avenue
Fort Worth, TX 76102
(817) 335-4041

Alternatives In Motion
20619 Aldine Westfield Road
Humble, TX 77338
(713) 821-6508

Andrel Adoptions
3908 Manchaca
Austin, TX 78704
(512) 448-4605

Angel Adoptions of the Heart
2715 Bissonet #221
Houston, TX 77005
(713) 523-2273

Atlantis Foundation
2800 NASA Road One,
 Suite 1406
Seabrook, TX 77586
(281) 326-1201

Bethany Christian Services
 of North Texas
10310 N. Central Expressway,
 Building III, Suite 360
Dallas, TX 75231-8627
(214) 373-8797
Fax: (214) 373-4797
Toll Free: (800) 650-6226
www.bethany.org
info@bethany.ord

Blessed Trinity Adoptions, Inc.
8503 Havner Court
Houston, TX 77037
(713) 855-0137

Bright Dreams International
2929 Carlisle, Suite 255
Dallas, TX 75204
(214) 740-0234

Buckner Adoption and Maternity
 Services, Inc.
4830 Samuell Boulevard
Dallas, TX 75228
(214) 381-1552
www.buckner.org

Buckner Baptist Children's Home
129 Brentwood Avenue
Lubbock, TX 79416-1601
(806) 795-7151

Buckner Baptist Children's Home
5200 South Buckner Blvd
Dallas, TX 75227
(214) 321-4535

Caring Choices, Inc.
10301 Northwest Freeway,
 Suite 508
Houston, TX 77092
(713) 688-5200

Catholic Charities
2300 West Commerce Street
San Antonio, TX 78207
(210) 734-5054

Catholic Charities
3520 Montrose
Houston, TX 77006
(713) 526-4611

Catholic Counseling Services
P.O. Box 190507
Dallas, TX 75219-0507
(214) 526-2772

Catholic Family Service
P.O. Box 15127
Amarillo, TX 79105
(806) 376-4571
Fax: (806) 345-7947

Catholic Social Services of Laredo
P.O. Box 3305
Laredo, TX 78044
(210) 722-2443

Child Placement Center
2212 Sunny Lane
Killeen, TX 76541
(817) 690-5959

Children & Family Institute
4200 S. Freeway, Suite 614
Fort Worth, TX 76115
(817) 922-9974
Fax: (817) 922-8151

Children's Home of Lubbock
P.O. Box 2824
Lubbock, TX 79408
(806) 762-0481

Chosen Heritage - Christian
 Adoptions
121 N.E. Loop 820
Hurst, TX 76053
(817) 589-7899

Christian Homes
P.O. Box 270
Abilene, TX 79604
(915) 677-2205
Fax: (915) 677-0332
Toll Free: (800) 592-4725
www.christianhomes.com
christianhomes@abilene.com

Christian Homes of Abilene
3435 Pine Mill Road
Paris, TX 75460
(903) 785-7701

Christian Services of East Texas
1810 Shiloh Road, Suite 1305
Tyler, TX 75703
(903) 509-0558

Christian Services of the
 Southwest
6320 LBJ Freeway, Suite 122
Dallas, TX 75240
(214) 960-9981

Counsel for Adoption Resources
1201 South W.S. Young Drive,
 Suite F
Killeen, TX 76541
(817) 690-2223

Cradle of Life Adoption Agency
245 N. Fourth Street
Beaumont, TX 77701
(409) 832-3000
Fax: (409) 833-3935
Toll Free: (800) 456-8001

DePelchin Children's Center
100 Sandman Street
Houston, TX 77007
(713) 861-8136
Fax: (713) 802-3897

El Paso Adoption Services
905 Noble
El Paso, TX 79902
(915) 542-1086
Fax: (915) 544-7080

El Paso Center for Children
3700 Altura Boulevard
El Paso, TX 79930
(915) 565-8361

Friends Adoptions International
700 S. Friendswood Drive, Suite B
Friendswood, TX 77546
(713) 992-4677

Gladney Center for Adoption
2300 Hemphill Street
Fort Worth, TX 76110
(817) 922-6088
Fax: (817) 922-6040
Toll Free: (800) 452-3639
www.gladney.org
info@gladney.org

Great Wall China Adoption
5555 N. Lamar Blvd., Suite H-135
Austin, TX 78751
(512) 323-9595
Fax: (512) 323-9599
www.eden.com/~gwcadopt
gwcadopt@eden.com

Guadalupe International
 Adoptions
16822 Avenfield
Tomball, TX 77375
(281) 370-8808

High Plains Children's Home and
 Family Services, Inc.
P.O. Box 7448
Amarillo, TX 79114-7448
(806) 622-2272

Homes of Saint Mark
3000 Richmond Avenue,
Suite 570
Houston, TX 77098
(713) 522-2800
Fax: (713) 522-3769

Hope Cottage, Inc.
Circle of Hope
4209 McKinney Avenue,
Suite 200
Dallas, TX 75205
(214) 526-8721

Hope for Tomorrow
1305 Early Boulevard
Early, TX 76802
(915) 646-4673

Hope International
311 N. Market Street, Suite 300
Dallas, TX 75202
(214) 672-9399
Fax: (214) 939-3001
www.hopeadoption.com
smilburn@hopeadoption.com

Inheritance Adoptions
P.O. Box 2563
Wichita Falls, TX 76307
(817) 322-3678

International Child
Placing Agency
P.O. Box 112
Los Fresnos, TX 78566
(210) 233-5705

J&B Kids, Inc. Placing Agency
Route 1, Box 173 F
Yorktown, TX 78164
(512) 564-2964

LDS Social Services-Texas
1100 W. Jackson Road
Carrollton, TX 75006
(972) 242-2182

Lena Pope Home, Inc.
4701 West Rosedale
Fort Worth, TX 76107
(817) 731-8681

Los Ninos International Adoption
Center
1600 Lake Front Circle
The Woodlands, TX 77380-3600
(713) 363-2892
Fax: (713) 297-4191
www.losninos.org
jerichsen@LosNinos.org

Loving Alternatives Adoptions
P.O. Box 131466
Tyler, TX 75713
(903) 581-7720

Lutheran Social Services
314 Highland Mall Blvd,
Suite 200
Austin, TX 78752
(512) 459-1000
Fax: (512) 452-6855

Lutheran Social Services
of Texas, Inc.
4200 Westheimer, Suite 285
Houston, TX 77027
(713) 521-0110

Marywood Children and
Family Services
510 West 26th Street
Austin, TX 78705
(512) 472-9251
Fax: (512) 472-4829
Toll Free: (800) 251-5433
www.marywood.org
marywood@eden.com

Methodist Children's Home
1111 Herring Avenue
Waco, TX 76708
(254) 750-1260

New Life Children's Services
19911 Tomball Parkway
Houston, TX 77070
(713) 955-1001

PAC Child Placing Agency
4655 S.Farm Market 1258
Amarillo, TX 79118-7219
(806) 335-9138

Placement Services Agency
P.O. Box 799004
Dallas, TX 75379-9004
(214) 387-3312

Read Adoption Agency, Inc.
1011 North Mesa
El Paso, TX 79902
(915) 533-3697

Smithlawn Maternity Home and
Adoption Agency
P.O. Box 6451
Lubbock, TX 79493
(806) 745-2574

Spaulding for Children
710 North Post Oak Road,
Suite 500
Houston, TX 77024
(713) 681-6991
Fax: (713) 681-9089

Tejano
6901 Brownwood Street
Houston, TX 77020-5319
(713) 675-7790

Texas Baptist Children's Home
P.O. Box 7
Round Rock, TX 78664
(512) 388-8256

Texas Baptist Home for Children
P.O. Drawer 309
Waxahachie, TX 75168
(972) 937-1321

Texas Cradle Society
8600 Wurzbach Road, Suite 1110
San Antonio, TX 78240
(210) 614-0299
www.texascradle.com

Unity Children's Home
12027 Blue Mountain
Houston, TX 77067
(713) 537-6148

**Adoptive Parent Support
Groups**

Adopted Friends
6610 Sharpview
Houston, TX 77074
(713) 777-5461

Adopting Children Together
8330 Meadow Road, Suite 218
Dallas, TX 75231
(214) 373-8348

Adopting Children Together
P.O. Box 120966
Arlington, TX 76012-9066
(817) 465-1825

Adopting Children Together and
North American Council on
Adoptable Children
Representative
1701 Los Prados Trail, P.O. Box
120966
Arlington, TX 76012-9066
(817) 265-3496
Fax: (817) 795-6009

Adoptive Families of Romanian
Children
1403 Nails Creek Drive
Sugarland, TX 77478-5360
(903) 763-4683

Adoptive Families Together
P.O. Box 1591
Sugar Land, TX 77487
(713) 668-9733

Adoptive Parent Support
  Services157 Trillium Lane
San Antonio, TX 78213
(210) 525-0095
Fax: (210) 525-8312

Austin Kids from All Cultures
4508 Sinclair Avenue
Austin, TX 78756
(512) 467-9177

Circle of Hope
c/o Hope Cottage
4209 McKinney
Dallas, TX 75205
(214) 526-8721

Council on Adoptable Children
808 Woodlawn
Harker Heights, TX 76548
(254) 690-3317

Council on Adoptable Children
  and North American Council
  on Adoptable Children
Route 2, Box 77-F
Edinburg, TX 78539
(956) 383-2680
Fax: (956) 381-2177

Council on Adoptable Children
  and North American Council
  on Adoptable Children
Representative
808 Woodlawn Drive
Harker Heights, TX 76543
(254) 690-3317
members.aol.com/nacac

Council on Adoptable
  Children of Austin
1201 Slaughter Ln.
Austin, TX 78745
(512) 282-0188

Council on Adoptable
  Children of Dallas
7411 La Sobrina
Dallas, TX 75243
(972) 701-0409

Council on Adoptable
  Children of East Texas
21404 Lake Haven
Chandler, TX 75758
(903) 849-2286

Council on Adoptable
  Children of Houston
207 Lakeside Dr.
Channelview, TX 77530
(281) 452-1599

Council on Adoptable Children
  of Texas, El Concilio
1712 Gardenia
McAllen, TX 78501
(956) 383-5611

Council on Adoptable Children of
  the Texas Panhandle
P.O. Box 3700
Amarillo, TX 79116
(806) 358-6211

Council on Adoptable Children,
  Coastal Bend
4322 Wood River Dr.
Corpus Christi, TX 78410
(512) 387-6699

Families for Russian and
  Ukrainian Adoptions
Houston, TX
(281) 469-7560
BKGates@aol.com

Families for Russian and
  Ukrainian Adoptions
1204 West Lilly Lane
Arlington, TX 76013
(817) 795-6703
cellis@swbell.net

Families Through Adoption
P.O. Box 190507
Dallas, TX 75219-0507
(214) 526-2772

Family Counseling Service
1635 N.E. Loop 410, Suite 601
San Antonio, TX 78209
(210) 821-5980

Forever Families of El Paso
P.O. Box 3182
El Paso, TX 79925-3182
(915) 594-2427

Friends and Families of Adoption
4117 Norcross
Plano, TX 75024

Heart Words
4054 McKinney Avenue,
  Suite 302
Dallas, TX 75204
(214) 521-4560

Jewish Children's and
  Family Services
12500 N.W. Military Highway
San Antonio, TX 78231
(210) 302-6920
BnLBarocas@aol.com

Life Matters
5025 N. Cental Expressway,
  Suite 3040
Dallas, TX 75205
(972) 496-3697

Limiar: USA
111 Broken Bough
San Antonio, TX 44236
(210) 479-0300
Fax: (210) 479-3835
www.limiar.org
limiarusa@aol.com

National Adoption Network
P.O. Box 2130
Coppell, TX 75019
(214) 335-0906
Toll Free: (800) 246-4237

Open Arms
1306 Hitherfield Drive
Sugar Land, TX 77478-2486

Parents Aiding and
  Lending Support
3709 Canterbury
Baytown, TX 77521
(713) 427-7293

Post Adoption Center
  of the Southwest
8600 Wurzbach Road, Suite 1110
San Antonio, TX 78240
(210) 614-0299

Romanian Cousins
382 Bedford Drive
Richardson, TX 75080
(972) 448-8002

Single Adoptive Parent
  Support Group
12751 Whittington,
  Apartment 136
Houston, TX 77077
(713) 496-2855

Stars of David International Inc.
Houston Chapter
49098 Braeburn Drive
Bellaire, TX 77401-5316
www.starsofdavid.org
starsdavid@aol.com

Search Support Groups

Adoptee Liberty Movement
  Association (ALMA)
P.O. Box 11273
Killeen, TX 76547

Adoptee Liberty Movement
Association (ALMA)
Austin Satelite
811 Graceland
Houston, TX 77249

Adoptee Liberty Movement
Association (ALMA)
P.O. Box 200392
Austin, TX 78720-0392
(512) 335-8982

Adoptee Liberty Movement
Association (ALMA)
Dallas/Ft. Worth Chapter
P.O. Box 560375
The Colony, TX 75056
(214) 601-6893

Adoptee Liberty Movement
Association (ALMA)
P.O. Box 1424
Plainview, TX 79072

Adoptee Liberty Movement
Association (ALMA)
P.O. Box 191
Spring Branch, TX 78070

Adoptee Liberty Movement
Association (ALMA)
P.O. Box 468
Riverside, TX 77367

Adoptee Liberty Movement
Association (ALMA)
P.O. Box 720301
McAllen, TX 78504
(210) 682-8748

Adoptees, Adoptive/Birth Parents
in Search
4208 Roxbury
El Paso, TX 78704
(915) 581-0478

Adoption Search and Reunite, Inc.
Box 371
Pasadena, TX 77501
(713) 477-0491

Adoption Triad Forum
Box 832161
Richardson, TX 75081

American Adoption Congress
State Representative
P.O. Box 832161
Richardson, TX 75083
(972) 699-8386
Fax: (972) 699-1269
AliciaKLa@aol.com

Birthparents/Adoptees
Support Group
4038 Clayhead Road
Richmond, TX 77469

Child and Family Resources
2775 Villa Creek, #240
Dallas, TX 75234

DFW Adult Adoptee
Support Group
5025 N. Central Expressway,
Suite 3026
Dallas, TX 75205
(972) 414-3639
cldemuth@aol.com

DFW Birthmother Support Group
5025 N. Central Expressway,
Suite 3026
Dallas, TX 75205
(972) 414-3639
cldemuth@aol.com

DFW Triad Support Group
1311 N. Washington Avenue
Dallas, TX 75203
(972) 414-3639
cldemuth@aol.com

Hope Cottage Adoption Center
4209 McKinney Avenue, #200
Dallas, TX 75205
(214) 521-4673
Toll Free: (800) 944-4460
www.dallas.net/~adoption

Love Roots Wings
10432 Achilles
El Paso, TX 79924
(915) 821-7253

Marywood Post Adoption
Services
510 W. 26th Street
Austin, TX 78705
(512) 472-9251

Orphan Voyage
1305 Augustine Court
College Station, TX 77840
(409) 764-7157

Orphan Voyage of Houston
5811 Southminster
Houston, TX 77035
(713) 723-1762

Post Adoption Center of the
Southwest
8600 Wurzbach Road, Suite 1110
San Antonio, TX 78240-4334
(210) 614-0299

Search and Support Group of
DePelchin Center
100 Sandman
Houston, TX 77007
(713) 802-7724

Searchline of Plano
3944 E. Bark Boulevard
Plano, TX 75074

Searchline of Texas
1516 Old Orchard
Irving, TX 75061
(214) 445-7005

Texas Coalition for Adoption
Resources and Education
TxCare
P.O. Box 832161
Richardson, TX 75083-2161
(713) 721-3845
Fax: (972) 699-1269
www.txcare.org
txcare@txcare.org

TEXAS LAWS RELATED TO ADOPTION: QUESTIONS AND ANSWERS

In Texas, a preadoption report is given to the adoptive parents, which provides the health, social, educational, and genetic history of the child and the child's biological family.

Can an attorney serve as an intermediary?
No.

Is advertising permitted?
Yes.

Who must consent to the adoption?
1. Both birth parents
2. A managing conservator, if appointed; a conservator is a person or agency who retains all the rights and powers of a parent to the exclusion of other parents

When can consent be taken from birth mother (father), and how long after the consent is signed can it be revoked?
Consent cannot be taken until forty-eight hours after birth and is irrevocable if the consent designates the Department of Human Services as managing conservator.

The consent must specifically state that it is irrevocable for a certain time period, up to sixty days. During this period of time the adoptive couple or adoption agency must file the adoption petition in order that the birth parents' rights be terminated. It is in the adoptive couple's best interests to include the entire sixty days on the consent form, so that there is plenty of time for the court to terminate the birth parents' rights.

Termination of rights can also be done by court appearance by the birth parents within ten days of filing.

What are the birth father's rights?
There is no consent required of a birth father who has abandoned the child with no means of identification or who does not file an admission of paternity within a reasonable time frame. If the birth father cannot be found, his rights can be terminated by publication of notice of the adoption proceedings; termination will occur after a certain time period has elapsed if he does not respond. Texas law also states that if a birth parents leaves a child in custody of another with no intent to return and without providing adequate support for the child, then consent is not required and that birth parent's rights can be terminated.

If a birth father is out of the picture, you may want to file his termination of parental rights before the birth. Also, his rights cannot be terminated until five days after publication of the notice begins. This way, once the child is born, the paperwork is completed.

What fees can adoptive parents pay?
Medical, legal fees, and reasonable counseling fees are permitted. In an independent adoption, no living expenses can be paid; such fees can only be paid through an adoption agency.

Where does the adoption hearing take place?
The adoption hearing may take place in the court of the county where the adoptive parents live, the child lives, or where the agency is located.

How are familial and stepparent adoptions different from nonbiological adoptions?
In a relative or stepparent adoption, the preadoption report on the child's background and status is not required.

Can a nonresident finalize an adoption in this state?
Yes.

UTAH

State Adoption Specialist

Utah Department of
Human Services
Division of Child and Family
Services
LeRoy Franke
120 North, 200 West
Salt Lake City, UT 84103
(801) 538-4078
Fax: (801) 538-3993
www.dhs.state.ut.us/
hsadmini.lfranke@state.ut.us

State ICPC Administrator

Utah State Division of Child and
Family Services
Adoptions/ICPC
120 North 200 West
Salt Lake City, UT 84145-7107
(801) 538-4100
Fax: (801) 539-3993

State Adoption Exchange/State Photolisting Service

Department of Human Services
Division of Child and Family
Services
P.O. Box 45500
Salt Lake City, UT 84145-0500
(801) 538-4100

Northwest Adoption Exchange
600 Stewart Street, Suite 1313
Seattle, WA 98101
(206) 441-6822
Fax: (206) 441-7281
Toll Free: (800) 927-9411
www.nwae.org
nwae@nwresource.org

The Adoption Exchange
610 East South Temple, Suite 40
Salt Lake City, UT 84102
(801) 412-0200
Fax: (801) 412-0202

State Reunion Registry

Utah Department of Health -
Vital Statistics
288 North 1460 West
Salt Lake City, UT 84145-0500
(801) 538-6105

Licensed Private Adoption Agencies

An Act of Love
8300 South 700 East, Suite 201
Sandy, UT 84070
(801) 568-1771
Fax: (801) 568-1991

A Cherished Child Adoption
Agency
2120 Willow Park Lane
Sandy, UT 84093
(801) 947-5900

A TLC Adoption
191 West, 400 North
Spanish Fork, UT 84660
(801) 798-9363
Fax: (801) 798-9355
tlcadoptparry@aol.com

A.A.C. Adoption and Family
Network
8833 South 5170 West
West Jordan, UT 84088
(801) 282-3198
aacadopt@frii.com

Adopt an Angel
254 West 400 South, Suite 320
Salt Lake City, UT 84101
(801) 537-1622
Fax: (801) 359-6873

Adoption Center of Choice, Inc.
241 West, 520 North
Orem, UT 84057
(801) 224-2440
Fax: (801) 224-1899

Catholic Community Services
2570 West 1700 South
Salt Lake City, UT 84104
(801) 977-9119
Fax: (801) 977-8227

Children of Peace
715 East, 3900 South, Suite 203
Salt Lake City, UT 84107-2182
(801) 263-2111
Fax: (801) 262-2259

Children's Aid Society of Utah
652 26th Street
Ogden, UT 84401
(801) 393-8671

Children's House International
1236 North 150 West
American Fork, UT 84003
(801) 756-0587
Fax: (801) 763-8384
www.adopting.org/chi
chi4@aol.com

Children's Service Society
124 South, 400 East, Suite 400
Salt Lake City, UT 84111
(801) 355-7444
Toll Free: (800) 839-7444

Families for Children
P.O. Box 521192
Salt Lake City, UT 84152-1192
(801) 467-3413

Heart to Heart Adoptions, Inc.
P.O. Box 57573
Murray, UT 84157
(801) 270-8017

LDS Family Services
1466 N. Highway 89, Suite 220
Farmington, UT 84025-2738
(801) 451-0475

LDS Family Services
55 West, 100 North
Richfield, UT 84701
(435) 896-6446

LDS Family Services
625 East, 8400 South
Sandy, UT 84700
(801) 566-2556

LDS Family Services
1400 West State Street
Pleasant Grove, UT 84062
(801) 796-9509
Fax: (801) 796-9528

LDS Family Services
95 West, 100 South, Suite 340
Logan, UT 84321
(435) 752-5302

LDS Family Services
1525 Lincoln Avenue
Ogden, UT 84404
(801) 621-6510

LDS Family Services
294 East, 100 South
Price, UT 84501
(435) 637-2991

LDS Family Services
10 E. South Temple, Suite 1200
Salt Lake City, UT 84111
(801) 240-6500
Fax: (801) 240-5508

LDS Family Services
4250 West 5415 South
Kearns, UT 84118
(801) 969-4181

LDS Family Services
2480 East Redcliff Drive
St. George, UT 84790
(435) 673-6446

LDS Family Services
1190 North, 900 East
Provo, UT 84604
(801) 378-7620

LDS Social Services
2202 North Main Street,
Suite 301
Cedar City, UT 84720-9790
(435) 586-4479

Legacy International
Adoptions, LLC
3198 Hampton Court
Salt Lake City, UT 84124
(801) 278-3066

Premier Adoption Agency
952 South Freedom Boulevard
#26
Provo, UT 84601
(801) 808-9738

Wasatch International Adoptions
2580 Jefferson Avenue
Ogden, UT 84401
(801) 334-8683
Fax: (801) 479-1301
www.wiaa.org/
info@wiaa.org

West Sands Adoption and
Counseling
461 East 2780 North
Provo, UT 84604
(801) 377-4379

**Adoptive Parent Support
Groups**

Adoption Connection of Utah
Salt Lake County Complex, 21st
South State Street
Salt Lake City, UT 84470
(801) 278-4858

Adoptive Parent Support Group
of Utah
645 East, 4500 South
Salt Lake City, UT 84165
(801) 264-7500

Adoptive Parent Support Group
of Utah
950 East 25th Street
Odgen, UT 84401-2626
(801) 629-5800

Adoptive Parent Support Group
of Utah
150 East Center Street, #5100
Provo, UT 84606-3157
(801) 371-1028

Catholic Community Services
Parent Support Group-Waiting
Families
2570 West, 1700 South
Salt Lake City, UT 84104
(801) 977-9119

Children's Service Society
124 South, 400 East, Suite 400
Salt Lake City, UT 84111
(801) 355-7444

Families for African-American
Awareness
11039 South Longdale
Sandy, UT 84092
(801) 455-5000

Families for Children and North
American Council on
Adoptable Children State
Representative
P.O. Box 521192
Salt Lake City, UT 84152-1192
(801) 467-3413
members.aol.com/nacac

Families Involved in Adoption
170 St. Moritz Strasse
Park City, UT 84060
(801) 647-0961

Friend to Friend
50 South, 300 East
Pleasant Grove, UT 84062
(801) 785-1480

Hand in Hand
3516 West, 12600 South
Riverton, UT 84065
(801) 254-8773

HOPE of Utah
945 South, 200 West, #20
Provo, UT 84601
(801) 373-0777

LDS Social Services
13897 South, 1835 West
Bluffdale, UT 84065
(801) 254-0188

Parents for Attachment (PFA)
603 West 3750 North
Pleasant View, UT 84414
(801) 782-2727

Search Support Groups

Adoption Connection of Utah
7th South, 2nd East, Job Service
Building
Salt Lake City, UT 84770
(801) 278-4858

Adoption Forum
3177 Cherokee Lane
Provo, UT 84604
(801) 371-1028

American Adoption Congress
State Representative
672 E. 2025 South
Bountiful, UT 84010
(801) 298-8520

Beyond Adoption
c/o Weber County Library
2464 Jefferson, Conference Room
Ogden, UT 84403
(801) 627-6193

LAMB
c/o St. Paul's Church
300 South, 900 East
Salt Lake City, UT 84101
(801) 298-8520

UTAH LAWS RELATED TO ADOPTION: QUESTIONS AND ANSWERS

Can an attorney serve as an intermediary?
Yes.

Is advertising permitted?
Yes.

Who must consent to the adoption?
1. The birth mother
2. The birth father, if he is married to the birth mother, or if he has demonstrated a significant commitment to the child
3. The child placement agency, if involved

When can consent be taken from birth mother (father), and how long after the consent is signed can it be revoked?
Consent cannot be taken until at least twenty-four hours after birth. The consent is irrevocable once signed.

What are the birth father's rights?
Although 1995 legislation reduced birth fathers' rights, their rights must still be terminated by court. No consent is needed if the birth father has not established paternity by filing an action in court, provided support for the birth mother during her pregnancy or for the child after delivery, or made an effort to maintain a parental relationship with the child.

What fees can adoptive parents pay?
Attorneys or other intermediaries cannot charge for locating a birth mother. A statement of all fees for legal and medical and living expenses paid must be filed with the court before the final adoption.

Where does the adoption hearing take place?
The hearing may take place in the court of the county where the adoptive parents live.

How are familial and stepparent adoptions different from nonbiological adoptions?
Generally, no home study is required in stepparent and familial adoptions. In a stepparent adoption, the child must reside with the petitioning parent for more than twelve months, instead of the six months required in other adoptions.

Can a nonresident finalize an adoption in this state?
No. However, residency can be established.

UTAH CODE ANNOTATED SECTION 78-30-1 TO 78-30-9 AND 78-3016,3 (1997)

VERMONT

State Adoption Specialist

Department of Social and
  Rehabilitation Services
Diane Dexter
103 S. Main Street
Waterbury, VT 05671
(802) 241-2142
Fax: (802) 241-2407
www.state.vt.us/srs/adopt/
  adopt.htm
ddexter@srs.state.vt.us

State ICPC Administrator

Vermont Department of Social &
  Rehabilitation Services
Social Services Division
103 South Main Street
Waterbury, VT 05676
(802) 241-2131

**State Adoption Exchange/State
  Photolisting Service**

Northern New England Adoption
  Exchange
Department of Human Services
221 State Street, State House
Augusta, ME 04333
(207) 287-5060

State Reunion Registry

Vermont Adoption Registry
103 South Main Street
Waterbury, VT 05671
(802) 241-2122
www.state.vt.us/srs/adopt/roots.htm

**Regional/District Public
  Agencies**

Vermont Department of Social
  and Rehabilitation Services,
  Barre
255 N. Main Street, Fourth Floor
Barre, VT 05641-4160
(802) 479-4260

Vermont Department of Social
and Rehabilitation Services,
Burlington
1193 North Avenue
Burlington, VT 05401-2776
(802) 863-7370

Vermont Department of Social
and Rehabilitation Services,
Newport
100 Main Street, Suite 230
Newport, VT 05855-1293
(802) 334-6723

Vermont Department of Social
and Rehabilitation Services,
St. Albans
20 Houghton Street, Room 211
St. Albans, VT 05478-2216
(802) 527-7741

Vermont Division of Social
Services, Bennington
1 Veterans Memorial Drive
Bennington, VT 05201-1999
(802) 442-8138

Vermont Division of Social
Services, Brattleboro
232 Main Street
Brattleboro, VT 05301-2879
(802) 257-2888

Vermont Division of Social
Services, Hartford
Gilman Office Center #3
White River Junction, VT 05001-
2090
(802) 295-8840

Vermont Division of Social
Services, Middlebury
84 Exchange Street
Middlebury, VT 05753-1105
(802) 388-4660

Vermont Division of Social
Services, Morrisville
Route 1, Box 929
Morrisville, VT 05661-9724
(802) 888-4576

Vermont Division of Social
Services, Rutland
20 Asa Bloomer Building, 88
Merchant's Row
Rutland, VT 05701-9409
(802) 786-5817

Vermont Division of Social
Services, Springfield
1 Hospital Court
Bellows Falls, VT 05101
(802) 463-3450

Vermont Division of Social
Services, St. Johnsbury
42 Eastern Avenue
St. Johnsbury, VT 05819-2688
(802) 748-8374

**Licensed Private Adoption
Agencies**

Acorn Adoption Inc.
278 Pearl Street
Burlington, VT 05401-8558
(802) 865-3898

Adoption Advocates
521 Webster Rd.
Shelburne, VT 05482-6513
(802) 985-8289

Adoption Resource
Services, Inc.
1904 North Avenue
Burlington, VT 05401-1315
(802) 863-5368

Adoptive Families for Children
26 Fairview Street
Keene, NH 03431
(603) 357-4456
Fax: (603) 352-8543

Angels' Haven Outreach
P.O. Box 53
Monkton, VT 05469
(802) 453-5450

Bethany Christian Services
Box 331
Jericho, VT 05465
(802) 899-2486
www.bethany.org
info@bethany.org

Child and Family Services of New
Hampshire
99 Hanover Street
Manchester, NH 03105-0448
(603) 668-1920
Fax: (603) 668-6260
Toll Free: (800) 640-6486

Friends in Adoption
44 South Street, P.O. Box 1228
Middletown Springs, VT 05757-
1228
(802) 235-2373

www.capital.net/com/fia
fia@vermontel.com

Friends in Adoption
The Maltex Building, 431 Pine
Street, #7
Burlington, VT 05401-4726
(802) 865-9886
www.capitol.net/com/fia
fia@vermontel.com

LDS Social Services
547 Amherst Street, Suite 404
Nashua, NH 03063-4000
(603) 889-0148
Fax: (603) 889-4358
Toll Free: (800) 735-0419

Lund Family Center
76 Glen Road, P.O. Box 4009
Burlington, VT 05406-4009
(802) 864-7467
Fax: (802) 546-6216
Toll Free: (800) 639-1741
www.lundfamilycenter.org

Lutheran Social Services of New
England
261 Sheep Davis Road, Suite A-1
Concord, NH 03301
(603) 224-8111
Fax: (603) 224-5473
www.adoptlss.org/
Intladopt@aol.com

MAPS International
400 Commonwealth Avenue
Boston, MA 02115
(617) 267-2222
Fax: (617) 267-3331
www.mapsadopt.org/

Vermont Catholic Charities
24 1/2 Center Street
Rutland, VT 05701
(802) 773-3379

Vermont Catholic Charities
351 North Avenue
Burlington, VT 05401-2921
(802) 658-6110, Ext: 312
Fax: (802) 860-0451

Vermont Children's Aid Society
32 Pleasant Street
Woodstock, VT 05091
(802) 457-3084
www.vermontchildrensaid.org/
children/adoption.htm

*Vermont Children's Aid Society
79 Weaver Street, P.O. Box 127
Winooski, VT 05404-0127
(802) 655-0006
Fax: (802) 655-0073
*www.vermontchildrensaid.org/
   children/adoption.htm*

Vermont Children's Aid Society
128 Merchants Row, Room 501
Rutland, VT 05701
(802) 773-8555
*www.vermontchildrensaid.org/
   children/adoption.htm*

Wide Horizons For Children
Main Office
38 Edge Hill Road
Waltham, MA 02451
(781) 894-5330
Fax: (781) 899-2769
*www.whfc.org/
info@whfc.org*

Wide Horizons For Children
P.O. Box 53
Monkton, VT 05469
(802) 658-2070
*www.whfc.org/
info@whfc.org*

**Adoptive Parent Support
Groups**

Casey Family Services
7 Palmer Court
White River Junction, VT 05001-
3323
(802) 649-1400

Casey Family Services
60 South Main Street
Waterbury, VT 05676
(802) 244-1408
Toll Free: (800) 607-1400

Department of Mental Health
   Children's Services for
   Respite Care
103 South Main Street
Waterbury, VT 05671
(802) 241-2214

Family Life Services
72 Main Street
Vergennes, VT 05491
(802) 877-3166

Friends in Adoption
Buxton Avenue, Box 7270
Middletown Springs, VT 05757

Future in Vermont
1904 North Avenue
Burlington, VT 05401
(802) 863-5368

North American Council on
   Adoptable Children
   Representative
28 Webster Road
Shelburne, VT 05482
(802) 985-3972

Vermont Children's Aid Society
   Lifetime Adoption Project
P.O. Box 127
Winooski, VT 05404-0127
(802) 655-0006
Toll Free: (800) 479-0015

Search Support Groups

Adoptee Liberty Movement
   Association (ALMA)
P.O. Box 257
Milton, VT 05468

Adoptee Liberty Movement
   Association (ALMA)
RD 2, Box 2997
Vergennes, VT 05491

Adoption Alliance of Vermont
17 Hopkins Street
Rutland, VT 05701
(802) 773-7078

Adoption Alliance of Vermont
91 Court Street
Middlebury, VT 05753
(802) 388-7569

Adoption Alliance of Vermont
107 Twin Oaks
South Burlington, VT 05403
(802) 863-1727

Adoption Alliance of Vermont
104 Falls Road
Shelburne, VT 05482-0641
(802) 985-2462

Adoption Resource Service, Inc.
1904 North Avenue
Burlington, VT 05401
(802) 863-5368

Adoption Search/Support
   Network
RR 1, Box 83
East Calais, VT 05650
(802) 456-8850

American Adoption Congress
   State Representative
RR 1, Box 83
E. Calais, VT 05650
(802) 456-8850
Beleaf4U@aol.com

B & C Search Assistance
   of Vermont
P.O. Box 1451
St. Albans, VT 05478
(802) 524-9825

Beacon of Vermont
5 Calo Court
St. Albans, VT 05478
(802) 527-7507

Beacon of Vermont
Box 152
Bakersfield, VT 05441-0152
(802) 758-2369

VERMONT LAWS RELATED TO ADOPTION: QUESTIONS AND ANSWERS

Can an attorney serve as an intermediary?
Yes.

Is advertising permitted?
Yes.

Who must consent to the adoption?
1. The birth parents, if married to each other, or
2. The birth mother, if the child is born out of wedlock or if the husband is not the child's biological father
3. The child placement agency, if involved

When can consent be taken from birth mother (father), and how long after the consent is signed can it be revoked?
Consent cannot be taken until seventy-two hours after birth. If it is taken in court and if stated on the consent, it is irrevocable. If irrevocability is not stated, the birth parents have fifteen days to revoke their consent. According to a staff person at the Interstate Compact office, the birth parents can go to court for termination of their rights within days after the child's birth. The court prefers the birth father to be present; however, this is often not possible, or he may refuse.

What are the birth father's rights?
A birth father has full paternal rights. His rights cannot be terminated unless he provides a consent or it can be shown that he has abandoned his rights to the child to be adopted. Vermont law also states that a birth father's rights can be waived if he does not acknowledge paternity at the time of the adoption hearing, or if he has executed a notarized statement denying paternity or disclaiming any interest in the child to be adopted with an acknowledgment that his statment is irrevocable when signed.

What fees can adoptive parents pay?
Payment of medical, legal, and some living expenses are permitted. The Department of Social and Rehabilitation Services may charge a fee of up to $535 for conducting a home study.

Where does the adoption hearing take place?
The adoption hearing takes place in the court of the county where the adoptive parents live. If they do not live in the state, the hearing takes place where the child placement agency is located.

How are familial and stepparent adoptions different from nonbiological adoptions?
In a stepparent adoption, the process is simple and an out-of-court consent is permitted. In a relative adoption, no home study is required under the present law.

Can a nonresident finalize an adoption in this state?
Yes, but only an agency adoption.

VIRGINIA

State Adoption Specialist

Virginia Department of Social
  Services
Brenda Kerr
730 E. Broad Street
Richmond, VA 21219-1849
(804) 692-1290
Fax: (804) 692-1284
www.dss.state.va.us/famserv.html
bjk@dss.state.va.us

State ICPC Administrator

Virginia Department of Social
  Services
730 East Broad Street
Richmond, VA 23219-1849
(804) 692-1270
Fax: (804) 786-0455

**State Adoption Exchange/State
  Photolisting Service**

Adoption Resource Exchange of
  Virginia (AREVA)
Virginia Department of Social
  Services
730 E. Broad Street
Richmond, VA 23219-1849
(804) 692-1280
Toll Free: (800) 362-3678
www.adopt.org/va/browse.htm
lxl2@dss.state.va.us

**Regional/District Public
  Agencies**

Alexandria Department of Social
  Services
2525 Mt. Vernon Avenue
Alexandria, VA 22301
(703) 838-0700
Fax: (703) 836-2355
suzanne.chis@ci.alexandria.va.us

Bristol Department of Social
  Services
621 Washington Street
Bristol, VA 24201-4644
(540) 645-7450
Fax: (540) 645-7475
*local520@localagency.dss.state.
  va.us*

Charlottesville Department of
  Social Services
P.O. Box 911
Charlottesville, VA 22902-0911
(804) 970-3400
Fax: (804) 970-3555
lawsonb@ci.charlottesville.va.us

Chesapeake Bureau of Social
  Services
P.O. Box 15098
Chesapeake, VA 23328-5098
(804) 382-2000
Fax: (804) 543-1644
jrb550@localagency.dss.state.va.us

Clifton Forge Department of
  Social Services
P.O. Box 58
Clifton Forge, VA 24422
(540) 863-2525
Fax: (540) 863-2532
smh560@localagency.dss.state.va.us

Danville Department of Social
  Services
P.O. Box 3300
Danville, VA 24543
(804) 799-6543
Fax: (804) 797-8818
mwf590@localagency.dss.state.va.us

Franklin City
Department of Social Services
City Hall Annex, 207 W. Second
  Avenue
Franklin, VA 23851-1713
(757) 562-8520, Ext: 250
Fax: (757) 562-8515
lao620@localagency.dss.state.va.us

Fredericksburg Department of
  Welfare and Social Services
P.O. Box 510
Fredericksburg, VA 22404-0510
(540) 372-1032
Fax: (540) 372-1157
jfp630@localagency.dss.state.va.us

Galax Department of Social
  Services
P.O. Box 166
Galax, VA 24333-0166
(540) 236-8111
Fax: (540) 236-9313
slc640@localagency.dss.state.va.us

Hampton Department of
  Social Services
1320 LaSalle Avenue
Hampton, VA 23669
(804) 727-1821
Fax: (804) 727-1835
wcredle@city.hampton.va.us

Harrisonburg-Rockingham
  Department of Social Services
P.O. Box 809
Harrisonburg, VA 22801-0809
(540) 574-5100
Fax: (540) 574-5127
ddd165@localagency.dss.state.va.us

Hopewell Department of Social
  Services
256 E. Cawson Street
Hopewell, VA 23860-2804
(804) 541-2330
Fax: (804) 541-2317
net670@localagency.dss.state.va.us

Lynchburg Division of Social
  Services
P.O. Box 2497
Lynchburg, VA 24501
(804) 847-1551
Fax: (804) 847-1785
mcj680@localagency.dss.state.va.us

Manassas Department of Social
  Services
8955 Center Street
Manassas, VA 20110-5403
(703) 361-8277
Fax: (703) 361-6933
jeo683@localagency.dss.state.va.us

Manassas Park Department of
  Social Services
1 Park Center Court, City Hall
Manassas Park, VA 20111
(703) 335-8880
Fax: (703) 335-8899
vck685@localagency.dss.state.va.us

Newport News Division of Social
  Services
6060 Jefferson Avenue
Newport News, VA 23605
(804) 926-6422
Fax: (804) 926-6118
sec700@localagency.dss.state.va.us

Norfolk Division of Social
Services
220 W. Brambleton Avenue
Norfolk, VA 23510-1506
(804) 664-6000
Fax: (804) 664-3275
svp@localagency.dss.state.va.us

Norton Department of Social
Services
P.O. Box 378
Norton, VA 24273-0378
(540) 679-4393
Fax: (540) 679-0607
wls720@localagency.dss.state.va.us

Petersburg Department of Social
Services
P.O. Box 2127
Petersburg, VA 23804
(804) 861-4720
Fax: (804) 861-0137
dpd730@localagency.dss.state.va.us

Portsmouth Division of Social
Services
1701 High Street
Portsmouth, VA 23704-2417
(804) 398-3600, Ext: 7100
Fax: (804) 393-5058
bjw740@localagency.dss.state.va.us

Radford Department of Public
Welfare
208 Third Avenue
Radford, VA 24141-4706
(540) 731-3663
Fax: (540) 731-5000
lab750@localagency.dss.state.va.us

Richmond City
Department of Social Services
900 E. Marshall Street
Richmond, VA 23219-2383
(804) 780-7430
Fax: (804) 780-7441
mevans@ci.richmond.va.us

Roanoke City
Department of Social Services
215 W. Church Avenue, Room
307
Roanoke, VA 24011
(540) 853-2591
Fax: (540) 853-2027
cqg770@localagency.dss.state.va.us

Suffolk Department of Social
Services
P.O. Box 1818
Suffolk, VA 23439-1818
(757) 539-0216
Fax: (757) 925-6354
lrh800@localagency.dss.state.va.us

Virginia Beach Department of
Social Services
3432 Virginia Beach Boulevard
Virginia Beach, VA 23452-4420
(804) 437-3201
Fax: (804) 437-3300
dms810@localagency.dss.state.va.us

Waynesboro Department of
Social Services
P.O. Box 1028
Waynesboro, VA 22980-1028
(540) 942-6646
Fax: (540) 942-6658
rjy@820@localagency.dss.state.va.us

Williamsburg Bureau of Social
Services
401 Lafayette Street
Williamsburg, VA 23185
(757) 220-6161
Fax: (757) 220-6109
pwallenti@ci.williamsburg.va.us

Winchester Department of Social
Services
33 E. Boscawen Street
Winchester, VA 22601-0762
(540) 662-3807
Fax: (540) 662-3279
kam840@localagency.dss.state.va.us

**Licensed Private Adoption
Agencies**

ABC Adoption Services, Inc.
4725 Garst Mill Road
Roanoke, VA 24018
(540) 989-2845

Adoption Center of Washington
Suite 101, 100 Daingerfield Road
Alexandria, VA 22314
(703) 549-7774
Fax: (703) 549-7778
Toll Free: (800) 452-3878
www.adoptioncenter.com
info@adoptioncenter.com

Adoption Center of Washington
Suite 1101, 1726 M Street, N.W.
Washington, DC 20036
(202) 452-8278
Fax: (202) 452-8280
Toll Free: (800) 452-3878
www.adoptioncenter.com
info@adoptioncenter.com

Adoption Home Studies and
Placement Services Inc.
TIA Adoption Connections
207 Park Avenue, Suite B-4
Falls Church, VA 22046
(703) 536-8523

Adoption Service Information
Agency, Inc. (ASIA)
7659 Leesburg Pike
Falls Church, VA 22043
(202) 726-7193

Barker Foundation
327 West 21st Street
Norfolk, VA 23517
(757) 626-1841

Barker Foundation
1495 Chain Bridge Road,
Suite 201
McLean, VA 22101
(703) 536-1827
Fax: (301) 229-0074
Toll Free: (800) 673-8489
www.barkerfoundation.org
bfinfo@atlantech.net

Bethany Christian Services
1924 Arlington Blvd., Suite 102
Charlottesville, VA 22903-1533
(804) 979-9631
www.bethany.org
info@bethany.org

Bethany Christian Services, Inc.
1406 Princess Anne Street
Fredericksburg, VA 22401-3639
(540) 373-5165
Fax: (540) 373-6463
www.bethany.org
info@bethany.org

Bethany Christian Services, Inc.
287 Independence Boulevard,
Suite 241
Virginia Beach, VA 23462-2956
(757) 499-9367
Fax: (757) 518-8356
www.bethany.org
info@bethany.org

Bethany Christian Services, Inc.
10378-B Democracy Lane
Fairfax, VA 22030-2522
(703) 385-5440
Fax: (703) 385-5443
www.bethany.org
info@bethany.org

Catholic Charities of Hampton
Roads, Inc.
4855 Princess Anne Road
Virginia Beach, VA 23462
(757) 467-7707

Catholic Charities of Hampton
Roads, Inc.
1315 Jamestown Road, Suite 202
Williamsburg, VA 23185
(757) 253-2847

Catholic Charities of Hampton
Roads, Inc.
Windsor West Prof. Ctr., 12829-
A Jefferson Avenue, Ste. 101
Newport News, VA 23602
(757) 875-0060

Catholic Charities of Hampton
Roads, Inc.
1301 Colonial Avenue
Norfolk, VA 23517
(757) 625-2568

Catholic Charities of Hampton
Roads, Inc.
Churchland Medical &
Professional Center, 3804
Poplar Hill Road, Suite A
Chesapeake, VA 23321
(757) 484-0703

Catholic Charities of S.W.
Virginia, Inc.
830 Campbell Avenue, S.W.
Roanoke, VA 24016
(540) 342-0411

Catholic Charities of the Diocese
of Arlington, Inc.
5294 Lyngate Court
Burke, VA 22015
(703) 425-0100

Catholic Charities of the Diocese
of Arlington, Inc.
612 Lafayette Boulevard, Suite 50
Fredericksburg, VA 22401
(540) 371-1124

Catholic Charities of the Diocese
of Arlington, Inc.
3838 N. Cathedral Lane
Arlington, VA 22203
(703) 841-2531

Catholic Charities of the Diocese
of Arlington, Inc.
1011 Berryville Avenue, Suite 1
Winchester, VA 22601
(540) 667-7940

Catholic Charities, Arlington
Diocese
131 South West Street
Alexandria, VA 22314
(703) 549-8644

Children's Home Society of
Virginia, Inc.
1620 Fifth Street, S.W.
Roanoke, VA 24016
(540) 344-9281
www.chsva.org/

Children's Home Society of
Virginia, Inc.
4200 Fitzhugh Avenue
Richmond, VA 23230
(804) 353-0191
www.chsva.org/

Commonwealth Catholic
Charities
New River Valley Office -
Carilion St. Albans Center
Attn: The Family Place,
P.O. Box 3068
Radford, VA 24143

Commonwealth Catholic
Charities
3321 South Crater Road, Suite C
Petersburg, VA 23805
(804) 778-4820

Commonwealth Catholic
Charities
3901 Melvern Place
Alexandria, VA 22312
(703) 256-4530

Commonwealth Catholic
Charities
1024 Park Avenue, N.W.,
P.O. Box 826
Norton, VA 24273
(540) 679-1195

Commonwealth Catholic
Charities
1512 Willow Lawn Drive
Richmond, VA 23230
(804) 285-5900
Fax: (804) 285-9130

Commonwealth Catholic
Charities
302 McClanahan Street, S.W.
Roanoke, VA 24014
(540) 344-5107

Coordinators/2, Inc.
Suite B, 5204 Patterson Avenue
Richmond, VA 23226-1507
(804) 288-7595
Fax: (804) 288-7599
Toll Free: (800) 690-4206
members.aol.com/C2ADOPT
C2ADOPT@aol.com

Datz Foundation
311 Maple Avenue West, Suite E
Vienna, VA 22180
(703) 242-8800
Fax: (703) 242-8804
www.datzfound.com
datz@patriot.net

Families United Through
Adoption
102 Lide Place
Charlottesville, VA 22902
(804) 923-8253

Family and Child Services of
Washington, D.C., Inc.
5249 Duke Street, #308
Alexandria, VA 22304
(703) 370-3223

Family Life Services
1971 University Blvd.,
Building 61-B
Lynchburg, VA 24502
(804) 582-2969

Frost International Adoptions
Suite 205, 5205 Leesburg Pike
Falls Church, VA 22041
(703) 671-3711
Fax: (703) 671-0355
Toll Free: (888) 823-2090
www.frostadopt.org
Thogan@Frostadopt.org

Holston United Methodist Home
for Children
18146 Lee Highway
Abingdon, VA 24210
(540) 628-1023

Holy Cross Child Placement
Agency Inc.
6723 Whittier Avenue, Suite 406
McLean, VA 22102
(703) 356-8824

Jewish Family Service of
Tidewater, Inc.
United Jewish Community Center
of the Virginia Peninsula
2700 Spring Road
Newport News, VA 23606
(757) 489-3111

Jewish Family Service of
Tidewater, Inc.
5520 Greenwich Road, Suite 202
Virginia Beach, VA 23462
(757) 473-2695

Jewish Family Service of
Tidewater, Inc.
7300 Newport Avenue
Norfolk, VA 23505
(757) 489-3111

Jewish Family Services, Inc.
6718 Patterson Avenue
Richmond, VA 23226
(804) 282-5644

Jewish Social Service Agency,
Inc./Adoption Options
7345 McWhorter Place, Suite 100
Annandale, VA 22003
(703) 916-0186

Loving Families, Inc.
101 S. Whiting Street,
Suite 302A
Alexandria, VA 22304
(703) 370-7140
Fax: (540) 341-0923
www.alovingfamily.org
LovingFam@aol.com

Lutheran Family Services, Inc.
2609 McVitty Road, S.W.,
P.O. Box 21609
Roanoke, VA 24018-0574
(540) 774-7100

Lutheran Social Services of the
National Captial Area Inc.
9506-A Lee Highway
Fairfax, VA 22031
(703) 273-0303

New Family Foundation
11350 Random Hills Road,
Suite 600
Fairfax, VA 22030
(703) 273-5960

Pearl S. Buck Foundation Inc.
T/A Welcome House
9412 Michelle Place
Richmond, VA 23229
(804) 740-7311

Rainbow Christian Services
6004 Artemus Road
Gainesville, VA 22065
(703) 754-8516

Russian Immigration
Services Inc.
2715 Grove Avenue
Richmond, VA 23220
(804) 353-3293

Shore Adoption Services, Inc.
113 Holly Crescent, Suite 102
Virginia Beach, VA 23451
(757) 422-6361

United Family Service of Virginia
205 South Main Street
Harrisonburg, VA 22801
(540) 564-0046

United Methodist Family Services
of Virginia Inc.
4621 Carr Drive
Fredericksburg, VA 22408
(540) 898-1773

United Methodist Family Services
of Virginia, Inc.
715 Baker Road, Suite 201
Virginia Beach, VA 23462
(757) 490-9791

United Methodist Family Services
of Virginia, Inc.
3900 W. Broad Street
Richmond, VA 23230
(804) 353-4461
Fax: (804) 355-2334
www.northva@umfs.org/
info@umfs.org

United Methodist Family Services
of Virginia, Inc.
6335 Little River Turnpike
Alexandria, VA 22312
(703) 941-9008
Fax: (703) 750-0621
www.northva@umfs.org/
info@umfs.org

Virginia Baptist Children's Home
and Family Services
700 E. Belt Boulevard
Richmond, VA 23224
(804) 231-4466

Virginia Baptist Children's Home
and Family Services
7100 Columbia Pike
Annandale, VA 22003
(703) 750-3660

Virginia Baptist Children's Home
and Family Services
8309 Orcutt Avenue
Newport News, VA 23605
(757) 826-3477

Virginia Baptist Children's Home
and Family Services Mount
Vernon Avenue
P.O. Box 849
Salem, VA 24153
(540) 389-5468

Adoptive Parent Support Groups

Adoption Resource Exchange for
Single Parents (ARESP)
8605 Cameron Street #220
Silver Spring, MD 20910

(301) 585-5836
Fax: (301) 585-4864
www.aresp.org
arespinc@aol.com

Adoptive Families of Central
Virginia
111 Cavalier Drive
Charlottesville, VA 22901
(804) 978-2835

Adoptive Families of Northern
Virginia
Merrifield, VA 22116-3408

Adoptive Families of Northern
Virginia
6315 Gromley Place
Springfield, VA 22207
(703) 242-1125

Adoptive Family Group of Central
Virginia
6404 Westchester Circle
Richmond, VA 23225
(804) 775-4348

Adoptive Parent Resource
Network of Virginia
10261 Queensgate Road
Midlothian, VA 23113
Toll Free: (800) 772-3253

Annandale Adoption and
Attachment Partners
4300 Evergreen Lane, Suite 300
Annandale, VA 22003
(703) 658-7103

Association for Single Adoptive
Parents
P.O. Box 3618
Merrifield, VA 22116-9998
(703) 521-0632

Association of Single Adoptive
Parents
408 Henry Clay Road
Ashland, VA 23005
(804) 798-2673

Barker Foundation Parents of
Adopted Adolescents Group
7945 MacArthur Boulevard, Suite
206
Cabin John, MD 20818
(301) 229-8300

Blue Ridge Adoption Group
7887 Hollins Court Drive
Roanoke, VA 24019
(540) 890-5813

Celebrate Adoptions, Inc.
P.O. Box 11604
Burke, VA 22009

Center for Adoption Support and
 Education, Inc. (C.A.S.E.)
500 W. Annandale Road
Falls Church, VA 22046
(703) 533-7950
www.adoptionsupport.org
caseadopt@erols.com

Fairfax Adoption Support Team
 (F.A.S.T.)
12011 Government Center
 Parkway
Fairfax, VA 22035
(703) 324-7639

Families for Private Adoption
P. O. Box 6375
Washington, DC 20015-0375
(202) 722-0338
www.ffpa.org

Families for Russian and
 Ukrainian Adoptions
Central Virginia
P.O. Box 1591
Mechanicsville, VA 23116
(804) 730-4276
centralvirginia@frua.org

Families for Russian and
 Ukrainian Adoptions
P.O. Box 2944
Merrifield, VA 22116
(703) 560-6184
www.frua.org

Families Like Ours
Washington, DC
(202) 488-3967

Families of the China Moon
1907 Boardman Lane
Richmond, VA 23233
CaryCH@aol.com

Families Through Adoption
1420 Cobble Scott Way
Chesapeake, VA 23322
(757) 482-8330

Families with Children from China
9803 Clyde Court
Vienna, VA 22181
(703) 281-9188
www.catalog.com/fwcfc

Friends of Children Services
2312 N. Wakefield Street
Arlington, VA 22207
(703) 528-6159

Korean Focus for Adoptive
 Families
1906 Sword Lane
Alexandria, VA 22308
(703) 799-4945
www.helping.com/family/pa/kfaf.htm
koreanfocus@hotmail.com

Latin America Parents
 Association of the National
 Capital Region
P.O. Box 4403
Silver Spring, MD 20904-4403
(301) 431-3407
www.lapa.com
joet@highcaliber.com

North American Council on
 Adoptable Children
 Representative
Route 1, Box 417
McGaheysville, VA 22840
(540) 289-9535
members.aol.com/nacac

North American Council on
 Adoptable Children State
 Representative
400 Farmer Street
Petersburg, VA 23804
(757) 861-4720
members.aol.com/nacac

Open Adoption Discussion Group
22310 Old Hundred Road
Barnesville, MD 20838
(301) 972-8579
msaasta@hotmail.com

People for the Adoption of
 Children
7908 Chowning Circle
Richmond, VA 23294
(804) 747-6633

People Places
1215 N. Augusta Street
Staunton, VA 24401
(540) 885-8841

Romanian Children's Connection
1206 Hillside Terrace
Alexandria, VA 22302
(703) 548-9352

Stars of David International Inc.
Metro DC Chapter
c/o The Datz Foundation, 311
 Maple Avenue West
Vienna, VA 22180
(703) 242-8800
Fax: (703) 242-8804
Toll Free: (800) 829-5683
www.starsofdavid.org
datz@patriot.net

United Methodist Family Services
 Adoptive Parent Support
 Group
6335 Little River Turnpike
Alexandria, VA 22312
(703) 941-9008

Virginia One Church, One Child
1214 W. Graham Road, Suite 2
Richmond, VA 23220
(804) 329-3420
Fax: (804) 329-3906

Virginia Peninsula Adoptive
 Parents Group
17385 Warwick Boulevard
Lee Hall, VA 23603
(804) 599-8962

Search Support Groups

Adoptee Liberty Movement
 Association (ALMA)
P.O. Box 4328
Glen Allen, VA 23058
(804) 750-2335

Adoptee Liberty Movement
 Association (ALMA)
Greater Richmond Chapter
10321 Capilano Place
Richmond, VA 23233
(804) 750-2335

Adoptee-Birthparent Support
 Network (ABSN)
P.O. Box 8273
McLean, VA 22106-8273
(202) 628-4111
www.geocities.com/Heartland/
 Flats/3666/ABSN.html
absnmail@aol.com

Adoptees and Natural Parents
949 Lacon Drive
Newport News, VA 23602
(757) 874-9091

Adoptees in Search
P.O. Box 41016
Bethesda, MD 20014
(301) 656-8555
Fax: (301) 652-2106
AIS20824@aol.com

Adoptees/Birthparents
Self-Help Group
603 14th Street
Virginia Beach, VA 23451

Adoption Resource Group
8094 Rolling Road, Suite 125
Springfield, VA 22153
(703) 440-5771

Adult Adoptees in Search
P.O. Box 203
Ferrum, VA 24088-0203
(540) 365-0712

Barker Foundation Adult
Adoptee Support Group
7945 MacArthur Boulevard,
Suite 206
Cabin John, MD 20818
(301) 229-8300

Barker Foundation Birthparent
Support Group
7945 MacArthur Boulevard, Suite
206
Cabin John, MD 20818
(301) 229-8300

Catholic Charities of the Diocese
of Arlington Birthparent
Support Group
5294 Lyngate Court
Burke, VA 22015
(703) 425-0100

Concerned United Birthparents
(CUB)
DC Metro Branch
P.O. Box 15258
Chevy Chase, MD 20815
(202) 966-1640
www.webnations.com/cub
LEC9@aol.com

Parents and Adoptees In Search
2500 Lauderdale Drive
Richmond, VA 23233
(804) 744-2244

VIRGINIA LAWS RELATED TO ADOPTION: QUESTIONS AND ANSWERS

In Virginia in a private placement adoption, the birth family and the adoptive family must exchange identifying information.

Can an attorney serve as an intermediary?
Yes.

Is advertising permitted?
Yes.

Who must consent to the adoption?
1. Both birth parents
2. The child placement agency, if involved

When can consent be taken from birth mother (father), and how long after the consent is signed can it be revoked?
In an agency adoption, consent can be taken ten days after the child's birth and can be revoked fifteen days after signed or twenty-five days after birth, or until adoptive placement, whichever is later.

In an independent adoption, a consent hearing takes place within ten days of filing the petition, or as soon as is practical. The hearing can take place in the county where the adoptive parents live, where the birth mother lives, or where the child was born. If the birth parents live outside of Virginia, the consent hearing may take place in the birth parents' state of residence, as long as the proceedings are first instituted in a Virginia court so that the Virginia court has jurisdiction over them.

Parental consent is revocable before the final adoption if it was given under fraud or duress, or if both the adoptive parents and birth parents agree to revoke it.

A birth father who is not married to the birth mother at the time of the child's conception or birth does not need to give a consent in court. He must be provided notice of the adoption proceedings, or he can sign a consent that waives further notice of adoption proceedings.

If the birth parents place a child and both birth mother and father do not show up in court (without good cause and after being given notice), the court may grant the adoption petition without their consent if the court finds it is in the child's best interests to do so. (Virtually all birth mothers do go to court, however.)

What are the birth father's rights?
When a birth father's consent is required and he has not consented, he must be given notice of the termination hearing and/or the adoption hearing. The hearing may be held after the birth mother's hearing. If the birth father does not respond within twenty-one days after personal notice of the hearing or ten days after an Order of Publication (notice of the adoption proceedings placed in the legal notices section of the newspaper), then the hearing can be held and his rights can be terminated.

If the birth father's consent is required but the court can also determine that the consent is withheld contrary to the child's best interests or cannot be obtained, the court will approve of the adoption as long as notice was provided to the birth father. Many judges will not permit a birth mother to refuse to name the birth father except in extreme situations such as rape.

What fees can adoptive parents pay?
Medical, legal, and transportation costs are permitted. Reasonable living expenses, including maternity clothes, can be paid if the birth mother's physician states that she cannot work. All fees must be disclosed to the court.
Where does the adoption hearing take place?
The adoption hearing takes place in the court of the county where the adoptive parents live or where the child placement agency is located.

How are familial and stepparent adoptions different from nonbiological adoptions?
Generally, in a stepparent adoption, a hearing may not be required and is up to the court's discretion. In consensual stepparent adoptions, home studies are not necessarily required. In addition, relatives up to the fourth degree are now given special relative adoption status. These include the child's great aunt and uncle. In general, in a familial adoption no postplacement supervision is required. Also, no hearing is required before the court for qualified relative adoptions.

Can a nonresident finalize an adoption in this state?
Yes, but only in an agency or agency-identified adoption.

Source: Code of Virginia Annotated Sections 63.1-220 to 63.1-238.5 (1997)

WASHINGTON

State Adoption Specialist

Washington Department of Social
and Health Services
Division of Children and Family
Services
Lois Chowen
P.O. Box 45713
Olympia, WA 98504
(360) 902-7919
Fax: (360) 902-7903
www.wa.gov/dshs/ca/ca3ov.html
chlo300@dshs.wa.gov

Washington Department of
Social and Health Services
Division of Children and
Family Services
Pam Caird
P.O. Box 45713
Olympia, WA 98504
(360) 902-7919
Fax: (360) 902-7903
www.wa.gov/dshs/ca/ca3ov.html
caip300@dshs.wa.gov

State ICPC Administrator

Washington Department of Social
& Health Services
14th & Jefferson, P.O. Box 45711
Olympia, WA 98504-5710
(360) 902-7984
Fax: (360) 902-7903

State Adoption Exchange/State Photolisting Service

Northwest Adoption Exchange
600 Stewart Street, Suite 1313
Seattle, WA 98101
(206) 441-6822
Fax: (206) 441-7281
Toll Free: (800) 927-9411
www.nwae.org
nwae@nwresource.org

Washington Adoption Resource
Exchange
600 Stewart Street, Suite 1313
Seattle, WA 98101
(206) 441-6822
Fax: (206) 441-7281
www.nwae/org
nwae@nwresource.org

Regional/District Public Agencies

Washington Department of Social
and Health Services
Community Service Office,
Wenatchee
P.O. Box 3088-B4-1
Wenatchee, WA 98801
(509) 662-0577

Washington Department of Social
and Health Services
Spokane DCFS
1313 N. Atlantic, Suite 2000
Spokane, WA 99201-2746
(509) 363-4601

Washington Department of Social
and Health Services
Community Service Office,
Spokane East
P.O. Box TAF C-40-B32-1
Spokane, WA 99220
(509) 536-1283

Washington Department of Social
and Health Services
Community Service Office,
Spokane Central
1427 W. Gardner Avenue
Spokane, WA 99201-9979
(509) 458-4404

Washington Department of Social
and Health Services
Community Service Office,
Everett
840 N. Broadway, N31-1
Everett, WA 98201
(425) 339-4817

Washington Department of Social
and Health Services
Community Service Office, Pasco
P.O. Box 931-B11-1
Pasco, WA 99301
(509) 545-2411

Washington Department of Social
and Health Services
Community Service Office,
Colville
Tri-County Community Services,
Route 3-B33-1
Colville, WA 99114
(509) 684-5261

Washington Department of Social
and Health Services
Community Service Office,
Olympia
P.O. Box 45715
Olympia, WA 98504
(360) 753-1029

Washington Department of Social
and Health Services
Community Service Office,
Vancouver
P.O. Box 751-S6-1
Vancouver, WA 98666
(360) 696-6111

Washington Department of Social
and Health Services
Community Service Office, Post
Angeles
1020 East Front Street, P.O. Box
2259
Port Angeles, WA 98362-0292
(360) 417-1474
Fax: (360) 417-1461

Washington Department of Social
and Health Services
Community Service Office,
Moses Lake
1620 Pioneer Way, P.O. Box 1399
Moses Lake, WA 98837
(509) 766-2200
Fax: (509) 766-2338

Washington Department of Social
and Health Services
Community Service Office,
White Salmon
P.O. Box 129-B20-1
White Salmon, WA 98672
(509) 773-6583

Washington Department of Social
and Health Services
Community Service Office,
Alderwood
19000 33rd Avenue, West
Lynnwood, WA 98036-4705
(425) 672-1269

Washington Department of Social
and Health Services
Community Service Office, Omak
South 130 Main
Omak, WA 98841
(509) 422-0082

Washington Department of Social
and Health Services
Community Service Office, Kelso
P.O. Box 330-S8-1
Kelso, WA 98626
(360) 577-2169

Washington Department of Social
and Health Services
Community Service Office, King
South
P.O. Box 848-N43-1
Kent, WA 98032
(425) 872-2686

Washington Department of Social
and Health Services
Community Service Office,
Bremerton
3423 6th Street, Suite 217
Bremerton, WA 98312
(360) 478-4690

Washington Department of Social
and Health Services
Community Service Office,
Centralia
2428 Reynolds Road
Centralia, WA 98531
(360) 748-2263

Washington Department of Social
and Health Services
Community Service Office,
Seattle Central
2809 26th Avenue, South, N56-1
Seattle, WA 98144
(206) 721-4892

Washington Department of Social
and Health Services
Community Service Office,
Aberdeen
P.O. Box 189-B14-1
Aberdeen, WA 98520
(360) 533-9293

Washington Department of Social
and Health Services
Community Service Office,
Puyallup Valley
1004 E. Main Street, N51-1
Puyallup, WA 98371
(253) 593-8600

Washington Department of Social
and Health Services
Community Service Office,
Tacoma DCFS Center
1949 S. State Street
Tacoma, WA 98405
(253) 593-2600

Washington Department of Social
and Health Services
Community Service Office,
Sunnyside
P.O. Box 818-B54-1
Sunnyside, WA 98944
(509) 839-2752

Washington Department of Social
and Health Services
Community Service Office, King
Eastside
14360 S.E. Eastgate Way, Suite
40-1
Bellevue, WA 98007-6462
(425) 455-7148

Washington Department of Social
and Health Services
Community Service Office,
Burien
15811 Ambaum Boulevard, S.W.,
N44-1
Seattle, WA 98166
(206) 433-1336

Washington Department of Social
and Health Services
Community Service Office,
Yakima
P.O. Box M2500-B39-1
Yakima, WA 98909
(509) 579-2269

Washington Department of Social
and Health Services
Community Service Office,
Toppenish
P.O. Box 470-B50-1
Toppenish, WA 98948
(509) 865-2805

Washington Department of Social
and Health Services
Community Service Office, Walla
Walla
P.O. Box 517-B36-1
Walla Walla, WA 99362
(509) 527-4370

Washington Department of Social
and Health Services
Community Service Office,
Smokey Point
P.O. Box 3099-B65-1
Arlington, WA 98223
(360) 653-0500

Washington Department of Social
and Health Services
Community Service Office,
Shelton
P.O. Box 1127-B23-1
Shelton, WA 98584
(360) 427-0136

Washington Department of Social
and Health Services
Community Service Office,
Bellingham
1720 Ellis Street
Bellingham, WA 98225
(425) 647-6100

Washington Department of Social
and Health Services
Community Service Office,
South Bend
P.O. Box 87-B25-1
South Bend, WA 98586
(360) 875-1236

Washington Department of Social
and Health Services
Community Service Office,
Yakima/Kittitas
P.O. Box M2500-B69-1
Yakima, WA 98909
(509) 454-4282

**Licensed Private Adoption
Agencies**

Adoption Advocates
International
401 E. Front Street
Port Angeles, WA 98362
(360) 452-4777
Fax: (360) 452-1107
aai.lbee.com
aai@olympus.net

Adoption Facilitators, Inc.
8624 N.E. Juanita Drive
Kirkland, WA 98034
(425) 823-3060

Adventist Adoption and
Family Services
1207 E. Reserve Street
Vancouver, WA 98661
(360) 693-2110

Americans Adopting Orphans
Suite 2001, 12345 Lake City Way
Seattle, WA 98125
(206) 524-5437
Fax: (206) 527-2001
www.orphans.com/
aao@orphans.com

Americans for International Aid
and Adoption (AIAA)
P.O. Box 6051
Spokane, WA 99207
(509) 489-2015
www.rainbowkids.com/aiaa.html
aiaateri@aol.com

*Bethany Christian Services
902 N. State Street, Suite 102
Bellingham, WA 98225-5010
(360) 733-6042
Fax: (360) 733-6216
www.bethany.org
info@bethany.org

Bethany Christian Services
10510 Bridgeport Way, S.W.,
Suite 2
Lakewood, WA 98499-4830
(253) 983-9250
Fax: (253) 983-9212
www.bethany.org
info@bethany.org

Bethany Christian Services
19936 Ballinger Way, N.E., Suite D
Seattle, WA 98155-1223
(206) 367-4604
Fax: (206) 367-1860
www.bethany.org
judith@bethany.org

Catholic Children and Family
Services of Walla Walla
Drumheller Building, Suite 418
Walla Walla, WA 99362
(509) 525-0572

Catholic Children's Services of
Northwest Washington
1133 Railroad Ave, Suite 100
Bellingham, WA 98226
(360) 733-5800

Catholic Community Services
100 23rd Avenue South
Seattle, WA 98144
(206) 323-1950

Catholic Community Services
1918 Everett Ave
Everett, WA 98201
(425) 257-9188

Catholic Community Services
Southwest Yakima
1323 S. Yakima Ave
Tacoma, WA 98405
(253) 383-3697

Catholic Family and Child Service
1023 Riverside Ave
Spokane, WA 99201
(509) 358-4260

Catholic Family and Child Service
of Wenatchee
23 S. Wenatchee, #209
Wenatchee, WA 98801
(509) 663-3182

*Catholic Family and Child
Service of Yakima
5301-C Tieton Drive
Yakima, WA 98908
(509) 965-7108

Catholic Family and Child
Services
2139 Van Giesen
Richland, WA 99352
(509) 946-4645

Catholic Family Services
P.O. Box 672
Moses Lake, WA 98837
(509) 765-1875

Children's Home Society of
Washington, Northeast Area
4315 Scott Street
Spokane, WA 99203
(509) 747-4174
www.chs-wa.org/
chswa@chs-wa.org

Children's Home Society of
Washington, Northwest Area
3300 N.E. 65th Street, Box 15190
Seattle, WA 98115-0190
(206) 524-6020
www.chs-wa.org/
chswa@chs-wa.org

Children's Home Society of
Washington, Southeast Area
1014 Walla Walla Avenue
Wenatchee, WA 98801
(509) 663-0034
www.chs-wa.org/
chswa@chs-wa.org

Children's Home Society of
Washington, Southwest Area
P.O. Box 605
Vancouver, WA 98666
(360) 695-1325
www.chs-wa.org/
chswa@chs-wa.org

Children's Home Society of
Washington, West Central
Area
201 S. 34th
Tacoma, WA 98408
(253) 472-3355
www.chs-wa.org/
chswa@chs-wa.org

Church of Christ Homes for
Children
30012 S. Military Road
Federal Way, WA 98003
(253) 839-2755

*Faith International Adoptions
535 E. Dock Street, Suite 208
Tacoma, WA 98402
(253) 383-1928
Fax: (253) 572-6662

International Children's Care
2711 N.E. 134th Way
Vancouver, WA 98686
(360) 573-0429

LDS Social Services of WA
200 North Mullan Road
Spokane, WA 99206
(509) 926-6581

Lutheran Social Services
6920 220th Street, S.W.
.Mountlake Terrace, WA 98043
(425) 672-6009

Lutheran Social Services of
Washington and Idaho
433 Minor Avenue, N.
Seattle, WA 98109
(425) 672-6009

Lutheran Social Services of
Washington and Idaho
Symons Building, Suite 200
Spokane, WA 99204
(509) 747-8224

Lutheran Social Services of
Washington, Southeast Area
3321 Kennewick Ave
Kennewick, WA 99336
(509) 735-6446

Medina Children's Services, Black
Child Adoption Program
123 16th Avenue
Seattle, WA 98122-0638
(206) 461-4520
Fax: (204) 461-8372
www.medinachild.org/
medina@medinachild.org

New Hope Child and Family
Agency
2611 N.E. 125th St.
Seattle, WA 98125
(206) 363-1800
Fax: (206) 363-0318
www.newhopekids.org
info@newhopekids.org

World Association for Children
and Parents (WACAP)
P.O. Box 88948
Seattle, WA 98138
(206) 575-4550
Fax: (206) 575-4148
www.wacap.org
wacap@accessone.com

Adoptive Parent Support Groups

Adoption Resource Center of
Children's Home Society
4315 Scott Street
Spokane, WA 99203
(509) 747-4174

Adoption Resource Center of
Children's Home Society of
Washington
3300 N.E. 65th Street
Seattle, WA 98133
(206) 524-6020

Adoption Support Group of
Kitsap County
11869 Olympic Terrace Avenue,
N.E.
Bainbridge Island, WA 98110
(206) 842-7122

Adoptive Parents of Walla Walla
103 E. Main Street
Walla Walla, WA 99362
(509) 529-8557

Advocates for Single Adoptive
Parents
11634 S.E. 49th Street
Bellevue, WA 98006
(425) 644-4761

Advocates for Single Adoptive
Parents - N.W.
5706 N.E. 204th Street
Seattle, WA 98155
(435) 485-6770

Circle of Love
East 2423 Fifth Avenue
Spokane, WA 99202
(509) 534-2000

Families for Russian and
Ukrainian Adoptions
4917 Northwest Esther Street
Vancouver, WA 98663
(360) 750-1852
cavies@worldaccessnet.com

Families for Russian and
Ukrainian Adoptions
WA
(206) 322-6135
rsolomon@iqc.apc.org

Families Through Adoption of
Washington
25310 217th Place, S.E.
Maple Valley, WA 98038
(425) 432-4543

Families with Children
from China
12224 210 Place, S.E.
Issaquah, WA 98027
(253) 271-9932
www.catalog.com/fwcfc

Goldendale Adoptive
Parent Group
Box 404
Goldendale, WA 98620

KIN
14803 Ash Way
Lynnwood, WA 98037
(425) 743-3049

Mt. Vernon Friends of WACAP
1598 McLean Road
Mt. Vernon, WA 98273

North American Council on
Adoptable Children
1229 Cornwall Avenue, #206
Bellingham, WA 98225
(425) 676-5437
members.aol.com/nacac

Okanogan Valley Adoptive
Parents
P.O. Box 3002
Omak, WA 98841
(509) 826-2820

One Church, One Child and
North American Council on
Adoptable Children
Representative
451 S.W. 10th Street, Suite 120
Renton, WA 98055-2981
(425) 235-4472
Fax: (425) 235-4863
Toll Free: (800) 882-4453

Spokane Consultants in
Family Living
South 1220 Division
Spokane, WA 99202
(509) 328-6274

SSAFE
3325 Agate Height Road
Bellingham, WA 98226
(360) 671-6516

WACAP Parent Group
South 509 Union Road
Spokane, WA 99206
(509) 924-0624

Search Support Groups

Adoptee Liberty Movement
Association (ALMA)
5208 Hyada Blvd., N.E.
Tacoma, WA 98422
(253) 927-1856

Adoptee Support Circle/Assoc. of
Confidential Intermediaries
3107 Maple
Port Angeles, WA 98362
(360) 452-2212

Adoption Resource Center of
Children's Home Society of
Washington
3300 N.E. 65th Street
Seattle, WA 98133
(206) 524-6020

Adoption Resource Center of
Children's Home Society of
Washington
4315 Scott Street
Spokane, WA 99203
(509) 747-4174

Adoption Search and Counseling
Consultants
6201 15th Avenue, N.W., #P210
Seattle, WA 98107
(206) 782-4491
www.reunionagency.org

B.I.R.T.H.
3018 28th Avenue, S.E.
Olympia, WA 98501
(360) 754-6249

Lost and Found
3232 Laurel Drive
Everett, WA 98201
(425) 339-1194

Open Arms
6816-135 Court N.E.
Redmond, WA 98052

Touched by Adoption
1105 Colonial Drive
College Place, WA 99324
(509) 529-1245

Tri-Cities Adoption Search
2130 Hoxie Avenue
Richmond, WA 99352
(509) 546-0363

Washington Adoptees Rights
Movement (WARM)
20 Hall Avenue
Yakima, WA 98902

Washington Adoptees Rights
Movement (WARM)
9901 S.E. Shoreland Drive
Bellevue, WA 98004

Washington Adoptees Rights
Movement (WARM)
P.O. Box 2667
Olympia, WA 98507

Washington Adoptees Rights
Movement (WARM)
5950 Sixth Avenue, South, Suite
107
Seattle, WA 98108-2317
(206) 767-9510

Washington Adoptees Rights
Movement (WARM)
408 S.W. 175th Place
Seattle, WA 98166-3758

Washington Adoptees Rights
Movement (WARM)
E. 303 Paradise Road
Spangler, WA 99031

Washington Adoptees Rights
Movement (WARM)
1119 Peacock Lane
Burlington, WA 98233

WASHINGTON LAWS RELATED TO ADOPTION: QUESTIONS AND ANSWERS

Can an attorney serve as an intermediary?
Yes.

Is advertising permitted?
Yes, but only through a Washington licensed agency and with verification of a completed home study in compliance with Washington law. Those outside of Washington cannot advertise in Washington newspapers.

Who must consent to the adoption?
1. Both birth parents
2. The child placement agency, if involved

When can consent be taken from birth mother (father), and how long after the consent is signed can it be revoked?
In general, consents can be taken before birth, but the order terminating rights cannot be entered with the court until forty-eight hours after birth or signing, whichever is later. The birth mother must appear in court to testify as to her consent. The birth father does not have to appear, but his consent can be brought before the court. Once entered into the court, the birth mother's and the birth father's consents are irrevocable.

What are the birth father's rights?
The birth father must consent or be given notice by serving him with summons or notice personally, or by publishing a notice of the adoption proceedings in the legal notices of a newspaper if his whereabouts are unknown. He does have an opportunity to object and have a hearing on his parenting abilities to show the court that it would be in the child's best interests to be parented by him. His rights can be terminated if it can be shown that he failed to perform his parental obligations, showing a substantial lack of regard for them

What fees can adoptive parents pay?
The legal and agency fees must be reasonable and should be based on time spent in conducting preadoption home studies and preparing the report. Living expenses must be approved by the court. At the adoptive parent's request, this fee can be reviewed.

Where does the hearing take place?
The hearing takes place in the court of the county where the adoptive parents live or the child lives.

How are familial and stepparent adoptions different from nonbiological adoptions?
They are essentially the same, except that the home study may be streamlined or waived.

Can a nonresident finalize an adoption in this state?
Yes.

SOURCE: REVISED CODE OF WASHINGTON. SECTIONS 26.33.020 TO 26.33.410 (1997)

WEST VIRGINIA

State Adoption Specialist

West Virginia Department of
  Health and Human Resources
Laura Harbert
350 Capitol Street, Room 691
Charleston, WV 25301-3704
(304) 558-7980
Fax: (304) 558-4563
www.wvdhhr.org/pages/
  bcf/cf-social.htm
lharbert@wvdhhr.org

West Virginia Department of
  Health and Human Resources
Carolyn Phillips
350 Capitol Street, Room 691
Charleston, WV 25301
(304) 558-7980
Fax: (304) 558-8800
www.wvdhhr.org
carolynphillips@wvdhhr.org

State ICPC Administrator

West Virginia Department of
  Health & Human Resources
350 Capitol Street, Room 691
Charleston, WV 25301-3704
(304) 558-1260
Fax: (304) 558-4563

**State Adoption Exchange/State
  Photolisting Service**

West Virginia Department of
  Health and Human Resources
West Virginia's Adoption
  Resource Network
350 Capitol Street, Room 691
Charleston, WV 25301
(304) 558-2891
Fax: (304) 558-8800
www.adopt.org
lgoodman@wvdhhr.org

State Reunion Registry

West Virginia Mutual Consent
  Voluntary Adoption Registry
West Virginia Department of
  Health and Human Resources
Office of Social Services, 350
  Capitol Street, Room 691
Charleston, WV 25301
(304) 558-2891
Fax: (304) 558-8800
lgoodman@wvdhhr.org

**Regional/District Public
  Agencies**

West Virgina DHHR - Region II-
  Putnam District
P.O. Box 660
Teays, WV 25569
(304) 757-7843

West Virgina DHHR - Region IV-
  Raleigh District
407 Neville Street
Beckley, WV 25801
(304) 256-6930

West Virgina DHHR- Region III-
  Hardy District
112 Beans Lane
Moorefield, WV 26836
(304) 538-2391

West Virgina DHHR- Region I-
  Ohio District
407 Main Street
Wheeling, WV 26003
(304) 232-4411

**Licensed Private Adoption
  Agencies**

Adoption Services, Inc.
28 Central Boulevard
Camp Hill, PA 17011
(717) 737-3960
Fax: (717) 731-0517
www.adoptionservices.org/
mail@adoptionservices.org

*Adoptions From The Heart
7014 Grand Central Station
Morgantown, WV 26505
(304) 291-5211
www.adoptionsfromtheheart.org
adoption
  @adoptionsfromtheheart.org

Burlington United Methodist
  Family Services
P.O. Box 370
Scott Depot, WV 25560-0370
(304) 757-9127
Fax: (304) 757-9136
Toll Free: (800) 296-6144
adoption@zoomnet.net

Burlington United Methodist
  Family Services
Route 3, Box 346A
Grafton, WV 26354
(304) 265-1338
Fax: (304) 757-9136
bumfs@westvirginia.net

Burlington United Methodist
  Family Services
Route 4, Box 240B
Keyser, WV 26726-9413
(304) 788-2342
Fax: (304) 788-2409
bumfscbf@access.mountain.net

Childplace, Inc.
2420 Highway 62
Jeffersonville, IN 47130
(812) 282-8248
Fax: (812) 282-3291
Toll Free: (800) 787-9084
www.adoption.com/childplace/
childplac@aol.com

CHILDPLACE, Inc.
5101 Chesterfield Avenue, S.E.
Charleston, WV 25304
(304) 344-0319
www.adoption.com/childplace/
cplace@iglou.com

*Children's Home Society of
   West Virginia
165 Scott Avenue, Suite 106
Morgantown, WV 26505
(304) 599-6505

Children's Home Society of West
   Virginia
P.O. Box 5533, 316 Oakvale Road
Princeton, WV 24740
(304) 425-8428
Fax: (304) 425-8438

Children's Home Society of West
   Virginia
1145 Greenbriar Street
Charleston, WV 25311
(304) 345-3894
Fax: (304) 345-3899
members.aol.com/nacac
www.arcchs@americaonline.com

Commonwealth Catholic
   Charities
302 McClanahan Street, S.W.
Roanoke, VA 24014
(540) 344-5107

Family Service Association
P.O. Box 1027 Steubenville, OH
   43952
(740) 283-4763
Fax: (740) 283-2929

LDS Social Services
4431 Marketing Place,
   P.O. Box 367
Groveport, OH 43125
(614) 836-2466
Fax: (614) 836-1865

Voice for International
   Development and Adoption
   (VIDA)
354 Allen Street
Hudson, NY 12534
(518) 828-4527
Fax: (518) 828-0688
*members.aol.com/vidaadopt/
   vida.html*
vidaadopt@aol.com

**Adoptive Parent Support
   Groups**

Adoptive Parent Support Group
1465 Dogwood
Morgantown, WV 26505
(304) 599-0598

Appalachian Families for
   Adoption
P.O. Box 2775
Charleston, WV 25330-2775
(304) 744-4067

Latin America Parents
   Association of the National
   Capital Region
P.O. Box 4403
Silver Spring, MD 20904-4403
(301) 431-3407
www.lapa.com
joet@highcaliber.com

North American Council on
   Adoptable Children
1511 Byng Drive
South Charleston, WV 25303
(304) 744-9602
members.aol.com/nacac

Parents Adopting and Learning to
   Support
301 High Street
Belington, WV 26250
(304) 823-3015

Search Support Groups

ALARM Network
37 21st Street
McMechen, WV 26040
(304) 232-0747

Reunite
P.O. Box 694
Reynoldsburg, OH 43068
(614) 861-2584

WEST VIRGINIA LAWS RELATED TO ADOPTION: QUESTIONS AND ANSWERS

Can an attorney serve as an intermediary?
Yes, as long as fees are related to services rendered.

Is advertising permitted?
Yes.

Who must consent to the adoption?
1. Both birth parents.
2. If a birth parent is under eighteen, the court must approve the consent and appoint a
   guardian.

When can consent be taken from birth mother (father), and how long after the consent is signed can it be revoked?
Consent cannot be given until seventy-two hours after the child's birth and may be
revoked within ten days if the adoptive parents are in-state residents or up to twenty days
if they are from out of state, unless the term "irrevocable" is written onto the consent.

The consent shall be before a county clerk and two witnesses. If the birth parent is a
minor the consent shall be executed before a judge.

It is generally recommended that an out-of-state couple adopting a child born in West Virginia provide documentation, such as consents, that complies with both West Virginia law and the state laws of the adoptive parents.

What are the birth father's rights?
Notice of the adoption proceedings is given to any birth father who has exercised parental duties, unless the child is more than six months old and the birth father has not asserted his parental rights.

What fees can adoptive parents pay?
Payment of legal, medical, and adoption agency fees or fees to other persons is limited to cover fees-for-services only. All fees must be approved by the court.

Where does the adoption hearing take place?
The adoption hearing takes place in the court of the county where the adoptive parents live.

How are familial and stepparent adoptions different from nonbiological adoptions?
The preadoption home study is not required in a relative adoption. Closeness in age cannot be the sole factor in denying an adoption in stepparent adoptions.

In some stepparent adoptions, some grandparent visitations may be granted.

Can a nonresident finalize an adoption in this state?
No.

WISCONSIN

State Adoption Specialist

Wisconsin Department of Health
   and Family Services
Christopher Marceil
P.O. Box 8916
Madison, WI 53708-8916
(608) 266-3595
Fax: (608) 264-6750
www.dhfs.state.wi.us/children/
   adoption/index.html
marceil@dhfs.state.wi.us

State ICPC Administrator

Wisconsin Division of Children &
   Family Services
ICPC Unit
P.O. Box 8916
Madison, WI 53708
(608) 267-2079
Fax: (608) 264-6750

State Adoption Exchange/State Photolisting Service

Wisconsin Adoption Information
   Exchange
1126 S. 70th Street, Suite N509A
Milwaukee, WI 53214-3151
(414) 475-1246
Fax: (414) 475-7007
Toll Free: (800) 762-8063
www.wiadopt.com
wiadopt@execpc.com

State Reunion Registry

Division of Children & Family
   Services
Special Services Section
P.O. Box 8916
Madison, WI 53708-8916
(608) 266-7163
www.dhfs.state.wi.us/children/

Regional/District Public Agencies

Wisconsin Division of Children
   and Family Services, Milwaukee
235 W. Galena Ave.
Milwaukee, WI 53212
(414) 374-4663
Fax: (414) 289-8561

Wisconsin Division of Children
   and Family Services,
   Northeastern Region
200 N. Jefferson, Suite 411
Green Bay, WI 54301
(414) 448-5312

Wisconsin Division of Children
   and Family Services,
   Northeastern Region
485 S. Military Road
Fond du Lac, WI 54935
(920) 929-2985

Wisconsin Division of Children
and Family Services,
Northern Region
2811 Eighth Street, South,
Suite 70
Wisconsin Rapids, WI 54495
(715) 422-5080

Wisconsin Division of Children
and Family Services,
Northern Region
1853A N. Stevens, P.O. Box 697
Rhinelander, WI 54501
(715) 365-2500

Wisconsin Division of Children
and Family Services,
Southeastern Region
141 N.W. Barstow Street,
Room 209
Waukesha, WI 53188
(262) 521-5100

Wisconsin Division of Children
and Family Services,
Southern Region
3601 Memorial Drive
Madison, WI 53704-1105
(608) 243-2400

Wisconsin Division of Children
and Family Services,
Western Region
610 Gibson Street, Suite 2
Eau Claire, WI 54701
(715) 836-3399

Wisconsin Division of Children
and Family Services,
Western Region
4003 Kinney Coulee Road, N.,
Suite 1
La Crosse, WI 54601
(608) 785-9453

**Licensed Private Adoption
Agencies**

Adoption Advocates, Inc.
2601 Crossroads Drive, Suite 173
Madison, WI 53704
(608) 246-2844
Fax: (608) 246-2875

Adoption Choice
924 E. Juneau Avenue, #813
Milwaukee, WI 53202-2748
(414) 276-3262

Adoption Option
1804 Chapman Drive
Waukesha, WI 53186
(262) 544-4278

*Adoption Services of Green Bay
& The Fox Valley
911 N. Lynndale Drive, Suite 2-C
Appleton, WI 54914
(920) 735-6750

Bethany Christian Services
2312 North Grandview
Boulevard, Suite 210
Waukesha, WI 53188-1600
(262) 547-6557
Fax: (262) 547-3644
Toll Free: (800) 238-4269
www.bethany.org
info@bethany.org

Catholic Charities,
Diocese of Madison
3311 Prairie Avenue
Beloit, WI 53511
(608) 365-3665

Catholic Charities/ Diocese of
Milwaukee
2021 N. 60th Street
Milwaukee, WI 53208
(414) 771-2881
Fax: (414) 771-1674

Center for Child & Family
Services, Inc.
4222 W. Capitol, Suite 104
Milwaukee, WI 53216
(414) 442-4702

Children's Home Society of
Minnesota
2230 Como Avenue
St. Paul, MN 55108
(651) 646-6393
Fax: (651) 646-0436
Toll Free: (800) 952-9302
www.chsm.com
info@chsm.com

Children's Service Society of
Wisconsin
201 Ceape Avenue
Oshkosh, WI 54901
(920) 235-1002

Children's Service Society of
Wisconsin
1212 S. 70th Street
Milwaukee, WI 53214
(414) 453-1400

Community Adoption Center
3701 Kadow Street
Manitowoc, WI 54220
(920) 682-9211
Fax: (920) 682-8611

Evangelical Child and Family
Agency, District Office
1617 S. 124th Street
New Berlin, WI 53151
(262) 789-1881
Fax: (262) 789-1887
Toll Free: (800) 686-3232

Hope International Adoption and
Family Services, Inc.
421 S. Main Street
Stillwater, MN 55082
(651) 439-2446
Fax: (651) 439-2071

LDS Social Services
1711 University Avenue
Madison, WI 53705
(608) 238-5377

Lutheran Counseling and
Family Services
3800 N. Mayfair Road
Wauwatosa, WI 53222-2200
(414) 536-8333

Lutheran Social Services
1101 W. Clairmont Avenue,
Suite 2H
Eau Claire, WI 54737
(715) 833-9466

Lutheran Social Services of
Wisconsin and Upper Michigan
647 W. Virginia Street, Suite 300
Milwaukee, WI 53204
(414) 325-3222

Pauquette Children's Services, Inc.
315 W. Conant Street
Portage, WI 53901-0162
(608) 742-8004
Fax: (608) 742-7937

Special Beginnings
237 South Street, #101
Waukesha, WI 53186
(262) 896-3600

Special Children, Inc.
910 North Elm Grove Road, #2
Elm Grove, WI 53122
(262) 821-2125
Fax: (262) 821-2157

Van Dyke, Inc.
1224 Weeden Creek Road
Sheboygan, WI 53081-7850
(920) 452-5358
Fax: (920) 452-5515
*www.execpc.com/romanian_
adoption_assistance/*
raa@execpc.com

Adoptive Parent Support Groups

Adoption Adventure
920 12th Avenue West
Ashland, WI 54806
(715) 682-9070
kswanson@ncis.net

Adoption is Forever
3305 W. Justin Street
Appleton, WI 54914
(920) 734-1153
JM11654@aol.com

Adoption Odessey
1416 Cumming Avenue
Superior, WI 54880
(715) 394-6617

Adoption Resource Network
P.O. Box 174
Coon Valley, WI 54623
(608) 452-3146

Adoptive and Foster Families
  Support Group
N. 348 Hwy 89
Columbus, WI 53925
(920) 623-3551

Adoptive Families of Greater
  Milwaukee
15385 West Glenora Court
New Berlin, WI 53151
(262) 860-0940
shale@execpc.com

Adoptive Families of Wisconsin
N. 12652 Hwy M
Galesville, WI 54630
(608) 582-4254

Adoptive Moms
  Discussion Group
Jewish Community Center, 6255
  N. Santa Monica Boulevard
Whitefish Bay, WI 53217
(414) 964-4444

Adoptive Parent Group of
  Southern Wisconsin
1408 Vilas Avenue
Madison, WI 53711
(608) 251-0736
Fax: (608) 251-6856
Mauri@IOL.com

Camp Bo Bae - Korean Culture
  Camp
Korean American Children's
  Culture Circle
W. 339 S. 5348 Prairie View Drive
Eagle, WI 53119
(262) 392-9857

Catholic Charities - Diocese of La
  Crosse
128 South Sixth Street
La Crosse, WI 54601-0266
(608) 782-0710
Toll Free: (800) 227-3002
www.catholiccharitieslax.org
info@catholiccharitieslax.org

Catholic Charities - Diocese of
  Madison
3577 High Point Drive, Box
  46550
Madison, WI 53744-6550
(608) 365-3665
Fax: (608) 365-1279
Toll Free: (888) 485-7385
cathchar@execpc.com

Central Wisconsin Support Group
P.O. Box 451
Colby, WI 54421
(715) 223-4581
magnus@pcpros.net

Club Peru
5476 North 37th Street
Milwaukee, WI 53209
(414) 466-1108

Families from Columbia
718 Marcks Lane
Luxemburg, WI 54217
(920) 845-2075
gary_bloch@msn.com

Families of Russian and Ukranian
  Adoptions (FRUA)
Wisconsin Chapter
7257 Countryside Drive
Franklin, WI 53132-8760
(414) 297-9000
Fax: (414) 423-1481
www.frua.org
FRUASA@aol.com

Families Through Adoption
616 Zimbal Avenue
Sheboygan, WI 53083
(920) 457-3473

Families United Through
  Adoption (FUTA)
297 Saint Augustine Road
Colgate, WI 53017
(414) 628-4559

Families with Children from
  China
850 North 119th Street
Wauwatosa, WI 53226
(414) 453-4480

Families with Children from
  China
21150 Stratford Court
Brookfield, WI 53045
(414) 784-4404
Holly.Winters@midata.com

Family Services of Northeast
  Wisconsin, Inc.
300 Crooks Street
Green Bay, WI 54301
(920) 436-4360, Ext: 1345
Fax: (920) 432-5966
Toll Free: (800) 998-9609
www.familyservicesnew.org
fsinfo@familyservicesnew.org

Fox Valley Friends in Adoption
N. 1611 Prairie View Drive
Greenville, WI 54942
(920) 757-6149

Heart Holders
2637 Pennwall Circle
Fitchburg, WI 53711
(608) 274-7967

HOPE
2218 Inverness Drive
Waukesha, WI 53186
(414) 548-3574
Fax: (262) 548-3589
freddy@pitnet.net

Interracial Families
  Network/Family Enhancement
2120 Fordem Avenue
Madison, WI 53704
(608) 231-1490

Just for Dads
KAY Foundation
P.O. Box 46160
Madison, WI 53744
(608) 273-2888
Fax: (608) 273-2876
www.kayfoundation.org
kainz@chorw.net

Just in Time for Kids
KAY Foundation
P.O. Box 46160
Madison, WI 53744
(608) 273-2888
Fax: (608) 273-2876
www.kayfoundation.org
kainz@chorw.net

Lakeshore Adoptive Families
1460 Iris Drive
Manitowoc, WI 54220
(920) 682-1647

NAMASTE
Wales, WI 53813
(414) 968-5464

NICA Parent Group
2809 North 56th Street
Milwaukee, WI 53210
(414) 445-5088

Ours Through Adoption of
  Northeast Wisconsin
150 Falcon Hill Court
Green Bay, WI 54302
(920) 435-2626

Ours Through Adoption of
  Southeast Wisconsin
8601 S. Glen Forest Court
Oak Creek, WI 53154
(414) 764-8764
mramich@earthlink.net

Paraguayan Adoptive Parents
7474 Oak Hill Court
Verona, WI 53593-9726
(608) 845-8823

Parents Through Korean
  Adoption
516 Harvest Lane
Verona, WI 53593
(608) 845-3518
Shariandjohn@aol.com

Reactive Attachment Disorder
  (RAD)
1919 N. 52nd Street
Milwaukee, WI 53208
(414) 476-4140

RESOLVE of S.E. Wisconsin
P.O. Box 13842
Wauwatosa, WI 53213-0842
(414) 521-4590
wiresolve@rocketmail.com

SideKicks
11672 Mascot Avenue
Cashton, WI 54619
(608) 654-7607
Fax: (608) 269-1850
tabby37@elroynet.com

Special Needs Adoption Network
1126 South 70th Street,
  Suite N509A
Milwaukee, WI 53214
(414) 475-1246
Fax: (414) 475-7007
Toll Free: (800) 762-8063
www.wiadopt.org
wiadopt@execpc.com

Special Needs Adoption Network
  and North American Council
  on Adoptable Children
State Representative
1126 S. 70th, Suite N 509A
Milwaukee, WI 53214
(414) 475-1246

Special Needs Adoptive Parents
  (SNAP)
5209 Airport Road
Stevens Point, WI 54481
(715) 341-5291

Stars of David International Inc. -
  Milwaukee Chapter
Jewish Family Services
1360 North Prospect Avenue
Milwaukee, WI 53202-0393
(414) 390-3800
Fax: (414) 390-5808
www.starsofdavid.org
starsdavid@aol.com

Support Group for Foster and
  Adoptive Parents
3577 High Point Road
Madison, WI 53744
Fax: (608) 821-3125
Toll Free: (888) 485-7385

United Family Organization
6676 Round Lake Road
Rhinelander, WI 54501
(715) 282-6870

United States Chilean Adoptive
  Families
1239 East Broadway Street
Waukesha, WI 53186
(262) 547-0671

Waiting to Adopt Support Group
680 Wolcott Street
West Bend, WI 53090
(414) 334-0424
dmiske@hnet.net

Wisconsin Association of Single
  Adoptive Parents
4520 N. Bartlett Avenue
Shorewood, WI 53211-1509
(414) 962-9342

Wisconsin Attachment Resource
  Network
P.O. Box 236
Dousman, WI 53118
(262) 965-5170
www.w-a-r-n.com
ruder@w-a-r-n.com

Wisconsin Single Parents of
  Adopted Children
403 Vilas Avenue
Nekoosa, WI 54457
(715) 886-5572
annehand@wctc.net

Search Support Groups

Adoption Information and
  Direction
P.O. Box 516
Stevens Point, WI 54481-0516
(715) 345-1290
www.uwsp.edu/acad/psych/dh/
  aidinf.htm
dhenders@fsmail.uwsp.edu

Adoption Information and
  Direction
P.O. Box 875
Green Bay, WI 54305
(920) 336-3005

American Adoption Congress
  State Representative
4308 Heffron Street
Stevens Point, WI 54481
(715) 345-1290
Fax: (715) 345-7830
firework@coredcs.com

Search
908 North Superior Street
Appleton, WI 54911
(920) 739-7444
jkbogie3@aol.com

WISCONSIN LAWS RELATED TO ADOPTION: QUESTIONS AND ANSWERS

Private adoption is allowed in Wisconsin, but an agency must conduct a home study and provide counseling to the birth parents.

In an interstate independent adoption, an agency must serve as the child's guardian from the time the child is placed with the adoptive couple to the time the adoption is finalized (about six months after consent is signed). Also, an agency must provide counseling to a birth mother in an independent adoption. Contact the ICPC office for written procedural information.

Can an attorney serve as an intermediary?
No, but the attorney is allowed to pass names along such as a friend might do, as long as no fees are charged.

Is advertising permitted?
No.

Who must consent to the adoption?
The birth parents must consent.

When can consent be taken from birth mother (father), and how long after the consent is signed can it be revoked?
A birth mother must have her rights terminated in court after the birth; there is no revocation period. A birth father who is not married to the birth mother and who does not appear in court with her may sign a written consent in front of a notary, and his consent is thereafter filed with the court at the time of the birth mother's hearing. Once the hearing takes place, he cannot revoke his consent.

What are the birth father's rights?
Generally, a birth father has the right to be notified of the court hearing. This can be done by notifying him personally or by publication of the adoption proceedings in the legal notice section of the newspaper if his whereabouts are unknown. If he appears and contests the adoption, he can be represented by an attorney at public expense.

What fees can adoptive parents pay?
A birth mother can be reimbursed for medical, legal, and agency expenses. With court approval, a birth mother may also be reimbursed for maternity clothing, travel, and child care. She must get a statement from her employer and her physician stating that she cannot work.
Living expenses up to $1,000 can be paid if necessary to protect the health and welfare of mother and unborn baby.

Where does the adoption hearing take place?
The adoption hearing take places in the court of the county where the adoptive parents live or where the child lives.

How are familial and stepparent adoptions different from nonbiological adoptions?
A child may be placed with a relative without a court order.Generally, in a stepparent or relative adoption, the termination of parental rights and adoption can take place at the same hearing; in other adoptions there is a six-month waiting period from termination of rights to the adoption finalization. Also, a screening is conducted instead of a full home study.

Can a nonresident finalize an adoption in this state?
No.

WYOMING

State Adoption Specialist

Wyoming Department of
Family Services
Maureen Clifton
2300 Capitol Avenue,
Hathaway Building, 3rd Floor
Cheyenne, WY 82002
(307) 777-3570
Fax: (307) 777-3693
dfsweb.state.wy.us/CHILDSVC/
TOC1.HTM
mclifton@state.wy.us

State ICPC Administrator

Wyoming Department of
Family Services
2300 Capitol Avenue,
Hathaway Building
Cheyenne, WY 82002-0490
(307) 777-3570
Fax: (307) 777-7747

**State Adoption Exchange/State
Photolisting Service**

The Adoption Exchange
14232 East Evans Avenue
Aurora, CO 80014
(303) 755-4756
Toll Free: (800) 451-5246
www.adoptex.org
kids@adoptex.org

**Regional/District Public
Agencies**

Wyoming Department of Family
Services, Albany
710 Garfield Street, Suite 200
Laramie, WY 82070
(307) 745-7324
Fax: (307) 742-8848

Wyoming Department of Family
Services, Big Horn
616 Second Avenue, North
Greybull, WY 82426
(307) 765-9453
Fax: (307) 765-2330

Wyoming Department of Family
Services, Campbell
1901 Energy Court
Gillette, WY 82716
(307) 682-7277
Fax: (307) 686-1889

Wyoming Department of Family
Services, Carbon
Third and Buffalo, Carbon
Building
Rawlins, WY 82301
(307) 328-0612
Fax: (307) 328-2801

Wyoming Department of Family
Services, Converse
530 Oak Street
Douglas, WY 82633
(307) 358-3138
Fax: (307) 358-4238

Wyoming Department of Family
Services, Converse
925 W. Birch Box 26
Glenrock, WY 82637
(307) 436-9068

Wyoming Department of Family
Services, Crook
102 N. Fifth, P.O. Box 57
Sundance, WY 82729
(307) 283-2014
Fax: (307) 283-1606

Wyoming Department of Family
Services, Fremont-Lander
201 N. Fourth
Lander, WY 82520
(307) 332-4038
Fax: (307) 332-4806

Wyoming Department of Family
Services, Fremont-Riverton
120 N. Sixth East
Riverton, WY 82501
(307) 856-6521
Fax: (307) 856-7937

Wyoming Department of Family
Services, Goshen
1618 E. M Street
Torrington, WY 82240
(307) 532-2191
Fax: (307) 532-4666

Wyoming Department of Family
Services, Hot Springs
403 Big Horn
Thermopolis, WY 82443
(307) 864-2158
Fax: (307) 864-2651

Wyoming Department of Family
Services, Johnson
381 N. Main
Buffalo, WY 82834
(307) 684-5513
Fax: (307) 684-7966

Wyoming Department of Family
Services, Laramie
1710 Capitol Avenue
Cheyenne, WY 82002
(307) 777-7921
Fax: (307) 777-5190

Wyoming Department of Family
Services, Lincoln
631 Washington Box 1336, Afton
Plaza
Afton, WY 83110
(307) 886-9232
Fax: (307) 886-3101

Wyoming Department of Family
Services, Lincoln South
1100 Pine Avenue Box 470
Kemmerer, WY 83101-0470
(307) 877-6670
Fax: (307) 877-4332

Wyoming Department of Family
Services, Natrona
851 Werner Court
Casper, WY 82601
(307) 473-3900
Fax: (307) 473-3967

Wyoming Department of Family
Services, Niobrara
905 S. Main Box 785
Lusk, WY 82225
(307) 334-2153

Wyoming Department of Family
Services, Park
109 W. 14th
Powell, WY 82435
(307) 754-2245

Wyoming Department of Family
Services, Park
1301 Rumsey Street
Cody, WY 82414
(307) 587-6246
Fax: (307) 527-7183

Wyoming Department of Family
Services, Platte
975 Gilchrist
Wheatland, WY 82201
(307) 322-3790
Fax: (307) 322-4125

Wyoming Department of Family
Services, Sheridan
16 W. Eighth Street
Sheridan, WY 82801
(307) 672-2404
Fax: (307) 672-8948

Wyoming Department of Family
Services, Sublette
111 N. Sublette
Pinedale, WY 82941
(307) 367-4124
Fax: (307) 367-6774

Wyoming Department of Family
Services, Sweetwater
1682 Sunset Drive
Rock Springs, WY 82901
(307) 382-5916
Fax: (307) 382-5917

Wyoming Department of Family
Services, Teton
P.O. Box 547
Jackson, WY 83001
(307) 733-7757
Fax: (307) 733-2165

Wyoming Department of Family
Services, Uinta
350 City View Drive, Suite 206
Evanston, WY 82930
(307) 789-2756
Fax: (307) 789-2165

Wyoming Department of Family
Services, Uinta
111 West Owen, Box 848
Lyman, WY 82937
(307) 786-4011
Fax: (307) 787-6359

Wyoming Department of Family
Services, Washakie
1700 Robertson
Worland, WY 82401
(307) 347-6181
Fax: (307) 347-6184

Wyoming Department of Family
Services, Weston
1517 W. Main
Newcastle, WY 82701
(307) 746-4657
Fax: (307) 746-2588

**Licensed Private Adoption
Agencies**

Casey Family Program
130 Hobbs Avenue
Cheyenne, WY 82009
(307) 638-2564
Fax: (307) 632-5251

Catholic Social Services
P.O. Box 1394
Gillette, WY 82716

Catholic Social Services
P.O. Box 1026
Cheyenne, WY 82003-1026
(307) 638-1530
Fax: (307) 637-7936
Toll Free: (800) 788-4606

Catholic Social Services
P.O. Box 2247
Casper, WY 82602
(307) 237-2723

Catholic Social Services
P.O. Box 1281
Cody, WY 82414
(307) 587-6694

Focus on Children
125 Dayton Drive
Cokeville, WY 83114-0323

(307) 279-3557
Fax: (307) 279-3444
*www.focus-on-children.com/
Adopt@Focus-on-Children.com*

Global Adoptions
50 East Loucks, Suite 205
Sheridan, WY 82801
(307) 674-6606
Fax: (307) 672-7605
*www.globadoption.com
adoption@wave.sheridan.wy.us*

LDS Social Services
905 Meadow Lane
Cody, WY 82414
(307) 587-9413

LDS Social Services
7609 Santa Marie Drive
Cheyenne, WY 82009
(307) 637-8929

Wyoming Children's Society
P.O. Box 105, 716 Randall Ave.
Cheyenne, WY 82003-0105
(307) 632-7619
*www.nbsweb.com/adoption/
wcs@nbsweb.com*

Wyoming Parenting Society
P.O. Box 2468
Jackson, WY 83001
(307) 733-6357
Fax: (307) 733-9304
wyadopt@silverstar.com

**Adoptive Parent Support
Groups**

Adoptive Parent Group of
Cheyenne
Wyoming Children's Society
714 Randall
Cheyenne, WY 82001
(307) 686-6412

Northern Wyoming Adoptive
Parents and North American
Council on Adoptable
Children State Representative
P.O. Box 788
Basin, WY 82410
(307) 568-2729

Search Support Groups

Adults Affected By Adoption
1203 E. Sixth Street
Cheyenne, WY 82003
(307) 635-6843

WYOMING LAWS RELATED TO ADOPTION: QUESTIONS AND ANSWERS

Can an attorney serve as an intermediary?
Yes. However, attorneys generally do not bring birth parents and adoptive parents together. Because the population of Wyoming is only 400,000 and it is the ninth largest state, such a service is difficult to offer in such a sparsely populated area.

Is advertising permitted?
Yes.

Who must consent to the adoption?
1. Both birth parents if the birth father is known
2. The head of the child placement agency if involved

When can consent be given by birth mother (father), and how long after the consent is signed can it be revoked?
Consent cannot be given until the child is born. Once signed, the consent is irrevocable.

What are the birth father's rights?
The birth father's consent is not needed if the birth mother does not know his name, or if he has been given notice of the hearing and has not responded within thirty days after receiving notice of the child's birth, or if he has abandoned or deserted the child, or if he has failed to contribute to the support of the child for one year or more, or if he has failed to pay at least 70 percent of court-ordered support for a period of two years. A putative father also has no right to contest the adoption unless he has asserted paternity or registered with the birth father registry.

If he does object to the adoption and has shown an interest and responsibility in the child within thirty days after being notified of the birth, then the court will decide whether his objections are valid, and his assertions of paternity timely, as well as what would be in the best interests of the child.

What fees can adoptive parents pay?
Medical, legal and living expenses can be paid. An accounting of them must given to the court.

Where does the adoption hearing take place?
The adoption hearing takes place in District Court. Adoptions are usually finalized in about six months.

How are familial and stepparent adoptions different from nonbiological adoptions?
A medical report is not required in a stepparent adoption.

Can a nonresident finalize an adoption in this state?
No. According to ICPC guidelines, a petitioner must be a resident of Wyoming for at least sixty days.

SOURCE: WYOMING STATUTES SECTION 1-22-101 TO 10220116 AND 1-22-201 TO 1-22-203 (1997)

Chapter 2: Agency Adoption

1. Flango, Victor E., and Karen R. Flango. "How Many Children Were Adopted in 1992?" *Child Welfare*, Vol. LXXIV, No. 5, Sept./Oct. 1995. We also gained some information from a personal interview with Karen Flango, who, with Victor Flango, is with the National Center for State Courts in Virginia. The Center is currently collecting data from the states to record the number of adoptions per year. Also, see "FactSheet on Adoption," a publication of the National Council for Adoption, 1930 Seventeenth Street, N.W., Washington, D.C. 20009-6297 202/238-1200. This organization collects and publishes adoption data.

Chapter 6: Who Are Birth Mothers, Fathers, and Grandparents?

1. Cocozzeli, Carmelo. "Predicting the Decision of Biogical Mothers to Retain or Relinquish Their Babies for Adoption: Implications for Open Adoption." *Child Welfare League of America* Vol. LXVIII, No. 5, Jan/Feb 1989.
2. "FactSheet on Adoption." National Council for Adoption, pp. 1–2. Also, see Resnick, Michael D. "Studying Adolescent Mothers' Decision-Making About Adoption and Parenting" in *Social Work*, Jan/Feb 1984.
3. "FactSheet on Adoption," National Council for Adoption, pp. 1–2.
4. "Black Women Are Not More or Less Likely To Place a Child for Adoption: An Empirical Analysis of Adoption." *Economic Inquiry*, Vol XXXI, Jan. 1993, pp. 59–70.

Chapter 9: Openness in Adoption

1. Kraft, Adrienne D., et al. "Some Theoretical Considerations on Confidential Adoptions." *Human Services Press*, 1985 pp. 13–21.
2. *Ibid*, p. 150.
3. Blanton, Terril L., and Jeanne Buckner Deschner. "Biological Mother's Grief: The Post-adoptive Experience in Open Versus Confidential Adoption." *Child Welfare*, Vol 69, No. 6, Nov./Dec. 1990, pp. 525–535.
4. Phillips, B. Lee. "Open Adoption: A New Look at Adoption Practice and Policy in Texas." *Baylor Law Review*, Vol 43:407, 1991, pp. 407–429.

Chapter 10: Special-Families: Special Considerations

1. Mattes, Jane. *Single Mothers By Choice*. New York: Random House, 1994, p. 10.
2. *Ibid*, pp. 22–23.
3. Crain, Connie, and Janice Duffy. *How to Adopt a Child*. Nashville, Tenn.: Thomas Nelson, 1994, pp. 121–137.
4. Gilman, Lois. *The Adoption Resource Book*. New York: HarperCollins, 1992, p. 29.
5. Crain, Connie, and Janice Duffy. *How to Adopt a Child*. Nashville, Tenn.: Thomas Nelson, 1994, p. 126–127.

Chapter 11: Relative and Stepparent Adoption

1. Flango, Victor E., and Karen R. Flango. "How Many Children Were Adopted in 1992?" *Child Welfare*, Vol. LXXIV, No. 5, Sept./Oct. 1995. We also gained some information from a personal interview with Karen Flango, who, with Victor Flango, is with the National Center for State Courts in Virginia. The Center is currently collecting data from

the states to record the number of adoptions per year. Also, see "FactSheet on Adoption," a publication of the National Council for Adoption, 1930 Seventeenth Street, N.W., Washington, D.C. 20009-6297 202/238-1200. This organization collects and publishes adoption data.

2. Melina, Lois. "Relative Adoptions Have Benefits, But Also Have Unique Challenges." *Adopted Child*, Vol. 12, No. 2, February 1993, pp. 1–4.

3. Sawyer, Richard J., and Howard Dubowitz. "School Performance of Children in Kinship Care." Academy for Educational Development, Washington, D.C., published in *Child Abuse and Neglect*; Vol. 18, No. 7, July 1994, pp. 587–597.

4. Personal interview with Ann Sullivan of the Child Welfare League.

5. Foster, Maurice Esq. "Adoption by Grandparents." *State Court Journal.* Vol 18, No. 1, Summer 1994, pp. 27–31.

6. Downey, Douglas B. "Understanding Academic Achievement Among Children in Step-Households: The Roles of Parental Resources, Sex of Stepparent, and Sex of Child." *Social Forces*, Vol. 73, March 1995, p. 875.

7. Adamec, Christine, and William L. Pierce. *Encyclopedia of Adoption.* Facts on File, New York, 1991, p. 272.

8. Downey, Douglas B. "Understanding Academic Achievement Among Children in Step-Households: The Roles of Parental Resources, Sex of Stepparent, and Sex of Child." *Social Forces*, Vol. 73, March 1995, p. 875.

9. Schur, William M. "Adoption Procedure." *Adoption Law and Practice*, Vol. 4, No. 1, December 1994, pp. 26–27.

Chapter 12: International Adoption

1. Personal interview with Melinda Garvert.

2. Jenista, Jerri Ann. "Adoptions from Africa." *Adoption Medical News*, Vol. I, No. 2. Nov./Dec 1995, p. 2.

3. Verhulst, Frank C., Monika Althaus, Versluis den Bieman, and Sophia J. Herma. "Damaging Backgrounds: Later Adjustment of International Adoptees." Children's Hospital, Dept of Child Psychiatry, Rotterdam, Netherlands. Printed in *Journal of the American Academy of Child and Adolescent Psychiatry*, Volume 31, No. 3, May 1992, pp. 518–524.

4. Reynolds, Nancy Thalia. *Adopting Your Child*. North Vancouver, Canada: Self-Counsel Press, 1993.

5. Verhulst, Frank C., Monika Althaus, Versluis den Bieman, and Sophia J. Herma. "Damaging Backgrounds: Later Adjustment of International Adoptees." Children's Hospital, Dept of Child Psychiatry, Rotterdam, Netherlands. Printed in *Journal of the American Academy of Child and Adolescent Psychiatry*, Volume 31, No. 3, May 1992, pp. 518–524.

6. Boer, Frits, Versluis den Bieman, J. M. Herma, and Frank C. Verhulst. "International Adoption of Children with Siblings: Behavioral Outcomes." Leiden University, Dept of Child and Adolescent Psychiatry, Netherlands. Published in *American Journal of Orthopsychiatry*, Vol. 62, No. 2, April 1994, pp. 252–262.

7. Van Gulden, Holly and Lida M. Bartels-Rabb. *Real Parents, Real Children: Parenting the Adopted Child*. New York: Crossroads, 1994, pp. 177–180.

8. *Ibid*, p. 179.

9. Kirkland, Judy. *Washington Metroplitan Area RESOLVE Newsletter*, March 1987.

Chapter 13: A Brief Overview of Canadian Adoption

1. Wine, Judith. *The Canadian Adoption Guide: A Family at Last.* Toronto: McGraw-Hill Ryerson, 1995.

2. *Ibid.*

3. Personal interview with spokesperson at the British Columbia Adoptive Parents Association.

4. Daly, Kerry J. and Michael Sobol. "Adoption In Canada: A Profile." Taken from a study prepared for the Royal Commission on New Reproductive Technologies. *Transition*, September 1992, pp. 4–5.

5. Wine, Judith. *The Canadian Adoption Guide: A Family at Last.* Toronto: McGraw-Hill Ryerson, 1995.

6. Shinyei, Marilyn E., and Linda Edney. "Open Adoption in Canada." *Transition*, September 1992, pp. 8–10.

7. Wine, Judith. *The Canadian Adoption Guide: A Family at Last.* Toronto: McGraw-Hill Ryerson, 1995.

8. Personal interview with Claire-Marie Gagnon, formerly of the Federation des parents adoptants du Quebec.

9. Wine, Judith. *The Canadian Adoption Guide: A Family at Last.* Toronto: McGraw-Hill Ryerson, 1995.

10. *Ibid.*

11. Personal interview with Claire-Marie Gagnon, formerly of the Federation des parents adoptants du Quebec.

12. *Ibid.*

Chapter 14: Adopting a Toddler

1. U.S. Department of Health and Human Services, Administration on Children, Youth and Families, Children's Bureau, Adoption and Foster Care Analysis and Reporting System (AFCARS)

Chapter 15: Special Needs Adoption

1. Kroll, Joe. "Waiting Children Still Wait." *Adoptalk*, Summer 1995, p 1.

2. Glidden, Laraine M. "Adopted Children with Developmental Disabilities: Post-placement Family Functioning." *Children and Youth Services Review*, Vol. 13, No. 5–6, 1991, pp. 363–377.

3. Rosenthal, James A., and Victor Groze. "Behavioral Problems of Special Needs Adopted Children." *Children and Youth Services Review*, Vol. 13, No. 5–6, 1991, pp. 343–361.

4. Fahlberg, Vera. *Common Behavioral Problems*, Michigan Department of Social Services, 1987.

5. Keck, Gregory C. *Adopting the Hurt Child.*

6. *Ibid.*

7. *Ibid.*

8. Kroll, Joe. "Waiting Children Still Wait." *Adoptalk*, Summer 1995, p 1.

9. Crain, Connie. " 'What I Need is a Mom': The Welfare State Denies Homes to Thousands of Foster Children." *Policy Review*, Vol. 10, No. 73, Summer 1995, p. 40.

10. McDonald, Thomas P., Alice A. Lieberman, Susan Partridge, and Helaine Hornby. "Assessing the Role of Agency Services in Reducing Adoption Disruptions." *Children and Youth Services Review*, Vol. 13, No. 5–6, 1991, pp. 425–438.

11. Adamec, Christine. "Rip-offs." *The Adoption Advocates NEWSletter* Vol. 3, No. 9, September 1995, p. 5.

12. Kroll, Joe. "Waiting Children Still Wait." *Adoptalk*, Summer 1995, p 1.

13. Groze, Victor, Simeon Haines, Mark Barth, and Richard P. Case. "Barriers in Permanency Planning for Medically Fragile Children: Drug Affected Children and HIV Infected Children." Case Western Reserve University, Mandel School of Applied Social Sciences. *Child and Adolescent Social Work Journal*; Vol. 11, No. 1, February 1994, pp. 63–85.

14. Lewert, George. "Children and AIDS." Columbia Presbyterian Medical Center, Dept of Social Work Services. *Social Casework*; Vol. 69, No. 6, June 1988, pp. 348–354.

15. Laws, Rita. "Between the Lines: How to Read a Waiting Child Description." *Adoptive Families*, Sept/Oct 1995, pp 34–35.

16. Chamberlain, Patricia, Sandra Moreland, and Cathleen Reid. "Enhanced Services and Stipends for Foster Parents: Effects on Retention Rates and Outcomes for Children." Oregon Social Learning Center. *Child Welfare*, Vol. 71, No. 5, September/October 1992, pp. 387–401. See also Tim O'Hanlon. *Adoption Subsidy: A Guide for Adoptive Parents*, published by New Roots, An Adoptive Families Support Group. February, 1995.

17. Bussiere, Alice and Ellen C. Sega. "Children With Special Needs." *Adoption Law and Practice*. Matthew Bender and Company, 1994.

18. *Ibid.*

19. *Ibid.*

20. Widermeier, Jeannette. "Adoption Subsidy Q & A." *Adoptalk*, Winter '96 pp. 7, 12

21. O'Hanlon, Tim. *Adoption Subsidy: A Guide for Adoptive Parents*, published by New Roots, An Adoptive Families Support Group. February, 1995.

22. *Ibid.*

23. *Ibid.*

24. McKelvey, Carol, and JoEllen Stevens. *The Adoption Crisis: The Truth Behind Adoption and Foster Care.* Golden, Colorado: Fulcrum Publishing, 1994.

25. Woodmansee, Carol. "Life Book." *Foster Care Connection*, Vol. 1, No. 5, October 1995.

26. Goetting, Ann, and Mark G. Goetting. "How Parents Fare After Placement." Western Kentucky University, *Journal of Child and Family Studies*, Vol. 2, No. 4, December 1993, pp. 353–369.

27. Bussiere, Alice and Ellen C. Sega. "Children With Special Needs." *Adoption Law and Practice*. Matthew Bender and Company, 1994.

Chapter 16: Transracial Adoption

1. Personal interview with Beth Hall of Pact, An Adoption Alliance and Pact Press, in San Francisco, California.
2. "All In the Family." *The New Republic*, January 24, 1994, p. 6.
3. Hayes, Peter. "Transracial Adoption: Politics and Ideology." Iowa State University, *Child Welfare*, Vol. 72, No. 3, May/June 1993, pp. 301–310.
4. Bartholet, Elizabeth. "Where Do Black Children Belong? The Politics of Race Matching in Adoption." University of Pennsylvania Law Review. Volume 139, No. 5, May 1991, pp. 1163–1256.
5. Kennedy, Randall. "Orphans of Separtism: The Politics of Transracial Adoption." *The American Prospect*, Spring 1994, pp. 38–45.
6. Bartholet, Elizabeth. "Where Do Black Children Belong? The Politics of Race Matching in Adoption." University of Pennsylvania Law Review. Volume 139, No. 5, May 1991, pp. 1163–1256.
7. *Ibid.*
8. *Ibid.*
9. Vroegh, Karen S. "Transracial Adoption: How It Is 17 Years Later." Paper published by Chicago Child Care Society, pp. 55.
10. Bowen, James S. "Cultural Convergences and Divergences, The Nexus Between Putative Afro-American Family Values and the Best Interests of the Child." *Journal of Family Law*, Vol. 26, 1988, pp. 487, 502.
11. Forde-Mazrui, Kim. "Black Identity and Child Placement: The Best Interests of Black and Biracial Children." *Michigan Law Revue*, No. 4, February 1994, pp. 925–967.
12. Mahoney, Joan. "The Black Baby Doll: Tranracial Adoption and Cultural Preservation." *UMKC Law. REV.* Vol. 59, No. 85, 1991, pp. 487–501.
13. Kallgren, Carl A., and Pamela J. Caudill. "Current Transracial Adoption Practices: Racial Dissonance or Racial Awareness?" Pennsylvania State U, *Psychological Reports*, Vol. 72, No. 2., April 1993, pp. 551–558.

Chapter 17: The Home Study

1. Johnston, Patricia Irwin. *Adopting After Infertility.* Indianapolis: Perspective Press, 1992, pp. 186-187.
2. Adamec, Christine. *There ARE Babies to Adopt.* New York: Kensington Press, 1996.
3. *Ibid.*

4. *Adoptalk*, publication of the North American Council on Adoptable Children, St. Paul, Minn., Fall 1996, p. 5.
5. *National Adoption Reports*, newsletter from the National Council for Adoption, Washington, D.C., July 1996.

Chapter 18: Adoption Expenses

1. "The New Adoption Tax Credit." From *Adoptalk*, publication of the North American Council on Adoptable Children, St. Paul, Minn., Fall 1996, p. 5.
2. "Common Questions on The Adoption Tax Credit." from *National Adoption Reports*, newsletter from the National Council for Adoption, Washington, D.C., Sept/Oct 1996, pp. 8, 9.

Chapter 19: Healthy Mothers, Healthy Babies

1. "Recommendations of the U.S. Public Health Service Task Force on the Use of Zidovudine (AZT) to Recuce Perinatal Transmission of Human Immunodeficiency Virus." The Center for Disease Control and Prevention, *Morbidity and Mortality Weekly Report*, Vol. 43, August 5, 1995, p. 194.
2. *Ibid.*
3. Hotchner, Tracie. *Pregnancy and Childbirth.* New York: Avon Books, 1984. p. 117.
4. Melina, Lois. "Prenatal Drug Exposure Affects School-Age Child's Behavior." *Adopted Child*, Vol. 15, No. 1, January 1996.
5. Chasnoff, Ira. "Guidelines for Adopting Drug-Exposed Infants and Children." Published by the National Association of Perinatal Addiction, Dept. of Research and Education, 1994.
6. Yolton, Kimberly A., and Rosemary Bolig. "Psychosocial, Behavioral, and Developmental Characteristics of Toddlers Prenatally Exposed to Cocaine." University of Tennessee, Dept of Pediatrics, *Child-Study-Journal*, Vol. 24, No. 1, 1994, pp. 49–68.
7. Cook, Paddy Shannon, et al. "Alcohol, Tobacco, and Other Drugs May Harm the Unborn." Published by the U.S. Department of Health and Human Services, 1990.
8. Gonzalez, Nilda M., and Magda Campbell. "Cocaine Babies: Does Prenatal Exposure to Cocaine Affect Development?" *Journal of the American Academy of Child and Adolescent Psychiatry*, Vo. 33, No. 1, 1994, pp. 16–19.

9. Melina, Lois. "Prenatal Drug Exposure Affects School-Age Child's Behavior." *Adopted Child*, Vol. 15, No. 1, January 1996.

10. Schneider, Jane "Assessment of Infant Motor Develpments." Presentation at NAPARE conference in New York City, Aug 10, 1988.

11. Yolton, Kimberly A., and Rosemary Bolig. "Psychosocial, Behavioral, and Developmental Characteristics of Toddlers Prenatally Exposed to Cocaine." University of Tennessee, Dept of Pediatrics, *Child-Study-Journal*, Vol. 24, No. 1, 1994, pp. 49–68.

12. Barth, Richard P. "Adoption of Drug-Exposed Children." University of California School of Social Welfare, Child Welfare Research Center, *Children and Youth Services Review*; Vol 13., 1991, pp. 323–342.

13. Chasnoff, Ira. "Guidelines for Adopting Drug-Exposed Infants and Children." Published by the National Association of Perinatal Addiction, Dept. of Research and Education, 1994.

14. Cook, Paddy Shannon, et al. "Alcohol, Tobacco, and Other Drugs May Harm the Unborn." Published by the U.S. Department of Health and Human Services, 1990.

15. Abrams, Richard S. *Will It Hurt the Baby?* Reading, Mass.: Addison-Wesley, 1990, pp. 168–169.

16. Cook, Paddy Shannon, et al. "Alcohol, Tobacco, and Other Drugs May Harm the Unborn " U.S. Department of Health and Human Services Rockville, MD 1990.

17. *Ibid.*

18. Abrams, Richard S. *Will It Hurt the Baby?* Reading, Mass.: Addison-Wesley, 1990, pp. 168–169.

19. Cook, Paddy Shannon, et al. "Alcohol, Tobacco, and Other Drugs May Harm the Unborn " U.S. Department of Health and Human Services Rockville, MD 1990.

20. *Ibid.*

21. *Ibid.*

22. *Ibid.*

23. *Ibid.*

24. Jenista, Jerrri Ann. "Health Status of the 'New' International Adopted Child. *Adoption Medical News*, Vol. II, No. 6, June 1996, p. 3.

25. Jenista, Jerrri Ann. "Chronic Heptatitis B: Medical Mangagement Issues." *Adoption Medical News*, Vol. I, No. 2. November/December 1995.

26. Nelson-Erichsen, Jean, and Heino R. Erichsen. *How to Adopt Internationally.* The Woodlands, Texas: Los Ninos Inernational Adoption Center, 1993, p. 58.

27. Hostetter, Margaret, and Dana Johnson. "Medical Concerns for International Adoptees." *Report on Intercountry Adoption*, 1996, pp. 50–51.

28. Sweet, O. Robin, and Patty Bryan. *Adopt International.* New York: Farrar, Straus and Giroux, 1996, pp. 107–108.